SURVIVAL

SURVIVAL

THE ULTIMATE PRACTICAL GUIDE TO STAYING ALIVE IN EXTREME CONDITIONS AND EMERGENCY SITUATIONS IN ALL ENVIRONMENTS, ANYWHERE IN THE WORLD

ANTHONIO AKKERMANS • PETER G. DRAKE
BILL MATTOS • ANDY MIDDLETON

southwater

CONTENTS

This edition is published by Southwater,
an imprint of Anness Publishing Ltd,
108 Great Russell Street, London WC1B 3NA;
info@anness.com

www.southwaterbooks.com;
www.annesspublishing.com;
twitter: @Anness_Books

If you like the images in this book and would like
to investigate using them for publishing, promotions
or advertising, please visit our website
www.practicalpictures.com for more information.

A CIP catalogue record for this book is available
from the British Library.

Publisher: Joanna Lorenz
Editorial Director: Helen Sudell
Project Editors: Sarah Ainley, Neil Champion,
Melanie Halton, James Harrison, Ann Kay
and Catherine Stuart
Production Controller: Ben Worley
Contributors: Anthonio Akkermans, Neil Champion,
Harry Cook, Bob Durand, Bill Mattos, Andy
Middleton Bob Morrison and Anne Charlish,
Book design: Michael Morey, Nigel Partridge
and Lisa Tai
Jacket design: Nigel Partridge
Illustrators: Peter Bull, Samantha J. Elmhurst, George
Manley, Patrick Mulrey and J.B. Illustrations
Photography: Mark Duncalf, Tim Gundry,
Helen Metcalfe, Martin Milner, Mark Wood
and Ray Wood

INTRODUCTION
by Debra Searle MBE

Survival is necessary only when the environment becomes unfamiliar to us and we are far beyond our comfort zone, battling with situations outside the realms of our previous experience. Sometimes, this onset of unfamiliarity is something we have been preparing for – a trip into the wilderness, for example, or rowing across the Atlantic as I did. At other times, a situation may take us completely by surprise. An otherwise relaxing holiday might be put to the test by perilous weather, by injury or sickness, or even – in one of the more extreme cases – by an actual threat of physical violence. Few of us have a death wish, but if we should ever find ourselves in one of the situations described in this book, we may not feel able to fight for survival if we became overwhelmed by fear, or if we were pitched against Mother Nature

– the ultimate battle. When we are sapped of all of our energy and reserves the only thing we have left to fight with is our minds.

THE WILL TO SURVIVE

Over the years much research has been conducted into why it should be that some people can survive a life-threatening situation when others in the same situation are overwhelmed. Often it is not the strongest or those with the best equipment who make it, although these things undoubtedly make a big difference. Unequivocally, the same conclusion is always reached: the difference between living or dying lies in the mind. The power of the mind, the resilience of the human spirit, an unshakable optimism and a mental readiness to handle the unexpected are vital to our survival.

Naturally some people have these qualities in abundance, but not all. Happily there are skills that can be learned to help us achieve the necessary mental strength. Just as we can repeat movements, like the running action or biceps curl, to make our bodies physically fitter, so the same principle can also be applied to the mind. But as with getting our bodies fitter, we have to work at it and repeat the action to increase our performance.

Rowing across the Atlantic was always going to be a test of mental strength, but, despite meticulous preparation, I still encountered situations I had not prepared for. Two weeks into the journey, I had to have

▼ *Debra Searle has honed her mental survival skills both as a sports psychologist and as an extreme sports participator.*

▲ *Water is essential to survival – never more so than when in short supply. Finding water and ensuring it is safe to drink are among the core skills discussed in this book.*

my rowing partner rescued, and as a consequence I rowed the Atlantic alone for three months in an 8m/24ft plywood rowing boat. During the voyage I had to survive many hazardous situations, such as hurricanes, attack by sharks and almost being run over by a supertanker.

The conclusion I have drawn from my experience on that and many other expeditions is that training the mind allows us to cope with situations that take us way beyond any mental or physical pain threshold we may have set ourselves, and that these mental skills, once learned, can be applied to all survival situations. It therefore makes sense to look at these now, at the start of this book, before you read on.

The two most important mental strength-building skills that can be developed can be summed up in two words – visualization and attitude.

VISUALIZATION
It may sound like psychobabble at first, but visualization is certainly not just for elite athletes. The idea is that by mentally imagining doing an action we can train our bodies to carry out that action without actually moving or completing it for real; therefore a thought alone can produce a physical response. An example of this that we can all experience is imagining sucking on a slice of lemon. When we do we get a rush of saliva to the mouth yet there is not a real lemon in sight! Our minds have just induced a physical response to the thought. Visualization is the most powerful survival tool we

can ever develop because often we cannot replicate an actual situation in order to practise surviving. However, if we can use our minds to rehearse mentally how we will respond, our minds and bodies will be trained and automatically know what to do if and when the situation arises.

I spent time before, and even more time during, my row across the Atlantic doing mental risk assessments of all the things that could go wrong and be potentially fatal. Running these "movies" in my head allowed me to rehearse life-threatening situations, such as fixing the watermaker in a big storm or surviving a collision with a whale, in which the key was to respond positively and correctly. Practising the physical response to a threatening situation without fail every time I visualized it meant that I did not even have to think about what to do when such a situation really arose. My body instinctively seemed to know exactly what to do.

Visualization increased the speed of my reactions and provided me with an effective response. It sounds extreme, but this type of mental exercise should be practised every time we face a new challenge likely to test our wits. We then gain confidence from knowing that, should that "worst case scenario" arise, we can rely upon our instincts and inner strength to assist us.

Not only can visualization help us achieve the right physical response, it is also incredibly powerful for eliminating fear. Let's face it – any survival situation

▲ *The* Troika Transatlantic *was Debra Searle's (formerly Veal) home for 3½ months as she made a solo crossing of the Atlantic. She faced the mental challenge of survival alone on such a long journey, as well as the fear of the boat being hit by whales or supertankers, or of being attacked by sharks.*

is likely to be terrifying, but if we can remain calm we are likely to be able to analyse, prioritize and plan a response amid the chaos and confusion. When visualization is used in this way it is like watching a scary movie for the second time. The first time you put the DVD in the machine and press Play you find yourself jumping at the scary bits

▼ *A positive mental attitude and ability to dig deep for inner strength are key to survival, as well as being able to adapt.*

▲ *If a fire broke out in your home, would you know how to get everyone out safely? Using visualization to help you to anticipate escape scenarios will enable you to cope that much better in a live situation.*

because you don't quite know when they are going to happen. But when you put the DVD in for a second viewing and press Play you don't jump when you get to the scary bits, because you have seen it all before and know that it is coming.

We often feel fear because we don't know what is going to happen next, but if we can visualize some of the possibilities by running our own "movies" in our heads we can eliminate some of the fear. We simply press Play when the situation arises.

THE POWER OF VISUALIZATION

Perhaps one of the most powerful ways to use visualization is as a means of developing that eternal optimism and hardness of human spirit that is so vital for survival. It is also possibly the simplest form of visualization to develop, for all you really need to do is visualize that one thing that is worth living for, and direct all your thought toward this, shutting out fear and worry.

We all have something to live for – something we love more than anything else. Maybe it would be to hold your child again, drive your car, watch your favourite football team win a home game… Whatever it may be you just have to visualize it using every sense in your body and imagine how amazing it will feel to do that again. For me it was the moment when I was finally going to row into a marina on the other side of the Atlantic and see all my friends and family waiting there to greet me.

I used to imagine it in so much detail, using every sense in my armoury. I could see myself walking up to my mum and giving her a huge hug. I would imagine her familiar smell, then what I would say to my twin sister and what she would say to me, and I would imagine seeing my brother in those scruffy shoes that he always wears. It used to take me an hour to imagine that moment, though in reality it was going to last only a few minutes. When I was lonely, scared or in pain it made the time go faster and it stopped me from giving up.

CHOOSE YOUR ATTITUDE

The one element common to many of the scenarios in this book is that we don't have a choice about being in these life-threatening situations. We can attempt to avoid them but some are unavoidable. For example, we have little choice about being involved in a kidnap, a terrorist attack or a natural disaster. Often the situation will be totally out of our control. If this is the case then it is vital to be able to recognize those things that you do have a choice about, rather than wasting time and energy worrying about those things that you have no control over. You may not be able to change the

▼ *Vigilance is the new buzzword of urban survival following the wave of terrorist alerts on public transport.*

DEBRA SEARLE MBE

Debra and her then husband Andrew took part in the Ward Evans Atlantic Rowing Challenge at the end of 2001, but the sudden onset of her husband's phobia meant that he had to be rescued, leaving Debra to face the 5,000km/3,000-mile challenge alone. This she did with incredible bravery, completing her voyage in Barbados after 112 days and gaining universal respect. Her transatlantic adventure became the talk of the media and an inspiration for other people battling against the odds in every area of life.

▲ *Terrorism has changed the way in which we view our chances of survival and how we can prepare ourselves against the unexpected. An obvious example after 9/11 is airport and airline secuirty.*

situation but you can always change the way in which you are responding to it. You can always "choose your attitude".

"Choose your attitude" is more than just a motto – it is a way of life. For this Atlantic rower it was a case of picking an attitude over breakfast every

morning at sea, but it had to be a positive one. Negative attitudes had been banned from on board the rowing boat. So optimism might be the attitude of the day, and a list of all the things there were to be optimistic about had to be formulated. The result was a pretty upbeat feel about what the day might bring, which in reality was crazy considering the situation. There was in fact every reason to have a rotten attitude at sea – being

desperately lonely, scared and not sleeping for more than 20 minutes at a time for fear of collision with a ship or attack by sharks. Rowing for three days might achieve about 50km/30 miles, but then overnight a storm would hit and push the boat back 60km/40 miles. But the key to survival was refusing to dwell on how bad the situation was, and choosing a positive attitude, because that was the one thing about which I had a choice.

▼ *Fortunately, we can learn survival skills such as self-defence for use out on the street when we find ourselves most vulnerable.*

THE KEYS TO SURVIVAL

This book is divided into three major categories that make certain basic assumptions about circumstances The first part looks at the challenges posed by camping and wilderness travel, and offers guidance on how to equip yourself and your travelling companions for a sustained period of outdoor living. From making wise decisions about kit and supplies to camping in comfort or taking on extreme sports, the maxim "be prepared" is central to the process of planning, realizing and relishing the trip of a lifetime.

The second part of the book rehearses strategies for coping when your expedition turns into

more than you bargained for – namely, when you are stripped of resources and forced to survive on the bare essentials of your environment. This might involve finding food and water in seemingly barren conditions, creating a shelter from snow or sand, or treating illnesses without proper medical supplies.

The setting for the third and final part is the everyday urban environment. Whether at home, in the workplace, navigating city streets on foot or taking public transport to a destination, the objective here is to hone instincts and achieve the "best response" when an everyday situation suddenly turns dangerous.

CAMPCRAFT AND TRAVEL

OFF THE BEATEN TRACK

As little as fifty or so years ago, the wilderness areas of the world were places that few people, except the indigenous inhabitants, had any means of exploring. They were virtually the exclusive reserve of a small group of explorers, scientists and travellers, who needed either the backing of large commercial companies or research organizations, or had private means. Today all this has changed. There are now many companies offering adventure holidays, and the relatively low cost of air travel has brought the remotest parts of the world within the reach of many more travellers. The huge number of travel programmes on television have made such places seem familiar, while newspaper articles and guidebooks deliver detailed information on almost every country of the world.

The democratization of travel has meant that the pressure on sometimes fragile environments has increased a hundredfold, so that enthusiastic travellers are in danger of destroying

▼ *Mountain regions offer the adventurous traveller some of the hardest challenges, but also some of the greatest rewards.*

the very places they have set out to see. In some cases national authorities have been forced to impose rules and regulations on people wishing to go to these wilderness areas. In some ways this defeats the wish of people to get back to the simpler, more natural life of the wilderness, but it is a balancing act that must be achieved in order to protect the natural world.

A SHRINKING WILDERNESS?
As an example of this, we only need to visit the base camp area of Mount Everest, where once two or possibly three national expeditions camped each year. Now there are commercial companies taking groups of people up the mountain at a time, and producing large amounts of rubbish and waste in what was once a pristine environment.

In the 1960s you could still visit Mount Kenya or Kilimanjaro, hire your own porter and simply set off up the mountain, so long as you gave your name to the local authority or national park. Now you have to buy into a package that provides you with accommodation, guides, porters and food, taking away much of the fun of

▲ *Travelling on horseback gives you the freedom to roam, and to appreciate all the sounds, smells and sights of the landscape.*

planning your own expedition. But because of the number who wish to climb these mountains, there has to be some sort of control or the very wilderness that everybody is seeking could soon disappear.

PREPARING FOR THE TRIP
The era of fast, cheap world travel has, ironically, brought its own set of problems for the adventure traveller. You can leave London or New York and be in the African bush or on the Arctic tundra within 24 hours, but you may not always be prepared either physically or mentally for the environment you find yourself in. This was not the case in the past, when travel was slower and gave one time to adjust to new environments and acclimatize to the cold, heat or altitude. However, there is much that you can do before you travel in terms of training and planning to allow you to make the most of your trip, whether you are travelling on foot, by boat, with animals or in a vehicle.

This part of the book sets out some of the skills you will need to plan your visit to the wilderness, to stay there comfortably and safely and to enjoy these unique environments. There is

▲ *Carrying all your camping equipment on your back allows you to travel along remote and beautiful paths and stop where you like.*

▼ *The leisurely pace of river travel by kayak or canoe offers a unique approach to a region and a close-up view of nature.*

practical advice on physical preparation before you leave, and on essential equipment for the expedition.

ADVENTURE SPORTS

Of course, there are those for whom the excitement of living outdoors is not quite enough. The chapter on Getting Around and Adventure Sports looks at some of the more innovative ways to travel between destinations, whether you are traversing a rocky cliff as part of a challenging hike, biking across mountainous terrain, navigating coastal waters and rivers by canoe, or journeying through the desert on camelback. Step-by-step guidance anticipates the physical demands of each activity, and how to avoid their possible pitfalls, such as tiredness, blisters or dealing with unruly pack animals. Coverage of some of the basic techniques helps to pinpoint what it takes to succeed in these exciting pursuits so that, when it comes to actually practising them, many

requirements will already be familiar. Remember that, with all of these activities, you should be realistic about the risks involved, and seek the proper trained supervision wherever necessary.

TRAVEL IN SAFETY

However, and wherever, you decide to travel, do remember that all of the wilderness areas of the world are very special and, in many cases, a shrinking asset. The chapter on campcraft looks at ways to create a base camp that is both efficient and environmentally sound. You should be able to leave a site saying that you left it no worse and, if possible, a little better than you found it. This basic respect for nature should inform all of the choices you make on your trip. From recognizing natural hazards to making the most of your resources, this new wisdom will make your journey more rewarding, and enable you, if only for a brief spell, to experience the sheer wonder of the world's great open spaces.

PLANNING & PREPARATION

Good planning is the key to a successful trip and anticipation is a big part of the pleasure of travelling. Careful preparations mean that everything should run smoothly and problems can be coped with rather than turning into crises. Don't make your plans so rigid that you can't enjoy the unforeseen: be prepared to take a different path or follow up an exciting opportunity that presents itself during your trip.

Planning your trip

Some degree of planning is necessary for any kind of trip. The complexity of your planning will depend on factors such as the remoteness of the area, the size of the group, and the length of the trip, but there are several decisions that have to be made in advance for even the most straightforward of outings.

Start the planning by thinking of the type of trip you want to take. When you have decided what this is, you can start to think about the destination, the people who will be going with you, the route, the means of travel, and the length of time you will be away.

You may not be able to make final decisions without doing some research, using maps, guidebooks or the internet, and you may need to adapt or change your plans as you gather information about what is involved. This is why planning is so important. The more thoroughly you think through your ideas and construct your plan, the less chance you have of encountering unexpected problems during your trip.

DOMESTIC TRIPS

If you are going on a walking week somewhere in your own country, then choosing your destination and your travelling companions, finding out train times or planning a car journey, calling the local tourist information office for information about campsites and buying suitable maps are the key tasks. You will have to consider what type of clothing and equipment you are likely to need, and if you do not own some of the items already, you may have to borrow or buy them. It is important for safety and comfort that your clothing and equipment are suitable for the climate, and some research into the kind of weather you can expect will prove invaluable.

Depending on the activities you are planning, you may need to buy additional insurance or brush up your skills with some training. Health concerns may need to be addressed, and you should familiarize yourself with basic first aid skills.

▲ A day's kayaking can give you a new perspective on an area, so check out the range of activities available at your destination.

◀ Find out about the terrain and expected weather conditions – how you cope with these is central to the success of your trip.

FOREIGN TRIPS

If you are going further afield, your planning may involve booking trains, ferries or planes, obtaining permits to walk or climb, hiring transport or obtaining paperwork for your vehicle, as well as obtaining visas, vaccinations and an international driving licence – all in addition to the things you need for a domestic trip.

If you are hoping to travel part of your route by cycle, horse or canoe, some practice sessions are a good idea to ensure that potential problems are identified and sorted out before you are out in the field. A cycle touring trip, where the bike is loaded with heavy gear, is very different from a day's cycling in the countryside; and even if you can already ride a horse, if you are planning an expedition on horseback, you need to know how to feed and

PLANNING AND PREPARATION CHECKLIST

12 months ahead
- Decide on the destination, route and aims of the trip.
- Decide on the group members.
- Think about transport options.
- Think about the activities to be undertaken.
- Carry out your risk assessment.
- Seek permission from countries or places to be visited.
- Produce an outline budget.
- Produce an information sheet on the area to be visited.

10–12 months ahead
- Hold the first meeting for the group.
- Finalize the dates of the trips.
- Check that all members have passed any medical examinations required
- Finalize the details of any activities to be undertaken.
- Agree the dates of any training sessions.
- Have a camping weekend with all the people going on your trip.

8–10 months ahead
- Finalize the list of equipment needed.
- Draw up a personal equipment list.
- Arrange insurance (medical, personal, third party indemnity, and so on).
- Draw up an outline menu and food requirements.
- Book any ferry crossings, flights, rail tickets, campsites or hotels.
- Appoint a home contact.

4 months ahead
- Check all passports and other travel documentation.
- Obtain any visas required.
- Start any vaccination programme required.
- Finalize food and menus.
- Finalize the itinerary for the trip.

1 month ahead
- Obtain any additional paperwork.
- Pack all non-perishable food.
- Gather together, check and pack all equipment.
- Check and make ready any vehicles

you will be using.
- Send any freight ahead.
- Change money and buy travellers' cheques, if using.

1 week ahead
- Complete all vaccination programmes; start to take malaria tablets, if appropriate.
- Check all equipment and food against lists.
- Go through the complete itinerary with the home contact.

1 day ahead
- Check your tickets.
- Check your kit and make sure you have packed everything.
- Check with the airport, ferry port or train station that there has been no change or delay to your transport plans.
- Make sure your hand luggage does not have anything in it that will cause you problems at airport security checks.

care for the horses at night. If you are travelling to a remote area and will be a long way from professional medical services, your first aid preparations need to be substantial. You may have to follow a vaccination programme before you travel, and you will need to take considerably more with you in your first-aid kit. In terms of first aid skills, a wider knowledge is invaluable for expeditions to remote areas or involving higher-risk activities, such as mountaineering: in the event of an accident, your chances of survival are far greater if you know what to do.

For such an expedition, planning should start at least 12 months before the trip. The checklist shown above is one that you may find useful. It is only a starting point, and you may find that you can leave some of the items out and/or add some of your own.

▶ *An off-road cycling trip can be hard going, and a programme of fitness training may be necessary for several months before you travel.*

First thoughts

There are many different aspects to consider when organizing a trip in the wilderness, and numerous detailed plans need to be made. The enormity of the project can seem very daunting when you first begin to think it through, but if you break the task down and deal with each aspect one by one, the planning will be easier to manage and you will soon find that you have resolved all the issues.

▼ *Children can greatly enjoy a trip to the wilderness, but make sure you make your plans for the trip with them in mind.*

THE TEAM

If you are choosing a team, think about the number of people that will work best for the activities you are planning. If it is a large group, it may be a good idea to have a designated leader. Choose your travelling companions with care and bear in mind that people react in different ways to the pressures of life in the wilderness. The group needs to be compatible, with roughly equal levels of fitness. Encourage individuals to talk about what they hope to gain from the experience: taking on board everyone's comments

and establishing objectives is the first step in the organizational strategy. If team members do not know each other in advance, plan a trial camping weekend to see how you all get along. For more information, see the section Getting your team together, 20–21.

BUDGET

Once your plans have been drafted, you need to work out a realistic budget. It is important to do this early on so that you can amend your plans to fit the budget if the total works out to be more than you want to spend. Do not underestimate costs and include a contingency fund of at least 15 per cent of the total. For more information, see the section Planning the budget, 22.

INSURANCE

Never overlook insurance, and make sure you are covered for the activities you are planning, as well as for your life, health and possessions in the area you are visiting. See also the section Money and Insurance, 23.

EQUIPMENT

A list of personal and group equipment can be drawn up only once you have chosen the team and decided where you are travelling to, when you are going, and what you are going to do when you get there. For information on what to take with you, see the chapter on Equipment, 44–95.

MEDICAL PROVISIONS AND FITNESS

If you are in doubt about whether there will be reasonable access to medical help in the area you are travelling to, you may prefer to have someone in the team with reliable first aid knowledge; discuss the most appropriate type of training with your team. Check if you need vaccinations or any particular medication, such as malaria tablets, and consider what level of fitness the team will require for the activities you have planned. For more information, see the section Medical preparations, 30.

PLANNING FOR A GROUP

You may be planning a trip for an existing group of people – your family, for example – and this might mean that you need to accommodate a fairly wide range of abilities and interests.

- If you're travelling with children, make sure you know their limits and don't push them too hard.
- Keep your plans flexible and be ready to compromise: tired, irritable children will wreck everyone's day. If you are crossing time zones, give children plenty of time to adapt.
- Build some rest days into your itinerary. The strongest, fittest members of the group can use these days for additional, more challenging excursions if they wish, returning to camp to meet up with the group in the evening.

TRANSPORT

Consider how best to transport the team and all of its equipment to your destination. Bear in mind that the means of travel will affect the amount of luggage you can take with you.

If your trip is being planned as a simple loop, starting and finishing in the same place, you can drive to the location and leave your car (or hire car) for when you get back, or you may be able to arrange a pick-up from a family member or friend. Depending on the size of the group, you may find it easier (particularly with a group of young people) and more enjoyable to hire a multi-seater vehicle and travel together, rather than make your own way there in individual cars.

If you are planning to travel by public transport, check that there is a connecting service all the way to the start of the route, and work out how you will get there if there isn't. If you require seat reservations – which is advisable for a larger group of people – you will need to book early. Be prepared for departure delays or cancellations, with a contingency plan and a budget in case you are faced with unexpected accommodation costs. Check that you will be able to carry bulky equipment such as bicycles or kayaks and all the related gear. If travelling by plane, find out about the weight allowance and the penalty that you will be liable to pay if you exceed it. For information on taking your car abroad, see the section Vehicle-related paperwork, 28–29.

▲ *Some team members may see the trip as a chance for relaxation, while others may be making plans for an action-packed adventure. Find out what individuals expect to gain from the trip so that you can plan accordingly.*

▼ *Travelling by plane will affect the amount of equipment you can carry, so your means of transport should be one of your first decisions.*

Getting your team together

Having the right people in your team will add to the enjoyment of your trip and will help to make it a more valuable experience. Suitable travelling companions are as important as the right equipment, and they need to be given just as much thought.

CHOOSING AN OBJECTIVE

Whether you are planning a trip with family members, or with friends, or as part of a team of new acquaintances, encourage people to communicate their expectations and goals for the trip before you go, and try to synchronize these goals into a common objective for the team. A shared objective is a good incentive that will encourage cohesion in the group. Spend time discussing likely situations and deal with concerns until you have a clear objective that you can all feel happy with, and one that is well within the capabilities of everyone.

CHOOSING TEAM MEMBERS

If you have an idea for a trip and are now choosing others to go with you, pick people with whom you get along and who have a level of experience similar to your own. Make sure they are compatible with each other, and seem happy with the idea of teamwork and group decision-making, and that they share your objectives for the trip.

If you need individuals with specific skills, such as first aid, be clear about their level of skill and check that their training is up to date; if it is not, ask them to take a refresher course.

A similar level of physical and mental fitness across the team is important. It may seem unkind to reject someone because of ill-health or injury, but an unfit person can slow down and even endanger the whole group. If conditions will be demanding, consider whether individuals are up to the challenge, or will turn out to be complainers.

PROMOTING TEAM SPIRIT

- Encourage team members to write a list of personal goals while you are still at the early planning stages, and try to build their aims into the schedule to encourage their commitment.
- Get an agreement on rules from the whole group before you set off, to avoid misunderstandings and conflict on the expedition.
- A trial camping weekend is a good way to see how a new group gets on together. It will encourage team bonding, and will also identify any problem personalities while there is time to do something about them.

▼ *A shared agenda, common goals and compatible personalities among the team are key features for a successful trip.*

▶ *Good communication is essential, and leaders need to talk to the group at least once a day to keep everybody informed.*

LEADERSHIP

For a trip involving a large group of people, it is a good idea to have a leader. This person can be self-appointed or chosen by the group, but he or she must command sufficient respect to be able to direct the group under good and bad conditions. The leader role is especially important with a group of children, or when travelling in unfamiliar or difficult terrain, or if the planned activities require a specific skill or experience.

With a group of adult friends, the leadership role can be informal, but for a group of above 20 people, a bigger leadership structure may be needed, and other team members can be asked to take responsibility for particular concerns, such as driving or first aid.

Communication

This is the most important skill a leader can exercise. A leader needs sound judgement and has to be able to lead discussions and communicate effectively, delegate tasks, and act as a mediator in the event of disagreement or conflict. Communication is especially important when people are in difficult conditions and possibly suffering stress and panic. If communication fails, members will at best become dissatisfied and the whole trip may become an unhappy experience. At worst, the group may come to grief.

Personality problems

A clash of personalities needs to be sorted out as soon as possible (preferably before you leave if you spot it that soon). If the group starts to break up into cliques, its common objective will become more difficult to achieve. Fun bonding activities, such as team games, can help to restore team spirit.

Always avoid showing favouritism. If it is noticed, some individuals may feel undervalued, and it could act as a spark for bad behaviour or aggression.

POSSIBLE ROLES FOR TEAM MEMBERS

The list below gives an idea of the different areas of responsibility that exist within a team. You may need only some of these in your group.

Deputy leader

To take over from the leader if anything happens to him or her before or during the trip.

Quartermaster

To be responsible for all equipment and food, and for looking after and issuing these throughout the trip.

Field treasurer

To approve the final budget, record all expenditure in the field and make sure the money lasts for the duration of the trip; may also be in charge of safeguarding funds and valuables.

Head of camp kitchen

To appoint a daily team and organize a rota to carry out food preparation, cooking, and washing-up duties, to oversee those duties and to draw up appropriate daily menus.

Medic or first aider

To treat team injuries and illnesses during the trip, and to look after the group first-aid kit; for larger groups, to keep a record of allergies or intolerances and any prescription medication being taken by anyone in the team; to record any illness or accidents that happen during the trip and the treatment given; could also be responsible for pre-expedition medical check-ups, vaccination programmes and fitness sessions.

Navigator

To look after and carry the maps and compass, to advise on the planning of the route, and to ensure that all team members follow the correct route.

Translator

To communicate on behalf of the group when travelling in a foreign country with a native language different to your own. Someone who can understand a handful of phrases and key words is enormously useful.

Planning the budget

The first task when you are planning the finances for a trip is to work out how much money you will need. The next task is to decide how the money is going to be spent. For both of these processes you will need a budget. The budget outline here is a starting point to which you can add or subtract headings to suit your trip.

BEING REALISTIC

Make your budget realistic and err on the side of caution, so that you can be confident you will be able to pay for all aspects of the trip. If you are worrying about money while you are away, your enjoyment will suffer.

Plan your budget in advance to give you time to research the costs fully. If you cannot get confirmed prices, get as many estimates as you can. Note the best price (lowest) and the worst price (highest) and budget in between the two. Ideally, the budgeted figures will

▲ *Even a simple backpacking trip involves costs, and you need to think about every aspect of the trip to plan a useful budget.*

work out just about right or too high. If they don't, you will have to dip into your contingency fund to cover basic expenditure, such as food, transport and accommodation, and there will be less money available for an emergency that necessitates a sudden change of plan.

BANK FEES

If you need to buy foreign currency, plan for bank charges for money changing and for transferring money abroad. If you have opened a bank account for the trip, budget for the charges that apply to any account.

FOOD AND EQUIPMENT

If travelling by public transport, check that you will not exceed the baggage allowance on your ticket, as this can incur charges. Goods can be freighted, but this can be expensive, and getting through customs can be costly in terms of money and time. Find out if it would be cheaper to buy food and equipment at your destination.

CONTINGENCY

Like insurance, this is essential. Allow at least 15 per cent if your trip will include vehicle transport, as you may need to pay cash for mechanical repairs.

BUDGET OUTLINE

Administration
- Postage
- Telephone/fax/ internet charges
- Publicity
- Passports and visas

Equipment
- Buy
- Hire

Training
- Canoeing or kayaking/ horse riding/cycling/ skiing
- First aid

Transport
- Plane/ferry/train/bus/taxi
- Vehicle hire
- Animal hire

Freight
- Equipment
- Vehicles

Insurance
- Personal
- Vehicle

Bank charges
- Currency changing
- Bank transfers

Food
- Buy at home
- Buy abroad

Field expenses
- Living costs
- Hire of guides/local people
- Fuel
- Customs and port duty
- Gifts
- Miscellaneous

Post-expedition expenses
- Administration
- Photography

15% contingency fund

Money and insurance

When planning any kind of expedition, you need to consider the safest and most convenient way of carrying money. Make sure you have adequate insurance cover for all of your planned activities.

MONEY

There are a number of ways to take the money you will need in the field. Try to pay for as much as possible in advance, so that you do not have the additional risk of carrying large sums of money with you.

Travellers' cheques

These are far less tempting to thieves because they can be used only with a passport as proof of identification. Buy travellers' cheques in the currency of your destination or, if these are not available, in the currency most acceptable there. A mixture of small and large denominations is the most useful. People and businesses in rural areas and in some developing countries do not accept travellers' cheques as payment, and it will be necessary to take cash in the local currency with you as well.

Cash restrictions

In some countries, in order to control the income generated by tourism, it is necessary to change a certain amount of money per person into the local currency, and you may not be allowed to change it back again or to take it out of the country. Find out if such rules apply at your destination before you travel, and budget accordingly.

Credit cards

You may not be able to use credit cards outside larger centres of population or international hotels, and check service charges and exchange rates before using credit cards to withdraw cash from ATMs abroad. Company credit cards are available for services such as car hire. International car hire companies issue them, and anything spent on the card is billed to you in your own currency, which makes it easier to check what has been spent.

INSURANCE

Standard holiday insurance will cover your needs for most trips, but you may need to take out specialist insurance for more adventurous activities.

Personal accident insurance

Standard holiday insurance will usually include a pay-out for personal accident claims, but ensure that it gives adequate cover for death, loss of a limb or sight.

Medical insurance

If you are going to an area with inadequate or non-existent medical services, air ambulance cover will be essential. You may also require separate rescue insurance if you plan to be in a remote or mountainous area, or if you are sea-touring in a canoe or kayak.

Baggage insurance

Most holiday insurance policies include an amount for delayed or lost baggage. Expensive items such as cameras and jewellery should be properly insured; avoid taking valuable items that are not necessary for the trip. Household insurance may cover some items, but always read the small print on your policy before you travel.

Credit card insurance

Always be insured against the loss or theft of credit cards because cards are such an obvious target for thieves.

▼ *Even if you intend to carry travellers' cheques and credit cards, you should still take some cash in small denominations.*

Note the telephone number of the lost or stolen card department of your card issuer and keep it with you in a safe place, separate from your credit card.

Hazardous pursuits insurance

Winter sports, mountaineering, boating, diving, big game hunting and other hazardous pursuits usually require specific insurance, even if you are not travelling abroad. Check the details of your standard holiday insurance policy to see what it will and will not include. As there is a greater risk of injury with these activities, insurance is essential.

Third-party insurance

It is sensible to have this in case, for any reason, you harm, or even kill, someone, or cause damage to their property. Third-party insurance is usually included in standard holiday policies, but check before you travel.

Vehicle insurance

If you are hiring a vehicle or taking your own with you, make sure you have sufficient cover for the country you will be driving in, as well as any countries you may need to drive through to get there.

Light aircraft insurance

If your plans include flying in a light aircraft, check that you are covered with your personal accident insurance. If you will be flying the aircraft yourself, it may count as a hazardous pursuit and require separate insurance.

Risk assessment

As a member of a team, you have a responsibility to yourself and to the other members of your team. It is essential to assess the possible risks that any activity undertaken on the trip could bring, where team members might be harmed and how high the level of risk is.

WHY ASSESS RISK?

Risk assessment is the evaluation of an activity to determine what could go wrong, who could be hurt and what could be done to manage the identified problems. Accidents will happen, but efficient risk assessment will reduce the potential for accidents and enable lessons to be learned from near misses and actual incidents.

IDENTIFYING HAZARDS

Mentally step back from the activity and look at it from a fresh point of view, concentrating on those aspects that could result in serious harm. Ask people who are unfamiliar with the activity what they think, as they might identify areas not immediately obvious to a regular practitioner. Equipment manufacturers' instructions may also help you to identify hazards and risks.

You should take into account other potential hazards, too, including natural disasters, extreme weather conditions, acclimatization to high altitude, dangerous wildlife and the safety of

▼ *A good guidebook can highlight potential dangers in a region, but check foreign office websites for the latest and most reliable information.*

local drinking water. If mountain rescue services could be needed, check that they will be available. Be aware of medical/health hazards and make sure that everyone has had the necessary inoculations. A good guidebook should be able to provide this information. Your journey may take you into a politically unstable area, where civil war, guerrilla warfare, kidnapping for ransom, or terrorist activity may be a threat. Foreign office websites will usually have the most up-to-date and reliable information.

When undertaking any activity, those most obviously at risk are the participants and their instructors, but you also need to gauge the potential for harm to those waiting to take part, spectators and passers-by.

EVALUATING RISK

Having identified the separate elements of the activity, you need to assign a level of risk to each element. Grade the level of risk from high to moderate or low, and take into account the past history of the activity, which may include actual incidents as well as any near misses.

▲ *An off-road mountain biking trip seems like a low-risk activity, but the potential for injury is high, especially for novices.*

A change of operating technique, additional equipment or increased training might be all that is needed to reduce the level of risk and therefore improve safety, without eliminating the

▼ *Guerrilla warfare presents a serious risk to personal safety: it is advisable to change your plans if this appears to be a hazard.*

element of challenge. Check the small print of your insurance policies (personal, vehicle and group policies) to be sure you have a level of cover that reflects the risk involved.

▲ Basic training before the trip is advisable for activities such as canoeing, where some knowledge of the skills will improve safety.

▼ Fitness and discipline are important in mountain country or on rough terrain, where careless accidents can easily happen.

RECORD KEEPING
Keep records of when equipment and facilities to be used by your team were acquired (new or used), their service history, any repairs or changes, and incidents that happen on your trip. The records should be made available to any other people who may wish to use the equipment in the future.

ASSESSMENT PROCEDURE

- Look at the hazards.
- Decide who may be harmed and how.
- Evaluate the risks arising from the hazards and decide whether existing procedures are adequate or if more should be done.
- Record your findings.
- Consult your risk assessment during your trip, and revise as necessary.
- Review your assessment after your trip and revise as necessary.

Personal paperwork

Paperwork may not be the most exciting part of travel, but it is vitally important. If you arrive at a border or get stopped by the police, you could be in real trouble if you do not have the correct personal documents.

PASSPORT

Make sure you have at least six months of life left on your passport if you are going to a country where you require a visa. Most visas will require at least a half page and in many cases a full page of your passport, so make sure you have sufficient pages empty in your passport.

Some countries issue passports with more than the normal number of pages in them, so if you are completing lots of international travel, especially to countries that require visas, it is worth considering getting one of these. Otherwise, if the normal one runs out of pages before it has expired, you will have to pay for another passport.

VISAS

These are a way for a country to control who gets into it and, in some cases, to make money from visitors and tourists. Visa regulations are constantly under review as immigration policies change and are revised from time to time.

You should telephone the embassy of the country you wish to visit while you are still in your own country, or contact its website on the internet, to find out if you will need a visa.

Visas for which you need to make an application can be obtained from the relevant embassy in your own country, either in person or by post. Depending on your nationality, your reason for travel and your destination, the issuing time can vary from hours to weeks. If you are sending your passport and visa application, plus the fee, by post, make sure you use a registered postal service and make a note of your passport number or photocopy the information pages of your passport before you post it. To get into some countries, you will also need to be sponsored by someone already living and working there. Always make sure you read the requirements of a visa very carefully because if you get it wrong and are refused entry, you may never be allowed a visa again.

If you are already abroad, you will usually be able to get your visa from the appropriate embassy in a neighbouring country. This can take time: in some cases, up to several weeks. Do not lose your patience with the embassy system or its staff; it will not speed up the process and it could lead to further delays, if not a refusal of the visa.

This is one instance where it pays to plan ahead. Decide if you are going to visit any country for which you need a visa while you are planning your trip. This will allow you plenty of time to apply for the visa(s) while you are still at home.

◄ *Keep your passport and other papers secure, not only while travelling but also between trips, as they have a high value on the black market.*

DRIVING LICENCE

Take a photocopy of your national driving licence, even if you know that you need an international driving permit to drive abroad. A national licence with your photograph on it will be accepted by most car hire companies abroad as a form of identification and proof of your ability to drive.

INTERNATIONAL DRIVING PERMIT

This document is recognized worldwide as proof that you hold a valid driving licence in your own country. The international driving permit (IDP) does not have to be carried as a legal requirement for foreign drivers in every country, because many countries recognize each others' licences, but it is intended to help motorists driving abroad, where licence requirements can vary widely, and it can be an advantage to be able to produce it if you run into difficulties with the transport authorities. It may also be a useful form of pictured identification in the case of a lost or stolen passport.

The international driving permit is printed in 10 languages – the five official languages of the United Nations (English, French, Spanish, Russian and Chinese) plus German, Arabic, Italian, Swedish and Portuguese. It is available, on payment of a small fee, from motoring organizations in the country in which your national driving licence was issued.

RECORD OF VACCINATIONS

Medical organizations and even some airlines now issue booklets in which you can record all the vaccinations you have had and when you had them. These are a convenient reminder to keep vaccinations up to date and they may also provide some sort of proof, if they are in a semi-official booklet, to a border guard or local doctor that you have received the vaccinations. If you do not have a booklet, note the vaccinations you have had and when you had them on a piece of paper and keep it with your passport.

INTERNATIONAL CERTIFICATE OF VACCINATION

Also known as the Yellow Card, this is internationally recognized proof that you have immunization against certain diseases, including measles, mumps, rubella, typhoid, hepatitis A, yellow fever and polio – all of which are recommended if you are travelling to developing countries or to rural or undeveloped areas of developed countries. It is issued by the doctor or medical organization that gave you the vaccination. Make sure the certificate is properly filled in and date-stamped with the official stamp of the centre, otherwise it may not be accepted. In some countries, you may be asked for the certificate at the border; if you do not have it, you will usually be offered the vaccination on the spot – to be administered by non-medical staff working in poor conditions and with a risk of dirty needles – or no entry.

INTERNATIONAL CAMPING CARNET

This document is issued by camping organizations worldwide, and has your passport details added to it. At many campsites you may be able to hand it in instead of your passport, which allows you to keep your passport for changing money, cashing travellers' cheques or any other reason, including peace of mind. Campsites are not obliged to accept the carnet in place of your passport, so find out in advance what the policy is at the campsites you intend to use.

CURRENCY DECLARATION

In some countries, a declaration of foreign currency has to be filled in at the border. This covers high-value items such as cameras and jewellery as well as money. Though it won't always happen, the documents can be requested when you leave the country, to check you haven't sold the items, so fill them in correctly and do not lose them.

▲ *Visa requirements vary widely between countries, depending on your nationality. Check foreign office websites for the latest information regarding what you need.*

▼ *If you are planning to paddle on rivers or lakes, check that the water has unlimited public access and you are not trespassing on private land, particularly when you are abroad or unfamiliar with local by-laws.*

Vehicle-related paperwork

If you are planning to take a vehicle abroad with you, you should allow time to assemble all the relevant paperwork that is needed in addition to your national and international driving licences. In some countries, you could run into serious difficulties if you are stopped by the police without the correct documentation, and a lack of adequate insurance could be disastrous in the event of a breakdown or accident.

Vehicle-related documents are usually issued by driving organizations in your own country. If you are unsure about what you will need contact one of these organizations for up-to-date advice before you travel.

REGISTRATION DOCUMENTS

These documents will be required to prove ownership of the vehicle you are driving if you are stopped by the police or if you try to cross a national border.

INSURANCE PAPERS

Always carry the original paperwork for the insurance cover you have in your own country, and make sure the policy is valid. If you are taking your vehicle abroad, international insurance is available from national motoring organizations and insurance companies.

Additional protection is provided by the Green Card, which is recognized in over 40 countries (mostly in Europe, but including Russia, Iraq and Iran) as part of a United Nations system to protect motorists abroad. The Green Card does not provide insurance cover but is proof that the requirements for third-party liability insurance in the countries for which the Green Card is valid are covered by the motorist's insurance policy in their own country. Contact motoring organizations in your own country to find out if you are eligible and for further details.

INTERNATIONAL CERTIFICATE FOR MOTOR VEHICLES

This is a vehicle passport and is valid for one year. It gives the registration document information in a number of different languages. Although the number of countries that accept it is limited, it is worth having for its translation of the information about the vehicle – which you may find useful if you need to visit a garage for mechanical repairs and you don't speak the local language. It also provides a way of recording your vehicle entering and leaving a country.

LETTER OF AUTHORITY

If you are driving a vehicle of which you are not the owner, such as a hire car, you will require a letter from the owner or the hire company stating your registration details, that you have their permission to drive the vehicle, and in what countries you will be travelling.

CUSTOMS CARNET

In some countries, you will be required to have a customs carnet to take a vehicle from one country to another, and to avoid having to pay customs duty on the vehicle. When you arrive at the border on leaving or entering, your papers will be checked and you will be asked to put up a bond – ostensibly to cover the cost of the customs duty, although the bond can be up to several times the cost of the

◀ *There are many advantages to travelling in your own vehicle, but you could run into difficulties without the correct paperwork.*

vehicle – before the carnet will be issued. Contact the relevant embassy before you travel to find out if a customs carnet is needed and how much the bond will be.

COPIES OF PAPERWORK

Take photocopies of all vehicle-related paperwork and keep them separate from the originals, so that if the latter are lost or stolen, you will still have proof of your entitlement to drive the vehicle. It may also be useful to carry a few passport photographs in the vehicle, as well as photocopies of the information pages of your passport.

If you are carrying valuable, bulky or unusual equipment in your vehicle, it can be a good idea to have a list of the items to produce when crossing borders. If you can get the list stamped in advance by the embassy of the country you are entering, it can help to smooth your way through customs.

▲ *Vehicle-related documents can be kept in the car, but store them in a safe place away from other gear, and keep copies separately.*

▼ *It can be useful to carry an itemized list of valuable equipment, such as work or study equipment, to produce at border crossings.*

Medical preparations

Part of your preparation before the trip is to find out which medical issues might affect the team and how you should protect yourselves. The medical problems you are most likely to encounter will vary depending on your destination. Follow the advice given in up-to-date guidebooks to the region you are visiting and contact specialist medical organizations for current advice and guidelines.

Your family doctor will be best placed to answer any questions relating to your current physical health and how it may be affected by, for example, changes of diet or extreme climatic conditions. A vaccination programme can guard against some of the endemic

disease hazards, while specialist clothing or sleeping nets will help to protect you from the insects that carry the diseases. In other cases, you will be able to avoid ill-health or injury by knowing of potential risks and adapting your behaviour accordingly. You also need to know what medical facilities and emergency services will be available in the area you are visiting, and if you will be entitled to use them free of charge.

VACCINATIONS

Before you leave, everybody going on the trip should have all the vaccinations specifically required for the area you are travelling to, which could include

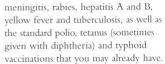

HEALTH WARNING

Some health conditions can cause serious complications while you are away. You are advised to seek medical advice about the suitability of your trip if any of the following conditions apply to you:
- Existing serious injuries
- Asthma
- Epilepsy
- Migraine
- Pregnancy
- High blood pressure
- Heart disease
- Cancer
- Contagious diseases

meningitis, rabies, hepatitis A and B, yellow fever and tuberculosis, as well as the standard polio, tetanus (sometimes given with diphtheria) and typhoid vaccinations that you may already have.

Individual team members must be responsible for checking whether they need boosters of previous vaccinations, but you may need to provide the relevant information and remind them to make sure they are adequately protected. If you are travelling with children or young people, liaise with their parents or guardians to get vaccinations organized. Everyone should make sure that all the necessary vaccination certificates are in order.

Depending on your destination, malaria tablets may be necessary, and you will need to find out well in advance about when to start the course of tablets. Your family doctor or travel agent may not have this information or be fully up to date, and it may be preferable to contact a medical organization that specializes in endemic and tropical diseases, and has the latest information available for travellers. Many airline companies also offer a vaccination advisory service.

◀ *A good level of health and physical fitness will make a walking trip more enjoyable, and can help to safeguard you against injury.*

CHECK-UPS

Have a full medical check-up before you travel if you are going away for a long time, or if you are travelling to a developing country or to an undeveloped region of a developed country where the medical services may not be as good as they are at home, or if you know that medical care will be very expensive.

If a qualified doctor or medic is to accompany you on the trip, they could be asked to carry out check-ups on team members. Individuals should also be asked to fill in a questionnaire regarding their past medical history, any prescribed medication they currently take, and any drugs or foods to which they are allergic.

The parents or guardians of children or young people should be asked for this information on their children's behalf, and should sign a form giving permission for medication to be given to the child in an emergency.

Ensure that all team members have a reasonable standard of physical fitness. This will help them to acclimatize to the more difficult living conditions outdoors, and will make them less prone to injury. Anyone in doubt about an ongoing health issue should talk to their own doctor before they travel. If you feel that an individual's condition could pose a risk to the rest of the team you may need to ask them to drop out.

DENTAL CARE

Persistent toothache will spoil your trip and if you are going to be away for more than a couple of weeks neglected tooth decay could lead to an abscess, infection and even blood poisoning. Have a dental check-up before you travel if you have not visited the dentist recently, and leave enough time for any treatment that proves necessary to be completed before you travel. If you are going to a high altitude or to a very cold country, local climatic conditions can bring on severe toothache in any unfilled cavities.

▶ *Learn as much as you can about the conditions you will be living in, and think about how this will impact on your health.*

HEALTH WARNING

Your personal safety is at risk if you do not take adequate measures for existing medical conditions or against contracting disease.

▲ *If you are heading for a remote area where you know that medical services will not be available, you must make sure you take with you all that you need for any existing medical conditions, as well as an adequate stock of first aid supplies and medication for everyday ailments.*

Medical and first-aid kits

The size and type of your first-aid or medical kits will depend on the nature of your expedition, the amount of time you will be away and the standard of your first aid or medical training.

If you will be doing a range of activities during the course of your trip, or will be travelling in different climates, you may need a greater range of first aid items or even a number of different kits to be fully prepared. Larger groups will have the capacity to carry a more comprehensive medical kit, kept in a vehicle or at the base camp, which caters for everything up to minor operations. Even so, basic first-aid kits still need to be carried by individuals, so that they can give first aid care in the field.

WHAT TO INCLUDE

When deciding on the size of the kit and what to put in it, think about the conditions in the area, the potential for risk of the activities being planned and the kind of accidents that may happen.

If you feel you need informed advice about what to include for an informal trip or with a small group, buy a standard first-aid kit and take it to your family doctor or to a specialist organization; ask them for suggestions of additional items and non-prescription drugs to include. One such item may be an emollient cream such as zinc and castor oil, which is useful for common skin conditions such as sweat rashes.

Larger groups may have a designated first aider or medically trained person, whose responsibility it will be to compile an appropriate medical kit. A standard kit will then be all that individual team members need to carry as part of their own personal equipment.

If you are travelling to a part of the world where AIDS is a major threat, or where you are not sure of the standard of medical care, include a sterile needle kit in case injections are needed. Keep the contents sealed in the case provided, so that they remain sterile and if your luggage is opened by customs officials or police you cannot be accused of using the needles for drugs.

Whatever the size of your medical or first-aid kit, make sure that all items are kept clean and are clearly labelled and easy to identify. If you need to use the kit in an emergency situation, you will want to find what you are looking for quickly.

Before your trip, attend a first aid course or a refresher course to learn or brush up on procedures for the following medical conditions. (For more information, see the chapter Life-saving First Aid, 488–507.)
- Resuscitation
- Recovery position
- Choking
- Shock
- Drowning
- Bites and stings
- Wounds
- Animal, reptile and insect bites
- Burns and scalds
- Sprains
- Fractures
- Effects of hot weather and cold weather

STANDARD FIRST AID ITEMS

- Plasters and adhesive dressings
- Sterile dressings
- Gauze pads
- Crêpe bandages
- Thermometer
- Small pair of scissors
- Sterile scalpel
- Safety pins
- Disposable gloves

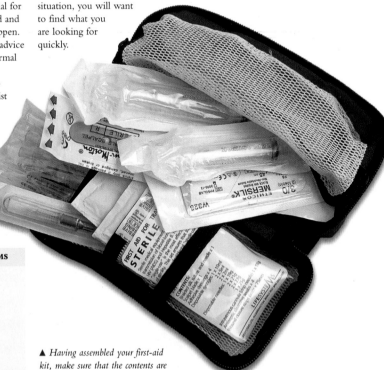

▲ *Having assembled your first-aid kit, make sure that the contents are labelled and well organized, and that the kit is always kept clean and dry.*

FIRST AID PRINCIPLES

Know your kit

It is immediately reassuring for an injury victim if you can produce a well-equipped first-aid kit when you give them treatment. It will also help you to handle the situation with confidence if you know that you have certain essential items with you. However, it is vital that you are familiar with the items in your kit. This includes knowing what they are, what to use them for, and how to use them correctly.

Practical knowledge

The casualty will feel calmer if you can dress and bandage an injury quickly and professionally, but if you become flustered and need to keep unwrapping the bandage to start again, they will start to panic.

Think on your feet

Nothing in your first-aid kit is as important as your ability to act swiftly and improvise with whatever materials you have to hand, while constantly reassuring the casualty to prevent panic.

Making contact

Communication with the outside world can be a key factor in dealing with a serious first aid situation. Focus on making the best use of whatever is available – passers-by, telephones or air and sea rescue services. Learn the international signalling codes, and be confident that you can give an accurate grid reference to locate your exact position. One day, somebody's life may depend on it.

FIRST AID TRAINING

At least one person in the team should have a good standard of up-to-date basic first aid training, but all team members can be encouraged to familiarize themselves with key first aid skills. There is no doubt that the more people in the team with first aid training, the safer the trip will be for all.

If the risk assessment has highlighted any particular areas of risk associated with your destination or activity, consider what specific training the first aider may need, such as how to treat snake bite, hypothermia, frostbite, heat stroke, dehydration or drowning. For health issues relating to specific activities, it's sensible to contact a specialist organization for advice and possible additional training.

Find out as much as possible about the medical facilities available at your destination. This kind of information is available from guidebooks, tourist information services and possibly from the relevant embassy. You will need to know the standard of local hospitals, where the nearest major towns and cities are, and the quickest way to get to them from a rural area; whether there is a 24-hour accident and

emergency facility and how good it is, and how you would go about getting an airlift rescue if someone became seriously ill or injured. The more basic and inaccessible the medical facilities, the more comprehensive your medical kit and training need to be.

▲ *Activities such as cycling introduce injury risks that can be prepared for if they have been identified in your risk assessment.*

▼ *Accidents can happen in any situation, and you need to be aware of the potential hazards in the environment you will be in.*

Physical fitness

The level of personal fitness you should have for your trip will depend on what the trip entails. If you are planning some mountain biking or white-water canoeing, for example, you will need a more advanced level of fitness than if you are planning low-level walking, though you should still be physically fit and mentally prepared.

If you are travelling as part of a team, remember that you have a responsibility to the other team members to stay as fit and healthy as you can. One person's ill health or lack of fitness may cause problems and could endanger the rest of the group. Regular, gentle exercise every day for at least a month before the trip will help to protect you against illness and injury.

ALL-ROUND FITNESS AND PERFORMANCE

To achieve a level of all-round physical fitness appropriate for camping trips and outdoor activities, the following components are essential: endurance; strength; flexibility; speed; agility; balance; coordination; and reaction time. Of these, endurance and flexibility are the most relevant here.

◀ *Cycling is good cardiovascular endurance training, and is very effective for the large powerful muscles in the thighs.*

▲ *Swimming provides an excellent workout, building stamina and promoting all-round fitness without straining any of the muscles.*

ENDURANCE

This means being able to continue physical activity for a long time, and it is the most important component of fitness. The fitter the person, the greater the level of endurance. There are two different types of endurance: cardiovascular and muscular.

Cardiovascular endurance

This involves the lungs, the heart, the blood and the blood vessels. It is the ability to exercise the whole body for long periods of time without running out of breath or becoming tired.

To build up your cardiovascular performance, work out a plan to undertake a series of fairly vigorous physical exercises that will make the heart work harder. Swimming is an excellent form of fitness training because it exercises muscles throughout the body. Particularly good are the backstroke and the butterfly, as these give a good workout to the back

▶ *Running will help to build up your stamina, but wear suitable footwear to protect yourself against impact injuries.*

and shoulder muscles, which can be difficult to exercise by other means. Cycling and running are also very good for improving all-round fitness and stamina, and they are especially good for the big thigh muscles. As part of your exercise plan in the build-up period up to a month before your trip, do some regular training in the boots or other clothing you will be wearing on the expedition, in order to get used to them. Wearing a backpack that is packed with the same weight as you will carry on your trip is very useful.

Muscular endurance

This is the ability to use the same muscles repeatedly without getting tired. Different activities require skills in different areas and therefore the development of different muscles and joints. For example, a walking and climbing trip needs strength in the upper and lower parts of the legs. If you need to carry your own camping and cooking equipment in a pack on your back, the shoulder muscles will also need to be strong. A canoeing trip, by contrast, needs strength in the arms, shoulders and chest, while a cycling trip needs strong upper and lower legs and strong arms and shoulders.

▲ *Diagonal crunches, from the elbow to the knee, will help to tone the stomach muscles and increase upper-body strength.*

You can tone your muscles and improve body strength in many ways. You may find it convenient to join a fitness club, where there is professional equipment, and follow a simple but regular programme of targeted action, supplemented with regular walking carrying a backpack. Alternatively, press-ups, pull-ups and stomach crunches are good exercises to prepare you for outdoor activities, and these can be done at home without the need for fitness clubs or sports equipment.

▲ *(Top) The simple press-up is an exercise to build short, powerful muscles in the pectoral, biceps and triceps areas of the body.*

▲ *(Above) You may find that by supporting your weight with your knees, you will find it easier to do press-up repetitions.*

▼ *Pull-ups are a good way to promote arm strength. Build up the number of repetitions as your muscles get stronger.*

TESTING YOUR FITNESS

Regular exercise will improve your fitness and endurance and make you feel better and livelier in every way. You will soon notice the difference in your general health, but some simple tests can help you measure your progress and provide extra motivation to keep going.
- As aerobic exercise strengthens your heart it will pump more slowly and efficiently. To take a step test, step on and off an exercise bench or step about 30cm (12in) high. Step up with one foot, placing it fully on the step, follow with the other, then step down with one foot followed by the other. Maintain a steady pace for three minutes, then check your pulse immediately.

An average rate for a man might be between 100–110 beats per minute and between 110–120 for a woman. Compare your results over time to see how your heart rate drops as your fitness improves.
- Measure upper body strength by doing press-ups. Simply do as many repetitions as you can to the point of exhaustion. Keep a record of your total and aim to beat it.
- Measure abdominal strength by doing stomach crunches: see how many you can do in one minute.
- Measure lower body strength with squats: do as many as you can, working at a steady pace, and see how your score builds up as you work out regularly.

▶ *A gentle jog along a beach is just one way to warm up your muscles before you begin a programme of stretching exercises.*

FLEXIBILITY

Stretching and mobilizing joints and muscles is a vital way to increase your range of movement and to prevent muscle strain. Always start a stretching programme with 15 minutes of gentle warm-ups, such as a brisk walk with your arms swinging, a game of frisbee, or a jog, to prepare your body for sudden exertions and minimize the risk of muscle injury.

Practise simple stretches on their own to achieve a good all-round level of flexibility, or practise them after endurance training to increase the benefit of a workout. Start at the top of the body, with stretches for the head and neck, and work down towards the legs and feet. Never bounce to increase your range of movement, but extend yourself gently to the limit of comfort. Hold each stretch for at least 15 seconds before relaxing. The longer you stretch your muscles after a workout, the more flexibility you will attain.

▼ *Stand with your feet apart, and one hand on your hip. Raise your other arm above your head and lean slowly across to gently stretch your side. Repeat on the opposite side.*

▼ *Stand with your feet together, then bend one leg back from the knee and grasp the foot to stretch the hamstring and quadriceps. Repeat with your other leg.*

▼ *Stand with your feet together, then bend forwards, keeping your back straight, and raise your arms above your back. Join your hands together and hold for 15 seconds.*

▶ *Having confidence in your ability to cope with difficult challenges makes you more likely to achieve your goals.*

MENTAL FITNESS

Strength of mind comes from within and is founded on your belief in yourself to cope with any situation you find yourself in. Knowing that you have prepared well helps you to overcome mental anxiety, and feeling that you are strong and fit, and that your physical strength can see you through times of difficulty, means that you are less likely to feel anxious about living outdoors.

Preparing in advance for emergency situations is invaluable. Training will make you more able to cope with hardship and difficult conditions, both physically and mentally, and it will improve your awareness of your abilities and limitations, which will increase your confidence. In the rare event that something does go seriously wrong, it will make you less likely to panic.

MENTAL PREPARATION

Some people who are well prepared physically for a trip do not perform well when they get into the field. This is largely due to a lack of mental preparation, which leaves them unable to adjust to their new surroundings or unprepared for what they are going to see or come into contact with.

Some people find the lack of privacy in camp a problem; others are upset by the poverty or sickness they may see around them in a developing country, or the smells and sounds they will encounter. Some people find it threatening to sleep out in the open and prefer to be in a tent: if one isn't available, they may not sleep well.

Many such problems can be eased by finding out as much as possible in advance about the area and culture you are going to, and trying out new experiences before setting off, such as cooking over a wood fire for the first time, or doing a difficult climb. These things can seem strange and threatening when you first do them, but will seem less so the next time. It is usually fear of the unknown that makes us most uncomfortable, not the experience itself.

FOOD AND TEAM MORALE

Food plays a key role in team morale when you are living outdoors, where the evening meal is a welcome treat at the end of a long, tiring day in the field. A healthy appetite is a sign of a positive attitude, and if the team is eating, it is also receiving the energy supplies it needs for strenuous activity.

However, eating with gusto is not easy after several days on a diet of dehydrated food. This kind of food can cause constipation, which means discomfort, and the lack of flavour can make it very unappealing. If the team doesn't eat properly, energy levels get depleted and individuals can become lethargic and irritable; this makes team spirit sink further still, and problems can flare up as individuals become discontented.

Make sure the team knows what food rations to expect, so that they can prepare themselves mentally for any hardship. Let them try out the rations at a trial camping weekend, and consider how you can improve the food if you feel it may have a negative effect on the team's morale.

Travelling as a group

A group expedition involves a great deal of organization to ensure that everyone has a safe and enjoyable trip. The purpose of the trip and an itinerary need to be agreed by everyone before you travel. This is important even for recreational holidays if the trip is to live up to individual expectations and you are to avoid disputes.

ORGANIZING GROUP MEMBERS

The larger the group, the greater the potential for chaos and confusion, and, not surprisingly, this is especially true with a group of children or young people. Travelling in large numbers can cause problems at ticket offices and check-in desks during the journey, where other passengers can become annoyed by the delays caused by a large group in front of them. Group leaders should remind everyone to get money, passports and tickets ready in plenty of time when approaching a border.

If your group is large, having a list of everyone's names, addresses, dates of birth and passport numbers will help when booking into accommodation or passing through borders. A list of just their names will also be useful for checking that everybody is present when you change modes of transport.

If the group is travelling by public transport, brief everyone on where they are heading and arrange a meeting point at the destination, so that if anyone does become separated, they will still be able to find the rest of the group.

You will quickly learn as the trip progresses which people take much more time to get ready than others, or never seem to have the necessary documents to hand. If they are not to hold up the others, they must be encouraged to be prompt and prepared. Other members of the group can be asked to help make sure they are at the right place at the right time.

GROUP IMPACT

If you are travelling in a group, and especially if you are acting as leader, it is important to remember that you have a responsibility not only to keep the group harmonious and happy, but to make sure that everyone respects the places and people you are visiting. Groups, especially large ones, can have a substantial impact on fragile environments, and a lack of understanding of the region's culture may cause distress and anger among local people, so good discipline is essential in camp. Before setting off, relay all the information you can about your destination to the team, and make sure everyone agrees to the standards of behaviour they will follow, to make the most of the experience for the whole group.

DISPUTES

No matter how big or small the party, and how well you know each other, disagreements and personality clashes during the trip are almost inevitable. Having a clear objective for the trip and an itinerary that has been mutually agreed by the group will help to keep these to a minimum, but deal with them quickly when they occur, before the group starts to break into factions.

CONTINGENCY PLAN

Have a fall-back plan that includes suitable accommodation should you need it at connection points on your journey, in case travel delays mean you miss a connection and are forced to make an unscheduled overnight stop. While individual travellers or a small group can usually be accommodated at short notice, a large group can run into problems if, for example, the flight arrives late, and the vehicle-hire

◀ *For the journey to run smoothly, allocate responsibilities among team members, such as looking out for particular items of kit.*

company has closed for the day. Keep phone numbers for the places you are booked into to hand, in case you need to inform them of any changes. Even if things are going to plan, it is a good idea to give your accommodation a call to make sure all is well for your arrival.

KEEPING VALUABLES SAFE

If you are staying in one place for any length of time, try to find a trustworthy individual or organization who will allow you to use their safe. The valuables of an entire group – including passports, travel tickets, expensive items such as jewellery and larger sums of money – can add up to a treasure chest for an opportunistic thief, and for peace of mind it is better to know they are stored safely under lock and key.

LOST LUGGAGE

Luggage can and does go missing when travelling, especially on public transport, and this is particularly likely with group travel because individuals tend to be less attentive of shared group equipment than they are of their own

belongings. It can help to make one or two people responsible for counting bags at each connection point, to make sure everything travels with you to your destination. If luggage is lost or delayed by an airline, you may have the complication of trying to arrange for it to be sent on to your destination.

▲ *With a large amount of gear and a big camping area, the potential for chaos at a group camp is huge. Encourage individuals to store their own kit tidily when not in use.*

▼ *Essential items of group kit, such as maps or cooking equipment, should be made the responsibility of one or two individuals.*

Travelling with young people

For a family camping holiday with your own children, you need to think about how the children will cope with the physical demands of living outdoors and how living in the wilderness may affect their spirit. Be ready to adapt your plans if the children appear uncomfortable or unhappy with the daily routine. Otherwise, as a parent, your responsibilities will be no different to those on any other family trip.

When you take a group of children or teenagers on an organized trip, you and any other leaders are responsible for them the whole time they are away from home. Much of the advice on travelling in a group will apply here, but your position of authority and your ability to deal with young people will make this a different type of challenge.

GROUP EXPEDITIONS

There should be at least one adult to every six young people, and if your programme includes activities that are potentially hazardous, or if the group members are under 15 years old, then the ratio will have to be higher. If there are children in the group with special needs, the number of adults has to be assessed on a case-by-case basis.

LEADING YOUNG PEOPLE

The challenges of outdoor living and adventure can be particularly beneficial for children and young people, but youth leaders need to be sure that they minimize the risks inherent in such activities and fulfil any legal requirements arising from their responsibilities. Guidelines are published by national and local education authorities, as well as international youth organizations such as Young Explorers Trust and the Scout Association.

PRE-TRIP MEETINGS

The agenda for the trip needs to be established with a series of meetings before you set off. The children's parents will want to feel informed and confident that their children are in safe hands. These meetings also allow the leaders to identify problematic issues while there is still time to amend plans.

Introductory meeting

Arrange a meeting early in the planning stage at which you can give the group and their parents or guardians detailed information about the area you will be visiting and even some training in the activities you hope to carry out there. This may also be the first time the group members meet each other. Explain the rules of behaviour for the trip and detail what will happen to any member who behaves badly.

Collect next-of-kin contact details from each person, as well as three passport photographs. If the group is travelling abroad you will need photocopies of passports and birth certificates in case any passports get lost. You will also need to talk through your insurance policy for the trip.

Ask the parents or guardians of any members under the official adult age to sign a consent form stating that you can authorize medical treatment in the event of an emergency. You also need medical information from every person, including details of any medication and any allergies to drugs or foodstuffs, as well as details of foods that they cannot eat on medical or religious grounds. If the group is travelling abroad, you will need to check that everyone has had the appropriate vaccinations.

Final meeting

Have a final meeting before you leave to run through the final risk assessment and explain what you are doing about the risks highlighted, pass on any last-minute information and answer any questions. Finally, introduce the liaison agent, who will be the point of contact between the group and the parents or guardians while you are away.

DURING THE JOURNEY

For a group of up to 12 children, have a rota so that one leader is in charge for a set time while the others relax. Larger groups of children (say, more than 20) are easier to handle if they are divided up into small units, each with its own leader, during the journey.

◀ *An early morning meeting to talk about the plans for the day ahead will make everybody in the team feel involved.*

If travelling by boat or train, or while waiting at an airport, and if the children are old enough to be trusted to behave sensibly on their own, they can be allowed time without adult supervision. Find a fixed point, such as a café, where a leader will be and where passports, tickets and luggage can be left, and ask each child to report in every hour. Keep a list of names to hand so that you can check everyone off as you change modes of transport.

DURING THE EXPEDITION

Start each day with a half-hour briefing session on the day's events, and give children the chance to ask questions or express concerns about any aspect of the trip. How much the children can achieve in one day will vary according to their age, physical strength and the type of activities planned. Base your schedule on past expeditions with young people of the same age, and be prepared to revise it if the group does not respond well to the challenges or if unforeseen weather conditions make the original plan untenable.

Deal with instances of bad behaviour immediately. Repeated bad behaviour may result in a child being sent home, but this is a last resort since a leader will have to accompany them, involving extra costs and the temporary lack of a leader.

▲ *Activities such as skiing should be within the capabilities of the child to avoid them becoming anxious or uncooperative.*

▼ *Allow time for rest and play to make sure young children do not over-exert themselves.*

Travelling alone

Many people love the freedom of travelling alone and relish facing new challenges and seeing new places with just themselves for company. If you hate the thought of group travel, with all the organization involved, the inevitable personality clashes and the lack of spontaneity, then it is worth considering this option.

The greatest advantage of travelling alone is that you have the flexibility of being able to change your plans as and when you want to, without having to consult anybody else. However, there are disadvantages to solo travel, and it is worth bearing in mind the following points when deciding whether or not to take a camping trip on your own.

BEING SELF-SUFFICIENT

If you are backpacking, you will have to carry everything yourself, including all of your camping and cooking equipment, so select lightweight gear and avoid taking unnecessary items. If you don't already own your equipment, try to borrow or hire as many of the expensive items as you can, or else kitting yourself out will be very costly. Make sure you know how to use all of your equipment correctly – including putting up your tent on your own – and learn how to carry out emergency repairs and maintenance.

TRAVEL COSTS

Unless you are travelling in your own vehicle and sleeping at a campsite, you may have to pay more for your trip, as ferries and organized trips will often charge a single-person supplement, especially if you want your own cabin or hotel room. If travelling on your own by train in parts of the developing world, bear in mind that a first-class ticket is worth considering from the point of view of safety and comfort.

KEEPING IN TOUCH

Make a point of phoning someone at home on a regular basis, perhaps at the same time each week, to let them know you are well and what your plans are for the days ahead (emailing is less reliable as the service is not available everywhere). If travelling in a developing country on your own, consider making your country's political representative in the country aware that you are there.

ACCOMMODATION

The thought of waking up on your own in the middle of the wilderness may seem appealing, but think very carefully about whether you want to be this isolated. Unless you are an experienced camper, a designated camping area may be a better option. Not only is there more chance of finding drinking water and washroom facilities, there will also be like-minded people nearby should you need help or advice, and it will usually be safer. If you are planning to stay in a hostel or hotel on your own, check guidebooks or ask at a tourist information office to find out about the character of the area. When travelling alone it is usually safer to choose accommodation in a better part of town.

▼ *Lone travellers have the flexibility to please themselves and change their plans at will if new opportunities arise.*

▲ *Women travelling alone are easy targets for sexual harassment. Be aware of this and make reducing the risk your top priority.*

◄ *Travelling without backup from other people makes you more vulnerable, so plan carefully to minimize the risks.*

SOLO ACTIVITIES

If you are planning a walking, cycling, horse riding or driving trip on your own, tell someone what you are doing, the route you are taking and when you expect to return. If you have an accident, they may be your only hope of help. Think very carefully about the wisdom of snow walking, climbing or mountaineering on your own, especially if there is a chance of bad weather. Some activities, such as kayaking and canoeing, should never be done solo. If you want to visit a famous site, consider joining an organized tour or getting a group of like-minded people to go together. It will be cheaper and it could be safer than going alone.

DRUG SMUGGLING

As a lone traveller, be careful whom you make friends with and never accept parcels or gifts unless you know what is in them, especially if you are passing through a national border. There are a number of people in prison around the world who carried a parcel for a "friend" that turned out to contain drugs or other contraband.

WOMEN TRAVELLERS

Observing local codes of behaviour is a matter of courtesy for all travellers, but for women it is easy to send out the wrong message, especially when travelling alone in countries where an unaccompanied female may be an unusual sight. Outside Europe, Australia and the United States, skimpy or tight clothes, including trousers, are generally inappropriate. Check the conventions before you go and always dress conservatively in loose-fitting, presentable clothes.

All lone women may face some sexual harassment. Take the same precautions you would at home: don't wander up dark alleys alone or accept drinks from strangers; find another woman to sit next to on a bus or train. If you are groped, don't get involved in an angry confrontation but get the attention of onlookers, who will probably rush to your defence. Avoid eye contact with men in public places: wearing dark glasses can help. Time your arrival in a new place during the day, so you are not wandering about late at night: travelling by night can be a good idea if it means you reach your destination in the morning.

On the plus side, local people – women particularly – will be more likely to offer you hospitality. They might assume that a male traveller can cope alone, while you need a helping hand, and they won't see a lone woman as a threat.

Be prepared for your periods to be irregular – changes in time zones, stress and exhaustion can affect them – and remember that stomach upsets can interfere with oral contraception. Sanitary protection may be hard to buy locally, and tampons with applicators are more hygienic in the absence of clean water to wash your hands. Be aware of cultural attitudes – in some countries menstruating woman are forbidden to enter religious buildings or to touch, or even go near, food, so be discreet.

BASIC EQUIPMENT

Commercial travel equipment is now so developed that it is possible to travel in the backcountry for several weeks in considerable comfort. However, some items are expensive and may be too specialist for your needs. The key to being well equipped is to take what is necessary. Do not carry more than you have to: this is especially important if you are backpacking, but even if you are transporting your gear by vehicle, it will hamper your progress if you are overloaded with luggage.

Choosing your equipment

Having the correct basic equipment is important for your comfort and safety. When assessing what you need, you should consider the climate and terrain of the area you are visiting and the activities planned. You also need to know how you are going to carry your gear, as this will affect the amount of weight and bulk you can manage.

HOW TO ACQUIRE EQUIPMENT

Outdoor equipment suppliers sell for every possible climate and terrain, so if you are buying new items for your trip, consider what design features will serve you best to help narrow the choice. Many items are expensive, and most people build up their equipment over a number of years to spread the cost. If this is your first trip, try to borrow as much as you can from friends or a local walking or activity group. That way you will also gain from the experience of others, who will be able to tell you what is and what is not important. Have an understanding in writing with the owner on what items cost and how you will compensate them for lost, stolen or damaged items, and make sure you are sufficiently insured.

▼ *Wearing a helmet, gloves and suitable clothing and footwear is important for any cycling trip, even if the distance is short.*

CLOTHING AND FOOTWEAR

The purpose of outdoor clothing is to keep you comfortable in the weather conditions you experience on your trip. It cannot be stressed enough that clothes need to be appropriate for the climate you will be operating in. Besides this, clothes need to be durable and quick drying, lightweight and low in bulk – this is especially important if you are carrying your gear in a pack on your back. Footwear has to protect your feet from water, mud, sand and rocks, while still enabling you to carry out your activities safely. Never be tempted to compromise your safety and comfort for fashion: it will make your trip a miserable one and may even put your life in danger.

PERSONAL AND GROUP CAMP KIT

Your camp kit is the core items of equipment that you take with you on any trip to the wilderness, such as a compass, map, water bottle, wristwatch, cooking equipment and wash kit. Some items, such as a compass, are essential and you shouldn't set off without them. Other items, such as an inflatable pillow, are luxuries that you can do without if your weight/space allowance is limited. Group kit may include study materials, or catering-size cooking equipment. For more information, see the sections Personal camp kit (60–63) and Group camp kit (66–67).

BASIC SURVIVAL KIT

In an emergency situation, having a few key items can make the difference between life and death. For advice on what to include in the kit, see Basic Survival Kit (64–65).

TENTS

Probably the most expensive item on your list will be a tent, so be clear about what sort you need. The perfect tent is weatherproof, spacious, easy to pitch, light and compact to carry, but few tents are all of these things and you will have to reach a compromise. See the section Choosing a tent, 68–71.

▲ *For backpacking trips you need cooking and sleeping equipment that is light in weight and designed to be packed up small.*

SLEEPING EQUIPMENT

The right sleeping gear can mean the difference between a good night's rest and a bad one. Consider where and in what conditions you will be using your sleeping bag, then buy the best one you can afford. For more information, see the section Sleeping bags, 72–75.

BACKPACKS

A backpack has to allow you to carry your equipment in comfort, and what sort of backpack you need will depend on your activities and how much you need to carry. Features such as hip belts, padding, frames or side straps can be very useful but they can also add weight and cost. See also Backpacks and carrying equipment, 78–81.

TOOLS

When living outdoors it is very useful to have some tools with you, even if your tool kit consists of nothing more than a penknife. Check with the police to see if any of your tools are illegal. If you have a machete, large knife or flares, for example, you may be able to own them but not carry them around in public. Anything that is classed as a firearm will need an official firearms certificate. See also the section Tools, 88–89.

BASIC HIKING AND CAMPING EQUIPMENT CHECKLIST

The following kit list is for a walking and camping trip lasting 3–4 weeks in a temperate climate:

Clothing and footwear
Underwear
Thermal vest, long johns and
    long-sleeved undershirt
Cotton T-shirts
Cotton socks
Woollen socks
Short-sleeved shirts
Long-sleeved shirts
Woollen sweater or zip-up fleece
Long cotton trousers
Shorts
Lightweight waterproof jacket
Windproof jacket
Waterproof overtrousers
Walking boots
Spare boot laces
Lightweight trainers or flip-flops
Swimwear
Sturdy belt
Fleece or woollen gloves
Fleece or woollen hat
Wide-brimmed sunhat
Sunglasses
Towelling sweat rag or head scarf
Set of smart clothing plus suitable
    footwear
Nightwear

Personal equipment
Compass
Maps
Wristwatch
Water bottle and case
Whistle
Cotton money belt
Kitbag or backpack
Day sack
Tent
Sleeping bag
Sleeping mat
Small stuff sacks and garbage bags
Penknife
Flashlight and spare batteries
2 x plates or set of army mess tins
Mug
Knife, fork, spoon
Dish towel
Pan scourer

Can opener
Travel wash or soap flakes
Clothes pegs (pins)
4m/13ft washline
Small folding camp chair
Walking poles

Wash kit
Towel
Soap
Toothbrush
Toothpaste
Steel mirror
Hairbrush or comb
Shampoo
Sanitary protection
Razor and shaving foam
Lipbalm
Deodorizing foot powder
Zinc and castor oil cream
Sunscreen
Insect repellent
Pocket tissues
Wet wipes
Washbasin plug

Miscellaneous items
Passport
Travel tickets
Cash, travellers' cheques, credit card
Vaccination certificate
Repair kit
Camera, spare batteries and film
Mobile (cell) phone
Binoculars
2 x spare passport photos
Photocopies of paperwork
Notebook, pen and pencil

Personal first-aid kit
Adhesive dressings (plasters),
    various sizes
Paracetamol tablets
Blister kit
Travel sickness tablets
Sterile dressings, various sizes
Triangular bandage
Roller bandages
Small pair of scissors
Thermometer
Tweezers
Safety pins
Disposable gloves

For more extreme weather conditions, add the following items:

Hot climate extras
Personal water purifier
Malaria tablets
Insect repellent bands and head net
Mosquito net and frame
Camp bed or hammock
Cotton liner for sleeping bag
Shade sheet
Machete
Extra water bottle

Cold climate/snow extras
Thermal underwear
Down or fleece zip-up jacket
Water- and windproof jacket and
    overtrousers, or fibre-pile
    one-piece suit
Balaclava
Inner or liner gloves
Fleece or woollen mitts
Outer mitts
Knee-length gaiters
Snow shoes or snow boots
Crampons
Climbing harness
Ice axe
Bivvy bag
Space blanket

For trips involving paddling or cycling activities, add the following items:

Kayaking or canoeing extras
Boat and paddles
Buoyancy aid or Personal flotation
    device (PFD)
Helmet
Thermal or cotton T-shirt
Thermal or cotton trousers
Cagoule and waterproof trousers
Technical sandals, lightweight trainers
    or neoprene boots
Spraydeck (spray skirt) (kayaks only)
Waterproof kit bags and containers

Cycling extras
Cycle
Helmet
Gloves
Lightweight trainers

Clothing for temperate climates

Temperate zones worldwide include Europe, North America and New Zealand. Average temperatures range from –14–37°C/5–100°F. This climate has warm summers with rain showers and cold, wet winters, which can turn to snow at high altitudes. Although the weather is not extreme, it is changeable, and controlling your body temperature will require you to take off or put on clothing. What to wear in winter is covered in Clothing for Cold and Wet Climates; here we deal with clothing for the spring, summer and autumn.

LAYERING SYSTEM

In a temperate climate, clothing is best worn in a layering system to give maximum flexibility. Several thin layers of clothing that trap air between them will keep you warmer than one thick garment. If you become too hot, lower your body temperature by removing layers or opening zips or buttons to allow warm air to escape and cool air to enter. If you feel cold, add a layer or refasten zips and cuffs. If it rains, put your waterproofs on straight away so that you do not get your lower layers wet, and take them off when it stops raining, so that you do not overheat.

▼ *Dress for the conditions you expect, and have with you clothing and equipment in case the weather worsens significantly.*

First layer

Cotton underwear can be worn with either a cotton vest or T-shirt in the summer. It may be cold enough to wear long johns and a long-sleeved undershirt in the spring or autumn.

Second layer

Choose a long-sleeved shirt that will allow you to roll the sleeves up or down as the weather conditions dictate. In warm weather, a cotton shirt will keep you cool, while a woollen shirt will give warmth for the cooler spring and autumn months. Trousers should be loose-fitting and made of cotton or synthetic fibres. Shorts can be worn, but take a pair of trousers with you in case the weather suddenly worsens.

Third layer

A lightweight fleece jacket or a woollen long-sleeved sweater can either be worn or carried in your rucksack, as the conditions dictate.

Outer layer

This climate will certainly be wet at times, and you will need a waterproof, windproof jacket – preferably one with cuffs inside the sleeves, a comfortable neck seal and a good hood to protect the head. Waterproof overtrousers should always be carried. It will be a great advantage if this layer is made of

▲ *A good windproof and waterproof outer layer is essential in temperate regions, where sudden rain showers can be expected.*

a breathable fabric, either synthetic or natural; non-breathable fabrics can cause you to overheat and sweat, and will be uncomfortable to wear.

ACCESSORIES

A brimmed sun hat or baseball cap will protect your head from the sun, while a woollen hat can be pulled down over your ears to keep you warm when it is cold or windy. A scarf made of towelling or wool and worn wrapped around the neck may be useful in the cooler spring or autumn. Carry a pair of woollen or fibre-pile mitts in your pack to keep your hands warm when you stop for rest breaks.

FOOTWEAR

Wear walking shoes, lightweight boots or leather walking boots, depending on the conditions. Even on a warm summer day, footpaths can be wet and muddy, and wearing short gaiters over your boots, or longer lightweight knee-length gaiters, will keep your lower legs clean and dry. Socks should be made of cotton or wool; wear one or two pairs.

◀ *Lightweight cotton trousers are comfortable to wear and will dry quickly if they get wet.*

◀ *Wear a lightweight fleece zip-up jacket or a woollen sweater for a warm, cosy layer beneath your waterproofs.*

▼ *A cotton T-shirt makes a practical undergarment for any time of year.*

▼ *Carry woollen mitts in your rucksack to put on when you make a rest stop for any length of time.*

◀ *Fibre-pile gloves are water-resistant and warm, and will allow you to use your hands far better than mitts.*

◀ *A fleece hat is excellent head insulation and can be kept in your rucksack ready to be pulled on if the temperature drops.*

▶ *Gaiters attached to your boots will keep your lower legs dry and clean if conditions are wet and muddy underfoot.*

▲ *A woollen scarf worn around the neck and tucked inside your outer layer will effectively keep out chilly draughts.*

▼ *A cotton sunhat will protect the head from strong sun. Air vents in the hat will keep you cooler and reduce sweating.*

▲ *A folded towel worn around the neck will absorb sweat in hot temperatures.*

Clothing for hot and dry climates

Hot and dry environments are found in parts of the United States, Australia, Africa, and the Middle East. Typical terrain includes deserts and open plains, with a temperature range from -6–50°C/ 20–120°F. Local people in this climate favour loose-fitting clothing that does not constrict the airflow around the body. Rather than the flexible layering system of clothing worn in temperate climates, the key to comfort in hot, dry climates is good ventilation and protection from the sun.

Clothing should be made of strong, hard-wearing fabrics as even deserts have vegetation with thorns, and these can tear at clothing. Choose breathable natural fibres, such as cotton or wool, to encourage airflow and keep you cooler, and light colours, preferably neutrals, such as khaki or green, which do not show the dirt as much as white.

UNDERWEAR

Choose underwear made of cotton because of its breathable qualities; men may prefer to wear boxers to avoid chafing in the crotch area. A cotton T-shirt worn under the shirt will keep you warmer in the winter, when

▼ *The intense sun and lack of shade can cause real problems in the desert, and your clothing is your main form of protection.*

SUN PROTECTION

In a hot, dry climate the sun is your worst enemy and you will need to give your body protection from it for your comfort and safety. A high-factor sunscreen (minimum SPF 25) and a good sun hat, one with a wide brim or a peak and neck flap, are necessary if you will be outdoors in the heat of the day.

temperatures can go down to below freezing, even in the desert. At any time of year, if you are sweating a lot, wear a cotton T-shirt underneath your shirt to absorb the sweat.

SHIRT

A lightweight cotton shirt with long sleeves and buttoned cuffs will allow you to wear the sleeves rolled down to protect your arms from sunburn. A shirt with large breast pockets allows you to keep to hand items that you may need often during the day, such as a compass, camera or sunscreen.

TROUSERS

Wear lightweight cotton trousers that are loose in the crotch and long enough to be tucked into your boots. This is how you should wear them

▲ *A windproof cotton gilet can be added on top of your shirt to keep out cool winds in the evenings, after the sun has gone down.*

when walking on loose rocks and sand to avoid getting debris inside your socks and boots, which can cause friction against the skin and can lead to blisters. A sturdy trouser belt made of leather or heavy webbing is useful for carrying heavy items that you will need frequently, such as your water bottle. Large pockets on the trouser leg can be used to carry maps. A double thickness of material on the knee area will protect the trousers from wear.

JACKET

Take a lightweight windproof jacket for the summer and a heavier, cold-weather coat for the winter, when temperatures can drop quite severely. It does rain in the desert, and a waterproof jacket with a hood, or a waterproof poncho, will prove very useful. Some ponchos can also double up as groundsheets.

ACCESSORIES

Wear a wide-brimmed sun hat or some form of headgear at all times in extreme heat to cover your head, the back of your neck and your ears. This is especially important during the heat of the day. Deserts can be very windy

▲ *A cotton shirt with long sleeves that can be buttoned up will allow you to keep your arms covered to protect them from the sun.*

▲ *Choose loose-fitting cotton trousers in a neutral colour, and wear them tucked into your boots to prevent sand getting in.*

▲ *Carry a lightweight cotton windproof jacket in the summer, and a heavier jacket for the cooler winter months.*

places, so make sure there is a sturdy chin strap to prevent the hat blowing away. Eyelet vents around the brim give ventilation and help to keep the head cool. It is so important to keep your head covered in intense sunshine that you should carry a spare hat just in case you lose one.

Protect your eyes from the glaring sunlight with dark sunglasses that offer a good standard of protection from ultraviolet rays. If you are driving, you may prefer to wear sturdy goggles, as these will offer more protection from the blowing, gritty dust of deserts and open plains. Carry at least one spare pair of sunglasses in case you lose or damage the ones you are wearing.

A bandana, small towel or towelling sweat rag, tied loosely around your neck, is very useful for wiping sweat from your face and neck, and will help to keep the sun off the back of your neck (prolonged sun on the back of the neck can cause sunstroke.)

If you are travelling by horse, mule or camel or if you are driving, you may want to wear cotton gloves to prevent the backs of your hands getting sunburned. In the cool winter months, lightweight leather gloves are warmer.

FOOTWEAR

Wear lightweight cotton socks, and take a clean pair for every day or make provisions for washing them, as your feet will sweat and this can cause discomfort. Specially designed boots are available for deserts and extremely dry terrain. These have lightweight suede uppers, which allow feet to breathe, as well as high sides to keep out the sand, and robust soles to protect feet from the rocky terrain. Regular leather walking boots are too heavy, and the non-porous uppers will cause the feet to sweat.

▼ *This wide-brimmed cotton sun hat gives ideal protection from strong sun, with the air vents encouraging air flow to reduce sweating.*

▼ *A cotton baseball cap can be worn with the brim shading the face or turned around so that the cap peak protects the back of the neck.*

▲ *A sturdy leather belt can be used to hang items that you need quick and easy access to, such as a water bottle, compass or map.*

▲ *Good quality sunglasses should be worn at all times when the sun is at its most intense. Attach them to a sturdy cord worn around the neck.*

▼ *Lightweight driving gloves will protect the hands from sunburn if you will be spending several hours a day driving in the sun.*

◀ *A lightweight cotton bandana worn loosely around the neck will help to absorb sweat from the neck.*

Clothing for hot and wet climates

High temperatures and humidity make hot and wet environments very difficult places in which to live comfortably. Hot and wet regions worldwide are found in the equatorial zones of South America, North America, Africa, Asia and parts of Australia. Average temperatures range from 20–30°C/68–86°F. Local vegetation in a hot, wet climate will usually be jungle; many plants and trees will have thorns, and some will have poisonous leaves. The important thing is to keep your body completely covered from head to toe to protect yourself from these very hostile surroundings.

Everything you wear in a hot and wet climate should be made of cotton, because as a breathable fabric it will help to keep you cool and it will dry quickly. Take two sets of clothing, so that you have one set for the day when you are working or travelling, and another clean, dry set to change into when you make camp in the evenings.

Your spare set of clothing must be kept in a waterproof bag if you are carrying all of your gear inside your rucksack during the day, otherwise the humidity alone will make it damp. Depending on the duration of your trip, you can make provision for washing your clothes while you are away to avoid having to carry huge amounts of clothing with you.

UNDERWEAR

As in a hot, dry environment, you will find that cotton underwear is the most comfortable in hot and humid weather. Choose items that fit well and avoid anything restricting that limits movement. Simple designs are best,

▲ *The jungle environment is uncomfortable and dangerous, with high humidity and a range of very threatening plants and insects.*

▼ *Head-to-toe protection is needed at all times in a hot, wet climate; always wear your boots when crossing a jungle river.*

INSECT PROTECTION

Cover your hands and neck with insect repellent, but take care not to put repellent near your eyes; do not put it on your forehead either, as sweat will wash it into your eyes. Repellent bands can be worn on your wrists, but should be reproofed every few days. You can also put insect repellent around the tops of your boots and around the eyelets of your boots and the air vents of your sun hat. Do this when you take rest stops, as the repellent will get rubbed off as you travel through the undergrowth. A head net offers good protection from insects. Put it on over your hat but only when you stop, as it cuts down visibility and can get torn as you move through dense vegetation.

▲ *A lightweight cotton shirt, with long sleeves that can be securely fastened, will offer good protection from plants and insects.*

▲ *Choose loose-fitting cotton trousers in a serviceable neutral colour. Trousers with large leg pockets are particularly useful.*

▼ *A wide-brimmed hat will protect your head from the vegetation and insects; choose a hat with air vents and a sturdy chin strap.*

▲ *Wear lightweight cotton socks inside your jungle boots, and try to change your socks every day to keep your feet comfortable.*

▼ *Knowing what conditions to expect and equipping yourself accordingly is the secret to dressing suitably in the jungle environment.*

as the more details there are, the greater the risk of chafing. A lightweight cotton vest or T-shirt can be worn underneath your shirt to absorb sweat.

SHIRT
Choose a long-sleeved cotton shirt in a neutral colour and wear it buttoned down to the wrist to protect your arms from the vegetation and insects. You will find it useful to choose a shirt that has large breast pockets in which to keep the smaller items, such as insect repellent, that you will want easy access to throughout the day. There is no need for a jacket in a hot, wet climate, where the high temperature is constant and any kind of wind or breeze is rare.

TROUSERS
Your lower body should be well covered with loose-fitting trousers, worn tucked inside your socks and boots to protect the legs and feet from insects. Anything kept in the trouser pockets will become wet during your activities from sweat and the humidity, so keep essential maps and paperwork in waterproof pouches in order to protect them.

ACCESSORIES
Always wear a sturdy sun hat to protect your head and face from vegetation and insects. A brimmed cotton hat is ideal; air vents will encourage ventilation and reduce sweating, and a chin strap will prevent the hat getting knocked off your head by low-hanging undergrowth. A cotton bandana or towelling scarf tied loosely around your neck is useful

for wiping sweat from your face, which you will need to do almost continuously, and it will also protect your neck from sunburn. A bandana or scarf will help to prevent insects crawling inside the collar of your shirt.

FOOTWEAR
The wet, uneven surface of the jungle floor means that adequate footwear is essential. Jungle boots are better than walking boots because they are designed for the conditions (see the section Footwear, 58–59).

Clothing for cold and dry climates

Cold and dry environments are found at high altitude in Europe, North America, Canada, South America, Asia and Africa, where conditions include rocky terrain as well as snow and ice. Average temperatures range from -56–18°C/ -81–65°F. In this environment your aim is to dress sufficiently well to keep warm, but not so well that you overheat.

LAYERING SYSTEM

To achieve a balanced body temperature, you will need to use the flexible layering system of clothing, which allows you to put on or take off layers depending on the conditions and your activities.

First layer

This should be a long-sleeved thermal vest and long johns, made from natural or synthetic materials, which cover the whole of the body except for the hands and feet. The garments should fit close to the skin without being tight and restrictive, and there should be a good overlap at the waist to avoid exposing the skin. Carry at least one spare set of first layer clothing.

▼ *Snow and ice are often a feature of cold, dry climates, but the sun can also get hot, and your clothing needs to give flexibility.*

Second layer

Choose either a long-sleeved button-up insulated shirt and heavy-duty trousers, or a one-piece fibre-pile suit with a high collar and elasticated cuffs to keep your neck and wrists well protected. A shirt and trousers will allow you to roll the sleeves up and down to control your body temperature; not all one-piece suits will allow you to do this, so try to find one that does. The second layer can be made of synthetic or natural materials, but the advantage of natural fabrics is that they will "breathe" and absorb moisture (in the form of sweat) from the body. Items that need to be kept at a temperature above freezing, such as your compass, should be carried in a buttoned-up pocket in this layer, where they will be easily accessible.

Third layer

If you are on a walking trip and will be able to stop to take off and put on items of clothing as and when you need to, choose a woollen sweater or a lightweight fleece jacket. However, if you are planning an activity where you are not going to be able to change your clothing easily, it will be more convenient to wear fibre-pile salopettes with a fibre-pile mountain shirt, or

a one-piece down or fibre-pile suit. These overlap at the waist to keep you warm where other clothing can be disturbed with movement, while still allowing ventilation at the chest and shoulders to reduce heat loss and discomfort through sweating.

Outer layer

This should be a zip-up waterproof jacket and a pair of overtrousers, which should be breathable, windproof and water-resistant. The jacket sleeves should come down over the wrists and upper hands so that they overlap the gloves, and it should have a large hood with a wire-structured visor, which will help to keep the front of the hood in place even in high winds. Large pockets with fasteners will be useful.

ACCESSORIES

Wear fibre-pile headgear or a woollen balaclava. Both of these will cover the head as well as all of the neck and ears. For extra protection in extremely cold conditions, you can wear a lightweight silk balaclava underneath the outer one.

Like the rest of the body, the hands should be covered with a number of layers. This can mean as many as three pairs in extreme cold conditions: first a pair of silk gloves, then woollen or fibre-pile mitts, then an outer layer of wind- and waterproof mitts, which will cover the join between the outer jacket and the second-layer under-mitts.

FOOTWEAR

Wear two pairs of woollen socks, one of which should be long enough to be pulled over the lower part of your thermal leggings to form a seal, so that no skin is exposed to the air.

Suitable footwear can mean leather mountain boots covered with insulated overboots or gaiters that come up to your knees, or plastic snow boots. Make sure that your socks and boots do not fit tightly, as this will restrict the blood circulation and can make your feet feel even colder and more susceptible to frostbite.

◀ *A lightweight fleece jacket should make up part of the third layer of clothing, and can be put on or taken off as the conditions dictate.*

▲ *Cotton trousers can be worn with a shirt tucked inside. Zip-up pockets will allow you to carry any items that you need often.*

▼ *A windproof and waterproof jacket with a hood that covers the whole of your head is your first line of defence against the cold.*

▼ *Fibre-pile mitts are waterproof and make a good outer layer to protect the hands.*

▲ *Waterproof overtrousers give protection from rain or snow showers. Take them off as soon as the showers stop to prevent sweating. Zips on the lower leg make the trousers easier to put on over boots.*

▼ *A woollen balaclava fits snugly over the head and neck, giving good protection for the ears, and as a further advantage it will not blow off in high winds.*

▼ *A cotton shirt can be worn as part of your second layer of clothing, and the full-length sleeves can easily be rolled up if you become too hot.*

▼ *Fleece gloves can be worn on their own or beneath fibre-pile mitts in cold conditions.*

Clothing for cold and wet climates

Cold and wet climate zones worldwide include the polar regions, Greenland, Iceland and northern Scandinavia and Russia. Average temperatures range from –42–21°C/–34–70°F. This climate is probably the most challenging and dangerous for human beings because the moisture in the air will actively destroy the insulation properties of clothing. The effect is to rapidly reduce the body temperature, leading to a very real risk of hypothermia, which, if it isn't treated in time, can be life-threatening.

LAYERING SYSTEM

Clothing should be worn in a system of layers so that you can add on and take off items as the weather conditions dictate. It is also essential to consider which materials will offer the best insulation when wet. Clothing that is completely waterproof is not suitable for strenuous walking or climbing as it will not allow body sweat to escape. Instead, the sweat will be absorbed into your clothing, and in extremely cold temperatures it can quickly freeze.

▼ *Activities such as skiing will make you sweat, and this will cause a chill unless the moisture can be absorbed by your clothing.*

First layer

The clothing that sits next to the skin must be able to absorb sweat from the body as well as any moisture (such as rain water or melted snow) that seeps down from the outer layers of clothing, while still retaining its insulating power. A long-sleeved thermal top and thermal long johns made from wool or a fibre-pile material will offer a base layer that is both absorbent and insulating.

Second layer

This middle layer is the same as that recommended for cold and dry climates: a loose-fitting long-sleeved cotton shirt and trousers, or a one-piece fibre-pile suit with a high collar and elastic cuffs that will keep the neck and wrists protected and warm. The advantage of a one-piece suit over a shirt and trousers is that it will not become dislodged at the waist, so that no skin is exposed during strenuous activities. A woollen scarf, or even a towel, worn around your neck will stop rain or melting snow running down your neck and back, and will keep the shoulders warm. Items that need to be kept warm and dry should be carried in this layer, in a waterproof pouch inside a pocket.

▲ *Children will be very vulnerable to the conditions in a cold and wet climate, so make sure they are appropriately protected.*

Third layer

The recommendations for this layer are the same as for cold and dry climates: a woollen sweater or a lightweight fleece jacket, an all-in-one suit such as fibre-pile salopettes worn with a fibre-pile mountain shirt, or a one-piece down or fibre-pile suit with a high collar and elastic cuffs. One-piece suits should be coated in a lightweight, water-repellent fabric. Synthetic fibre pile is extremely effective in cold and wet conditions because it retains its insulation properties when wet, whereas natural down does not. Furthermore, if down is allowed to become wet frequently, it will lose its insulation properties permanently.

Outer layer

Wear a zip-up waterproof jacket and a pair of full-length overtrousers that are breathable, windproof and water-resistant. The length of the jacket will depend on the activities you are planning: a knee-length jacket will offer more warmth and protection, but a shorter, waist-length jacket is less restrictive for more strenuous walking or mountaineering.

▶ Fibre-pile long johns are warm and will quickly absorb body sweat, but they do need to be kept dry to be effective.

▼ Fibre-pile salopettes can be worn with a fibre-pile mountain shirt to make a highly protective and insulating third layer.

▲ A long-sleeved thermal vest top will give good insulation worn next to the skin if it is kept dry; it is less effective when wet.

ACCESSORIES

Keep your head, neck, shoulders and ears well protected with a woollen or fibre-pile balaclava. For extra insulation in conditions of extreme cold, a lighter silk balaclava can be worn beneath. Gloves should also be worn in up to three layers – first, fine silk gloves, then woollen or fibre-pile gloves, then waterproof outer mitts. It is a good idea to have your mitts attached to your jacket with a strong cord, so they cannot be lost or blown away if you take them off.

FOOTWEAR

Wear two pairs of thick woollen socks and a pair of leather mountain boots protected by insulated over-boots or heavy-duty knee-length gaiters. For very deep snow and ice conditions, you may prefer to wear plastic snow boots, which are specially designed with a thermal inner boot inside a plastic outer boot. Crampons attached to the outside of your boots will give a better grip when walking on snow and ice.

▼ Knee gaiters will help to keep water and snow out of your boots and protect your legs from the cold temperatures.

▼ A woollen balaclava gives good protection for the head and neck. Cover it with the hood of your jacket to keep it dry in a rain or snow shower.

▼ Metal crampons can be attached to leather walking boots or snow boots to give you a surer grip underfoot in icy conditions.

▶ Plastic snow boots are better equipped than regular leather walking boots to stay waterproof and provide a good grip in snow or ice conditions.

▼ A woollen scarf tucked snugly into the neck of a shirt or one-piece suit will prevent rain water or snow running down your back.

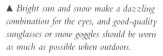

▲ Bright sun and snow make a dazzling combination for the eyes, and good-quality sunglasses or snow goggles should be worn as much as possible when outdoors.

Footwear

Your footwear is going to be one of the most important items of your kit, both for your comfort and for the protection of your feet. Boots need to fit properly, and they must be comfortable. If you have bought them new for your trip, you need to make sure they have been broken in before you use them.

BREAKING IN NEW BOOTS

Although a pair of new boots may feel comfortable in the store when you buy them, they will need to be properly broken in before use. This loosens up the uppers and moulds the insides to the shape of your feet, so as not to cause soreness. Experienced walkers say that it takes at least 160km/100 miles to break in a pair of leather walking boots, and 80km/50 miles to break in a pair of lightweight fabric boots.

SUITABILITY

A wide choice of footwear is available, but you need to make sure that what you wear on your feet is suitable for the terrain and climate and any activities involved. Boots have been designed for specific terrains, such as mountain or desert or jungle. These boots are not meant to be interchangeable, and wearing inappropriate footwear will not give your feet adequate protection and can put you at risk of injury.

PROTECTING YOUR BOOTS

Your walking boots are likely to be one of the most expensive items of your kit and as such you will want them to last for as long as possible. In order to keep them waterproof and resistant to damage, all boots should be coated in a protective waterproofing compound before you set off. Leather boots or shoes should be given two coats of oil, dubbin or a product recommended by the manufacturer. For fabric boots use a recommended silicone-based product, which can be either sprayed or rubbed on to the boot.

LIGHT WALKING

If you know you will be walking mostly on well-maintained tracks or footpaths, and you can expect the weather to be mild and dry, with dry, firm ground underfoot, you can wear leather or fabric walking shoes instead of boots. Many people find these more comfortable than boots, especially in warm weather. Walking shoes can be pulled off your feet in wet and muddy conditions and they do not offer much in the way of ankle support, but the advantage is that they dry out quickly when wet.

▲ *Modern lightweight fabric boots are comfortable to wear and ideal for fine-weather walking conditions.*

▶ *Leather boots are durable and give good foot protection for cross-country walking.*

▲ *Do not expect the same pair of boots to be suited for every walking trip as boots are now designed to handle specific conditions.*

For low-level walking in wet or dry weather, or across open country, where you can expect the ground to be waterlogged and slippery, you can wear either lightweight fabric boots or leather walking boots. Fabric boots are a modern alternative to the leather boot. They are light and comfortable to wear, while still offering good ankle support, and the treads on the soles provide a good grip. Leather walking boots are the classic multi-purpose choice. These are more durable than fabric boots, and they have a better resistance to water if regularly reproofed.

HIGH GROUND AND MOUNTAINS

If you will be walking on high ground, conditions underfoot will be unstable and you need to think carefully about your footwear. Leather walking boots or leather mountain boots, which have sturdier soles, will give good protection from the rough, often rocky, terrain. The boots should be well insulated to keep the feet warm, and they should have a sewn-in tongue to prevent water or snow getting inside.

DESERTS

Boots designed for the desert will protect you from the tough scrub and insects. The uppers are usually made of suede or light canvas, but the soles should be stout and strong, as there may be very sharp thorns on the ground. Some have smooth or ribbed soles. The pattern on the sole does not matter, unless you intend to do mountaineering or some other activity.

▲ *Heavier leather mountain boots will be needed if you are walking above the snow line.*

◀ *Desert boots have lightweight uppers and a strong sole to protect the feet and ankles from thorny plants and sharp stones and rocks.*

JUNGLE

Boots designed for jungle environments have strong rubber soles to keep out the wetness of the jungle floor, and canvas uppers that allow the feet to breathe and will dry quickly. The boots lace high above the ankle to allow the trousers to be worn inside the boot and protect the legs from leeches and other insects. Look for boots with one-way air vents, which allow water to drain out but prevent insects getting in. A sewn-in tongue will also stop insects getting to your feet. The tread pattern on the soles has wide, deep cleats to give a good grip in the wet, muddy conditions.

▲ *Gaiters will help to keep the lower legs warm and dry in cold, wet conditions.*

▶ *Jungle boots grip well, dry quickly and allow the feet to breathe, but will keep out insects.*

SNOW AND ICE

In many areas of the world you will encounter snow on high ground year-round. If the snow is deep, or if there is ice as well as snow, the ground will be extremely unstable, and your boots will have to be robust enough to take metal crampons in order for you to walk safely without sliding.

If you know you will be walking through deep snow, consider plastic snow boots. These comprise a thermal inner boot inside a plastic outer boot. The thermal inner boot gives heavy insulation for extreme cold conditions, and these boots are designed to hold the foot rigid while using crampons, allowing you to make a more stable foothold. However, like ski boots, the plastic outer boots are very inflexible and will make any kind of movement very awkward. It will often be preferable to wear snow boots when walking on snow and ice, especially if using crampons, but you should be prepared for this lack of flexibility.

One useful advantage is that the thermal inner boots can be detached and worn on their own at camp, inside the tent, if the weather is too cold to wear only socks.

▲ *Overboots are laced up over walking boots. They are useful for snow and ice conditions, and can be worn with crampons.*

▼ *Plastic snow boots consist of a thermal inner boot inside a plastic outer boot, and are excellent for use in deep snow.*

Personal camp kit

There are several core items of equipment that you will need to complete ordinary daily tasks while you are away. These items are known as your personal camp kit. You may feel that some of the items listed here are not relevant for your trip, and there may be other items you do need, but this list makes an excellent starting point when you first begin to pack.

COMPASS

Each person needs to have their own compass, but it is not enough just to carry it, you must also be confident that you can use it correctly. A compass is an essential aid to navigation, and if you get separated from the rest of your team it may be your only way of finding your way back to safety. Most people find the protractor compass easier to use than the prismatic type. Take good care of your compass, and keep it near to hand, either in a buttoned-up pocket, or attached to a belt or strong cord and worn around your neck. See also the sections The compass (100–101) and Using a map and compass (102–103).

MAP

A good map is essential when you are in the wilderness, but it will only be useful if you know how to read it. A planimetric map shows road systems and towns and is a useful tool when planning your transport route, but to learn about the shape of the land you need a topographic map, which is the standard map for wilderness travel. Choose a map with a scale larger than 1:100,000, because this will show land features in the amount of detail you need for accurate navigation. Take care of

▼ The compass is one of the most important items of your kit. Be sure you know how to use it properly and always keep it safe.

your map: have it neatly folded open at the right area as you travel, and keep it in a waterproof map case if the weather is wet or windy. See also the sections Reading a map (98–99), and Using a map and compass (102–103).

WATER BOTTLE

Drinking water is essential for survival, and when travelling in the wilderness you will need to carry all the water required between water sources. Buy good quality water bottles because you risk serious problems if your bottle leaks and you lose all your supply when you are a long way from a water source.

Bottles are available in a range of sizes: quart/pint sizes are the most useful because they are not too heavy to carry when full. An attached bottle cap is best because it cannot get lost; caps that you drink through are very prone to leakages.

WATER PURIFIER

These are widely available from outdoor suppliers, and you will need to carry one if you are travelling in an area where the purity of the drinking water is in doubt. Fill the bottles with water and leave for 15 minutes, then pour the water through the bottle cap, which acts as a sterilizing filter. The filtered water will be fit to drink.

◄ Impure water is poured into the filter of this water purifier and pure water drips into the bottle below.

MONEY

While travelling keep your cash and your passport in a cotton money belt, strapped under your clothing so that it is out of view but still readily accessible. As insurance, keep an emergency fund of low denomination bills in a separate part of the belt from your main money.

Your choice of currency will depend where you are travelling to, but also remember to carry currency for any countries you will be passing through on the way to your final destination. If travelling to parts of the developing world with a minor local currency that is not available in your own country, a supply of US dollars can be extremely useful. Take around US$100 in $10 and $1 bills. US dollars are accepted in most parts of the world.

WRISTWATCH

It is tempting to do away with the trappings of urban life when in the wilderness, but you should always wear an accurate wristwatch. Besides showing the time a watch can be used as a simple check that you are on course on your route. When travelling check the time when you reach scheduled rest points to make sure you are in line with the day's plan; if you haven't reached a checkpoint by a certain time, it could be an indication that you have taken a wrong turning.

▼ Use a wristwatch set to local time to check you are where you expected to be on your route and to measure travel speeds.

▶ *Choose a flashlight that is as small as possible and waterproof as part of your kit.*

◀ *A Swiss Army penknife is compact and includes some valuable features.*

FLASHLIGHT

A small hand-held flashlight is useful for inside the tent or to read a map in dim light or darkness. If you have the space in your pack, take a head torch as well, as this will allow you to work with your hands free – if you have to put up a tent or change a cycle tyre in the dark, for example, or in an emergency situation at night.

BATTERIES

Unless you are sure you will be able to buy them while you are away, carry plenty of spare batteries for use in electrical items, such as torches and radios. Include both alkaline and lithium batteries in your kit. Alkaline batteries cost less than lithium batteries and they are more widely available, but lithium batteries run for longer and can be used in much colder temperatures. Dispose of used batteries with care. Do not burn them or bury them in the ground because the iron they contain can leach out into the earth; take them with you or dispose of them in a garbage bin.

PENKNIFE

If you do not have the space for a comprehensive tool kit, a good penknife such as the Swiss Army knife can be almost as useful. Carry it in your main kit bag before a flight (you will not be able to travel on a plane with a penknife in your hand luggage), then transfer it to your person when you arrive.

EATING EQUIPMENT

Take two plates, one of which should be a deep bowl type, or a set of army mess tins. The advantage of the latter is that you can use them for cooking as well as eating. You will also need a mug (about 300ml/½ pint capacity). Consider the pros and cons of plastic equipment versus enamel and aluminium. Plastic is light and less likely to burn you if filled with hot food or liquid, but it can melt if left too near to a direct heat source. On the other hand, enamel and aluminium are hardwearing, but they are heavier than plastic and can get very hot when filled with hot food

▲ *A set of army-style mess tins provides equipment for cooking and eating, and can still be packed away neatly after use.*

◀ *Each person will need their own mug, bowl, plate and cutlery. Sturdy plastic equipment will avoid mouth burns from hot food.*

or liquid. Your knife, fork and spoon should be made of aluminium or toughened plastic. Buy special camping cutlery if you can as it will be lighter and less bulky than kitchen cutlery.

TENT

A tent provides you with protection from the elements and a sheltered place to rest and sleep. Tents are available in a range of shapes and sizes, many with features designed for specific conditions. Choose a tent that is suitable for the climate and terrain you are visiting, and if you are backpacking, consider how heavy it will be to carry. Get used to putting up your tent before you go, and take extra tent pegs and a guy line with you. See also the section Choosing a tent, 68–71.

▲ *Your sleeping bag should be stored properly when not in use and you should not allow it to get wet.*

SLEEPING BAG AND MAT

Choose a sleeping bag that is suited to the climate because otherwise you will spend your nights too warm or too cold, and in extreme conditions this could be dangerous. You can also carry an insulated sleeping mat to put underneath your sleeping bag. The bag provides your home comforts while you are living outdoors, so look after it well and do not allow it to get wet. If it does, make it a priority to dry it out as soon as you can. For more information, see the section Sleeping bags, 72–75.

▼ *Your washbag should contain everything you need for your personal hygiene regime.*

WASH KIT AND TOWEL

Besides the usual soap, toothbrush and toothpaste, facecloth and hairbrush or comb, your camp wash kit should include shampoo, a nail brush, a pair of nail scissors, and a razor and shaving foam if needed. All of this should be stored in a compact waterproof bag. If you are going to be away for more than a few weeks, have a comprehensive wash kit in your main rucksack and a smaller wash kit of essential items that you can carry around with you. Take both a bath and a hand towel. A supply of flat-packed toilet tissue may also be appreciated. You may wish to add a sunscreen, a lipbalm and some insect repellent, all of which can melt or leak and will need to be securely wrapped inside a plastic bag in the wash bag. Many women prefer to take their usual sanitary protection products with them as these can be hard – if not impossible – to find when you need them in remote areas or developing countries. Even if you do manage to find what you need they may be very expensive.

◀ *A camera and film can be included in your personal kit to give you a valuable photographic record of your trip.*

▲ *A mobile (cell) phone will help you to stay in touch with contacts at home as long as you are able to recharge the battery.*

ELECTRONIC EQUIPMENT

A radio is not an essential item but it can help to make longer trips more enjoyable. If you are travelling abroad and do not expect to have access to a television or the internet, a short-wave radio will enable you to pick up local and international radio programmes.

Other gadgets that you may want to take with you include a camera and film so that you can record your trip. A mobile (cell) phone can be useful, although it can be difficult to pick up a signal in remote or mountainous areas, and if you are travelling abroad you will need to carry a plug adaptor and charger so that you can recharge the battery while you are away.

▲ *Carry a bath towel for bathing or showering, and if your storage capacity allows it carry a hand towel as well.*

▼ *A packet of paper tissues has many uses, so keep a good supply as part of your wash kit.*

▲ *Include a sunscreen of at least SPF 25, especially if you will be in snow or bright sun or at high altitudes.*

FIRST-AID KIT

Include a basic first-aid kit for your individual needs. This should contain some waterproof plasters in various sizes, some sterile gauze wound dressings, medication for diarrhoea, aspirin or paracetamol (acetaminophen), indigestion tablets and a few sachets of rehydration powder to be put in water. A small pair of scissors, a sterilized scalpel blade and a crêpe bandage are useful extras.

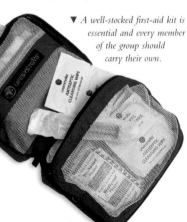

▼ *A well-stocked first-aid kit is essential and every member of the group should carry their own.*

◀ *A pair of binoculars is a non-essential item but one that you will appreciate if you have the space to carry them.*

▼ *A repair kit that includes basic sewing items will allow you to make emergency repairs in the field.*

BINOCULARS

A pair of binoculars is very useful for life in the outdoors, and as long as you are happy to accommodate the extra weight, they can add to the experience of the trip. With a pair of binoculars you can scan ahead along your route for possible hazards; watch wildlife without disturbing them; get a close-up of distant flowers or vegetation; check out a possible campsite without walking to it; or judge the best place to cross a river from a high viewpoint. Keen birdwatchers may prefer to carry a substantial pair of binoculars but for most people a pair of mini-binoculars will be adequate.

PERSONAL JOURNAL, NOTEBOOK AND WRITING MATERIALS

Paper is easily damaged if it gets damp, so carry stationery items in a waterproof pouch. It is worth keeping a travel journal to log your impressions and activities on a long trip; you will find it immensely enjoyable to read long after you have returned home. A notebook and pencil are useful for writing notes or memos for other group members.

REPAIR KITS

A mending kit can be as small as a matchbox but it should contain thread and needles and one or two spare buttons of different sizes, plus darning wool for socks and a few safety pins and a small pair of scissors. Lightweight, compact repair kits are now widely available from outdoor suppliers.

If you wear spectacles, it is worth bringing a spectacle repair kit so that you can carry out minor repairs. You can buy lightweight emergency reading glasses in a tube, which would be better than nothing if your normal glasses get broken or lost.

CLOTHES WASHING KIT

If you will be away for more than a few days and will need to wash and dry your clothes while you are away, you will need a small phial of detergent or travel wash, a washing line and some clothes pegs (pins). Roll up the washing line and pack it together with the other kit items in a plastic bag.

VALUABLE EQUIPMENT

If you are carrying expensive items of equipment, make sure they are covered by your travel insurance. Keep a list of key items to check in transit and before leaving camp.

TRAVEL GAMES

Carrying a selection of games is a good idea to provide entertainment in the evenings or on rest days, or to fill the hours during long journeys or travel delays. If you are staying at a base camp and transporting your equipment by vehicle you will be able to fit in board games or even bat and ball games or skittles, and, if you are backpacking, a pack of playing cards can be carried without adding much weight or bulk.

Avoid carrying expensive electronic games that can be easily damaged and may be a temptation to thieves. If you are travelling with a group of young people it may be an idea to organize group games, perhaps with an educational theme; think these through before you travel and remember to include the necessary props, such as pencils, pens and notebooks.

◀ *A pack of playing cards will provide entertainment at camp in the evenings and in case of travel delays.*

▼ *Along with a phial of detergent, carrying a washing line will mean you are equipped for washing and drying clothes.*

◀ *A notebook and pencil takes up very little room and will prove useful for recording thoughts and writing notes.*

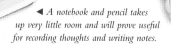

Basic survival kit

If you are travelling in the wilderness it is highly advisable to carry a survival kit. The purpose of the kit is to keep you alive for 24–72 hours if you find yourself lost or injured without shelter, fire or water. It can quite literally mean the difference between life and death.

The survival kit must be carried on your person at all times to be sure it is there when you need it, so keep it small and light; attaching it to a sturdy belt around the waist is ideal. The contents should not be used for any other reason. It should be checked often and items replaced as necessary. Keep the kit in a waterproof pouch bag or in a small tin with a tight-fitting lid.

Your priority in a crisis will be to:
• Protect yourself from the elements
• Make a fire
• Carry and purify water to drink
• Signal your position
• Find your way
• Perform simple first aid

It is important to practise basic survival skills using the equipment in your kit, so that you will know what to do if a situation does arise.

MAKING A SHELTER
Your first priority in a survival situation is to construct a shelter for warmth and to give you a refuge while you take stock of your position.

Space blanket
A lightweight blanket, known as a space blanket, can be used in three ways: to keep warm, with the reflective silver material preventing body heat from escaping and deflecting it back to the body; as a horizontal shelter to reflect the sun's heat away from you; and as an A-shaped shelter to keep you dry from rain.

▲ *A space blanket helps to retain body heat and can be used to deflect the sun's rays away from you.*

◄ *The orange-coloured bivvy bag is light, packs up small and can be a lifesaver in several different ways.*

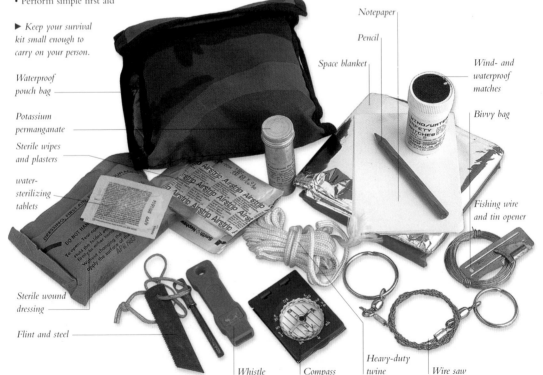

► *Keep your survival kit small enough to carry on your person.*

Waterproof pouch bag

Potassium permanganate

Sterile wipes and plasters

water-sterilizing tablets

Sterile wound dressing

Flint and steel

Whistle

Compass

Heavy-duty twine

Wire saw

Notepaper

Pencil

Space blanket

Wind- and waterproof matches

Bivvy bag

Fishing wire and tin opener

Bivvy bag

A large orange-coloured body-size heavy-duty plastic bag, known as a bivvy bag, has many uses yet is very light to carry. You can get into the bag as a way of keeping warm in cold and windy conditions; for a case of hypothermia, while you are waiting for help to arrive, one person can get inside the bag along with the casualty, using the body as an effective heat source to keep the casualty warm. In addition, the bivvy bag can be used as a groundsheet, or it can be used to signal to the air rescue services in an emergency situation: the bright orange colour makes it highly visible from the air, even in severe weather conditions.

▼ *A length of sturdy cord should be included as part of your main kit.*

Cord

If you need to construct a shelter, you will find parachute cord useful. Carry about 20m/66ft of the cord, packed inside your survival bag.

Wire saw

This packs up very small and is very effective for cutting through small to medium-size tree branches if you need to make a shelter or cut fire wood.

LIGHTING A FIRE

You can buy ready-to-use fire-making kits, or you can make your own. A flint and steel is the most effective homemade version, or you can carry a small amount of

▶ *Firelighting kits, available from outdoor suppliers, contain flint and steel, tinder and matches.*

cotton wool, in case you cannot find kindling, and a small magnifying lens for starting a fire from the sun, a disposable lighter and waterproofed matches (lifeboat matches, which burn in high wind and when wet, are the best). If using matches, keep the striking surface dry and carry an extra striking surface in your survival kit.

Candles

Tealight candles will take up very little room in your pack and can be used to light fires. Do not carry tallow candles as they will melt in hot weather.

CARRYING AND CLEANING
WATER

Once you have found a source of water, you need a container to carry it in. A plastic bag or a condom can be used for this purpose; a condom can hold over 9 litres/2 gallons of water. Put the condom full of water into a sock or knotted trouser leg for added strength and protection. Before drinking the water, you will need to purify it using water-sterilizing tablets. Include a small phial of potassium permanganate, which can also be used to purify water (it is also an antiseptic and can be used to light a campfire). See also the section Clean Water, 234–235.

▶ *Tealight candles burn easily and can be used to light a fire.*

▲ *Water sterilizing tablets are a vital part of your survival kit.*

SIGNALLING

Pack a small flashlight and a heliograph, and wear a whistle on a cord around your neck. A few sheets of paper and a pencil will allow you to leave messages for rescuers trying to track you. A bivvy bag will enable you to signal your location.

FINDING YOUR WAY

Carry a spare compass in your survival kit as back-up in case you lose or damage your first compass.

FIRST-AID KIT

The survival kit should include the following first aid items:
• Adhesive dressings (plasters)
• Sterile wound dressing
• Sachets of rehydration powder
• Salt tablets
• Crêpe bandage
• Sterile scalpel blade
• Darning needle
  • Length of thread or wool

FOOD

Your body can last for up to five days without food, whereas it will last only 24 hours without water. This makes eating your least immediate need in a survival situation. Including food in your kit is not practical but if you carry a length of fishing wire and plenty of fish hooks and sinkers you will be equipped to catch fish for eating.

▶ *Learn how to use fishing wire, hooks and weights for catching fish.*

Group camp kit

If you are going away in a large group, many of the items included in the kit will belong to the group rather than to individuals. For this reason extra care must be taken to ensure that group equipment, including tents, activity or study equipment and guidebooks, is treated with care and respect. If it gets damaged or lost, everyone will suffer.

SHARING RESPONSIBILITY

Large pieces of equipment used by the whole group, such as large sleeping tents or cooking stoves, will need to be looked after by several people in order to distribute the load, if they are being carried, and to share the task of putting them up and taking them down. It can help to allocate responsibility for items to individuals for the duration of the trip. That way everybody knows who has tent A and who has tent B and so on, and there is less chance that key parts, such as tent pegs, will be lost or left behind. If there isn't enough equipment to be allocated in this way, consider working to a rotation system, which will split the responsibilities evenly between group members.

MAPS AND GUIDEBOOKS

These are essential items and as such they should be kept at a central point at the base camp and issued only when

▲ *You may be able to buy equipment such as cooking pots cheaply at local markets at your destination to save you transporting it.*

needed. One person in the group could be made responsible for ensuring the maps and guidebooks are logged out properly and returned after use.

COOKING EQUIPMENT

For group expeditions it is usually easier to handle all meal times in one session, rather than have individuals trying to set

up their own stoves in the same area of the campsite at the same time. For larger groups a campfire offers an effective and more spacious method of cooking large quantities of food, and it means you do not need to transport cumbersome stoves and fuel supplies with you. You may not feel it is worth building a campfire for just one overnight stop but it is a good idea if the group is to stay at the campsite for several days; besides, it adds a lot to the wilderness experience to eat together around an open fire. If planning to cook over a wood fire, make sure that your cooking equipment is suitable for use over direct heat. If you try to use lightweight cooking equipment on a hot wood fire, you can melt the equipment or burn the food.

To prepare and cook food for a number of people at the same time you will need catering-size cooking equipment. If the area you are travelling to is not too remote and

▶ *So important is it that the group's map collection is well looked after that it may be worth making one person responsible for maps for the duration of the trip.*

▲ *Large-volume containers such as jerry cans will be necessary to provide water at a base camp for a big group of people.*

there will be access to local markets, you may be able to buy items such as pans, jerry cans, storage containers and utensils very cheaply. This will mean that you don't have to transport these bulky items to and from your destination, saving baggage space and possibly extra costs if you are travelling by plane and have a restricted luggage allowance. Once you have finished with the equipment you could simply give it away – to the people who run the campsite where you have been staying, for example.

FIRST-AID AND MEDICAL KITS

It is sensible to take a comprehensive first-aid kit if travelling in a large group; this should be in addition to the basic first-aid kits carried by individuals. It may be a good idea to have everyone in the group fill out a medical form that is kept with the first-aid kit; even on personal trips it is reassuring to have a list of individuals' allergies or medication to hand in case it is needed quickly.

Consider separating the group kit into clearly identified sections for emergency and non-emergency items, so that you can get to everyday treatments for blisters, cuts and

scratches or headaches without having to unpack the whole kit. This way it will be easier for group members to find what they are looking for in the kit, and medical items such as sterile dressings and bandages won't get misplaced or made dirty by being unpacked and repacked every day.

The group first-aid and medical kits should be kept in water- and dustproof containers to ensure that none of the items is found to be dirty or damaged when you need it. Make sure everybody knows where the first-aid kit is kept at camp and who is carrying it when on the move. For a large group it is a good idea to make one person responsible for the first-aid and medical kits, replenishing stock as needed and making sure the contents are kept in order. Ideally, the first-aider should have a good level of up-to-date first aid or medical training.

TOOLS

Make sure that someone in the group is responsible for any tools that the group is taking with them. Many of the tools you are likely to need, such as knives, machetes and axes, are very dangerous items and it goes without saying that this is a role for a responsible person; if the group members are children you may need to keep the tools locked up. The tool monitor can also be asked to make sure that the tools are in good working order at the end of the expedition, and that they are cleaned and stored ready for another trip.

▼ *An extensive medical kit will be necessary for a team of people; organize the kit into labelled packs so that you can find what you need easily.*

A QUESTION OF OWNERSHIP

If you are going on an expedition and have bought group equipment out of expedition funds (which may include contributions from the team members as well as from sponsorship or donations) you need to decide what you are going to do with the equipment when you return home. Are you going leave it in the area you have been travelling or working in, giving it away to local people or a local organization; or will you store it for a future trip; or are the members to be allowed to buy it – perhaps it could be auctioned off for charity – when the group gets back home? Discuss as a group at your pre-trip planning meetings and make a decision before you go.

▲ *A hands-free flashlight may be needed for field or study work, and will simplify the task of putting up tents in the dark.*

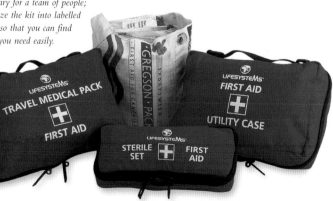

Choosing a tent

When you choose a tent, you will be faced with a huge selection of styles, colours, weights and sizes. To help narrow down your choice, and to make sure you end up buying what you do actually need, consider where and when you are going to use the tent, how you are going to carry it, what you are going to use it for and how many people it will need to sleep.

WHERE AND WHEN ARE YOU GOING TO USE THE TENT?

Consider the climate you can expect at your destination and the environment in which you are going to camp. In the African bush your tent will need to protect you from the heat and possibly from heavy rain; on a mountainside above the Arctic Circle your priority is protection from high winds.

▲ *Small robust tents are preferable for use in exposed sites or colder climates, with the lower volume of air space retaining the heat.*

▼ *In hot, dry climates choose a larger tent with more internal space that encourages air circulation and keeps the temperature down.*

▲ *The general-purpose ridge tent is suitable for climatic conditions anywhere in the world, and is available in a range of sizes.*

▲ *Some vehicles have been adapted to take a tent on the roof to give protection from wild animals attracted to the camp at night.*

▲ *A contemporary one-person tunnel tent. The hoop pole structure offers good floor space but will not withstand high winds.*

If you are going to a hot, dry climate try to allow for as much space in your tent as possible to encourage the air to circulate and keep you cooler. If you are backpacking you will need to consider the pros and cons of an airy tent against the extra bulk to be carried. Cotton and canvas materials will stand up to and protect you from the sun far better than synthetic materials. Strong ultraviolet light in the tropics can ruin nylon materials very quickly, and the thorns on many bushes and trees can destroy lightweight material.

TENT CRITERIA

The tent is your home while you are in the wilderness. Its main function is to provide a warm and dry place for you to sleep, but you may also need to cook inside it or use it as a shelter while you sit out severe weather conditions. The following criteria are essential:

• The tent should be big enough to allow sleeping space and adequate ventilation for all users and their kit.
• There should be enough height on the inside for everyone to sit upright at the same time.
• The flooring material needs to be robust enough to give protection from the ground; if it isn't you will need to carry additional matting if you are to sleep in comfort.

If the climate is hot and wet, and you visit in the rainy season, the tent may have to withstand weeks or months of heavy rain. Natural materials such as cotton or canvas will cope better with this type of climate.

In high mountains in a cold climate, you will want a small tent that will warm up quickly with your body heat and will be able to withstand high winds. A tent made from synthetic materials will be lighter, and therefore easier to carry, than a cotton or canvas one. It will also be stronger, with a sewn-in groundsheet, made of a substantial material, suitable for pitching on snow, ice and rocks.

In very extreme cold conditions you may find that the tent doors are better fastened by some other means than a zip, such as tied or velcro fasteners, because zips can freeze if it is extremely cold.

HOW TO CARRY THE TENT?

If you plan to transport your tent in the back of a vehicle, then weight or size will not be a major consideration. However, if you will be carrying the tent yourself, you will need to choose the lightest option possible (see the section on Lightweight camping, 186–187).

▶ *The geodesic dome tent is spacious on the inside, and if the sloping wall is pitched in the direction of the wind it is very stable.*

WHAT ARE YOU GOING TO USE THE TENT FOR?

Is your tent going to be used for backpacking, where you will set it up for the night, cook, sleep, then take it down and move on? Or are you going to set up camp and use your tent as a work place, eating, sleeping and general living area, perhaps staying for several days or weeks? Think about how you will use the tent and choose accordingly.

HOW MANY PEOPLE WILL THE TENT NEED TO SLEEP?

If your tent is going to be used in a base camp, decide how many people it will need to sleep, and how much room you will allow each person. If you have a mixed-sex group, they may prefer to be separated for sleeping, using either a divided tent or separate smaller tents. How much kit each person will have must also be taken into account if the kit is going to be stored inside the tent.

RIDGE TENT

This general-purpose tent is suitable for camping anywhere, from the back garden to the desert or jungle. The ridge tent has an upright pole or an A-shaped pole assembly at each end, and, in some cases, an additional ridgepole across the top. This adds extra weight but it also stabilizes the tent, and this could be important if you are likely to experience high winds. Some ridge tents have sloping ridges to cut down on weight.

The walls of the ridge tent are created by adjustable guy lines, which stretch the inner walls outwards,

KEY QUESTIONS

Before making any decisions, look at the styles available and talk to a reputable tent retailer before asking yourself the following questions:

• How heavy is the tent? Pick up a packed version to feel the weight for yourself.
• Are there additional features that are of no use but add to the cost?
• Is the stitching well done and are the guying and guy line points reinforced to take the strain?
• Are the poles strong enough for the job and would they support the material in strong winds?
• If the tent gets damaged in the field, can it be repaired quickly and easily?
• If it is a dome tent can you buy spare poles for it?
• How easy is it to pitch the tent, not just on a summer's day in a local field but also on a mountain in high winds in near darkness?
• How many people are required to pitch the tent?
• Is the tent material of good quality and will it stand up well to the conditions you are going to take it into?
• Will you need a two-skin tent, i.e. an inner tent with a fly sheet, and will the fly sheet need to come right down to the ground to offer you protection in wet and windy conditions?

supporting the tent and allowing you to utilize the whole of the floor space without touching the sides of the tent. This is important because if the inner walls touch the outer fly sheet and the fly sheet is wet, the dampness will soak through to the inner walls, causing water to leach inside the tent. A door at each end is the preferred choice, so that if you have to cook in a doorway due to intense cold or heavy rain you can choose the door opening that offers the most shelter from the prevailing wind and the elements.

▲ *A standard ridge tent is simple to erect and maintain even for most inexperienced campers, hence its continued popularity.*

BELL OR SINGLE-POLE TENTS

Bell tents have a single pole in the middle of the tent, while single-pole tents may have either a pole or an A-shaped pole assembly. Both designs are very stable in strong winds.

▼ *Large patrol tents are ideal for base camps but the size and weight of the canvas means they will have to be transported by vehicle.*

DOME AND GEODESIC DOME TENTS

These have a number of poles threaded into sleeves on either the inner or outer tent. The extra poles make these the most expensive types of tent to buy, and if your poles break you will need spares or splints to slide over the break.

The geodesic dome is more stable than the ordinary dome in bad weather, but it is difficult to pitch in high winds.

TUNNEL AND WEDGE TENTS

The tunnel tent is a cross between a ridge tent and a dome. It offers good floor space as the pole system is a series of hoops down the tent, but in high winds it can blow in and lose its shape. The wedge tent has most of the disadvantages of the tunnel and few advantages. Instability is a problem in bad weather as the large areas of material are a target for high winds.

▲ *Wedge and tunnel tents on display at an outdoor suppliers fair. The advantages of these tents are their small size and low weight, making them popular with backpackers. One disadvantage is the lack of headroom.*

▼ *Geodesic dome tents are one of the sturdiest tents available and will withstand even gale-force winds so long as the poles – which are threaded through the fabric to give the tent its shape – are not damaged.*

▼ *Large frame tents provide useful areas for study or group meetings at base camps, but several people will be needed to put them up.*

Sleeping bags

A comfortable, warm sleeping bag will give you the good night's sleep you need when living outdoors. Getting enough sleep is as important to your physical health and state of mind as eating, and the right bag is important.

All sleeping bags work by trapping air in their fillings; the air is warmed by the heat from your body and retained in the filling, insulating you against the cold. The more warm air a bag traps, the greater its insulating properties.

There is a huge variety of sleeping bags available, from inexpensive but basic simple-quilted versions to quality, down-filled double-quilted ones. The criteria to look for when choosing a bag are the method of construction, what material is used, what filling is used, how it is zipped, its size and whether or not it has a hood.

CONSTRUCTION

There are basically three different types of sleeping bag construction: simple quilting or stitch-through; box-wall; and double quilting.

Simple quilting or stitch-through

This method is usually used in the cheaper sleeping bags. They are not very effective at retaining warmth because warm air will be lost where the stitching goes through the fabric. These bags have a low temperature rating, making them suitable for warm summer weather, or for two consecutive seasons: spring and summer or summer and autumn.

Box-wall

Bags with this type of construction have a high temperature rating, and they may be suitable for two to three seasons, or even three to four seasons in a temperate climate. They come in three different forms.

- Box-wall construction, where the filling is contained within "boxes" to prevent the filling from moving about.
- Slant-wall construction, with slanted layers of overlapping fibres. This improves on the box-wall version by giving the filling more room to expand, filling with air for improved insulation and, therefore, warmth.
- V-baffle construction, which improves on the slant-wall construction by making sure there is always plenty of filling throughout the bag.

Double quilting

This is effectively two simple quilting or stitch-through-type sleeping bags put together and offset to eliminate cold spots. It usually has the highest-quality filling but is heavy to carry and may not be suitable for backpacking trips.

MATERIAL

Your choice of material for the shell depends on the type of environment and what time of year you will be using the sleeping bag:

- Cotton is ideally suited to high temperatures and humidity as it is a breathable natural fabric and will absorb sweat and feel comfortable.

Consider any kind of sleeping bag rating as a rough guide only as there is no standard rating system. Some manufacturers describe the number of seasons a bag may be suitable for. Others give temperature ranges; these may be the range of temperature in which the bag will feel comfortably warm, or it may be the temperature at which you will survive but won't feel warm.

- Nylon is better suited to cooler temperatures, where sweating is not likely to be a problem; some nylon sleeping bags have a cotton lining on the inside, which increases the comfort factor.
- Pertex is a good down-proofing material, which means that it stops the filling material from working its way through the fabric. It is also water-repellent (but not water*proof*), which makes it suitable for damp, though not wet, conditions, such as high humidity.

Military-type sleeping bags have a groundsheet sewn on to the underneath of the bag so they can be used directly on the ground, even without a tent or sleeping mat. However, these bags are often heavy and bulky and they can be difficult to clean. They are available from specialist outdoor stores that sell ex-military equipment.

▲ *Simple or stitch-through quilting is found in cheaper sleeping bags that are suitable for one or two seasons of the year.*

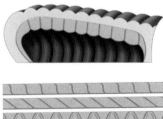

▲ *Box-wall construction comes in three forms: box-wall (top and main diagram), slant-wall (centre) and V-baffle (bottom).*

▲ *Double-quilting construction is effectively two simple or stitch-through bags put together and offset to better retain the heat.*

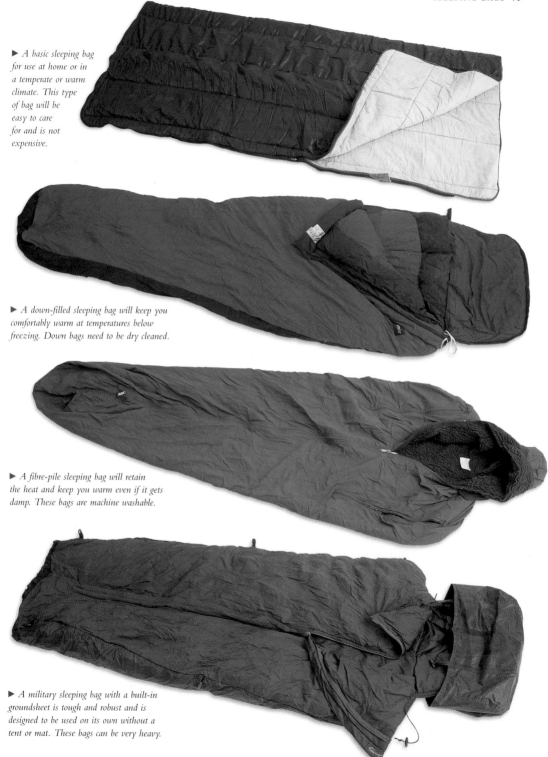

▶ *A basic sleeping bag for use at home or in a temperate or warm climate. This type of bag will be easy to care for and is not expensive.*

▶ *A down-filled sleeping bag will keep you comfortably warm at temperatures below freezing. Down bags need to be dry cleaned.*

▶ *A fibre-pile sleeping bag will retain the heat and keep you warm even if it gets damp. These bags are machine washable.*

▶ *A military sleeping bag with a built-in groundsheet is tough and robust and is designed to be used on its own without a tent or mat. These bags can be very heavy.*

FACTORS AFFECTING WARMTH

How warm your sleeping bag will keep you is dependent on a number of variable factors besides bag construction and filling:

- The climate, including the humidity level (high humidity makes the bag damp, and increases heat loss through conduction).
- Whether you are in a tent or shelter, or out in the open air.
- Whether you are on your own inside the sleeping bag.
- Whether or not you are using a sleeping mat underneath the bag.
- What clothes you are wearing.
- The shape of the bag, with a close-fitting bag being warmer.
- How much you have eaten, as food provides energy and heat.
- How tired you are, as it is more difficult to get warm when tired.

FILLINGS

The biggest difference between bags is in the type of filling and the thickness of it. The purpose of a sleeping bag filling is to trap air as insulation. The thicker the filling, and the more effectively it traps the air, the better the bag will be at keeping you warm.

Natural fillings

Feather-filled sleeping bags have one of three types of filling: down, feather, and down and feather mix.

Down

Pure down is the fluffy underplumage of ducks and/or geese. It is by far the lightest and warmest, weight for weight, of all bag fillings, and is comfortable over a greater temperature range. Down shapes itself around the body for a close, warm fit, unlike synthetic fillings, which tend to stand away from the body, leaving cold spots. Down is more compressible than synthetic fillings, so it packs up much smaller and won't get damaged when stuffed into a rucksack. The drawbacks of down are that it loses its insulation properties when wet, and takes a long time to dry out. It can also be damaged by damp storage. However, it is difficult to get a down bag wet in the first place, unless you drop it in water or sleep outside in the rain without shelter. This is especially so with modern shell materials, which are water-resistant and dry out quickly.

Although down bags are expensive, they can be expected to last much longer than synthetic bags – for up to 20 years if well cared for – and this makes them a more economical choice in the long term. They are most suitable for situations where warmth and space are at a premium, and are a particular favourite for cold conditions because of their comfort, weight and bulk.

Down/feather mix

A number of manufacturers mix duck or goose down and feathers together to make a cheaper filling (separating the feathers from the stalkless down plumules is very time-consuming and therefore expensive). The mixed filling has all the advantages of down: it is warm and comfortable, light to carry and easily packed up, although you do need more filling to achieve the same level of warmth. Check what proportion of down makes up the filling, as a greater amount of down means a warmer sleeping bag. There will usually be less than 50 per cent down in the mix.

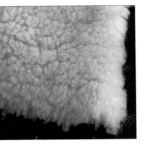

▲ *A fibre-pile filling will keep you warm even if it becomes damp or wet, and this may be crucial in a cold and wet climate.*

▼ *Duck or goose down is the most costly bag filling but it is also the most effective at retaining heat and it will last the longest.*

▲ *Synthetic bag fillings are cheaper than down and although they weigh more, they will perform better when damp or wet.*

▼ *Feather filling uses poorer quality feathers than down and requires more in weight and bulk to provide the same amount of heat.*

▼ *Many people find a down and feather mix a good compromise between cost and the ability to insulate effectively.*

▲ *At good outdoor suppliers you will be faced with a huge selection of sleeping bags. Always ask for advice if you feel confused.*

Feather

These are the bigger, stiffer feathers of ducks and geese, which you will be able to feel through the bag shell. A feather filling will not have the same insulation properties as down or the down/feather mix, and you will need at least twice as much filling to achieve the same warmth, but feather bags are less expensive and they can still provide a very comfortable night's sleep.

Synthetic fillings

These fillings don't have the natural lightness of down or feather fillings, and synthetic bags at the cheaper end of the market tend to be heavy, bulky and less soft. They are also less durable, as the synthetic filling starts to lose its insulation properties after only a couple of years. However, synthetic bags are inexpensive to buy. They perform well when wet and dry out quickly, and are machine washable. They are more tolerant of careless handling and damp conditions than down bags, and are perfectly adequate for situations where warmth, low weight and bulk are not your priority.

One specialist synthetic filling is fibre pile, which is a thicker version of the material used for fleece jackets. Fibre pile will retain its insulation properties when wet, it can be hung out to dry, and is machine washable. However, it is bulkier and heavier than other synthetic-filled bags, and it may not be suitable for lightweight camping. Fibre-pile fillings can be difficult to find in stores.

SIZE AND SHAPE

Try out the bag in the store to see if it is wide and long enough for you. A bag that fits close to your body will keep you warmer than a roomy one, but check it doesn't feel too restrictive. Better quality bags have a tapered shape.

ZIPS

Most bags have a zip of some kind to allow the bag to be opened out full, which makes getting in and out easy, and allows for ventilation. It is also useful for cleaning the bag. Zips can be full-length, half-length, or down one side and across the bottom. Any zip is a potential cold spot, though a quality bag will have a protected pad of filling under the zip. If a bag does not have a zip, it will be more difficult to get into but will weigh less.

HOOD

Some 20 per cent of body heat is lost through the head, and a bag with a hood retains warmth more effectively. It also makes a comfortable resting place for your head, and can be pulled up over your head to protect you from insects, such as flies or mosquitos.

SAFETY

Never leave your sleeping bag or liner on the ground for any length of time, even when it is rolled up, but pack it away in your rucksack. In temperate or hot countries, unroll your sleeping bag only just before you get into it to avoid any insects getting in with you.

▼ *Sleeping out without a tent can be great fun but do not sleep too near the camp fire or else you could damage your sleeping bag.*

Other sleeping equipment

Additional items can be added to your kit for a more comfortable night's sleep. Consider the cost of buying and transporting these extra items, as well as the additional weight and bulk if you are backpacking and have to carry them.

INSULATION AND PROTECTION

You may want to insulate yourself from the ground if it will be cold, hard or wet, or if there will be ants, snakes or spiders on it.

Camp beds

These come in all shapes and sizes and are heavy, so you will want to use them only if transporting your equipment by vehicle or pack animal. However, camp beds will get you right off the ground for a very comfortable night's sleep.

If you are going to use a camp bed, you will need some insulation beneath the sleeping bag, such as a mat, as the layer of air between you and the ground will become very cold at night. If you are going to an area where there will be mosquitos, consider setting up a frame around your bed for a mosquito net. When using a camp bed, always set it up on flat ground, so that you don't tip the bed over accidentally when turning over in the night.

Air mattresses

These require inflating by mouth or with an air pump, and this makes them time-consuming to set up. Air mattresses come in different sizes, colours and thicknesses. If over-inflated, they may feel hard and uncomfortable to sleep on.

An air mattress full of air becomes cold overnight, so in anything but hot weather, you will need extra insulation underneath you, such as an insulated mat. Be careful that the mattress does not get punctured by sharp stones on the ground or carelessly pierced by a knife or penknife, and do not drag it along the ground; carry a puncture repair kit so that if necessary you can make repairs in the field.

Self-inflating sleeping mats

When you unscrew the valve on one of these mats, air will be sucked in and it will inflate itself, though you can speed up the process by giving one or two puffs of air by mouth to start off with. Check for sharp stones or thorns on the ground before laying the mat out. These mats are best carried inside the rucksack to protect them from damage.

Insulation mats

These are the lightest and cheapest type of insulation, and they come in several thicknesses. If you are going to a very cold climate, a thick foam mat will provide good insulation but it will be heavy to carry and bulky. The great advantage with these mats is that you cannot damage them, except by putting them in direct contact with something

◄ *Metal frame camp beds are bulky and heavy but they do keep you off the ground and this will greatly improve your comfort.*

▼ *Insulation mats are available in a range of thicknesses and lengths, so choose one for the conditions you will be sleeping in.*

▼ *Self-inflating mats are convenient to use, but do not over-inflate them and watch for sharp stones or rocks on the ground beneath.*

▼ *A cotton sleeping bag liner will help to keep the sleeping bag clean and is easy to wash.*

▲ *A mosquito net is essential for tropical climates. Attach it to the inside of your tent and check daily for tears.*

very hot, which will melt them. Check for stones on the ground when you unroll your mat, which could give you an uncomfortable night's sleep.

NEWSPAPER

If you are lightweight camping without a sleeping mat, and are going to have to sleep on the ground with only the tent groundsheet for insulation, you can lay sheets of newspaper under your sleeping bag. You will need at least five to ten sheets of newspaper for effective insulation, but it is better than nothing if the ground is very cold or hard.

SLEEPING BAG LINERS

Whichever material you choose for the outer shell of your sleeping bag, you might want to consider buying a separate liner. This is a thin fabric bag, usually made of cotton or silk, which fits inside the sleeping bag. It does offer a little more warmth, but its main advantage is that it protects the sleeping bag from getting dirty on the inside,

▶ *Self-inflating sleeping mats can be rolled up neatly and strapped on to the outside of your rucksack during transit.*

and it can be washed more easily than the bag. In hot weather, you can sleep in the liner on its own, perhaps using your sleeping bag underneath it for padding, as you would a sleeping mat.

INFLATABLE PILLOW

Although it is not strictly necessary, an inflatable pillow weighs next to nothing and will add to your comfort during the night. It can also be used to give head and neck support on long journeys. Inflate the pillow by mouth at your campsite and deflate it after use, so that it can be folded up and packed with your tent bag or tucked into your rucksack.

▼ *An inflatable pillow is small and light enough even for backpackers to carry, and will improve your night-time comfort.*

Backpacks and carrying equipment

A backpack is used to carry food and clothing while on the move. It can be used to carry camping and cooking gear if you will be living outdoors and without any other means of transporting your gear. The backpack you need for a day's walking in warm weather will be very different to the one needed for a three-week camping trip through the mountains. As with any equipment, decide how you will be using the pack before you buy one.

Many modern backpacks are covered in straps, zips, gadgets and pockets, and these additional features will often add to the price. Rather than being dazzled by the apparent complexity of these backpacks, consider if you really need the extra features. Remember, too, that most people will fill whatever size backpack they have, which can make for a very heavy load, so the smaller the sack, the less temptation there will be to take too much gear.

All backpacks are claimed to be waterproof but some fabric materials are better than others, and it is a good idea to line the main compartment with a plastic bag to keep your gear dry. (You may prefer crucial items such as your passport or first-aid kit to be wrapped in additional sturdy plastic bags as a further safeguard.)

Main compartment

Lockable zip opening to main compartment

Smaller front compartment

Lockable zip opening to front compartment

Document pocket for quick-access items

Mesh side pockets

▲ *A day sack should be big enough to carry your waterproofs and a sweater, a survival kit, and enough food and water for the day.*

DAY SACKS

For a day's walking in the summer, a small, light day sack with a capacity of between 20 and 35 litres containing food and water, waterproof clothing and emergency supplies will be as much as you need. If your activities will involve mountaineering, ski touring or snow hiking, choose one of the larger day sacks of around 40 litres.

Additional features

Day sacks do not need a support frame because they are not designed to carry heavy loads. Even so, comfort is always important, and because a day sack sits directly against your back, padding on the outside is advisable so that any sharp contents do not dig into you.

In addition, when packing make sure you place soft items such as clothing against the rear of the pack to act as an extra cushion for your back.

In hot weather or during strenuous activities, wearing the sack may cause your back to sweat. To control this, many better-designed packs have a robust cotton panel on the back to absorb sweat; a cotton panel feels more comfortable than a synthetic one. Quality modern sacks are fitted with a high-wicking padded mesh back for improved ventilation to reduce sweating.

Day sacks do not usually have pockets on the outside because the main compartment is small enough to be easily accessible. There will usually be a pocket in the top flap, which is useful for holding maps and valuables.

Larger day sacks will come with a waist strap, and if you think you are going to do a lot of scrambling or steep country work, it is advisable to have one of these, otherwise the pack can move around as you climb, and this may affect your balance.

If you are planning to walk over difficult terrain, or are mountaineering, ski touring or snow hiking, choose a larger day sack with attachment points on the outside, which will allow you to fix on your walking pole, ice axe, skis or crampons, keeping your hands free.

Other features include compressible straps, which can be pulled tight to reduce the volume of an empty sack, a key-ring attachment and a top handle.

WHAT TO LOOK FOR IN A PACK

• The pack must be sturdy and comfortable, whatever its size.
• Webbing needs to be tough, in good condition and adjustable. This is especially important on larger packs as heavy loads can quickly weaken poor webbing.
• The outer fabric should be tough and fully waterproof.
• There should be a drawstring hood inside the main sack to prevent water leaking in and contents falling out.
• Outer pockets should have zips rather than straps or drawstrings.
• A comfortable waist belt is essential on any pack bigger than a day sack.

LARGE DAY SACKS OR OVERNIGHT BACKPACKS

These will come in the 35–55 litre range, and they may have a frame or may be frameless.

As you will be carrying a heavier weight than in a smaller day sack, look closely at the waist or hip belt to see if it is strong and well padded and has a quick-release buckle in case you need to jettison the sack quickly. Also check that the shoulder straps are well padded and that the straps can be tightened or slackened quickly and easily. The webbing on all straps should be well made and strong.

This type of sack can come with external pockets, usually one or two on each side, as well as an easy-access document pocket in the top flap for maps. Side pockets are very useful for keeping water bottles, fuel and other fluids or dirty items of kit away from your main kit to prevent damage in the event of leakage. Make sure zip-up side pockets are kept securely fastened when in use, so that nothing can fall out accidentally.

Whether or not you need a pack with a frame depends on how you will be using the pack and the type of loads you will be carrying. A frame adds extra weight to the pack but it will make heavy or bulky loads more comfortable to carry, and this is very important over long distances.

▲ *If you expect to carry heavy loads in a larger backpack you need to make sure that the waist belt is padded and the shoulder straps are intact and strong. If any of the stitching is loose before you set off, the straps may break under the weight of the load and this will make your trip very difficult.*

▲ *If fully packed a large backpack without a frame can cause sweating on the back in hot weather or during strenuous activity.*

▼ *Overnight backpacks will hold equipment for short lightweight camping trips or for day use if work or study gear is to be carried.*

Elastic holders for easy-access items

Hooded opening to main compartment

Front pocket for smaller items

Zip-fastening side pocket

Padded waist belt

Straps to carry equipment externally

EXPEDITION BACKPACKS

These packs are available in 55- to over 120-litre sizes. The smaller packs are ideal for lightweight walking, while the larger ones are for longer trips or trips to more remote areas; somewhere in between is usually enough for most people and most camping expeditions.

These packs can be expensive, so make sure the one you buy feels comfortable to wear and is suitable for the load you will be carrying.

Key features

Two or more external pockets is usual on expedition backpacks, with some packs having pockets that can be detached and used on their own as small day sacks or large belt pouches. Many modern packs have the main compartment divided so that your sleeping bag and clothes can be packed in the lower, smaller section, and the upper section can be used for general equipment. In better-quality packs, you will be able to open the zipped divider or remove it altogether to accommodate longer-length items.

Access is through the top of the pack, but zipped-front access to the divided compartments is increasingly common.

It is important that an expedition backpack is comfortable and fits well, as you could be wearing it every day for days if not weeks, travelling over difficult terrain and carrying heavy loads. The waist belt and shoulder harness must be padded and adjustable; a chest strap will hold the sack more firmly in position on your back.

External frame packs

If you have to carry boxes or oddly shaped loads into the backcountry using your backpack, tying them on to an external frame may be the best solution. The most useful frame designs will have a small step at the bottom to support the load from slipping down. If you will be walking in woodland, rainforests or jungles, where there is dense vegetation, choose a backpack with a frame that isn't too high above your head to avoid getting it caught in the tree branches and vines and making your progress more difficult.

▲ *The advantage of a frame backpack is that you can strap almost anything on to it, no matter how awkward the shape.*

CHOOSING A PACK FRAME

• A pack with an internal frame will be lighter than one with an external frame, and the pack will be less bulky for storage in transit or when not in use.
• External frames are stronger, which means they can carry a heavier load without causing damage to the backpack.
• External frames are more rigid and are especially good for awkwardly shaped and bulky items. In an emergency, a backpack with an external frame can be used as a stretcher to carry a sick or injured person to safety.
• External frames carry the load high up on your body, distributing the weight more evenly over the hip and back area.
• A good external frame is designed to allow air space between the frame and your back to minimize sweating caused by constant body contact with the pack.

Hooded opening to main compartment

Main compartment for large or heavy items

Side pockets for fuel or water bottles

External elastic straps

Padded waist belt

◀ *Modern expedition packs are designed to carry heavy loads conveniently and in comfort but they must be packed correctly.*

▲ *If carrying equipment by vehicle you can use a roofrack for bulky items to save space inside, but make sure the load is attached securely and protect it with a waterproof sheet in case of sudden showers.*

▲ *Pack animals can carry heavy loads but you must make sure that the weight is balanced on either side of the animal.*

PANNIERS

If you have to carry your gear on a bicycle, vehicle, motorbike or animal, you will need a set of panniers.

Cycle

Make sure cycle panniers are well secured and will not get in the way of the wheels or the chain of the cycle. Check that you have balanced the weight of the load as equally as possible between each side.

Vehicle or motorbike

Cars and vans can be fitted with roofracks to increase the storage space inside the vehicle. Motorbikes can be fitted with panniers that sit on either side of the bike, behind the saddle.

Animal

On animals, you will need some kind of frame or pannier bags, but these must sit comfortably on the back of the animal and not rub its back. Always check any pack animal's back at night for any signs of sore spots and treat

◀ *Panniers are essential for touring trips on a bicycle, and even then you will be very limited with the equipment you can carry.*

▲ *Equipment is loaded on a camel in a very specific way, and if you are planning to do it yourself you should ask your guide's advice.*

them immediately. Horses, mules and camels are capable of carrying heavy loads but do not overload an animal with equipment; the animal must always be able to move freely. Make it part of your routine at each rest stop to check that the load has not moved or become unsafe.

▶ *If travelling by plane and vehicle you may find conventional luggage more convenient than a backpack.*

Cooking stoves

There are five kinds of fuel suitable
for outdoor cooking stoves, and all
have their advantages and disadvantages,
including volatility, smell, ease of use
and cost. Which fuel you choose will
dictate the type of stove you can take,
though multi-fuel stoves, which use
more than one type, are available.

When planning your trip, consider
the type of conditions you need the
stove to operate in. Some gases will
not perform well in extreme cold
conditions and some fuels evaporate
quickly in very hot conditions, so it
is important to make a suitable choice.
Also note that in some countries you
may not be able to buy the right kind
of cylinder for your stove.

GAS
This is probably the most popular and
easiest type of stove to use, though the
fuel is potentially the most dangerous.
There are two types of gas (liquid
petroleum gas) available: butane (the
more usual) and propane (which will
operate in much lower temperatures).

▼ *Gas stoves are available in different sizes
but the most important feature for safe use is
a stable base to prevent it toppling over.*

◀ *The Trangia stove runs on
methylated spirits. It is windproof
and stable and includes its own
set of cooking pans and a kettle.*

When gas stoves are not being used,
they must be turned off and kept in a
well-ventilated area, away from sleeping
areas. If they do leak, they can build
up an invisible layer of gas that can
suffocate sleeping people and explode
when ignited.

METHYLATED SPIRITS
The most popular stove of this type is
the Trangia stove and cooking set from
Sweden, which is windproof and very
stable; some models also have a small
gas stove attached. These stoves come
in two sizes, and each comes with its
own set of cooking pans.

Methylated spirits (methyl alcohol)
burn very cleanly, but the flame
is almost invisible, so great
care must be taken when
lighting or refilling the burner.
It should be carried in a
specialized fuel bottle.

PARAFFIN
This burns in the form of a
vapour mixed with air, and it
will need to be primed or heated

▶ *A camp oven will allow you to bake
fresh bread at a base camp if you are able
to transport your gear by vehicle.*

▲ *A paraffin stove is cheap to run but it can
be difficult to use. You may need to practise
before taking it into the field for the first time.*

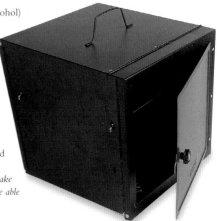

▲ *A petrol stove is versatile and easy to use but can be expensive to buy.*

▲ *A windshield can be fitted around a petrol stove to protect the flame and make cooking more efficient in windy weather.*

CARRYING SPARE FUEL

Make sure you have an adequate supply of fuel for your cooking stove. If you are travelling abroad you will need to check that the fuel for your stove is available in the country you are going to. If not, you may have to change the type of stove you are using, since most airlines, including all in Europe and the United States, do not allow gas or flammable liquids to be carried on planes.

▼ *Use sturdy metal containers for carrying petrol or paraffin supplies to your destination; use plastic containers for water only.*

with another fuel to bring it to the temperature where it will vaporize. Spilt paraffin will not evaporate and will leave an unpleasant smell. Always store it in a metal fuel bottle in case of leakages.

This kind of stove is cheap to run and burns well with a hot flame, but it is also the most complicated to use and can take a while to get used to. As a further disadvantage it will blacken cooking pans and clog burner jets.

PETROL

This burns in the form of vapour under pressure and will burn cleanly unless additives are in the fuel. Unlike paraffin, it does not need a secondary fuel to heat it to the required temperature.

Petrol is very volatile and the smell is strong and unpleasant. It must be stored in a special metal fuel container in case of leakages. If spilled it will evaporate quickly, especially if the weather is hot, and it will ruin food and stain fabrics if it comes into contact with them.

SOLID FUEL

This is available in two forms: tablet (Hexamine) and alcohol jelly. This type of fuel gives off strong and unpleasant fumes, and the flame is difficult to put out (although this can be an advantage in windy conditions) and hard to regulate. Solid fuel stoves must only ever be used in a well-ventilated place.

▲ *Solid fuel stoves were first designed to be used by the army. They are for one-time use only but are useful to carry in an emergency.*

WARNING

All stoves must be treated with care. When lit they use oxygen and give out lethal carbon monoxide, and must be used in a well-ventilated place. Make sure the flame is really out before filling a stove with fuel.

▼ *Solid fuel stoves are now available to the public and are excellent for use in windy conditions.*

Cooking equipment

What you need in the way of cooking equipment for a backpacking trip will be minimal, since the priority is to keep your pack weight down and the meals you eat will be basic. At a base or standing camp, you may have the capacity to set up a kitchen to feed a large number of people, who may be ready for better and more varied meals than they have had out in the field. This will require the type of cooking equipment used by a catering kitchen. For anything in between, the sort of equipment you take will depend on how easily you can transport it.

LIGHTWEIGHT CAMPING

When you are carrying your equipment on your back, you cannot afford to take more than what is essential. While the food you eat is important, its primary function is as a source of energy, and it is unlikely that you will eat as well

▼ *Individuals should carry their own set of cutlery. The advantage of folding sets is that they are very convenient to pack.*

as you would like to. The typical menu will consist of canned, pouch or dehydrated foods, which require little in the way of cooking except to be heated through. A set of mess tins is a practical choice for your equipment because the two tins can be used for both cooking and eating, and can be neatly packed, one inside the other, for storage. A folding aluminium cutlery set takes up little space and will double up as a set of cooking utensils. If you are taking canned foods you need to pack a can opener. Good penknives, such as the Swiss Army knife, can be used as improvised kitchen utensils. The tiny scissors and can opener on the knife will be useful, especially for overnight or ultra-lightweight camping, but for longer trips, a standard household can opener will be easier to use.

BASE CAMPS

Much more sophisticated meals can be cooked at a base camp, which may stand for several weeks while the team completes a schedule of activities or a course of study. Because a base camp is more permanent, and is not being dismantled and moved on a daily basis, it can be better equipped, with a wider range of sturdy cooking equipment and utensils. You will need to decide the kind of heat source you will be using before choosing your equipment.

COOKING POTS

Depending on how many people you are catering for, you will need a number of pots in a range of sizes, with some big enough to boil up to 9–13.5 litres/ 2–3 gallons of water. Make sure that all pots are kept clean both inside and out and that the handles are safe and in good working order. Having lids on the pans will reduce cooking times.

◀ *Mess tins pack away neatly with one tin inside the other. They were designed for army use but are now available to the public.*

How heavy your pots will need to be will depend on whether you are using stoves or fires for cooking; lightweight metal containers can be used on stoves, but never on an open fire (see the sections Cooking over a fire, 222–223, and Cooking on stoves, 224–225). Frying pans, in particular, need to be heavy duty because they are used at such high temperatures.

WATER CONTAINERS

Lightweight campers cannot carry supplies of water and must source it along the route. However, if weight is not an issue because you are travelling by vehicle to a base or standing camp or to a remote area or through a dry climate, you can carry large quantities of water in dixies. These robust containers, which hold several litres of water, are made of plastic and have a screw-top lid that makes them leak-proof. The flat-sided shape of some designs makes them easy to store at camp or during transit. Fuel can be stored in metal jerry cans, but do not carry water in metal containers.

▼ *When a fire of grass or twigs is lit in the base of a volcana kettle, the heat passes up a tube in the container to heat the water.*

◄ *Camp cookware can include a range of pots of different sizes and even an egg poacher.*

▶ *If you are catering for a group you will need cooking pots that hold large quantities.*

◄ *A pair of oven gloves is invaluable to protect your hands when holding a hot pan handle or lifting the lid of a steaming pot.*

OVEN GLOVES

If you are handling hot, heavy cooking pots and pans you will need something to protect your hands, especially if you are cooking over an open fire. A couple of pairs of oven gloves should always be kept in the cooking area of the camp.

MIXING BOWLS

You will need a number of bowls in different sizes for food preparation. Bowls can be either plastic or metal; plastic is lighter to carry but must be kept away from the heat source.

▼ *Your choice of cooking utensils will depend on how much weight and bulk you can carry, and the types of food you will be cooking.*

MEASURING JUGS

These are available in all sizes, so choose the size appropriate for your needs. In a base camp kitchen catering for a number of people one large jug (pitcher) and several medium- and small-sized jugs will be the most useful.

CHOPPING BOARDS

Separate plastic boards should be used for raw and cooked vegetables, fish and meat and bread. Ideally, the boards should be colour coded so that they are used exclusively for one type of food, such as red for raw meat, blue for fish, green for vegetables, and so on. This will prevent food contamination, which could spark an outbreak of food poisoning among the group.

◄ *Do not forget to carry a can opener if you will be eating canned foods.*

OTHER USEFUL ITEMS

If you will be cooking for a large number of people from a base camp kitchen, the following items will make your task a lot easier:

• Wooden spoons in different sizes; do not use chipped wooden spoons as these can carry bacteria.
• Two or three serving spoons.
• A large slotted or draining spoon.
• Sharp knives in a range of different sizes, including some serrated knives. Make sure they are kept sharp. Knives should be kept in the camp kitchen at all times and should never be used for any other purpose.
• A fish slice or metal spatula can be used to take delicate foods, such as fried eggs, out of pans.
• Ladles in different sizes for serving soups and sauces.
• Potato peelers and mashers, which can also be used for other root vegetables, such as carrots.
• A hand-held balloon whisk for mixing powdered sauces or soups into water.
• A catering-size can opener if you need to open catering-size cans.
• Sieves for draining rice, pasta and potatoes and other vegetables.
• Salt, pepper, sugar and sauces such as ketchup and mustard.

Additional gear

In addition to major items of gear such as backpacks, tents and cooking equipment, and personal gear such as wash kits, radios and flashlights, there are some items of kit that are not essential but may make your trip easier and more comfortable.

Lamps

A small gas lamp is a great advantage at camp when night falls. If you take one, make sure you carry extra mantles and pack the lamp well so you do not accidentally break the glass cover in transit. Like gas stoves, gas lamps cannot be carried on planes, but there are some good candle lanterns on the market and these make an effective alternative. Candle lanterns are not as bright as gas lamps, but you can transport them by plane.

▶ *A gas lamp is more convenient than a flashlight as a night-time light source.*

Never leave a lighted gas or candle lamp unattended in a tent, and do not sleep in a confined space with a gas lamp (even if it is turned off) in case it leaks.

Pillow

If you find it difficult to sleep without a pillow for your head, you could improvise by folding your dry clothing into a pillow shape to give you a more comfortable night's sleep, or you can take a cotton pillowcase with you to stuff your clothes into, so that your pillow will not disintegrate during the night. There are also small inflatable pillows and neck-rests that are quick to inflate and will pack up into almost nothing when the air is released. While these are not essential they can be worth taking for a little extra comfort that will mean the difference between a good night's sleep and an uncomfortable night.

Camp stool or chair

A stool or chair is a luxury item, but it does allow you to take a rest or eat your meals in comfort off the ground. Consider taking one only if your gear is being carried in a vehicle or on an animal; these are not suitable for lightweight camping trips. Camp stools or chairs are very useful for expeditions that will involve birdwatching or study activities that require you to sit still for lengthy periods of time.

Sitting mat

A sitting mat or a piece of foam, about 30 x 60cm/12 x 24in, such as an off-cut from an old sleeping mat, can be used to sit on when you make rest stops, protecting you from damp, wet or uncomfortably rocky ground.

◀ *Camp stools are made from a very lightweight aluminium and can be folded up for relatively easy packing.*

◀ *A neck-rest and eye mask will make your night's sleep or plane journey much more comfortable.*

▼ *A cotton or silk sleeping bag liner will help keep the main sleeping bag clean.*

▲ *A cotton pillowcase stuffed with spare dry clothing will form a perfectly adequate pillow that will increase your comfort at night.*

▲ *Sitting mats are available from outdoor suppliers. They are light enough for day-trippers and backpackers to use.*

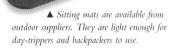

▼ *Pack a steel mirror in its waterproof pouch with your wash kit.*

Steel mirror

These thin pieces of shiny metal, which can be bought at most camping shops, make shaving and other toilet operations very much easier. If you can, keep the mirror in its own case or plastic envelope, so it will not get wet in your wash kit. The mirror can start to go rusty if it is wet most of the time.

Stove windshield

A number of stoves have their own small, in-built windshield, but you can buy a larger and more effective one made of cotton or aluminium. This weighs very little but it will make cooking much quicker and more efficient (you are less likely to waste fuel) and can be hugely useful if there is a chance you will need to cook outdoors in high winds.

▲ *Carry a hanging scale and use it to make sure your luggage is within your weight restriction.*

▲ *If you are a deep sleeper, you may want to carry an alarm clock to be sure you wake in time to make your daily schedule.*

► *Board games provide entertainment for relaxation times and can help to promote a good group spirit.*

Board games

These are impractical to carry on lightweight camping trips or where you are unable to accommodate large, bulky items, but otherwise board games can be carried to provide entertainment for evenings and rest days. If only one game is available for a group of people, divide the group into teams or even into a league table to introduce a spirit of competition and encourage team bonding. Pack any counters and dice in a secure bag because if these get lost the game will be unusable.

Alarm clock

If your wristwatch does not have an alarm setting and you think you will need an alarm call to wake you in the mornings, pack a battery-operated travel alarm clock to be sure you don't sleep right through until lunchtime.

Adaptor

If you travel abroad with electrical equipment that needs to be plugged into a mains socket, you may need to carry an adaptor. Try to find out this kind of information before you travel.

Hanging scales

If you are travelling by plane or with any weight allowance, carrying a set of hanging scales means that you can check you are not exceeding your limit and therefore avoid penalty fines.

Stretchers

These are lengths of reinforced elastic with a hook attached to each end. They can be put to any number of practical uses, from setting up a sheet as a shelter or attaching a mosquito net over your bed to securing a backpack with a broken zip. You can also use them for attaching equipment, such as a sleeping mat, to your pack.

▼ *Three- and two-pin plug adaptors will allow you to use electrical equipment in a mains socket abroad.*

▼ *Carry a good supply of stretchers: they can be rolled up small for easy packing and have a multitude of practical uses.*

Tools

Tools are usually heavy and bulky, so most will be restricted to use in a semi-permanent campsite, though some items are available in lightweight versions too. All tools should be kept dry, sharp and in good working condition, and they should always be checked before use for safety's sake.

SHOVELS
A number of long-handled shovels are essential multi-purpose tools for a base camp. If travelling by vehicle in a desert or wet environment, carry at least one shovel in case you have to dig the vehicle out if you get bogged down. One or two folding entrenching shovels are useful and take up little space. A small plastic trail trowel or shovel, which can weigh only ounces and fits easily into a backpack, will be useful for burying toilet waste.

MACHETES
These large, heavy-duty chopping knives are very useful if you need to cut a path through thick bush or jungle or clear a campsite of bush and scrub. When buying one make sure it has a good, heavy, sharp blade. You will need a sturdy leather sheath in which to store the machete safely when not in use.

▼ *A machete blade has to be kept razor-sharp for the machete to be effective.*

▼ *For safety a machete should be kept in a leather sheath when not in use.*

▲ *Axes are dangerous tools in the wrong hands. Make sure they are stored safely.*

▼ *Check your axe is sound before you start to use it.*

AXES
If your kit is to be transported by vehicle and you are going to a remote area you may want to carry a hand axe or a larger felling axe for chopping tree branches to make a camp fire or a temporary shelter.

SAWS
These are available in a range of sizes, and, for the less experienced, they are easier to use than an axe when cutting up wood. Lightweight campers can carry a small wire saw, which takes up little space and weighs next to nothing.

REPAIR KITS
Stoves and lighting equipment may need some level of maintenance while you are out in the field. Carry basic tools, such as a screwdriver, that will allow you to make repairs. Some equipment may require a specialized repair kit, so check this when you buy.

▲ *A leather mask on the axe head keeps it clean and protects the blade.*

DUCT TAPE
This is a strong adhesive tape that can be used to make temporary repairs on almost anything from tents to backpacks to vehicles. Take a large roll of tape, and store it in a lidded container or it will get covered in dust and sand.

◄ *A roll of duct tape is useful for all sorts of running repairs.*

▼ *Check that the saw blade is firmly fixed in the handle before you try to use it.*

▼ *Sharp knives are best carried in a leather sheath for safety. If your knife does not come with its own sheath, try to buy one for it.*

▼ *A Swiss Army penknife is as good as a tool kit, but the blades are small and relatively flimsy and need to be used with care.*

▼ *Folding knives are compact and safer to carry because the blade is protected by the handle.*

▲ *Carry a chain or wire saw in a container and oil it before and after use to keep the saw blade supple.*

▼ *You will need to carry a sharpening stone if you are using axes or saws.*

SHARPENING STONES

These are used to keep tools in good working order. All saws, axes, knives and machetes need daily sharpening to remain effective.

PENKNIFE

A penknife, such as a Swiss Army Knife or a Leatherman, is like a pocket-size multi-tool kit. Useful features to look for include straight and serrated blades of various sizes and scissors.

▲ *A multi-purpose Leatherman tool has a host of useful features, including several different blades, saws and scissors.*

TENT REPAIR KITS

These are available from outdoor suppliers. A typical kit will include several nylon patches, adhesive paste, spare guy ropes and a spare tent peg. Before applying a patch to repair a tear in the tent material clean the area to remove dirt and seal the edges of the patch with adhesive paste to hold it in place.

▼ ▶ *A folding shovel packs neatly away and is useful for digging trenches for camp fires or to dispose of waste.*

Caring for your equipment

Camping equipment can be expensive and your safety may depend on it, and it should be looked after if you want it to work properly. Repairs are best done when you return home at the end of a trip, while any faults or damage are still fresh in your mind. Clean, dry and repair the equipment before storing it, so that it is ready for your next trip.

TENTS

Before packing away your tent after a trip, check that the tent parts are present and in good working order. If the tent is made of a synthetic fabric and the seams are not taped, apply a sealant (available from outdoor equipment suppliers) and allow to dry before the tent is stored. If the tent has a mosquito net on the inside, check the net for holes and get these mended before you use the tent and a mosquito finds them.

STOVES

A badly maintained stove will not only be inefficient, it can also be dangerous. Never try to use a stove if you think something may be wrong with it. If you need to replace parts, use only genuine manufacturer's parts. Do not store a stove for a long period with fuel in the tank or with a partly used gas cartridge attached to it. Remove the fuel and store separately to the stove.

▲ *At the end of your trip check your pack for tears or damage to the zip and seams, and make repairs before you store it away.*

▼ *Wipe your cooking stove clean after every trip, but do this in a well-ventilated place and make sure the stove is switched off first.*

COMPASSES AND EQUIPMENT WITH ELECTRICAL COMPONENTS

Keep compasses away from magnetic fields, such as an iron or radio speakers. If you have a protractor compass (which is mounted on a clear plastic base) make sure the plastic is kept clean so that the markings can be seen clearly. Batteries should be removed from battery-powered equipment that is not to be used for some time as they can leak and cause corrosion.

BACKPACKS

When in use, try not to drop or drag a loaded backpack, and do not carry it by only one strap. When you return home after a trip, empty the pack and wipe it clean inside and out with a damp cloth and check the seams for tears and holes. Make sure it is dry

▲ *Backpacks should be wiped with a damp cloth after use. Allow the pack to dry out and then store it in a well-ventilated place.*

▼ *The plastic base of a protractor compass needs to be wiped clean after use to keep the base free of dirt and the markings readable.*

before storing away. If your pack is very dirty, wash it in soap flakes and water but do not use detergents as they can destroy the waterproofing properties of the fabric. Packs should be stored in a dry, well-ventilated place.

SLEEPING BAGS

With the exception of fibre-pile bags, all sleeping bags need to be cleaned carefully and they all take a long time to dry out thoroughly. If you have your bag dry-cleaned, air it for at least half a day before you use it to get rid of the fumes from the chemicals. If you wash your bag in a washing machine dry it flat as line-drying can damage the bag's construction. If you use a bag liner, be it silk or cotton, this should be cleaned according to the manufacturer's instructions at the end of every trip.

▼ *Remove the fuel cartridge from a cooking stove before you pack it away and store the two parts separately, preferably in the garage.*

Feather or down filling

It is safest to take a feather-filled bag to a dry-cleaners and ask them to clean it in the same way as they would a feather or down duvet. If you prefer to wash it, use a specialist product designed for the job, then dry the bag flat. While the bag is drying, break up the clumps of down. When almost dry, shake the bag to distribute the filling. When dry, store it by hanging it in a warm, dry place.

Synthetic filling

A synthetic bag should be hand-washed without detergents and dried slowly in a well-ventilated place or in a tumble drier on a low heat. Synthetic bags can also be dry-cleaned.

Fibre-pile filling

These are the easiest bags to clean. Just put them in your washing machine, using a soap-based powder rather than a detergent, and line-dry. Fibre-pile bags will dry very quickly.

FOOTWEAR

As expensive and important pieces of kit, footwear needs special care during your trip and when you return home.

During your trip

When you take off your boots at the end of each day, shake them and tap firmly together to get rid of loose dirt. Prise mud out from the treads with a penknife. Allow the boots to dry out as best you can: stuff the insides with scrunched up newspaper and leave overnight in the door of your tent or hang them outside if it isn't raining. Do not dry boots in front of a camp fire or in the hot sun because this can ruin the uppers.

At the end of the trip

Remove all traces of dirt and mud, then wash the boots in warm soapy water and allow them to dry naturally. All footwear needs to be reproofed in order to waterproof the uppers before

▲ *To dry wet walking boots, stuff the insides with sheets of newspaper or long grass and leave overnight in a dry place.*

further use; leather that isn't regularly treated with a wax or oil-based product will eventually dry out and crack. If your walking boots or shoes are made of leather give them two coats of polish, wax dubbin, oil or a recommended product before storage. If your boots are made of fabric use a recommended silicone-based product, which can be either sprayed or rubbed on.

CARING FOR WALKING BOOTS

1 With a boot on the end of each hand tap your boots together to knock off any loose pieces of mud and dirt.

2 Using a penknife or small stick, prise mud and dirt from between the treads on the underside of each boot.

3 Using a hard-bristled brush, firmly brush each boot all over to remove any remaining mud, dirt and dust.

4 Check that the laces on each boot are not frayed and replace if necessary. Wash the boots in warm soapy water.

5 Use your fingers or a soft cloth to apply an oil-based waterproofing product to leather boots or shoes.

6 Protect fabric walking boots with a silicone-based waterproofing product recommended by the manufacturer.

Preparing your equipment

Before setting off on any trip in the outdoors, whether it is a day's walking in your local area or a month-long expedition to another country, you should check the equipment you are taking with you. Any items showing signs of wear will need to be repaired or replaced. It is far easier to carry out major repairs at home, where materials and replacements are available, rather than out in the field.

CLOTHING AND FOOTWEAR

As well as making sure your outdoor clothing is suitable for the climate and planned activities, you need to check that key items such as shirts and trousers still fit you comfortably, especially if you have not worn them for a while – you may have put on or lost weight since your last trip. Check the condition of your clothing and repair as necessary, paying particular attention to zips and buttons as these

▲ *Protective sealants can be applied to the seams of clothing to strengthen the stitches and maintain the waterproofing qualities.*

are likely candidates to break or fall off under the pressure of use. If you are travelling in a group with a number of other people, you may want to mark personal kit and clothing with your name or an identifying mark.

Check that your walking boots are clean and in good working order. Stitching on the seams needs to be intact; if it isn't you could take the boots to a shoe repair shop or sew the stitching yourself using a bradawl or awl and a strong needle. Intact seams should be coated with a sealant to protect the stitches.

◀ *Ordinary boot polish can be used on leather boots but fabric boots will need a recommended silicone-based product.*

▲ *Always check the head and shaft of your axe. A head that comes loose when in use can result in a nasty, if not fatal, accident.*

Small splits in the leather or fabric uppers of boots can be repaired at home with an adhesive. A shoe repair shop may be able to patch up large tears, otherwise you will need to replace the boots: large tears will let in water or sand and dirt and they will worsen with use during the trip. Replace frayed laces and take at least one spare pair of laces with you.

Check that the sole is not coming away from the main boot; if it is you may be able to get it repaired at a shoe repair shop or you may need new boots. Reproof or polish leather boots before every trip (and again when you return home) to maintain the condition of the leather, and treat fabric walking boots with a silicone-based product.

CHECKING YOUR BOOTS

1 Check boot laces for damage or early signs of fraying that may cause them to break under the pressure of hard use. Fit new laces if needed and carry spares.

2 Check that none of the D-rings is bent or broken and make sure they are free of mud or dirt from previous trips, which may make it difficult to fit laces.

3 Look closely at the stitching all the way round each boot, and organize repairs for any that is loose. Apply a sealant to waterproof the stitches.

▼ *A small but well-equipped repair kit is essential if you will be away from home for some time.*

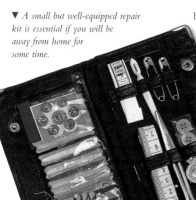

▲ *Gas stoves are awkward shapes but they can be packed into pouch bags designed for the purpose for easy storage and transit.*

battery, once you have checked it, reverse one of the batteries so as to break the circuit, which means the equipment cannot be switched on by mistake. Carry correctly sized spare batteries for all your equipment, including lithium batteries for camera or computer equipment.

CAMPING EQUIPMENT

Check that your tent has all its parts and enough pegs to put it up as well as some spare, and that everything is in working order. Look for holes or tears in the tent and groundsheet, and check that the guying points are in good condition. Check that your sleeping bag is clean and that the zip, if there is one, works properly.

COOKING EQUIPMENT

Try out your stove to make sure it is working and check you have sufficient fuel to last the duration of your trip unless you know for certain that you will be able to buy that particular type of fuel at your destination. If you are travelling by plane you will not be able to carry fuel with you, so part-used gas containers should be removed from your stove. Crockery and utensils should be clean and supplies of washing-up liquid and condiments replenished. Check that pan handles are not damaged, that pan lids fit properly, and that your water containers do not leak.

BATTERY-POWERED EQUIPMENT

Equipment that requires batteries should have had them removed when they were last used, as leaking batteries can cause corrosion. If this wasn't done and a battery has leaked, you may be able to remove any corrosion with an emery file or a piece of abrasive paper. (It will be a lot easier to do this now at home than in some cold field at dusk when your torch does not work.) Check all of the battery terminals for corrosion, and remove any that you find. If this is not successful the item may need to be replaced. Otherwise, put new batteries into the equipment and check that it works properly. If equipment requires more than one

▼ *Check that you have enough fuel for the trip. If you haven't used your stove for a while try it out to make sure it works.*

CARRYING EQUIPMENT

Your backpack should be clean, with all straps and/or zips undamaged. Repair any straps that appear to be loose or weak, paying attention to the waist belt and shoulder straps of large backpacks, which take the bulk of the weight. Apply a sealant to waterproof all of the seams.

▶ *Always make sure your first-aid kit has been properly restocked before setting out on a trip.*

▼ *Check the straps on your pack and make any repairs while you are still at home. Weak straps can break easily under pressure.*

▼ *Make sure the zips and seams on your pack are intact and apply a protective sealant to the seams to reinforce the stitches.*

Packing your gear

When packing your equipment, the first rule is to pack as lightly as possible without omitting any essential items. The second rule is to pack carefully, so that anything that you do not want to get wet is sealed in a waterproof wrapping, and anything that might break is adequately padded.

PERSONAL EQUIPMENT
The first step is to get your equipment together, based on a well-thought-out checklist. Lay out all of the equipment on the floor and check each item against the list. When you are satisfied that you have everything you need, go through it one more time to make sure you are only taking items that are useful enough to justify the weight and bulk they will add to your pack.

When you are ready to pack, wrap up all your small items in separate stuff sacks or packing cubes, or even sturdy plastic bags, so they do not get lost in a large kit bag or holdall.

Make a list of the contents of each sack and attach to the outside, so that when you are at camp, you will not have to open every sack to find what you are looking for.

Pack your sleeping bag with care and keep it in a waterproof bag or container, so that if your kit gets wet you will still have something dry to sleep in. Down and feather sleeping bags are highly compressible, and can be rolled up into small bundles without causing damage to the filling. Synthetic bags can lose their thickness, and therefore their insulation properties, when rolled, so pack them in as large a stuff sack as you have space for, and unpack them and shake them loose as soon as you reach your destination.

GROUP EQUIPMENT
Assembling shared group equipment in one place to pack means that you are less likely to forget key items. It also gives you the chance to check that you are not over the weight allowance if travelling by plane.

◀ *Waterproof plastic bags are useful for carrying sleeping bags and tents.*

▲ *Pack your backpack with heavier items at the top to keep the centre of gravity high and prevent the pack from pulling you backwards.*

PLANE TRAVEL
Equipment that will not be with you all the time during the journey should be locked or secured, and fragile items should be well protected against rough treatment by baggage handlers. Put sharp implements, such as knives, scissors, scalpels or razor blades in your kit bag rather than your hand luggage. These items are not allowed in the cabin of the plane, and if your hand luggage is searched, they will almost certainly be removed.

▶ *Waterproof rigid storage containers can be used for storing valuable or delicate items. They are ideal for use in kayaks or canoes.*

PACKING A VEHICLE

Make sure items are packed in boxes, crates or bags, so that they will not be able to fly about if you hit a bump or drive on rough tracks. If there are lots of parcels, label each one with the contents to make items easier to locate. Do not overload your vehicle, and keep the weight as near to the axles as possible.

Pack only light, bulky items on roof-racks as a top-heavy vehicle will turn over easily on rough ground. If using a roof-rack or trailer, pack all non-water-resistant items in waterproof containers or sturdy plastic bags, or cover the load with a tarpaulin sheet.

▲ *Stuff sacks and packing pods will help you to organize your personal equipment within a bigger backpack or kit bag.*

Fragile items should be protected with padding. Filled fuel containers should be kept well away from food, clothing, medical supplies and any source of flame, electric spark or direct heat. Put padding around fuel and water containers as these can puncture if jolted continuously on a rough track.

PACKING A BACKPACK

Pack your sleeping bag first, then your tent and waterproofs last, so that they are in the correct order of need when you come to unpack. Water bottles, maps, compasses and personal items, such as lipbalm, can be kept in side or top document pockets for easy access. Carry your stove and fuel in side pockets, away from food, clothing and your sleeping bag in case of leakage.

PACKING A HOLDALL

The most user-friendly holdall is a rectangular bag in which the top can be opened to allow you to see inside. Heavy items, such as books, should be packed in a layer at the bottom, with fragile items in the middle, and soft items, such as clothes or your sleeping bag, wedged in around them.

Maps, notebook and pencil in a waterproof wallet.

Warm sweater, hat and gloves, sunglasses and wash kit.

Food, eating and cooking equipment, tent, tent poles and pegs.

Sleeping bag, clothing, length of rope, bivvy bag.

First-aid kit, stove and fuel, water bottle and waterproof overtrousers.

◄ *Try to fit all your gear inside your backpack, as outside attachments are likely to get lost or damaged.*

NAVIGATION
& SIGNALLING

Knowing how to find your way in unfamilar territory is the most
important skill for wilderness travel and it is no exaggeration to say that
your life may depend on it. Learn how to use a map and compass before
the trip, and train yourself to think in navigational terms, developing an
awareness of nature and the landscape around you. This will help you
to follow your course and to correct yourself when you go wrong.

Reading a map

For thousands of years man navigated successfully all over the world over land and sea without the aid of maps. The luxury of accurate maps that we have become used to is a relatively recent development and really only goes back a couple of hundred years. The reassurance of accurate maps has made navigation as much more accurate art, but the ability to read maps well, interpret them and then apply the information gleaned from them, is still a skill that must be learned and developed for your own safety.

THE THREE NORTHS

Most national and regional maps are drawn with true north (the direction of the geographic North Pole) at the top. Large scale maps with a grid system, however, use grid north. The difference between grid north and true north occurs because a map is a flat illustration of the Earth's curved surface. In low to mid latitudes the difference between true and grid north can be disregarded, but at high latitudes it becomes significant. The third north is magnetic north. A compass needle

does not point to the geographic North Pole but to the magnetic North Pole, which is currently in Hudson Bay, northern Canada, and moves slowly but continually. All quality maps will have all three norths – true, grid and magnetic north – marked on them, along with the annual rate of change of the magnetic variation.

▲ *Geographical features in the landscape can be checked off against the map to make sure you are where you should be.*

LEARNING MAP SYMBOLS

A list of symbols used on the map is usually printed on it in a key. Symbols do vary from map to map so be careful to check before making decisions regarding route choice and distance. You should make yourself familiar with the symbols on the map you are using so that you do not have to continually refer back to the key. This makes map reading fluid and allows you to really see the land as you look at the map. An understanding of and ability to interpret contours is the most important skill of map reading. It is not an easy skill and needs practice to get it right.

If you are not familiar with map reading, spend time practising before your journey until you can read the map with reasonable accuracy. Look at a map of your local area – preferably an area with height variation in the form of hills, and including some natural and man-made features. Choose a route to follow on foot, looking at the contours to assess height variation and noting the features you would expect to find. Then take your map outdoors and follow the route to see how accurate you were.

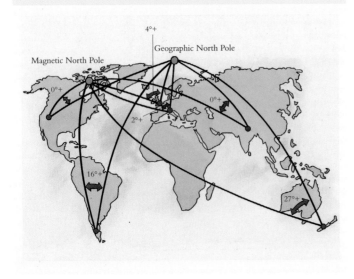

MAGNETIC VARIATION

4°+

Geographic North Pole

Magnetic North Pole

0°+

0°+

2°+

16°+

27°+

A PICTURE OF THE LANDSCAPE

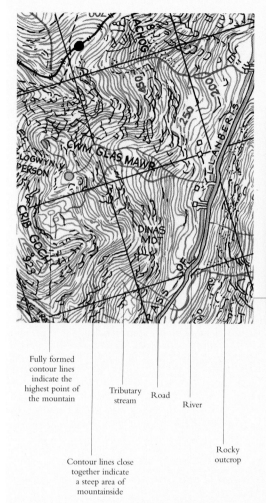

Fully formed contour lines indicate the highest point of the mountain

Tributary stream

Road

River

Contour lines close together indicate a steep area of mountainside

Rocky outcrop

The map and photograph do not bear much relation to each other at a quick glance. You must pick out and identify features in relationship to each other in order to relate the view to the map. Learning to make allowance for areas of land that are hidden from view and to get a grasp of scale are both very important. This is a simple exercise but it will help you to understand the basic principles of reading a map.

Start slowly, identifying features in the landscape and using their symbols to locate them on the map. Focus on one feature at a time, and note how the steepness of the hills is shown by the densely packed contour lines. As you progress, you will begin to see how closely the landscape in the photograph has been represented in pictorial form on the map.

FINDING YOUR LOCATION

Good navigators can always relocate quickly and accurately. It is always done by a systematic process of positively identifying and positively eliminating features in the surrounding landscape. The first thing to do is to orientate your map. This can be done visually by lining up the map with features that you can see around you, such as a forest or a lake, or by using your compass (see the section The compass, 100–101). Either way, your map will now be pointing north and mimicking the landscape. You can then set about finding features that fit with where you are and eliminating the places you could not possibly be. For example: you are standing on a steep, rocky slope that faces south, looking down on a stream with an S-bend and the stream is flowing east. This immediately eliminates all the slopes that don't face south and all streams that don't flow east. This may leave you with a few possibilities, but continue your process of elimination: how many of the other east-flowing streams have S-bends below a steep rocky south-facing slope? If you are unlucky and there are two you need only find one other distinct feature and you are sure to reduce your possible location to a single choice.

The compass

The development and use of compasses to help maintain direction of travel goes back thousands of years. Contrary to what a lot of people imagine, a compass needle does not point to the geographic North Pole but aligns itself along the magnetic field of the earth, pointing to the magnetic North Pole, which is currently situated in Hudson Bay in northern Canada.

Compasses were traditionally a swing needle housed in a round case with the 360 degrees of the circle and the cardinal points (north, south, east and west) marked in order to give a bearing. Later, sighting prisms were added to increase the accuracy of the bearing. In order to take a bearing off a map a protractor had to be carried to measure the angle of travel in relation to the North Pole. After the Second World War the Scandinavians came up with the combined instrument that is almost universally thought of today as a compass. This is a combination of a compass, protractor and a ruler.

The protractor compass is perhaps the most popular type of modern compass. It is a versatile navigation tool which allows you do the following:
• Orientate a map.
• Measure distances on the map.
• Work out a grid reference for the location where you are or for a specified location on your route.
• Take a bearing directly from the ground in front of you.
• Take a bearing from a map, apply magnetic variation (see the section Reading a map, 98–99), and follow the bearing to your destination.

LOOKING AFTER YOUR COMPASS

A compass is a delicate instrument that could save your life. Keep your compass safe, and do not drop it or stand on it. Keeping it strapped to your wrist or worn around your neck on a cord is a sensible option. Do not allow your compass to come into contact with a magnet as this could damage it and will drastically affect its accuracy.

▼ *The modern compass includes a sighting mirror, which allows you to set a bearing by sighting on a distant object in the landscape.*

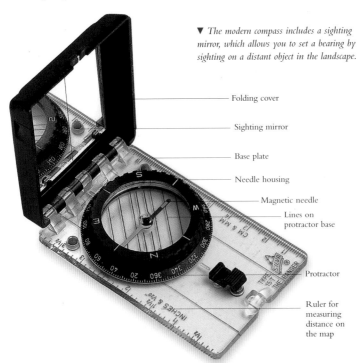

Folding cover

Sighting mirror

Base plate

Needle housing

Magnetic needle

Lines on protractor base

Protractor

Ruler for measuring distance on the map

A sewing needle that is repeatedly stroked in *only* one direction against a piece of silk will become magnetized and can be suspended on a piece of string or thread so that it swings to north. Top up often to maintain the magnetism. Stroking the needle with a magnet, if you have one, would be even more effective than silk. Stroke the metal in one direction *only*.

FINDING NORTH

Hold the compass flat in your hand and make sure there is no large source of ferrous metal nearby (this may act like a magnet and attract the compass needle, thereby affecting the accuracy of the reading). The red magnetic compass needle will point towards magnetic north. In order to find true (geographic) north, you will need to know the magnetic variation for the area where you are and apply this to the protractor. Depending on where you are on the earth you may have to add or subtract the variation: your map will be able to tell you which. Line up the red magnetic needle with the lines on the base plate of the protractor; the direction of travel arrow will now be pointing at true north.

FOLLOWING A BEARING

If there is an absence of line features along your route, such as a footpath, stream or ridge that you can follow to maintain your sense of direction, a compass bearing can act as a reliable substitute, providing a continuous guide to your direction.

Having established the bearing you wish to travel on, line up the red magnetic needle with the lines on the base plate of the protractor; the direction of travel arrow will now be pointing on your bearing. The bearing then has to be laid on to the ground: in other words, you have to identify a feature on the ground, such as a tree,

that is in line with the bearing when the compass is held flat in your hand, and walk towards it. Having arrived at the feature, you will need to repeat the process in order to move further along the route. Line up the red magnetic needle with the arrow on

◄ *The prismatic compass is so-named because it contains a prism, which allows for greater accuracy when taking a bearing.*

◄ *The button compass features a magnetic swing needle that shows your location in relation to magnetic north.*

the base plate to find your direction of travel, and choose a feature on the ground in that direction. Continue in this way until you reach your destination or are able to pick up a line feature along your route.

In poor visibility it is extremely easy to lose your way and you must avoid drifting off your bearing at all costs. You may have to use ground features that are very close to you to be absolutely safe, such as outcrops of rock or even tufts of grass. If you have other people in your group, you can send one party member ahead to the limit of visibility on your bearing, then ask them to stop and wait until the rest of the party has caught up before sending them off again. If visibility is so poor that you can barely see in front of you, it is an advantage to use a party member as a ground feature because if you call out to them, your voice acts as an indicator of direction and distance; by calling back to you they will be able to direct you to their position relatively easily.

▼ *The protractor compass has an in-built protractor, as well as a compass and ruler, which allows you to set an accurate bearing on the map.*

HOW TO CARRY A COMPASS

• All types of compass are sensitive to knocks and shocks, and all must be treated with care when you are on the move. Aim to keep the compass in some form of casing at all times. For easy access, keep the cased compass in the buttoned-up breast pocket of a shirt or jacket, or strapped to your wrist, or worn on a sturdy cord around your neck.
• If travelling by plane as part of the trip, carry your compass in your hand luggage to protect it from the pressure differences of high altitude, which may affect its accuracy. It also means you will not be without your compass if your luggage is lost or delayed.

LAYING A BEARING TO GROUND

1 Hold the compass with the direction of travel arrow pointing on your bearing. Select an object in the distance that is in line with your bearing. Walk towards it.

2 When you arrive at the object, repeat the process to continue along the route. Line up the red magnetic needle with the arrow on the base plate.

3 With the direction of travel arrow pointing on your bearing, select an object that aligns with the bearing and walk towards it. Repeat as necessary.

Using a map and compass

The essence of navigation is to be able to establish your position anywhere on the earth's surface and then be able to plot a course to another position. Armed with a map and compass a good navigator can confidently navigate in any conditions.

To navigate accurately you need to know your starting point; your direction of travel; and the distance you have travelled. People who get lost have almost always failed to keep track of these three key points, and having done so they then panic and wander around blindly. Re-establishing your position is a matter of quiet, logical observation and slowly proving to yourself that the features you can see in the surrounding landscape fit the position on your map.

SETTING A MAP TO NORTH

The ability to orientate a map so that it points north and therefore mimics the land is an easy but important skill. If you can recognize features then you can orientate the map visually. If this is not possible you can use your compass to orientate the map. First you must apply the local magnetic variation to

▼ *If used correctly a map and compass can help you plan a route, indicate distance and locate your position in the wilderness.*

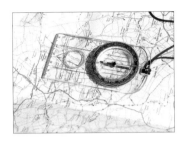

▲ *You need to orientate your map to the land before you set out on the route. Use your compass for this if visibility is poor.*

the compass, then place the compass on the map with the lines on the protractor running parallel to the grid lines on the map. Now move the map around until the red half of the compass needle is in line with the lines on the protractor and pointing north. Your map is now orientated.

MAP-TO-GROUND INTERPRETATION

Many navigators rely too much on the use of the compass. This produces a blinkered approach to navigating. The ability to navigate using the map alone gives you a much broader understanding of the landscape you are travelling through and also allows you

GLOBAL POSITIONING SYSTEM

GLOBAL POSITIONING SYSTEM

The global positioning system (GPS) is an important development in navigational equipment. It can be used for all outdoor pursuits, and is particularly popular for those that cover large distances in remote areas, such as kayaking, cycling, horse trekking and vehicle travel.

The GPS works by picking up transmissions from orbiting satellites and it will locate your position with great accuracy. Some models include an electronic compass and altimeter, which allow you to predict weather trends and plot your route.

However, like any electronic device the GPS is prone to damage and battery failure, and it should never be carried as an alternative to a conventional map and compass.

to reassure yourself that your course is the correct one. Travelling by compass bearing alone has no second check if things go wrong. Contour line interpretation is the most important skill of navigating and you should aim to regularly "tick off" contour features as you travel. By doing so you maintain a continual check on your position, direction of travel and distance. Then if you do go wrong, you can backtrack to the last point at which you knew you were on the right path, which will not be too far away, and restart from there.

SETTING A COURSE

Walking on a compass bearing becomes necessary in poor visibility, at night or on particularly featureless terrain, such as open plains or desert.

To take a compass bearing between two points on a topographical map with grid lines, place the long edge of the protractor base plate along the line between your starting point and your destination. Make sure the direction of travel arrow on the base plate is pointing the right way. Hold the map and compass base plate firmly

together. Now turn the protractor around until the lines on the base plate are parallel to the north grid lines on the map. Take the compass off the map and read your grid bearing at the base of the direction of travel arrow. Before you set off on your course you need to apply the local magnetic variation to the bearing. Holding the compass flat in your hand, move yourself around until the red half of the needle is in line with north on the protractor base. Your course is where the direction of travel arrow is now pointing.

ADJUSTING MAGNETIC NORTH TO TRUE NORTH

The red half of the compass needle points to magnetic north. Your map is drawn to grid north or, with small-scale maps, to true north. In all but very high latitudes the difference between true north and magnetic north is known as magnetic variation. This angle varies dramatically across the globe and, of course, can be easterly or westerly, depending on where you are on earth in relation to the magnetic North Pole.

For compass bearings applied to the ground to be the same as those taken from the map the bearing must be adjusted for magnetic variation. In Europe you will need to add the variation to your grid bearing but in many parts of the world you will need to subtract it. The amount of variation, the direction and the annual change will be printed on your map.

The above information applies if you are taking a bearing off a map and laying it on to the ground (identifying a feature on the ground that falls in the direction of your bearing so that you can use it as a visual guide to your direction). Often you will want to take a bearing off the ground to apply it back to your map – perhaps to check you are on the right route or to locate your position if you have left the route. If you are doing this then the variation needs to be applied in reverse: if when applying information from map to ground you need to add the magnetic variation, then to apply information from ground to map you will need to subtract the variation, and vice versa.

▲ *Magnetic variation needs to be added to, or subtracted from, the grid bearing taken from your map before you try to follow a course using your compass.*

WILD READINGS

Whenever you are using a compass, bear in mind that the proximity of large amounts of ferrous metal will affect the accuracy of the reading, giving you what is known as a "wild reading". Far worse, it could permanently damage the compass. Keep any magnetic or iron objects, such as work equipment, well away from the compass at all times.

SETTING A BEARING USING A MAP AND COMPASS

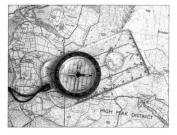

1 First connect your start and finish points with the edge of the compass base plate. Make sure the direction of travel arrow is pointing the right way.

2 Turn the needle housing around until the lines on the base align with the map grid lines. The arrow on the compass base should point to north on the map.

3 Add or subtract any magnetic variation. You now have a bearing to walk on as long as the magnetic needle and the direction of travel arrow are aligned.

Navigation by the sun, moon and stars

Modern man has so many distractions and gadgets that we often fail to notice all the help that nature can give us in finding our way around. There is no doubt that navigating by map and compass is efficient and accurate, but what happens if you are deprived of these tools, if you lose your map or damage your compass?

The heavenly bodies behave in predictable ways, predictions that were worked out by our ancient ancestors and have been used for navigation for centuries. In the event of lost or damaged equipment your ability to use the sun, the moon and the stars to monitor your direction could be a lifesaver, and it pays to commit a few basic principles to memory.

Practise each of the following natural navigation methods before you travel and afterwards use your map and compass to check how you did. Not only will it give you faith in the accuracy of natural signposts, it will also boost your confidence in your own abilities as a navigator. Seasoned navigators are aware of and actively read the signs provided by nature at all times, no matter how sophisticated their modern equipment. After all, the ability to navigate accurately is the most important bushcraft skill of all.

USING THE SUN
The sun rises in the east and sets in the west every day wherever you are in the world, so you may want to take note of obvious geographical features that are in line with the sunrise or sunset to give you a rough sense of direction for use throughout the day. The techniques outlined below are only useful if the sun is visible, but even with a heavy cloud cover it is usually possible to detect the lightening of the sky that happens at sunrise. This can then be noted for use later in the day.

In the northern hemisphere the sun will be due south at noon and in the southern hemisphere it will be due north. The techniques below are at their most accurate when carried out as near to local noon as possible.

Finding north and south using your wristwatch
To do this you will need a traditional analogue watch with two hands set at local time (without variation for summer daylight savings, which do not match real time) and held horizontally. If you are in the northern hemisphere, point the hour hand of your watch towards the sun. Imagine a line halfway between the hour hand and the 12. This line will be pointing roughly south. If you are in the southern hemisphere, point the 12 at the sun and an imaginary line between the 12 and the hour hand will give you a rough indication of north.

FINDING NORTH AND SOUTH USING A WRISTWATCH

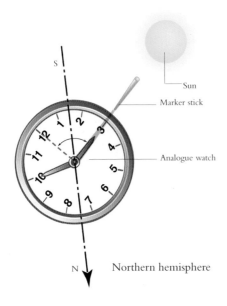

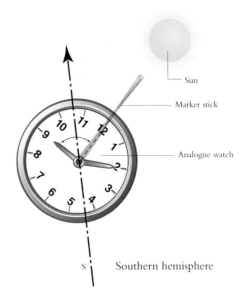

Sun

Marker stick

Analogue watch

Northern hemisphere

Southern hemisphere

SHADOW STICK METHOD

1 Plant a stick of 90–120cm/3–4ft and as straight as possible into a flat, open piece of ground. Mark the tip of the shadow that forms with a pebble.

2 Wait for about 15–20 minutes before checking the shadow. It will now have moved, so mark the tip of the new shadow with another pebble.

3 Lay a stick on the ground to connect the two pebbles. The line that it forms will give you an east–west reference, with the first pebble being west.

Finding east and west using the shadow stick method

This useful method, illustrated above, works well in open country when there is sunshine of any strength, and at any latitude or in either hemisphere.

Try to find a stick of the approximate length suggested above, and be sure to site it in ground that is not overlooked by trees, vegetation or any other tall objects that may obscure the shadow. Mark where the tip of the shadow falls over a 15–20 minute using two pebbles as shown, then join the two points together with a second stick to obtain your east–west reference.

If you will be in your location from the early morning for almost the entire day, you can try another method. Plant a stick about 90–120cm/3–4ft long and as upright as possible into the flat, open ground and mark the first shadow tip in the morning. Draw a smooth arc in the ground at exactly this distance from the stick, using the stick as the centre

point of the arc. As noon approaches, the shadow will shrink. During the afternoon, the shadow will start to lengthen again, and you need to mark the exact point where it touches the arc. Join up the two points to give an east–west reference, with the mark made in the morning being west.

SEASONAL VARIATION

It is a well-known fact that the sun rises in the east and sets in the west, but what is less well known is that the sun does not rise and set *exactly* in the east and west. There is some seasonal variation, and you may need to bear this in mind if you need to make decisions based on the general rule.

WHAT'S IN A SHADOW?

The way a shadow moves can indicate which hemisphere you are in: clockwise in the northern hemisphere and anticlockwise in the southern hemisphere. A shadow can also be used as a guide to both direction and the time of day.

USING THE SUN TO MEASURE TIME

1 To see how much light is left, extend your arm towards the sun. Each finger's width represents about 20 minutes.

2 Bend your wrist so your hand is horizontal and lower your hand so that it appears to "rest" on the horizon.

3 The sun is visible above three fingers. This means that it is about one hour after sunrise or before sunset.

▶ *A moon that is not hidden behind clouds may be able to direct you to reference points for north–south and east–west.*

USING THE MOON

Unlike the sun the moon has a highly variable pattern of visibility and it is far less bright than the sun. As a result its usefulness as a navigational aid is much more limited, particularly in cloudy conditions when the moon can be almost completely obscured.

The moon reflects the light of the sun and as the moon travels around the earth we see different amounts of its sunlit face, ranging from a sliver crescent through to a full moon. When the moon lies between the sun and the earth the side of the moon facing the earth has no sunlight so we cannot see it at all: this is called a new moon. It takes 29.5 days for the moon to travel round the earth.

If the moon rises before the sun has completely set, the visible side of the moon (which is the side illuminated by the sun) will be on the west. If the moon rises after midnight, when there is no sun, the visible side of the moon will be on the east. A basic rule to remember for an east–west reference at night is that if you can see the moon rising you are facing east, and if you can see it setting you are facing west. This will apply whichever hemisphere you are in.

Finding north and south using a crescent moon

If the moon is not full, and is not obscured by cloud, you will be able to work out a simple north or south reference during the night. Looking up at the moon, imagine a line drawn through the two tips of the crescent moon and continue the line all the way down to the horizon. If the two tips of the crescent are on the left, the point where the imaginary line meets the horizon will be roughly south in the northern hemisphere and roughly north in the southern hemisphere. If the tips of the crescent are on the

right the reverse is true, and the point at which the imaginary line meets the horizon will indicate north in the northern hemisphere and south in the southern hemisphere.

▼ *The diagram below shows how to find north or south using a crescent moon. The dotted line connects the tips of the left-hand moon and meets the horizon at a point that is south in the northern hemisphere and north in the southern hemisphere. The right-hand moon shows the other way a crescent moon can appear. Here, the dotted line intersects the horizon at north in the northern hemisphere and south in the southern hemisphere.*

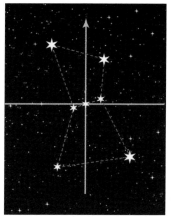

▲ *The North Star lies above the North Pole and can be found by running a line into the sky from the far side of the Plough's pan.*

▲ *An imaginary line drawn across the middle of the Orion constellation lies roughly east–west in the northern hemisphere.*

▲ *The Southern Cross will help you to find south in the southern hemisphere. Note the false cross of dimmer stars to the right.*

USING THE STARS

Because of the many and varied constellations, navigation by the stars is by far the most complex part of celestial navigation and therefore the most difficult to commit to memory. The constellations and individual stars visible from the two hemispheres differ, and this adds to the difficulty. Despite this, stars have been used for navigation for tens of thousands of years.

As the earth is constantly moving, note that the star constellations may appear upside down or sideways when compared to the above diagrams. Like the sun, star constellations always rise in the east and set in the west.

In the northern hemisphere

To find north, locate the North Star or Polaris, which lies over the North Pole. This is one of the brightest stars in the sky and the only one that appears to remain static. To locate it, first find the pan-shaped constellation known as the Plough or Big Dipper. Follow the two stars that form the far side of the pan for six times the distance between them; this will bring you to the North Star.

To find an east–west line, use the star constellation known as Orion or the Hunter. A line taken through the three stars that make up the Hunter's belt lies roughly east–west.

In the southern hemisphere

The North Star is not visible in the southern hemisphere and there is no equivalent star coveniently lying over the South Pole. Instead you can use the Southern Cross constellation. To find it, look towards the middle of the Milky Way where there is a dark area known as the Coal Sack. Straddling this area is the Southern Cross: four bright stars forming a cross plus a fifth fainter star and two bright pointer stars. (A false cross of dimmer stars lies to the right.) Follow the longest line through the cross and down four-and-a-half times its length, then look down to the horizon and that will be due south.

NAVIGATIONAL STARS

North Star Also known as Polaris and the Pole Star. Located above the North Pole it is a key reference for north. It is the only star that remains static; all other stars move around it.
The Plough Also known as the Big Dipper. It forms part of the large Great Bear star constellation.
Orion Also known as the Hunter. This rises above the Equator and can be seen in both hemispheres.
Milky Way A hazy band of millions of stars that stretches across the sky. In the middle of it is the Coal Sack.

MARKING YOUR DIRECTION

When using the moon and stars as navigational tools, do not forget that they will not be visible the next day when the sun has risen. If you are not planning to start on your course straight away during the night, you will need to mark the direction to give yourself a reference point for the morning. Mark your course with a stick or identify it with a prominent object on the horizon, so that you will know which way to go without your guiding moon and stars.

▲ *Remember to mark the direction with a stick or a pebble before daylight breaks.*

Other natural signposts

Nature provides us with endless clues to help us establish direction, which we can gather from the physical, animal and plant worlds. Natural signs will only provide an approximate direction and you may soon leave behind or lose the clue that is helping you, but if all else is unavailable you may be very grateful that you took the time to digest the following points. Ideally, you should hunt for a combination of signs to determine your direction.

THE WIND
Many parts of the world have consistent wind patterns where the prevailing wind will blow in the same direction for the whole year or part of the year. If you are able to find out this information in advance, you may be able to use the wind as an aid to orientation. Beware of the effect that land formations have on wind. For example, deep valleys or steep ridges can completely change true wind direction. The only accurate way to establish true wind direction is to look at the clouds in the free air.

Trees and bushes in exposed places will lean away from and be shaped by the prevailing wind. However, in some

▼ Trees in an open landscape can help you determine the wind direction, but by far the most accurate guide is the clouds up above.

areas of the tropics palm trees will grow into the wind; this goes against the general rule but the palm trees will still give an indication of wind direction.

The wind also leaves clues in sand and snow. Sand and snow drifts always form downwind of any obstruction.

▲ Find out about the direction of prevailing winds in the area you are travelling to: local people will often be able to tell you.

▼ Never trust the wind direction in steep valleys or canyons as land formations can have a severe effect on how the wind blows.

Wind blows up the sloping side of the drift before meeting the obstruction that causes it to deposit its load of sand or snow. So, from the direction the drift faces you can deduce which way the wind was blowing when it was formed.

VEGETATION

Plants need sunlight and water to survive, and analysing where and how well they are growing can help us to establish our direction. Because of the interplay between sun and water, you may have to think about which influences are the more dominant, depending on whether you are in a hot, dry country or cold, wet country. Mosses and lichens dry out quickly, and will generally grow on the cooler, damper sides of trees or rocks, away from the sun. In cold areas, larger plants and trees will dominate the warm sides of terrain and most plants will grow more prolifically on the sunward side. Having sorted this out think about which hemisphere you are in. Some plants, such as the North Pole Plant, which grows in South Africa, will lean to the north to take advantage of the sun. Many flowers move from east to west on a daily basis, following the sun as it moves across the sky.

▼ *Moss will grow on the northern side of trees in the northern hemisphere, and on the southern side in the southern hemisphere.*

▲ *Snowfall at the base of trees can show the direction of the prevailing wind, and you may be able to use this for navigation.*

SNOWY TERRAIN

If you are in or can see snow-covered terrain you will see that the snow cover is more extensive on land sheltered from the sun. Likewise, snow will be markedly deeper on land to the lee of the prevailing wind. It will depend on where you are as to which direction you can establish from these observations. You may already know whether or not the prevailing wind blows in the same direction year-round. If so, and you can establish the wind direction, you can orienteer yourself accordingly.

ANIMAL TRACKS

In dry country, if you see animal tracks following in one direction, it is likely they will be heading for a water source. This can also be true of flocks of birds, though the distances can be far greater. In very heavy vegetation, animal tracks can help in making headway and will often lead to more open country, which may allow you more visibility to plan your subsequent route.

ANT HILLS

In Australia, ants and termites build their nests in the form of mounds or thin blade-like structures. These are always orientated north–south, so that they can take full advantage of the sun's warmth in both the morning and the afternoon in winter; in the summer months the ant hill structures offer some shade from the intense sun.

▼ *Wildlife can be a very valuable source of information. Animal tracks on the ground may be able to lead you to a water source.*

Signalling

Before you embark on any expedition you must consider how you will get help should an emergency arise. You should make sure that others know your plans and route, so that they can take action if you do not return, but if you are ill, injured, lost or stranded in some way you may need to be able to signal to your potential rescuers.

There are two types of distress signal: those that use specialized equipment and those that rely on natural materials. If you are spending time in wild areas, you will find it useful to understand and be able to use both types in case you need them.

If you are going to a national park or wilderness area, you should find out in advance if there is any special system of distress signals that you need to use there, and make sure you and the rest of your party learn it. Alternatively, you may be required to carry a certain amount of specialized survival equipment while you are in the area, and this is likely to include any relevant signalling equipment.

▲ *A rescue helicopter may need to make a difficult or dangerous landing to reach you, so your signals to the crew must be clear.*

BASIC DISTRESS SIGNALS

If you need help you must be able to convey a message that anyone who sees it will understand. "SOS" (short for "Save Our Souls") is an internationally recognized distress signal. It may be transmitted using Morse code (three dots, three dashes and three dots) by the flashes of a mirror or flashlight, or by smoke signals, or it could be written on the ground as a visual message. The radio call "mayday" (from the French "m'aider") is understood worldwide.

You can also learn the international mountain distress signal, which consists of six flashes of a flashlight, six blasts on a whistle, or waving something for one minute, followed by a minute's silence. The signal is then repeated. The reply from anyone who sees it is three flashes, blasts or waves.

All these signals are taken seriously and you should use them only when you are in trouble.

VISUAL AND AUDIO SIGNALS

If rescue is likely to be coming in the form of a helicopter or plane, you will need to rig up a visual signal that is large enough to attract the attention of the crew. If your rescuers are likely to arrive by land, an audio signal, such as a whistle, will be more effective.

Obviously, any visual ground signals you decide to use must be arranged on sites in open ground, where they can be clearly seen from any direction. You will also need to set up different signals by day and by night, whereas audio signals are equally effective in daylight and darkness.

If you are in a vehicle of some kind, you should always stay with it, as it will offer you some shelter from the elements and you may need to protect yourself from wild animals, particularly at night. A vehicle is also a visual signal in its own right, as it is reasonably large and can be seen from the air, especially if you put bright objects on its roof and beside it. Finally, if you have told people which route you were planning to take, a rescue party will follow it when looking for you.

WHISTLES

Everybody in the party should carry a whistle at all times and should know the international mountain distress signal or any special signals you may

◀ *If you need to make a visual signal, choose an open area where you have a good chance of being seen from land and air.*

have been achieved when climbers in difficulty have phoned home to get relatives to contact the rescue services on their behalf.

PERSONAL EQUIPMENT

If you are in dense scrub or forest, lay your equipment out in a long line on either side of your position, so people looking for you on the ground will have more chance of finding you. Items of equipment can also be laid out on the ground in an open situation to form a visual signal to show an air crew your position.

SPECIAL SIGNALLING EQUIPMENT

A range of emergency equipment is available to help with signalling. You will probably not want to, or be able to, carry all these methods with you, so you need to decide which would be best for your situation.

Transmitters and rescue beacons
This traditional marine method of signalling is becoming far more common for use on land, but the transmitters can have a limited range and are reliant on batteries. Before you

▲ *A bright orange bivvy bag can be spread out to make a ground marker.*

▲ *A folded space blanket can be used to catch the sun's rays and flash an SOS signal.*

▶ *If you take a mobile phone, make sure you load it with all the relevant numbers, but you should use them only in a real emergency and not abuse the goodwill of the rescue services.*

have decided on. They are not only useful for attracting the attention of a rescue party, but can be used by any member of the expedition who strays off the path and gets lost.

MOBILE PHONES

In some countries you may be able to use a mobile (cellular) phone to make contact with the rescue services if an emergency situation arises. This can be a vital timesaver in cases of injury or sudden illness, though its availability should never lead you to lower your usual standards of safety precautions and the correct equipment.

You will need to know in advance the right numbers to call for help or rescue, though some spectacular rescues

▲ *A stand allows a flashlight or strobe light to be set up for signalling.*

▶ *Carrying a flashlight will allow you to send the international mountain distress signal.*

go into the wilds, arrange two times in the day when you will transmit if you are in trouble – say midday and midnight – then simply transmit for around 15 minutes at both of these times to give the recipients time to pinpoint your position.

Flashlight and strobe lights

A flashlight will allow you to flash a signal or to guide your rescuers to you. Once you switch on a strobe light, it will give a bright flash several times a minute and can be seen at night over great distances.

▼ *Strobe lights can be seen over long distances if they are placed in positions of good visibility.*

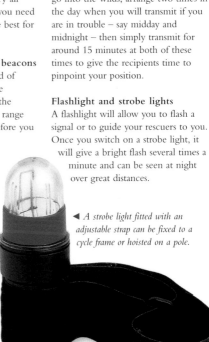

◀ *A strobe light fitted with an adjustable strap can be fixed to a cycle frame or hoisted on a pole.*

◄ The use of some types of flares requires the possession of a firearms licence, and they can be dangerous.

▼ Flares provide both a visual and an audio signal but should not be used without proper training.

Flares and smoke

These can be bought from specialized stores and ships' chandlers. Some may require a firearms certificate. Flares give both a visual and an audio signal, but they can be dangerous and need to be handled with great care, following the instructions that come with them. You should not let anyone handle them who has not been trained in their use.

Flare and smoke containers will become very hot during use, so wear gloves if possible when you are holding them.

Smoke is useful as a visual signal to attract help from the air or on the ground, though for ground rescue it will need to be on an exposed site that can be seen from a distance. If you do not have smoke containers with you, you can of course light a fire to create a plume of smoke.

Heliographs

A heliograph is a flat, shiny plate, usually silver-coloured, that uses light reflected from the sun to send a flashing light signal. A hole in the middle will help you to direct the sun's rays to the place you are trying to signal to. Heliograph signals can be seen from a great distance. They are quick and require little energy. However, they do need bright, sunny conditions.

By holding the heliograph in the direction of the sun and tilting it

▲ Tilt the reflector so that the sunlight shines on the plane, and keep it moving to attract the attention of the pilot.

▼ A heliograph is a good way of attracting the attention of a pilot too far away to see you, as it is visible over a long distance.

GROUND-TO-AIR CODE

This international code is designed to be laid out on the ground, using special panels or any natural materials you can find, such as branches, rocks or pebbles. You could also draw the symbols in sand or mud. Make them as large as you can so they can be seen clearly and interpreted correctly.

Some of the messages are particularly useful if you need supplies to be dropped but do not need rescuing, because they allow a plane or helicopter crew to decipher your needs without having to make a risky landing.

Serious injury – immediate evacuation

Need medical supplies

Need food and water

Negative (No)

Affirmative (Yes)

All is well

Unable to move

Am moving this way

Show direction to proceed

Do not understand

Need compass and map

◀ A whistle should be part of the basic survival kit of every member of the expedition.

downwards until the beam of sunlight hits the ground you can make sure you have it in the correct position. Move the panel to flash the light upwards to a passing aircraft or a distant position where a rescuer might spot it.

Water dye

If you are in a boat and need to send a distress signal, a water dye pack can be seen as soon as it is released into the water. The intense colour of the dye patch makes it highly visible, and it can be seen by air rescue more easily than a small boat.

Dye is a very effective way to mark your position on still water, such as on a lake. It is less effective on the sea, where the movement of the waves quickly causes the dye to dissipate and disperse.

Ground-to-air signal panels

Usually made of material in fluorescent colours, these panels can be laid out on the ground as a ground-to-air signal or on a hillside as a ground-to-ground signal. They should measure at least 180 x 75cm/6ft x 2½ft. They can be used to lay out the international ground-to-air code, which it is useful to know (see box).

NATURAL SIGNALS

If you are ill-prepared, or just unlucky, you may not have any specialized method of signalling to hand. You can, however, indicate your position by forming an "SOS" on the ground, or by marking out the relevant ground-to-air signal using part of your kit or any natural materials you can find, such as branches or stones.

You can dig or scrape "SOS" in the earth or snow, or in the sand on a beach. Make the letters as large as you can and build up the sides so that during the day the shadows cast will help the letters to stand out. On snow, you may be able to fill the base of the letters with wood, rocks or earth so that they will be clearer. If you have

fuel from a vehicle, sprinkle some of it along the letters and then light it at night if you hear a plane overhead.

If you use this kind of signal, make sure it is destroyed when you are rescued or if you move away, otherwise other rescuers may see it and endanger their own lives trying to find a non-existent survivor.

FIRES

A fire makes a good signal at night, and if you place boughs of fresh green foliage over the flames during the day it will produce dense smoke, which will make an effective signal both to the air and on the ground. Even if you are not using a fire to keep warm, you should have it prepared in advance, with plenty of fuel ready, so that you can light it quickly if you hear or see possible rescue coming.

▲ Have a fire ready to light if you hear rescuers coming, with some green foliage ready to put on it to create smoke.

▼ In misty conditions a smoke signal may not be seen, and you will not be able to reflect the sun, but a flashlight may work.

Signalling while on the move

It has already been stressed, and is worth recapping, that you should always communicate your travel plans to others prior to making a trip, and that, if travelling in a vehicle that has broken down, you should remain with it for as long as possible. However, even if you have taken these precautions, help may not come straight away, and you might find yourself stranded for a considerable period. This situation throws up new possibilities that must be considered extremely carefully, and discussed with other members of the group if you are not alone. With every decision you make, whether it is in siting a camp or leaving it to find food and water, you need to ensure that any rescue teams who reach the area will be able to find you.

LEAVING SIGNS FOR RESCUERS

It is all too common for people to leave a crash site without any indication where they were headed. It is best to remain near the crash site, but if the site cannot sustain you it may sometimes be necessary to move away.

In this case, it is vital that you leave clear signs behind, indicating the number of survivors, whether any are wounded and where you have gone.

Once you have arrived at a site that can sustain you well and you decide to settle and wait for rescue, make sure your site is clearly visible from the air. You can do this by making large signs on the ground with sticks or any other easily distinguishable material. If a sign is at any distance from the actual camp, make sure it indicates where the camp is by means of an arrow.

Another idea is to throw green plants and leaves on to the camp fire during the day, as smoke is a good

▼ If you draw signs on a beach it is very important that they are above the high tide mark, so they are not washed away in the surf. Rather than drawing in the sand, use rocks or branches, which show up clearly.

▲ Using stones, you can lay out signs on or beside the trail for rescuers to follow. These signs are mainly useful when leaving the site of an accident.

signal. At night you may want to light a large fire, depending on your resources. If you have plenty of fuel, one thing you can do is to construct three fires in a triangle with the corners approximately 10m/33ft apart.

▼ When abandoning a crash site you must leave signs that make it clear there are survivors, and show where you have gone.

LEAVING TRAIL SIGNS

STRAIGHT AHEAD	TURN RIGHT	TURN LEFT	DO NOT GO THIS WAY
ROCKS			
PEBBLES			
STICKS			
LONG GRASS			
NUMBER OF PACES IN DIRECTION INDICATED		I HAVE GONE HOME	

There are many ways to leave tell-tale signs for would-be rescuers that you have passed by this trail and to show your onward direction. Use rocks if possible, otherwise wood or even rooted grass and foliage.

ESSENTIAL SIGNALLING TO AN AIRCRAFT

▲ *Stretch out both arms as if to embrace the aircraft to ask the crew to fly towards you to pick you up.*

▲ *Stretch out both arms sideways, to signal to the pilot to hold the aircraft in a hover pattern.*

▲ *Palms down, arms outstretched, moving your arm up like a bird's wings, tells the aircraft to descend.*

▲ *Lower your outstretched arm as part of the bird-like movement to make it clear to the pilot it's safe to descend.*

▲ *With left arm outstretched, wave your right arm to make it clear that the pilot needs to move to your left.*

▲ *Continue waving your right arm deliberately and keep your left arm outstretched to maintain this signal.*

▲ *Placing both hands behind your ears indicates that your receiver is working.*

▲ *This signal indicates to the pilot that mechanical aid is needed.*

▲ *This tells the pilot that the safe direction to exit is to your left.*

▲ *Stretch out your arms in a particular direction and bend your knees, to show the area that is a safe landing zone.*

▲ *Moving both outstretched arms parallel above you from side to side says: "Do not try to land."*

▲ *Stretching your arms out in front of you and waving them up and down signals the word "yes".*

GETTING AROUND & ADVENTURE SPORTS

The wilderness areas of the world survive because they present a challenge to the traveller, whether of extremes of climate, ruggedness of terrain, the need to cross water or sheer distance from today's human settlements. Whether your mode of transport is by foot, by animals, by pedal bike or by paddle boat, these unique landscapes present the opportunity to learn and practise all kinds of new and exciting activities and skills.

Planning your day's travel

Before the journey begins you will have planned your overall route and, unless you are wilderness camping, will probably be aiming for specific locations for overnight stops. However, unforeseen events, particularly changing weather conditions, often mean that you need to establish the details of the route on a daily basis.

DISTANCE

Always plan to start your trip with a relatively short day, mileage-wise, and gradually build up to longer distances each day as you get used to carrying a full pack. Factor in either an easy day or a rest day every four to six days.

When planning a long-distance walk, most people tend to overestimate how far they can go. Most fit and experienced walkers will enjoy walking 16–24km/10–15 miles a day, though much will depend on the kind of terrain you are covering, and the weather conditions you can expect. If you will be carrying your cooking and camping equipment, then you should expect to achieve no more than 16km/10 miles a day, or even 13km/8 miles a day to begin with.

The appropriate distance for a day's travelling can vary even more when your journey is by bicycle, kayak or

▲ *When travelling by water, your daily route planning needs to take into account suitable landing and launch points as well as the distance you can paddle.*

canoe, or with animals or a vehicle. As with walking, much will depend on your level of experience, and on the terrain and climate.

WATER AND FOOD

An adequate supply of drinking water should be your first consideration. Establish whether water will be available at your campsites and along the route. This does not have to be drinking water, it could be water from rivers or streams that you can purify yourself for drinking and cooking. On mountains or in polar regions snow can be melted for water. On parts of your route where water will not be available, you will have to carry your own supplies. Top up your water containers whenever you have the opportunity. As you will be active, each person in the group should expect to

▶ *Fill your water bottle before you leave camp; if you have to refill the bottle use a water purifier.*

drink at least 4 litres/7 pints of water per day, or as much as 8 litres/14 pints in hot weather. Don't be tempted to carry sweetened or alcoholic drinks with you: they will

REST DAYS

Don't forget to rest during your journey. If you are exploring a new area it's easy to feel that a day not travelling is a wasted day. However, if you are moving under your own steam your body will rebel if you don't give it an adequate break from time to time.

In a group, individual members' needs for rest will vary, and the timing of rest days may depend on where you are: it makes sense to organize prolonged stops at interesting sights or in beautiful surroundings where everyone will be content to linger.

▲ *In mountains, where clouds come and go, always take the opportunity of checking your route when you get a clear spell.*

simply increase your need for water and could even lead to dehydration if your water supply is limited.

A substantial breakfast and evening meal, and a high-energy snack at midday, are the best combination on days when you will be active and away from camp during the day. Apart from adding to the weight of your pack, too much food in the middle of the day will make you feel sluggish in the afternoon while you digest your lunch. Choose trail snacks carefully: unsalted nuts, raisins, chocolate and oat-based cereal bars will provide a steady release of energy that will sustain you during endurance pursuits like walking or cycling. Avoid taking any foods that are too salty as they will simply make you thirsty.

▼ *Take high-carbohydrate snacks such as cereal bars or chocolate in your pack to maintain your energy levels during the day.*

CLOTHING

Do not overdress. If you set off feeling a little cold, within 15 minutes of starting out you should be feeling just about right. If you set off feeling warm, however, you will be too hot within 15 minutes. If you are in a temperate climate, be prepared for sudden changes in the weather.

Consider the type of terrain you will be travelling through. If you will be walking or cycling through lots of scrub or thick undergrowth, or if there are biting insects in the area, wearing shorts will mean cuts and grazes to your legs and insect bites.

In hot countries you may need to change from shorts to lightweight trousers as the sun's heat increases in order to protect your legs from sunburn. A wide-brimmed sun hat will protect the back of your neck from the sun.

If you are going to be walking over loose rock or sandy soil, some short gaiters over the top of your boots will stop small stones and soil getting into your boots. If the conditions are going to be very wet under foot, you will find knee-length gaiters useful to protect your boots and feet from the mud and water.

If you will be travelling in an area where it is likely to rain, pack your waterproofs at the top of your pack so you can get them out quickly if it starts to rain very suddenly. Items such as maps, guidebooks and a compass can

▲ *When packing your bicycle, always arrange the load carefully so that it can be controlled safely.*

be carried in a large pocket in your clothing or in a plastic document wallet on a cord around your neck. If you have to stop to take them out of your pack each time you need to refer to them, you will slow down the pace or the group and, if you are walking, will find it almost impossible to get into a good rhythm.

PACKING A DAY SACK

If you day's route is part of a longer journey you will be carrying your whole pack, but for a one-day outing from an established camp you can carry a smaller pack for the day's needs. These should include some emergency supplies in case of accidents or getting lost:

• Maps, compass and guidebooks
• Small first-aid kit
• Insect repellent and high-factor sun cream and/or sunblock
• Spare socks if walking
• Water
• Trail snacks
• Waterproof clothing
• Extra layer of warm clothing such as a fleece jacket
• A mobile (cell) phone may be appropriate in some situations

Walking: what you need

Most trips will involve some walking, even if the main activity is cycling or horse riding. A short hike is within most people's capabilities, but if you are going to walk 16–19km/10–12 miles or more a day with a pack on your back, daily for several days, your feet and body will suffer if you have not prepared yourself beforehand.

PREPARATION

If you are not an experienced walker and are expecting to find your walking trip quite demanding, try to get in some training walks as part of your preparation. Start with gentle walks of 3–5km/2–3 miles a day on easy-going terrain around your home or place of work. Build this up to 16–19km/10–12 miles walking on local footpaths once or twice a week wearing your boots and carrying your pack.

BUYING NEW BOOTS

When you go to a store to buy a pair of walking boots, take with you the socks you will be wearing on the trip. Always try the boots on before you buy. Make sure you have plenty of room to move your toes, but not so much room that your foot slips, which can cause rubbing and blisters. If you are unsure about what you need, ask a trained sales assistant to recommend the best boot for you and the conditions you are going to.

New boots need breaking in before you wear them for long walks, so that the inside of the boot is moulded to the shape of your foot. This is particularly important for leather boots. Lightweight fabric boots need less breaking in than leather ones, but you should still wear them around the house for a few days, for half an hour at a time, before going outdoors in them. Even then, wear them on short walks at first, gradually building up the distance.

Think about your overall physical fitness if you are overweight or out of condition, or if you have been ill or are recovering from an injury. On a backpacking trip, where you will be carrying all of your camping and cooking gear, including food and water, you will be carrying considerable extra weight on your feet and legs and putting a greater strain on your body, and you need to be sure that this won't cause health problems or severe discomfort, or aggravate existing injuries.

CARE OF YOUR FEET

Never underestimate the importance of comfortable feet on a walking trip; uncomfortable or sore feet can make your trip truly miserable, so it is worth taking care of them properly.

Harden your feet before a walking trip by rubbing them with surgical spirit (rubbing alcohol) after washing and drying. Concentrate on the ball of the foot, the toes and around the heel.

During the expedition, keep your toenails cut short, so that your boots don't press on them. Keeping your feet clean will make you more comfortable and washing them every day is advisable; not only does it make good hygiene sense, but it is also hugely refreshing to wash your feet when you return to camp at the end of the day. Dry feet well after washing, and check for sores or blisters before pulling on cotton socks and lightweight trainers or flip flops to wear around camp. Dust feet with an anti-fungal foot powder if they are prone to sweating.

Deciding on footwear

The most important criteria with walking boots is that they fit you properly. Badly fitting boots can cause

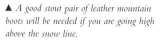

▲ *A good stout pair of leather mountain boots will be needed if you are going high above the snow line.*

discomfort and blisters, and this will be enough to ruin your day. Boots should give good ankle support, and this is especially important for mountain walking. Bear in mind that the same boots will not necessarily be suitable for every trip. For extreme conditions, such as snow and ice, jungle or desert, you will need specially designed boots, because the conditions underfoot are so harsh that your feet and lower legs need extra protection.

For a fine-weather walking trip on well-maintained paths and tracks, strong walking shoes might be just as good as walking boots. They may even be better, because they are not quite so enclosed and will allow your feet to "breathe" better, and this will improve your comfort in hot weather.

Treating blisters

Some people are more prone to blisters than others, but blisters are very likely to develop on a walking trip if your boots have not been adequately broken in, or if they are fastened too tightly, or if your socks have dirt or sand in the weave. Check your feet after your training walks or when breaking in your boots. Look for any red or pink areas where your boots might be starting to rub. If left unchecked, these could form blisters. Cover any sore areas with adhesive plasters or surgical tape before you wear your boots again.

If you get a stone in your boot or you can feel a fold in your sock while walking, stop immediately and remove your boot to take the stone out or straighten your sock before the friction starts to rub up a blister. If your boots continue to hurt as you walk and you think you are getting a blister, stop as soon as you can and treat the blister or the sore area before it gets any worse. If the skin is just beginning to rub, put a small moleskin patch on it. Moleskin patches are made from adhesive felt and are widely available from pharmacies and drugstores. They provide padding to take the pressure off the sore area as you walk.

If a blister has developed but you have to go on walking, you can drain it if you have a scalpel blade in your first-aid kit. Blisters can turn nasty if they become infected, so drain the blister only if you have a clean scalpel. Poke a small hole in the blister to allow the fluid to drain out, then cover with a clean plaster or moleskin patch to prevent dirt from entering the open blister, and refit your boots.

If you do not drain the blister, you should still cover it with a clean dressing. The aim is to protect the fluid-filled blister sac, so build padding with raised sides and a hole in the middle; do not cover the top of the blister as this will put pressure on the fluid-filled sac and may cause it to burst. Use a moleskin patch with a hole in the middle (or cut a small hole in a flat patch) and secure with plasters before refitting your sock and boot.

At camp, wash your feet and change the dressing on the blister. The next morning, make sure that the blister is well padded before you put on your boots and start walking.

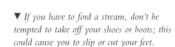

▼ *A specially prepared blister kit is useful on any walking expedition. Take action as soon as you feel a sore spot.*

▲ *You may be more comfortable with a backpack harness that allows some air to circulate between the sack and your back.*

Socks

Whether you wear two pairs of socks or just one thick pair, change them for a clean pair every day, washing the dirty ones as you go if you do not have enough clean pairs for every day. Walking socks should never have mends in them, as these cause friction against the skin and can lead to blisters.

WEIGHT OF YOUR PACK

How much weight adult men and women can carry comfortably will depend on their personal fitness levels, how many hours they will be carrying the load, and what sort of terrain they will be walking on. As a general rule, try to keep down the weight of your pack to under 11kg/25lb, as more than this is likely to turn a pleasant walk into an endurance march. With modern lightweight equipment and food rations, especially if you are sharing the burden of carrying equipment with others, your pack need not weigh more than this. If you are walking in hot weather, the amount of water you take with you will increase the weight of your load, and you may need to look at ways to reduce the overall weight of your camp kit to compensate for this.

▼ *If you have to ford a stream, don't be tempted to take off your shoes or boots; this could cause you to slip or cut your feet.*

Walking techniques

Everyone knows how to walk: it's not a skill you need to master from scratch before setting off on a trip, but there are some tips and dodges that can ease your way when walking on rough, steep or slippery ground, helping you to avoid accidents and putting less strain on your feet and joints. Developing an easy, elastic stride means that you expend less energy with each step, enabling you to walk longer distances with greater pleasure.

WALKING AS A GROUP

If you are walking as a group, especially if some members are inexperienced or young, aim to have one experienced adult walker at the very front of the party and another at the very rear so that stragglers don't get left behind.

If the group has more than ten people, you may consider splitting it into smaller parties, as it is not much

▼ In hostile country, keep your party close together and keep checking the route ahead to warn everyone of upcoming hazards.

fun walking as a long crocodile of people for several hours. It is also easier to keep control of a smaller group, making sure everyone keeps together, takes their rest stops at the same time, and does not wander too far from the footpath or route.

The lead walker, at the front of the group, should set the pace, and this should only ever be the pace of the slowest person in the group, although it should be steady. A particularly slow walker should never be left to walk on their own; other members of the group should take it in turns to walk with them to give encouragement. Some people will naturally walk faster than others, but if those at the front of the group do get some way ahead, they should stop and wait for the others to catch up. The front group should never get so far ahead that they cannot be seen by those at the rear.

This is critically important if not everyone in the group is equipped with a map and compass because those at the back may not be sure of the route to

▲ If the group gets split up when walking in remote locations, wearing bright clothing makes people easier to spot.

follow. The leader can also act as scout, watching out for obstacles or potential hazards and finding the best route across or around them.

While the group should be careful that the slowest walkers are not left behind, the latter need to do their best to maintain a steady pace. If they dawdle and linger, or demand too many stops, the whole group can become discouraged and impatient and the walk will not be a success.

WALKING EFFECTIVELY

There is one important way of making your walking more effective, less tiring and safer, and that is to take long strides. If you walk from the hips, rather than from the knees, your strides may be slower but they will be longer, and you will be able to put your feet down carefully and surely.

Each step you take uses up energy, so if you can cover 90cm/3ft with each stride instead of 60cm/2ft, you will be

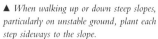

▲ *When walking up or down steep slopes, particularly on unstable ground, plant each step sideways to the slope.*

▲ *When walking in extreme conditions the party should keep close together, if necessary using a system of ropes.*

covering a lot more ground for the same energy output. It's a good idea to practise lengthening your stride during everyday walking so that it becomes natural to you.

WALKING UP AND DOWNHILL

When going uphill, take shorter steps than usual, and keep your body weight forwards, but try to keep to the same walking rhythm that you had on level ground. When walking downhill, again take short steps, keep your body weight back and bend your knees slightly, so that the shock of your downward motion is absorbed by your thigh muscles rather than your knees. Descending can be hard on the knees, especially if you are carrying a heavy pack, and you may want to take more stops to make it easier on your legs. Steep ascents and descents will be much easier if you walk in a zigzag.

DIFFICULT TERRAIN

If a slope is composed of sand, snow or loose material, such as scree, stand sideways to the slope and step sideways up or down it. Treat descents over wet grass, rocks or loose ground with care, as even walking boots with good grips can slip. Avoid walking over loose, large rocks and boulders, which may

become dislodged and start to fall. Walking poles will help you to keep your balance over uneven ground.

If walking over level snow, you may find the going easier with skis. In an open area, a group should walk in single file and within touching distance of each other, so that if there is a sudden blizzard that cuts visibility, you will know where everyone is. In a very heavy blizzard it is usually safer to stop and take shelter, but if you must keep walking, everyone should walk with one arm on the shoulder of the person in front of them.

THINK AHEAD AND LOOK AHEAD

Even if you are following a footpath, look at the features of the landscape around you, such as lakes, rivers or woodland, and check that it matches the landscape shown on your map to ensure you are following the correct route and are walking in the right direction. If you are at all unsure, take a compass bearing.

Always be on the lookout for the easiest route around possible hazards, such as boggy land, streams or unstable rocks, that some in the group may have difficulty with. If walking uphill, be prepared to descend a little if you have to in order to find a safer route

upwards, and vice versa. If you cannot see the whole course of a stream or river, do not use it as a route down a mountain, as water will take the shortest route, and this may be over a cliff. Likewise, when descending a hill, make sure you can see the whole slope, as some slopes end in cliffs.

COUNTRYSIDE ETIQUETTE

Respect the environment and other users of the countryside when walking, especially in a group.
- Give way to other walkers, cyclists and horse riders.
- Take all litter home with you.
- If you are walking over farmland where crops are growing or livestock are grazing, keep to footpaths, close gates behind you and do not touch or deliberately frighten the animals; if you are walking with a dog, put it on a lead (leash) and do not allow it to approach or worry livestock.
- If you have to walk on roads or tracks that have vehicles on them, walk facing the oncoming traffic, unless you are approaching a sharp bend when it is better to walk on the outside of the corner where you will be seen more easily by the oncoming traffic. Take special care if you come to a blind summit.

Daily walking routine

On a long-distance walk it may take you a few days to settle into a daily pattern of walking, striking a happy medium between feeling relaxed and enjoying a sense of achievement.

WALKING PROGRAMME

At what time you start and finish your walk is something for the group to decide between them according to personal preference, but it will also depend on where you are walking and at what time of year.

If you are walking in a temperate or arctic climate in the winter months, there will be fewer hours of daylight than in the late spring, summer or early autumn, and as you will not be able to walk for as long, you will not be able to cover as much distance. You may prefer to walk right through all the few hours of daylight there are before making camp, rather than stopping for lengthy rest stops mid-route.

If you are walking in a hot climate, you may wish to start your walk at dawn and finish in the late morning, around 11am, when the sun will already be very hot. You can either make camp then or rest up in the shade until the mid afternoon, around 3.30pm, when the day will start to cool down and you can move on again.

Try to divide up your day so that your lunch break comes roughly half way through the walk. This is for practical and psychological reasons: it makes sense to restock your energy levels with food and rest halfway through the day, and it makes the day's programme more balanced, so that you are not faced with an unpleasantly long afternoon walk after a short, easy stretch in the morning. You may want to make an exception if you prefer to have lunch at a particular site, such as somewhere with a view or shelter, or where you can replenish your store of water.

As a lone walker you will be able to fix your own routine and suit yourself how far you go and when you stop. However, it's still important to take regular rests and not try to walk too far in one day, as the result will be that you won't feel like walking at all the next day.

Provided you have confidence in your navigational skills, you will be free to change your plans and make detours at will. Without the distraction of fellow walkers you will be far more alert to your surroundings and the slow pace will give you time to observe all that is of interest in the landscape.

▼ *Get into a comfortable rhythm, but try to match your companion's pace to avoid the walk feeling like a forced march.*

REST STOPS

Try to keep these brief: a 5–10 minute stop every hour on the hour should be enough for most walkers, but be flexible if someone is having a bad day and needs to stop more often or for longer. In hot weather or if the walking is very strenuous and you are sweating a lot, take more stops to have a drink to avoid becoming dehydrated. If you are walking with children, you may need to build in more stops than this, depending on the age and strength of the children, but plan the stops before you set off and be firm with the children if they try to manipulate you to make more stops along the way: the more stops you make, the more difficult it is to get into a good walking rhythm. Likewise, it is a good idea to agree within the group that going to the toilet, drinking and checking the map will all take place during these hourly stops. If you need to drink as you walk, use one of the drinking systems in which you carry the water bag in your pack and drink from a tube leading from it.

When you stop for a long period, such as at lunchtime, or while waiting for slower walkers to catch up, put on an extra layer of clothing to make sure

▲ *Rocky terrain can be hard on the feet and especially on the knees. Be sure to take plenty of brief rests.*

▼ *From a high viewpoint on a good day you may be able to see many miles of the route ahead of you.*

you do not get too cold. If you take your boots and socks off while you rest, be careful not to get your feet too cold or even sunburned, and do not walk around bare-footed in case of thorns or sharp rocks.

When starting your walk after a stop, check the area in case a camp fire has not been put out properly, or items of kit or litter have been left behind.

TAKE EXTRA CARE WHEN TIRED

Be aware that at the end of the day's walk, when you will be feeling physically tired, your concentration can wander, and it is at this point that accidents are most likely to happen. Don't take short cuts from your route and avoid skipping rest stops in order to get to the campsite quicker: remember that the original schedule was carefully thought through in the first place, and if a rest stop was planned, it is probably needed.

SICK OR INJURED WALKERS

If someone in the group becomes injured or unwell on the walk, give them first aid attention straight away. Dress the injury or make them as comfortable as possible. If the casualty is unable to move, the group needs to work out how to fetch help. If the casualty can walk, they should be escorted by a fit person in the group, with the two walking in the middle of the group so as not to be left behind. You may well need to change your route to find the swiftest or easiest way back to camp or to find medical assistance.

Cycling: what you need

Cycle camping trips were traditionally confined to the road system until the arrival of the mountain bike opened up new possibilities of off-road routes not previously available to the cyclist.

CHOOSING A BIKE

A multi-speed touring bike is comfortable and speedy for road riding, but if you are planning to include rough tracks in your route a mountain bike is more rugged and reliable. Its fatter tyres and heavier frame make it harder work on tarmac and when climbing hills. Hybrid bikes, a compromise between the tough mountain bike and the fast, light tourer, are a versatile alternative.

If you are choosing a new bike, make sure its frame is the right size for you and check that the saddle is comfortable, as a bad saddle will ruin your trip. Buy the best tyres you can afford. The rear tyre will wear faster than the front one, so it can be a good idea to switch them around when they are partly worn.

Before any long trip your cycle should have a full service: if you can't do the servicing yourself take the bike to a specialized cycling shop.

SETTING UP YOUR BIKE

It's important to ensure that your bike is set up correctly to suit you. This means adjusting the position of the saddle and the handlebars for comfort and maximum pedalling efficiency. With the ball of your foot on the pedal

▼ *Cycling helmets are made of shock-absorbing foam that does not recover: replace any helmet that has suffered an impact.*

when it is at the bottom of its rotation you should have a slight bend in your leg. When you start pedalling, you should be able to reach the pedals without having to move your hips. If this is not the case you will need to change the height of the saddle.

You'll find that you can adjust your saddle backwards and forwards slightly, as well as tilting it up and down – experiment with this to see what feels most comfortable.

Handlebar height and reach is also a vital consideration. You don't want to be too stretched out as this puts strain on the hands, wrists, arms, shoulders and back, so again experiment with adjusting the bars to find the optimum riding position. If you're not sure how to do this your local bike shop will be able to help. If you are riding a mountain bike you may find that the straight handlebars offer too little variation in hand positions, so that your arms get tired and stiff. Drop handlebars on a touring bike avoid this problem, and you can buy extensions for mountain bike handlebars to give you an alternative grip.

CLOTHING AND EQUIPMENT

If you are planning a touring trip using a bike as transport, consider your clothing and equipment carefully. You need to keep the weight and bulk down, otherwise you may find the bike becomes too difficult to control. How much you can carry comfortably will depend on your bike and your level of physical fitness, but as a rule, aim to keep the combined weight of your gear below 11kg/25lb: about the same as a walker's backpack.

A WELL-FITTING HELMET

A good cycling helmet is a vital accessory, and modern helmets are so lightweight and aerodynamic you'll scarcely notice you're wearing one. Your helmet should fit snugly on your head when fastened, and not be able to move around or slide forward and obstruct your vision. The chin-strap shouldn't be too tight.

▲ *Padded cycling gloves will protect your hands from blisters caused by gripping the handlebars.*

▶ *Padded cycling shorts act as a cushion to make sitting on a saddle all day more comfortable.*

▲ *A cycling computer can be attached to your handlebars to keep you informed of speed, distance and route gradient.*

▲ *A cyclist's tool kit includes all manner of elements that could come in handy for emergency repairs during your trip.*

▲ *When weight is an issue, a compact multi-tool combining a range of knives, scissors and pliers can be invaluable.*

Clothing

It is possible to buy specialized bike clothing that will keep you warm (or cool) and dry in virtually any weather conditions. Check guidebooks and local information services to find out what conditions to expect.

Your basic kit should include a helmet, a waist-length waterproof cagoule top and waterproof trousers if you are likely to run into heavy rain. Thermal base layers can be worn beneath your waterproofs. Choose clothing that can be layered and is close-fitting, so it won't flap in the wind or get tangled up with the bike.

Padded gloves will protect your hands from blisters and will also soften the effect of vibration when cycling on rough surfaces. Padded shorts or cycling tights are specially designed for comfort and ease of movement; they

▼ *This pannier sits at the front of the bike, just below the handlebars. It should be used for items you need ready access to.*

are not essential, but are worthwhile if you are planning to cycle long distances. Otherwise, cotton trousers or leggings are appropriate as long as they fit neatly at the lower leg and will not catch on the chain. In warm weather shorts are ideal, but remember to protect your legs with sunscreen.

Some cyclists like to wear clip-in shoes, which attach to the pedals and make for more efficient pedalling, or toe clips; neither of these is strictly necessary. However, you should wear footwear with stiff soles, such as walking shoes: trainers are designed to absorb impact, and will compress with each pedal stroke, wasting your energy.

Luggage

For long journeys it is more comfortable to stow all your luggage on the bike rather than carrying a pack on your back. Use rear panniers strapped to a rigid carrier that keeps the weight evenly distributed over the back wheel. If this is not enough, add front panniers, but make sure they don't interfere with the front wheel or restrict your ability to steer the bike. The general rule when loading luggage is that the weight should be kept as low and as close to the middle of the bike as possible to maintain stability.

Bear in mind that the more kit you carry the harder your ride will be, and with heavily laden panniers your bike will become less manoeuvrable. You should keep items you may need during the day near the top of your panniers for easy access.

Spares and repair kit

Modern bikes are easy to maintain and relatively cheap to repair and service. If you are going to be away from cycle stores or suppliers for a week or more during your trip, you will need to carry a spare inner tube, a puncture repair kit, a multi-purpose spanner (US wrench), appropriate Allen keys (wrenches), brake blocks and at least one spare brake cable for the back brakes. (The rear brake cable is longer than the front one, so it can be used for either front or back brakes.) It may be worth carrying a spare tyre as well.

If you are travelling as a group, it will be useful if some of your spare equipment can be interchangeable between your bikes, so that you can spread the load. Make sure you have a serviceable pump for your tyres and a small pressure gauge to check the tyre pressures on everyone's bike each morning before setting off.

▼ *Your puncture repair kit should include patches of various sizes, adhesive, abrasive paper and chalk to mark the puncture site.*

Cycle training

Racing cyclists are generally considered to be some of the world's fittest athletes, and cycling certainly does get you fit. Yet you don't have to aim so high to plan an enjoyable trip.

BUILDING STAMINA

Whether you are riding on- or off-road you need to build up your training gradually. There is no point in achieving a massive ride on your first day if you are hardly able to get on the bike the next day.

If you are not used to riding a bike, or haven't ridden for some time, you will need time to get your muscles used to propelling a bike and your bottom used to being on a saddle. Regular short rides will build your strength and stamina and you can try a day's ride from home to see how far you can manage comfortably.

As with most sports, the best training for cycling is actually doing it. You can improve your general fitness by doing weights, running or swimming, but by spending more time

on your bike you will get fit just as well while at the same time becoming technically more efficient at cycling. Use your gears to get you up the hills – there is no point struggling in one gear if you have an easier one, and remember, you can always get off and walk to rest those leg muscles.

Families can enjoy cycling together both on- and off-road. Because bikes are so simple to use and maintain children find them easy to relate to and enjoy.

RIDING THE BIKE

Your riding technique will depend on where you ride. All cyclists should obviously be alert to their surroundings, but while a road cyclist's main concern is usually other road users, mountain bikers will find they need to keep a close eye on the rough terrain they're riding over. Always look well ahead and prepare for the rocks and roots you're about to reach rather than looking straight down in front of your wheel – by the time you see objects this close it's too late to take action to avoid them.

The main difference in technique between road cycling and off-roading is one of balance. When cycling down steep off-road sections, get out of the

▲ *When going uphill, if the trail is not too steep, riding out of the saddle uses energy less efficiently but produces more power.*

▲ *Mountain bikes can be safely ridden over small obstacles such as fallen tree branches or sizeable rocks that appear on your path.*

▼ *Familiarize yourself with gear-changing before you set off. Gears will only make pedalling easier if they are used correctly.*

▼ *Woodland tracks are bound to be crossed by roots; on descents, slow down before you reach them and rise out of the saddle.*

saddle and keep your weight over the back wheel of the bike. If cycling in a group make sure you do not bunch up when going downhill – the results can be disastrous.

Riding single-track paths can also be tricky and potentially hazardous so do practise on some narrow paths in your neighbourhood before planning a long trip off-road. Control is paramount so always stay focused and keep your eyes on the route ahead.

WORKING OUT A PROGRAMME

Keep your training sessions varied, alternating hard and easy days. Some trails, especially those at mountain bike centres, are graded for difficulty which means you can ensure you don't take on too much when you go out for a ride. Try to find trails that offer a variety of terrain – flat, undulating and hilly, both on- and off-road – as on a long trip you may encounter any of these conditions. When training on hills, vary the length and gradients of the slopes you attempt. Train in wet and windy weather, not just on fine days, so that you are fully prepared for all conditions.

Practise riding at a steady pace over different surfaces and concentrate on developing endurance rather than speed. When travelling you will want to appreciate your surroundings. You need to find a pace that you can maintain comfortably without feeling breathless and exhausting yourself.

RIDING SAFELY IN A GROUP

The ideal number for your cycling party is four. If anyone has an accident it is safer for two people to go off in search of help, not one, while someone else stays with the casualty. As everyone's abilities and stamina will vary within the group it is important to watch your pace and keep within the capacity of the group as a whole. Do not allow the group to become too strung out and always wait for each other at the bottom of steep hills. Take frequent rests, eat, drink and keep warm to avoid any risk of exposure. Finally, watch out for signs of exhaustion among your fellow riders.

PUNCTURE REPAIR

1 Take off the wheel. Make sure you keep all the nuts and bolts safe.

2 Using tyre levers, ease the tyre off the rim of the wheel.

3 Carefully remove the inner tube from the tyre, taking care not to damage the valve. Locate and mark the hole.

4 Gently brush the area around the puncture with abrasive paper to roughen the surface of the rubber.

5 Apply the glue, making sure you cover a large enough area around the puncture to secure the patch.

6 Put on the repair patch. Hold it down firmly for as long as required by the manufacturer's instructions.

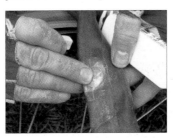

7 Dust the repair with chalk. Refit one edge of the tyre. Inflate the tube slightly and refit on the rim.

8 Use your thumbs to tuck the tyre edge back into the wheel rim and inflate the tyre fully.

Daily cycling routine

One of the advantages of travelling by bicycle is its portability. You can easily transport it by plane, boat, train or car, so you can plan your trip anywhere in the world.

PLANNING YOUR ROUTE

If you are a relative novice, it's wise to choose reasonably flat, well-maintained terrain rather than challenging hills. Beware of absolutely flat countryside, however, as you will have no shelter from the wind and pedalling will be hard if it is against you.

On- or off-road cycling allows you to explore and discover countryside you might never otherwise see. Because you travel so much more slowly than in a car, you have time to take in your surroundings, but because cycling is faster than walking, you can cover more ground. As your fitness develops you'll be amazed at the distances and hills you can tackle.

When planning your day's route, it is worth remembering that you will be able to cover a far greater distance than

▼ *In some places drivers may expect cyclists to get out of their way: don't argue with a truck in the middle of the road.*

your walking counterpart. You should reckon on about four times the distance of a walker: about 80–100km/50–62 miles a day. This makes it feasible to plan detours to particular places of interest: an extra 16km/10 miles in a day's cycling may be worthwhile to get the most from the trip, unless the route involves particularly strenuous ascents and descents.

If you are planning to take your bike cross-country, there are now guide books available to show trails and tracks in popular cycling areas. These trails are often graded according to their level of difficulty, and this will be useful if it is an area you are unfamiliar with. Bear in mind that a bike with 9–13kg/20–30lb of extra weight on it will be much less manoeuvrable than an unladen bike.

MAINTENANCE CHECKS

While on your trip, your daily routine should include checking your cycle at the beginning and end of each day. Use a gauge to make sure that the tyres are inflated to the recommended pressure. Inspecting the treads for embedded stones and other sharp objects may save you the trouble of repairing a puncture later on. Check that the chain and

▲ *When the going gets too rough for the most rugged bike its portability means that you can carry it across obstacles.*

gears are all working and well-oiled. Check the brakes: inspect the brake pads and adjust the tension in the brake cables if necessary. If the cables are too tight the brake pads will be touching the wheel rims; if they're too loose you won't be able to stop.

Check the height of the saddle periodically as weight and vibration may lead it to sink slightly over time. If you have marked the correct position on the post it is easy to restore. Check that the lights are working and do not need adjustment.

When you've finished your ride for the day, don't forget to clean and lubricate your bike (this applies especially to mountain bikers). If you leave the mud and grime on it will be harder to shift later, and it can cause damage to mechanisms such as gears and brakes, as well as causing rust to develop. Keeping the chain clean and free of grit will give you a smoother ride and lengthen the life of the chain and cogs. It should be lubricated each time it's cleaned.

DAY RIDES

On shorter day rides you won't need anything as big as panniers to carry your gear, but try to find a cycling-specific backpack. It should be big enough to store your repair kit, spare clothes and food and water for the day. Many backpacks are now fitted with a hydration system; they contain a bladder for carrying water with an attached drinking tube so you can drink while on the move. However, they can be difficult to keep clean if you use them for extended journeys.

LOADING THE CYCLE

Before setting off in the morning you'll need to stow your camping gear and other luggage on the bike, and doing this neatly and methodically every time is important for your comfort and safety. Make sure that most of the weight is over the back wheel, packed in the rear pannier bags. More gear can be placed on the rear carrier in between the panniers. If you are using front panniers, you must make sure they are packed neatly and will not interfere with the steering of the cycle. Check that all pannier bags are securely attached so they cannot interfere with the wheels once they are turning.

If you are carrying a tent, either strap it on the rear carrier or carry it in one of the rear pannier bags. Spare clothes and cooking equipment should also go at the back. In front will be your stove and food. Light, bulky articles such as your sleeping bag can go on top of the rear panniers.

You may have a pouch on your handlebars for those items that you will need during the day's cycling, such as your waterproofs, your map and compass, and a water bottle. A map board attached to the front of the bike saves time when navigating.

Ensure that all your gear is well secured, cannot interfere with your steering and is well away from the wheels. It is worth considering that most braking systems are designed to stop an unladen bike, so another of

▲ *Try out the cycle and your own fitness on a number of shorter day trips before you start on a long expedition.*

your regular safety checks should be to see how they perform when you are fully loaded.

STOPS AND BREAKS

If you're cycling in a group, agree on a schedule for regular rest stops, with time for a snack and a chance to consult the map for the next stage. If the group varies widely in fitness and skill, some members may set a considerably faster pace. Agreeing in

advance on stopping places will give everyone a chance to catch up. At the end of the day, the fastest cyclists can be persuaded to start setting up camp if they arrive at your destination early.

In hot weather, it may be preferable to have a really early start so that you're riding in the coolest part of the day. You can then take an extended break while the sun is at its hottest. Vary the pace of the trip by building in some easy days and rest days.

▼ *When cycling off-road, be considerate to other users of the countryside and try to minimize your impact on the terrain.*

Rock climbing: what you need

Rock climbing is a rewarding activity that can, once mastered sufficiently, be incorporated into a challenging hike. The most basic level of climbing is known as "bouldering" (either indoors or out) and requires few pieces of specialist equipment. You will need a pair of rock shoes and a chalk bag. You might also wish to wear a helmet when you start out on your climbing career. It is highly recommended that you do wear a helmet, but more experienced climbers will often choose not to. At the end of the day, it is a matter of personal preference, but there is no doubt that helmets have saved lives.

ROCK SHOES

The choice of footwear depends entirely on your sphere of activity. If you choose to boulder or climb only

▲ *A selection of footwear: two shoe styles, two boots and a slipper.*

▲ *"Bouldering", or climbing without ropes, is very much a social activity and though you may find that there will always be someone to "spot" you if you fall off, a crashmat can give reassurance.*

on indoor walls, a light and snug-fitting pair of slipper-style rock shoes is adequate. This type gives a high degree of sensitivity in feeling the holds on which you place your feet. This is advantageous to an experienced climber but the benefits may not be appreciated fully at a beginner level. Slipper-style shoes do not offer much in the way of support and protection

◀ *A chalk bag and chalk ball are essential items of kit, and should be obtained before embarking on basic training.*

for the feet, so if you intend to climb on more adventurous rock you will need to consider this factor and choose something more robust.

The sturdier and more supportive the shoe, the less sensitive it will be to standing on tiny edges or "smearing" (see Rock climbing terms, 137).

CHALK AND CHALK BAGS

The use of chalk to increase hand grip is widespread. Chalk absorbs moisture from the fingertips and allows the climber to hold on with greater confidence, which also means the climber endures that little bit longer. Chalk is available in block form and is broken into tiny pieces and carried on a waistband in a small pouch, called a chalk bag. This bag need only be big enough to get the fingers of one hand into at one time. Some indoor walls have banned the use of this type of chalk for reasons of health and safety: certainly, if you fall upside down, a deluge of chalk dust is likely to fall on to your belayer and pollute the air. Chalk balls go some way to alleviating this problem. These are chalk-filled secure muslin (cheesecloth) bags that are simply kept in the chalk bag itself. When squeezed, chalk is released through small holes in the muslin. It is also possible to buy very large chalk bags intended for communal use.

CRASHMATS

If you get really serious about your bouldering you might want to consider acquiring a crashmat. There are a number of types available, some of which fold up into quite small packages while still providing cushioning.

HELMETS

There are many different types available commercially. Most are made from plastic or fibreglass, although some new designs have used the cycle helmet model and use very light polystyrene. Things to look out for are weight (most people prefer light helmets), durability (some designs will only take one knock and should then be retired), and fit. They are designed to take an impact from above (in the event of falling stones) and the

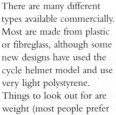

▲ *An example of a good all-purpose helmet.*

▲ *An ill-fitting helmet, giving poor protection.*

sides. If a helmet does sustain a major impact, it should be seen as damaged, and replaced.

CHOOSING A HARNESS

More than any other item of gear, harnesses present the widest variety of design and style. This can make it difficult to decide on the most suitable type for your chosen style of climbing. If you climb only on indoor walls and outdoors on sport climbs that are protected by in situ bolts, you will have little need for anything more sophisticated than the simplest and lightest harness available. For comfort, it is better to opt for a harness with a fixed-size waist belt and padded leg loops. You will not need to carry heavy equipment on the harness, nor are you likely to require it to fit over bulky clothing. However, if you plan to climb on high mountain routes, you might like to consider a fully adjustable harness. This will enable you to fit it over whatever clothing you need to wear for that particular climb.

BELAY DEVICES

The belay device is a safety mechanism that works via friction. It is fitted to the rope and used to prevent the climber going the full length of the rope should they fall. It is connected to the rope via a karabiner (see below). You should choose devices suitable for almost any climbing situation, either outdoors or inside, but note that some climbing walls stipulate the type of device that should be used. In Britain this is rarely the case, but there are many indoor venues in other countries that insist on a device that has a "fail-safe" mechanism such as the Petzl Gri-Gri.

▲ *A simple and inexpensive adjustable harness is fine for starting out. The best ones are light and comfortable to wear.*

Proper training in the safe operation of whatever device you use is essential and it is quite possible that on a first visit to an indoor wall you will be asked to demonstrate your belaying skills prior to being permitted to climb.

KARABINERS

A belay device needs a screwgate or "locking" karabiner, usually a HMS (or pear-shaped) one. This allows the rope to run smoothly through a belay device and lessens the chance of a tangle occurring or the rope jamming.

ROPES

These come in two main strengths: full (or single) and half (or double). A full rope can be used on its own, whereas a half rope must be used in conjunction with another half rope. Full ropes have

▲ *A well-padded harness for more sustained climbing. This will be comfortable and provide plenty of gear loops for equipment.*

traditionally been a thickness of 11mm/^{1}/$_2$in (although today this has been reduced to 9.8mm/^{2}/$_5$in, and half ropes 9mm/^{1}/$_3$in). In terms of length, you can buy standard 45m/148ft, 50m/164 ft, 55m/180ft and even 60m/197ft ropes. Obviously, bear in mind that the thicker and longer a rope, the heavier it will be.

You can also buy ropes that have been treated to repel water. These are useful for climbing outdoors but not necessary if you only climb indoors. This treatment inevitably puts the price of the rope up.

It is important to read the accompanying manufacturer's safety notes when you buy your rope. They will give a recommended life-span (dependent on how often you use it), and how many heavy falls it could take.

▲ *A belay device fitted with a screwgate or "locking" karabiner.*

CROSS–SECTION OF ROPE

core

outer sheath

◄ *Modern ropes are dynamic – they stretch. This property absorbs the energy of a fall. The inner core provides the greatest contribution to strength and elasticity, with the sheath acting as a protective cover.*

Rock climbing: warming up

Climbing is one of the more arduous activities invented to test joints and connective tissues, and preparing the body for the physical challenge makes the possibility of injury less likely. It also gives you time to prepare mentally, filtering out unrelated thoughts. As an overall rule your core stretches, which should be common to every climbing session, are the fingers and forearms, elbow tendon insertions, shoulders and neck. For steep rock, pay particular attention to your back and sides, and for lower angled rock, make sure you go through your leg stretches.

UPPER BODY STRETCHES

Starting with the hands, first perform some finger clenches, either with or without a grip exerciser (a multi-tiered spring device that can be clenched at the centre of the palm). This warm-up can be done while still sitting down, on the journey to the wall or crag. Then carefully work through each finger and thumb joint, stretching them in both directions using even pressure for approximately 6–8 seconds, and up to three times, each. Avoid sharp tugging.

Next, perform some elbow, forearm and shoulder stretches. Hold each stretch for 8–12 seconds and repeat three times before swapping arms. Beginning with the forearm, hold one arm out straight in front of you, clasp the fingers with your spare hand and bend your wrist and fingers back, so as to take up the tension on the flexor tendon insertion to the elbow. To stretch the shoulders, stand upright, grasp your elbow and bring your upper arm behind your head, applying gentle downward pressure to stretch the deltoid muscles. Then hold your arm out straight in front of you and pull it sideways across your body.

Finally, stretch the neck and back. Gently bend your neck to one side, back to the centre and then to the other side, to the front and then to the back, always returning to the centre first each time. Do not rotate your neck. Next, stand legs apart and slightly bent, then lean sideways stretching the leading arm over your head so as to feel the tension in your sides. Place the other hand on your hip or thigh for support. Finally, hold both arms out in front with hands clasped, then curl your arms and shoulders forward.

◄ *The thumb stretch.*

◄ *First joint finger stretch.*

▲ *Forearm stretch.*

▲ *Shoulder stretch (1).*

▲ *Shoulder stretch (2).*

▲ *Rear neck stretch.*

▲ *Upper back stretch.*

▲ *Side stretch.*

LOWER BODY STRETCHES

For warming-up purposes, lower body stretches can be kept to an absolute minimum. Choose one basic exercise for each muscle group, namely the groin, thighs, hamstrings and calves.

All these exercises can be performed while on the rock or wall to help you combine your flexibility work with an element of climbing technique. This provides a fun way of breaking up the monotony of a stretching routine.

It is worth consulting an elementary yoga or flexibility training manual for more detailed information. However, it is worth prioritizing the following flexibility exercises, which are especially good for the inner thigh.

THIGH AND QUADRICEPS STRETCH

Stand straight, bending one leg up behind you. Hold your ankle to keep it in position. To increase the stretch, gently push hips forward. Use the wall or rock face for support if necessary.

CALF STRETCH

Place both hands against the wall and stretch one leg out straight behind you, holding for a few second until you can feel the tension in the calf of your rear leg, and the thigh of your forward leg. Repeat with the other leg.

HAMSTRING STRETCH

Sit on the ground, stretching one leg out in front of you, and fold the other leg in so that the sole of that foot touches the inner thigh, opposite. Now gently ease your upper body forwards, holding your ankle for support.

▲ *You can also do this hamstring stretch by standing straight-legged and bending forward to touch the toes. Never bounce, but hold the stretch for 8–12 seconds.*

▲ *A good exercise to prepare you for rock-overs or high step-ups.*

▲ *This exercise stretches the relevant muscles for standing on small holds.*

▼ *Using an undercut hold on a crag. Warm up the fingers and forearms before a climb.*

PROGRESSIVE BUILD-UP

Now for the really important part. You are warmer, mobile and fully stretched, so the final stage is to subject your muscles and tendons to gradually increasing "overload" (climbing or climbing-related movements of heightened intensity). As a general rule, use longer sequences to prepare for endurance climbing and shorter programmes to prepare for bouldering. Try, also, to make the moves in your warm-up sequences specific to the crag or wall you are about to use. For example, warm up on steep rock if that's what you are mainly going to be doing. Your first movements should be so easy that you barely notice them; use these to relax, stretch out and to

tune in mentally to the sensation of climbing. Then, with the inclusion of intermittent rest, build up until you are almost ready for maximum effort. Once you reach this stage, stop and rest for anything between 6–15 minutes before you commence with the actual climbing session. It's worth taking a small drink and performing a light secondary stretch during this period.

One word of caution. While these techniques propose an optimum warming-up model for climbing, it is not intended as a comprehensive guide and should be adapted to suit the requirements of the individual. Above all else, you should warm up in a way that best suits your own mental and physical conditioning.

Rock climbing: technique

Regardless of your level of fitness or strength, technique is always the deciding factor in climbing. You can incorporate some aspects of technique into your basic training. They will help develop your flexibilty, as well as atune you to more difficult climbing moves. Establishing a repertoire of moves is an important aspect of mental training. These pages take you through some of the key techniques.

FROGGING

This is a technique that can be used to help bring your centre of gravity in close on vertical or overhanging rock. It is especially relevant where you have either one central foothold or two very close footholds. The idea is to push

▲ *Frogging – a technique that demands some flexibility.*

your hips in as close to the rock as possible by turning your legs out in a sort of ballet dancer's "plié" movement. The more flexible your inner groin, the better you will be at this. Frogging can provide that crucial means of resting when all else is letting you down.

THE EGYPTIAN

So named because of the extreme dropped knee posture that is adopted during these moves, the Egyptian is a useful and cunning method of keeping your centre of gravity as close to the rock as possible when climbing on steep ground. It applies to situations where you have two high footholds either side of you on rock which is usually in excess of 5 degrees over-hanging. The idea is to "twist into" the next move by dropping the knee on the same side as the hand that you are about to reach with (the passive side) and turning your body to face the hold that you are currently holding on with (the active side). This brings your hips in close and perpendicular to the rock and creates torque (force generated by twisting) between the footholds, which will reduce the loading on your arms.

▲ *The Egyptian – a good technique for use on steep or overhanging rock.*

▲ *Inner flagging is used when your inner leg is free to move.*

▲ *Outer flagging involves movement of the outer leg.*

FLAGGING

This is a subtle conterbalancing technique which can be used as a quick and efficient substitute for swapping feet. It applies mainly to situations on steep rock where you only have one central foothold and thus require that fine degree of balance to make the next move. The idea is to pass your free leg either inside you or behind you and hang your body straight down, so as to form a stable "tripod" position with your three points of contact. Then, having completed the move, rectify yourself so you are set up to move on.

SIDE HEEL-HOOKING

The basic heel-hook is well known and is useful for making traverses (see Rock climbing terms, below) on very steep

ground. However, the side heel-hook can be used far more frequently if the user is sufficiently creative and flexible. In situations where you have a large flat hold just to one side of your waist, simply lift your leg and rotate your foot outwards in such a manner that enables you to get the side of your heel on to the hold. Use the heel, and then when you're halfway through the move and have gained sufficient height, re-adjust to using your toe. Side heel-hooks can feel weird and insecure the first few times you try them, but like all rock climbing techniques you will feel more comfortable using them the more you are able to practise.

◄ *A heel-hook in action at an indoor climbing wall.*

ROCK CLIMBING TERMS

Overload is the term used to describe the healthy, desirable stresses and strains that are placed on the connective tissues and joints during physical training.

Intensity in climbing refers to the relationship between the length of climbing and the difficulty of the moves. For example a short boulder problem would be described as high intensity, whereas a long sea cliff climb would be seen as low intensity.

Circuits are sequences of moves which usually work their way across, diagonally or up and down an indoor or outdoor bouldering wall.

Timing refers to the ability of a climber to use neuromuscular co-ordination to pull up and catch a handhold at speed.

Primary pump is the act of climbing to deliberately induce a light burning cramp into your

forearms to prime them for a more severe pump later on in the session.

Traversing is the term used to describe any situation where the climber moves horizontally or diagonally to the right or left for a number of moves.

Smearing is a method of using the foot to generate friction against the foothold when the latter isn't good enough to ensure positive support.

Rock climbing: using your feet

Good footwork is one of the main foundations for good climbing. The skill of precise foot placement enables better balance and movement. Your legs are much stronger than your arms, and the more you learn to use them, the farther and longer you will be able to climb. Most beginners concentrate on where to put their hands, ignoring their feet entirely. This approach should be resisted. You must learn to trust your feet, even on the smallest of holds. The use of rock shoes, with their excellent friction properties, makes this much easier to do.

EASY-ANGLED ROCK
Find a really low-angled piece of rock, say about 25 to 30 degrees, and simply walk around on it. At this angle you will find that it's easily possible to manage without using your hands.

Take the opportunity to become acquainted with the superb friction properties of your rock shoes. Try standing on a small ledge of rock with the inside or outside edge of the shoe. Avoid high-stepping movements. Though there are times in rock climbing when you need to make a big step up, a good deal of energy can be saved by utilizing intermediate, perhaps smaller, footholds to reach a more secure one. Keep looking down at your feet and slowly begin to develop precision about where you place them. Each time you put your foot on a hold, it should be placed deliberately and, hardest of all, with confidence that it will stick in place. Try using only the friction between shoe sole and rock to create a foot-hold. This is known as "smearing" (see Rock climbing terms, 137, and the image directly below).

USING FOOTHOLDS
Having gained some confidence in the stickiness of the shoes, it's time to move on to techniques of standing on specific and obvious holds or ledges. Find a piece of rock that is a little bit steeper and where hands placed against the surface can be used for balance. Balance only, remember! You don't need to use them to pull up on just yet. It was once thought that climbing is more efficient and safer if you maintain three points of contact with the rock at all times, and lean out and away from the rock so that you have a clear view of your feet and the rock in front of you. While this may be useful for easier climbs, in the grand scheme of things, and when you progress towards more challenging climbs, it may serve to misdirect you and make your climbing experiences much less efficient.

▲ Economy of effort is essential in rock climbing. Try to avoid high stepping movements when taking those first steps or you may tire too easily.

▲ The technique of "smearing" the shoes over the rock surface is well illustrated here. Many brands of rock-climbing shoe promote their frictional capacity, and of course the more pliable the shoe, the easier it is to perform the technique. For this reason, newly-purchased "stiff" shoes do not always lend themselves well to smearing until they are "worn in". The hands can also be used to perform smearing where necessary.

▲ The feet are smeared and the hands are used mainly for balance, though some support may be gained by curling the fingers over the smallest of edges.

USING SMALL STEPS

It is a good idea to get into the habit of taking small steps up as you climb. This may mean using footholds that are not particularly good. However, it is better to use them and move up for better holds, rather than stretching too high to get to the better holds straight away. Over-reaching immediately puts you off balance and will also put a greater strain on your muscles.

Experiment at your local indoor wall or crag. Choose an easy route (either short, easy bouldering problems or a longer route – but use a rope and be belayed!). Try it first making big reaches with both hands and feet. Now do it again, but taking small steps and making smaller controlled moves. It should entail less effort and greater coordination.

▲ *Keep the hands low to avoid over-stretching the arms.*

▲ *Having made the step up, the next handhold is reached.*

EDGING

Look down towards your feet and try to pick out small or large edges, protrusions and depressions in the rock surface. Each one you find could be a foothold and you should try to use them all, even if it means taking 20 steps to gain a few feet of height. You will quickly discover that by using these features each placement of the foot gains greater security than if it was just smeared on to the hold. If you find an edge that is difficult or uncomfortable to stand on with the front of the shoe, experiment by turning your foot sideways and putting either the inside or the outside edge of the shoe on the hold. This technique will be instantly more comfortable, for the simple reason that you are able to gain more support from the shoe across its width than its length because there is a good deal more rigidity and less leverage across the sole. Using the sides of the shoe in this way is called "edging", and it is useful when moving on steep rock.

▶ *Using the inside and outside of the shoe means you can get more of your foot in contact with the rock, and will ultimately be more comfortable.*

Rock climbing: using your hands

Handholds are more easily seen, generally speaking, than footholds. They are at eye level, or thereabouts. However, they come in all shapes and sizes and at all angles. You will need to experiment to find the best usage.

JUGS, FINGERHOLDS AND SIDE-PULLS

Having gained some confidence with your feet, it's time to move on to the hands. We have already experimented a little with the hands for balance. Having an edge to curl your fingers over increases the feeling of security, but we are not yet ready to use holds to pull our body weight up the rock – that has to wait for much steeper occasions. To begin, select a section of rock at a 45–50 degree angle and long enough so that you can make several consecutive moves horizontally or at a slight rising diagonal across the surface.

This sideways movement is called "traversing" (see Rock climbing terms, 137). The benefits of traversing are that you don't need to climb too high above the ground and that movement can be more continuous.

Now you need to look not only at the positioning of your feet, but also to consider using your hands to make life easier. You will need to use a variety of handholds. The simplest ones to use are those that you pull on from directly below. No doubt these will sometimes feel large and occasionally so small that they might appear inadequate. Large handholds that you can curl all of the fingers of one hand over are usually called "jugs". In the past, climbers have referred to them as "thank God" holds for obvious reasons! Holds that you can only get half the length of your fingers on, or your fingertips only, are known as "fingerholds".

Having mastered these two types of handhold, you have a good enough technique to be able to climb most moderately graded rock. But other less obvious handholds exist, and to get the best out of them you will need to experiment. For example, a handhold found to lie vertically with the cliff face may at first seem useless. However, if it is pulled on from the side, with your feet positioned to keep you in balance, this type of hold will be found usable. They are called "side-pulls". Side-pulls are great holds to use when traversing, as they help you to pull your body across the rock and to transfer weight from foot to foot. As has been mentioned, the hands can also "smear" rock, and this is useful when a handhold is angled awkwardly. A canny climber will look for, find and use even the most obscure hold to aid progress, so don't dismiss anything lightly.

▲ *Holds over which you can comfortably curl your hand are sometimes called "thank God" holds. These are the most welcome holds to find on any climb.*

▲ *More examples of large handholds, this time inside and along the edges of a diagonal crack. Use your imagination when looking for holds to grip on to.*

▲ *Small fingerholds are surprisingly secure, particularly if there is an incut "lip" to the edge of the hold to make the grip easier.*

REMOVE RINGS AND WATCHES

It is always a good idea to remove your watch and any rings or other jewellery. Some types of handholds can be very taxing on your fingers and arms, and may cause damage to anything you happen to be wearing. Apart from scratches to your jewellery, you may also suffer damage to yourself if your jewellery becomes trapped. The forces involved could dent a ring into your finger, for example.

▼ *Leaning sideways off a hold will allow you to let go with one hand to reach upward and diagonally. In this case, the climber will be able to let go with the right hand and reach up to better holds above.*

THE WARM-UP SURVIVAL GUIDE FOR HANDS

• Always ensure that all the main finger grip angles are utilized during the warm-up: crimp, half crimp, and open hand. "Crimping" refers to the arching of the main finger joint while keeping the hands rigid, and is useful when you can only get the very tips of the fingers into a hold and need to generate your support from that point. If necessary, try to incorporate slopers (used when smearing the hands across sloping rock), pinches (shown by the image, right) or other more

specific types of fingerhold into the warm-up if you think they will be required during the climb.
• Try to climb fluidly, smoothly and in control and only attempt faster dynamic moves to recruit your power and timing towards the end of the warm-up.
• For longer endurance climbing, you will always climb better after incorporating a primary pump into your warm-up to open the capillaries and to activate your body's lactic acid transfer systems.

▲ *The art of pinching.*

Rock climbing: basic moves

The key to climbing efficiently is to be able to read the rock you are about to climb. This will require some imagination (what will it be like to be up there in that position?) and your past experience, and then devising moves for that particular climb.

CLIMBING MOVES IN SEQUENCE

To climb a section of rock, whether it is a traverse or straight up, you should try to look upon it as a sequence of interlinked movements. To link the movements successfully, you'll need to look beyond the section of rock immediately in front of you and determine where your sequence will end before beginning the next. Sometimes this will be three or four moves and sometimes considerably more. For example, if you have a clear view of a place where you think you can comfortably stand that is about 3m/10ft above, plan a sequence of moves to reach that point.

READING THE ROCK

To successfully plan a sequence of moves, you'll need to look very carefully at the availability of handholds and footholds over the section of rock. You will need to think ahead in terms of how you might use the available holds and in what order. An interesting insight into this takes place at indoor climbing competitions. A climber taking part in an indoor climbing competition is allowed to see the route they have to climb a little before they actually have to do it. They will stand at the bottom of the route and scrutinize the holds, trying to visualize where they will be when they get to certain points, how their weight may be distributed, where their hands and feet will be and what technique they might use to move up. They will break the route down into manageable sections. To some extent, all climbers with experience will learn to do this to a certain level to help them cope with the climb they are about to do. Quite often there are many different ways to

THE FIRST MOVES: FEET

1 The objective is clear – first you need to stand up on the right foot and gain suitable holds using the hands.

2 Pull your weight over on to the right foot and stand up. Keep as much weight on your right foot as possible.

3 Reach up with your right hand for the jug. Here, this sequence of three moves will gain you 1m/3ft in height.

link holds and moves together in a sequence. These variations depend on what you see, what you think you might be able to use, how far you can reach and your experience or ability to visualize the moves – often referred to as being able to "read the rock".

The way one person climbs a sequence is not necessarily the way that another might link it together, though it is quite right to say that having seen someone climb a piece of rock the next climber to attempt it has a distinct advantage.

THE FIRST MOVES: HANDS

4 In this sequence, notice how the feet change position but the left hand stays on the same hold.

5 The left hand remains in place to aid balance while an intermediate hold is taken by the right hand.

6 The left hand changes from a pull hold to a push hold and the feet can be comfortably moved higher, now that there is a secure hold for the right hand.

▲ *Grooves and corners should be straddled for comfort and energy-efficient climbing.*

USING A ROPE

When you first climb using a rope, you may feel differently about the whole experience of climbing. There is more to think about than simply making moves. The harness and rope may get in the way, but you will soon get used to them. At this stage, try to find a climb that is not too steep, that is well endowed with handholds and foot-holds, and which offers a diversity of rock features. By giving attention to these three factors you are assured of success. An ideal height for the climb would be around 10m/30ft. Ideals, of course, are rarely achievable! Before starting out on the climb, stand back and take a good look at the route you think you might take. Look for obvious ledges or breaks in the cliff face, places where you might be able to pause and rest to consider the remainder of the ascent. The knowledge that you gain from doing this can be used to break down the climb into short sections that are easier to cope with. Keep the final goal in mind, but don't let it hinder your ability to think calmly.

If you find that your calculated sequence doesn't quite work, take a moment to re-think. Do not just look at the rock immediately in front of your nose. Look to the sides of the line you are to take. Quite often there will be holds off to one side or the other that are not immediately obvious but that you can put a foot or hand on for maintaining balance or resting. They may not be quite the types of big holds you are looking for or expecting to find, but experimentation is quite likely to prove worthwhile.

Grooves and corners in the rock face are usually straddled with both feet and hands for comfort. This is called "bridging" and is a particularly restful and economic way to climb, because much of your body weight is supported by the feet and legs. Find places where you can experiment with taking one hand off, or even both, in order to gain a rest. Climbing on a top rope is totally safe, and though your weight might sag on to the rope, you'll not fall off in the truest sense – it'll only be a slump! Armed with this knowledge, you can forget those worries and concentrate on the task in hand.

Some people find it a useful exercise to climb the same route several times. Each ascent should become more efficient in terms of energy expended and you will learn a great deal about body movement and awareness. However, rock in all its infinite variety offers so many different combinations of moves that it is as well not to ponder for too long on any particular climb. After you have gained confidence from your first climb, you need to extend your experience to include widely differing styles of movement in order to make progress.

▲ *An easy-angled slab makes an ideal first climb. Slabs can be surprisingly tiring on the feet and legs, so try to vary the position of your feet frequently.*

Kayak and canoe touring: what you need

Kayaking and canoeing are very old methods of transportation and can vary from a pleasant paddle along a flatwater river or sheltered coastline to a fast and exciting paddle down a white-water river. The only interruption to a continuous, comfortable journey will be extreme rapids, weirs or non-navigable locks, when the boat will have to be carried overland.

CHOOSING A BOAT AND PADDLES
A huge number of kayaks are now available. They are all single-seaters. When choosing a kayak, check that it has sufficient buoyancy to float when full of water; the buoyancy should be distributed so that the kayak floats level when swamped. It must have a seat and a footrest to brace against, otherwise you will not be able to paddle properly.

Canoes are available as single- and double-seaters. A double canoe will accommodate two people, as well as all the supplies necessary for several days of touring. A double canoe can be paddled by one person, but putting two people in a solo canoe is a recipe for a swim. Canoes for three or more people are also available. Double canoes vary from expensive wooden models to cheaper alternatives made of synthetic materials, such as aluminium and polymers, which are more resistant to serious damage if you scrape them over rocks in low-water conditions.

Paddles need to be robust but as light as possible. They also need to be the right length: to check the length of a kayak paddle, stand it up level with your foot, and reach up to grasp the top blade. You should be able to do this comfortably with your arm slightly bent. A canoe paddle is always shorter than a kayak paddle because it has only one blade. Beautifully crafted wooden paddles have the nicest feel, but paddles with alloy shafts and plastic blades are a lot cheaper. If you are buying or hiring a paddle, try out a variety of models before deciding. Always carry a spare set of paddles with you in case of damage or loss.

▼ A white-water canoe is fitted with airbags to keep it afloat when full of water. These can be removed for paddling flatwater, and the space used to carry your gear.

▼ A modern white-water kayak suitable for beginners. This boat could also be used for paddling flatwater and sheltered stretches of coastal water.

▼ The correct length for a recreational kayak paddle is determined by your height and reach: this one is ideal. A canoe paddle is shorter.

SPRAYDECKS

A spraydeck (spray skirt) fits around your waist and over the cockpit, and is used with kayaks to prevent water from getting into the boat. It is not generally needed on flatwater, where the water is calm and there is little or no splashing. If you wear a spraydeck, it is essential that you know how to remove it easily, in case you need to exit the boat quickly in a capsize.

▲ *A thermal top worn with board shorts, a buoyancy aid and trainers are ideal clothing for fine-weather paddling.*

PERSONAL BUOYANCY

A buoyancy aid (personal flotation device or PFD) is vital to help prevent drowning and should be worn at all times when on the water, no matter how confident a swimmer you are. Choose a style that allows you to move your arms freely, and one that fits snugly and will not pull off when you are in the water. To check the fit, pull firmly upwards from the shoulders: if it can be pulled off, the straps need tightening.

HEAD PROTECTION

There is no legal requirement to wear a helmet, but it is advisable to wear one, especially for paddling on white water. Make sure it fits: a helmet that is too big can slip off and one that is too small can cause discomfort. Look for a helmet that carries a recognized safety mark.

CLOTHING

Your insulation requirements depend on the weather, so check the forecast before choosing your level of clothing. Whatever you wear should not be too heavy when wet for you to swim in. Polyester and polypropylene are better than cotton for warmth when wet.

If the water temperature is cold and the air chilly or wet, wear a thermal base layer made from polyester fleece or polypropylene, or wear a wetsuit. If wind-chill is an issue, and a wind- and spray-proof cagoule for upper-body warmth. Good features to look for in a cagoule are a waterproof fabric, neoprene cuffs, a comfortable neck seal and an adjustable waist. In fine weather, a T-shirt and shorts can be worn, with something warmer in case you capsize.

FOOTWEAR

You cannot paddle well in bulky, heavy footwear, but bare feet are not ideal, as you will need shoes that have a good grip on wet, muddy banks. Light pumps or technical sandals are light enough to swim in if you capsize. Wetsuit boots and water-sports shoes have good grips, and are padded and reinforced in all the right places, but this is specialized footwear and not strictly necessary for one-off paddlers.

▼ *Additional items might include a hand pump, knife, compass, VHF radio, transistor receiver, flares, sunscreen and a mobile phone.*

▼ *Suitable warm-weather footwear includes technical sandals, which are lightweight, comfortable and widely available.*

▲ *A cagoule offers good protection from the rain, but choose a close-fitting, waist-length style that allows full upper-body movement.*

▼ *A correctly fitting helmet sits on the head without sliding forward. A helmet that does not fit will not give adequate protection.*

▼ *Specialist water-sports shoes will keep the feet warm even when wet, and are a good investment if you plan to paddle frequently.*

Kayaking: warming up

Canals and lakes are good training areas when you are acquiring paddling skills, and will often be adjacent to suitable camping land. The one essential requirement before you begin is the ability to swim. You should be able to swim at least 50m/170ft in the clothes you will be wearing in the boat.

CROSS-TRAINING

Improving your general level of fitness will dramatically increase the fun you get from paddling, and reduce the likelihood of injury and tiredness. While paddling vigorously or over a long distance is itself an excellent all-body workout, extra non-paddling exercises such as swimming, cycling or running will benefit your cardiovascular system and build body strength before

your trip. Whatever cross-training you choose, do it in moderation but aim to exercise regularly – daily if possible.

Target specific muscle groups with toning exercises. The muscles in the thighs, abdomen, shoulders and back do most of the work in the boat, and performing press-ups, pull-ups and crunches therefore make good preparation for paddling.

WARM-UP ROUTINE

Start with some light exercise, such as brisk walking, swimming or playing with a frisbee, to warm up and raise your heart rate. Gently stretch each muscle group. Once afloat, take a short paddle then do some more stretches in the boat, leaning backwards and forwards and rotating the trunk.

SAFETY RULES

- Never paddle on your own.
- Always wear your buoyancy aid (personal flotation device).
- Warm up before paddling.
- Know where you are going and, if you do not know the river, check for any rapids.
- Cover any cuts or grazes with waterproof plasters before canoeing to avoid infection.
- Always secure the equipment that you are carrying in your boat.
- Always get help to move a canoe when on land.
- Make sure you wash your hands or take a shower after paddling and before eating.

STRETCHING IN THE BOAT

After your initial stretches on land, it is time to get used to being seated in the boat, where you can continue your warm-up routine with exercises that simulate more closely your movements while out on the water.

BEFORE GETTING AFLOAT

Exercises performed in the boat while you are still on land serve a dual purpose. First, you will be getting all the usual benefits of stretching, but specifically geared to the range of motion you have in the boat. Second, you are checking that you have good freedom of movement in the boat and in your paddling kit. If something is hurting, chafing or digging into your ribs when you do these stretches, get out now and solve the problem immediately.

TIPS

- Always stretch gently and progressively; never bounce.
- Only use your muscles to stretch; do not use weights or external forces, which will cause muscle strain and possible injury.

BOAT STRETCHES ON LAND

1 Check you can reach the right-hand side of the stern with your left hand.

2 Repeat the stretch, using your right hand, on the other side of the boat.

3 Extend fully backwards, so that you are stretching over the back deck.

4 Then, extend fully forwards, so that you are stretching over the front deck.

Getting into the kayak

The first thing to learn is how to get into the kayak while it is afloat. It is one skill that you may be able to practise on dry land, if you are sure that the boat is strong enough to take your weight on its hull, but is best practised at the water's edge.

Find a place to launch where the bank or jetty is not too much higher than the gunwale of your kayak. Place the boat on the surface of the water, making sure that it is sufficiently deep to keep you afloat after you climb in! If it is deep enough to capsize, ensure that it is also deep enough to get out of the boat when upside down.

Don't be tempted to tether the boat to the bank, which would make things very difficult if you capsized. It may be possible to step into the boat while holding on to the bank, simply pick up your paddle, and paddle away, but this can often be tricky. A useful technique is to place your paddle across the boat at the back of the cockpit, and hold on to it and the cockpit rim at the same time. The paddle blade will then be resting on the bank, and this will stop the boat floating away, as well as supporting the back deck of the boat. Don't attempt this if the bank is much higher than the kayak, however.

Now that the boat is afloat and you are holding on to it and the paddle, place one foot in the bottom of the boat, and make sure it is right in the middle before you put any weight on it. Transfer all your weight on to that foot and, still holding on to boat and paddle with one hand, place your other foot right inside the footwell of the boat and sit down on the back deck. Take a moment to get settled.

Finally, get your legs into position in the cockpit. Now you are ready to use your free hand to hold on to the bank, and can bring your paddle around in front of you ready to paddle away.

GETTING INTO THE KAYAK

1 Place the boat as close to the river bank as possible. Keep hold of the cockpit to stop the boat drifting away. Place the paddle across the back of the cockpit with holding the front.

2 Continue to hold the front of the cockpit as you climb into the boat. Put one leg in at a time. Steady yourself by holding on to the river bank with one hand and the boat with the other.

3 Once you are positioned over the cockpit, slide forward into the opening and get both legs in. You should still be holding the paddle and the river bank to steady yourself and the boat.

4 Bend your knees to get both your legs stretched out beneath the front deck. Continue to hold the paddle and the bank while you adjust your position. Bring the paddle to the front.

5 Now that you are sitting securely in the cockpit, get your posture right. This image shows the correct posture. The body is upright, maintaining a well-defined spinal "S".

6 If your posture and seating position are poor, you will not be able to paddle properly. A good indicator is whether the release handle of the spraydeck (skirt) is visible and within reach.

Capsize drill in a kayak

You cannot get into a boat unless you accept that you may capsize. Hence, you also need to learn the escape drill. It is a simple skill, but the sooner you learn it the better. Losing the fear of capsizing means you will enjoy paddling a lot more.

Most people realize that a kayak, by nature, is prone to capsize. Although this can be avoided, the beginner will not know how, and that is why everyone should know how to capsize.

If you try to get out of a kayak while it is in the process of capsizing, you run the risk of injuring yourself or ending up in a position where your head is underwater, but you cannot free yourself. It is better to wait until the boat has capsized and stopped moving, and then get out. It is quite hard to visualize what you will do when you are upside down, but remember that when you are in the water you will not

be so aware of it. Rather, everything will look and feel exactly as it does when upright, except, of course, that you will be holding your breath.

First, remove your spraydeck (spray skirt), if you are wearing one, by pulling up the release handle and letting go. Then, bang on the bottom or sides of the boat to attract attention. Lean forwards and push yourself out by placing your hands either side of the cockpit. You will naturally do a somersault in the water, breaking surface in front of the cockpit.

If you come up directly under the boat, do not worry because kayaks are so narrow that there is no way you will be stuck underneath. If you can open your eyes it helps, but you can easily escape blind. If possible, try to keep hold of your paddle, but this is often difficult. As soon as your head breaks surface, take hold of the boat and

paddle or swim to the bow or stern. From there you can swim the boat ashore. Alternatively, someone may rescue you and help you back to land, or put you back in your boat so that you can continue paddling.

You should practise the capsize drill every time you go kayaking, until you are extremely confident. Most people do it at the end of a session because emptying a boat is tiring, and you need to be fully warmed up before you drill.

With practice, you may be able to keep hold of the boat with one hand, and the paddle with the other. This can be very useful to rescuers, or if you need to try to get back in the boat on your own. In the long run, a paddler with these skills will be ready to learn how to roll as an alternative to capsizing, and will be determined to stay in the boat. But for the present, getting safely out of the boat is key.

CAPSIZE AND GET OUT (UNDERWATER VIEW)

1 Locate the spraydeck (skirt) release handle and pull off the spraydeck.

2 Bring your knees together, place your hands on each side and tuck forwards.

3 Push firmly away with your hands and you will find that you fall out of the boat easily.

4 From the cockpit, turn to one side. Hold on to the boat and paddle if you can.

TIPS

- Wait until the boat has capsized completely before you try to get out of the boat.
- Pull off your spraydeck (spray skirt) as a matter of urgency, using the handle at the front of the boat. Make sure that it has been released all the way to the cockpit before you try to move.
- Free both of your knees from under the deck at the front of the boat.
- Tuck your body forwards, with your knees pulled up to your chest in a foetal position; don't try to lie across the back deck.
- Aim to keep hold of your boat with one hand as you come up to the surface of the water.
- Don't try to get your head above the surface of the water until your legs are completely out of the boat because you risk getting into a tangle that could prove dangerous: learn the stages of a capsize in one sequence and keep to it.

CAPSIZE AND GET OUT (ABOVE WATER VIEW)

1 You are on flat water and are ready to begin the capsize drill. Keep your hands by your sides and take a deep breath.

2 Lean over to one side and capsize. At first, you may have to resist your body's natural instinct to right itself.

3 Remain sitting upright, at 90° to the boat, as you go over. It may help to place your hands on the sides of the boat.

4 It will help to keep hold of the sides of the boat as your head hits the water and goes under.

5 Wait in this position until the boat stops moving. You will feel it settle when you are completely upside down.

6 Once completely inverted, bang on the bottom or sides of the boat. This makes a loud noise and attracts attention.

▶ **7** Once out of the boat, go to one end and hold on to the grab handle. Take a moment to get your bearings, and then use your force to swim the boat towards the shore or your rescuer.

TIPS

- Only practise the capsize drill when there is an instructor or experienced rescuer on hand to help you in case you get into difficulties.
- Make sure the water is at least 1.2m/4ft deep. It is tempting to stay in shallow water, but this can lead to entrapment or injury.

Holding the paddle

How the paddle is held is critical if you are going to use it properly. This is because the correct grip enables the paddler to apply the maximum amount of force with the minimum effort.

Almost all kayak paddles are feathered (one blade at an angle to the other), which means that with each stroke you will turn the paddle to put the other blade in the water. One hand will be your control hand and will grip the paddle at all times. Allow the paddle shaft to turn in the other, non-control hand, gripping it only as you make the stroke on that side.

Find your best hand position by putting the middle of the paddle shaft on your head and shuffling your hands until your elbows make 90°, as shown in step 3, below. Make sure that your hands are equidistant from the blades

Hold the paddle out in front of you with your arms straight and horizontal, knuckles up. Grip the paddle with your control hand so that the blade on the control side is vertical, and the drive (concave) face is forward. If it is your paddle, you can mark your hand positions with tape.

Never be tempted to change your grip on the paddle once you've got it right. There are no significant advantages to shifting your grip, and you will find that any changes hamper the learning process. Learning is feedback related, and changing the grip means you have to start all over again.

MAKING THE FIRST STROKE

With all paddle strokes you should aim to put the whole of the blade in the water, but no more. There is no

advantage to the blade being deeper in the water, and it will not work properly if it is only half in.

When you make a stroke, you should always try to rotate your shoulders to give you as much reach as possible. This also means that much of the power for the stroke will come from your leg and torso muscles, leaving your smaller arm muscles to provide control and react to feedback during the stroke. Rotating the head is just as important. Before making a stroke, you should make sure your head is facing in the direction you want the boat to move in. So, for forward paddling, you must be looking at the horizon. If you want to turn the boat to the left or right, you should first turn your head in that direction. This helps the whole of your body make the strokes, and eliminates bad posture.

HOLDING AND USING THE PADDLE

1 Incorrect hold. You should never hold the paddle shaft off-centre.

2 Incorrect hold. Here, the hands are too close together on the shaft.

3 To find your correct grip, hold the paddle so that, with the wrist of the control hand straight, the drive face (the concave side of the blade) faces down towards the water.

4 Incorrect stroke. The blade is too deep in the water and the paddler's hand is too low.

5 Incorrect stroke. The blade is too shallow in the water – only half of it would come into play.

6 Correct technique: the paddle blade is submerged just deep enough to start a forward stroke.

Forward paddling

A good forward paddling stroke is a basic requirement, but it is not the easiest stroke to master. The main aim is to propel the boat forward while applying as little turning force as possible. Normally, if you make a stroke on one side, the boat will move forwards while turning away from the paddle blade that made the stroke. In order to minimize this effect, you should make the stroke as close to the boat as possible, with the paddle shaft as upright as possible.

Reach forward as far as you can, leaning from the hips but without bending your spine forward. You should be able to put the blade in the water about 2.5cm/1in from the boat, near your feet, and drive face back. When the blade is fully immersed, pull it back using your shoulders and torso,

straightening up your top arm to push the "air blade" to the side of the boat that the stroke is on. This will make the paddle vertical and a lot more comfortable for you.

Continue to pull the paddle blade through the water until it is level with the back of the seat. Try to resist the urge to pull with your bottom arm for as long as possible. When your arm finally does bend at the elbow, it will be time to extract the blade from the water. Keep this blade the same distance from the boat throughout the stroke.

As soon as the blade is out of the water, rotate your body the other way to make the next stroke on the other side. As you do so, you will have to rotate the shaft with your control hand; drop in the blade with the drive face pointing the same way as before.

FORWARD PADDLING TECHNIQUE

1 Begin the forward stroke by placing the blade as far forward in the water as you comfortably can do.

2 Drop the whole of the blade into the water and start to push away from you with your top hand.

3 The blade in the water follows the side of the boat, and the bottom arm stays fairly straight.

4 As the water blade passes your body, the top arm should be coming across in front of your face.

5 Finally, as you reach the end of the stroke, the air blade starts to come down towards the water.

6 Continuing this motion recovers the water blade, and you are ready to place the opposite blade in the water.

Backward paddling

Paddling backwards is in principle no different from paddling forwards, but it is more difficult to get the hang of.

Always back-paddle using the back of the blade. There is no need to turn the paddle around since its curvature actually helps you to make the back stroke, and because it is bad practice to change your grip.

It is not possible to keep the paddle shaft as vertical as you do for forward paddling, or to keep the blades so close to the boat, but this is what you should aim for. Make a big effort to rotate your shoulders as far as you can to place the blade behind you – this also helps you to glance behind and see where you are going. Push your paddle forward through the water with your arms fairly straight, and make the stroke as long as you can.

Most boats will turn during the back stroke so that you zig-zag a little. With a bit of practice, you can keep this to a minimum. Find somewhere where you will not crash into anything, and see how long you can keep going back in a straight line. It will teach you excellent control over the boat.

▲ *Incorrect method. Do not turn the paddle around like this.*

TIPS

- Think before you back-paddle: it may be quicker and easier to turn your boat and paddle forwards.
- Look over your shoulder at least every other stroke to avoid a crash.
- Pick out a feature behind you in the direction of travel, and focus on it whenever you turn around.

BACKWARD PADDLING TECHNIQUE

1 Rotate as far as you can to one side, and place the blade quite far back in the water behind the boat.

2 Drive the blade forwards through the water using your torso; do not use your arms for strength.

3 As you come around to face the front, straighten your arms, keeping the blade as close as you can to the boat.

4 Try looking behind you as you finish the stroke – rotating the body will help with this. It may seem difficult at first but will come with practice.

5 The stroke should end with the bottom arm straight and the blade still in the water in the area of the boat next to your feet.

6 As the blade comes out of the water, you can continue rotating to place the blade behind you on the other side and then repeat the action.

Stopping

Learning how to stop the boat quickly is important. Use this stroke if you are in danger of hitting something.

Begin by moving the boat forwards at a good pace. To stop, jab one blade into the water next to your body, as if to paddle backwards. The drive face should be pointing backwards with the shaft perpendicular. Resist the force on the blade, but as soon as you tense against that force and the boat begins to turn, jab the other blade in quickly on the other side. Repeat on the first side, and by the time you make your fourth jab, the boat should have stopped. Do the jabs quite aggressively, and switch sides when you feel the pressure on the back of the blade.

▶ *Stopping quickly in a fast racing kayak requires sharp jabs in the water.*

STOPPING TECHNIQUE

1 Jab the paddle in on one side, at 90° to the kayak rather than as you would for a normal stroke.

2 Pull the paddle out again as soon as you feel the pressure of the water on the blade and the boat begins to turn.

3 Drop the opposite blade in on the other side. Resist for a little longer this time, until the boat is straight again.

4 Returning to the side of the boat on which you started, make a longer back stroke this time.

5 Moving backwards this time, make a final stroke on the opposite side to straighten up the boat.

6 At the finish, you should be pointing in the same direction you were at the previous step, except with the boat still.

Canoeing: getting in and posture

To practice getting into the boat, it is best to start by finding a launching site where the river bank or jetty is low enough to let you step into the canoe without having to jump or climb in. Place the boat on the surface. The water should be deep enough to keep the craft afloat with your weight. If the water is deep enough to capsize in, make sure that it is also deep enough for getting out if the boat turns upside down.

Also consider how you are going to stop the canoe from floating away while you climb in. A useful technique is to place your paddle on the ground next to the boat, and keep one hand on it as you climb in. This is often easier than clinging on to a grass bank.

When the boat is afloat and you are holding on to both the gunwale (the strengthening rail running the length of the canoe on each side) and the paddle,

you are ready to get in. Place one foot in the bottom of the boat, and make sure it is right in the middle before you put any weight on it. Now gradually transfer all your weight on to that foot, and still holding on to the paddle if necessary, place your other foot right inside the footwell of the boat and gently sit or kneel down. Pick up the paddle and manoeuvre into your preferred sitting or kneeling position.

GETTING INTO THE CANOE

1 Keeping the canoe close to the bank, make sure that it is floating freely on the water and won't touch the bottom when you get in. Keep hold of the nearside gunwale and lay the paddle across.

2 Holding on to both gunwales and the paddle, put one foot in the middle of the canoe and transfer your weight on to it. Keep the other foot on the bank until you feel confident to step in.

3 When you are happy that the canoe is balanced and stable, bring your other foot into the boat, still holding the paddle across the gunwale, and using it as a support to balance the boat.

4 Supporting your weight using both of your hands, and still holding the paddle, settle yourself into your preferred sitting or kneeling position.

5 This show a good kneeling position. The paddler is kneeling with the buttocks resting on the seat and knees apart, spanning the width of the canoe.

6 An example of the correct seating position. The paddler is sitting on the seat, with the knees against the sides of the boat, giving good control.

Capsize drill in a canoe

If you are going to paddle a canoe it is important that you know what to do if it capsizes. The ability to swim is obviously important, but how you get out of the boat and handle yourself should be addressed as soon as possible.

If you try to get out of a canoe while it is capsizing, you run the risk of a gunwale cracking you on the head, or getting in a muddle. It is far better to get out once upside down, when the boat has stopped moving. Push away from the gunwale with your hands, keeping hold of your paddle if possible. As soon as your head breaks surface, take hold of the boat and swim to one end. You can then either swim the boat ashore, or try to turn it over.

A reasonably athletic canoeist can often right the boat and get back in unaided. Get alongside the upturned canoe, and take hold underneath. Push it up until the gunwales are about to break the surface, keeping it level. Tread water to maintain upward force. Finally, allow yourself to sink into the water and, as you come up again, push up harder on one side than the other, flipping the canoe over with the minimum of water inside. With a really light boat it is possible to throw it into the air and land it upright. Having righted the boat, push down the side nearest to you, and reach across to the opposite gunwale to steady the boat and haul yourself in.

TIPS

- If you know the boat is going to capsize, it is worth getting out if you have enough time. Only jump out of the boat if you are able to do so before it flips over.
- If you jump out before a capsize, you will be able to get back in without the difficulty of righting and emptying the canoe.
- By kicking off from the high side of the boat, you can often stop the canoe turning over.
- If the boat turns over, wait until it has stopped moving and is upside down before you get out.

CAPSIZE AND GET OUT

1 Starting from your usual paddling position, let go of the paddle with one hand and take hold of the gunwale of the boat. Lean over to one side until the boat overbalances.

2 Keeping hold of the paddle as you go over, allow the boat to capsize, still holding on to the gunwale. Wait until you are completely upside down and the boat has stopped moving.

3 Push away from the gunwale and kick away from the boat until your head breaks the surface of the water. Ideally you should still be holding the paddle. Take a hold of the boat.

4 Swim your way to the front of the boat, still keeping hold of the canoe and the paddle if at all possible.

5 Take hold of the front of the canoe, leaving it upside down. Attract the attention of the other paddlers.

6 Using the paddle, if you can, and your arms and legs, swim the canoe to the shore or to other paddlers.

Holding the paddle

You can only use a paddle properly if you are holding it correctly in the first place. This is because the correct grip enables the paddler to apply the maximum amount of force with the minimum effort. It is also important to hold the paddle in exactly the same way every time you use it. This is the only way for you to become familiar with the feel of the paddle in the water.

Canoe paddles have only one blade, with a T-grip at the other end. It is important to hold this T-grip with your top hand knuckle up and thumb under, and the shaft of the paddle with the other hand. If the paddle has a curved blade, you should grip the paddle with the bottom hand so that the blade has the drive (concave) face towards you. Hold the T-grip in one hand; place the other hand so that if the paddle is held horizontal in front of you, your hands are slightly further apart than your shoulders.

WHICH SIDE TO PADDLE ON?

In the early stages of your paddling practice, you are going to have to decide whether you are a leftie or a rightie – that is to say, whether you will paddle on the left-hand side of

the boat or on the right. Most people are able to paddle on either side, but have a preferred side. The only way to find out is by trial and error; whether you are right- or left-handed has very little bearing on the matter.

What is certain is that whichever side you are paddling on, you should try to keep to that grip. It is the principle of canoe paddling, as opposed to kayaking, that you should be able to do everything from one side of the boat, without changing sides. Expert paddlers use cross-bow strokes to put the blade in on the opposite side from their normal paddling side without altering their grip, but the easiest technique is to paddle on the on-side where possible, using a cross-bow stroke or two if necessary.

CORRECT USE OF THE PADDLE

Beginners often find what they imagine to be the easiest tasks actually the trickiest. Using the paddle is a very good example of this but, by following the guidelines below, and establishing good habits from the start, you should have no problems. For all paddle strokes you should aim to put the whole of the blade in the water, but no more. There

is no advantage to the blade being deeper in the water, and it will not work properly if it is only half in. Put the blade in until it is totally immersed; keep the paddle shaft visible.

When you make a stroke, you should lean forwards to give yourself as much reach as possible. This also means that much of the power for the stroke will come from your leg and torso muscles, leaving your arm muscles to provide control and react to feedback from the water. It is a misconception to think that canoeing is all about using arm muscles. If your technique is good, a vigorous paddle is more likely to leave you with tired, aching legs and stomach muscles.

As with kayaking, the canoe paddler must concentrate on is head rotation in order to make a stroke really effective. Before angling the stroke, make sure your head is facing in the direction you want to move in. So, with forward paddling, you must look straight ahead at the horizon. If you want to turn the boat to the left or right, first turn your head and shoulders to look that way. Such movements demonstrate how the whole of your body is key to making your paddling as efficient as possible.

▲ *An example of poor paddling technique. The blade not fully immersed in the water. This will not give you enough grip on the water to be able to drive the boat forward.*

▲ *Another common mistake is to position the paddle too deep. As a rule, you should never immerse the shaft of the paddle, and certainly not your hand!*

▲ *Paddling with a correctly immersed blade. The whole of the blade area is completely covered but only just, the paddle shaft is almost vertical and the hand is well clear.*

Forward paddling in tandem

A correct forward paddling stroke is a basic requirement if you want to be a good canoeist, but it is not the easiest stroke to master. In addition to the technique for moving forwards, you will inevitably have to learn how to paddle backwards, stop and steer. Learning to combine these techniques is a useful discipline that teaches you control and the ability to respond to feedback from the water – and will make you a much better paddler!

The main aim of forward paddling is to propel the boat forwards. It is important to apply as little turning force as possible, since by turning you are making your forward stroke less effective. Normally, if you make a stroke on one side, the boat will move forwards but it will also turn away from the paddle blade that made the stroke. In order to minimize this effect, you should make the stroke as close as you can to the boat, with the paddle shaft as vertical as possible.

If you are paddling a canoe alone, you will also have to use a technique to keep the boat in a straight line. This is called the J-stroke, and it is described on the next page. If two people are paddling tandem, their paddles will be on opposite sides of the boat, and the J-stroke will not be necessary because their turning effects on opposite sides will cancel each other out.

▼ *The lighter paddler should sit in the front of the boat when paddling tandem.*

TANDEM FORWARD STROKE
Begin with both paddlers reaching forwards as far as they can, leaning from the hips without bending the spine forwards. Both should put the blade in the water as far forward as possible, drive face pointing back. When the blade is fully immersed, it should be pulled back firmly, using the shoulders and torso, straightening the top arm, and keeping the T-grip on the side of the boat that the stroke is on. This will make the paddle as vertical as is comfortable.

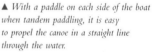

▲ *With a paddle on each side of the boat when tandem paddling, it is easy to propel the canoe in a straight line through the water.*

Continue to pull the blade through the water until it is level with your seat. Try to resist the urge to pull with your bottom arm for as long as possible. When it finally does bend at the elbow, it will be to extract the blade from the water. Aim to keep the blade the same distance from the boat throughout the duration of the stroke.

As soon as the blade is out of the water, lean forwards smoothly to begin another stroke. The less time the paddle is out of the water the more control you have, but if you lunge forwards too sharply it will stop the canoe in its tracks.

This is enough to move forward on flat water. If you want to take a canoe through white water with a partner, you will need to learn how to weave between the rapids using a forward sweep stroke. This is an advanced technique, not suitable for beginners.

Forward paddling alone

The J-stroke is the cornerstone of canoe paddling. Unless there are two people paddling the canoe on opposite sides, or you have an extremely straight-running craft, you will need this stroke to keep the boat going in a straight line.

The principle of the J-stroke is to perform a normal forward stroke but, at the end of the stroke, when the bottom arm is starting to bend, you must rotate your top hand outwards to point your thumb down. As a result, the drive face of the blade will then turn away from the hull of the canoe. This turns the stroke into a strong rudder, which arrests any turning force you may have inadvertently applied during the stroke. If you hesitate for a moment with the blade in this position, you will also be able to make fine adjustments to your course, by pushing or pulling the blade relative to the hull. Practise looking straight ahead in the direction of the travel when making the J-stroke, rather than at the paddle.

It takes a while to master the J-stroke. Persevere and learn to respond to the feedback from the blade. If, once you can do the J-stroke effectively, you find that some boats or conditions still make it difficult to paddle straight, there is a more powerful variation called the C-stroke. This is a J-stroke with a sharp pull of the drive face towards the hull at the very beginning, so that the blade creates a C rather than a J-shape.

TIPS

- Practise the J-stroke for as long as it takes you to feel comfortable with it: it's key to the good handling and control of a solo canoe.
- Use the J-stroke to keep yourself in line when you are happy with your general direction.

▶ *This paddler is using a J-stroke to keep his white water open canoe on course as he moves downstream.*

J-STROKE TECHNIQUE

1 Put the paddle in the water as far forward as possible, leaning forward to increase your reach.

2 Push with the top hand rather than pull with the bottom, and use your body as well as your arms.

3 As the blade passes your body, twist the paddle shaft so that your thumbs are pointing down. Unlike this paddler, you should aim to look straight ahead.

4 Keep the pressure on the paddle until the end of the stroke or else it won't work. It's a stroke with a twist, not a stroke followed by a stern rudder.

Backward paddling and stopping

Paddling backwards is in principle no different to going forwards, but it is a bit more difficult. As with kayaking, beginners will often try to change their grip on the paddle, which is a mistake.

The first thing to note is that you should back-paddle using the back of the blade. There is no need to turn the paddle around because any curvature actually helps you do the back stroke. It is bad practice to change your grip. It is not possible to keep the paddle shaft as vertical as you do for forward paddling, or to keep the blade so close to the boat, but you should try to do so as much as possible. Make a big effort to rotate your shoulders as far as you can to place the blade behind you; this also gives you an opportunity to look behind you to see where you are going.

Push your paddle forwards through the water with your arms fairly straight, and make the stroke as long as you can. Most boats will turn during the stroke, so you may have to turn the back face of the blade out at the end of the

▼ *Look where you are going when paddling backwards in tandem!*

stroke in a sort of reverse J-stroke, unless there are two of you paddling the canoe. Find somewhere safe where you will not crash into anything, and see how long you can keep going backwards in a straight line. It teaches you excellent control.

Don't be disappointed if you can't paddle backwards very far. It is a difficult technique to pick up, and can take a while to learn properly. Try to be as good at it as you can, but bear in mind that it is usually easier to turn the boat around and paddle forwards instead.

STOPPING

Getting an open boat to stop in a straight line is almost impossible because the boat will always turn towards the paddle. If you have room to let the boat turn sideways this will be the safest way to stop. If not, stick the paddle in the water as a brake, and, when the boat turns, sweep the paddle through the water in a wide arc to keep the boat straight. Repeat this action as many times as it takes to get the boat to sit motionless on the water. Tricky at first, it does get easier with practice.

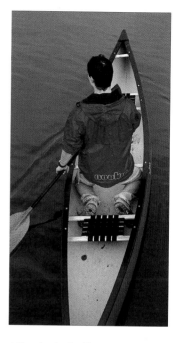

▲ *Rotating the shoulders as you place the blade behind you will help you make a more effective back stroke.*

Daily routine on a paddling trip

If you are taking your first canoe or kayak trip on a waterway, you will find that many waterside campsites provide excellent facilities and local farmers will rarely turn you down if you ask to camp on their land. Beware of animals in rural areas, particularly in spring as they will be protective of their young.

The tent you normally use for camping/backpacking will be fine. Always pitch it well above the water level of a river or lake as water can rise quickly. If the weather will be reliably fine, you could use your boat instead, rigging up plastic sheets or a groundsheet to make a shelter.

COOKING AND EATING

Although cooking on open driftwood fires gives a real sense of outdoor living, many places ban it or allow it in only designated areas. It is a good idea, therefore, to take a simple gas stove with a built-in flint, plus a few pans.

Ensure you take high-energy food supplies, as you will need them to power your muscles and generate warmth while paddling. There are plenty of instant savoury meals and desserts now available from outdoor shops in a wide variety of flavours; read the packaging to check on the calorific value. Chocolate and dried fruit make excellent snacks. Boil water on your stove to kill any bacteria.

KEEPING THINGS DRY

Your main concern when preparing to get afloat each day will be packing your belongings into the boat. All your equipment needs to be kept as dry as possible, which is not always easy in the case of rain or an inadvertent capsize.

Plastic waterproof drums, which come in a variety of shapes and sizes, are ideal for canoes. They are not too large to carry when loaded, and have easily re-sealable waterproof lids. Specialized waterproof bags are also convenient, as they pack slightly more easily in the boat. Buy different colours or ones with see-through sides, so that you do not keep getting out your dry underwear when you want your lunch.

▲ *A sea kayak has little storage space but offers the possibility of extended sea journeys into remote areas full of wildlife.*

When packing up your tent, make sure the poles and pegs are attached securely, or stow them separately in a special bag so that you do not lose them if you capsize.

Tying all your bags and equipment into the thwarts is always a very sensible decision, since any capsize could lighten your load instantly, and possibly disastrously.

▼ *The inside of a kayak is an enclosed space, which makes it difficult to pack. Kit needs to be divided between several bags.*

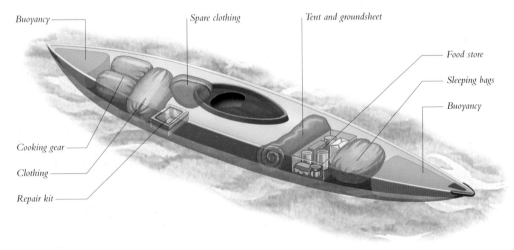

Buoyancy

Spare clothing

Tent and groundsheet

Food store

Sleeping bags

Buoyancy

Cooking gear

Clothing

Repair kit

▲ *Durable plastic containers, known as "BDHs", are ideal for storing small items that must be kept dry.*

▶ *Two paddlers carry their loaded sea kayaks down to the water. Hold the boat end grabs, one in each hand.*

PACKING

A double canoe can easily accommodate all the supplies and equipment necessary for days of cruising, but in a kayak the space is much more confined. Merely getting all your equipment into the boat can be difficult. Rather than keep your kit in one large bag, the secret is to use several small waterproof bags, known as dry bags, which can be packed more easily into the spaces available. Careful packing is essential.

With a canoe, the balance of the boat will determine how easy it is to paddle, so, taking into account the weight of the paddlers (usually, the heavier paddler sits at the back), try either to weigh or estimate the weight of the different bags, then distribute them evenly in the boat to achieve a level trim.

Pack everything into the boat in the reverse order to which you are likely to need it, and keep your map and compass, water bottle and snacks to hand. Most importantly, never have anything positioned in the boat that would impede your exit or that you could get tangled up in if you need to get out in a hurry.

▶ *More than one boat can be transported on a roof rack, and carrying them vertically reduces wind resistance. Both boats must be placed centrally between the roof bars.*

▶ *Use a roll-top dry bag for essentials such as phones, money and keys.*

▶ *Sea kayaks are equipped with watertight hatches, but you should put your belongings in waterproof bags in case of leaks.*

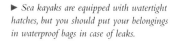

Travelling by horse: what you need

Horseback expeditions are a great way for families and non-walkers to visit remote rural areas. You need to think about how you are going to provide food and water for the horse, as well as for yourself, but, in general, this is an enjoyable way to travel, allowing you to ramble across the countryside, taking photographs and absorbing the wilderness scenery all around you.

CHOOSING YOUR HORSE

For a successful expedition on horseback, it is important to have the right horse. If you are hiring a horse from a trekking centre, find out how much experience he has of carrying riders and gear, and as much as you can about his personality. Some countries have their own training systems for trekking horses, so ask about the training your horse has had.

Get to know not only your own horse but also the other horses in your group trip, finding out which horse prefers to follow the others and which is the slowest traveller. Your pace will be dictated by the slowest horse. Find out if the horses you are going to ride are familiar with people who may have little or no riding experience, and if any packhorses you need are used to being loaded with the equipment you intend to use.

Ask about the stabling arrangements you will be expected to provide, and if the horses will be happy to spend the night outdoors in an unfamiliar area.

CLOTHING

There is little you need in the way of specialized clothing, but when choosing what to wear the keynote is safety.

In many countries, riders wear hard hats, securely fastened with a chin strap, as a matter of course, but this may not be a legal requirement, and you should check if a hat can be borrowed along with the horse, or whether you must take your own. A fall from a horse can be fatal, and a hard hat will always reduce the likelihood of serious injury.

Safe footwear is equally important. Riding boots, jodhpur boots or any leather boot with a smooth sole and a clearly defined heel will prevent the foot from sliding through the stirrup, or becoming caught in the stirrup in the

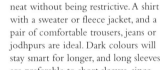

▲ *A wide-brimmed hat will cut out the glare of intense sunlight, but it offers little head protection in the event of a fall.*

event of a fall, which is a potentially fatal situation. Trainers and boots and shoes with ridged soles and little or no heel should never be worn for riding.

Clothes should be well-fitting and neat without being restrictive. A shirt with a sweater or fleece jacket, and a pair of comfortable trousers, jeans or jodhpurs are ideal. Dark colours will stay smart for longer, and long sleeves are preferable to short sleeves, since they offer some protection from nips from equine teeth. No matter how warm the weather, avoid wearing sleeveless suntops or beachwear.

▼ *The crash hat can be worn with a silk or velvet covering (back left and right); the riding hat (front) is traditional headgear.*

▼ *Short leather jodhpur boots can be worn on their own with riding trousers, or with half-chaps to protect the rider's lower leg.*

▼ *Long riding boots can be made of leather or rubber. The narrow shoe and low heel prevent the foot getting caught in the stirrup.*

◄ The essential grooming kit: (clockwise from far left) body brush and metal curry comb, dandy brush, water brush, rubber and plastic curry combs, hoof pick with brush, and cactus cloth.

▲ A saddle pannier is fitted to the saddle, positioned behind it, with the pockets hanging over the sides of the horse.

▼ A trail pad is a fleece numnah attached to a canvas cloth. The side pockets provide useful easy-access storage for smaller items.

Wear jackets and shirts buttoned up, as a flapping shirt can frighten a horse, and there is the danger that the shirt could become caught on a tree branch if you are riding through woodland. Some horses may be nervous of noisy waterproof fabrics. Long hair should be tied neatly to avoid scaring the horse or becoming caught. Prominent jewellery, such as earrings and bangles, can cause injury if they become caught up.

EQUIPMENT

Horses are powerful animals and they can carry a considerable weight, but hot weather and long distances are an additional strain, and it is still important to keep your camp kit light, so as not to overload the horse. As well as your own camp kit and clothing, you need to think about the horse's tack, a basic grooming kit, and, depending on how much grass you expect along the route, enough feed for the trip. If you will be in a remote area, carry a spare set of reins and spare stirrup leathers in case your first set become damaged.

PACKING THE HORSE

Panniers designed for horses are available, and these can be fixed over the back of the saddle. Make sure that no item of kit is sticking into the horse's back or side, and avoid having any equipment hanging off the saddle or pannier, as this could spook the horse. All of your gear should be packed into bags or rolls, and the weight of the load should be balanced on the horse.

PICKING OUT HOOVES

Picking up one foot at a time, use the hoof pick to scrape dirt and stones from the underneath of the hoof, working from the horse's heel towards the toe. After removing large pieces of debris, use the brush on the hoof pick to clean remnants of dirt from the triangular part of the hoof at the heel, known as the frog. The frog is sensitive and easily damaged, so work gently.

FITNESS AND TRAINING

A horseback trek is a far gentler way to visit the open country than walking or cycling, and physical fitness is not a priority. Also, you do not need to be an experienced equestrian as the horses are likely to be mild and steady and you will rarely break out of a trot. However, anyone who has never ridden is advised to spend some time on horseback before they go to make sure they feel comfortable in the saddle.

▼ If you are an inexperienced rider, taking a course of lessons before the trip will give you the confidence to perform the basic commands.

Daily routine on horseback

Taking care of the horses' needs is one of the main tasks on a mounted trek. The agenda for every day has to be planned with the horses in mind.

ON YOUR ROUTE

Spend some time working out your route before you travel, and ask advice from local people or riding institutions as to which trails will be suitable for horses, including where water will be available for the horses to drink. Try to keep to trails constructed with horses in mind, if possible. If you will be following a popular route, plan to take rest stops or breaks for lunch at areas where you will be able to tether the horses off the trail, so that they are not blocking the route for other users.

The etiquette of wilderness trails is that walkers, vehicles and cyclists all give way to horses. Not everyone you meet will be prepared to do this, however, so be on your guard when riding past other trail users, because sudden movements or noises, such as the revving of a car engine, can spook your horses. If you meet another horse party, then those coming downhill should give way to those going up.

▲ *Horseback treks are a hugely enjoyable way to travel across open country, but good planning and preparation are essential.*

SAFETY CHECKLIST

- Wear your own properly fitted hat, with the chin strap fastened, at all times when mounted.
- After a fall, replace a hat that has been subjected to impact.
- Wear safe footwear at all times when mounted and use the correct stirrup iron size – about 2.5cm/1in wider than your boot.
- Avoid riding on roads if visibility is poor or at night.
- Do not wear jewellery.
- Ride with your coat fastened, and don't take off a coat or sweater while mounted.
- If your eyesight is not perfect, wear soft contact lenses if possible. If not, ask your optician about the safest spectacles.

CAMP ROUTINE

Try to select a well-drained, level stretch of land, and picket the horses at least 60m/200ft away from each other and well away from any water, such as a lake or river, which they could contaminate with urine or droppings. Aim to make camp when there are at least two hours of daylight left, so that the horses have time to graze before it gets completely dark.

However tired you may be, you must deal with your horse before you tend to your own needs. Remove the saddle and bridle, and fit the headcollar, then groom him and provide him with food and water. Visually check the horse's head, body and hooves and run your hand over the back where the saddle has been, and down all four legs. Treat any sore spots immediately, using equipment from your equine first-aid kit. Clean out the hooves with a hoof pick, and brush off any mud from the legs and body, using a body brush.

The next morning, before refitting the saddle and saddle pannier or trail pad when tacking up the horse, check that there are no burrs or small sticks attached to the saddle area of the horse, which could cause sore spots on his back during the course of the day.

FEEDING HORSES

Unless you have had confirmation that grass or feed will be available for the horses at your camping ground, do not assume that it will be. Buy an adequate supply of appropriate horse feed from the organization that supplied the horses, or else provide your own.

If you decide to take horse feed with you abroad, check to see if there are rules and regulations about the kind of feed you can take into the country. You may need a certificate stating that

▲ *Your horse is your responsibility for the duration of the trek. If you make friends with him, he is more likely to cooperate.*

the feed is free of weed seed, as proof that there is no danger of contaminating the area with potentially poisonous or non-native weeds.

The horses will need to eat a good meal once a day. It doesn't matter what time they eat, but for convenience, it makes sense to feed them in the early evening, as soon as you have made camp, and before you prepare your own meal. Try to feed the horses at roughly

the same time every day and make sure there is enough water for them to drink. Horses do not need to drink purified water, but their water supply should be as clean as possible, free from chemical pollutants, rotting vegetation and litter.

WILD ANIMALS

If wild animals, such as bears, wolves, hyenas or big cats could be a danger to you or your horses, ask for a safety briefing before you set off from the organization you hire the horses from, and carry required safety equipment,

▲ *Choose a campsite where there will be space to tether the horses. If it doesn't have grazing land, you will need to carry feed.*

such as a rifle, with you. If it is a high-risk area, remember that food smells can attract animals from a great distance. Pack away unused food and burn food waste. Rather than leaving the horses free or hobbled to graze at a distance from camp, it is safer to keep them in camp, tied to a stock line.

▼ *Discipline is needed for horses and riders when travelling on horseback in large groups.*

Travelling with pack animals

If you are venturing into areas inaccessible to vehicles you must either restrict your baggage to the amount you can carry in a backpack or employ one or more pack animals to carry your load for you.

MULES AND DONKEYS
In areas of the world where the terrain is rocky and steep, the animals of choice for transporting people and heavy loads are mules or donkeys. Both have the ability to survive in conditions where horses and camels do not.

Mules have been used as transport animals for many centuries, though they have a tendency to be bad-tempered and stubborn, and may kick or bite if provoked. They therefore need firmer handling than donkeys. They are the stronger animal, and are capable of carrying up to 100kg/220lb if expertly loaded. They can travel at a good speed but have very wide backs, so riding them for long periods can cause discomfort. Donkeys are smaller and slower, carrying up to 50kg/110lb and requiring to be led on foot. They are gentler than mules, and are very sure-footed in mountain areas.

▼ *Donkeys are better suited to carrying gear than people, and travel at a pace slow enough to appreciate the wilderness.*

Animal handlers
It will usually be advisable to employ handlers to take care of any pack animals you are using. Unless you have experience of pack animals, dealing with them on your own can be difficult and time-consuming. The handlers will be familiar with the animals, and will know how much weight they can carry, what they need to eat and drink, and how long they need to rest; the animals are likely to respond better to the handlers than they will to you.

▲ *Mules are proverbially stubborn animals but will usually respond well if they are treated with kindness.*

This frees you up from taking responsibility for the animals and gives you more time to enjoy the trip. You will be grateful for this if the route is demanding and the living conditions

▼ *In this sort of rocky country it is better to hire mules or donkeys for use as pack animals rather than camels.*

difficult, but travelling with animal handlers does need to be thought through. If no one in your group can speak the handlers' language, you will need to employ someone who can speak to them on your behalf.

It will need to be agreed whether your team is responsible for providing food and water for the animals and their handlers while they are with you. If you are providing it, allocate it as needed, so that it doesn't all get consumed at the beginning. This is especially true of drinking water. If you are carrying the water you need for your entire trip, issue just the required amount each day (as you would to other team members) or you may find that water gets wasted and you could run out.

Checking equipment

If you are riding a mule, check the equipment that the animal will have on its back. Is the saddle comfortable to sit in? Are the stirrups in good condition? Are the pack frames suitable for the equipment you wish to carry?

Hiring agreement

Negotiate an agreement for use of the animals before you set off on the route. The agreement should include the costs to hire the animals, the services of their handlers, food costs for the animals and the handlers, plus any additional equipment you may have to provide or

ANIMAL HANDLING

If you travel without a handler, you will have to take responsibility for a pack animal yourself:

- Feeding and watering: once unloaded, the animal can either be let loose to graze, hobbled or picketed for the night.
- Grooming: caked mud and dust should be brushed out before loading. Hoofs need checking.
- Loading: Make sure the saddle is straight and the load equally weighted on both sides.
- Leading: it may take a few days to get animals going at a steady pace.

pay for, such as tents for the handlers and equipment for the animals.

Try to make the hire agreement with a reputable tourist organization, or in the presence of a respected local, such as the local chief, a priest at a mission station or the officer commanding the local police, to give you some back-up if there turns out to be a misunderstanding about what was agreed. It may also be wise to pay the handlers in their company, though pay only half upfront, keeping the second half back until you are safely back at base. If you have doubts about the trustworthiness of the animal handlers or owners, you may find that offering an additional sum if all goes well will help to make your trip go smoothly.

DOGS

Sled dogs have been working for centuries in Arctic and subarctic regions. In Alaska they were much used during the 1896 Gold Rush, proving far more hardy and reliable than ponies.

The dogs are bred to haul loads and work in teams, and are very sociable, strong and hardy. They have the highest metabolic rate of any mammal and require a large amount of fresh meat every day. Alaskan Malamutes are

▲ *Dog power enables you to visit the most remote wilderness areas, and sledding is an increasingly popular form of adventure travel.*

long-legged and ideal for pulling loads in deep, soft snow; Siberian Huskies are smaller but faster.

A team of seven dogs can travel about 32km/20 miles a day pulling a sled with a load of about 270kg/600lb – known as a "rig". The teams are carefully assembled: three leading dogs, usually female, are chosen for their intelligence; the middle pair are the speed-dogs and regulate the pace of the whole team; the two nearest the sled are known as the wheel-dogs – normally male, they provide the pulling power.

You can hire teams of dogs and sleds together with experienced handlers, or "mushers" (an Inuit term meaning "one who travels through snow on foot"). This gives you the option of travelling on skis alongside the teams, but the mushers can also offer training in sledding and dog handling. The dogs respond to shouted commands, such as "haw" to go left and "gee" to go right. The key to successful sledding is to relax and loosen up so that you take bumps and twists in the trail in your stride, rather than being thrown off.

Travelling by camel

Camels are ideal pack animals for the desert as they can go for long periods without needing food or water. However, camels are temperamental animals: they can bite and kick, and they get upset by strange people, so it is important to keep your distance and to carefully follow any instructions given by their handlers.

PLANNING YOUR TRIP

The camels will set the pace of your journey at around 6.5km/4 miles per hour. You will need to establish contact with guides and camel owners at your departure point, which is best done through personal recommendation. Once you have found a local guide you believe to be reliable, it is wise to let him choose the camels for you.

HANDLING CAMELS

When you first meet your camel, keep your distance and do not pet it, or you risk getting bitten or kicked. On the first morning, let the handlers do the loading, but assist by carrying loads over to them. If you want to help, ask the handlers what you should do.

Once you get more used to your camel and lose your fear of it, and vice versa, you can become more involved in handling it. Be firm and gentle, and if it tries to misbehave, stand your ground and correct its behaviour.

LOADING CAMELS

Your belongings are likely to deteriorate very quickly as they will be exposed in desert conditions and it is always possible that a camel will fall, roll over or shed its load. It is best to pack everything in hardwearing but pliable canvas bags that will not dig into the animal's skin. If you need to carry boxes containing such things as photographic equipment, make sure they are securely roped on top of the load with enough padding beneath to avoid injury to the camel. Water can be carried in skin containers that can be roped on either side of the camel. Make sure you have plenty of rope.

▲ *Use a muzzle if you do not want a camel to eat or if it is causing problems by trying to bite.*

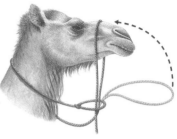

▲ *To fit the head rope, pass the end round the neck then bring a length of the rope through the loop and over the nose.*

▼ *The camel must kneel down to have the saddle fitted. If it tries to rise, hobble the front legs to prevent it.*

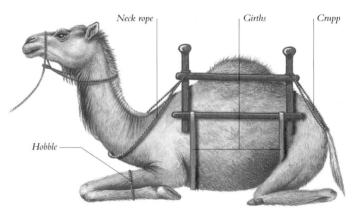

Neck rope | Girths | Crupp

Hobble

▼ *View of the saddle from the front. The padding must fit snugly to the shoulders and the saddle should not touch the spine.*

▼ *View of the saddle from the rear. The saddle should be at the front and completely clear of the camel's behind.*

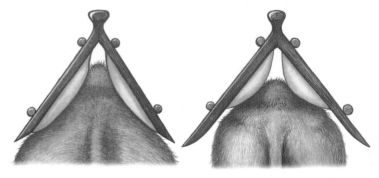

WHAT TO TAKE

- Comfortable boots. Though hot, they will protect your feet from sun and thorns. When riding a camel you will need to take them off to avoid chafing its neck.
- Loose-fitting cotton clothes and headgear for protection against sun and insects.
- Warm clothing: the night-time is very cold in the desert.
- A warm down sleeping bag and groundsheet. The sleeping bag can be used as extra padding on the saddle when riding.
- Sunglasses to protect against glare.
- Sunscreen or sunblock.

Try not to make any sudden movements or sounds around the animal when loading, and always be alert to what the camel is doing: they do not like being loaded so may attempt to bite or kick.

Fit the head rope first, then couch the camel (make it kneel down) to the command of "too". If it tries to rise, hobble it before fitting the saddle. The load must be of equal weight on both sides and tied up as high as possible.

DURING THE TREK

Camel treks usually take place in hot and dry desert climates. Because of this, the trek will start at first light so that the day's distance can be covered before the heat is at its most intense: at midday until the early afternoon. Aim to trek for the first two hours without breaks in order to cover as much ground as possible while the temperatures are relatively low; as it gets hotter, you can stop for five minutes every hour.

The animals should be checked every now and then to make sure that the saddles and their loads are not loose or slipping, otherwise the camels may develop sores on their backs and/or you may lose your kit.

There should always be a handler at the front to lead the train and one at the rear to watch out for any kit that falls off a camel's load. Always keep within eyesight of your camels and handlers, as they know the route and it is very easy to get lost in bush country.

MAKING AND BREAKING CAMP

Camp should be made around lunchtime to avoid walking in the heat of the day and to give the camels the six hours they need for browsing before they are brought in for the night. Ideally, choose somewhere upwind of where the camels will be spending the night, as they do smell. Check all the camels each evening with your head handler to make sure they are properly hobbled and to check for sores or tender spots. These must be treated before you start your trek the next day.

▲ *Camels like to proceed in order: some animals like to be in front while others will prefer to follow.*

▼ *Camels are able to eat and live off almost any kind of scrub, but need several hours of grazing each evening.*

Vehicle transport

If you are going to use one or more vehicles on your expedition, you have to decide what type you will need and whether you are going to ship your own out to the expedition area or hire what you need there.

For off-road expeditions in remote areas you should take at least two vehicles, ideally three, so that if one breaks down it can be towed to safety. You will need four-wheel drive if you are intending to drive in boggy or sandy conditions. At the expedition area you will need to pay attention to loading and maintenance. You should be confident that you can service the vehicle yourself, and if necessary attend a vehicle maintenance course before setting off.

TAKING YOUR OWN VEHICLE

The downside of taking your own vehicle out to the expedition area is that you will be faced with all the costs and bureaucracy involved in this process. The upside is that you will have a vehicle that you know will be in good working order, with all the necessary spares and tools, and which you are confident of driving.

HIRING A VEHICLE

If you are hiring a vehicle from a local company, look it over first to check all the tyres, suspension, steering, lights and brakes, and ask to take it on a test drive. Choose your vehicle carefully: a long wheelbase will give you more space but will lack manoeuvrability; the most powerful vehicles will cope with any terrain but will use a lot of fuel. Petrol engines are lighter and more powerful than diesel, but the latter

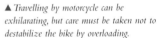

▲ *Travelling by motorcycle can be exhilarating, but care must be taken not to destabilize the bike by overloading.*

cope well in very low gear so are more reliable in rough terrain. They use less fuel, and diesel fuel is often very much cheaper than petrol.

In some countries you must have a driver, whereas in others you will have the choice of driving the vehicle yourself. The advantages of having a local driver are that he will know the country, will be used to driving on its roads and can be your interpreter. The disadvantages are that you lose a seat in the vehicle, you may not get on with the driver, or even understand him, and he may not be prepared to follow your route. Make sure you can work together before you hire him and the vehicle, and promise a good tip if the trip goes well.

SPARES AND MAINTENANCE

Check that you have a spare wheel with a good tyre on it that is inflated, a jack and a tyre spanner (wrench). Also make sure that the hirer has provided any other items that are required, such as a fire extinguisher,

◀ *When hiring vehicles make sure you have thought through the conditions you will be driving in so that your transport is suitable.*

first-aid kit and warning triangle. If you are going to be off-road for any time, you should also have spare oil, inner tubes for the tyres and a puncture repair kit including tyre levers, along with a full set of tools.

Always keep your fuel tank as full as you can, and never pass up the chance of buying fuel. If it is not clean, use a large funnel with a filter in it to filter the fuel before putting it into the tank.

Each night when you have finished your driving for the day, inspect the whole vehicle, especially the tyres, oil level, radiator fluid level and so on.

LOADING

How you load the vehicle is important, and if you are going off sealed roads you should keep your loading down to about three-quarters of the manufacturer's recommended limit.

DRIVING AT NIGHT

Be wary of driving at night in developing countries, as many vehicles have faulty lights and vehicles may be parked or abandoned without any warning lights or signs.

DRIVING IN DIFFICULT TERRAIN

Err on the side of caution: drive slowly and if necessary stop and check the state of the road or track ahead on foot. Stay in the middle of muddy tracks, taking care not to spin the wheels or ground the engine on rocks. Use four-wheel drive except when on firm road surfaces. If you do get bogged down in mud or sand, try reversing out or get your passengers to push. Failing this, dig in front of the wheels to create a gradual slope and try to go gently forwards. Lay down wood, canvas or anything that will help the wheels grip.

MOTORCYCLES

In temperate regions a motorcycle can be an attractive option if you are travelling alone. A heavy-duty bike will be able to cope with almost any terrain but will need constant servicing: wash it daily and check all the connections.

The amount of luggage you can take will be strictly limited, and will need to include spare parts and tools. Keep the

heaviest weight above the rear wheel and don't load too much on the back as it could destabilize the front wheel. Side panniers should be as slim as possible to reduce wind resistance.

If you are travelling in areas where motorcycles are unfamiliar, take extra care around other road users.

▲ *Snow chains should be fitted either on all four wheels or on the rear wheels only. Make sure the tyres are at the right pressure otherwise the chains will damage them.*

▼ *Getting your vehicle out of heavy mud is a skilled job and should be practised before you embark on a trip.*

Public transport

You will almost certainly use public transport at some stage of your journey, whether just to get to your starting point or to complete most of your travel. Its quality varies greatly from country to country. In some you will find a modern, well-organized, integrated transport system, while in most developing countries the trains, ferries and buses may be crowded and uncomfortable. It is a good idea to take your own food, water and toilet paper.

PLANES

The overbooking of plane seats is a universal curse, but in some developing countries you may arrive at an airport only to find that your flight has been oversold by 50–70 per cent, with no system of seats going to those who booked first. This may leave you with no option but to bribe your way on to the flight. If you are tempted to use a local charter airline or private plane instead, check first to see if your travel insurance policy will cover you for this type of transport.

▼ *If you use small local boats for river trips, make sure they are safe and have a life jacket on board for each passenger.*

TRAINS

In many countries you will be offered up to three classes of travel. If you are making a long journey, and especially if this involves travelling overnight, it is worth paying to travel in either first or at least second class, as third class will probably have uncomfortable seats and will be very crowded.

If you are travelling on your own in developing countries, it is generally better to travel in first class as you will benefit from more space and comfort

▲ *Be on time or early for check-in when flying or you may find that you do not have a seat on the plane.*

and there will be more staff. On long journeys, check in advance to see if sleeping facilities are available. Be warned that sleeping cars may be filled on a first-come first-served basis, and

▼ *If you are travelling by ferry it is a good idea to have a contingency plan in case you arrive late at the port and miss your boat.*

▲ If you are travelling by train on your own or overnight, it may be worth paying the extra fare to go first class.

the sexes are not always segregated. Keep your luggage with you at all times. Lock your window closed at night so that nobody can get in at stops.

LOCAL FERRIES

Usually, ferry companies offer a number of different classes. These range from first class, where you will have a cabin, to third class, where you may have to fight for a space on the open deck. In developing countries, ferries may get grossly overcrowded, carrying little or no safety equipment, especially for the deck passengers. Bear in mind that by travelling first class you will attract the attention of fellow passengers, and you should lock your cabin at night.

Some ferries can be seasonal due to the height of the river as a result of the dry or wet season, so check if your travel plans depend on a ferry trip.

BUSES

In developing countries buses are the mainstay of most transport systems. They range from new, air-conditioned vehicles to buses that would have been old when you were born. In hot countries, many buses will leave around dawn to take advantage of the cool part of the day. Be early for your bus but expect long delays, as it may wait until it has filled all its seats before departing. You will usually be asked to put your luggage on the roof rack, so make sure you carry anything valuable with you.

Long-distance trips by bus can be a good way to meet fascinating local people as well as seeing the landscape at speed. Travelling with an open mind and an open ticket may lead you on some unexpected adventures.

LOCAL TAXIS AND MINIBUSES

If you use a taxi, either find out the rate and then watch the meter, or negotiate a price before the journey. Local minibuses are the cheapest form of transport in some parts of the world, but can become very overcrowded and are often involved in accidents.

▼ Greyhound buses criss-cross the United States and are much used by backpackers as a cheap way to explore the country.

CAMPCRAFT

While camping you are at the mercy of natural forces, and your activities
will be dominated by the times of sunrise and sunset, changes in the
weather, the lie of the land, the nearest water and the supply of fuel.
Your comfort will depend on your skills in choosing a suitable site,
erecting a shelter, building a fire and establishing a smooth routine.
When you leave there should be no trace of your stay.

Choosing a campsite

There are very few perfect campsites, so when choosing a site you will probably have to compromise to some extent. Obviously your priorities will vary depending on how long you are going to stay there, and how large your camp will be, but it is a good idea to have some general principles in mind during the selection process so that you know what to look out for.

RECONNAISSANCE

For a long-term campsite, particularly for a large group, you will need to plan ahead and may have already visited the site before the group arrives. If you choose a site on private land you will need the landowner's permission to camp. However, whether you are looking at an established site or scouting in the wilderness, the points to check are the same.

WHEN TO LOOK

If your campsite is to be an overnight stop on the trail you should start to look for a suitable place at least two to three hours before it gets dark. By that time you will need to have settled in and pitched your tents and your food preparations should be well under way. Be prepared to stop short of your intended destination for that day if you find a spot that looks ideal. You may even want to backtrack a little if you do go on but the terrain ahead fails to offer further viable sites.

WHAT TO LOOK FOR

Try to avoid extreme conditions of any kind. In hot countries you will find it a great advantage to have some natural shade on your campsite. In colder areas your priority is likely to be natural shelter from wind. Always try to find a site that is well drained; this usually means looking for a reasonably high site. Not only will you avoid marshy, damp ground, but you will also not

▲ *In hot countries shade on your campsite will be a great advantage. If you want to use a popular site you will need to book ahead.*

find yourself in a pocket of cold air during the night. If it is windy, you will need space to pitch your tents with the doors facing away from the wind.

It will be an advantage if the site has its own water supply but you should always check to see where the water

comes from. Just because local people drink it, it does not mean it is safe for you to drink. Unless you have good evidence to the contrary, you should always regard water as contaminated and treat it accordingly. Don't be tempted to camp too near a water

▼ *Camping by a river can be noisy. Make sure that, if it floods, your camp is high enough above the river not to be affected.*

▶ *Make sure you set up your camp well above the high-tide mark if you are camping near tidal water.*

CAMPSITE CHECKLIST

Check to see if the site is protected from the prevailing wind and that there is a readily available water supply. Once these criteria are satisfied, assess the following points, depending on your area and situation:

- The ground is reasonably level and flat, and is not covered with sharp stones or pieces of wood that could damage your groundsheet or sleeping mat.
- The land is not in a hollow, where a pocket of cold air could collect during the night.
- The land is not in a dried-up watercourse, which could flood without warning.
- The ground is neither boggy nor likely to become boggy.
- You have checked to see if you need permission to camp and have agreed any fees to be paid.

- You are happy that you can drive your tent pegs into the ground or that you can anchor the guy lines in some other way.
- There are no branches or unsafe trees near your tent site or dry-stone walls or other loose stones that are near enough to collapse on your tent or you while you are asleep.
- If the site is near to water, it is well above the flood level of a river or the high-tide mark at the coast, and there is no danger of crocodiles.
- There are no insect nests nearby and no holes or bushes where snakes may live.
- In a hot climate, there is adequate shade from the sun.
- You are not too near a source of water or a patch of wetland that will attract insects and animals during the night.

- There is a plentiful supply of wood for your fire. Unless you have permission, you should use only dead wood or wood lying on the ground.
- The camping area has not previously been used by domestic animals or livestock, which could have left ticks and other insects on the ground.
- There are no domestic animals or livestock in the field and no obvious signs of game trails going through the camp.
- In the mountains, your campsite is protected from a snow avalanche or rock falls from above.
- If the ground is covered in snow, you have stuck a ski pole or stripped tree branch into the snow to see if the ground is firm all over your site, with no hidden crevasses.

source, such as a stream, as it may attract clouds of biting insects in the evening, and may be a place where animals come to drink.

In an area where there is the possibility of attack by bandits or a track record of theft from tourists, it

can be worth calling at a local police post and asking them for advice on where you can camp safely. They will sometimes offer you a site in their own compound. If you are camping in a place – or travelling through the area – for any length of time, try to

build and maintain good relationships with the local people, especially the community leaders. You may find that during your stay you need their help obtaining supplies or settling disputes between yourselves and other local people or traders.

▼ *Trees with seriously undermined roots might be felled by a high wind, so it could be risky to camp near them.*

▼ *If you have to camp among trees check that there are no rotten or broken branches above the area where you pitch your tent.*

▼ *Get some local knowledge about the site: a watercourse may be subject to flooding in the event of heavy rain many miles away.*

Camp layout

The layout of your camp will be dictated by the site you have chosen, the climatic conditions, the size of the camp and personal preferences. There are, however, some golden rules that should be followed for the sake of the safety and well-being of the campers.

POSITIONING TENTS
Try to pitch the tents with their back into the prevailing wind. If possible, use either a belt of trees or bushes to form a natural windbreak. If hot weather conditions make shade important then choose a place under some trees, but remember that falling twigs and branches will be likely. Make sure your sleeping area is well away from the cooking area and toilet area, and upwind of them if there is a prevailing wind.

TOILETS
If there are no permanent toilets on the site, construct a toilet area downwind of the tents and away from sleeping and cooking areas, with natural screening or a bivvy bag or groundsheet for privacy. You can dig a hole in the ground with a trowel or knife for solid waste, covering it with soil after use and burning toilet paper. Have a separate urination point. Alternatively, you can dig a large ditch to make a latrine, covering it with soil each time it is used. Note that latrines can become a breeding ground for germs unless the soil covering is applied religiously after every use.

USING WATER WISELY

If your camp is near a stream or river use the water systematically:
- Collect water for drinking and cooking upstream of the site. Make sure you are also upstream of animals' drinking spots.
- Wash yourself midstream.
- Wash dishes downstream, scraping food remnants off before rinsing. You can wash clothes downstream but do not use detergent as it will pollute the water.

WASHING AREA
If you are going to have an area dedicated to washing clothes, keep this away from the cooking and sleeping areas. Site any clothes lines well away from where people will be walking, especially at night.

WHERE TO SITE A FIRE
If you are going to have a fire, light it well away from the tents, as sparks can fly out and burn holes in the material. Also make sure it is downwind of the tents, on a flat area well away from trees and bushes.

KITCHEN
Site the food preparation area some distance from where you will be sleeping, so that if an animal is attracted by the smells of food during the night, you will not be disturbed. Also, any flies attracted to your cooking will be well away from your sleeping area. If you can, have an extra tent near the

▲ *A campsite under trees has the advantage of being shady, but you risk twigs and branches falling on your tent.*

cooking area for the storage of food. Do not keep food inside a tent where anyone is sleeping.

SOCIAL CENTRE
Choose an area away from the sleeping and cooking areas where you can set up a working and/or social area in which people can sit and talk or work. This area will become the social centre of the camp. Make sure that everyone accepts responsibility for keeping this shared area clean and tidy.

PARKING AREA
A large campsite will probably be accessible by road or track. If your group is travelling by vehicle, allocate a parking area and make it clear that vehicles cannot drive around within the camp itself, which could be dangerous.

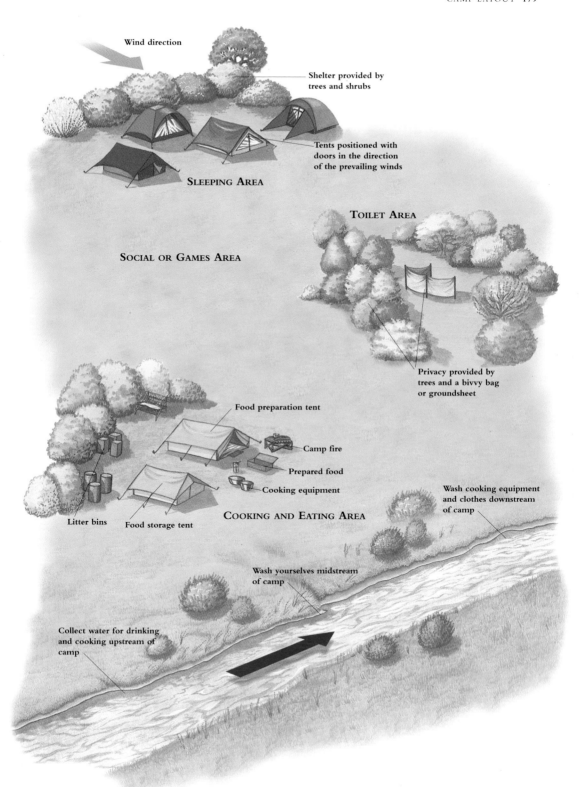

Wind direction

Shelter provided by
trees and shrubs

Tents positioned with
doors in the direction
of the prevailing winds

SLEEPING AREA

TOILET AREA

SOCIAL OR GAMES AREA

Privacy provided by
trees and a bivvy bag
or groundsheet

Food preparation tent

Camp fire

Prepared food

Cooking equipment

Wash cooking equipment
and clothes downstream
of camp

COOKING AND EATING AREA

Litter bins   Food storage tent

Wash yourselves midstream
of camp

Collect water for drinking
and cooking upstream of
camp

Erecting tents

Once you have checked your site for suitability you can get on with erecting your tent. No matter what kind of tent it is, you will need to follow the same system of erection. You should refer to the manufacturer's instructions, especially if this is the first time you have put the tent up, but your memory may also need refreshing if there has been a long gap since you last did it.

It's a wise precaution to practise erecting and striking your tent before you go away (you can do this in the garden or a local open space), so that you iron out any problems and can do the job quickly. On the expedition

▶ *The geodesic dome (shown here without the outer tent) is very strong, but if any of the poles break it will lose its strength.*

ERECTING A DOME TENT

1 Check that you have all of the tent parts. If the inner tent needs to be attached to the outer tent, do it now. Make sure that all zips are closed.

2 Assemble the poles and thread them through the sleeves in the tent. It is easier to push them: pulling them may pull the pole sections apart.

3 Now place the ends of the poles in the fastenings provided in the lower part of the tent so that they put the whole of the tent under tension.

4 Peg out the inner tent. Always push the pegs in at an angle away from the tent. This prevents the pegs from being easily pulled up by the wind.

5 Peg out the outer tent and check to see that the inner tent is attached correctly. If you need to reposition a peg, use another peg to pull it out.

6 Peg out all the remaining guy lines. Gather up any remaining pegs, place them in the tent bag and stow the bag inside the tent.

there may be days when weather conditions are bad and you are forced to pitch your tent in windy or rainy weather, or even in the dark, so the more familiar you can become with the procedure in advance, the better. If you erect the tent using the same procedure each time it will become automatic.

If you are using a tent made of cotton, it is better to pitch it and get it thoroughly wet, then let it dry out naturally before using it.

CHECKING THE SITE

The first thing to do is to check the piece of ground on which you intend putting the tent. Make sure it is flat and does not dip in a way that will mean water collects there if it rains. Is the

▶ *The traditional ridge tent is still widely used on expeditions. It is simple to erect and will withstand a lot of bad weather.*

ground soft enough for you to drive the tent pegs into it? Is it reasonably sheltered from the wind but not too near anything that might crash down on to it, such as a dead tree? When you are happy with the lie of the land, the

next thing is to make sure that there are no sharp objects that could damage the groundsheet, such as stones and twigs. Clear anything of this kind from the site and if necessary remove or flatten any small humps.

ERECTING A RIDGE TENT

1 Take the tent out of the bag and check to make sure all the parts are present, then lay out the inner tent on the ground and peg down the corners.

2 Assemble the frame over the inner tent. Check the poles before fitting them together as incorrect connections can be hard to unfasten.

3 Attach the inner tent to the poles using the fittings provided. Place the flysheet over the poles and where necessary attach to the inner tent.

4 Peg out the guy lines on the flysheet, starting with the four corners. Make sure all the door zips are closed while you do this.

5 Complete the pegging out of all pegging points and guy lines. The flysheet should be tightly stretched and should not be touching the inner tent.

6 Undo the door zip for ventilation and tie at the sides to secure. Adjust the guy lines so that the walls of the flysheet are clear of the inner tent.

ASSEMBLING THE PARTS

If it is a new tent, read the instructions and check that you have all the parts. With most tents, you will put the inner tent up first, but do check the instructions about this. First assemble the poles and get the pegs out of their bag. Then, depending on the type of tent, start your pitching routine. Make sure all the doors are closed when pitching the tent. If you cannot erect your tent on your own, make sure other people are available to help.

Many modern tents, especially geodesic domes, have quite thin poles. To strengthen them, wrap tape around each pole where it fits into the next joint. This will stop the joints splitting in high winds.

▶ *The weather may be calm when you put your tent up, but always use all guy lines provided in case it changes for the worse.*

ERECTING A FAMILY TENT

1 Take the tent out of its bag and check with the instructions that you have all the parts – the pegs, inner and outer tents, poles and guy lines.

2 Lift the poles forming the main assembly to pull the tent up into position.

3 Lock the joints in the poles to create the tent frame.

4 Slide any additional poles into their sleeves. Assemble the porch area, taking care not to damage either the tent fabric or the poles.

5 Peg out the sides of the tent, sticking the tent pegs firmly into the ground and angling them to pull the guy lines away from the tent.

6 If your tent has a separate inner it may be necessary to attach it at this stage, then peg it out. Add the flysheet and peg out all of the guy lines.

ERECTING A PATROL TENT

1 Take the tent out of its bag and check that you have all the parts.

2 Spread the main tent out, upside down, on the ground.

3 Place the ridge pole in the sleeve or loops provided in the main tent.

4 Push the spikes on the two uprights into each end of the ridge pole.

5 Push the spikes through the reinforced holes in the tent canvas.

6 Pull the canvas back over the poles and attach the main guylines.

7 With someone at each end holding one of the poles firmly, lift the tent into an upright position.

8 Peg out the main guy lines so that the frame of the tent will stand up on its own.

9 Now make sure the door flaps are closed, either by lacing them together or by closing the zip.

10 Peg out the walls. Check they will be under the roof so that rain will clear them when it runs off the roof.

11 Peg out the side guy lines of the tent to create the walls.

12 Check the whole tent. If it does not have a sewn-in groundsheet, lay out the groundsheet inside the tent.

Base camps

For a long or large-scale expedition exploring challenging and inaccessible terrain or requiring a large amount of equipment, it is usually necessary to set up an initial camp to act as a semi-permanent support structure. From this "home base" more lightly equipped expeditions can set off, for instance to trek through wilderness, climb a mountain or conduct an archaeological survey. The base camp acts as a communications hub and supply store. It is likely to be sited in an area that is accessible by motor vehicles and can generally offer a reasonably high degree of comfort.

Setting up this more elaborate kind of camp is naturally a much more complex operation than setting up a small temporary camp. You will probably be using heavier and bigger tents, your cooking area will be of a more permanent nature and you will need to construct a toilet area and make provision for rubbish disposal.

CAMP ROUTINE

You will find it useful to draw up a simple and sensible set of rules that everyone is able to follow. If there are a lot of people in the camp, you may want to post up a programme each day listing meal times and any planned events or meetings. It is also a good idea to have either a lights-out time or

a quiet time, so that those who want to sleep can; you should also try to implement this rule if your camp is set up near other people, who will not want to be kept awake.

CAMP SECURITY

If you are a large party with people coming and going, perhaps sometimes overnight, make sure you have a system of knowing who is where and who will be in camp when. This will not only act as a general safety feature, letting you know where all the members of the group are at any one time, but will also aid with planning the catering.

▲ *A base camp may need to include many different components. Draw up a logical plan for its layout before pitching any tents.*

If there will be times when all or most of the members of the expedition are going to be away from the camp it is a good idea to employ a local person to act as a guard. Even when the camp is not empty, your equipment should not be left lying around in case it is stolen or damaged.

▼ *Long-stay camps need to be supplied with well-maintained and carefully sited toilet and washing facilities.*

BURNING WASTE

Not all waste will be suitable for burning on the camp fire, and a large long-term campsite may require an incinerator, which should be carefully sited well away from the tents. This could be an ordinary galvanized incinerator of the kind intended for garden waste, or you could make one by piercing holes all around an oil drum or metal bin and siting it over an open fire. The ashes should be removed regularly and buried in a pit used for solid waste.

▲ *A daily discussion and briefing involving all the group members will help to keep the base camp running smoothly.*

▲ *A large camp will probably require one or two designated cooks to provide regular meals for the whole party.*

KITCHEN

Hygiene should be a priority in the food preparation area in a large camp. Make sure your kitchen area is kept thoroughly clean and that all waste is properly disposed of each day so it will not attract animals and insects. With a lot of people living together, poor hygiene can quickly result in everyone getting ill, especially in hot countries.

Wash all the cooking pots and equipment in hot water each day. Try to have some hot water on your fire or stove all the time so that people arriving back from activities can always have a hot drink or even some hot water to wash in.

If possible, rig up some sort of structure that enables you to store your eating and cooking equipment, and all your food, off the ground. This is useful and more hygienic than leaving them on the ground. Some kind of table or raised surface also makes the preparation of food much easier if you are cooking for a large group. All fresh food should be stored in sealed containers or cool boxes.

If you are using a fire to cook on, make sure your woodpile is kept tidy

and well stocked. Your reserves of water should always be kept covered and should be well marked to show which water is for drinking and which is for washing.

BURYING WASTE

In a camp that will be occupied for some time it is particularly important not to leave any waste lying around. Waste food will encourage wild animals to scavenge in the camp and will attract flies. If you are allowed to do so on your site, dig two pits at least 60cm/2ft deep: in one you should dispose of any solid waste, such as flattened cans; the other is for the disposal of any cooking or waste water.

Each time you put anything into the first pit, cover it with soil to prevent insects from feeding on the waste. Make sure this pit is well marked so that nobody steps in it. If you are going to bury cans or other packaging, burn and flatten them first.

Place a layer of bracken or grass over the top of the second pit to filter out any scraps of food that may be in the cooking water. This covering should be burnt or buried every day.

A large base camp may need to accommodate the following specific areas, whose siting needs to be planned before you start pitching the tents:

- Camp fire: should be central but downwind of the tents.
- Woodpile: near the fire. The wood, especially the kindling, will need a cover to keep it dry.
- Chopping area: next to the woodpile, and clearly marked out to avoid accidents.
- Kitchen area: should be sheltered, fairly near the camp fire and away from the tents, and ideally near the water supply.
- First aid tent: in a large base camp everyone should know where to find the first-aid kit in an emergency situation.
- Storage: should be conveniently sited depending on its use. If you do not have a dedicated first aid tent, keep the first-aid kit near the door of a storage tent.
- Toilets: should be downwind of the site and screened off, but not so far away from the tents that people are tempted to use a nearby bush instead.

Lightweight camping

This form of camping is so-called because the weight of your camping gear is cut to a minimum, allowing you to transport it under your own steam. All the equipment you use will have been selected because it is made of lightweight material and made to be either carried in a backpack or packed into a canoe or cycle pannier bags.

MINIMIZING YOUR LOAD

Lightweight camping can be an end in itself, although most people use it as a means of carrying out some other kind of activity, such as walking, cycling or paddling in the countryside. The real enthusiasts believe that you should be able to go away for, say, a weekend's expedition on your own taking kit weighing no more than 9kg/20lb. Getting your load down to this level requires practice and experience. However, if you are travelling with another person the target is much

▼ *Lightweight camping gives you the freedom to explore inaccessible areas that few others will be able to reach.*

easier to reach, as much of what you take, including your tent, stove, fuel and cooking equipment, will be shared between you.

CHOOSING EQUIPMENT

If it is to combine the high performance you need when camping with extremely lightweight and compact design, all your equipment needs to be of the best quality. This means it will not come cheap, and you may well find that you have to carry more weight to begin with and acquire better, lighter pieces of kit over time. Very lightweight equipment tends also to be more susceptible to damage; you will need to treat it with care and maintain it well, following the manufacturers' instructions.

Much of the art of travelling light lies in the care with which you choose what to take. Thinking very carefully about where you are going and the kind of terrain you will be travelling over will help you to avoid carrying unnecessary items. The more trips you do, the better you will know how

Overloading a cycle, kayak or canoe can make it dangerously unstable, and, if you are walking, carrying too heavy a load will be wearisome and spoil your trip.

Your equipment should weigh no more than 11kg/25lb and, with some care, you should be able to get it down to 9kg/20lb.

When you have all your equipment together, consider how you could reduce its weight.
- Is everything you have essential?
- Do you need to carry the containers some of the equipment may be packed in?
- Do you need all the things in your washing kit? Could you cut the soap in half and take a smaller tube of toothpaste?
- Do you need a knife, fork and spoon, or could you get by with just a spoon?
- Do you really need all the clothes you are thinking of taking?

much is really essential. After every lightweight camping trip, put all your gear into three piles: "used a lot", "used sometimes" and "never used". Retain any items from the last pile that are your safety equipment, then get rid of the rest.

At the same time, make a list of any items you wished you had taken, so that you can add these next time. Soon you should get your kit down to the minimum weight possible.

TENTS

Single-skin tunnel tents made of waterproof, breathable material with a minimal frame of flexible poles are lightweight but pricey. Even lighter are bivvy bags, which dispense with a frame and simply form a waterproof covering for your sleeping bag.

Although lightweight tents can be strong and robust you will need to be careful, especially with the tent's groundsheet, which is likely to be very thin. If you pitch on a sharp piece of wood or rock you may damage it. One way around this is to place your sleeping mat on the ground before you pitch the tent over it, so you can still have the warmth of the mat to lie on but your groundsheet will be protected.

COOKING EQUIPMENT

If you are a really lightweight camper, your cooking equipment will be very basic, which means that you will have to choose your food and utensils carefully, perhaps cutting the latter down to just a knife and a spoon.

If you are cooking on a single stove and using dehydrated foods, make sure you will have enough cooking pots. Choose a pan with a close-fitting lid that will double as a frying pan. Remember to check on the cooking times of packaged food: the longer the cooking time, the more fuel you will need. If you are going to carry food, take it out of its outer packaging but keep the cooking instructions.

Each of these things individually may save only grams/ounces, but added together they represent a significant weight saving.

▲ *Choosing a site with a good view may mean that it is exposed. Be sure that your lightweight tent will withstand the wind.*

▼ *If you have to pitch your tent on very stony ground, protect your groundsheet with your sleeping mat.*

LIGHTWEIGHT EQUIPMENT

For a three-day trek in a temperate climate it should be possible to take the following gear per person without exceeding 9kg/20lb:

- Shirt, trousers, socks, underwear
- Fabric or leather walking boots
- Windproof jacket
- Woollen or fleece sweater
- Waterproof jacket and trousers
- Hat and gloves
- One-person tent, or bivvy bag and groundsheet
- Sleeping bag and insulated mat
- Lightweight backpack
- Canister stove and lighter
- Cooking fuel
- Cooking pot/mug and lid
- Spoon and knife
- Water bottles and purifier
- Food and food storage bag
- Whistle
- Wristwatch
- Map
- Compass
- First-aid kit
- Basic survival kit
- Sunglasses and sunscreen
- Insect repellent
- Wash kit

Camp safety and hygiene

When camping, you should be even more aware of safety and hygiene than you are at home, particularly if you are in some remote area where help may be hard to summon. For this reason, all camp members should prioritize their own and each other's health and safety.

TIDINESS

A basic rule to go by is that a tidy camp is a safe camp. On this basis, always try to have as much as possible packed away before you go to sleep each night, leaving out only those things that you may need during the night and first thing the next morning.

Never leave axes, knives or saws lying on the ground at any time, as someone could seriously hurt themselves if they fell on or over one of these. Keep all tools stored away when not in use: apart from the safety issue, this means that everyone will know where to find them. Finally, never tie a rope or washing line between trees in a position where someone is likely to walk into it. At night, mark any such line by putting something light-coloured over it.

FIRE SAFETY

If you are cooking on a wood fire, make sure your woodpile is safe and that your fire cannot spread from the fire area. Use an existing fire pit if there is one on your campsite, and be very careful not to start a forest or brush fire in dry weather. Keep a bucket of sand or soil near the camp fire to use as a fire extinguisher in an emergency.

If you are cooking on a gas stove, do not cook in a sleeping tent and make sure that all gas is stored away from fires and sleeping areas and out of direct sunlight. Never change a gas cylinder in a confined space, and never put an empty cylinder on a fire.

When you eventually strike camp and put the fire out, make sure it is completely extinguished before leaving.

HYGIENE AND SAFETY TIPS

- Whatever task you are doing in camp, tidy up as you go along.
- If you are leaving camp do not leave open fires, stoves or gaslights alight and unattended.
- If cooking in the porch of your tent make sure you have a good level area for your stove.
- Try not to eat food in a sleeping tent as crumbs and scraps will attract animals and insects.
- Keep all drinking water covered and mark it clearly to differentiate it from non-drinking water.
- Store all inflammables well away from fires and out of direct sunlight. Do not store fuel in sleeping tents.

▼ *In a large camp, pitch tents with enough space between them so that walkways are clear of guy lines and tent pegs.*

▲ *The highest standard of hygiene should be maintained when preparing food in camp. Dispose of kitchen waste scrupulously.*

FOOD PREPARATION

Allocate a specific area of the camp site for the preparation of food and keep it scrupulously clean. Always wash your hands in clean, purified water before preparing food and wash dishes and utensils promptly to avoid attracting flies. In hot weather, cook and eat fresh food such as fish as quickly as possible

▼ *Sleeping under the stars has appeal in warm climates, but also presents hazards in the shape of camp fires and insect bites.*

after bringing it into camp, and don't keep cooked food standing around cooling, as bacteria will proliferate.

WASTE DISPOSAL

Dispose of all waste food by burning and burying it as soon as possible (see also Base camps, 184–185). If you cannot bury it, pack it into a plastic bag and put it in a bin as soon as possible. Never store waste near the sleeping area, and never leave food uncovered because it will attract wild animals.

TENT HYGIENE

If you are camping in the same area for more than one night, try to keep your tents tidy, clean and aired, if the weather allows. If your tents do not have sewn-in groundsheets, lift the walls each day to air them. If they do have sewn-in groundsheets, open the doors and sweep out the tents each day. Turn your sleeping bag inside out and air it for an hour or so each day, preferably in the sun. Afterwards roll it up until you need it so that nothing can crawl into it before you do.

TOILETS AND WASHING

Dig a hole or latrine for solid waste and cover it with soil each time it is used. Have a separate urination point. To make sure the used water from your washing area cannot run straight into a river or lake, dig a soakaway channel so that the dirty water will be filtered through the ground first.

▲ *When using chopping or cutting tools make sure you have no obstacles or people around you who might get hurt.*

▲ *Keep your wood-chopping axe sharp with a Carborundum stone: a sharp blade is safer than a blunt one.*

▼ *Always cook outside a tent, though you can use the porch to shelter the stove, and never store stove fuel inside a sleeping tent.*

Personal hygiene

Although personal cleanliness is always important, it becomes even more vital if you are travelling in a foreign country, particularly a developing one, since you may be exposed to many diseases and illnesses to which you have no natural immunity. If you are travelling in a group it is also in everyone's interest that you should all stay as clean and fresh as possible.

BODY

Wash yourself all over at least once a day if you have access to water. The best time to do this will usually be in the early evening when you have returned to camp or pitched your tent and are changing out of your day clothes. Pay special attention to the armpits and groin area, which can suffer painful sweat rashes if not kept clean, and don't forget your ears.

If washing water is in short supply, be careful of the amount of creams and lotions you apply. If they build up on your skin they may begin to block the pores, which could lead to infection.

▼ *When you are active in the wilderness it is even more important to pay attention to personal hygiene than at home.*

FEET

Never walk around bare-footed. You may tread on a thorn or something else that gets stuck in your foot, or on an insect that bites you, which will make subsequent walking difficult. At best, you will make your feet dirty.

At the end of the day, take off your boots as soon as you reach camp and make washing your feet a priority. Be careful if you are drying them near an open fire: it is easy to burn them. Make sure they are clean and dry and check them for blisters. If you are in a wet environment, put anti-fungal foot powder on them. If you are in a hot, dry climate, dress any cuts or abrasions immediately to stop them developing into desert sores. Try to wear clean, or at least different, socks each day.

▲ *A purpose-made waterproof wash bag will help you organize all your toiletries and keep them clean and easy to find.*

Hang wet boots on sticks to dry overnight, or stuff them with newspaper if available. Removing the laces and insoles will help them to dry more quickly. Don't try to dry leather boots quickly by the fire or in the sun, as fierce heat will crack the leather.

TOILETRIES

If you will be away in the field for a long time, working from a base camp, take all your personal toilet materials in a purpose-made wash bag. If you leave your base camp for a night and weight is a factor, use a smaller bag, or an ordinary plastic bag, for the small amount you will need while you are away. Keep your toilet bag clean and tidy, with the lids well screwed on tubes and containers to avoid leakage. Avoid glass containers, which may break if your bag is roughly handled; flimsy ones, which may burst if squashed; and pressurized aerosols, which can explode and are not allowed on aircraft.

MANAGING YOUR CLOTHES

The number and type of clothes you take is a personal decision and will depend on the nature of your trip and the weather conditions, but you will have to compromise between travelling light and having enough changes of clothes.

- Wash clothes whenever you have the chance, rather than waiting until all your clothes are dirty.
- Take a length of washing line and a few pegs (pins) to help with the drying of clothes.
- Clothes made of natural fibres are usually more comfortable; they retain their insulation properties better when wet and will absorb sweat in hot conditions.

▲ *If water is available, try to wash any dirty clothes whenever you get the chance – at least every other day.*

EYES

If you are travelling in a very dusty environment, take some eyewash solution or contact lens solution with you and give your eyes a good wash out each evening.

If you normally wear contact lenses, consider wearing glasses instead if you are travelling to a hot, dry area. Contact lenses can cause inflammation if dust gets into the eye when you are taking the lens out or putting it in, or when wind blows dust around.

TEETH

When cleaning your teeth, remember to use purified or sterile drinking water. Do not use tap or river water to rinse your mouth unless you are absolutely sure it is clean and free from pollution.

CLOTHING

An adequate supply of clean and dry clothing is important for your health and comfort, but if you are travelling light your wardrobe will be minimal so you will need to wash clothes whenever you have the opportunity. You will find that wearing loose-fitting

underwear made of natural materials is comfortable and less likely to rub or cause irritation or sweat rashes.

Keep all your clothes as clean as possible. When washing them is a problem, wear one set during the day, keep another set for the evening and, if you have enough clothes, keep a separate set to sleep in. If water is limited the most important items to wash are your socks: if you keep them in good condition they will help to keep your feet in good condition, but they must be thoroughly dry before you wear them again.

You should try to wash dirty clothes at least every other day, if water is available. Use either some travel wash, which works in both salt and fresh water but can still pollute a water supply, or an environmentally friendly soap, which will wash both you and your clothes but not harm the water supply.

If you are in a wet environment, keep your sleeping and

▶ *In hot weather wear cool, loose-fitting cotton clothing that will wick sweat away from your body and give some protection from the sun.*

camp clothes dry in a waterproof bag and change from your wet day clothes when you return to camp.

In dry, dusty conditions try to keep all clean clothing packed in stuff bags or plastic bags so that they stay free of dust and grit. If you roll your clothing rather than folding it, it will stay less creased. Have a separate bag for dirty clothing so that you do not get clean and dirty items mixed up.

Take a sewing kit so that you can repair any tears in clothes as soon as you notice them to avoid them getting worse, but beware of darning holes in the feet of socks, as walking on the stitching may cause blisters.

Camp fires

To make a camp fire you need tinder and kindling as well as fuel. Tinder and kindling have separate functions. Tinder is used as a firestarter, to kick-start the burning of kindling, which in turn is used to ignite the fuel. Lighted kindling on its own could be used to light fuel, but setting the kindling alight first with tinder means that you need much less of a flame initially to start the camp fire fuel burning. This could be important in wet or humid conditions or where you are finding it difficult to light a flame.

Tinder

Any material can be used as tinder so long as it is highly combustible, and the best tinder will need only a spark to set it alight. Avoid using highly flammable materials such as aerosol spray cans, as these can explode when ignited and the explosion will be difficult to control.

It is a good idea to take your own tinder with you, storing it in a small waterproof container. Manmade tinder materials can be bought from outdoor suppliers, but there are many natural materials that are readily available – free of charge – outdoors. Keep an eye out for new tinder supplies as you follow

SOURCES OF TINDER

- Silver birch bark
- Crushed dry, fallen tree leaves
- Crushed dry, fallen fir cones
- Dry, fallen pine needles
- Dry, fallen seed heads
- Short lengths of dried grass
- Any plant down
- Fine wood or bark shavings
- Bird down
- Dried, powdered fungi
- Short newspaper strips
- Short waxed paper strips
- Short strips of rubber car tyre
- Cotton wool
- Camera film
- Cotton fluff from clothing
- Charred natural fabric, such as cotton or silk

CHOOSING FUEL AND KINDLING

▲ *Dry, crisp leaves make excellent kindling for a fire; or try pine needles and dry grass.*

▲ *Pine cones can be used as fuel if dry, but they do not kindle as well.*

▲ *Twigs and small branches make ideal kindling providing they are dry. Break them into a manageable size before use.*

▲ *Dry bark found on the forest floor can be used as kindling. Do not strip bark from trees because it can cause considerable damage.*

your route, even if you do not need them that day. If the weather is dry you can store the materials in a waterproof container until needed. In wet weather you can dry damp materials inside your tent or at the side of the camp fire – not so close that they catch fire – until they are dry enough to be stored.

Kindling

Materials used for kindling are types of wood. The best materials are small, dry twigs and sticks. The soft woods flare up quicker than hard woods (those that contain resin burn particularly well), but they can produce sparks and will burn very fast, which means that you may need more of them to light a large camp fire. Kindling should be bigger than tinder in order to encourage a high flame, but it should be smaller than the fuel wood, so that it can be packed between the pieces of fuel.

Avoid collecting kindling straight from the ground as it will be damp and will take longer to burn. Carry it with

FIRE STICKS

Firesticks are kindling that has been "feathered" to make it catch fire more quickly. To prepare a firestick from a dry twig, make small shallow cuts down the length of the twig with a knife. Then tease out the fronds so that they bend outwards to catch the flame more easily.

you in a waterproof container if possible; if you have to use damp wood as kindling, shave off the outside and use the inner part, which will be dry.

Using tinder and kindling

When your camp fire is ready to light, ignite the tinder using a match, lighter, artificial flint striker or traditional flint and steel. When it is burning, hold the tinder against the kindling. As the flame takes hold and rises, pack the kindling in between pieces of fuel wood on the camp fire, which should start to burn.

CHOOSING WOOD

If you are planning to use a camp fire to cook your meals, you will be relying significantly on wood as your fuel supply, so find out as much as you can about the burning properties of the wood available in the area before you travel. Know how to identify the wood you need, and make sure you are equipped with the right tools to deal with it.

Some woods, such as telegraph poles and treated fencing or building timbers, are dangerous to burn because they contain chemicals that give off a toxic smoke: do not use these even if you see them lying on the ground and are sure they are unwanted debris. Natural woods can also be unsuitable: bamboo can trap water in its stems, and this may explode when heated on the fire.

Different woods burn in different ways. Some burn faster than others and produce varying amounts of heat, making them particularly suited to different methods of cooking – those that burn quickly are better for boiling and those that burn slowly and give out a lot of heat are better for roasting. Knowing the character of your wood fuel will help you to use it in a more efficient way, reducing the quantity of fuel you need and the amount of time spent sourcing it. Be prepared to use different types of wood on your fire if you plan to boil some ingredients and roast others for the same meal.

Hard woods are generally regarded as the best woods for roasting or grilling foods because they burn hot and for a long time (avoid using willow unless it is very dry because it has a high water content and therefore burns poorly). Soft woods burn quickly and for a shorter amount of time, and are best used for boiling.

Whatever the type of wood, it must be dead and well dried if it is to burn well (one exception is ash, which burns well whether it is dry or green). Wood picked from the ground will be damp, and this will burn with an unpleasant amount of smoke and not enough heat (the fire's energy is used up drying out the wood). Instead, look for dead wood that is caught up in branches: a vertical position means it will be drier.

HARD WOODS

▲ *Apple and cherry burn well and give off a pleasant and sweet smell. They grow in sunny areas of temperate climates.*

▲ *Holly is found in woodland areas in temperate and cold, dry climates. Holly and yew burn equally well whether green or dry.*

▲ *Narrow-leaved ash usually grows in wet temperate conditions so it will need to be well dried before it can be burned.*

▲ *The silver birch grows in mountainous regions of temperate climates. It lights easily and the bark makes good kindling.*

SOFT WOODS

▲ *Cedars and other coniferous trees make excellent kindling and good fire fuel, giving out a lot of heat.*

▲ *Horse chestnut is common to cooler temperate climates. Like all softwoods, it burns quickly and gives out a lot of light.*

▲ *Small-leaved lime is common to warm temperate and hot, dry climates. It is not easy to light but will give off a good heat.*

▲ *Cones from spruce and any other coniferous tree can be used as a fuel but will not burn with much of a flame.*

SITING A CAMP FIRE

Good preparation is essential for a successful camp fire. To choose the site, look for a place where you are not going to damage any overhanging trees or will risk setting scrubland on fire. Always be aware of these dangers when your fire is burning.

No matter which kind of fire you build, you must have a good supply of fuel. This will usually be wood, but dried animal dung can also be used if wood is not available, though it will not burn as well.

When you have finished with the fire and are leaving the site, leave as little trace as possible. Remove burnt remains of wood from around the fire, bury the ashes and level the ground. If you had to cut out an area of turf to make the fire, replace it before you leave. There is more on the different types of camp fire in chapter nine.

TYPES OF COOKING FIRE

Camp fires have different purposes. Some are best used to give warmth, while others are better for cooking, with some of these suited to large-scale cooking and some for smaller pots. A pyramid fire, for example, is easy to build and good for warmth, but if you want to cook on a fire, you need to add some form of structure on which you can safely put cooking pots.

The reflector fire is one of the most complex and time-consuming to build, but it is an effective cooking fire and will cater well for groups using several large pans. It has a wall of wood or clay at one end, which reflects the heat back into the fire. It can be used for any method of cooking and is ideal for roasting food, such as meat or fish.

The hunter or trapper fire has a more basic structure and is most effective for boiling. It is made by

placing two logs parallel to each other, about 30cm/12in apart but close enough for your pans to be balanced securely. Lay the fire in between the logs, starting with tinder, then adding kindling and finally the wood fuel. Make sure the logs cannot move either outwards or inwards, wedging them firmly in place with rocks if necessary.

If there is a strong wind, consider building a trench fire as this will shelter the flame below ground level. To build a trench fire, dig a trench 90cm/3ft long and 30cm/1ft wide, and line the base with a layer of rocks. Lay your fire on top, surrounded by a ring of rocks. Pans can be placed on top of the rocks, or foods such as meat can be cooked on a spit constructed from whittled tree branches and positioned over the fire in the trench. Ideally, the trench should be angled so that the prevailing wind can blow down it to give a draught.

BUILDING A REFLECTOR FIRE

1 If you are constructing the fire on an area of grass, remove the turf from an area about 1 x 0.75m/3 x 2ft. Store it for later replacement.

2 Lay a raft of dry, thick sticks across the cleared area to protect the fire from the damp soil beneath.

3 Drive two stout sticks into the ground leaning away from the fire and lay a wall of logs or strong sticks against these to form the reflector.

4 When you have completed the fireplace check that it is stable.

5 Place some dry kindling in the middle of the raft of wood. Set light to the kindling and add small twigs to get the fire going.

6 Once you have built up the fire and got it going, the wall at the back will reflect the heat back into the centre to give you more heat for cooking.

Alternative shelters

There may be occasions when you either do not have a tent or you are unable to use the tent you have, but you still need a shelter to protect yourself from the elements. A tent groundsheet can be used to form a makeshift shelter, or you could construct an A-frame shelter from tree branches. Further options for building shelters in snow, jungle and other extreme environments are explored in chapter eight.

When choosing the site for a natural shelter, consider whether the ground will be waterlogged if it rains heavily. Cover the floor with a layer of bracken, ferns, heather or any other vegetation available. This will insulate you from the ground and will make you more comfortable; use only dry vegetation and shake it first to get rid of insects.

GROUNDSHEET SHELTER

If you have a groundsheet, or a sheet of ripstop nylon, and a length of cord, tie the cord between two trees about 3m/10ft apart, and place the sheet over the cord. Then take the corners of the sheet and either peg them into the ground or tie a guy line to each corner and guy them out. This will provide you with the simplest of shelters, but it will be considerably better than a night in the open air, especially in windy or rainy conditions. Make sure the sheet comes down to 45–60cm/18–24in from the ground, or driving rain will soak you. The waterproof bivvy bag included in the survival kit (see page 64) can also be used to construct an emergency shelter if a groundsheet is not available.

A-SHAPED NATURAL SHELTER

If you do not have a groundsheet big enough to make a shelter, you will have to rely on natural resources. Find two convenient trees and rest a long branch or piece of wood between them, about 1.2m/4ft from the ground. Make sure you secure it very well, using either cord or natural vines, so that it will take the weight of the frame you are going to build.

Now lean some tree branches on the long branch at 30–45cm/12–18in intervals to form an A-shaped shelter. Fill in the gaps of the structure with bracken, ferns or large leaves, starting at the bottom and working up, in the same way that a roof is tiled. If it rains, the rain will run down and off the sides and will not seep inside.

BUILDING A GROUNDSHEET SHELTER

1 Look for a fallen branch and place it between two trees about 1.2m/4ft from the ground, wedging it into the trunks or securing it with cord or rope.

2 Unpack the groundsheet of your tent (or use your bivvy bag or space blanket) and throw it over the suspended branch.

3 Arrange the groundsheet so that it hangs over both sides of the branch, coming down at least 45–60cm/18–24in off the ground on each side.

4 Take one corner of the groundsheet and peg it out with a tent peg, or guy it with a guy line, or weight it down with a heavy log or rock.

5 Work around the other three corners, securing the groundsheet firmly in place with tent pegs, guy lines, or heavy logs or rocks.

6 With the four corners secured, the completed shelter will provide basic but effective protection from driving wind, rain or snow, or from an intense sun.

Useful knots

The following knots have been found to be useful for life in the wilderness. It is a good idea to practise them so that they can be tied as second nature. They are designed to be tied with natural fibre rope, and may not be as successful with synthetic ropes.

FISHERMAN'S KNOT OR WATER KNOT

This is used to join two ends of a rope together to form a loop, such as a sling, or to tie two ropes of similar thickness together. It is not secure enough to be used for tying climbing ropes together, or any ropes that are to bear a heavy weight.

1 Lay the two lines parallel, tying an overhand knot with one end around the standing part of the other. Turn the half-completed knot end-for-end.

2 Tie an identical overhand knot with the other end. Pull first on both ends to tighten the knots, then on the standing parts to tighten the knot.

BOWLINE

This creates a non-slip knot in a rope. It can be used to make a loop at the end of a rope, or a waist loop for a climbing rope, when you do not have a climbing harness.

To make it more secure, once you have tied the knot, finish it off with two half hitches. It can become less secure if the rope is very stiff, or wet and slippery.

1 Bring the working end across the standing part of the rope to form an overhand loop.

2 Rotate the hand clockwise and so produce a smaller loop in the standing part of the rope.

3 Ensure that the working end points upwards, from back to front, through the smaller loop.

4 Lead the end behind the standing part, then tuck it back down through the small loop from front to back.

5 Arrange the bowline with a long end (longer than shown) and secure further, if necessary, with tape or a half hitch.

CLOVE HITCH

This can be used to suspend a light object at right angles to the suspension point or to tie a boat to a pole. The pull of the clove hitch must be steady, because the knot can work loose if it is not under tension. It can also jam if it becomes wet. If the knot has to last for any length of time, tie the two ends together to secure it more permanently.

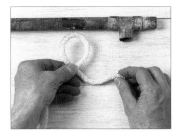

1 Hold the rope in a straight line and make an overhand loop of any size at any convenient point in the line.

2 Add an underhand loop further along the line, so that there is now a pair of loops consisting of two opposing halves.

3 Arrange the two loops so that they are the same size and close together in the line of rope.

4 Rotate the two loops a little, at the same time, in opposite directions, in order to position them so that they overlap precisely.

5 Insert the rail, spar, rope or other foundation through both of the loops and pull on either one or both ends to tighten the resulting hitch.

ROUND TURN AND TWO HALF HITCHES

This is a strong and secure knot or hitch, which can be used to secure a rope to a pole or ring, tow a broken-down vehicle or secure the guy lines of a tent. It will even make a haulage knot for securing a load or climbing. Before you trust a heavy weight to the knot, check the condition of the rope: if it feels soft and amenable, it is worn out and should not be used.

1 Take a turn around the anchorage of the pole or ring and bring the working end alongside the standing part. Apply a single half hitch by tying an overhand knot with the working end of the rope.

2 Add an identical second half hitch and draw the two snugly together to complete this dependable knot.

REEF KNOT OR SQUARE KNOT

This knot does not jam and can easily be untied. It is used for tying together two ends of rope or, in a first aid situation, two ends of a triangular bandage or sling. It is strictly a binding knot, reliable only when pressed against something else or tied in both ends of the same material. If any strain on the knot comes from an angle, it can turn into a slipknot.

1 Bring two ends of rope together, left over right. Tie a half-knot: the two entwined parts will spiral to the left. Bring the ends together, right over left.

2 Tie a second half-knot. The two entwined parts will now spiral to the right, opposite to the first half-knot.

SHEEPSHANK

The sheepshank's main use is to take the slack out of a fixed rope or line. It can also be used to shorten a length of rope or to bridge a damaged section, but the rope must be kept under tension, otherwise the knot can come undone.

1 Fold the rope and fold it once again, shortening it as required, into a shallow S-shape with two loops.

2 Make an incomplete overhand knot – known as a marlinspike hitch – in one standing part.

3 Pull the adjacent loop through the marlinspike hitch in a locking tuck that goes over-under-over the rope.

4 Turn the half-finished knot end-for-end and make another marlinspike hitch in the other standing part.

5 Insert the remaining loop over-under-over, securing the hitch, then tighten both ends of the knot until they are snug. Ensure that the load falls equally on all three standing parts; if one is damaged, it must lie between the other two and be slightly slacker than them.

DOUBLE SHEET BEND

This knot is used to bind two ropes of different thicknesses, or where one or both ropes are made of wet or slippery material. Check that the ends of both ropes are on the same side of the knot, otherwise it will be unsafe.

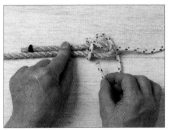

1 Create a loop in the end of one of the ropes. Take the second rope and tuck it up through the loop. Bring the end beneath the loop in the first rope.

2 Tuck the working end beneath itself so that both short ends are located on the same side of the knot. Bring the working end around and beneath the loop and its own standing line once again, keeping it to the right of the original pass. Finally, tuck the end through alongside the initial tuck to complete the double knot.

PRUSIK KNOT

This slide-and-grip knot is used to attach a sling, strap or loop to a main rope in order to hoist or lower a weight. The sling is tied with a fisherman's knot to the main rope, which will need to be secured at each end. The main use of the Prusik knot is as a rescue knot for ascending or descending with a rope – for example, out of a crevasse. The knot allows the sling to be slipped up or down the main rope when not under strain, but will jam tightly if suddenly jerked or strained.

1 Make a loop with part of an endless sling and lay over a climbing rope. Bend over and down behind the rope.

2 Pass the standing part of the sling through the working loop.

3 Pull some slack out of the initial loop and take it up and over the climbing rope once more.

4 Take the working loop back down behind the climbing rope again.

5 Tuck the remainder of the standing part through the wrapped loop and tighten the knot.

SIMPLE SIMON OVER

This knot is good for general camping use. It is especially effective in slick synthetic lines and, once mastered, it can be tied easily. It has rarely appeared in print, but it merits being more widely known as it is a secure knot and a very useful one to have at your disposal when faced with tying slippery, synthetic lines in a howling gale out in the field.

1 Make a bight in one of the two lines to be joined. Bring the working end of the other line over it. Tuck the working end down through the bight.

2 Bring the working end out to the left (in this instance), then take it over both bight legs and, in a snaking "Z" track, back again beneath them.

3 Lay the end back over its preceeding part (the "over" of the knot name).

4 From the outside of the bight, tuck the working end up and through and finally lay it alongside its own standing part. Tighten, working the slack out.

SIMPLE SIMON UNDER

This is a variation of the Simple Simon Over knot, above. It is more secure than the Over knot and it will cope better with dissimilar cord sizes and textures. To make the Under knot, first complete steps 1 and 2 of the Over knot.

1 After bringing the working end of the line back beneath both bight legs, tuck it beneath its preceding part (the "under" of the knot name).

2 From the outside of the bight, tuck the working end up through and finally lay it alongside its own standing part. Slowly work the slack out of the knot.

VICE VERSA

Some intractable materials – such as wet and slimy leather thongs or bungee (elastic) shock cord – are difficult to keep in place and will slither out of other bends. The Vice Versa is one way to keep these kinds of rope lines securely in place. The various tucks and turns that make up this knot are the secret of its very reliable strength and security.

1 Lay the two lines to be joined parallel and together.

2 Take the working end of the line on the right-hand side and bring it beneath the other standing part.

3 Pass the end over the other line and then tuck it beneath itself.

4 Take the other working end on the left-hand side, passing over the first of the two lines. Now bring the second working end back beneath the other line and up past the front of the knot (with no tuck).

5 Cross the right-hand end over the left-hand end and tuck it through the left-hand loop alongside its own standing part. Similarly, take hold of what has become the right-hand end. Tuck the remaining working end through the right-hand loop alongside its own standing part. Gently pull on all four emerging lines at once to securely tighten this knot.

Using an axe

Axes are useful for cutting down trees, removing branches and cutting up timber. As long as the axe is sharp and in good working order and you are aware of the dangers, accidents should not happen. Dress appropriately, with jackets and shirts fastened up to avoid them flapping around and getting caught, and wear strong footwear; do not wear open-toed sandals or bare feet.

Trees should never be felled or branches lopped unless you have the express permission of the landowner.

MAINTENANCE
Sharpen a blunt axe on a Carborundum stone, which can be used either wet or dry. Replace a split handle and check the axe head to see that the wedge is tightly fitted in and there are no chips out of the blade. After use, clean the blade and cover it before storing.

▼ When cutting branches from the trunk of a tree, start from the base and work upwards (left); do not work downwards (right).

▼ When chopping a log, weaken the log with a V-shaped cut by first making one cut from the right and one from the left.

▼ When splitting a log in half, position the log to be cut on a large log to raise it off the ground, and secure the log to be split with your foot before you start to swing the axe.

▲ Carry an axe with the blade in the palm of your hand, facing outwards and away from your body in case you should fall over.

CLOTHING
Make sure your clothes are neat as loose clothing could get caught as you swing the axe. Protect your feet with leather walking boots or walking shoes; you should not have bare feet or wear flip-flops or open-toed sandals.

PREPARATION
Before starting work, clear the area all around, including smaller overhead branches, or the axe may catch. Check that the ground you are standing on is firm and clear of obstacles. Make sure that nobody is within at least two axe-plus-arm lengths away from you. This is not just to avoid hitting someone but also to avoid wood chips flying up into their eyes as you chop.

CHOPPING DOWN A TREE
Decide where you want the tree to fall, and make a cut facing in that direction. On the other side of the tree, start to cut through the tree above the first cut. Remove any low branches that can be easily reached on the side away from the direction of fall, chopping parallel to the trunk rather than towards it. This should encourage the tree to fall

▲ You should always wear stout footwear and close-fitting clothes when working with an axe or any other sharp tool.

in the correct direction. When the tree is about to fall, shout "Timber!" and move to one side, so you will not be caught by the bottom of the tree swinging back or up. You can also use your axe for cutting and splitting the tree trunk into logs.

▼ Make sure you have a clear area around you before starting to use an axe to chop logs, in case of any flying wood chips.

Using a saw

Saws can be used for any wood-cutting job, and they do not leave the same amount of wasteful wood chips and debris as an axe. A high level of safety is required, as with an axe, because a saw has the potential to be a highly dangerous instrument.

MAINTENANCE

Before use, check to see that the blade is tight in the handle and that the teeth are sharp. Check from time to time that the teeth are not becoming clogged with wood shavings or resin from the wood. After use, clean the blade to remove wood shavings, and pack it away clean and dry. Keep the saw well oiled or greased to prevent rust. When not in use, mask the blade, either by using a plastic clip or mask or by tying a length of robust sacking around the saw several times.

CLOTHING

Wear jackets and shirts buttoned up and generally avoid wearing loose items of clothing, as the teeth of a saw could easily catch in them. Sturdy gloves will protect your hands in the case of the saw slipping, and may make it easier to grip the wood; mittens restrict your fingers and will not give you a firm enough grip.

TRIMMING A TREE

A saw can be used for cutting up small timber and is ideal for trimming a tree before or after it has been felled. Trim

▼ *When felling a tree the first, lower cut needs to be made on the side on which you want the tree to fall.*

the tree from the bottom and work upwards. Hold the tree with a tight grip, keeping your fingers well away from the moving blade.

FELLING A TREE

Make the first cut in the direction you want the tree to fall, then make the second cut on the opposite side of the tree, above the first cut. Work slowly until the blade has made a good deep cut in the wood. If at any time you feel tired, stop for a break. If you are using a two-handed or two-person saw, put your main effort into the pull stroke.

▲ *Rest the timber you are cutting on a secure base and get someone to hold it if necessary: never try to saw on the ground.*

Once you are about a quarter of the way through, push above the saw cut to take the pressure off the blade. If the saw blade jams, do not force the blade out. If necessary, take the blade out of the saw handle and work it out slowly, using a little oil or grease.

▼ *When two people are using a saw together, each of them should only ever cut on the pull stroke.*

Striking camp

When it comes to striking camp, it is important to have a proper system for dismantling everything so that everyone knows what they are doing. How complex the job is will depend on whether you are taking down a small overnight camp or a large base camp. The most important thing is to clear the campsite so as to leave no trace of your presence after you have gone.

OVERNIGHT CAMPS

If the weather is fine, dismantle your tent first and hang it up to air while you are dealing with everything else. Pack all the rest of your gear into your backpack, then fold up your tent and add it to your pack.

If it is raining, pack your backpack first, while you are inside your tent, then pack the tent and add it to your pack. Make sure you dry the tent at the earliest opportunity (see below). When

▼ *In a large camp set up a system and have somewhere where you can stow equipment and baggage that has already been packed.*

▲ *Ideally, pack the tent away when it is dry and clean. If you have to put it away wet, unpack it and dry it as soon as you can.*

you have finished packing, spend a little time walking around the site to see if anything has been left lying around before you depart.

BASE CAMPS

The size of this type of camp and the number of people concerned will make dismantling the camp a more complex operation. Make sure that everybody is involved and knows which jobs they

▲ *The tent poles should be counted and checked for any damage, then packed away in their own bag.*

have to do, and when. It is a good idea to keep one tent up until everything else is done, so that as you take the other tents down and pack up your cooking and other equipment, and any constructions such as clotheslines, you can put everything in this tent. If it rains, this will also stop all your kit getting wet. Alternatively, have a large groundsheet ready to spread over the kit that has been packed if the weather becomes stormy.

STRIKING TENTS

As with pitching tents, the way in which you take the tent down will depend on the type of tent, but there are some general rules that should be followed for all of them. If you are taking down a large tent, make sure there are enough people working with you to take it down safely, so that the tent is not damaged.

When you strike your tent you may need to pack it up while it is wet. If you leave it for more than a few days, however, a cotton tent may become mildewed and a synthetic tent can start to smell (its cotton inner will also become mildewed), so get it dried as soon as possible.

If the tent has a sewn-in groundsheet, clean the inner tent thoroughly then turn the inner tent over to make sure the groundsheet is dry and clean. If not, let it dry then clean the groundsheet with a cloth.

▲ *Clean all your pegs so that they are ready for use next time. Make sure none has been left in the ground before you go.*

Make sure all the tent pegs are clean and straight and ready for use next time, and that you have the right number. Also check that all the guy lines and pegging points are in working order and any zips are working.

When you have taken down the tent, make sure that all the different parts, such as poles and pegs, are together in their respective bags before packing them away in the main bag.

COOKING AREA

Make sure you fill in all the pits you have dug. If you have been using a fire, make sure it is out and that the fireplace has been filled in and the ground covering replaced.

TOILETS

If you have set up your own toilets, make sure that all waste products are well buried, holes or trenches are filled in and the ground cover is replaced. All screening materials, unless they are naturally growing in the area, should be removed.

If you have dug a latrine and used it for some time, mark the site before you go so that others following you will not use the same site.

WASTE

Either burn all the waste and bury the residue, or take it away with you. Never leave plastic bin liners full of waste at a site, as animals will quickly

rip them open, allowing the contents to blow away. If the animals try to eat the plastic, it can kill them.

Finally, it is a good idea to walk around the site once everything has been taken down and packed to see if any items of kit, any tent pegs or pieces of litter have been left lying about. There is nearly always something.

▲ *If the weather is dry and sunny, turn your groundsheet over to dry it off and clean it before packing up your tent. Pack your other equipment while it is airing.*

▼ *Make sure all your equipment is clean and dry before you pack it so that it is ready to use when you arrive at your next stopping place.*

NUTRITION & FOOD

Whatever kind of expedition you are planning, food will play an important part in its success. If you are using up a lot of energy trekking, cycling or climbing, you will need hearty meals at the beginning and end of each day to keep up your strength, and communal cooking and eating in camp can be a great morale booster even in harsh conditions. Without the modern conveniences of refrigeration and hot water on tap, rigorous attention to food hygiene is vital.

Nutritional needs

When you're at home you can choose what to eat from a vast range of different foods. Assuming you have a healthy appetite, eating a wide variety of foods you like should ensure that you get a balanced diet. When travelling, however, you need to pay more attention to the details of nutrition: you may be coping with a different climate and unfamiliar foods; it may be more difficult to buy and prepare food; and if you're taking part in strenuous activities you'll need to keep your energy levels high. Poor diet quickly leads to fatigue and even illness. And if you're looking after children it's crucial to make sure the meals you provide supply all their needs.

There are five main elements in a balanced diet: carbohydrates, proteins, fats, vitamins and minerals, and water.

CARBOHYDRATES

Plants store their energy in the form of carbohydrates, so these foods are derived mainly from plant sources such as cereals, vegetables and fruit. There are two groups: simple and complex.

The simple carbohydrates are sugars. The body finds these easy to absorb, and they provide instant energy (if not used straight away they are stored as

glycogen). Fruits are a good source, and dried fruits are a convenient, lightweight option for travellers. However, sugars provide fewer calories than other foods and if you eat too much your body will react by producing insulin to reduce your blood sugar level, leaving it lower than before. If you need a quick energy fix, combine sugary foods with other foods to avoid this energy dip.

Complex carbohydrates, which are derived from starchy foods such as bread, rice and beans, have to be

▲ Pasta is a complex carbohydrate food, which means it is digested slowly and will provide energy over a long period of time.

broken down into simple sugars before the body can use them, but provide the bulk of its energy needs. Because they are digested slowly they provide the sustained fuel you need for endurance pursuits like walking, climbing, cycling or kayaking.

Try to get most of your daily carbohydrates from unprocessed foods and whole grains, which also supply essential vitamins and minerals, rather than stoking up on refined foods. When travelling abroad, remember than every locality has a staple grain: check it out and base your diet on that.

PROTEINS

As well as providing energy, proteins supply amino acids. These are the body's building blocks, essential for growing and repairing tissue as well as manufacturing enzymes, hormones and antibodies. For this reason, children need plenty of protein, as do adults recovering from illness or injury.

Complete proteins, which contain all the essential amino acids, are derived mainly from animal products such as meat, fish, eggs and dairy foods. Grains and beans usually contain incomplete proteins, and vegans and vegetarians

---

CELLULOSE FOR SURVIVAL

Grain products such as bread and cereals provide cellulose, otherwise known as fibre, in your ordinary diet. Your body is unable to break down cellulose, so it has no value as a nutrient. It travels through the body unchanged until it is eliminated as a waste product. It does, however, aid in the digestion of food, and is therefore an essential part of the diet. Deprived of cellulose, the body's system works too slowly and the result is constipation. When grains are not available, you should replace them by eating more vegetables, which also contain a certain amount of fibre.

WATER

Drinking enough water is crucial to the optimum functioning of all of the body's systems: digestive, absorptive, circulatory, and excretory. It is also needed to maintain the correct body temperature. Even mild dehydration soon produces symptoms such as irritability, nausea and headache.

Although water makes up about 75 per cent of our bodies, we have no means of storing it. All of the fluid that is lost through breathing, sweating, urination and digestion has to be replaced on a regular basis. About 3 litres/5 pints is the very minimum daily requirement.

◄ *Fresh fruit, such as apples, provides important vitamins. If fruits will not be available, or if they may be unsafe to eat, take a multivitamin supplement to boost your diet.*

► *Eggs provide your body with protein and fats and can be used for a huge number of dishes.*

---

who do not eat animal-derived foods need to combine grains and beans with other foods to ensure that their diet is complete. For example, a combination of beans with brown rice, nuts and seeds forms a complementary protein.

FATS

You need a certain amount of fat in your diet, especially when you are active. Fats are the most concentrated source of energy available, giving nearly three times the energy of

▼ *When planning children's meals, choose foods that you know they will eat and allow for a higher calorie intake per day.*

carbohydrates weight-for-weight. High-fat foods include dairy products such as milk and cheese, and oils, but also egg yolks and nuts.

VITAMINS AND MINERALS

A balanced diet that includes fresh fruit and vegetables will provide the minerals and vitamins you need, but the body cannot store these essential nutrients and if you feel you may not get enough fresh food while travelling, take a multivitamin supplement with you. Salt is vital, but it is easier to take too much than too little – your body will tell you if you need more by craving salty food.

HOW MUCH SHOULD YOU EAT?

Just being out of doors makes most people hungry. Everyone's appetite is different, but if you are going to be active all day you will clearly need to eat more than usual. If you are going to be carrying your food with you, you will need some idea of how much more that might be.

An average man, living and working in average conditions, has an energy requirement of about 2,500kCal (for the average woman, who is smaller, the figure is lower). Engaging in a strenuous activity such as hiking, paddling or climbing raises this to about 3,500kCal. In extreme cold

weather conditions it takes extra energy to keep the body warm, so the average man's total needs may be as much as 5,000kCal – in other words about twice his intake in normal daily life.

If you apply this rough calculation to your own usual food intake – or that of any children you are catering for – you can get a reasonable idea of how much extra food you need to keep you going when active. When choosing food for children, bear in mind their likes and dislikes to make sure they eat well.

▼ *Expect an increased appetite when living in the wilderness, especially if your activities are fairly strenuous and the climate is cold.*

Planning your food

Carefully chosen rations are vital to the success of a trip, and it is important that everyone eats a balanced diet. At the planning stage you can decide what types of rations will be used and how they will be prepared at the camp and in the field, and find out about any special dietary requirements.

TYPES OF RATION

There are four different types of food you can eat when camping. These are fresh food, dry food, ready-to-eat meals in pouches and canned food. Their advantages and uses are described in detail on the following pages.

Unless you are travelling in the most arid and remote terrain, you are likely to use a combination of the various types of food during your trip – for instance, enlivening the dry food you take with you with fresh items bought locally. The different rations available will suit different stages of the trip:

▼ *Lightweight rations may be needed in the field. They should be easy to prepare and require the minimum of equipment.*

Cooking and eating is a central aspect of camp life, and it is important to make it as enjoyable as possible, even at times when the range of available food is limited.

• As well as asking about special dietary needs, try sending out a food preference form in advance so that people can tell you which foods they particularly like.
• Take some special luxury foods with you, including items that are group members' favourites. These can be brought out on a special occasion, such as reaching the expedition's goal or somebody's birthday, or at a difficult time when the party needs a lift.

• In transit, pre-packed picnic food or eating in cafés may be best.
• At camp, plenty of storage space, good cooking facilities and no need to carry the food mean that fresh and canned food may be eaten.

▲ *Try to include as much fresh food in your diet as possible when it's available and you have the means to prepare it.*

• When you are out in the field or on activities everything has to be carried on your back, and so dry and pouch meals are ideal.

Whatever type of food you use, always bear in mind that you are responsible for disposing of any waste, such as empty wrappers and cans.

PLANNING RATIONS

When planning your food, consider whether there are any constraints on the amount or type of food you are going to use during the trip, such as:
• weight
• bulk
• fuel
• the size of your party
• packaging
• cooking time
• ease of cooking
• cost

Will it be easy to buy local food during your journey? If so, this will help to make the packaged food you take more palatable; if not, you'll have to think harder about the flavourings and seasonings you can carry with you.

When you are planning your menus, don't forget to choose food that you and the other members of the group actually like: don't take anything you wouldn't normally eat just because it is in freeze-dried or pouch form – if you don't eat it at home, it won't seem any more appealing in camp.

SPECIAL REQUIREMENTS

Check in advance with all the members of your party in case anyone has specific dietary needs that will affect your catering plans. If anybody going on the trip has special requirements due to food intolerance or allergies, moral or religious beliefs, it is important that you know this at the planning stage so that you can accommodate their needs.

FOOD BUDGETS

Work out the food budget for your trip by basing it on a figure per person per day and adding an amount for contingency. You will need to arrive at this figure through a combination of educated guesswork and thorough research about your destination; running out of money for food would be disastrous, so the food budget needs to be as accurate as possible.

If you are cooking for a large number of people you will benefit from economies of scale. Bear in mind, too, that food costs will be lower in developing countries than in the developed world. Your food budget will need to be higher if you are a small group, and much higher if you are expecting to eat some of your meals in cafés and restaurants.

FOOD PACKING

If you decide that you are going to use pre-packed rations, make sure they contain everything you will need for the length of time covered by the ration. Apart from the food itself, each package should include toilet paper, a can opener (if cans are included), matches, salt and cooking instructions for everything in the package.

If you are planning a large and complex expedition involving different camps and locations, it is a good idea to mark all the food packages clearly before you leave, to make sure that the right rations go to the right locations. Again, make sure you include any utensils needed to use the food, such as a can opener, in the package destined for each location.

Use a simple marking system that everyone will understand without needing to refer to you – in case you

are not around when they are being loaded on to your transport. Be careful of colour coding as some people are colour blind.

Try to keep packaging materials to a minimum, as you will have to find a way of disposing of them when you have used the contents. Make sure the package is secure, but don't make it too hard to get into as there is nothing worse, after a hard day, than having to fight to get at your food.

If food is going to be carried on the back of a pack animal you may need to pad any sharp corners of boxes or containers. If your rations are to be carried in a vehicle they will need to be packed to withstand jolting in transit, especially on unmade roads.

IMPORTING FOOD

If you are travelling overseas you may be thinking of carrying food from your own country with you, possibly in advance of your arrival. Before doing so, it is worth finding out about any import regulations and restrictions, and the costs this will entail. You may find that carrying food with you rather than sending it to your destination in bulk is a cheaper and easier option.

▼ *Pasta is a good filler: light to carry and quick to cook, it is a nourishing source of carbohydrate.*

▼ *Chocolate is just one of a range of favourite foods that can be carried as a luxury item and given out as a treat.*

▼ *Food supplies for a large expedition need to be clearly labelled before the packing begins to make sure that they are transported to the correct destination.*

Local foods

One of the most enjoyable aspects of travel is being able to sample the foods of the country you are visiting, but food can carry disease and it is important to make sure that eating local foods, either served in restaurants or prepared at your campsite, does not make you ill and spoil your trip.

AVOIDING FOOD POISONING

Whether you are at home or abroad, it's important to eat fresh food that has been properly cooked, but whatever the quality of the food it can be contaminated by external sources, such as dirty water, dirty hands or flies.

In many countries the mains water is not reliably clean, so it is best to avoid uncooked food such as salads, which may have been washed in it. Avoid ice cubes in drinks and if you have doubts about the cleanliness of plates and glasses, drink from the bottle through a straw and leave the bottom layer of food on the plate.

Make sure you wash your own hands scrupulously before preparing food or eating with your fingers and avoid food handled by others who you feel may not have been so thorough. Flies may

▼ Eating local food is an exciting part of the whole experience of travel, but make sure you only eat well-cooked dishes.

settle on food that is left standing on buffets, and chutneys or sauces left open on the table are especially likely to be contaminated.

EATING OUT

Try to find out where the local people eat, as these places will almost certainly offer the best-value food, and they will give you an authentic introduction to local cuisine and culture. In popular, busy restaurants the ingredients are more likely to be completely fresh and cooked dishes won't stand around waiting to be eaten.

In countries with unreliable food hygiene standards the locals' stomachs may be stronger than yours. If they eat from stalls beside the road or in market places, which may not be hygienic, you should be wary of following their example, as the food could give you diarrhoea or dysentery. For the same reason, avoid buying any cold food displayed in shops, and eat only ice creams sold sealed in packaging and made by well-known firms.

When eating in local restaurants, ask to watch the food being cooked and ask for yours to be cooked well. Be careful of shellfish and meat, which may have gone off before being cooked. Shellfish are especially risky as they may contain concentrations of

▲ Be careful of food that is on open display in restaurants; choose popular places where the dishes are unlikely to hang around long enough to be contaminated.

toxins. Ideally, eat only those shellfish that you have seen alive before they go into the cooking pot.

AVAILABILITY AND PRICES OF LOCAL FOODS

Unless you are taking all your food with you, you will need some idea of what types of food you can buy in the area you are going to and what are the local delicacies, as well as the prices. This information can be obtained either on a reconnaissance trip from a local contact or from an up-to-date guidebook. The price of seasonal foods may fluctuate, but you will at least have a general idea.

COOKING LOCAL FOODS

Fresh vegetables, salad ingredients and fruit need to be well washed in a weak solution of antiseptic and then rinsed in purified water before they are eaten. If you don't have time for this process – for example, if you want to snack on

▲ *In hot countries all fresh food – such as fish and meat – should be cooked and eaten on the day it is bought.*

a piece of fruit while visiting a local market – choose a piece of fruit that you can peel before you eat it and make sure the peel is intact before you buy. Make sure your hands are clean when you peel it.

Avoid watermelon and watercress in countries where food hygiene is suspect, as both of these foods contain large amounts of water and can make you very ill if they have been grown under conditions of poor hygiene.

OBSERVING LOCAL CUSTOMS
If you are lucky enough to be invited to eat with local people, make sure you understand the customs of the region. In some countries it is important to use only the right hand to handle your food, as the left is considered unclean; in others you may cause offence by showing your hosts, or the people you are eating with, the soles of your feet, so you should keep them flat on the floor or tuck them under you if you are sitting on the floor. You may find that if you eat everything on your plate it will immediately be filled again, or your host may serve you with particular delicacies which it would be impolite to refuse, even if you don't like the

look of them. As a tourist, it is up to you to find out which rules of etiquette apply in the region you are visiting, and to observe them.

DIET RESTRICTIONS
Your research when planning your trip will highlight any dietary restrictions that apply at your destination, but if you have specific dietary needs, especially if these are for health reasons, you should make a point of finding out specific information and asking direct questions. In some parts of the world, eating strictly vegetarian meals may be difficult, especially when eating in cafés and restaurants. Foods produced for vegans can be even more difficult to find in some countries, as will, for example, organic, gluten-free or diabetic foods. In other parts of the world, vegetarian food will be the only option. Other foods, especially different types of meat, will have taboos attached to them in different parts of the world, usually for religious reasons.

DRINKS
Tea and coffee, which require water to be boiled, are safe to drink, but you should stay away from unpasteurized milk, non-bottled water and locally made cold drinks. It is safest to stick to brands that are internationally recognized, and to make sure that the

seal on the bottle or can is unbroken when you buy the drink.

Alcohol will not be openly available in many countries because it is against the prevailing religion or local customs. In some of the more extreme regimes, it can be a criminal offence to drink or be in possession of alcohol. If you arrive at the border of such countries with alcohol in your baggage, it can be confiscated and you can be fined or refused entry into the country.

▲ *Unpasteurized milk may carry harmful bacteria and should be avoided in areas where hygiene standards are unreliable.*

Dry foods

The main advantage of dry foods is their lack of weight, especially if you have to carry large amounts of food on your back. The taste, however, is not as pleasant as that of fresh or tinned food, or even pouch meals, so they may require some extra ingredients to make them palatable.

Despite being lightweight, these meals do require hot water to rehydrate them. If you plan to cook over a wood fire, with a water source nearby, then you will need only a pan, but if these options are not available, you will need a stove, water and a pan, plus fuel, all of which are heavy items.

There are two types of dry food: air-dried and freeze-dried. As with all food, you get what you pay for. You can cut the cost by buying in bulk and packing individual portions in small, well-sealed plastic bags. If you do this, make sure the contents of the bulk container are well mixed up first.

AIR-DRIED FOOD

The food is placed in a drum and the moisture is removed by passing hot air through it. This system has been used for many years and is very simple, but it does tend to destroy the cell structure of the food, so that when it is reconstituted it tends to be rather mushy. In addition to changing the texture of the food, it can also affect the taste adversely.

FREEZE-DRIED FOOD

This newer, more expensive, process can be used to prepare both fresh and cooked food. The food is flash frozen, which means that it is frozen very rapidly so the water in it forms ice crystals. The food is then put into a vacuum at very low temperatures and the ice crystals are drawn off as water vapour. When reconstituted, the results look and taste far more like the original.

IMPROVING THE TASTE

It is a good idea for people to sample any dried food you intend using on your expedition to find out the best way to cook it and to see if the tastes are acceptable. Adding spices or fresh foods, such as onions or other vegetables, will improve the flavour.

If you have time, allow the dried food to soak for some time before you start to cook it. Also use more water than the manufacturer's instructions suggest, to ensure that the food is properly rehydrated. Make sure you cover the pan while the food is soaking, so that nothing is able to fall or crawl in before you start cooking.

You may be able to vary your diet by eating dried fruit and even dried meat and fish, depending on the country. Wash these thoroughly before you use them, and be wary of any that are not packaged.

▲ *If there is time before the meal, add water to the dried food and leave it to soak for a while before starting the cooking process.*

HEALTH CONCERNS

If you are living almost totally on reconstituted dry food, you may begin to suffer from constipation. Include plenty of dried fruit in your diet to help avoid this, and drink plenty of water. Also, if you are going to use this type of food almost exclusively for a long time, you may need to take some sort of mineral supplement to create a balanced diet.

If you are short of water, never be tempted to eat dried foods that have not been reconstituted, as they will use up body fluids that you cannot afford to lose.

PREPARING DRY FOODS

1 Empty the packet of dried food into a cooking pot and give it a stir to break up any lumps.

2 Add clean water and leave to soak if possible. You will need more water and longer cooking times at high altitudes.

3 Cook over a gentle heat, stirring, to avoid scorching. Cook thoroughly to allow time for complete rehydration.

Canned and pouch foods

Cans and foil pouches offer many of the same advantages: the food is of fairly high quality, it can be eaten cold if necessary, and it has a long life. Pouch meals have now taken the place of cans in military rations, where their reduced weight is a great advantage.

CANNED FOOD

The advantage of this form of processing is that it is suitable for almost any food, and, unless the can is punctured, it should be edible. If, however, the can is bulging, it means that bacteria are at work and it should be thrown away. Most canned food now comes with a sell-by date on it. The food is usually already cooked

so it can be eaten cold straight from the can in an emergency, though it usually tastes better heated. Vegetables and fruit usually come in their own syrup or brine and will require less water in the cooking process, but the weight of the liquid adds to your load.

Although many cans have a ring pull, these can snap off, so everyone should have a can opener. Write the contents on the cans with a permanent marker pen, so that if the label comes off, you know whether you have rice pudding or stew for supper.

When you have eaten the food, you should either take the empty cans with you or burn them first and then bury them at least 90cm/3ft underground.

POUCH FOOD

The main advantage of these ready meals is that they can just be dropped into boiling water and left for 10–15 minutes to heat, then taken out, torn open and either eaten straight from the pouch or poured on to a plate. As with cans, pouch food can be eaten cold in an emergency because the food is already cooked.

Further advantages are that more than one kind of meal can be prepared at the same time in the same pan, and

◀ A number of companies offer chemical heating units that can be used to heat both canned and pouch food in an emergency.

portion control is easy because most pouches contain one portion. Finally, when you have finished cooking, there are no dirty pans to wash up.

The main drawbacks are that the pouches are not as strong as cans and usually have to have an outer case or covering to protect them from being punctured. Also, at present, most of the meals packaged in this way are stews and casseroles, which can be rather monotonous, though more varieties are coming on to the market every year. Finally, this kind of food is probably the most expensive to buy.

▼ If you intend to use canned food extensively, make sure everyone on the expedition has a can opener.

PREPARING POUCH FOOD

1 Fill a pan large enough to hold the pouch with water and bring it to the boil on the stove.

2 When the water is boiling, drop in the pouch and boil for 10–15 minutes. Several pouches can be heated at once.

3 Either eat the food from the pouch or pour the contents into a bowl. Be careful, as the pouch will be very hot.

Packing your food

Well-prepared rations will be carefully packed and clearly labelled, with full instructions for their use included in the package. The contents will vary depending on the climate, the type of activity being undertaken and the method of transport. All packaging should be as lightweight as possible, but the food should be packed securely so that it is not crushed and stays dry and free from contamination.

PREPARING RATIONS

The food you are going to use on the expedition will come in its own packaging, and you will have to decide whether to keep it in this or repack it in special ration packs, perhaps with a set menu for each day. If you decide to dispense with the original packaging, remember to keep the cooking instructions and details of any special storage conditions. If cans are included, include a can opener in the package. You may also need to add such items as toilet paper, salt, pepper and matches.

You may need to pack some rations for specialized uses, such as high-altitude or lightweight rations. Make sure these are clearly marked in a way that will be understood by everybody, or you could end up with the wrong rations going to the wrong place.

RATION PACKS

- The ideal ration pack should be self-contained for the period it is designed to cover.
- The ration pack should include clear instructions on how to cook all the food in the pack.
- It should be packed in suitable packaging to withstand the climatic and travelling conditions it will be exposed to.
- The pack should be easy to get into and use.
- The contents, or the type of ration, should be marked on the outside of the pack in a way that is easily read and understood.

FOOD CONTAINERS

If you are carrying a small amount of food for a weekend backpacking trip, use a series of rigid plastic resealable containers, which will keep the food away from the rest of your kit and protect it from being crushed or soaked, or from coming into contact with stove fuel and so on. Such items as washing-up liquid and cooking oil can be carried in small plastic bottles with screw tops.

Make sure the food containers you choose have tight-fitting, airtight lids to help keep the food fresh. If you buy them in graduated sizes they can be stored neatly inside each other

▶ *Whenever possible, buy fresh fruit and vegetables locally to supplement your pre-packed rations.*

▲ *Double-check your rations, as when you next open the packages you may not be in a position to make any additions.*

when not full of food. Buying them in different colours may be helpful, to give you some idea of what is inside each container, but make sure all food

containers are well labelled with the contents. Keep cooked and raw meats in separate containers, well apart to prevent cross-contamination, and in camp make sure they are covered at all times to prevent flies settling on them. Never leave any food containers open when you are camping or you could attract animals or insects to your food. Keep food containers out of the sun and packed away when not in use.

PACKING RATIONS

Your mode of transport will be a major factor in deciding how much weight and volume you can carry and how you will pack the food.

If you are going to carry all your food in a vehicle, weight will be a relatively unimportant factor and it should not be difficult to keep your food stores dry. However, if you are intending to travel on dirt roads, the way you pack your food will be important: it needs to be kept well away from fuel in a strong box, which is securely wedged in so it will not jump about in the vehicle.

If you are travelling with one or more pack animals, both the weight and the method of packing will be important to ensure that the animal is not overloaded or unevenly loaded. Any packaging with sharp edges will need to be well padded to stop it

- Check all canned and pouch food before you pack it to make sure that the containers are sound and unpunctured.
- Check the sell-by dates of pre-packaged food.
- Make sure all your food containers have airtight, close-fitting lids with no splits.
- Never pack raw meat or fish in a way that would allow it to cross-contaminate cooked food.
- If you buy fresh food in hot countries, don't store it at all: cook it on the day you buy it.
- Do not store any food in direct sunlight or on the ground.

CARRYING WATER

Water is a heavyweight item, but it is vital to carry enough at all times, and there are many types of water carrier on the market.

- If you use water bags, make sure they are well protected from sharp objects or rubbing, as either may cause the bags to leak.
- Check for leaks in the bags at the end of each day's travel.
- If you need to purify your water, mark each container as it is purified. You can do this using a

▼ *Collapsible water containers are useful but after a lot of use they may eventually split along the folds. Check older ones for leaks before you use them.*

piece of coloured cord or tape tied to the handle.

- If you are using a lot of jerry cans to carry water, number them so that you can keep track of how many you have used and use the cans in sequence.
- If you use canvas water bags you can keep your water cool by hanging them outside your vehicle or on the side of pack animals. This is due to the evaporation of water from the walls of the bag.

▼ *Water bags are available in all sizes and when not in use they take up very little space, but they can be punctured when full if not treated with care.*

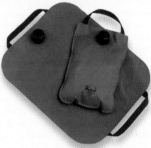

rubbing the animal's skin and developing sores. If you are carrying food in a canoe or kayak, you will need to make sure it stays dry and the space available will be limited. Pack food inside

waterproof containers and wedge or strap them tightly into the boat. When backpacking, weight will be the most important factor, and you need to adopt the principles of lightweight camping.

▶ *Plastic containers will keep food safe from water and insects.*

Planning your outdoor kitchen

If you are a lightweight camper, your kitchen will be little more than a fire or stove sited a little way from your tent. If you are establishing a camp on one site for more than a week, however, it will be worth planning the layout of your camp kitchen, and you may even want to build some simple structures to make your life easier.

ESTABLISHING THE COOKING AREA

The first thing to do is to fence the cooking area off in some way so that people cannot just wander through it unawares and get in the way of the cook. If there are children in the camp you may want some way of deterring them from getting too near the stove or helping themselves to the food while you are preparing it. Your store tent and woodpile, and any structures you build for the kitchen area, will all help to establish its boundaries.

Next, choose where you are going to put your cooking site, be this a stove or fire. If there is a suitable natural feature such as a flat rock, use this as your base; otherwise, if you can, build a framework off the ground as the base for the fire, so that when you are cooking you will not have to bend over all the time. Make sure this framework is substantial and will not wobble or

▲ *A safe cooking fire is spacious and well thought out. Large timbers around the fire provide both a safety barrier and seating.*

collapse once you have built the fire and loaded it with cooking pots. Allow some space for the cooks to stand. If you are using a fire, keep the woodpile well stocked, but make sure it is kept tidy, as leaving pieces of wood around could cause people to trip over them.

You will need to put your store tent near the cooking area, but don't have it so near that it gets in the way of the people doing the cooking.

PROTECTING THE KITCHEN

You may choose to build one or two structures in the kitchen area to keep eating and cooking equipment off the ground. If you construct a simple table you can use it to prepare all your food and also as a serving area, and some form of dresser will keep the cooking equipment tidy and help to demarcate the kitchen area. If your campsite has trees growing around it, they

◄ *In a long-term base camp the kitchen will be easier to organize if you can set up some kind of dresser to keep all your cooking equipment together and off the ground.*

can be useful in several ways, though you should not build your fire or site your stove too close to them. Leafy trees will provide shade for keeping food cool, and in a hot climate they will also offer welcome shade for the cook, to offset the heat of the fire. You can also use any branches within reach as racks on which to hang utensils, mugs and food. It makes sense to store as much off the ground as you can, to keep things clean and make them easier to find, and to clear the area where you are preparing any food.

THE EATING AREA

In a large camp it's a good idea to establish a designated eating area to help keep the rest of the site tidy and free of food debris. If you are in a place where it rains regularly, you might consider it a good idea to have a shelter over both your fire and the eating area. Discourage people from eating in their tents as crumbs and spilt food may act as a lure for animals later on. You will need to dig two waste pits near the kitchen (see the section Base camps, 184–185) or have two bags, one for dry waste and one for wet waste. Insist that everyone disposes of all waste responsibly.

▲ *A mug tree is useful for keeping mugs clean and organized. On a campsite it can be the branch of an actual tree.*

THE CAMP PANTRY

If you have a store tent, all dry and packaged food can be kept in it, but fresh food will need to be kept as cool as possible. For this you can use a hanging camp pantry. You can buy these in various styles, but you can also make one with a few pieces of wood, a length of muslin (cheesecloth) or nylon mesh, and some cord. Hang the pantry from a rope slung over the

▼ *By constructing a fire or stove stand you will save yourself a lot of bending down, but you must make sure that it is very stable and will not collapse when loaded with fuel and heavy cooking pots.*

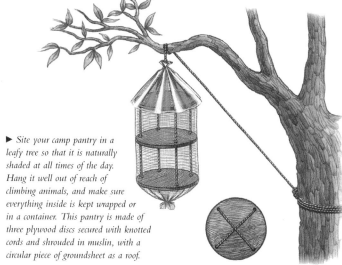

▶ *Site your camp pantry in a leafy tree so that it is naturally shaded at all times of the day. Hang it well out of reach of climbing animals, and make sure everything inside is kept wrapped or in a container. This pantry is made of three plywood discs secured with knotted cords and shrouded in muslin, with a circular piece of groundsheet as a roof.*

branch of a large tree and make sure it stays in the shade for as much of the day as possible. Any food that you keep inside it should be well wrapped up or packed in an airtight container.

BEAR BAGGING

In case the camp is visited by animals attracted by the smell of your fresh food, the pantry and any other bags containing food should be hung far enough away from the trunk of the tree to prevent them climbing to get to it. This is particularly important if you are camping in bear country. Unless you can hang your food around 4m/13ft high and 3m/10ft away from the trunk you may lose it all to a hungry bear. You should also hang food downwind of your camp so that if any bears do want to investigate it they don't need to pass you to get to it.

To rig up your bag or pantry, weight the end of a rope with a small rock tied into a bag and toss it over a high branch, keeping hold of the other end. Lower the rope until you can reach the rock, which you can discard. Tie your food bag

to one end of the rope and use the other end to haul it up to a suitable height. Make the end of the rope fast around the tree trunk.

If you are camping in an area with no trees, this arrangement will not be an option for you. In this case, try to avoid the need to store fresh food at all by taking dehydrated, pouch or canned food supplies instead. If you do have to keep fresh food at ground level, use thick double wrapping to mask the smell of the food, and avoid any particularly smelly foods if you don't want to risk attracting animals to your camp. Pack the food in sealable plastic containers and don't keep it inside or around your sleeping tent.

▼ *Empty food cans should be cleaned out or burned, then squashed and taken away from the site when you leave, or buried at least 60cm/2ft underground.*

Food hygiene and storage

You will be faced with many hazards in the wild, so the last thing you should do is add to them by failing to practise sound food hygiene. If you are part of a group, bear in mind that everyone's health depends on the whole group taking equal care in this respect. If any members of an expedition do not follow the basic rules of food safety, they risk causing bouts of diarrhoea or even a serious case of food poisoning.

FOOD PREPARATION
Make sure that anybody preparing or cooking food washes their hands

▼ *You should have separate chopping boards for different types of food to prevent any cross-contamination.*

▲ *Be scrupulous about washing your hands before you start to prepare food, whether it is to be eaten raw or cooked.*

▲ *All the plates, cups and bowls from which you eat should be properly washed in hot water after each use.*

frequently. Keep raw and cooked foods separate during preparation, and, if possible, use different chopping boards and utensils for each type. If you cannot do this, make sure they are thoroughly washed before changing from one type of food to the other. For more advice on the preparation of food, see Local Foods, 212–213.

CLEANLINESS
Cooking pans, plates, cups and cutlery must be washed thoroughly in hot water after each meal, and with antiseptic added to the water every three or four days, if possible. To cut down the possibility of spreading infection, each person should use only their own eating equipment and drink from their own mug or water bottle.

In a base camp or semi-permanent camp kitchen, use an antibacterial fluid to disinfect all working surfaces and utensils at least every three or four days. In hot climates this

▲ *Make sure all your cooking equipment is thoroughly cleaned and disinfect everything every three or four days.*

should be done every day. Make sure that all dishcloths and drying towels are washed regularly.

Check that wooden cooking utensils are kept clean and in good condition. If they get chipped or badly scored, discard them and buy new ones as they are likely to harbour germs.

SERVING FOOD
Well-cooked, piping hot food will be safe to eat, but if it is left to sit around at a lower temperature, bacteria will start to multiply. For this reason, if you are going to serve a lot of people, call them before you take the food off the fire, so that it is still very hot when it reaches their plates.

Serve each dish using a different spoon, if possible, and clean up any

◄ *Specialized lightweight equipment is excellent for backpacking expeditions but may not be robust enough for use in a larger base camp.*

▲ *Although it is bulky, a large plastic bowl for washing dishes will be useful in camp.*

▲ *Collapsible mesh covers are invaluable for keeping flies off dishes of food.*

▲ *A weighted fabric cover can be used to protect dishes of all sizes from flies.*

spillages as soon as they happen. If you have to touch any prepared foods – including bread – wash your hands first: this applies whether you are serving it or picking it up to eat.

Finally, keep all food covered until you are ready to serve it, and, if the food is cold, get it ready and serve it in the shade.

DRY FOOD STORAGE

All items should be stored in a cool, dry, well-ventilated place, raised off the ground. Try to make sure your storage is bird- and rodent-proof and never leave food containers open. If you do not have a lid for a pot use a piece of muslin (cheesecloth) to cover it.

▼ *Proper serving implements, such as ladles and large spoons, are essential if you are catering for a large camp.*

No food should be kept in a sleeping tent at a base camp. If you are on a lightweight camping trip this is less easy to arrange, but you should pack all your food away in containers or put it in your backpack.

If you buy dried fish or meat from local traders in tropical countries, make sure you wash it well before eating it. It may well have been dried out in the sun, which will have allowed flies and other insects to settle on it.

FRESH AND COOKED FOOD STORAGE

Unless you are cooking in a semi-permanent base camp and have some form of refrigeration or effective cool boxes, do not keep either fresh or cooked foods for long periods, and never for more than 24 hours in a hot country. Keep all food out of the sun

and covered with muslin to keep flies away, and never store cooked and uncooked food together.

If you are camping within reach of local markets or food producers, try and buy all your fresh food daily, then you can cook it straight away and storing it will not be a problem.

As an alternative to going to the market, you may have local traders coming to your camp or base. If you want to use this arrangement, make sure you stipulate a time and place, as you will not want a succession of people turning up throughout the day trying to sell you food.

If you can, try to spread your purchases around a number of different traders when you are visiting a Third World country. Your money will make a big difference to small farmers and traders in the locality.

SERVING MEALS

- As well as the cooks, people serving food must have the highest standards of cleanliness, both personally and with the equipment they are using.
- Serving food should not be a free-for-all. Either ask everyone to sit down and serve them where they are going to eat or get them to queue up so that you can serve the food on to their plates: don't let them use their own spoons.
- Make sure all your serving equipment is clean and you use a separate implement for each pan.

Cooking over a fire

Most cooking is more successful when it is done on a good bed of hot embers rather than over a fire with lots of flames. So this means preparing the fire by burning a good amount of fuel until it has died down to a bed of embers, then placing your pots safely either directly on the fire or on its surrounds.

HEAVY-DUTY POTS
Use heavy-duty cooking pots when cooking on a fire. If your pots and pans are too thin and flimsy they will not heat evenly and the food inside is likely to burn. The fire may also damage the cooking pots themselves, especially if you are cooking directly on the fire. If you have constructed a structure to support the pots (see the section Camp fires, 192–195), they will be exposed to less intense heat.

Have a padded oven glove or something similar to lift pots off the fire, as the handles may become very hot. Be careful when lifting pots on or off the fire that you do not get smoke in your eyes, as this could lead you to drop the pot.

If a pot is extremely heavy, use two people to lift it off the fire and warn others in the cooking area to get out of the way while you are doing so.

PROTECTING COOKWARE

If planning to cook on open fires, coat the outside of cooking pots with a paste made up of washing powder and water, and allow it to dry before putting the pots on the fire. When you come to wash the pots, this coating will wash off with the layer of soot on it.

▲ *Make sure the pot is completely stable when you put it on the fire, and will not fall over during cooking.*

You may lift the pot by pushing a stick through the handle with one person on each side, but if you use this method make sure the stick is strong enough and will not break when the full weight of the pan and contents is brought to bear.

On a windy day, be careful that ash from the fire does not blow into your cooking pots or food.

PLANNING COOKING TIMES
Before you start cooking, think about the way you are going to use the fire: for instance, you may need access to the hottest part of the fire to grill some meat, while pots are simmering gently over a cooler part, so make sure you can reach everything easily. If you are cooking a meal with a number of different elements, consider which foods will take longest to cook, and start with these.

If you want to cook a number of dishes all at the same time, and have enough people, you can make one person responsible for each dish, making sure it is ready on time and does not burn.

KEEPING EMBERS HOT
Once you have constructed your fire (see Camp fires, 192–195), and it is burning, don't forget it while you are cooking. If the bed of embers starts to cool down, you may have to stop cooking and burn some more wood. Since stopping the cooking process is

▼ *When you put a pan on the fire, try to arrange the handle so that it is shielded from the fiercest heat.*

▶ *Woodland will supply shelter and fuel for your camp fire, but be careful to choose a site for the fire that is not too near the trees.*

rarely ideal, a better solution is to use part of your fire, where you have the bed of embers, for cooking, and keep a wood-burning fire stoked on another part to create a steady supply of hot embers that you can rake across when you need them.

Make sure you have a good supply of wood for the fire, as you will not want to have to hunt for more wood halfway through cooking a meal.

CAMP OVEN

If you have a camp oven, place it at one end of the fire and bank earth or sand around it to make it secure and keep it at a constant temperature. The door should face away from the fire so that food can be put in and taken out easily and safely.

Remember that, as in most ovens, the temperature will be higher in the upper part than in the bottom. You do not want fire directly under the oven, as this can turn the bottom of the oven into a hot plate and cause anything left on this to burn.

▼ *Let the fire die down to a bed of glowing, ash-covered embers before cooking on it, so that food cooks rather than burns.*

COOKING IN THE CAMP FIRE

It can be great fun to cook a meal using the minimum of utensils, though this is not usually practicable if you are catering for a large number of people. With this type of cooking it is particularly important to have a good bed of embers and no flame on your cooking fire. You can use aluminium foil to keep food moist and protect it from burning on the outside, and from getting covered with ash.

You need to make sure that everything is cooked thoroughly when using this method. One secret is to cut everything into fairly small pieces or thin slices. If you are using ingredients such as potatoes or apples, try to cut them into pieces that are all of roughly the same size, so they cook evenly.

Be careful not to burn yourself when putting things on the fire, or taking them off.

FIRE SAFETY

Make sure everyone using the camp fire follows these rules:
- Site the fire well away from trees and other vegetation.
- Never throw wood on a fire, but place it on gently.
- Always have water available in case you need to put it out.
- Never allow people to mess about around a fire, especially when it is being used for cooking.
- Keep the area around the fire clean and tidy.
- Keep the woodpile well clear of the fire.
- If you have pans of water or food on a fire make sure someone is looking after them.
- Use an oven glove or padded glove to take pans off the fire.

Cooking on stoves

If you are going to use a stove for cooking, you will need to decide how many burners you need, or even how many stoves if the party is a big one. A single-burner stove will be the lightest to carry, but meals will be limited and slow to prepare.

USING STOVES SAFELY

Make sure you always operate a stove of any kind in a well-ventilated area and never store any fuel in or near a sleeping tent. This is especially important if you are using a gas stove. Never change a gas cylinder in a confined space or near a naked flame. If you need to remove it to dismantle the stove, leave it to cool first then take off the cylinder quickly and check that it has sealed itself and is not leaking.

A stove will not burn as hot as a fire, so you can use much lighter pans on it. If the stove is burning on full power,

▲ *Always set up your stove on a flat, stable surface to ensure that it will not tip over while it is in use.*

▲ *In windy conditions use a windshield, either a purpose-made one or something like a log, a rock or another piece of equipment.*

USING A GAS STOVE

1 Outside (not in a confined area) attach the gas cylinder to the burner.

2 Light the stove by turning on the gas and applying a flame.

3 Let the stove cool if dismantling it, and remove the cylinder quickly.

USING A METHYLATED SPIRIT STOVE

1 Assemble the stove and place it on a flat, level surface. Fill the burner.

2 Carefully light the methylated spirit (methyl alcohol).

3 Extinguish the flame by placing the screw top over the burner.

however, the food may still burn if you don't watch it carefully.

If it is very windy, either use your stove's windshield or improvise one using something from your kit or natural materials such as logs. Make sure you don't position anything so close to the stove that it catches light.

When you have finished cooking, turn the stove off. If you need to dismantle it, let it cool down before doing so, and give it a good clean

▼ *A double-burner gas stove is a more efficient way to cater for a large group.*

before packing it away. If it requires special tools to maintain it, make sure they are packed with the stove for easy access when you need them.

COOKING ON A SINGLE-BURNER STOVE

If you are backpacking and have just a single-burner stove, you will have to plan your cooking carefully, as you will not be able to cook anything that requires more than one pan per course.

Before you start cooking, make sure that your stove is in good working order with plenty of fuel. To avoid wasting any fuel, do all the food preparation before lighting the stove. Once the pan is on top, the stove may become top-heavy and unstable, so do not leave it unattended.

COOKING ON A MULTI-BURNER STOVE

If you are cooking on a multi-burner stove, perhaps with a grill as well, you should be able to cook the sort of

meals you do at home. Unless you have an oven in which to keep things hot, remember to plan your cooking so that all the different parts of the meal are ready at the same time.

Only the cooks should be around the stove and cooking area. This is particularly important if you are having to cook in a tent or confined space, where someone could kick or knock over the stove and food, which could be very dangerous.

▼ *The army mess tin is designed to be used with the army solid fuel stove.*

USING A SOLID FUEL STOVE

1 Open the can of fuel, remove the foil covering and assemble the stove.

2 Light the fuel. If it is in gel form, be careful not to get any on your hands.

3 Extinguish the flame using the lid and leave to cool before packing away.

USING A PETROL STOVE

1 Make sure the fuel tank is full and assemble the stove.

2 Give the tank several pumps with the plunger and turn the valve.

3 Light the stove. After cooking, turn off the burner and release the valve.

Lightweight camp menus

If you are going to have to carry all your food on your back, in cycle panniers or in a canoe, your main concern is likely to be the lightness of your food rather than its variety. Nevertheless, after a week or so eating the same freeze-dried dishes, you may feel your priority was wrong. Beyond pre-packaged, freeze-dried meals there is plenty of lightweight food on supermarket shelves, and with a little imagination you can devise interesting and appetizing menus for each day.

When choosing your food, consider how many cooking pots and burners you will have to cook on. You should also take the time to read the cooking directions on the food packets. Some soups, for example, take just a few minutes to cook, whereas others can take 20 minutes, meaning that you will need to use (and carry) extra fuel.

BREAKFAST

If you want to be up and on the move quickly, a bread roll with jam may be as much as you have time for. If you have a camp fire, the bread can be toasted over the fire. There are plenty of muesli (granola) and other cereals on the market that are ideal for a speedy breakfast, but for these you will need milk or yogurt. In cold weather you can warm yourself up with instant porridge (oatmeal), which can be mixed

▼ *If you use aluminium or enamel eating equipment be aware that they get very hot when filled with hot food.*

with either hot water or milk. You can buy it packed in individual portions for camping, and in different flavours such as cinnamon and apple or maple syrup and brown sugar.

If you want a more substantial cooked breakfast to keep you going through the day, you could heat a small can of beans, or beans with sausage, and eat that with bread. A more expensive option might be a suitable recipe in the form of a pouch meal.

Make sure you have plenty to drink at breakfast time. It doesn't matter if your drinks are hot or cold, but you could have hours ahead of you where you will be losing fluid by walking or working.

◀ *A mug of soup, hot baked beans and an instant pudding can be prepared using the smallest stove in just a few minutes and they make a warming and sustaining meal.*

LUNCH

If you are on the move during the day you will probably want only a brief break at lunchtime and won't want to eat anything that will slow you down. Lunch will usually be in the form of a high-energy snack meal that will need very little preparation and will be easy to eat. Nuts, fruit, chocolate and energy bars are the sorts of foods that will give you this high energy but will not require the body to over-exert itself digesting them.

DINNER

The evening meal will be your main meal of the day, when you have made camp at the end of your journey, or finished work. It should be a substantial three-course affair.

The first course can be a packet of instant soup, which just needs hot water poured on to it. The main course might be either a dehydrated meal or a pouch meal. If you're eating fish or meat, make sure you also have plenty of carbohydrates, in the form of rice, instant mashed potatoes or pasta, with it. All of these are easy to cook and light to carry.

The final course can be something like an instant pudding or fruit cooked with custard, both of which can be bought in dehydrated form. If you buy one of the varieties that just need hot water added to make them, you will save yourself the trouble of having to wash up one of the cooking pans you used for the main course.

COOKING DEHYDRATED FOOD

- Do not eat dehydrated food without adding the correct amount of water: it will dehydrate you.
- Add extra water at high altitudes.
- Soak ingredients such as dried vegetables in the cooking water before you start to cook them, to improve rehydration.

- Cook over a gentle heat, and keep stirring as the food cooks to avoid burning.
- Taste before adding any salt, as some dry foods are very salty.
- Get water boiling before adding rice or pasta.
- Thicken liquids with instant potato mash, raw eggs, grated cheese or powdered milk added at the end of cooking.

◀ *Dried pasta is quick to cook and provides a substantial evening meal. Bring a pan of water to the boil and tip in the pasta. Leave to boil for about 12 minutes, stirring occasionally, then drain and add to your chosen sauce. Heat through and serve.*

TRAIL SNACKS

Because of time constraints, or by preference, you may decide to snack during the day rather than stop for a meal break. The food you choose to take with you will be a matter of personal preference but it will also be dictated by the sort of climate you are travelling in. In hot countries, for instance, chocolate or anything with chocolate in it will melt and be very messy. Nuts, dried fruit, dried meat, biscuits and cheese are all suitable for eating on the move. Avoid salty foods that will simply make you thirsty. Some high-energy bars may not be to everybody's taste, so try them out before you set out on your expedition.

If you do decide to eat trail snacks make sure that any wrappings are not thrown away: put them into your pocket until you find a waste bin to throw them away.

◀ *Dried fruit and nuts are high-energy snacks and are easy to eat on the trail.*

▼ *Cereal bars are sustaining and can be substitutes for breakfast if necessary.*

▲ *Chocolate gives a quick burst of energy but it can make you thirsty.*

PACK SIZE

Although it is a more expensive way to buy food, you may consider buying some things packed in individual portions, including coffee, sugar and creamer. These little packs will help with portion control and, as many are plastic, they will offer some protection against wet, damp, dust, sand and insects. The downside is that you have more packaging to get rid of.

The alternative is to pack up your own individual portions. Apart from specially sealed pouch meals, you can repackage cereals, pasta, soup and pudding mixes in light, small freezer bags, which you can recycle later to carry away litter. Don't forget to add labels to your packages identifying the ingredients and including any necessary cooking instructions.

DRINKS

Tea, coffee and drinking chocolate are all light and easy to carry, and adding sugar to hot drinks will increase your calorie intake.

The most important drink is of course water. If you are living mainly on dehydrated food, it is important to make sure you are drinking enough fluid during the day, especially if it is hot and you are working hard. You can buy supplements from chemists which you can add to your water bottle, to put back into the body many of the trace elements which you will be losing if you are sweating a lot.

ADDITIONS TO YOUR MENU

If you come across berries on bushes or other natural fruit, or carry some dried fruit with you, this can turn a rather bland dehydrated pudding into a great treat. If you pick wild fruit, you must always be confident that you have identified it correctly before you eat it, especially when travelling abroad, and be sure you know that it is edible and not poisonous. If you do find ripe berries to pick, try to avoid bushes growing beside busy roads as they tend to get coated with pollutants from the exhaust of passing vehicles. No matter where you get your wild food from, wash it before you eat it.

Base camp cooking

Cooking in a base or standing camp offers many more opportunities than cooking in a lightweight camp. You will probably have more than one stove, a greater variety of cooking utensils and, most importantly, access to a wider range of ingredients. It will be easier to obtain fresh food, and as weight will not be a limiting factor if you have vehicular transport, using convenient but heavy canned food will not be a problem.

The type of dishes you offer will depend largely on where you are and what your programme for the day will be. If most people leave camp for the day, for example, breakfast will need to be more substantial than if you are also providing a cooked lunch.

BREAKFAST

If you are in a hot climate you may not want a cooked breakfast, especially if you are going to have a substantial lunch in camp. If, on the other hand, you are in a temperate or cold country and are going to be in cold weather or doing physical work all day, you may want a cooked breakfast of several courses. This might begin with fruit or cereal, muesli (granola) or porridge (oatmeal), followed by either a cooked meal such as bacon and eggs, or bread/toast with fruit jams or honey.

Try to offer fruit juices as well as tea, coffee or hot chocolate with breakfast (and all other meals), as they are a healthy addition to the diet as well as providing extra fluid.

LUNCH

This will usually be the lightest meal of the day, but people returning to base camp after a morning's exertion may well be quite hungry. Food needs to be quick and simple but sustaining. A good option is soup, sandwiches and either hot or cold drinks. Try to include some fresh fruit with the meal if it is available.

▲ A good breakfast is important if you are going to be active during the day.

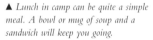

▲ Lunch in camp can be quite a simple meal. A bowl or mug of soup and a sandwich will keep you going.

DINNER

This will usually be the main meal of the day, a more elaborate, three-course affair to be lingered over and enjoyed at the end of the day.

Soup will usually be the first course. If you are using soup powder, try to add some fresh vegetables if they are available to make the soup more nourishing and improve the flavour.

The main course will probably be some kind of meat or fish accompanied by rice, potatoes or pasta and some fresh vegetables. Cooking meat or fish in a stew is the easiest way of preparing these foods at camp, particularly if you are catering for a large number of people who may not all be ready to eat at the same time.

Remember to include some spices and other flavourings in your food supplies so that you can give some variety to the camp diet, which might otherwise tend to be bland. With these you can turn a stew into a curry, a chilli or perhaps a sweet and sour dish, depending on taste. But be careful that you do not spice the food to such extent that some people will not eat it. If you find that some people do and others do not like certain spices, you

▲ *The main meal of the day can be eaten in the evening and should be a fairly substantial and relaxed meal.*

can either cook dishes in two different batches, one spiced and one not, or stick to plain recipes and leave people to add their own flavourings.

Desserts can be as varied as your ingredients and cooking skills allow. If you decide to fall back on such things as instant puddings from packets, you can liven them up by serving them with fresh or canned fruit.

KEEPING FOOD HOT
When you are cooking for a large number of people one of the biggest problems is to serve hot food hot but not burned. One way to achieve this is to have a large pan of simmering water on the fire or stove with a large dish on top. As the food is cooked, it can be placed on the dish and covered with a lid. The heat will be gentle enough to keep everything hot without burning or drying out, and the water can be used later for washing the dishes.

If you have to serve such things as fried eggs and you can only cook say six or seven at a time, then only call for that number of people to receive their food. This way they get all their food hot and you do not have great queues waiting with only half their food served and getting cold.

CLEANING UP
Do not allow your standards to slip just because you are cooking and eating outdoors. In your base camp, there should be no reason why you have to eat all courses of your meal from the same plate or bowl. If you do not have enough plates or bowls, you can quickly wash up between courses.

Make it a strict policy to check that eating and serving surfaces are kept clean and free of food scraps and spills.

SHARING THE COOKING
In a large base camp it is sensible for one or two people to take responsibility for planning and providing meals. This makes it easier to work out how you are going to use your rations and avoids confusion about who is cooking dinner. On the other hand, everyone in camp should be ready to lend a hand preparing ingredients, watching cooking pots, building and fuelling the fire, serving food and cleaning up after meals. You may want to arrange a rota so that you know you always have some help, and don't get too many people hanging around the kitchen area when you are busy cooking.

It is quite possible that various members of the party, apart from the designated cook, will have a particular culinary skill. They may be especially good at cooking fish or making bread, or spicing a curry, so always be open to offers to take over the cooking of a particular course or even a whole meal. But make sure a guest cook doesn't squander your entire stock of, say, lemons or cheese in one fantastic dish: insist that they tell you what they are going to make so that you know it will fit in with your other plans for the meal, or the day's cooking.

COOKING EGGS

Apart from the fact that they are fragile and need to be carefully packed for travelling, eggs are the perfect camp food: popular, adaptable, nourishing, cheap and

quick to cook. As well as frying and boiling and scrambling them, try baking them in potato skins in the embers of the fire, or stirring them into hot soup, Asian-style.

▼ *Scrambled eggs need careful cooking. Keep stirring and watch them constantly to avoid overcooking them.*

▼ *Fried eggs take only a couple of minutes, so cook them at the last minute when the rest of the meal is ready.*

Base camp sample recipes

The following recipes will give you an idea of the varied and interesting meals you can achieve when cooking on a simple stove or open fire. Any of these dishes could be cooked at a base camp, where you are likely to have more time and equipment, as well as access to canned and fresh food. Each recipe will serve 6–8 people.

MAIN MEALS
Dishes that can be cooked from start to finish in a single pot make the best sense for camp cooking,

Fish Hotpot
675g/1½lb fish, such as cod or plaice
30ml/2 tbsp vegetable oil
250g/9oz hard cheese, grated
450g/1lb tomatoes, sliced
500g/1¼lb boiled potatoes or 300g/11oz
*   boiled rice, to serve*

Wash and cut the fish into 3cm/1¼in squares, and pour a little oil over them. Grease the pan. Put the fish in the bottom, cover with a layer of cheese and then some sliced tomatoes. Repeat these layers until all the ingredients have been used. Cover tightly and cook slowly for 20–30 minutes.

▼ *A cheesy fish hotpot makes a warming yet light main course.*

▲ *Corned beef is an invaluable standby for camp cooking as it is already cooked and just needs to be heated through.*

Spaghetti and Corned Beef
1 onion, chopped
30ml/2 tbsp vegetable oil
350g/12oz corned beef
400g/14oz chopped tomatoes
400g/14oz spaghetti in tomato sauce
50g/2oz hard cheese, grated
500g/1¼lb boiled potatoes, 350g/12oz
*   cooked and drained pasta or fresh crusty*
*   bread, to serve*

Heat the oil in a frying pan and gently fry the onion until soft. Dice the corned beef and add to the onion with the chopped tomatoes and spaghetti. Simmer gently for 5 minutes. Sprinkle with cheese and serve with potatoes, pasta or bread.

▲ *Chilli con carne is a camp fire classic, warming and easy to eat. Keep the heat gentle so that everyone enjoys it.*

Chilli Con Carne
15ml/1 tbsp vegetable oil
450g/1lb minced (ground) beef
1 large onion, chopped
400g/14oz chopped tomatoes
400g/14oz cooked and drained red kidney
*   beans or baked beans*
1 beef stock (bouillon) cube
375ml/13fl oz water
5ml/1 tsp chilli powder
300g/11oz boiled rice or fresh crusty bread,
*   to serve*

Heat the oil in a large pan and fry the beef until brown. Stir in the onion, tomatoes and kidney beans. Crumble in the stock cube and pour in the water. Bring to the boil and simmer for 5 minutes. Add the chilli powder. Simmer gently for 30 minutes, stirring occasionally. Serve with boiled rice or chunks of bread.

COOK'S TIPS

- Be inventive: by adding some fresh vegetables and imaginative seasoning you can transform the flavour of quickly prepared canned ingredients.
- When making stews, choose fresh ingredients that cook quickly, such as fish and minced (ground) meat, to save time and fuel.
- Cut vegetables into small chunks for speedy cooking.

▲ *Any meat and potatoes left over from dinner can be appetizingly fried up for a quick lunch dish the following day.*

Leftover Hash
50g/4oz/4 tbsp butter
450g/1 lb cooked potatoes, grated
450g/1 lb cooked leftover meat
½ onion, grated
300g/11oz can sweetcorn kernels
salt and pepper to taste

Melt the butter in a heavy frying pan, then add the potatoes, meat, onion and corn and mix well. Season to taste and brown over a medium heat.

DESSERTS
Proper desserts, not just a portion of fresh fruit, will be much appreciated and will satisfy hefty appetites.

Fruit Fritters
150g/5oz self-raising (self-rising) flour
25g/1oz granulated sugar
1 egg, beaten
175ml/6fl oz milk
115g/4oz fruit (cooking apples, bananas, pineapple, pears or oranges)
vegetable oil, for frying
caster (superfine) sugar, for sprinkling

Mix the flour and sugar in a bowl. Add the beaten egg and milk to make a thick batter. Peel, core and grate the apples, or slice or dice other fruit, and add to the batter. Pour some oil into a pan so it is at least 1cm/½in deep. Once the oil is hot, cook spoonfuls of the batter mix until golden. Sprinkle with caster sugar and serve hot.

▲ *Crunchy syrup-coated cornflakes make a satisfying contrast with soft stewed apples in this easy-to-make dessert.*

Ginger and Rhubarb Crumble
8 sticks rhubarb
sugar or honey, to sweeten
water
20 ginger biscuits (cookies)
50g/2oz butter
natural (plain) yogurt or double (heavy) cream, to serve

Cut the rhubarb into chunks and put them in a pan with the sugar or honey and a little water. Stew gently until soft. Crush the biscuits in a plastic bag. Melt the butter in a pan and stir in the crushed biscuits. Divide the rhubarb between serving bowls and sprinkle the crumble over the fruit. Serve with natural (plain) yogurt or cream.

▼ *Fruit fritters can be made using any fresh fruit you have available. Serve them freshly made and piping hot, sprinkled with sugar.*

Swiss Apples
800g/1¾lb cooking apples (or you could use pears, or canned fruit such as peaches or apricots)
50g/2oz sugar
40g/1½oz butter
15ml/1 tbsp golden (light corn) syrup
cornflakes
double (heavy) cream, natural (plain) yogurt or custard, to serve

Peel, core and slice the apples, then cook them in a little water with the sugar before placing them in serving bowls. If using canned fruit, drain off a little of the juice or syrup and divide between the serving bowls. Melt the butter and golden syrup together in a large pan, then stir in enough cornflakes to use up all the syrup mixture. Serve this on top of the fruit with cream, yogurt or custard.

▼ *This quick alternative to a baked crumble topping is made with crushed ginger biscuits and butter, and goes well with rhubarb.*

Cooking without utensils

Preparing a meal with the minimum of equipment can be an enjoyable challenge, and it is an integral part of lightweight camping. Learning how to do it does, however, also have a more serious purpose: if you can make a meal in this way, it could save your life in an emergency. For this kind of cooking you will need to be able to light a wood fire and let it burn down to give you a good bed of embers.

BREAD
There are a number of ways of cooking simple loaves. Unleavened bread needs to be shaped into fairly thin loaves as it is heavier than bread made with yeast. It should be eaten soon after cooking, but is delicious when freshly cooked.

Mix about two cupfuls of flour – self-raising (self-rising) gives a lighter result but plain (all-purpose) can be used – with a pinch of salt and water to make a thick dough. Knead the dough and shape it into a number of small loaves, about 2.5cm/1in thick and 7.5–10cm/3–4in wide. Place them on a clean, flat rock that has been heated in

▼ *If you are camping on the coast, you can bake freshly caught shellfish over heated pebbles. Dig a pit approximately 90cm/3ft square and 30cm/1ft deep, and line the base with the stones, taking them part way up the sides. Build a mound of kindling in the centre and light the fire. After 45–60 minutes, carefully remove any dying embers using a long-handled fire-resistant tool, and douse them with water. Arrange the seafood over the hot pebbles and bake for 1–2 hours.*

the fire. (Make sure you brush the ash off it first.) Leave it for 20 minutes, turning halfway through. Check to see if the bread is cooked through by breaking one of the loaves open. Alternatively, roll the dough into a sausage shape and wrap it around a stick that has had its bark removed. Hold it over the fire and cook for about 10 minutes, then slide or twist it off the stick and fill the centre with fruit, honey or just butter.

EGGS
Hollow out the centre of a large potato and break an egg into it. To stop ash getting on the egg, place a piece of potato over the top of the hollow. Put the potato in the ashes of the fire and leave for about 20 minutes. If you want to eat the potato as well as the egg, wrap it in foil to protect it from the fire. Alternatively, break the egg into half an orange skin, and leave to cook for about 10 minutes.

MEAT
For a meal in a parcel, slice a couple of large potatoes and place these on some foil. Put some raw meat on the potatoes, and on top of the meat put sliced carrots and then more potatoes. Double-wrap the whole parcel in more foil, place it in the embers and rake more embers over the top of the parcel. Leave it to cook for about 30 minutes

▼ *If you want to use the pit again and have some newspaper to hand, cover it to keep it dry. Seaweed can also be used to do this.*

▲ *If you cut an orange in half and scoop out the flesh, you can use the skin as a container in which to bake an egg.*

before opening the parcel. You can use some large, thick cabbage leaves as wrapping for this dish instead of foil.

If you have no foil, cut your meat into cubes, thread them on to a stick from which the bark has been removed, and roast over the fire.

If you catch a rabbit, kill, clean, gut and skin the animal, wrap it in fresh green grass and then cover the whole parcel with some clay made from mud and water. Bake this in the embers for about one and a half hours, then remove it, break open the clay shell and clean off the grass.

FISH
If you catch fish yourself, you can cook them straight away and be sure that they will be absolutely fresh and

▼ *Meat and vegetables can be threaded on to straight sticks to make simple kebabs for roasting over the fire.*

▲ *Mussels can be cooked in their shells, but take particular care to ensure that they are fresh and from a safe source.*

▲ *Tough, fibrous leaves make ideal parcels for cooking food. Depending on climate and terrain, cabbage or banana leaves are among the most effective of this type of packaging.*

delicious. Gut each fish and open it out flat, then place it on a smooth, medium-size stone that has been heated

in the fire. Now place this stone on the embers and allow the fish to cook for about 15 minutes or until done. Insert a knife tip in the thickest part of the flesh – as soon as it comes away from the bone it is ready to eat For a step-by-step guide to this technique, see Building a fire for cooking, 326.

DESSERT

Take a large apple and cut out the core, then fill the hole with sugar, adding some dried fruit such as raisins or sultanas (golden raisins) if you have them, and wrap in foil. Place the parcel in the embers for 15–20 minutes. Be careful when you open the foil and eat the apple because it will be very hot.

▼ *You can make a whole meal by wrapping meat and slices of fresh vegetables up together in a secure foil parcel.*

▼ *Baked apple is an easy dessert: just remove the core, stuff with dried fruit and sugar, and wrap in foil.*

▼ *Baked banana is simple and delicious. Use a spoon to scoop it out of the skin, which will turn black as the fruit cooks.*

Clean water

When living outdoors, clean water will be the most important single item that will determine where you can go and for how long. You may have to plan your route and campsites to take into account the availability of water. See also page 334 for advice on finding a safe water suppply in remote terrain.

FINDING WATER
The first thing to do is to look at the countryside around you for signs of streams, rivers, lakes or the sea. If you are in the desert, look for vegetation, which requires some water to survive. Also look in dried-up watercourses or at the base of cliffs, as water has previously flowed here, and even if you cannot see it you may find it by digging down 60–90cm/2–3ft.

▼ *It is a good idea to equip yourself with more than one method of treating your drinking water.*

▲ *For your own safety you should always treat all water as potentially contaminated, even when travelling in wild areas.*

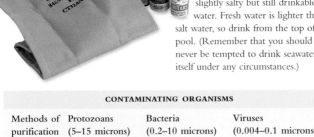

If you are near the coast, by digging above the high water line you will soon find a little pool of slightly salty but still drinkable water. Fresh water is lighter than salt water, so drink from the top of the pool. (Remember that you should never be tempted to drink seawater itself under any circumstances.)

In rivers with lots of silt, the deeper down you get your water, the cleaner it will be, as most of the silt and debris travels in the top layer of fast-moving water. Remove any remaining silt and debris before purifying the water by pouring it through either a finely woven, sock-shaped filter bag or an ordinary sock filled with a layer of sand and then a layer of small pebbles.

▼ *A Millbank filter bag will remove some impurities from water, but not all.*

CONTAMINATING ORGANISMS			
Methods of purification	Protozoans (5–15 microns)	Bacteria (0.2–10 microns)	Viruses (0.004–0.1 microns)
Boiling	Kills	Kills	Kills
Iodine	Does not kill all	Kills	Kills
Chlorine	Not effective on larger micro-organisms	Kills	Kills
Silver	Does not kill all	Kills	Does not kill all
Filters	Eliminates	Eliminates if pores are small enough	Does not eliminate
Purifier	Kills	Kills	Kills

▲ Boiling water kills all impurities and is the best way to make sure that it is safe for all purposes, including drinking.

PURIFYING WATER

The chart on the opposite page shows the benefits and disadvantages of all the methods of cleaning water. Once it has been purified, drinking water should always be kept in clean, sealed containers, labelled to avoid confusion.

BOILING

The safest way to purify water is to boil it vigorously for at least 5 minutes and allow it to cool before drinking. If, however, you want water quickly or in large quantities, you might choose another method.

CHEMICAL TREATMENTS

There are three different chemical agents currently used to treat water: iodine, chlorine and silver. When using any of these, always read the directions on the packet or bottle as in some cases an overdose can be harmful.

Iodine

This is available in liquid form or as tablets. After treatment with iodine, the water should be left to stand for 20–30 minutes. Neutralizing tablets can take away most of the smell and taste.

Iodine should be used on a short-term basis only, and should be avoided by pregnant women, children or anyone with a thyroid condition.

Chlorine

This is easy to use and takes only about 10 minutes to sterilize reasonably clean water and 30 minutes for more suspect water. Neutralizing tablets are available to take away most of the swimming-pool taste of chlorinated water.

Silver

This may be less effective than the other chemicals, but is longer-lasting and leaves no taste. The sterilization process may take at least two hours.

▼ A water purifier is simple and quick to use. Fill with water and leave to stand before pouring out drinking water.

FILTERS AND PURIFIERS

A purifier both filters and sterilizes the water, giving safe drinkable water, whereas a filter only sieves the water, which then needs to be chemically treated or boiled. See also pages 338–341 for advice on treating water.

When choosing a filter, you need to know if it will filter enough water for the trip (you will need 2–3 litres/ 3½–5¼ pints per person per day in temperate climates, and up to 6 litres/ 10½ pints in extreme hot climates, more if you are working hard). You should also check to see how fast it works. For a purifier, you need to know how fast it works and whether the cartridge can be cleaned, or a new cartridge fitted. Disposable cartridges tend to be compact but involve more expense.

▼ Water filters need thorough cleaning and servicing after use or they can become ineffective.

NATURE & THE ENVIRONMENT

When you venture into the wilderness you immediately begin to form a very intimate relationship with it; even though the forces of nature are infinitely more powerful than you, you have a responsibility to protect the natural world and not to disrupt the fragile ecosystems you are visiting. By respecting the wild environment, you can help to preserve its integrity while travelling safely through it.

Personal safety

When going into the wilderness, your personal safety will be in the hands of yourself and the people around you. It is important that you plan carefully, refer to your risk assessment, prioritize good hygiene and emphasize to the team the importance of safe behaviour at all times, whatever the activity.

RISK ASSESSMENT

Keep the results of your risk assessment in mind throughout the trip and add to it or rewrite it as necessary. If your assessment concluded that equipment such as helmets and buoyancy aids (personal flotation devices) should be worn, then wear them, even if they are uncomfortable or get in the way. Contact specialized organizations for up-to-date advice on health and safety concerns in the area.

▼ *Establishing a set of clear safety rules that everyone follows will mean that you can all safely enjoy wild places.*

HEALTH

Steps to make sure you and your team are physically fit and mentally prepared for the trip should be taken before you set off; this is especially important if you are planning challenging activities. One or two people, if not everyone, in the team should have an appropriate level of experience for the activities. Going ahead with activities without the right amount of skill and experience in the team is foolish and will almost certainly result in an accident.

Check that your personal and team first-aid kits are well-stocked and that you know what's in them and how to use it. Any appointed first aider or medic should be up to date with their training. Encourage everyone in the team to pay close attention to their personal hygiene, and at camp in the wilderness, make sure you have improvised facilities that enable them to do so. This should avoid unnecessary bouts of diarrhoea, or worse.

▲ *When chopping wood make sure there is a clear area around you so that no one will be hit when you swing the axe.*

PROTECTING YOUR HEAD

You are at risk from falling rocks wherever there are cliffs or steep slopes. If you are climbing, wearing a helmet can increase your safety, not only from falling rocks but from falling equipment dropped by other climbers!

Any falling object can cause serious injury, especially if you are not wearing a helmet. For instance, in tropical countries many people are killed and injured by falling coconuts. The answer, of course, is not to walk under coconut trees unnecessarily, and the same could be said of cliffs and steep slopes. However, if you are taking part in a climbing expedition, the important thing is to be sensitive to the potential dangers and ready to protect yourself from falling rocks at all times. When climbing, be careful to keep your equipment secure for the safety of those below.

▲ *Every party should include at least one person with a medical qualification or comprehensive training in first aid.*

▲ *When you are cooking, make sure all cooking pots are supported in a stable, level position and cannot be knocked over.*

▲ *If you are going on a canoeing or kayaking trip, every member of the party should know how to cope with capsizing.*

SAFETY AND EQUIPMENT SUPPLIES

Always make sure your basic survival kit is with you at all times. Check that your personal equipment and clothing are suitable for the worst possible conditions you could encounter, and during the trip check it regularly to make sure that everything is in good working order. Carry out repairs as soon as damage occurs.

SAFETY RULES

Work out a simple but comprehensive set of safety rules, which everybody in the party agrees to sign up to, and then stick to them. While you are travelling you may see other people, including local inhabitants, who are not following the rules you have drawn up regarding drinking water, for instance, but these people will be immune to many bacteria that could cause you illness. Or they may not be, and may end up suffering from diseases and illnesses that you would not want to contract, so don't be swayed by their example.

STAYING SAFE

Many mountaineering accidents happen on the descent, on relatively easy ground, when climbers, who are relieved to be away from the dangerous terrain they have coped with, forget to concentrate fully on the last stage of their climb. On any kind of expedition, silly accidents may happen at base camp or in safe areas, because people have started to relax. It is vital that every team member is aware that they need

to concentrate on safety all the time, not just at the testing times when they might be in personal danger.

▼ *Before you set out through unfamiliar terrain, find out about potential risks such as poisonous snakes and insects.*

Looking after the environment

Part of the reason so many of us want to visit and enjoy the wilder parts of the world, or just our own local countryside, is for peace, beauty and quiet. So, when planning your trip, be it a weekend's hike or an expedition of many weeks, make sure you don't spoil the very aspects of the countryside that you have gone to enjoy.

CONSIDERATION FOR OTHERS

Remember that many people live and work in the area that you are visiting, so respect their homes and land and don't do anything to disrupt their lives. Never park your vehicle in a place that will obstruct gateways or access roads, and always ask permission before setting up camp.

If you are canoeing down a river and people are fishing, do your best to avoid them and not to disturb the river any more than you have to.

RESPECT FOR COUNTRY LIFE

If you are walking or riding in a national park, or another area where there is an established path system, stay on the paths to avoid causing soil erosion. Similarly, keep to footpaths when crossing farmland, though in this

▲ *Avoid disturbing livestock when walking through pasture land; stick to recognized footpaths and close gates behind you.*

case you should do this to avoid damaging crops or frightening livestock. Make sure you refasten any gates you have to open to go through, avoid damaging fences, hedges and walls by climbing them, and keep any dogs under proper control.

Be very careful if you light fires, as these can easily get out of control, especially in hot, dry, windy weather.

Dispose of every scrap of litter by putting it in bins, burning or burying it, or taking it home with you.

LEAVING NO TRACE

The responsible traveller, according to the saying, should take only memories and leave only footprints. This applies equally whether you are going for a walk in the countryside, setting up a camp in the wilderness, or visiting a distant country with a culture and economy that is vulnerable to the effects of foreign tourism.

▼ *Be extremely careful whenever you light a camp fire or use matches, as bushfires can destroy a wilderness area extremely quickly.*

▼ *Dispose of your litter responsibly: the debris left by a large base camp can have a devastating effect on the natural environment.*

▲ *Be considerate of the resident wildlife: don't set up camp near a nest or obvious feeding site, disrupting their lives.*

PROTECTING WILDLIFE

Never be tempted to feed wild animals, however much they may invite it. The practice can make them dependent on humans for food, with the result that when you move on they will lose their food source. It can also lead them to lose their natural fear of humans. With large animals this might mean that their behaviour around other people eventually becomes dangerous and they will have to be destroyed.

It is illegal to bring wild animal products into many countries. If you are tempted to buy animal skins, ivory, eggs or any other animal products, make sure that what you buy has a certificate saying it has been farmed at a recognized centre, otherwise it will almost certainly have been poached from the wild. Note that it is illegal to buy rhinoceros horn products anywhere in the world.

If you are near or on a beach, try to avoid doing any damage to coral and underwater life in general, and do not buy shells, shell jewellery, and coral or turtle products. Buying such goods will encourage the local people to continue destroying their local environment and wildlife for economic reasons.

RESPECTING INDIGENOUS CULTURES AND CUSTOMS

Before travelling to a new region or country, read a good guidebook to find out as much as you can about the local culture and customs. As well as enriching your experience of your trip, this could avoid the embarrassment of doing the wrong thing or inadvertently insulting people you meet.

If you are travelling abroad, be aware of the national religion and of the attitude towards religion in the country. If the national language differs from your own, try to find the time to learn something of it. Even if you have only mastered the basics by the time you go, your efforts to speak to the local people in their own language will always be

▼ *Don't be tempted to buy seashells offered by local traders, as continued collection can damage the natural marine environment.*

▲ *If you are lucky enough to see wild animals, don't feed them or encourage them away from their normal habitation.*

appreciated. Wearing the correct clothing is also important to avoid giving offence, especially in Muslim countries but also in the religious buildings of many faiths, so find out about this and other customs before you go, and be sure to follow them.

If you wish to take photographs of local people, their homes and belongings, always ask permission and be prepared to pay for the privilege. You should be especially careful when taking pictures of women. In general, treat people with the respect you would expect to receive yourself.

▼ *If foreign travel introduces you to new cultures, consider yourself a guest in someone else's home and respect what you see.*

Natural hazards: vegetation

You can be at risk of serious injury from some of the plants and trees you may find in the wild. Your skin may be stung or pierced by thorns, or you could become ill after eating a poisonous plant or mushroom. For further guidance, see the section on Edible plants, 344.

THORNS AND SEEDS

Many plants have thorns that can be painful if you walk into or on top of them. They can also snag your clothes or go through the soles of your boots. Never walk around barefoot, and when you make camp check the ground where you are planning to pitch your tent, and the surrounding area, for thorns on the bushes growing nearby or on the ground.

Many seeds in the tropics are equipped with sharp barbs intended to get caught in animals' fur. If you tread on these and they get into your boots, they can work up into the skin of your feet and may set up an infection.

INSECT DEFENCE SYSTEM

Some acacia trees in Africa have a mutually supportive relationship with insects such as ants. The tree provides nourishment for the insects and the

ants provide defence against browsing animals. So, if you brush against or touch the tree, a large number of ants will appear from galls on the branches and attack you.

FUNGI

There are far more safe and edible fungi than there are poisonous ones, but some of the species that are toxic are extremely dangerous. The deadly Amanita species, such as the Death Cap and the Destroying Angel, are white, mushroom-shaped fungi that could be mistaken for edible mushrooms unless

▼ *African acacia bushes are protected not only by their savage thorns but by colonies of ants that live on their branches.*

◄ *Brown Roll-rim is a very common mushroom but is severely toxic, with effects similar to leukaemia.*

you know the distinctive signs to look for. These include a cup, or volva, at the base of the stem, a ring around the stem, and white gills. The poisonous Fly Agaric, with its distinctive red and white cap, is easier to identify.

With fungi (as with all wild food), it is sound advice to eat only those species that you are absolutely sure you can identify correctly. It is preferable to go out in the field with an expert, or with a reliable book, to learn how to recognize the most worthwhile edible species. Anything that you cannot positively identify should be left alone.

POISONOUS PLANTS

A good rule of thumb is never to eat or put near your eyes any plant that has a milky sap, such as spurge or members of the buttercup family. There are also a number of plants, such as poison ivy and poison oak, that can cause a burning rash on your skin if you touch

▼ *The Fly Agaric (Amanita muscaria muscaria) is easy to recognize — and avoid — because of its distinctive colouring.*

the leaves. These and many other irritant plants can be particularly dangerous if you touch them with your hands then rub your eye, when the blistering may cause permanent damage to your sight.

Some common trees of temperate regions, such as the yew and the laburnum, have berries or seed pods that are deadly poisonous. The sap of some members of the mangrove family, known as Blinding Mangroves, can cause blindness if it gets near the eyes.

Any plant that smells of bitter almonds or peaches should be avoided, and mature bracken becomes poisonous as it gets older. As with fungi, it is imperative that you should not eat any part of any plant you cannot identify.

MANGROVES

These salt-tolerant trees grow on the edge of tidal creeks in tropical regions, and their knotted roots, which become immersed in water for part of the day as the tide ebbs and flows, create a rich habitat for many plants and animals.

Although the trees themselves are unlikely to cause you harm, they attract colonies of shell-dwelling mussels, which can be razor sharp and will cut your feet and legs badly if you try to walk through them. It will always be easier to find another way to or from the water than trying to get through an area of mangrove forest. These forest belts can also be home to salt-water crocodiles and snakes, so you should take great care when visiting them.

NUTS AND FRUITS

The fruits of many plants and trees are good to eat and, where edible, make excellent energy foods, but you should be aware that some nuts and berries that are good to eat may closely resemble others that are poisonous. A good example is the sweet chestnut, which is delicious roasted, and the horse chestnut, which is inedible. Sweet chestnuts are easily recognizable by their spiny, hedgehog-like husks.

Many tropical fruits look inviting when ripe, and you may even see animals eating them, but you should not regard anything as safe unless you know exactly what it is.

If you have children with you, don't let them pick fruits on their own. If they do make a mistake, they will be more severely affected by any toxin.

▲ *Mangroves are vibrant tree-based habitats that attract a vast array of wildlife, from fish and molluscs to birds and reptilians. They do conceal certain hazards, however.*

▲ *Horse chestnuts, or conkers, are poisonous and should never be confused with the sweet chestnut. If in any doubt at all, do not eat.*

COOKING SWEET CHESTNUTS

1 Slit the skins of the chestnuts to stop them bursting as they heat up, then tip them into a pan of boiling water and cook for about 20 minutes.

2 Drain the chestnuts and peel off the outer skins as soon as they are cool enough to handle. You may need a knife to peel off the inner skin.

Natural hazards: wildlife

Depending on where you will be travelling, you may come across any number of wild animals, reptiles, insects and sealife, all of which could harm or even kill you. Taking sensible precautions, including vaccinations, being aware of the creatures' habits, and staying alert to the dangers will help to protect you against attacks.

MAMMALS

All wild mammals will avoid human contact and will attack only if they feel they are in danger, if you startle or frighten them and do not allow them a means of escape. Most attacks happen when humans encounter animals accidentally, so it makes sense to create plenty of noise and let them know you are in the vicinity.

Females can be just as aggressive as males, and are far more so when they are protecting their young. The sensible course is to avoid getting too close to any wild mammal and never to try to touch them – especially foxes, deer, bears and large cats.

Bears will not seek you out, but may be attracted to your camp if they smell your food. Keep everything edible well

▲ *All female animals will defend their young, and in the case of lionesses this can make them very dangerous indeed.*

sealed and away from your tent to avoid tempting them. See page 246 for advice on handling a bear attack.

If a large predator does start to approach you, you should retreat slowly to safety. Do not turn and run away, as this may trigger its instinct to chase after its prey.

SNAKES

A snake will attack a person only if stood on or threatened, and then only if it cannot get away. Many snakes hunt at night, so always carry a flashlight if you are walking around in the dark.

▲ *The hippopotamus inhabits African waters and will attack humans if it cannot see another way of escaping from them.*

RABIES

In countries where rabies is still prevalent, domestic animals as well as wild animals can be infected. The main symptoms of rabies are excessive salivation and irritable and aggressive behaviour. Have the vaccination before you travel and avoid touching any animal.

▼ *Brown bears are more likely to avoid you than to attack, but a female may become aggressive if she is defending her cub.*

▼ *Deer are usually retiring, but mature stags become aggressive during the mating season and should not be approached.*

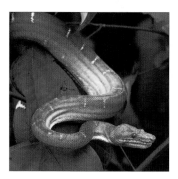

▲ *As snakes feed on rodents they are a useful means of pest control. They pose a threat to humans only if disturbed.*

▲ *Learn about the snake species that are native to the area you are travelling in, and be aware of where you may find them.*

▲ *Even if you are confident that a snake species is not venomous, you should always leave the handling of snakes to an expert.*

There are far more non-venomous snakes than venomous ones. Constricting snakes are not venomous but can give a nasty bite, which will often become infected. Only the largest constrictors, including boas and anacondas, would attack humans. See Treating snake bites, page 248.

LARGE REPTILES

Only the largest lizards, such as the Nile monitor lizard and the Komodo dragon of Indonesia, are a threat to humans. Crocodiles, found in the tropical fresh waters of Africa, Asia and Australia, are extremely dangerous and should always be avoided if seen as many are capable of moving at high speed. See page 247 for the best course of action if you are attacked.

▼ *The estuarine crocodile of South-east Asia and northern Australia is the largest and most dangerous member of the family.*

INSECTS

The mosquito carries a number of diseases, including malaria and yellow fever. In addition to the protection offered by vaccination, you should dress appropriately, sleep under nets and use a good mosquito repellent when travelling in tropical regions.

Bees, wasps and hornets can be life-threatening if you develop an allergic reaction when stung, or disturb a nest and are stung many times. Make sure you do not camp near their nests.

Ticks, mites, lice, flies, tapeworms and roundworms can cause discomfort at best and illness at worst. Avoid walking barefoot and don't sit or camp where livestock have been. Scorpions and poisonous spiders are indigenous to South America, Africa, Asia and

▼ *In tropical areas, check before you sit down or put your foot into a shoe: scorpions like dry, dark places and may surprise you.*

Australia. Be on your guard, look at what you are picking up and where you are sitting. They are usually encountered hiding in shoes and clothing. See pages 248–9 for advice on how to deal with the various threats posed by insects.

WATER CREATURES

Stonefish fire venom from their dorsal fins if you stand on them, and their sting can be lethal. Box jellyfish are equally dangerous: they are hard to see in the water, and usually sting swimmers who brush up against their tentacles unknowingly. Sharks are native to temperate and tropical waters. The great white has a fearsome reputation, but this is often because humans are mistaken for seals.

▼ *Jellyfish are found worldwide: beaches littered with dead jellyfish bodies will indicate a swarm in that stretch of coast.*

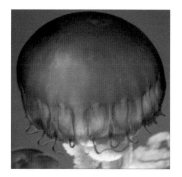

Surviving wild animal attacks

Most stories about the dangers of large mammals are sensationalized and very few people are threatened by them, even in the wilderness. However, most mammals will fight if cornered, threatened or protecting their young. Lone herd animals like elephants, rhinos and buffalo – perhaps self-exiled or driven away by their fellows – are unpredictable animals and may be inexplicably aggressive. If stalked or attacked by a wild animal, your reaction to the threat may greatly improve your chances of survival.

BEARS

There are a number of different types of bear, and much of the received wisdom about the differences in their behaviour appears to be unreliable. It's wise therefore to consider all bears as very dangerous animals. Polar bears will hunt and eat humans and are practically invincible unless you have a powerful firearm, but sometimes they will be scared off by loud noises. Other bears do not predate upon humans and will only attack if they feel threatened, or if they are competing for food. Therefore, don't have food or sweet-smelling items

▼ *Never surprise a bear – on the trail let them know you're around by talking, singing or clapping loudly. If you do find one confronting you, let him know you know he's the alpha male. Don't look aggressive. If a bear is trying to intimidate you, be intimidated. Remain calm and unstressed, appear submissive, and make soothing noises if you can.*

MAKING A BEAR BAGGY

1 Throw your rope over a high branch of a solid tree, and get hold of both ends. It may help to weight the end of the rope or use a specialist throw line.

3 Haul the bag until it is 4.5–6m/ 15–20ft off the ground. Stand to one side of the branch so you don't pull the rope off the end or get it snagged.

2 Tie your food stash to one end of the rope. Try to keep the package sealed to avoid unwelcome interest from fauna of all kinds.

4 Tie off the loose end of the rope to the tree trunk using a reliable knot (see Useful Knots, pages 196–201) that won't come undone with tugging.

in the open in bear country, don't approach bears, and don't approach carcasses of other animals that a bear might regard as dinner.

If you are approached by a bear, remain calm and motionless and make soothing noises if you can. Don't ever try to outrun a bear as it can cover 50m/55yd in three seconds from standing. If it attacks, try to scare it off with loud noises or pepper spray if you have these options. Otherwise, curl up

in a ball and wait for the bear to accept that you are no longer a threat. It may attack your prone form anyway, but play dead at all costs.

DOGS AND OTHER CANINES

Canine animals come in many guises around the world, including dogs, wolves, hyenas, dingos and jackals. Their bites are generally infected with bacteria and parasites and they may carry rabies, which is usually fatal.

BEAR BAGGY VARIATION

1 You need about 15–20m/50–65ft of strong rope or nylon cord. Select two sturdy trees at least 3m/10ft apart from any vertical support and at least 3.5m/12ft tall. Tie one end of rope to a tree. The other end is for lowering/raising.

2 Tie a loop in the rope to connect the food bag securely. Then, with a rock or stone tied to the loose end, fling the rope over a branch of the second tree and pull. This will raise the food at least 3.5m/12ft off the ground.

Despite what you may feel, these animals don't as a rule predate upon humans, but they do fight in defence of territory, their young, or their status. Their aim is to win a power game, not to inflict damage. The bites inflicted by canines under these circumstances are more like nips and lack the ferocity of a full-on attack. An appropriate reaction, like leaving the scene – which removes the threat to their territory – will usually be enough to make them back off. An excessive reaction that threatens the life of the canine may cause an escalation of violence as the animal switches to full fight mode. It then applies as much force as it can with the only weapons it has, basically four small canine teeth driven by powerful jaws and strong neck muscles.

FIGHTING BACK

If any dog, particularly a hunting animal like a wolf, adopts a full fighting approach, your reaction must be extreme. If you attempt to flee the animal will bring you down, constantly improve its grip, and shake its head to inflict maximum pain and damage, until the trauma overcomes you.

Fight back aggressively. If it has your arm in its mouth, slam your arm to the back of its jaws. Use the gripping, squeezing technique shown left to inflict sufficient pain and stress on the animal to make it give up and retreat, allowing you to escape. If you don't do this with conviction, the wolf will quickly regrip, moving the bite to a more critical or damaging area. Finally, the wolf will begin to shake its head violently, causing more damage, blood loss, and ultimately death. It is therefore important that your grip on the animal is out of range of its jaws and very powerful. If it does have a part of you in its mouth, you should continue to try to squeeze and crush it.

CROCODILES AND ALLIGATORS

If you are attacked on land punch, kick and poke with anything to hand (including your fist) at the eyes and nose. Punching the nose might also get it to release its grip on you. In the water you must prevent it from rolling you over underwater and drowning you – its normal killer blow. Try to keep its mouth shut so it can't hold, shake or crush you, and try to pull away.

▼ *Canines are fast and aggressive, with sharp teeth. More often their approach is part of a complex power game and you can gain the upper hand without conflict.*

▼ *If you have to fight a wolf or aggressive dog, turn it around so you're grasping it across its back before squeezing its body as hard as you can with your arms and legs. This may encourage it to back down.*

BIG CATS

Unlike canines, big cats have the additional weapons of dexterous and powerful limbs and claws, making them powerful predators. If a big cat were to attack you, you wouldn't stand a chance without a firearm or similar weapon. If you should meet a big cat on your travels do not run. Keep still, facing the animal, and make yourself as "big" and imposing as you can. Extend your arms and raise your jacket over your shoulders. If your size looks imposing this may deter the cat. Don't crouch or show fear as the cat will pick up your defencelessness.

HIPPOS

Stay away from hippos at all costs as they are far more dangerous than most of the scarier looking animals we all fear. They might not be predators but they are vicious fighters and commonly attack people, overturning boats, especially when with their young. They weigh up to 3,600kg/8,000lb and can gallop at 30kph/18mph, which is fast enough to catch you. The one consolation is that they can't jump, so that might give you some escape plan.

SNAKES

Most snakes are not venomous but all can inflict a nasty bite. In addition, some are powerful constrictors. No snake will go out of its way to hunt humans but most will fight if cornered or threatened. The usual cause of an

attack is when we stumble over them unawares. This can be avoided by making a noise to alert the snake of our presence and taking care not to disturb holes and trees where they might nest.

The striking distance of snakes is usually exaggerated – they can rarely manage more than half their length, less for a large snake. Even a 3.5m/12ft cobra will only strike over a 1m/3ft range. Although snakes have astonishing reflexes and lightning-quick strikes, they cannot outpace a running man.

SURVIVING A SNAKEBITE

Under half of all bites from poisonous snakes actually inject venom, but you should assume the worst. If possible, someone should kill the snake for later

▲ *Aggressive behaviour may simply be territorial defence if you're lucky. Back off slowly, facing the cat.*

identification. Try to keep the victim calm as this will slow the spread of venom more than anything. If you have one, attempt to suck out the poison with a venom pump, though opinion is divided over whether these actually work. Trying to suck out the venom orally is harmless to the person doing it but almost certainly ineffective. Don't cut the wound, which only exposes more blood vessels to the venom.

If, by the time you act, the victim has become envenomated (poison has spread through the bloodstream), he or she is likely to die unless medical attention is received. Tingling, facial numbness, cramp, palpitations or breathing problems are all indicators of possible envenomation – however, these could also be symptoms of the shock and anxiety associated with the attack.

The best chance of survival is to get the victim to hospital, ideally with the dead snake. A hospital may have the right antivenins, which are snake-specific and need to be refrigerated so are unavailable in the field.

Beware of snakes in cars. It is common for them to curl up in the engine bay or passenger compartment, then become startled by human intervention and respond aggressively. Always check for unwanted hitchers.

DEALING WITH SNAKEBITES

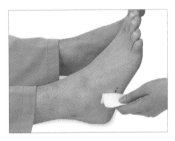

1 The distinctive twin pinholes of a snakebite. Angle the body so that the bite is below the victim's heart so that any venom has to travel "uphill".

2 Assume it is venomous even if it isn't. Clean away any excess venom, and immobilize the affected area. If you can, take the victim to hospital.

INSECTS

Multiple stings from a swarm of bees, wasps or hornets can be fatal to humans, and even a single sting can in some people cause a massive and, if untreated, lethal allergic reaction (see anaphylactic shock, below). If you are being attacked, plunge through dense undergrowth or vegetation in order to brush away the insects. Bee stings break off in the wound and should be removed as soon as possible. Other types of sting do not, but this allows the insect to sting repeatedly.

Other dangerous stinging insects include some caterpillars that have stinging hair, and certain types of ant. Bulldog ants found mainly in Australasia have particularly nasty stings, and a Tasmanian variety of these called the "Jackjumper" is known to cause potentially lethal allergic reactions in many people, even those not normally allergic to insect venom (see anaphylactic shock). African driver ants, known locally as "Siafu", do not have a sting but a vicious non-toxic bite, and swarms of them will attempt to eat almost any animal. Humans attacked by large numbers of them usually die by suffocation after their lungs have been invaded by thousands of ants. The best protection from ants is to drive them away with fire.

The stings of almost all insects can be treated with moist tobacco, ammonia or a paste of baking powder. These remedies also work for stings

▲ *Remove leeches with a hot flame or salt. Remove the whole animal. Clean thoroughly with antiseptic.*

from scorpions and other invertebrates. Scorpions have a sting in their tail and are quite aggressive. Most of them are fairly harmless, but some do have a powerful sting that can cause illness and even death. Always shake out your bedding, clothes and boots before use and pack them away as soon as you have finished with them. The venom of scorpions can be sucked out more effectively than that of snakes. In the tropics, apply coconut meat to the infected area.

ANAPHYLACTIC SHOCK

Some bites or stings (such as wasp venom) can cause anaphylactic shock, a severe and sometimes fatal allergic reaction. The symptoms are breathing difficulties, fainting, itching, swelling of the throat or other mucous membranes and a sudden drop in blood pressure.

These reactions are often so severe as to be fatal. Treatment is an appropriately dosed adrenaline (epinephrine) injection – if the casualty is prone to such attacks, he or she may be carrying an auto-injector.

TICK-BORNE DISEASES

The most common (and most often ignored) danger from insects in temperate climates comes from ticks. They carry various diseases but Lyme disease is the one to watch out for. In most places the risk is low, but up to one third of ticks in the USA carry it.

Once on your body, the tick will dig into your skin to feed on your blood. After about 12 hours it will release its barb by injecting saliva to dissolve the tissue around the bite. It is this saliva that may contain bacteria or viruses.

If you contract Lyme disease you may or may not find a "bull's-eye-like" rash, which is usually not itchy, and you may have flu-like symptoms such as headache, fever, stiff neck and sore joints. If the infection spreads, it can affect the heart, nervous system and joints. In some cases it can ultimately be fatal. Treatment is with antibiotics; there is no vaccine.

Remove a tick as soon as you spot it and don't leave it to fall off by itself. In high-risk areas, check for ticks every 12 hours. Burning it off with a cigarette will only encourage the tick to inject saliva. Instead, grab it with tweezers and pull it straight out.

▲ *Using a branch or long stick to thrash in front of you will flush out snakes in thickets. Watch where you put your hands.*

▲ *If you are chased by a swarm put your shirt or jacket over your head as that's where they'll try to sting you. Run for cover.*

▲ *Do not jump into a pool or running water. The swarm will just hover and sting you as you surface.*

Understanding the weather

When planning a trip, the weather can be of vital importance, so it is sensible to learn what all the terms and symbols shown on a weather map and referred to on a radio forecast mean. Knowing the highest and lowest temperatures for the area you are travelling to, and the expected rainfall for each month, is also very useful.

ISOBARS

Meteorologists measure the atmospheric pressure at internationally agreed times, every three hours. After plotting these readings on maps, they draw lines known as isobars, which link places of equal pressure.

The closer these lines are to each other, the higher the wind speed will be, because they show that the pressure values are changing quickly over a relatively small area. The isobars on a chart form the shapes of concentric rings which indicate areas of low pressure (depressions or cyclones) and high pressure (anticyclones).

▼ *Low-pressure areas, indicated by closely spaced concentric circles of isobars, are often associated with warm or cold fronts.*

FRONTS

A weather front is marked as a heavy line on the chart, with either small triangles (a cold front) or semicircles (a warm front) on it. A front marks the edges of air masses of different origins and at different temperatures.

A warm front indicates that warm air is advancing and rising over cold air. This usually leads to a bout of heavy rain, followed by a rise in temperature. A cold front shows that cold air is replacing warm air at ground level. This leads to a short spell of heavy rain followed by much brighter weather with showers and gusty winds.

DEPRESSIONS

These may be described as low-pressure areas or cyclones in the northern hemisphere. When pressure falls, the winds blow in an anticlockwise direction (clockwise in the southern hemisphere), often bringing rain.

ANTICYCLONES, OR HIGHS

In anticyclones, winds blow clockwise in the northern and anticlockwise in the southern hemispheres. They are indicated on a weather chart by areas

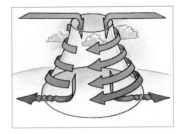

▲ *In an anticyclone, air is descending, compressing and warming. Clouds tend to evaporate and winds are generally light.*

▼ *In a depression, air is rising, expanding and cooling. Water vapour condenses, forming clouds and leading to rain or snow.*

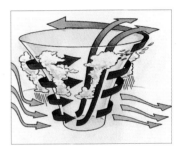

of widely spaced isobars. The pressure is high and the winds are light. Highs bring sunny weather in summer, cold and foggy conditions in winter.

WIND

The speed of winds is measured in knots, but a system called the Beaufort scale is also used to describe the kind of wind indicated by the wind speed.

Regarding wind temperature, as a general rule, summer winds that have come over a landmass will be warmer and drier than those that have come over the sea. In winter, winds that have travelled over a large landmass will be colder than those that have travelled over the sea. In the northern hemisphere, winds from the north will be colder than those from the south, and in the southern hemisphere the reverse is true.

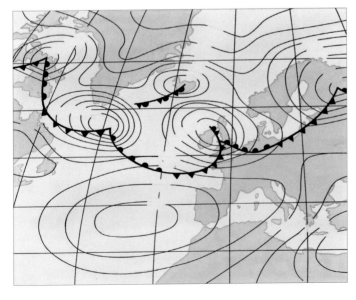

▲ *Cirrocumulus clouds signify a blue sky and fair weather. They often follow a storm.*

▲ *Altocumulus clouds predict fair weather. They will often follow a storm shower.*

▲ *Cumulus clouds indicate fair weather if widely separated; they may produce showers.*

▲ *Stratocumulus clouds covering the sky mean light showers which dissipate quickly.*

▲ *Heavy rain or snow is signified by the dark low cloud cover known as nimbostratus.*

▲ *Stratus clouds look like hill fog. Although not a rain cloud they can produce drizzle.*

BEAUFORT SCALE OF WIND FORCE

Beaufort number	General description	Sea criterion	Landsman's criterion	Velocity in knots
0	Calm	Sea like a mirror	Calm; smoke rises vertically	Less than 1
1	Light air	Ripples with appearance of scales form but without foam crests	Direction of wind shown by smoke drift but not wind vanes	1–3
2	Light breeze	Small wavelets, short but pronounced; crests look glassy and do not break	Wind felt on face; leaves rustle; ordinary vanes moved by wind	4–6
3	Gentle breeze	Large wavelets; crests begin to break; foam of glassy appearance; scattered white horses	Leaves and small twigs in constant motion; wind extends light flags	7–10
4	Moderate breeze	Small waves become longer; fairly frequent white horses	Raises dust and loose paper; small branches are moved	11–16
5	Fresh breeze	Moderate waves take pronounced form; many white horses; chance of spray	Small trees in leaf begin to sway; crested wavelets form on inland waters	17–21
6	Strong breeze	Large waves form; white foam crests more extensive; probably spray	Large branches in motion; whistling in telegraph wires; umbrellas used with difficulty	22–27
7	Near gale	Sea heaps up and white foam from breaking waves is blown in streaks in direction of wind	Whole trees in motion; inconvenience felt when walking against wind	28–33
8	Gale	Moderately high waves of greater length; edges of crests break into spindrift; foam is blown in well-marked streaks	Breaks twigs off trees; impedes progress when walking	34–40
9	Strong gale	High waves; dense streaks of foam along direction of wind; wave crests topple; spray may affect visibility	Slight structural damage (chimney pots and slates removed)	41–47
10	Storm	Very high waves with long overhanging crests; foam in great patches is blown in dense streaks along wind direction; surface takes on white appearance; visibility affected	Trees uprooted; considerable structural damage occurs	48–55

Hot weather

A basic understanding of the weather is invaluable when you are pursuing any kind of outdoor activity, but you also need to know what to do in extreme environmental conditions. It is not always obvious how to respond to extreme heat and humidity, or to lightning, and many people end up endangering themselves by doing the wrong thing.

In many hot countries, all the weather is extreme. When it rains, very large amounts of water can be deposited in a short space of time. When the wind blows, it is with destructive force. Of course the sun can burn your skin in a short time, even (in fact sometimes especially) on overcast days.

You must always remember that in some places there are large temperature variations. Maritime climates (that is, in places near the sea) can have a fairly constant temperature day and night. In contrast, in the central areas of large continents the temperature may be 40°C/104°F or higher in the daytime but drop below 0°C/32°F at night.

SUN

Prolonged exposure to the sun in any climate will lead you to suffer from sunburn, especially at high altitude or in the tropics or in ozone depleted regions like the Antarctic on the tip of South America. Wear appropriate clothing, sunscreen and/or sunblock to protect your skin. The short-term effects of sunburn can be painful, and the long-term ones fatal, so you must simply not allow it to happen.

HYDRATION

In a hot and humid environment, such as a rainforest or during a monsoon season, your biggest danger is heatstroke and/or dehydration, although you may be surrounded by water. You will be perspiring at the maximum rate possible for your body, but the perspiration will not evaporate from your skin in the 100 per cent humidity. This means that your body does not cool down, so it

continues to sweat as much as it can to try to achieve this. But it makes no difference to your temperature and you lose water at an incredible rate. All you can do in this situation is keep drinking the coldest water you can safely use, to keep hydrated and try to reduce your core temperature.

STORMS

You should find out about and understand any predictable local weather conditions. In hot climates, storms often occur nearly every day as the land heats up, and you should take care not to be caught out. Especially avoid being on the water in a boat, whether travelling by canoe on a lake,

▲ *A cyclone is a funnel of whirling wind that produces extremely low pressure at its base, which acts like a giant vacuum cleaner.*

or at sea. If you are caught by a storm while afloat, tie everything down and try to keep the centre of gravity of the boat as low as possible. In the event of a wreck or capsize, try to stay with your craft if you can.

You can often predict the onset of electrical storms by the presence of cumulonimbus and anvil clouds, often massing together. Beware if you find yourself downwind of these cloud formations – this means the storm is coming your way. Storms triggered by heat tend to hit in the afternoon or early evening, but they can happen at any time. Such storms often bring with them heavy rain or hailstones.

Even if lightning is not hitting the ground and endangering personnel, you should be aware that electrical activity in a storm can damage navigation gear such as GPS, and knock out communications equipment, so this could endanger your party.

Lightning

If you are out in the open space of a desert or savanna, a lightning storm can be very impressive but it is also very dangerous. If the lightning is very close and you feel you are in danger of being struck, crouch down, with your head as low as possible, and put your hands over your head.

You are in more danger from lightning if you are near trees or any upward pointing object. You are also in great danger if you are on water. Surprisingly, however, on land you are safer in the open, as long as you curl up as described. One of the safest places to be is in a car.

Bushfires

Lightning is frequently the cause of bushfires. If one starts near you, or is coming towards you, and you cannot get out of the way, find an open space and consider burning your own firebreak, but remember that fire can jump quite large distances. If you have to escape a fire, remember that it travels upwards: rather than going up to a ridge, stay down in a valley.

Be warned that the fire will flush out all sorts of animal life, so be careful of snakes and larger animals being forced out to share your space. If the fire is near your camp, make sure you get well away from all gas canisters and similar inflammable materials.

Hurricanes, tornadoes and typhoons

There is little you can do in the face of storms of this magnitude, except to hide from them. Don't stay inside a building that could be destroyed by the storm. The best protection is a safe basement of a very solid construction.

Dust and sandstorms

Desert areas are normally windy places, but if the wind becomes strong enough, it starts picking up first the surface dust and then, as it gets stronger, particles of sand. These storms can last from a few hours to a number of days, and if you are caught in one you can become disoriented. In any area where you are going to encounter blowing sand and dust, make sure your eyes and ears are protected with goggles and maybe a headscarf or headdress.

Driving can become very dangerous, as you will be disoriented and unable to see where you are driving. You should stop and park the vehicle with the engine facing away from the prevailing wind. Close all heating/ air-conditioning vents to stop the sand being drawn inside the vehicle.

If you are with animals, turn their backs to the wind while you sit out the storm. Camels should sit down, but horses, mules and donkeys will stand.

▼ *If lightning is striking the ground near you during a storm, don't be tempted to shelter under trees as they may be struck.*

SEASONAL EFFECTS

Many tropical countries have very distinct wet and dry seasons, and transport and logistics may be affected in the wet season due to roads and bridges being washed away, and routes blocked by landslides.

Rain

A violent downpour on dry, baked land may have effects some 36–54km/ 20–30 miles away. The rain will run off into a dried-up river system that may have been dry for many months, and can turn it into a raging torrent in just a few hours.

This can be very dangerous if you are camped or are walking in a dried-up watercourse. It may be that no rain has fallen where you are and you will therefore not expect a flood.

Mud and landslides

Landslides may be the result of heavy rain and they can be even more destructive than a flood. If it is still raining, never try to walk or drive through one, since where one slide has happened, another can follow.

Cold weather

If you are travelling in or to countries where the temperature rarely rises above freezing, such as those in polar regions at any time, at high altitude, or inshore in very large continents during the winter, you must know how to survive in blizzards, avoid avalanches, and move safely across snow and ice.

Intense cold can damage the lining of the lungs, so always cover your nose and mouth and breathe through a scarf or something similar so that the air is slightly warmed before you inhale it. You are also in danger from hypothermia and frostbite, so make sure all your clothing and equipment is up to scratch.

BLIZZARDS
In a blizzard, heavy snow is accompanied by strong winds. In extreme cases, the driven snow fills the air and can reduce visibility to less than a metre/yard. It can also cause drifting and very quickly build up large drifts, which can close roads and even cover tents or buildings.

If you are caught in a blizzard, always seek shelter and be prepared to sit it out, even though this may take several days. If you are inside a tent when the blizzard strikes, you may have

▲ *Fast-falling snow quickly transforms the landscape, and if it is combined with a high wind, deep drifts can soon build up.*

to dig your tent out occasionally to stop the weight of snow from collapsing it. Also, make sure the snow is not blocking up your ventilation, as people have suffocated in tents or snow holes when the snow has blocked the door or ventilation holes.

AVALANCHES
There are two main types of avalanche: powder snow and slab. Powder snow avalanches usually consist of newly fallen snow and can be very destructive, mowing down whole forests and villages. Slab avalanches are particularly liable to fall in the spring melt. They move more slowly at the edges and the base than in the centre. They also can be very destructive and their weight can crush anything in their path.

Before you visit a cold country, you should find out if the area is prone to avalanches and know what signs to look for that will tell you when there is a high risk of one occurring. These include rapid snowfall, leading to a buildup of more than 30cm/12in new snow, and sudden rises in temperature.

ICE
Be cautious when approaching any expanse of frozen water, as the ice can be anything from 1m/1yd to only a few centimetres/inches thick. If anyone does fall through the ice, they must be got out as soon as possible and treated for hypothermia (see also Cold-weather effects, 258–259). Anybody going to the person's rescue should beware of becoming another casualty.

Remember that thin ice could be covered by snow. When this is possible you will have to make slow careful progress, checking as you go. Walking on skis or snowshoes can reduce your likelihood of breaking the ice.

If you are on steep ground and start to encounter ice, and cannot avoid it, put on a pair of crampons if you have them. If not, pull a spare pair of socks over your boots, which will give more grip than ordinary soles.

Ice can be a hazard for travellers in vehicles as well as on foot. The ice you can see on a road or track is not your greatest problem, however: it is the ice that may be hidden under a light covering of snow or slush that will cause the accident.

▼ *Navigation can be much more difficult when you are travelling through a snowy landscape where visible landmarks are few.*

ALTITUDE

As you gain altitude the air becomes colder. This is because the air pressure is less, and so the air is less compressed. On a clear day the temperature might typically decrease by 1°C/2°F per 100m/330ft of altitude. If you are under or in cloud, this fall might be reduced to about 0.5°C/1°F as a result of the heat that is released by the condensation process.

TEMPERATURE INVERSION

This usually occurs after a clear night in the mountains. The mountain tops become very cold, and this cools the air in contact with them. The air is now heavy, and rolls down the mountain to make the valleys very cold, forcing the warm air of the valley back up the mountains.

SUNBURN

Even in a cold climate prolonged exposure can result in sunburn, especially in ozone-depleted regions such as the Antarctic on the tip of South America, and you should take all usual precautions to protect your skin.

▶ *It is dangerous to approach an iceberg: a boat may be capsized by turbulence if the berg moves, or underwater ice may ram it.*

▼ *Thick snow may mask watercourses, but you should take extreme care when crossing ice in case you fall through and get wet.*

WIND CHILL

Inanimate objects, including thermometers, are not affected by wind chill, so although a thermometer may accurately measure the air temperature, the combined effect of the temperature and the prevailing wind may have a serious effect on the human body, leading to conditions such as hypothermia and frostbite.

Wearing layers of clothing helps to insulate the body, trapping layers of warm air, while cutting down the penetration of the wind and preventing it carrying away heat.

Hot-weather effects

The effects of the heat on those not used to it can be dangerous, ranging from a bad case of sunburn to life-threatening heatstroke. Staying out of the sun, wearing cool cotton clothing and drinking plenty of fluids are good preventive measures. Other threats to the health in tropical countries arise from water-borne diseases, such as bilharzia, which can be contracted from just a splash of water: avoid swimming in rivers and lakes where there may be any danger of infection. You should have all the necessary vaccinations before you travel, but the commonest infections encountered in hot climates are those contracted from contaminated food and drink or mosquito-borne diseases such as malaria.

SUNBURN

If you are overexposed to the sun without adequate protection you risk getting sunburnt, and it can happen

▼ *Treat heat exhaustion before it turns into heatstroke by getting the person to rest in a shady place and cooling them down.*

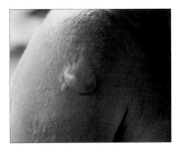

▲ *An extreme case of sunburn can cause blistering of the skin. Treat as you would a burn and seek medical help immediately.*

anywhere: you should always make sure you are well protected. You will be particularly susceptible to sunburn if you are fair-skinned and from a temperate latitude. Those with fair or red hair are most at risk and some parts of the body are particularly vulnerable, such as the nose, the back of the neck and shoulders, a bald scalp and the tops of the feet.

Sunburn can make you extremely uncomfortable and can do lasting damage to your skin, increasing the risk of skin cancer. In more extreme cases, it may mean you are unable to continue your trip, so take it seriously and be prepared.

Treatment If the skin is bright red and sore and feels hot to the touch, get the person out of the sun, either indoors or in the shade. Cool the affected area of skin using cold compresses or by immersing it in cold

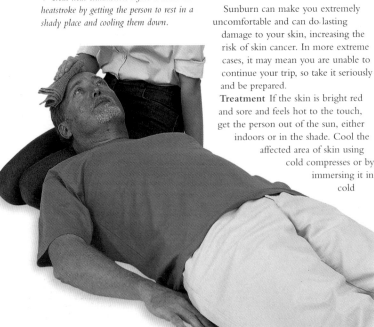

water for at least 10 minutes. Apply calamine lotion or any product that has been designed to soothe and moisturize sunburnt skin (many are now available from pharmacies and drugstores). Give the patient plenty of water to drink and encourage them to lie still, keeping the affected area uncovered, if possible, although a loose cotton covering could be used if preferred. If the skin has blistered, treat in the same way as for a burn and seek medical help.

HEAT EXHAUSTION

This is a particular health risk in hot, humid areas, and people are especially subject to it if they are taking part in strenuous exercise in the sun. It is caused by the loss of salt and water through excessive sweating.

The symptoms of heat exhaustion are headache, dizziness, confusion, nausea and sweating, with clammy skin and rapid breathing.

Treatment Move the person out of the sun to somewhere cool, then lay them down with their feet raised. Raise their head while they drink water, followed by a saline solution (1 tsp salt per litre/1¾ pints water). Always seek medical help.

PROTECTING SKIN FROM BURNS AND BITES

All exposed skin needs to be covered with sunscreen to protect against the burning effects of the sun's UVB rays. But you should also apply it to skin that will be under thin clothing, as it may not be an effective screen against UVA rays, which can cause long-term damage.

The brand of sunscreen you choose needs to give protection against both UVA and UVB rays. Apply it 30 minutes before going outside and re-apply it regularly, even in cloudy weather. Look for a protection factor of at least SPF 25, and at least SPF 40 if you are at altitude, on snow or in water, when you should use a water-resistant brand. The protection factor applies only to the burning UVB rays; UVA protection may be indicated by a star system.

Insect repellent also needs to be applied regularly. The standard chemical repellent is DEET, which is available as a liquid, spray, gel or stick. This guards against all biting insects, including mosquitoes. Take care not to get it near the eyes or mouth – spray it on your hands then apply it to your face with care – and don't get it near cuts or grazes, or apply it to skin that will be covered by your clothing. Insect repellent can also be sprayed on to clothing. If you can't bear the smell of DEET, try using natural plant oils such as citronella, eucalyptus or lavender.

Sleeping under specially designed insect netting at night and wearing clothing made from closely woven fabrics, fitted at the wrists and ankles, can help to minimize the use of chemical repellents.

HEATSTROKE

Formerly called sunstroke, heatstroke can follow heat exhaustion, but it can also come on very quickly, leading to unconsciousness within minutes. It is a serious condition that involves the failure of the body's heat control mechanism and can lead to death if the temperature is not lowered.

The symptoms are similar to those of heat exhaustion, but the body temperature will go over 40°C/104°F and there will be little or no sweating.

SKIN CANCER

It is now established that the risk of skin cancer and skin damage is increased by both exposure to the sun over a long period and episodes of acute sunburn. Moles and pigmented areas of the skin should be examined regularly and you should consult a doctor if you notice changes such as a patch increasing in size, developing an irregular outline, showing variations in colour from brown to black within the area, itching, becoming inflamed or bleeding.

The person will therefore have dry, rather than clammy, skin. They will be very restless, behave irrationally and have a lack of coordination. They may experience headache and delirium, and can become unconscious.

Treatment The priority is to cool the person down quickly. Move them somewhere cool, lay them down and remove their clothing. Cover them with a wet sheet if available, or sponge them with cold water, until their temperature falls to 38°C/100.4°F. Contact the emergency services for help or get the victim to hospital as quickly as possible.

HEAT OR SWEAT RASHES AND PRICKLY HEAT

These complaints of the skin in hot countries are often brought on by tight clothing or where the clothing rubs the skin. They can be avoided by wearing loose-fitting clothes of pure cotton, taking frequent cool showers without using soap and drying the body carefully. If rashes do flare up, soothe them with calamine lotion.

TRAVELLER'S DIARRHOEA

This is usually caused by food poisoning, eating unusual foods or drinking contaminated water, and may be accompanied by vomiting. Symptoms will usually pass within a few hours, but if they continue, or the person starts to pass blood and has a fever, seek medical help.

Treatment Encourage the person to drink plenty of fluids, including rehydrating solutions, to ward off dehydration caused by fluid loss.

▲ *Heat exhaustion is caused by the loss of salt and dehydration that results from excessive sweating, so the victim should be given water and a weak saline solution to drink.*

Cold-weather effects

The risk of frostbite and hypothermia is always present in cold conditions, and the risk increases if there is a wind blowing, since the wind-chill factor can bring the temperature down still further. The onset of hypothermia is the commonest cause of calls to the emergency rescue services, but snow blindness, sunburn, frostbite and trench foot may also develop in cold conditions.

SNOW BLINDNESS

This is a temporary form of blindness caused by the intensity of the sun's rays on snow or ice. A mild case can cause the eye to become red and inflamed; an extreme case can cause permanent damage to the sight. To avoid snow blindness, wear sunglasses or goggles.

SUNBURN

If you are on snow or ice or at altitude, you are in increased danger of sunburn. The snow and ice can reflect the sun's rays and cause burning of the skin on the nose and chin. You must cover all exposed skin or use a high-factor sunscreen (at least SPF 40) or sun block.
Treatment See the section Hot-weather effects, 256–257.

▼ Offer a hypothermia victim a warm drink such as sweetened tea to raise their body temperature. Do not give alcohol.

FROSTBITE

In icy conditions frostbite can affect any bare skin. All the extremities of the body, such as the face, nose, ears, hands and feet, are most commonly affected. To avoid frostbite, wear loose clothing, mittens rather than gloves, and a woollen balaclava type of headgear. Try to keep your clothing dry and keep moving your fingers and toes to keep the circulation going.

The signs of frostbite are prickling pain and numbness. If you are in a group, work in pairs to check each other's extremities, looking for pale, hard and stiffened skin, changing to white, then blue and finally black.
Treatment Remove gloves or boots, then warm the affected area slowly, either by placing it somewhere warm, such as in the patient's armpit, or putting it in warm water, before bandaging it. Support the limb in a raised position and seek medical help if necessary.

▲ Someone suffering from hypothermia will become confused. Get them to shelter, wrap them in extra layers and stay with them.

TRENCH FOOT

This is caused when the feet are wet for long periods in very cold conditions, from 0–10°C/32–50°F. It can become a serious complaint if the conditions continue for a long time, as the blood vessels can become constricted, cutting off circulation, which could lead to losing a foot or limb through gangrene.

The feet become uncomfortably numb, cold and heavy and the affected area may swell up and feel prickly or tingling. The toes and ankles are stiff and walking is difficult. Trench foot can be prevented by moving around, keeping the feet dry and loosening footwear to allow good circulation. Changing out of wet footwear should be a priority on arrival in camp.
Treatment As for frostbite.

EFFECTS OF ALTITUDE

The various stages of altitude sickness generally affect climbers at different heights:

- Acute mountain sickness (rare below 2,450m/8,000ft): comes on quickly; headache, nausea, dizziness, shortness of breath.
- High-altitude pulmonary oedema (rare below 3,000m/10,000ft): fatigue, dry cough, headache, fever, rapid heartbeat, blue lips.
- High-altitude cerebral oedema (rare below 3,350m/11,000ft): severe headache, noise in chest, lack of coordination, loss of vision, hallucination.

HYPOTHERMIA

Prolonged exposure to the cold, especially in windy and wet conditions, can cause hypothermia, which occurs when the body cools down to a temperature below 35°C/95°F.

As the body temperature falls, the person will start to shiver, then become confused and lethargic and act in strange ways. They will complain of fatigue and may suffer from visual disturbance, slurred speech and cramp. Their skin will be pale and clammy. The final stage of the condition, when the body temperature drops below 26°C/79°F, is unconsciousness followed by death from cardiac arrest. All members of a party must keep checking each other for the symptoms.

To avoid hypothermia, make sure you are well insulated with a protective windproof layer over your warm clothing. You should eat well, drink plenty of water and stay active.

Treatment Wrap the person in a blanket and cover their head. Move them to a sheltered place and put them in a sleeping bag, bivvy bag, space blanket, or anything similar. Call for medical aid or send someone to fetch help, but do not leave the victim alone. Warm them with a hot drink if possible and some easily digested, high-energy food. Keep talking to them to cheer them up. Give mouth-to-mouth resuscitation if they stop breathing.

ALTITUDE SICKNESS

Mountain or altitude sickness can range from a bad headache and sickness to life-threatening pulmonary or cerebral oedema (fluid in the lungs or brain). It is caused by climbing mountains over 3,000m/10,000ft too quickly.

At high altitudes the atmospheric pressure is lower and the air thinner than at ground level, so that less oxygen gets into the bloodstream. The body is able to adjust to this, up to a height of about 5,500m/18,000ft, but it needs time to do so. The first noticeable symptoms are usually breathlessness and a need to slow down, but a more severe attack of altitude sickness may result in severe headache, chest discomfort, loss of appetite, nausea, vomiting, disorientation, confusion, difficulty with balance and a dry cough. Altitude does not have the same effect on people each time they climb: escaping altitude sickness on one expedition does not mean you will avoid it at a later date.

To avoid the condition, you should climb large peaks slowly (no more than 300m/1,000ft a day) even if you are fit enough to ascend more rapidly. If possible spend a few days at a moderate height (around 2,500m/8,200ft) to acclimatize to that level before beginning a further climb. Dehydration aggravates the condition, so it is important to drink plenty of fluids while climbing.

▲ *The extremities are most prone to frostbite in cold conditions. Warm cold, numb hands by placing them in the armpits.*

Treatment If someone starts to show any of the symptoms of altitude sickness, they should be taken down to a lower altitude as fast as possible, especially if the condition comes on very quickly. The symptoms should disappear after a few days, but if they continue to worsen after this partial descent, the victim needs to get medical help urgently as this indicates pulmonary or cerebral oedema.

▼ *A bivvy bag should be carried as part of the basic survival kit. It will help to retain body heat in an emergency situation.*

Dehydration

This occurs when there is insufficient water in the body, or when the body loses large quantities of water quickly and the fluid cannot be replenished. Dehydration is a medical emergency. It can be fatal, and should be treated as soon as the symptoms are noticed.

Severe dehydration can occur with excessive heat and sweating, through a lack of food and fluid intake, or because of prolonged vomiting or diarrhoea. It is very likely to occur through sweating if you are doing strenuous exercise in a hot climate, if climbing at high altitudes, or trekking cross-country. It is particularly common in the elderly, and in infants and young children, often as a result of diarrhoea, when it will occur rapidly.

PREVENTION
To prevent dehydration, you need to drink enough fluids to replace those lost. If the human body loses as little as 10 per cent of its natural fluid level, it can start to shut down and will need hospital treatment to restore its natural balance, with the victim being put on a drip in order to be rehydrated.

If you are sweating a lot, you will be losing not only water but also salt and, in small quantities, a number of the body's trace elements. The salt and

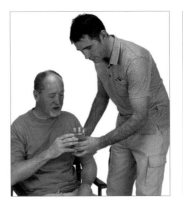

▲ *Encourage the casualty to take small sips of drinking water as soon as they start to notice the effects of dehydration.*

▲ *If you feel deydrated but drinking water is unavailable, loosen or remove clothing and stop your activities to seek shade.*

trace elements need to be replenished as well as the fluids if you are going to continue to function normally.

On average, an adult who is walking or exercising for several hours each day needs to drink at least 3 litres/5¼ pints of fluid in a mild climate, rising to over 6 litres/10½ pints in hot temperatures or if at a high altitude or doing any strenuous physical activity that causes severe sweating. If you drink less than this, you are at risk of dehydration.

SYMPTOMS
An early sign of dehydration is thirst, and in an extreme case you may be unable to quench your thirst no matter how much you drink. Another early symptom is a headache, as the blood vessels in the head constrict due to lack of fluids. Lightheadedness may follow.

You may notice that your urine becomes darker in colour and there is less of it. In the later stages of dehydration, there may be feelings of drowsiness, restlessness and confusion about where you are and what you are doing. Abdominal or muscle cramping are also common.

◄ *Hydration backpacks, ideal for cycling and other endurance sports, contain a water reservoir with a drinking tube attached.*

Treatment
As soon as you notice the symptoms of dehydration in yourself, move indoors or into the shade, and drink as much fluid as you have available or until you no longer feel thirsty. If you suspect a member of your group is dehydrated, encourage them to move to a cooler area and give them something to drink.

What to drink will depend on where you are and what is available. Water alone is not ideal, because it can pass straight through the body. Adding 20–25ml/4–5 tsp of salt and 5ml/1 tsp of sugar per litre/1¾ pints of water is better because it will help to replenish the body's water and salt level. Good alternatives to a sugar and salt solution

SEVERE DEHYDRATION
Seek immediate help for anyone who displays any of the following symptoms due to dehydration:

• Vomiting and/or diarrhoea
• Seizures
• Fast, weak pulse
• Fast breathing
• Sunken eyes
• Lack of tears
• Wrinkled fingers and toes
• Dry mouth

If drinking fluid supplies are limited and you need to stave off thirst, there are steps you can take that will help you handle the psychological effects of thirst. This will allow you to focus more efficiently on sourcing water or fluid supplies.

- Suck on something small and smooth, such as gum, a nut or pebble, or a chunk of raw onion.
- Conserve body fluid and reduce sweating by making only calculated moves. In a hot climate, move in slow motion.
- Regulate your clothing. In a hot climate, reduce sweat evaporation by keeping all skin covered; in a cold climate, reduce sweating by loosing/removing clothing.
- Rest or sleep as often as possible, in the shade in a hot climate.
- Do not eat anything if you have nothing to drink; avoid eating proteins if fluids are limited; eat fruit, sweets, crackers and plants.
- Rub the hands, face and neck with a pad soaked in sea water, urine or alcohol, if available.

include a rehydration solution (available from pharmacies and drugstores) that has to be made up with water, an isotonic glucose drink, flavoured gelatin in liquid form, a carbonated drink that has been allowed to go flat, clear broth or diluted fruit juice. All of these will do the job equally well, but caffeinated drinks should be avoided as they are diuretic and can thus aggravate the problem. Drink at least 200ml/8fl oz of fluid every hour and avoid eating solid foods for 24 hours. Make sure that any water used to make up a water-based drink has been purified and is free from contamination. Otherwise, the bacteria in contaminated water may cause vomiting, and this will further increase the fluid loss.

If a severely dehydrated person cannot or will not take a drink, if the thirst cannot be quenched and the symptoms persist, or if there are any complications, seek medical help.

DEHYDRATION IN CHILDREN

Children suffering from diarrhoea can become dehydrated very quickly. A young child showing symptoms of dehydration, should be given fluids to drink but be careful how much salt you give them: give no salt at all unless they are severely dehydrated, in which case emergency medical help should be sought urgently. For an infant, give as much fluid as they can drink and seek medical help straight away.

VOMITING

If someone is vomiting as a result of dehydration, their condition is serious and you should get medical help. If the vomiting is due to another known cause, such as a digestive upset, but is a potential cause of dehydration, a rehydration solution may help if they can keep it down. Get them to sip the fluid very slowly rather than attempt to drink down a whole water bottle or cup at once, which they may not be able to manage.

A child who is vomiting should be given a small sip (about a teaspoonful) of fluid every 10–20 minutes. You can increase this amount gradually if the fluid stays down.

DIARRHOEA

Mild diarrhoea is characterized by frequent loose, watery bowel movements, and in more severe cases there may also be stomach cramping, tiredness, thirst and/or streaks of blood in or on the stools. Common causes of diarrhoea include food poisoning, certain medications, emotional stress, excessive alcohol consumption, and viral and bacterial infections.

In its mildest form, diarrhoea brings inconvenience and discomfort but it is not dangerous so long as the fluids lost can be replaced. Encourage the individual to drink two glasses of drinking water each time they open their bowels to maintain their level of body fluid.

If the person cannot or will not drink liquids, the replacement of fluids will not be possible and dehydration will result. Hospitalization will then be necessary to restore the body fluids. If the diarrhoea persists for longer than a day or two medical attention should be sought.

▼ *Climbing at high altitudes increases the risk of dehydration. Planning proper water supplies is vital from the outset.*

Surviving acts of nature

Being prepared for an earthquake or hurricane is the best way to survive one. Discuss the possibilities with your family and colleagues so you have a plan if disaster strikes. Always check radio and local area networks (internet) as well for disaster area advice.

EARTHQUAKE

If you are affected by an earthquake, stay calm. Don't run or panic. If you're indoors, stay there. If you are out of doors, remain outside. Most injuries occur as people are entering or exiting buildings. If possible take cover under something that will protect you from being hurt by falling masonry or other building materials or structures – under a table or upturned sofa, or next to a solid wall. Stay away from glass, windows or outside doors. Put out any fires and stay away from utility wires and anything overhead.

    If you're in a car, stop carefully and stay in the vehicle until the shaking ceases. It's a good safe place to be. Do not stop on or under a bridge or flyover, nor under overhead cables or street lights. Look out for fallen debris.

▼ *Earthquakes can shatter constructed objects as easily as natural ones – don't think you are safe anywhere, but in particular avoid bridges and flyovers.*

▲ *Looking down into this volcano's crater we can see a low-energy eruption taking place. A column of steam rises high into the air, and hot ash is billowing out, but there is no sign of an explosion or pyroclastics.*

VOLCANO

Many volcanos are harmless, described by geologists as either extinct or dormant. However, an active volcano always has the potential to erupt and cause catastrophic damage. Most volcanic eruptions are slow affairs, quite unlike the ferocious explosion of Mount St Helens in Washington, USA, in 1980. Usually the eruption produces only slow-moving rivers of ash or lava and a variety of poisonous gases. That makes them extremely dangerous if you are in their path, but relatively easy to escape from. There is also a more insidious danger from vast quantities of odourless carbon monoxide which can collect in still valleys (or basements) and which can lull you into sleep, followed by oxygen deprivation and death.

    Stay away from lava flows even if they seem to have cooled. Move directly away from the volcano and do not shelter in low-lying areas. If a volcano explodes, the land for miles around can be devastated and all landmarks eradicated. You will find yourself stumbling around an unrecognizable, smoking landscape in incredibly severe heat, perhaps being bombed by a variety of pyroclastics (objects, often molten, launched high into the sky by volcanic eruptions).

    The only real form of protection from the latter type of eruption is to have had enough warning not to be in the area when it happens.

▼ *Lava flows may be slow-flowing but they travel with molten intesity. Get well away from the locality.*

Volcanoes usually "grumble" for a long time before erupting, and science can warn of the danger. If you do find yourself there when it happens, all you can do is move directly away from the eruption as fast as possible, using far-away landmarks to help you navigate.

TSUNAMI

On 26 December 2004 an earthquake under the sea in Indonesia triggered a series of deadly waves which fanned out across the Indian Ocean and crashed on to shores – some as high as 20m/65ft – from Asia to Africa, killing over 140,000 people and leaving millions desititute. It brought to everyone's consciousness the word "tsunami", the

Japanese word for tidal wave. They are not in fact caused by the tides but by earthquakes, landslides and volcanic eruptions – anything causing massive displacement of water. A tidal wave is not like an ordinary wave. It is more like a sudden increase in water level spilling across the ocean, and usually has several sequential wave fronts.

If you hear of an earthquake, a tidal wave might well be heading your way from the quake zone. Do not stay in low-lying coastal areas if this occurs. Sometimes the waters recede from the coast minutes before a tidal wave arrives. If this happens, put curiosity aside and run as fast as you can for high ground.

▲ *This tsunami sign warns of a risk. Heed the warning especially if the water suddenly recedes dramatically. Head inland and uphill.*

▲ *A tsunami can occur anywhere in an ocean that has undersea geological movement. The coastline affected might be calm or, as seen here, quite rough water.*

▲ *Before a tsunami the waters will often recede – this is the classic warning signal and the time to run for the hills, not to stroll on to the beach to pick up stranded fish.*

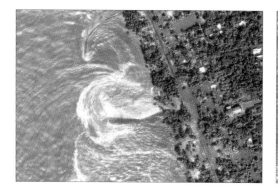

▲ *As the water surges back on to the shore a thousand tonnes of water crashes down on each metre of beach. In this whitewater zone the waves reached 10m/33ft.*

▲ *The water will continue to surge on to the land, moving much farther inshore than any normal tide, floods or storms, and demolishing almost everything in its path.*

FLASH FLOODS

It is important to know whether you are in an area that might be prone to flooding, and how high you are above typical flood levels, so that you are in a position to respond accordingly if a flood warning is issued.

If significant flooding is imminent, do not stack sandbags around the building to keep water out. Water beneath the ground may collect around the foundations and cause the entire building to "float" upwards causing structural damage. It is usually better to allow the flood water into the lower levels of the house. If you know it will flood anyway, consider deliberately flooding the basement to equalize the pressure inside and out.

• Switch off the electricity supply at the main distribution box.

• Store drinking water in clean, sealed containers since the water supply may be contaminated for some time to come.

• Disconnect any electrical appliances that cannot be moved, and decamp upstairs with any other possessions.

▼ *If you have to hang on to a tree or other fixed object in moving water, make sure you do it from the downstream side, as shown.*

▶ *If you have to, you can drive through flooded water. Work out where the shallowest water is – in this case it seems to be on the right, but it pays to check first.*

GROUP CROSSING A FLOODED RIVER

1 Find a place with anchor points (trees or rocks) and let a strong swimmer cross with two ropes. Check for any hidden dangers downstream or upstream.

2 Once across, tie a line between the two banks. The others can now haul their way across the water. A second, hand-held rope gives extra grip.

3 Equipment can be attached to the fixed rope with a karabiner and hauled across in a similar way. Make sure you keep both ends of the haul rope safely at either bank unless the river is narrow enough to throw the gear across.

4 The last member of the party can untie everything from the departure bank and be hauled across safely by the rest of the group. This is the most dangerous part, so this person should be strong and confident in the water.

▲ *Storms of any kind can cause trees or pylons to fall on to buildings, roads or cars. Avoid going out during a storm and keep an eye on vulnerable parts of your house.*

DRIVING THROUGH FLOODS

When driving through flood waters, put the car in low gear and drive very slowly. Try to avoid water splashing up into the engine area of petrol cars and affecting the ignition system. If practical, disconnect any electric cooling fan in the engine bay and remove any low-level mechanical one – this will stop the fans throwing water over the engine. Diesel vehicles are unaffected by water as long as water doesn't enter the engine through the air intake/air filter or the fuel tank through the filler or breather pipe. Be aware of these two. Remember brakes may not work well when wet.

Try to check the depth of water by having someone walk ahead tethered to a rope. A well-sealed car may begin to float in only 60cm/2ft of water – it could be very dangerous if the car starts floating away. Be certain the level is no higher than your knees or a car's wheels.

DEFENSIVE SWIMMING TECHNIQUES

If swimming in fast-moving water, maintain a defensive swimming posture with feet up and downstream (*see below*). Look ahead for obstructions. A current of 5–6.5kmh/3–4mph can pin you irrevocably to railings or fences causing almost certain drowning – be ready to swim out of the way of any such obstructions. Do not try to grab lamp posts or anything similar – you will just hurt yourself. If you're going to hit something try to fend off with your

▲ *You can get on to the roof of your house by going upstairs and pushing off some tiles from the inside – this will be much safer than going outside into the flood waters.*

feet and push around it to one side, whichever way more of the current is going. Wait for an opportunity to swim into an eddy or the safety of shallow water. Do not try to stand unless the water is under 30cm/12in deep.

If possible wear a buoyancy aid (personal flotation device). Do not enter buildings that may be damaged by flooding unless necessary. Do not approach people in trouble in the water until you have calmed them down and ensured that they won't endanger you. It is common for rescuers to be injured or even drowned by relieved victims climbing on them to get out of the water.

TACKLING THE CURRENT

▲ *You need a strong staff to give you triangular support – vital so you don't get carried away by the current.*

▲ *If you get caught in the current go feet-first and keep your head above the water with your feet and backside raised.*

▲ *You are only as secure as your weakest link so be extra vigilant if you use a human chain to pull partners across.*

HURRICANE

Fuelled by the ocean, hurricanes are extremely powerful winds generated by tropical storms moving up the coastline. They do not last long once they begin to swing inland, but they are immensely destructive in coastal areas. If you are living on high ground and have not been instructed to flee, stay indoors. Secure anything that might blow away and board up all windows. If there is a lull in the storm be aware that you might be in the eye of the hurricane and the severity might increase again. Away from home, do not shelter in your car. It would be better to lie in a ditch, but if there is nothing consider hiding under your car.

▲ There is little you can do in the face of a hurricane except to hide from them. Don't stay inside a building that could be destroyed by one, such as this timber-built house.

TORNADO

A tornado is a funnel-shaped storm capable of tremendous destruction with wind speeds of 400kph/250mph or more. Damage paths can extend to 1.6km/1 mile wide and 80km/50 miles long. If you see a tornado, try to move out of its way at right angles to the

▼ The safest place in the wake of a tornado is underground in a tunnel or basement. Outside, get into a ditch or depression to shelter from the wind and flying debris.

▲ In any lightning storm keep away from hill brows, lone boulders, anything tall. Sit on any dry insulation such as rubber-soled shoes. A dry coil of rope is good insulation.

direction it seems to be travelling. Cars, caravans and mobile homes are usually tossed around by tornadoes so head for a more solid shelter. If there is no escape, lie flat, sheltered in a ditch if possible. If you are indoors, follow the same rules as for hurricanes.

LIGHTNING

If caught in an electrical storm, get inside a large building or a vehicle with a metal roof. Don't touch any electrical items. If you can't get to safety, avoid being a vertical pinnacle, or being near to one. Stay low. Get away from open water. Put down objects like walking sticks or golf clubs. Stay away from small sheds or stuctures in open ground. If in a forest, find an area where the trees are small and close together.

If you are hopelessly exposed and feel a build up of energy, tingling spine or hair standing on end, drop to the ground and curl up. Those struck by lightning can be handled immediately. Quick resuscitation is essential – for further advice, see chapter 17 on life-saving first aid. Some people who seem unhurt may need attention later – check everyone for burns at the extremities and near to metal buckles or jewellery.

STORM ACTION

Abnormal weather conditions such as hurricanes and typhoons will be forecast on the radio, television and internet. Heed any advice – in coastal areas you might need to abandon your home and move inland to higher ground. Otherwise stay at home, bring in loose objects from the garden, barricade the windows, put away valuables, and gather together emergency supplies, including water. If the storm hits, head for the basement or under the stairs, or hide under furniture. Keep listening to the forecasts.

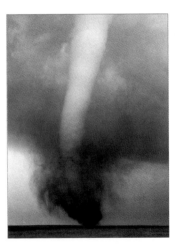

▲ *Lightning and trees don't mix – stay away from them. Make for low, level ground and jettison any metal objects on you.*

▲ *Get out of water fast if there is lightning. Anything wet reduces insulation. If you are trapped bend your head down and hug your knees to your chest.*

FOREST FIRES

In dry forests or brush, do not start any kind of fire or leave optical items like glasses anywhere that could magnify the sun's rays and start a fire. If you see or hear of a fire, try to stay upwind of it and get away.

Do not try to outrun a forest fire if it is close. Make for the nearest water and get into it, keeping yourself soaked and away from anything on shore that might burn. Rocks may become very hot and the water might warm up, but the water will not get hot enough to harm you unless it is a huge fire and a very shallow or stagnant stream or pond. Avoid smoke inhalation by making a mask from some clothing

▲ *Bushfires generate a lot of smoke and people can die from smoke inhalation before the fire front reaches them. It's safer to be in a building than in a vehicle or on foot, and though a building can burn down, cleared ground around the building may survive the passage of the flame front unscathed.*

or similar. The fire may deprive the area of oxygen so remain still and breathe normally to conserve it.

If you cannot get to water, you might try to clear an area around you of flammables. This will only save you in a small bushfire, not a huge forest fire where you need to run for safety. Remember also to stay outside and out of hollows and caves.

ESCAPING FOREST FIRES

1 Check the smoke to see the wind direction and run away from that. The flame front can travel at 8kph/5mph.

2 Head for any natural fire break such as a stream. Stay in the water, where you should be safe from leaping flames.

3 If the fire is getting really close and scorching, lie as low as you can in the stream and stay there for safety.

Natural hazards: landscapes

The best way to protect yourself from any danger is to be aware of how and when it might happen, and to know how to cope if it occurs. Crossing rivers or open water, walking on ice and snow, and exploring caves and forests are all potentially dangerous activities, but a cautious, sensible and informed approach should keep you out of harm's way.

QUICKSAND

What appears at first to be solid ground can trap the unwary. Whether it is boggy ground or a special combination of sand and fine dust in dry areas, it is generically known as quicksand.

Avoid any kind of boggy ground, or if you must cross it, try to step only on substantial plants or rocks. If you do find you are sinking too fast to escape, stop struggling immediately and lie back with your arms spread out. You will almost certainly be able to "float" in this position, with your weight spread evenly, until help arrives; if it feels all right to do so you may be able to swim slowly to more solid ground.

ESCAPING QUICKSAND

In tropical conditions walk with a strong stick or pole – then if you sink in quicksand (sand saturated in water), you can lie on your back on the pole and "relax". Keep your hips on the pole and your body will float as it is less dense than the sand. If you struggle you will sink deeper. Quicksand is rarely deeper than a few feet. Spread yourself out and backreach for dry land.

If you need to cross bogs or quicksand and there is nothing to step on, improvise by using ladders or even backpacks to help spread your weight.

RIVER CROSSINGS

Many people have drowned attempting to cross what appeared to be quite innocuous rivers, and they are far more dangerous than they appear. Check up and down the river for the best place to cross. Remember that if the water is fast-flowing you will not be able to cross water more than knee-deep without roped assistance, unless it

▲ *An active volcano can be a spectacular sight but you should not venture near the crater without consulting local experts.*

is deep enough to swim and not turbulent. To fall down in fast-flowing water when wading is very dangerous. Face downstream on your back and keep your feet up. Do not try to stand up again until the water is so shallow you come to a halt.

▼ *In mountainous terrain, take care to select a site for your camp that is safe from potential rockfalls or avalanches.*

▲ *Despite their obvious appeal to the adventurous, caves can be extremely hazardous places and, if large, deep or complex, should only be entered by experienced cavers, or under supervision.*

▲ *No matter how scenic, the beach can be a dangerous place. Deep water, offshore winds, sea currents and riptides all present real risks.*

If you are trying to walk across a river, check the depth with a stick if necessary, and be extra careful with your footing. Untie the waist belt on your backpack so that you can ditch it, or better still rope the backpacks across the river once someone is safely on each side. Roping people across is good, but you must *never* tie anyone on to the rope – rely on holding/belaying the rope only.

SEA CURRENTS

The currents in the sea are not normally as strong as they can be in rivers, but be aware that they may be too strong to swim against. Currents can be caused by the tide, longshore drift, or other local effects, but make sure you know about them. Ask local people if you don't understand what conditions might prevail. Remember that tidal currents may reverse twice a day, or four times a day in some island environments, and that the combinations of wind with current or wind against current can represent entirely different sea states. For more information, see the section Survival at the seashore, 466–467.

GLACIERS, CREVASSES AND CAVES

You should never be on a glacier unless you are an experienced mountaineer. You must always be roped up in groups of three, and be fully equipped with mountain rescue gear, which you must be practised in deploying in case anyone falls into a crevasse.

If you are entering a cave, you should bear in mind that animals often live in them, and you may be

▼ *Don't pitch tents too close to a river: it may look tranquil in dry weather but rivers can rise very quickly when the rain falls.*

cornering a creature that could become aggressive. Even if you do not meet the inhabitants, a number of diseases can be caught from the droppings of birds, bats and other animals, so be careful what you touch and always wash your hands before handling food.

If the cave is a deep or complex system, use a foolproof system to ensure that you can find your way back out again. And if the cave opens on to the sea be aware of tidal variation. Many people have been trapped when their only escape route has been filled with water by the rising tide.

Surviving arctic conditions

If you travel or trek in arctic or alpine regions, as long as you are able to provide the basics of shelter, heat, water and food – as covered in chapters eight to 11 on bushcraft – you should be able to survive the extreme conditions for days or weeks at a time. Sometimes, though, things go wrong and that's often to do with the surface that you are travelling across giving way.

AVALANCHES
Around 95 per cent of people who are caught in avalanches are caught by a slide triggered by themselves or their group. Avalanches are more likely after recent heavy snow falls or after heavy rain. Be aware of your surroundings and take heed of the obvious warning signs – evidence of recent slides, signs of recent high winds or snow drifting, shooting cracks in the snow and snow collapsing around where you put your weight. If you do get caught out:
- Drop everything and run to one side of the advancing snow.
- Try to use a front crawl-style swimming stroke to keep above the snow as it carries you. Many survivors have said that being caught in an avalanche is similar to being caught in a large wave at the beach.
- Keep your mouth shut to avoid being suffocated.
- Just before you come to a halt, place

your hands over your face and try to create an air pocket.
- If you are buried, the snow around you will probably be packed solid and you won't know which way up you are. If you can, dig a small hole in the snow around you and spit in it. The saliva should head downhill, showing you which direction is up. Then start digging your way out.
- Your best chance of survival comes if somebody has seen where you disappeared under the snow. Sniffer dogs and individual beacons are also effective aids.
- Avalanche beacons are built into a lot of winter sports equipment and

▲ *People on foot on a snow-covered glacier. Crevasses and other hazards abound so they are tied together in threes for optimal safety.*

clothing. Make sure you have one if you are going off-piste or into the backcountry.

INJURIES IN ICY CONDITIONS
Blood loss is more severe in cold weather since the blood runs thinner and takes a long time to clot. Also, loss of blood is an even more serious matter since it is blood that carries heat around the body. You can bandage wounds to check the bleeding, but loosen these as soon as possible in case

▲ *If an avalanche overtakes you, swim with it just as though it were a surge of water, battling to stay near the surface at all times.*

▲ *Beware of slopes of about 40 degrees. Snow does not gather on slopes steeper than 50 degrees while lesser slopes are more stable.*

▲ *Never ski off-piste without checking the local avalanche forecasts for your area, and never ski alone.*

of frostbite. If you can, elevate the wound and apply direct pressure to stop any bleeding. In extreme cases of bleeding from a limb, if you cannot stop the bleeding you must make the difficult decision to apply a tourniquet and accept that this may result in the loss of the limb due to frostbite and lack of blood.

Survivors in freezing conditions can become dehydrated just as easily as they do in hot ones. Although there is fresh water all around in the form of ice and snow, the obstacle is often the energy required to gather enough, or the lack of fuel to melt it. Do not simply eat handfuls of snow since this will cause further dehydration rather than curing

it. Any dark surface that absorbs solar heat can be used to melt ice and snow without using precious fuel. Try to arrange it so that the melt water drains into a container ready for use.

CROSSING ICE

Take care when crossing or walking on ice. That seasonally frozen-over lake or canal might appear strong and easily capable of taking your weight, but it only needs one weak spot for you to find yourself in bitterly cold water, which can knock the breath out of you, put you into a spasm and sap your strength within minutes. If things go wrong, follow the advice below.

▲ *If you fall into freezing water move as swiftly as you can for land. Roll on the ground to absorb the icy water. Change into several layers of dry kit.*

ESCAPING FROM ICE

1 If you fall through ice, you will be knocked out of breath and your body will curl up with shock. It's important to get your arms and chest out quickly.

2 If the ice is cracking, don't load one spot with your hands or elbows. Stretch your arms out wide, keep flat to the ice and try to roll out.

3 If you manage to free yourself, stay flat on the ice and drag yourself clear, making sure that you don't put too much weight on one spot.

4 If you can't free yourself, shout for help. You can survive for 15-20 minutes, so don't panic. Any rescue must be from the lake's edge.

DRESSING FOR EXTREMES

Don't run the risk of being underdressed in freezing or heavy snow conditions. If you find that you must go out, dress apropriately:

- Several thin layers of clothing is better than one thick layer since it allows you to control the temperature by adding or removing layers.
- Inner layers should be insulating materials, while outer layers should be wind- and waterproof.
- Do not wear tight base layers as these hamper blood circulation and reduce the amount of warm air that can be trapped next to the body.
- Wear a lot of socks. If your boots aren't big enough to allow this it might be better to improvise some footwear that does allow a lot of insulation to be worn.
- Keep clothes dry so that they can serve their intended purpose: to maintain body temperature by insulating it from the cold.
- Don't allow yourself to get too hot. If you sweat profusely you will get very cold as soon as you start to perspire.
- Keep your hands head and feet protected from the cold at all costs. Do not take off your hat, gloves or boots outside even if you feel warm enough.

WILDERNESS SKILLS

ADAPTING TO EXTREME TERRITORY

By far the biggest problem people face when thrust into a survival situation is not how to find food or water, but how to cope mentally with the situation. Suddenly they have to rely on their instincts, and a whole range of powerful and conflicting emotions can surface. Psychologists generally agree that there is a classic sequence of reactions to any traumatic event, or variations of those emotions:

• **Shock** You are unprepared for what's just hit you. You have difficulty processing the information.

• **Denial** As a survival mechanism, you may now acknowledge your situation, but you refuse to believe it is true. You continue to say, "No, this can't be happening to me."

• **Anger** You become enraged over your situation. You are upset that things aren't the way they were, and you're scared that you'll never get back to normal.

• **Blame** Blaming others for your situation makes you feel better but makes little rational sense.

• **Depression** This is internalized anger. You search for some way to

▼ The most inhospitable environment can yield clues for survival. Green shrubbery indicates a water source in a desert.

make your stress more manageable.

• **Acceptance** Now you are getting "real". You are facing reality, however wild and remote it appears to be.

• **Moving on** Mentally you begin to redress the balance and think about your situation and how you are going to survive, not just for the next few hours but the next few days and weeks.

▲ Solve each problem as it arises. Once a problem has been fully resolved, you are free to move on to the next issue.

DON'T PANIC

In a survival situation, feelings of helplessness can turn into depression and loneliness very quickly. One of the greatest and most difficult emotional states to deal with is panic. Panic can cause you to perform irrational actions that can worsen the situation you're in. In extreme circumstances, failure to remain calm can even endanger your life, just because you didn't have the presence of mind to make the right decisions. Most of the time, you won't even realize you're panicking.

The first step to beating panic is to recognize the fact that you may panic if you don't take steps to prevent it. When you are in an unnerving situation it is important to take things step by step and to give yourself a chance to assess your situation properly. The second step is to sit down for a moment, take a few deep breaths, and think about your most urgent difficulty. Avoid the trap of adding all your problems one on top of the other until they become one gigantic problem. Rather, concentrate on solving the most pressing dilemma. After this issue is resolved, move on to the next. Take it one step at a time.

MAKE THE MOST OF WHAT IS AROUND YOU

There is a wealth of knowledge that, if applied correctly, could make a dramatic difference to your immediate circumstances and ultimate survival chances. The natural environment can be ferocious, but it can also offer salvation. Even if you are down to the last of your original supplies, you can still make a temporary shelter from materials such as dead wood, dead leaves – even tightly-packed snow. Being able to tell the difference between poisonous and edible plants, knowing where to look for water, or understanding what it takes to get a fire going in just about any terrain or climate could buy you the time you need to work out the next step, or wait for rescue. The important thing is to make your environment as inhabitable, efficient and self-serving as possible. Don't neglect basic principles such as

▲ *In a survival situation with another person or a group, a lot of emotional comfort can be shared between individuals.*

hygiene and safety, even when other priorities seem greater. When things are already tough, unnecessary illnesses caused by poor cleanliness will only undermine strength and morale, just when you need these the most.

SURVIVAL STRATEGIES IN A GROUP, OR WHEN ALONE

There is safety in numbers and obvious physical advantages in having someone else with you, especially if you are injured or weak. But there are other advantages to being in a group when

you are in a survival situation. The greatest is that there are more individuals to take care of the necessary tasks of day-to-day living. Not only do many hands make light work, but the various individuals in the party are bound to have different strengths and weaknesses. If you are someone who is very good at building a shelter but less proficient at finding wild edibles, for instance, being part of a group allows you to put all your efforts into providing an effective group camp, while feeling secure that other people in the group will provide other necessities, such as food, water and fire.

There are also a few disadvantages, however. Now you have to provide not only for yourself, but for the whole group. If you are the only one with any survival skills, or if there aren't many supplies available, it can be very hard to ensure that the whole group is well hydrated, fed and comfortable. It may also happen that one member of the group is injured and needs taking care of. As the saying goes, the chain is only as strong as its weakest link. As soon as you can, build a list of group priorities (see left) and discuss these with your companions. This will enable you to evaluate what needs doing most urgently, and by whom. Overall, the sense of purpose generated by a collective strategy will be a real boost to everyone present: put simply, having something to do will detract from the difficulty of the situation.

If you are on your own in the wilderness, one of the most difficult problems to overcome will be loneliness, which can quickly lead to feelings of hopelessness, panic and then desperation. Overcome this by drawing up a list of priorities and sticking to it. Keep focused on the task in hand and drive away negative thoughts whenever they creep into your head. Take strength and confidence from each task you complete. In fact, most of the techniques covered in this part of the book can be performed alone – it is just that some may take a little longer. Wisdom, and a strong mental attitude, will pull you through, even when the odds seem really stacked against you.

GROUP PRIORITIES

Remember these key pointers to ensure that your group is well prepared to face the challenges ahead.
- Choose a leader. This should be the person with the greatest skill, who must be able to carry the responsibility, acting as chairperson rather than as dictator. As leader, you must take responsibility for the situation and organize any tasks that need to be completed; listen to all the ideas the group bring forward and help them come to any decisions that need to be made. Sometimes this may not be possible, and you will have to make decisions and assign tasks, for instance in the case that only one of your group has the relevant knowledge.
- List all the tasks needed to ensure immediate survival and share them out among the group members.

- Find out what each individual's strong points are, so that tasks can be put in the most able hands. Some tasks will have to be done by everyone working together, such as building the group shelter.
- Keep each other up to date on the progress the group is making, and make sure everybody is still OK. Promote a feeling of mutual dependence within the group, so that everyone is there for the whole group and no one feels left out. Make sure that people who have difficulty with certain tasks get help.
- Make an inventory of all the items in everyone's possession. In the case of a crash, try to rescue as much from the wreckage as possible: anything from electrical wires (to use as cordage) to the stuffing in the seats (for insulation).

SHELTER

The first basic requirement of survival is shelter, to protect yourself from the elements. Whether it is to help you survive a single night or for a longer period, a shelter offers you a place in which you can feel safe physically and, just as importantly, psychologically. A good shelter will provide protection against rain, snow, heat and unwelcome wildlife, while allowing you to conserve your body heat and energy and to rest, recuperate and recover. Though the principles of erecting shelters in the wilderness are simple, building one can be hard work. If you try to take shortcuts, your well-being and perhaps your survival may be compromised. If you build your shelter soundly, you will be safe and secure night after night.

Choosing a place to shelter

Finding a place to shelter from the elements should be your first priority in any survival situation. Fire can also give some protection from the elements, but it may be hard to make a fire if you are unequipped. Take the hypothetical example of trekkers in the wilderness who have forgotten this and spend most of the day trying to get a fire going with a bow drill. When they finally realize that their first priority should have been shelter rather than fire, they have spent too much time and energy on trying to make a fire, and no longer have time to build a shelter. They have to spend the night freezing without either a fire or shelter.

SHELTERING NEEDS AND WANTS
If you consider for a moment what you have in a modern house, the list can be overwhelming. Amenities such as flowing water, electricity, toilets and so on make modern life pleasant, but you can survive without them – you don't really *need* them. When thinking about a natural shelter, it is important to distinguish your needs from your wants.

An emergency shelter will normally be small enough to conserve your body heat, and it should be thickly insulated

▼ *If you are travelling across the frozen Arctic tundra, knowing how to build a snow shelter could save your life if you lose your way or there's a sudden snowstorm.*

so heat can't escape and rain can't get in. Conversely, in a hot climate it will need to provide shade from the sun and should be slightly larger with lighter insulation.

When erecting an emergency shelter it is important to preserve energy and time. Ask yourself first, "What are my needs?" The answer is that whatever the environment you find yourself in, you need protection from its extremes. This could mean any of the following:
• cold
• heat
• the sun
• wind
• rain
• dangerous animals
In some circumstances, you may need protection from all of the above. Think about where you site your shelter, and the direction in which it faces, so as to minimize exposure to such extremes.

SHELTER FOR EMOTIONAL SURVIVAL
A shelter can be built entirely with your bare hands, without the need for tools or cordage. A good shelter can keep you alive by conserving your body temperature, so it is not essential to keep a fire alight through the night. Apart from physical safety, it is also emotionally important to have a shelter. It is a place you can call home, where you can sit down to think about your

▲ *If you have no tools, it's possible to make a shelter entirely with your bare hands.*

situation. It is a refuge where you can stay safe in a wild environment. It also gives you a base from where you can venture out to get food, water and fuel.

USING A NATURAL SHELTER
There may be situations where you are forced to find some sort of natural shelter. You may not have time to build anything late in the evening, or you may be ill or weak from hunger.

A natural shelter can be anything in nature that will protect you from the elements. A fallen tree that still has all its leaves and branches can protect you

▼ *The roots of a fallen tree will give some shelter from rain and wind, and can be used to support your own construction.*

from the worst of the wind and rain. Big clumps of vegetation may offer you the opportunity to quickly bend the stems and leaves over yourself. In some environments, you may find caves or natural hollows that can be stuffed with vegetation to insulate them.

If you are stranded in a sandy desert, you might have to bury yourself in the sand to protect your body from the sun during the day. In most situations, however, especially in cold weather, you should try to insulate yourself from the ground in any way you can, as it can quickly sap all your body heat.

It is likely that spending the night in a natural shelter will be the most uncomfortable night you ever spent, but the main objective is to stay alive. You can improve on your shelter, or build a new one, the next day.

FINDING THE RIGHT LOCATION

Consider the points on this checklist when deciding where to build a shelter.
- Ensure that there are plenty of shelter-building materials around you. Dragging them over a long distance can cost hours of unnecessary labour and waste your precious energy.
- Make sure you are close to water, but not in the floodplain of a stream. To avoid contaminating the water, build your shelter at least 30m/33yd away from the bank of a river or stream. This also prevents too much dew from falling on your shelter in the morning.
- Check for any dead branches in overhanging trees, which could fall on your head or damage your shelter. Check for the possibility of an avalanche or rockslide.
- Ensure you are not building your shelter on top of an anthill or other animal shelter.
- Try to find areas that are naturally protected from severe weather, but avoid building deep in the woods. Deep woods take a long time to dry out, and don't get much sun. Try to stay on the leeside, or sheltered side, of woods, mountains and other such protective features in the landscape.
- If you intend to have a fire, ensure you look out for fire hazards such as overhanging boughs, peat-like soil or dry grasses.

WHERE TO FIND A NATURAL SHELTER

▲ Woodland offers some protection from wind and rain, and there will be plenty of debris to insulate your shelter.

▲ Try to make sure there is no heavy dead wood above the site. Remove it and pile it up for firewood, or move to a safer location.

▲ Natural caves are always a good option, though you must be careful of other creatures that may have the same idea.

WHERE TO BUILD A SHELTER

▲ When looking for a site to build a shelter, try to find a place where there is plenty of raw material within easy reach.

▲ Make sure the site is not below a possible landslide. If you have no choice, let the slide happen before you build.

▲ You will need access to water, but beware of choosing a low-lying site in case rain upstream causes the water level to rise.

Building a debris hut

In many wilderness environments, there is plenty of debris such as dead leaves and brushwood available, and a debris hut is the ideal short-term shelter. It is small and well insulated to conserve heat and protect you from the rain. The debris hut is such an effective shelter that it can keep you warm in temperatures well below freezing. It can also be built entirely with your bare hands, so no tools or cordage are needed. The debris doesn't have to be dry, and in a survival situation green material could be used instead.

The debris hut creates a maximum amount of dead air to keep heat in the shelter. It forms a cocoon around you, ensuring that your body is not heating up unnecessary empty space.

AN ADAPTABLE HUT
A debris hut can be adapted to suit the most difficult scenarios as long as you stick to the guidelines shown here. You need to gather as much debris as possible in the shortest amount of time – when your life is on the line, every minute counts. You'll need a thickness of about 1m/3ft around the sides (except the opening) – use a stick to help you judge the amount of debris you've added and pack it down as much as possible.

Fill the interior with the driest, fluffiest material you can find. If there is a lot of fern or bracken around, use

▼ For the framework of the debris hut you will need a strong ridge pole, about 2.5m/8ft long, and two strong Y-sticks, like this one, each about 60cm/2ft long.

it as a top layer inside the shelter. It smells nice, and does not poke into your body. Make sure you pack it in well. When you bed down in the shelter, you will automatically squeeze the excess debris into the corners and the foot-end, forming a cocoon around your body.

Put some branches over the shelter to stop leaves blowing away. Slabs of bark or a layer of moss will help to stop rain getting through. You will also need to fashion a door by weaving a "bag" from flexible stems and filling it with leaves. You can pull this bag into the entrance behind you to seal it. Trying to seal the entrance with a pile of leaves

▲ The debris hut takes the form of a dome, which is perfect for shedding water.

is really cumbersome, and ineffective. Once the bag of leaves is in place, use debris from inside to plug any holes.

Don't worry about cutting off the fresh air supply by plugging the door. There will still be plenty of air flowing in through the leaves. Just make sure you go to the toilet before you crawl in and get snug, as it takes a long time to get in and out of this shelter.

▼ In order to retain heat, make the entrance of the shelter just big enough to shuffle into backwards, lying flat on your belly.

BUILDING A DEBRIS HUT

1 Lie down on the ground and mark out a line around your body, about a hand's width away from you.

2 Dig a pit about 30cm/12in deep in the marked area. If the weather is very cold, try to dig down even more.

3 Create a "floor" over the ground by laying branches along the bottom of the pit, running from head to foot.

4 Create another layer by placing a second row of branches crossways over the first layer. Keep it sturdy and even.

5 Fill up the hole with the driest debris you can find. This layer should be at least 15cm/6in deep.

6 For the frame, plant two Y-sticks at the two corners of the head end, leaning them against each other.

7 Rest a long ridge pole on the Y-sticks, extending to the foot end.

8 Add branches to each side of the frame, lining them up vertically.

9 Fill up both sides of the framework with sticks, then pile debris over them.

10 Pile the debris over the shelter to a depth of about 1m/3ft on all sides, leaving the opening clear.

11 Fill the interior with the driest, fluffiest material you can find. Fern or bracken makes an aromatic top layer.

12 Use pliable green shoots to make a 1m/3ft tunnel for the entrance and cover them thickly in debris.

Building a stacked debris wall

The stacked debris wall is a shelter component that can be used in many different ways. It is simply a double row of poles driven into the ground and woven together with brushwood, with a thick wad of insulating debris between them, so it can be straight or curved, tall or short.

You can use this technique to build a small survival shelter for one person or adapt it to a large construction for a group, perhaps building a number of shelters around a central fire, which will help to retain and reflect heat. It can also be used in other ways – as a hide for hunting, for example. A small semicircular version can be built around the back of a fire as a heat reflector.

THE RAW MATERIALS

To build this kind of wall you'll need plenty of poles. Their length will depend on how high you need the wall to be, but for a shelter they should generally be about 120cm/4ft long.

You'll need a heavy rock to hammer the poles firmly into the ground. You will also need a lot of material to weave the sides, such as semi-flexible brushwood, though in a survival situation you might need to use fresh, green material if there is no dead wood available. You'll also need plenty of debris, which can be of any kind, wet or dry, as long as it creates air pockets.

CONSTRUCTING THE WALL

Having decided on the site for the wall, hammer the first line of poles as deeply as possible into the ground, about 30cm/1ft apart. The second row should be parallel with the first, about 50cm/20in away to allow for plenty of insulation. You might want to put an extra pole at each end of the wall so you can weave around the ends too.

Weave brushwood loosely along the rows to make the sides of the walls. Now all that remains is to pack the space in between with debris.

As a possible variation, you could weave one side of the wall tightly for strength, for example if it is to form the inside of the shelter. If you also weave the outer side tightly you can plaster the wall with "survival cement" (a 50:50 mix of dry grass and sticky mud) or clay. Another option is to build two side walls at each end of the wall, thereby giving you protection from wind blowing in from the side. You could also add a roof using Y-poles to support the front where it's not resting on the wall.

The stacked debris wall is an amazingly strong construction when it is built properly, and a tightly woven wall can last for years. If you ensure that the roof slopes gently you won't even need too much debris to make it more or less waterproof.

▼ *Building a stacked debris wall rather than a complete shelter may save time, but you will need a fire to keep you warm all night.*

BUILDING A STACKED DEBRIS WALL

1 Lay two long branches on the ground or mark two lines indicating where the poles are going to be driven in.

2 Hammer strong, straight poles into the ground 30cm/12in apart, following the first line.

3 When the first row is completed, make a second one parallel with it, about 50cm/20in away.

4 Hammer in a pole between the rows at each end of the wall to stop debris spilling out when you pack the wall.

5 Weave flexible shoots or brushwood between the poles to give the structure stability and hold the debris inside.

6 To neaten the inside of a shelter, or if you intend to plaster the wall, make the weaving really tight.

7 Once all the weaving is completed, fill the whole cavity with debris.

8 Pad the debris down well, checking that there are no large gaps.

9 Plastering the wall with survival cement will help it reflect more heat.

10 To construct a roof over the wall, place Y-sticks in front of the two ends and inside each end of the wall.

11 Place a ridge pole along the top of the wall and a second in front of it; lay sticks across the two ridge poles.

12 Place a good thick layer of debris over the top. A layer 50cm/20in thick should keep out moderate rain.

Building a long-term shelter

All over the world, primitive shelters are built in the round. There are several good reasons for this. When a fire is lit inside (in the centre) the heat can reach everywhere in the shelter, and the walls will reflect all of it right back. In a square shelter, the distribution of heat tends to be uneven, resulting in cold corners. If there are several people in a round shelter, everyone gets an equal share of heat. Round shelters are also stronger than square ones, and they are easier to build.

UPGRADING YOUR SHELTER

Once all the basics of survival are taken care of and you have supplies to last you for a week or more, if you have time and materials available you can consider making your existing shelter more comfortable. Remember though, that you don't want to waste resources

and energy building a shelter that is larger than you need.

To improve on your shelter use the stacked debris wall technique. This

▲ *A long-term shelter can make life a lot more comfortable. Because this can take a long time to build, it is important that all essentials should be taken care of first.*

BUILDING A LONG-TERM SHELTER

1 First make the fireplace. Dig four trenches to carry air to your fire pit and build a hearth with large stones.

2 Cover the trenches with sturdy sticks, so that soil will not fall through and eventually block the tunnels.

3 Pack a layer of soil over the sticks, so that you can walk over the floor without disturbing the oxygen tunnels.

4 Use a line and two sticks, planting the first stick in the central fireplace, to mark out the perimeter of the shelter.

5 Place two markers where the doorway will be. When building the wall, leave this space open.

6 Start the wall by driving 120cm/4ft poles into the ground, following the circle, keeping them 30cm/1ft apart.

means you'll need to collect plenty of poles and weaving material. In this case the roof will be supported by four Y-sticks in the centre, each a good 2m/6ft long. They will need to be very thick and sturdy: the poles shown here are about 12.5cm/5in in diameter. You will also need four sticks to connect the Y-poles in the centre, creating a square. These will also need to be very strong and about 1m/3ft long.

PLANNING THE SHELTER

Think a little about how large you really need your shelter to be. If you are on your own you should go for a diameter of about 3m/10ft: this gives plenty of space for one person and will be easy to heat. Don't overestimate the space you need: a group of six might plan a shelter about 5m/16ft across, but this could accommodate nine.

Before you start building the walls you should construct the fireplace. The fire will burn better if oxygen reaches it from underneath, and you can achieve this by digging four trenches in the floor, one from each direction, from the walls to the centre.

The easiest way to mark the line of the wall is with a line and two sticks. Drive one stick into the centre of the site and tie a cord to this. Measure the required radius and attach the second stick at this point. Now walk around the centre, keeping the line taut and drawing a circle on the ground with the point of the stick.

Next, decide where you want the door. Traditionally, doors face east to catch the morning sun, and this makes sense because it is a mental and physical boost to be woken up by the sun shining through the doorway (assuming you can leave this open). It also allows the sun to dry out any dampness inside the shelter during the morning. If your shelter faces west you may find you wake up a lot later because it seems darker inside.

BUILDING AND FURNISHING

When the poles for the walls have been pounded in you will get a much clearer idea of the size of your shelter. You might even want to build some basic furniture in the shelter now, before the walls and roof are finished, because it is harder to bring materials inside once the shelter is complete.

Consider making a low platform for your bed. Otherwise, if you intend to sleep on the ground, put down a layer of rushes or twigs, then throw about 20cm/8in of debris over this, to keep you well insulated from the ground.

Once you are happy with the interior, you can complete the debris wall by weaving flexible material through the two rows of poles and filling the space between them with debris. You should make sure that the wall is about the same height as your head when you are sitting inside the shelter – about 120cm/4ft – to enable you to sit against it with a straight back.

7 Once the first circle is complete, hammer in the second circle of stakes about 30cm/1ft outside it.

8 Hammer in the four Y-pole roof supports to form a central square; try to orient them on the entrance.

9 Weave brushwood between the poles to create two circular walls with an empty space between them.

10 Fill the area between the woven walls with debris, making sure it is packed in tightly.

11 Use four stout branches to connect the central Y-poles: these must be strong enough to support the roof.

12 Lay sturdy poles from the wall to the central square: these will support a thick layer of debris for the roof.

Before you begin to add the debris, hammer a number of sturdy Y-shaped poles into the ground between the two woven walls. You can connect these with strong branches later on to act as the outer supports for the roof. If you don't do this, the sides of the shelter will gradually sink as the weight of the roof compresses the debris wall.

BUILDING THE ROOF

When the wall is finished, you can connect the four Y-poles in the middle with the four strong branches you selected for this. Make sure that these branches are really sturdy: they should be capable of carrying three times the weight of the roof when you first assemble it. In the lifespan of the shelter, you will be adding more debris as it compresses, and it will also get very wet regularly when it rains. These factors can add a tremendous amount of weight to the roof of your shelter.

Now you can start building the roof by laying thick, sturdy poles from the wall to the Y-pole square in the centre of your shelter. Make sure the poles stick out a little on both the square and the wall. However, you should leave a large enough hole in the centre for smoke from the fire to escape. Depending on how much wind is

FIRE HAZARD

A note of warning. A shelter built of debris is basically one giant bundle of tinder. Take great care to keep your fire under control and watch that embers don't suddenly burst into flame. Even if you come out of it unharmed, if your shelter burns down hours of hard labour will have been wasted.

---

likely to reach your shelter, your smoke hole should be around 20-30cm/8–12in wide at least.

At the doorway, lay some extra sturdy poles at each side of the door, then lay a very thick branch across the entrance so you can put roof poles there too. When you cannot fit any more poles on to the square of branches in the centre, fill up any remaining gaps in the roof with smaller sticks and branches, until all the major holes are covered.

DEBRIS FOR THE ROOF

All you have to do now is add a thick layer of debris to the roof. Depending on the angle of your roof and the size of the material you are using for this, you may have to weave a layer of supple twigs through the poles to stop debris from sliding down the roof.

A good 60cm/2ft layer of debris on top of the poles and twigs will be needed to stop the rain soaking through into the shelter. Ensure the debris goes all the way from the smoke hole across the whole width of the wall (this is why the roof poles should overhang the wall).

If you find the roof is too high for you to reach the centre in order to pile on the debris, you can leave out the poles at the entrance temporarily, to

---

▲ *Once all the roof poles are laid, you can finish the roof by placing a thick layer of debris on top, leaving the smoke hole open.*

enable you to throw the material on to those difficult spots from there. Once the roof is completely covered with debris, smooth it out and add some heavier branches to stop the material from blowing away in the wind.

FINISHING OFF THE SHELTER

There are a few things you can do with a primitive shelter to make it more comfortable. Obviously all the building materials you've gathered will be full of small creatures, so one of the most important tricks is smoking out your shelter before you move in, to get rid of all the insects that are now inside it.

You can create a lot of smoke by placing a few embers in a fireproof container and then throwing on some damp, green materials that will produce a thick, pungent smoke. Try using fresh pine needles or sage if they are growing in the area. When the container is smoking furiously, place it inside the shelter for about half an hour. Keep the entrance closed so all the smoke goes through the debris.

Once you are living in your shelter you will want any smoke from your fire to escape through the central smoke hole. You can help to direct it out of the hole by weaving a little square "lid" the same size as your smoke hole. Place this upright next to the smoke hole, facing into the wind. The contraption will act like a funnel, allowing the smoke to escape from your shelter before it's caught by the wind, and stopping the wind blowing smoke back into the hole.

The smoke-hole cover can be made in many different ways. The easiest is to use an animal skin, if you have one, stretching it over a square framework of flexible branches woven together. Keep in mind that the hide will shrink as it dries and expand when it gets wet.

In heavy rain, the cover can be used to close the smoke hole, though you will not be able to have a fire inside the shelter if you do this, as the smoke will have no way out.

▲ *If you are carrying cordage and a tarpaulin, you can rig up a hammock between two trees. This way you can sleep off the ground, which will help you to keep warmer overnight if you haven't got the time to build a proper shelter. Once you've built your shelter, a hammock provides a comfortable alternative on warm, dry nights.*

SMOKING OUT INSECTS AND BUGS

1 Put a few burning embers in a fireproof container.

2 Add a handful of fresh spruce needles or sage to encourage smoking.

3 Put the container in the hut and seal the entrance for about 30 minutes.

MAKING A SMOKE-HOLE COVER

1 Cut some flexible branches to the size of the opening you need to cover. Plant a row of them in the ground about 7.5cm/3in apart.

2 Weave more flexible branches from side to side to construct a sturdy frame. You can make it stronger by tying the corners with some cordage.

3 Finish the cover by tying an animal skin or some large leaves over the frame. In this case, a rabbit skin was just the right size for the smoke hole.

Snow shelters

In winter conditions snow can be used to build an emergency shelter. It has long been used to build shelters by the military of northern countries. The Swedish army, for instance, has built large snow shelters for vehicles and also for use as field hospitals.

When you are trekking in this kind of climate, having the skill to build a proper snow shelter can save your life in the event of a snowstorm. If you lose your way or your equipment fails – for example if your skidoo gets broken – building a snow shelter enables you to protect yourself from the cold.

▼ *In Antarctica this perfect four-person shelter was built from a hundred blocks hewn with the most valuable tool – a saw.*

Protection from the wind is most important, since a high windchill factor can create dangerously cold conditions that quickly lead to death.

When selecting a site for a shelter in a snow-covered environment, keep in mind that the easiest way to build a shelter is by digging into the snow rather than building it up in walls. Look out for places where snow has drifted, or dig around trees and other natural "funnels" where the snow has concentrated and is at its deepest. Of course, there may be situations when you are forced to build rather than dig to create a shelter.

There are three main types of snow shelters, each suited to particular kinds of snow: the igloo is designed for hard snow, the quinze for powdery snow, and the snow cave, or "drift cave", for drifts. While a lot of different designs and variations are possible, there are a few important things to keep in mind in all cases.

PROVIDING AN AIR SUPPLY

You need to ensure you are protected from the cold, and you want to be insulated, but you also have to make sure there is sufficient ventilation to allow fresh air inside your shelter. When the heat from your body warms the shelter the surface of the snow will melt slightly, forming an airtight seal, so you must cut vents and check them regularly to prevent a build-up of carbon dioxide in your shelter.

WINDCHILL

Wind speed in MPH	40	30	20	10	0	-10	-20	-30	-40
	Air temperature in °F								
	Comparable windchill temperature								
0-4	40	30	20	10	0	-10	-20	-30	-40
5	37	27	16	6	-5	-15	-26	-36	-47
10	28	16	4	-9	-21	-33	-46	-58	-70
15	22	9	-5	-18	-36	-45	-58	-72	-85
20	18	4	-10	-25	-39	-53	-67	-82	-96
25	16	0	-15	-29	-44	-59	-74	-88	-104
30	13	-2	-18	-33	-48	-63	-79	-94	-109
35	11	-4	-20	-35	-49	-67	-83	-98	-113
40	10	-6	-21	-37	-53	-69	-85	-100	-116

Little effect on windchill, little danger of frostbite | Increasing danger of frostbite | Great danger of frostbite

▲ *Once an igloo is completed, melting snow inside will make the joints airtight. The entrance should be a tunnel under the wall, allowing cold air to sink and flow away.*

▲ *Wind can make the air feel much colder than the recorded temperature, and as its strength increases the effect is multiplied.*

KEEPING DRY

When you are building a shelter with snow there is a great danger of your clothes getting wet. When the weather is very cold this is unlikely, but at temperatures higher than -15°C/5°F it can be a serious problem. In all temperatures mittens get wet easily. You should also try not to work yourself into too much of a sweat. It is one thing trying to keep warm when you are dry, but quite another to stay warm when wet.

IGLOOS

If you are in the high Arctic, tundra or other open snow-covered terrain where the temperature is below −5°C/23°F, it is relatively easy to dig or cut snow for a shelter, and the low temperature will ensure that the walls of your structure will stay safely in place. If you are stranded on hard-packed snow you can cut blocks and build an igloo. This makes a comfortable, long-term shelter, though you should bear in mind that it will take time to build and you need a saw or knife to cut the blocks.

Start by marking out a circle on a flat area of compacted snow. For a two-person igloo you will need a circle of

about 2.5–2.8m/8–9ft diameter. As you cut the snow blocks, lay them on their long edges in a rising spiral, stepping them slightly so that most of the weight of each block is on the blocks beneath it. When you have completed the dome shape, the inside should be smoothed so that the "steps" inside do not start to drip water as the inside temperature rises. The outer wall should be covered with loose snow to fill all the cracks and make the igloo windproof. It is best to dig a tunnel under the wall for the entrance, but if this is not possible it can be cut straight through the wall and covered with a rucksack or a block of snow.

BUILDING AN IGLOO

1 Cut blocks of hard-packed snow 60 x 40 x 20cm/24 x 16 x 8in and use them to form a circle around the hole you cut them from.

2 Cut away the tops of the first few blocks at an angle to the ground and build up the walls in a spiral. Cut an entrance hole under the wall.

3 Make the blocks lean into the igloo a little more in each row, to create a dome. Trim the last block from inside to fit exactly into the central hole.

Building a quinze shelter

The quinze shelter looks a little like the better-known igloo, but it is constructed in a different way and is suitable for areas of powdery snow. Obviously when snow is in this condition it has no structural strength and it would be impossible to cut the kind of blocks you would need to build an igloo.

The quinze is made by collecting snow into a pile, which is then left to harden by recrystallizing before the structure is hollowed out from the inside. Making a snow pile of a usable size takes about an hour. You then need to wait for about another hour if the temperature is at least −10°C/14°F. At higher temperatures up to two hours will be needed.

PLANNING THE QUINZE

For a two-person quinze the snow pile should be about 1.8m/6ft high, 2.5m/8ft wide and 3m/10ft long. If you need to accommodate more people, add another 80cm/2ft 6in per person.

Unless time is short because night is falling, the work of piling the snow should be done quite slowly to avoid the diggers getting overheated and sweating. A shovel is ideal for the purpose, but in an emergency situation snowshoes, a billy can or a frying pan can be used to scoop up the snow.

Before you start to make the pile, mark out the area of the shelter and tread the floor to compact the snow.

▲ *If the snow is loose, as it is in northern forests, taiga, boreal forest and coniferous forests, and the temperature is below −5°C/23°F, you can build a quinze.*

CREATING THE SHELTER

On to this floor, arrange rucksacks and any spare gear, bushes and any other bulky material you can find, forming a compact heap. This will help to create the basic dome shape, and will reduce the amount of snow you need to shovel on to the pile. The gear can be removed later. Cover the heap with a layer of snow at least 1m/3ft thick and leave it to harden.

Once the snow has recrystallized, your gear and any other material you have used can be dug out again from the side. You can then enlarge the shelter by digging out from the inside, but you must be very careful that you don't dig away too much and weaken

◀ *Very cold conditions present the dangers of frostbite and hypothermia. If you feel cold, do not fall asleep at any cost. Try to stay warm by moving around, sing songs and keep busy attending to your equipment.*

USING A QUINZE

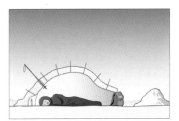

1 The temperature inside should be below freezing, so the snow is dry. Do not make a fire inside a quinze.

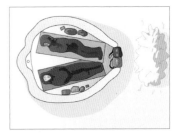

2 Make a small shelf for a candle in the wall near your head. As long as the candle burns there is enough oxygen in the quinze.

the walls. To avoid this, find some sticks and trim them all to the same length – at least 30cm/12in. Poke them at regular intervals into the outside of the snow pile. When you come to dig away the snow from the inside, you will hit the ends of the sticks and know that it is time to stop digging. When the main shelter is complete, you can add a tunnel, digging a trench where

the entrance tunnel is going to be so that the cold air sinks below the level at which you are sitting or lying. It is important to make the entrance just large enough to crawl through. You can use the snow you have dug out of the shelter to create a windbreak outside the entrance. The door should be plugged with snow or a rucksack before you go to sleep.

VENTILATION

The snow walls will be airtight, so you must cut a hole in the roof for ventilation to avoid the possibility of carbon dioxide poisoning. Keeping a candle burning inside the quinze will tell you that there is enough oxygen. The best place for the candle is a small niche in the wall at the end of the shelter, near the sleepers' heads.

BUILDING A QUINZE SHELTER

1 Work out the rough dimensions by lying down and drawing a circle around the users (this is a three-person quinze).

2 Tread down the floor to compact it, then make a pile of powdery snow at least 3m/10ft wide and 1.8m/6ft high.

3 When the pile is complete, tap down the surface with the flat of the shovel to compact the snow.

4 Wait an hour for the snow pile to recrystallize so that it is hard enough for you to begin hollowing it out.

5 Meanwhile, cut some 30cm/1ft long sticks and poke them into the snow to an equal depth all around the pile.

6 When the snow is hard enough, cut out a small doorway. Pile up the snow on the windward side of the hole.

7 Hollow out the shelter, bringing the snow out through the door. When you meet the ends of the sticks, stop digging – the wall is 30cm/12in thick.

8 The roof should be dome-shaped. Make a 10cm/4in diameter ventilation hole in the roof to avoid the danger of carbon dioxide poisoning.

9 Close the doorway using snow or a rucksack, or a plastic bag filled with snow or clothes. You can also make a little shelf for a candle in the wall.

Snow caves and other shelters

If weather conditions worsen suddenly or the light is failing, there may be very little time available to build a snow shelter. In these situations look for natural hollows, perhaps with overhanging trees, that will offer some protection from the wind, or a large drift into which you can dig to make a cave. Tools for cutting snow and ice are an essential part of your survival equipment when you are travelling in arctic terrain, but in an emergency other items, such as skis or cooking pots, can be used to dig a trench or cave. Keep things simple – smaller shelters tend to retain their warmth longer and take less time to build.

SNOW TRENCH

The simplest one-person snow survival shelter is the snow trench, also known as a "snow grave". Its main purpose is to keep out the wind. At its most basic, it involves digging a slit trench in the snow with whatever tools are available, adding a roof and then covering it with an insulating layer of snow.

Having dug the hole, dig down another 60cm/2ft at one end. When you make the roof from branches and snow, site the entrance opening above the deeper part of the pit. Lay branches and other material on the higher part of the shelter to form an insulated seat.

If the bottom of your pit reaches the ground, you can light a fire here, but if the snow is very deep this won't be possible. Even without a fire, the cold air will sink down into the deeper part of the shelter, leaving the higher part, warmed by your body, slightly warmer.

▲ *In coniferous forest there is plenty to build an improvised shelter with. A lean-to of spruce branches, with a fire in front of it, makes a good shelter. Make sure that there are logs or foliage insulating you from the ground, and that your fire doesn't melt snow on overhanging branches.*

BUILDING A SNOW TRENCH

▲ *For a quick survival refuge, dig a trench about 1m/3ft deep and wide and 2m/6ft 6in long. This one has a roof made of packed snow blocks.*

▲ *If wood is available, lay some branches over the trench, leaving one end open, and cover the roof with 30–60cm/1–2ft of snow.*

▲ *By adding brushwood to the sides and piling up the snow you dig out on either side, you can make an insulated shelter in which you can sit.*

▲ *When trekking in arctic conditions, it's vital to carry an emergency survival kit containing a snow saw, ice axe and shovel.*

SNOW CAVES

A snow cave requires a depth of snow of at least 2m/6ft. While the simplest of trenches can be built in under half an hour, a snow cave takes far more time and effort to complete – allow at least three hours to build a basic cave. You'll need digging tools, and because digging will make you perspire, you should remove one of your inner garments before you start digging so that you have something dry to put on when you have completed your shelter.

▲ *Digging your snow cave near the top of a slope means the snow you dig out will naturally fall away from the entrance.*

In a large bank of drifted snow, dig a cave starting about 2.5m/8ft above the bottom of the drift: this saves energy as the shovelled snow simply drops down the hill. You should then tunnel slightly uphill so that your snow cave is higher than the door. In a small drift you may have to hollow out a shallower cave and close up the front with blocks of snow.

As with all shelters, don't forget the ventilation – your survival depends on it. Also, erect a clear marker outside so that potential rescuers can find you.

▲ *If the snow is very deep you can dig directly down and then tunnel sideways under the snow surface.*

▼ *If you are in a group you can dig a number of snow caves in a large drift.*

BUILDING A SNOW CAVE

▲ *Make a temporary shelter in a shallow drift by hollowing out the snow, then closing the entrance with snow blocks and making an airhole.*

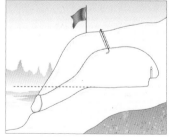

▲ *On a slope, the sleeping area in a drift cave should ideally be higher than the entrance tunnel so that the warmer air stays inside.*

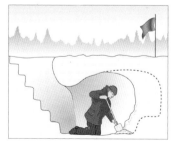

▲ *Despite the flat terrain, the snow here is deep enough to be able to dig down then sideways to make the cave. Ventilation will need to be added.*

Finding shelter in the desert

Deserts pose their own unique problems. Most of these are due to the immense heat present in many deserts during the day. This leads to a lack of vegetation, so that there are few materials to work with when you need to build a shelter. So what do you do when there are no resources in the area around you? What if there is nowhere to dig, nowhere to find wood or scrub, no water and no food? The answer sounds very stark, but it is very simple. If you cannot get to an area where there are resources, you will die.

Deserts actually force you to deal with two extremes: apart from the searing heat of the day, the second is the intense cold of the night, when the temperature can fall very rapidly.

DAYTIME SHELTER

During the day, your main concern will be shade. If you have the materials to hand, a roof or canopy will help you to keep cool. The story is rather different at night, when you need insulation. Most of the time in the desert, however, you'll be travelling

A desert rock face makes a natural windbreak and radiates heat at night.

through the night. This means that you will only need shelter during the day, to protect you from the sun while you sleep. In many situations, it is not necessary to build anything.

Shade can often be found under trees or, if there are no trees in the area, you may be able to find caves to hole up in. Just remember that animals

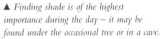

Finding shade is of the highest importance during the day – it may be found under the occasional tree or in a cave.

need the same things you do, and may also be sheltering in these nice cool spots. Always check for scorpions, snakes and the like. When you rest in the shade of trees or shallow caves, keep in mind that the sun moves through the day, so be careful about falling asleep in a shady area that may not be so shady any more in an hour's time. It's easy to get burned while you are asleep. As a last resort during the day, you can dig yourself in under the sand, which may be slightly cooler.

SITES TO AVOID

Take great care in choosing a safe site for your shelter. In many desert areas, flash floods can occur during the rainy season, because the rain falls so heavily that the hard, dry ground does not have time to absorb it all. The water will then just run off the surface and collect in rivers.

These floods can become very large in no time, appearing with little or no warning, often as a result of rain falling far away. Sometimes you will find a

▲ *A shallow cave may provide just enough shelter from the sun. Keep in mind that the shade in such a cave may not last all day.*

▼ *A heat-stress index combines the effects of high temperature and humidity to show how much stress your body might be under.*

river where five minutes before there was only cracked earth. These "temporary" rivers can have amazingly strong currents, so it is a good idea to stay away from areas that resemble river beds, the bottoms of canyons, places right at the foot of cliffs and other low-lying areas. It is also important to keep away from areas where rock falls and landslides may occur, as these can be quite common.

USE THE NIGHT-TIME

Heat and lack of water can wear you down very quickly, so you should try to travel at night and rest in the shade during the day. This way you will at least avoid exercising in extreme heat, which will only worsen your physical condition further. Unless it is absolutely necessary, it is advisable even to build your shelter and find your

firewood during the night, or at least in the evening and early morning, while it is relatively cool. If in doubt, have a look at what the local animals are doing: where do they find shelter, when do they use their shelter, when do they come out to feed, and where do they find water?

The table below explains the stress placed upon the body in different types of heat. The higher the number, the more stress your body is under and the more dangerous your position is. For instance, if the temperature is 40°C/105°F and the humidity is 50 per cent this means that your body has a stress factor of 135, which is very high. This number is located in the "Extreme danger" zone, meaning that heatstroke is very likely if you continue to be exposed to the heat. Exercise in such conditions heightens the risk.

HEAT-STRESS INDEX

Temp in degrees F	Relative humidity														Heat-stress index
	10%	20%	30%	35%	40%	45%	50%	55%	60%	65%	70%	75%	80%	90%	
70	65	66	67	67	68	68	69	69	70	70	70	70	71	71	
75	70	72	73	73	74	74	75	75	76	76	77	77	78	79	I Caution 80-89°F
80	75	77	78	79	79	80	81	81	82	83	85	86	86	88	
85	80	82	84	85	86	87	88	89	90	91	93	95	97	102	II Extreme 90-104°F
90	85	87	90	91	93	95	96	98	100	102	106	109	113	122	III Danger 105-129°F
95	90	93	96	98	101	104	107	110	114	119	124	130	136	•	
100	95	99	104	107	110	115	120	126	132	138	144	•	•	•	
105	100	105	113	118	123	129	135	142	149	•	•	•	•	•	
110	105	112	123	130	137	143	150	•	•	•	•	•	•	•	IV Extreme danger greater than 130°F
115	111	120	135	143	151	•	•	•	•	•	•	•	•	•	
120	116	130	148	•	•	•	•	•	•	•	•	•	•	•	
125	123	141	•	•	•	•	•	•	•	•	•	•	•	•	
130	131	•	•	•	•	•	•	•	•	•	•	•	•	•	
135	•	•	•	•	•	•	•	•	•	•	•	•	•	•	
140	•	•	•	•	•	•	•	•	•	•	•	•	•	•	

• Beyond the capacity of the atmosphere to hold water

I Caution 80-89°F	**Effect**: fatigue possible with prolonged exposure and/or physical activity
II Extreme 90-104°F	**Effect**: heat cramps and heat exhaustion possible with prolonged exposure and/or physical activity
III Danger 105-129°F	**Effect**: heat exhaustion, heat cramps likely; heatstroke possible with prolonged exposure and/or physical activity
IV Extreme danger greater than 130°F	**Effect**: heatstroke highly likely with continued exposure

Building a desert shelter

When you need a shelter in the desert and a suitable natural feature such as a cave is not available, you will have to build something.

Remember that "small is beautiful" and avoid spending energy on any unnecessary space even if you feel you really want it. Try to make sure the shelter can be well sealed, whether you are occupying it or not, as dangerous animals may try to spend the day there too, especially if you build an underground shelter. This means trying to create a door that fits the entrance snugly, and making sure there are no exposed openings.

USING HOT ROCKS

The most basic method of surviving the cold hours is to find a slope facing the sun, with plenty of rocks lying about. Pick up the hottest rocks you can find, and build some sort of wall around the site where you are going to spend the night. To get most benefit during the night, you should build the wall in such a way that the side of the rock that has been baking in the sun faces you when the wall is complete. The rocks will radiate their heat for much of the night.

If you are in a sandy area, you can dig down into the sand slightly and build the rock wall inside the hollow. Such a shelter could see you through the night. However, it would have to be broken down in the morning and built again in the evening to make it work a second night. You can use the same technique, however, as a natural central heating system in a more permanent shelter.

PIT SHELTERS

In an area of sand or soil you can construct an underground pit shelter. It needs to be about 1m/3ft deep, but don't make it larger than you need: you should just have space to lie down.

You may have to support the sides of your shelter by building walls inside the pit, so you will need to find branches or rocks You will also need two sturdy beams at the sides of the pit to support the roof. There will be a considerable amount of weight on top of the roof, and you need to make sure your shelter won't cave in during the night.

Use clothing, shrubs or flat rocks to fill all the gaps between the sticks, before adding a deep layer of sand. The main problem with this shelter is fashioning a door to prevent heat escaping and animals coming in.

BUILDING A ROCK WALL SHELTER

1 When building a rock wall shelter to keep you warm overnight, find a south-facing slope.

2 A shallow cave like this is ideal. As it is south-facing, the walls of the cave will retain the heat of the sun.

3 Use any rocks you find strewn about on the slope, which will have been baking in the sun for most of the day.

4 Build a wall using these rocks, leaving just enough space for you to lie. Make sure the hot side of each rock is facing into the shelter.

5 Try to enclose the entire hollow apart from an entrance, which can be located either at the foot or the head end of the shelter.

6 It is important to make this shelter as small as possible, so that your body nearly touches the hot rocks and there is less space to heat.

BUILDING A SAND PIT SHELTER

1 You need to be in an area where there is sand or soil that you can dig and some wood or shrub.

2 Mark out an area for the pit, which should not be more than 30cm/1ft longer and wider than your body.

3 Start digging the pit, using any tools you have or your bare hands. It will need to be about 1m/3ft deep.

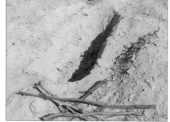

4 If the soil is sandy, you may have to build retaining walls inside the pit to prevent the sides collapsing.

5 Even if the soil is not sandy, you will need to lay two beams alongside your pit for the roof to rest on.

6 Gather some strong branches and lay them across the pit to begin constructing the roof.

7 Leaving an opening near the head-end, pile flat rocks on the sticks.

8 Cover the rocks with sand or soil to form the ceiling.

9 Try to eradicate all the gaps, so sand can't fall through into the pit.

10 Place a good layer of sand over the rocks as insulation. Form a slight dome over the area, so any water can run off.

11 Make sure you leave an opening that runs the entire width of the shelter and is large enough to squeeze through.

12 The shelter needs to be easy to spot, both for yourself when out roaming, and for potential rescuers.

Building a jungle shelter

In the jungle, the main concern is often rain. The shelter you will make has to withstand the rain, offering you a well-protected, dry spot inside. Palms are usually very abundant in rainforests, making their leaves the ideal material for your shelter. Bamboo is another natural tropical material you can adapt to build a workable shelter. The shelter shown here uses cohune palm leaves.

MAKING THE LEAN-TO FRAME

You will need six poles, each about 2–3m/6–10ft long, to make the frame on which the roof will rest. Drive two poles into the ground about 2–3m/6–10ft apart. Another pole is then tied to the top of these uprights. You can use any kind of vine as cordage to tie the frame together; the bark of various

▲ *A woven palm-leaf structure makes an ideal roof and walls. The shelter will be more comfortable if you raise the floor surface to avoid the jungle damp and the myriad insects.*

COVERING A ROOF WITH PALM LEAVES

1 Locate a suitable palm tree. The cohune palm has large divided leaves that can be arranged like thatch to channel water off the roof.

2 Use a machete to chop down the stems of the palm and trim the fresh leaves. You will need enough leaves to set closely together on the frame.

3 Split each palm leaf in two all the way down its length, starting from the tip. If you try to split it from the thick end it may break.

4 The next stage is to collect enough vines to use as cordage. This will then be used to tie the frame together and to tie on the leaves.

5 Starting from the bottom of the frame, lay the halved leaves crossways with the fronds hanging down, and alternate the direction of the leaves.

6 The last palm leaf to go on the frame should be unspliced. This will provide an "eave" to channel the raindrops away from the front of the shelter.

forest species is also suitable. The three remaining poles are arranged at an angle from the ground to the crossbar to form a lean-to frame.

WEAVING THE PALM LEAF ROOF

Cut down some palm leaves from a tree (you'll need quite a few) then splice the palm leaves in half: this is easy to do by splitting the tip of the stem and working your way down. Splice most of the leaves before you start attaching them to the frame.

The split palm leaves are laid on top of the wooden frame, starting at the bottom. Arrange them so that the

▲ *Tropical rainforest provides an abundance of raw materials with which to build shelters. The main challenge is keeping dry.*

fronds hang down, directing the water to the back of the roof. Use alternate sides of the leaf each time to create a good watertight "cross-hatching". Once a full row of palm has been placed on the frame, tie it to the bars and add the next layer, until you have covered the whole structure. If you wish you can extend the top of the roof a little in front of the uprights when building the frame, to keep the rain off the front of the area.

You can use the same palm leaves to make yourself a comfortable mat to sleep or sit on inside the shelter. Lay them in alternate directions, as before, for maximum comfort.

▲ *A machete, or parang, is a sharp slashing bushcraft tool for the jungle. Look for handles with riveted plate grips and always sheath the blade when not in use.*

▲ *Bamboo is one of the jungle's most versatile plants. It is a rich source of food and its exceptionally strong wood is used to construct everything from chairs to bridges.*

BUILDING A TROPICAL A-FRAME SHELTER

1 Lash two branches or bamboo poles together to make an A-frame and erect it against a tree for support. Set up a second A-frame about 2.5m/8ft away.

2 Secure a long branch in the V-shaped tops of the A-frames. Tie two poles to the sides and lash a groundsheet around them to make a raised bed.

3 Spread a tarpaulin over the top of the frame to protect the bed from the rain, and keep the roof taut by tying the corners to surrounding trees.

Hygiene and waste disposal

In any kind of survival situation personal hygiene is critical, especially in avoiding the possibility of cross-infection. It is a common misconception that primitive peoples are less clean that we are, when in fact, in many so-called primitive societies, cleanliness and hygiene are as important as they are in Western society.

There are a host of natural alternatives to soap, shampoos, brushes and toothpastes that are used by primitive societies the world over, and knowledge of these can be useful in a survival situation. A little preparation is needed to produce many of these items, so they may not be a priority for you. In a long-term situation, however, it is well worth spending some time and effort making toiletries.

TOILET PAPER

"What can I use instead of toilet paper?" is probably the question most frequently asked regarding hygiene. There are many things in nature that can be used for this purpose. In fact, anything you can find around you will work when you really need it. A good solution is a combination of dried and wet moss. Use the wet moss first to clean yourself and then use the dried moss to dry off. Some people prefer it the other way around, which, they say, works in a refreshing way.

When there is not a lot of moss around, or in an emergency, you can pick some large leaves from nearby plants. Again, use fresh green leaves first, followed by some barely dead leaves. You should always make sure the

leaves you choose are not poisonous or irritating to the skin. Some people use the inner bark from trees, but getting it entails quite a lot of work.

DEALING WITH HUMAN WASTE

Whatever method you prefer for dealing with waste, observe the following basic rules:

• Always make sure you dig your toilet facility at least 25m/27yd away from your fresh water source, so that there is no chance of contamination.

• Dig the hole to a minimum depth of 45cm/18in.

• Always cover your waste with soil immediately, and when your pit is full, or if it starts to smell even after a layer of soil has been added, fill in the rest of the pit and make another one.

▼ *A good example of a discreet latrine, sited well away from the living area.*

▼ *Make sure your toilet hole is deep so that waste will not be detected by animals.*

▼ *Wash your hands to help prevent unhealthy bacteria entering your body.*

DIGGING A LATRINE

1 If you are staying in an area for a while, dig a latrine at least 25m/27yd away from your fresh water source, to a minimum depth of 45cm/18in.

2 You can make the latrine more comfortable by placing a log or two over the pit. Gather mosses and leaves so that "toilet paper" is always at hand.

3 Each time you use the latrine, add a layer of soil to keep smells at bay. Adding some charcoal from the fire will also help to mask any smells.

▲ *In a survival situation you must stay well hydrated. Food is important in the long term, but is not needed as much as fluids.*

• When using paper, always burn the paper afterwards. Paper can lie around for many years to come and will spoil the environment quickly.

• Make sure none of the items you keep in your pockets can accidentally fall in. Having to fish your knife out of your latrine is very unpleasant.

• As always, wash your hands and wrists when you have finished.

DIAPERS AND MENSTRUAL CARE

Most native peoples use dried moss for feminine hygiene, but very soft, well tanned animal hides have also been used for this and for babies' diapers. Some native peoples make pads from cloth filled with absorbent material such as moss or bulrush (cattail) fluff. Hygiene is important because menstruating women may otherwise attract unwelcome attention from bears.

▲ *Never use soaps or shampoos when washing in streams, lakes or rivers, even if they are labelled as biodegradable. Contrary to the manufacturers' claims, these products will not degrade completely and even a small percentage of soap in the water may destroy the environment.*

A NATURAL DIARRHOEA REMEDY

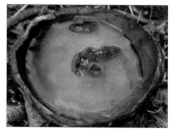

1 A decoction of oak bark is a good remedy for diarrhoea, slow-healing wounds, or throat and gum infection.

2 Pound the bark and put it in a bowl, then cover it with fresh water, put it on the fire and bring it to the boil.

3 When it has boiled for 3–5 minutes, remove from the fire and allow to cool before drinking like a tea.

MAKING NATURAL SANITARY TOWELS

1 Diapers or absorbent sanitary pads can be made by collecting a supply of dry, springy moss.

2 Put a pile of moss into the middle of a clean piece of cloth or soft, thin buckskin and fold in the edges.

3 This makes an absorbent pad that has many uses. The cloth or buckskin can be washed and re-used.

Making soaps and toiletries

One of the things most often forgotten on trips and outings, but often needed, is soap. It is quite easy to make in the wild and can be a great aid to hygiene, especially in a survival situation.

If you do have biodegradable soaps or shampoos with you, you should be aware that they need soil in order to degrade. So dig a pit at least 25m/27yd away from the water source, to avoid contaminating it, and pour all your washing water into this.

The ingredients you need to make a basic soap are as follows:
• Wood ash or charcoal (which contains alkali).
• Water.
• Oil or fat (either animal or vegetable fat will do).
• Pine resin or needles (these are not essential but will make the soap slightly antibacterial and give it a nice smell).

You will also need some kind of strainer or filter, such as a piece of cloth, to strain the ash out of the water. Always use a stick rather than your hand to stir the ash in the water, since wood ash and water create a very strong alkaline solution that can burn your skin.

Once all the water has boiled off the mixture you will have a good, serviceable soap. You can make it stronger or weaker by changing the percentages of ash, oil and pine resin.

YUCCA-BASED SOAP

Another common way of making soap is by pounding the roots of yucca plants. You get a froth when pounding the plant, which contains a lot of saponin, a lathering substance. The soap that comes from this froth is best used as a shampoo.

TOOTHPASTE

If dogwood or birch are growing in the area, you can chew on one of their fibrous twigs to create a toothbrush. You can use water mixed with wood-ash as toothpaste, but rinse your mouth very well after use to ensure that this doesn't irritate your gums.

A very effective mouth rinse can be made by pounding pine needles in water, then filtering it. The water will smell of pine and be slightly antiseptic.

NAIL AND HAIRCARE

Other aspects of hygiene that are taken for granted are cutting nails and hair. The easiest method of keeping your nails short is to file them regularly on a smooth stone. The stone should have the texture of an emery board. Filing nails may take a long time, but it is preferable to breaking them when they

MAKING A BASIC SOAP

1 First wait until the campfire has cooled down, and collect some charcoal from its centre.

2 Grind down the pieces of charcoal using a stone until you have a fine black powder.

3 Mix the charcoal with water. Stir well, and then strain it through a filter and reserve the water.

4 Heat up some oil or fat and mix the filtered water into it. Bring the mixture back to the boil.

5 Pound a handful of pine needles and add them to the mixture. Boil until all the water has evaporated.

6 Take the mixture off the fire, allow it to cool down and you are left with a good, mildly antiseptic soap.

are too long. Unless you have access to a very sharp, hard stone such as flint or obsidian, it may be easiest just to leave your hair to grow.

If you do have access to obsidian, sharp flakes can even be used for shaving. However, it is important to be extremely careful if you try this, as obsidian can be far sharper than a metal blade and the flakes can cut you easily, since they are not protected as in a modern razor and are often irregular. It may be better not to shave than to run the risk of cutting yourself.

▶ *If you have any small cuts or wounds, you can keep them clean and help them heal by making an oak bark compress. Simply make a decoction of oak bark by boiling it in water, and soak a wad of moss in the liquid when it's cooled down. Secure this over the wound using cordage or a bandage made from cloth or buckskin.*

MAKING AN ANTISEPTIC MOUTHWASH

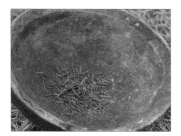

1 Gather a handful of fresh pine needles and put them in a bowl.

2 Use a clean stone to pound and grind the pine needles.

3 Add boiling water, leave to infuse for five minutes, then strain.

MAKING A NATURAL SHAMPOO

1 Dig up a yucca root and trim off the shoots. Scrape off all the soil and cut the root into short sections.

2 Collect a clean rock to use as a mortar and a smaller clean stone to use as a pestle. Then pound the root.

3 Pounding the yucca root produces a lather, which is perfect for use as a shampoo as well as a regular soap.

Maintaining health and safety

As mentioned previously, it is wise to carry a small survival kit with you at all times. If you find yourself stranded in the wilderness without supplies, however, don't panic: it does not mean you can't do anything to help yourself or others. In addition to disposing of waste and maintaining a hygienic environment at camp, there are some common ailments that can be treated in a wilderness survival situation using the plants and wildlife you may find around you. Remember also that some illnesses and injuries can be kept at bay simply by avoiding unnecessary risks.

MINOR CUTS
By far the most widespread plant of this kind, with many uses, is plantain. Many people use the crushed leaves to relieve the irritation of insect bites. Historically, however, plantain leaves were chewed into a pulp and used to treat minor cuts. Plantain tea is also very helpful for soothing a cough. It is made by putting approximately 10ml/ 2 tsp of dried leaves in a mug of boiling water and leaving them to infuse for 10 minutes (see below).

COLDS WITH FEVER
Elder is a common shrub, or more rarely a tree, that grows in many areas with temperate climates; it is familiar as the source of elderberry wine, which is said to prevent winter colds. The

flowers, fresh or dried, can be made into an infusion, in much the same way as plantain leaves, which will help to cool a fever and alleviate the symptoms of a cold. Elder leaves help to repel biting flies and mosquitoes, and an infusion of the leaves can be dabbed on the skin for this purpose.

▲ *A useful healing plant, plantain can help to treat wounds and soothe bites.*

CREATING A CACHE

Avoid harvesting any plants or killing any animals in the immediate vicinity of your camp. Move at least 100m/110yd away from your camp before looking for what you need. This way, you are not only leaving your immediate area intact, you are also creating an emergency cache. If you were to fall ill, it would be a relief to find edible plants growing right outside your shelter.

▲ *Mosses can be used to bandage wounds and control bleeding. Some, such as sphagnum moss, have antiseptic properties.*

▲ *Wounds need to be tended to and direct pressure to wounds needs to be applied if there is any bleeding.*

MAKING A NATURAL COUGH MIXTURE

1 Dried plantain can be used to brew a good anti-cough tea. Put a handful of dried plantain leaves in a bowl.

2 Boil some water and pour it over the leaves. Then let the leaves steep in the hot water for about 10 minutes.

3 Remove the plantain leaves from the bowl and the cough mixture is ready for use.

When gathering wood, never break branches over your knee or by jumping on them. It is easy to underestimate the strength of the wood and to hurt yourself. Always do the work with sharp tools or by burning them to the right length in a fire (which is a more efficient use of your energy anyway).

Be careful where you put your feet when exploring the surroundings, and take as little risk as possible. Sometimes it's better to go around difficult terrain than to cross it. Safety should always be uppermost in your mind when there is no one on hand to give you medical treatment if you are ill or injured.

PREVENTION IS BETTER THAN CURE

Common sense will tell you that the best way to treat illness or injury is to prevent it. You don't want to wound yourself by being careless with a knife, for instance, especially when in an accidental survival situation, since adding to your problems will cause your situation to deteriorate faster.

▲ *When bleeding is controlled and shock has been dealt with, it is time to tend to non-life-threatening wounds like fractures.*

Ensure that sharp implements are used and stored correctly so you don't accidentally stab yourself. When using tools such as knives or axes, it is vital that your body is never in the path of the tool or a splinter of stone or metal.

RESPECTING NATURE

There is a balance to strike between reducing your impact on the environment as much as possible, and staying alive. For example, if you life is not in immediate danger, you can build your shelter using only dead material, but if you life depends on it, the conservation rules have to give way. if you have to survive the night and there is not enough debris to shelter you, you shouldn't hesitate to cut down live branches and leaves to use as insulation.

In a non-life-threatening situation, it is important to take care of the environment you live in. If you have to cut down particular trees or plants for use in your shelter or for other purposes, always try to find those trees that are in competition with others, so that your action benefits them. Try to pick trees and plants growing in places where they seem less likely to thrive. This kind of "caretaker" attitude could actually improve the area where you find yourself. If survival forces you to kill an animal for food (see chapter 11, Bush Tucker, 354–365) then make use of everything there is to glean from that particular animal – meat for food, bones for tools, hide for clothing – leaving nothing to waste.

▲ *When you are shaping wood, carve smoothly and slowly, with the blade facing away from your body.*

▲ *Never turn the blade of the knife towards your hand or body, and make sure the path of the knife is clear of obstruction.*

▲ *Never break a branch of wood over your knee in case it is stronger than it looks and you hurt your leg.*

▲ *Jumping on a piece of wood could damage your ankle. If you can't cut it, burn it through to achieve the correct length.*

FIRE

Creating a fire without recourse to matches or a lighter is one of the most crucial survival skills you can master. Once a fire is built and lit it gives warmth, provides light during the long dark hours of night, enables you to cook food, sterilize water and make tools, and helps to keep your spirits up. Starting a fire using friction is not an easy task, and the various techniques require a lot of skill. Even then, being able to conjure a burning ember by rubbing sticks together is only half the skill. Tinder does not burn for long, so it is equally important to know how to build a fire that lights with the smallest flame and stays lit.

Fire for survival

Of the four basic building blocks of survival, the need for fire may seem least urgent, but you will often need to start a fire even before you can think about water. The reason for this is that even in the most remote places on earth, water may not be safe to drink unless it is purified first. In addition to bacteria, viruses and other natural contaminations, there may also be chemical pollutants in the water. These could have come from a plane dumping its fuel, farmers spraying insecticide on their fields, illegal dumping or the discharge of chemical waste farther up a watercourse. There are many possible ways for water to be contaminated, but many of the risks can be reduced or eliminated by boiling water before you drink it.

Apart from this vital procedure, fire allows you to create containers in which to carry water, and can help you shape tools to take care of your other needs. Fire will help you stay warm and comfortable. It will also ward off potentially dangerous wildlife and generally make the camp feel safer.

▼ *Knowing how to make a fire may be vital to survival, as water is often contaminated and needs to be purified by boiling.*

SITING A FIRE

Before you can even begin trying to make a fire, you have to consider the best location for it. There are a few important rules to remember:
• To make sure the fire starts easily and burns without too much smoke, you need to build it on dry ground. This is not always possible, however, and if the area is wet it is best to create a dry base using bark or large stones. Once the fire has caught and is burning brightly, the dampness or rain should not matter too much.
• If you can find a feature such as a large rock or a small dip in the ground, the natural surroundings will act as a windbreak and help to reflect the heat of the fire. If it is very windy but there are no natural windbreaks or hollows, you will need to site the fire below ground level in a trench, downwind from your shelter.
• As when choosing a site for your shelter, it is always a good idea to build a fire where there is plenty of material to use for fuel. You don't want to have to walk a long distance each time you need more wood for the fire.
• Before lighting a fire you must ensure that there are no flammable materials on the ground, such as dry leaves. In

▲ *Not only is a fire warming, but getting it to light can make you feel you have achieved something important. A fire also creates a sense of increased security.*

extremely dry regions, the roots of trees or accumulated underground debris could easily start smouldering and might eventually start a fire far away from the original site of the camp fire. When there are flammable materials on the ground you should clear an area at least 120cm/4ft across. Try to build the fire at least 2m/6ft 6in away from your shelter to make sure it stays safe: a debris hut can act like a gigantic tinder bundle.
• If the ground is wet or contains flammable materials such as tree roots, and you need to line the fire pit with stones, make sure they are not waterlogged otherwise you could end up having to protect yourself from exploding rocks (*see panel opposite*).
• Do not make the fire any larger than necessary, both to avoid accidents and to conserve fuel. Placing a circle of stones around the edge of the fire helps to define its size.
• Finally, make your fire in a location where you can watch it at all times.

CLEARING UP YOUR FIRE

When you go into the wilderness to practise your survival skills, it is important to leave the natural beauty of the area intact when you depart. This means that when you have finished with your fire you should remove all visible traces of it.

If you want to preserve the embers for the duration of your journey so that you can make a new fire somewhere else, scoop them up and put them into a non-flammable container, such as an old tin can. Make sure the fire is completely extinguished by dousing it with a lot of water, then check whether there is any warmth or smoke still emanating from it. If there is still a trace of heat or smoke, douse it again.

Ideally, all wood should have been burned away before extinguishing the fire, but if this has not been possible, remove and bury any half-burned

Here are some tips to help you make a small fire that will burn efficiently and keep you warm and comfortable.

- When you dig a pit for the fire, try to give it gently sloping sides. This will help to keep the burning materials gathered in the centre of the fire, making them burn longer and hotter.
- Build a horseshoe-shaped wall on the opposite side of the fire to where you are sitting. You should make this wall as smooth as possible, preferably using stones,

to help it reflect the heat back towards you. Keep the wall about 60–90cm/2–3ft away from the fire and about 90cm/3ft high.

- Another wall, or a natural feature you can sit against, will reflect the heat passing you. A grassy bank, a pile of logs or a stump would do fine instead of a solid wall.
- If you are in a larger group of people, you might want to build both walls far enough away from the fire for you all to sit inside them and keep your backs warm.

pieces of wood. Remove the ashes and scatter them around the area. Then remove any stones you used to border the fire, and fill in the pit with the soil you dug out of it. Camouflage the area

so it fits in with the landscape, for example by drawing the forest debris back over it. This way, the area will look pristine when another person passes through in the future.

PREPARING A SAFE, EFFICIENT FIRE

1 Locate a suitable piece of ground that is free of debris, or clear the site, then dig a shallow pit about 15–25cm/ 6–10in deep, with sloping sides.

2 Place rocks on the bottom of the pit, to help reflect any heat upwards. You can also line the far side of the pit to reflect the heat towards you.

3 Gather all the resources you need to start your fire and maintain it. In a desert area there may not be much available, but at least it will be dry.

4 Build a simple reflecting wall about 1m/3ft from the fire using rocks, logs or whatever you can forage, to reflect the heat back towards you.

5 A wall behind you will reflect any heat that passes you back in your direction. This is a highly efficent way of channelling the available heat.

EXPLODING ROCKS

Select the rocks you use at the bottom of a pit with care. You should never use stones that may have water trapped inside them, as this can turn to steam when the stones are heated up, leading to an explosion. To avoid this, never collect rocks from stream beds or from the bottom of valleys. It is not necessary to find completely dry stones, so long as they are not waterlogged.

Firelighters and fuels

All over the world people use numerous different fuels – including dried grasses, wood of many different trees and dried animal excrement – to start and maintain fires.

The first rule when gathering fuel is that it must be dry. This sounds obvious, but it may be very hard in some survival situations. It is also a good reason to gather plenty of fuel at the outset. You should have enough to last at least the whole night, as you don't want to have to go out to find more dry fuel in the dark or when it has started to rain.

▶ *Firewood needs to be as dry as possible, though larger pieces will burn even if damp once the fire is well established.*

▲ *Always try to collect dead wood that is still hanging in the trees to burn in your fire, as it will be drier and less smoky. For kindling purposes, the dead twigs in the left hand above are better for starting a fire than the leaves, even though they are dead.*

▲ *Use a flint or sharp stone to lift the bark off dead wood. The dry inner bark can be shredded into loose fibres to use as tinder.*

KINDLING FOR GETTING FIRES STARTED

▲ *Dry grass may burn well, but is not great as a fire starter because it will remain whole after burning, cutting off vital oxygen.*

▲ *The high oil content of dry gorse or furze means it catches light easily and burns well when used as kindling.*

▲ *Dry plant stalks can be shredded to form excellent tinder or can be used as kindling, though they often burn away fast.*

▲ *Dry seed heads are excellent for catching a spark. They will allow your ember to grow before you place it in the tinder.*

▲ *Dry leaves burn brightly but, just like grass, remain intact, often smothering the fire. Never use leaves to light your fire.*

▲ *Dry sticks are the material of choice to build your fire with. If they are thin they also make excellent kindling.*

THE IDEAL WOOD FOR FIRE

If possible, try to gather dead wood exclusively from standing trees, because when it has been lying on the ground for a while it will probably have soaked up moisture, with the result that it will create too much smoke when burned.

Five different grades of fuel are needed to make a fire, from tinder, to catch the first spark, to large logs.

TINDER

In a survival situation in which you need to light a fire by a friction method, and not with a flame from a match or lighter, tinder is the first and most important component. Basically, it is any soft, fluffy, dry material that will ignite from a spark.

You can use any fine, dry plant material, such as fluffy seed heads or the dry inner bark of dead wood. Fibre that you would normally use to make cordage is usually a great source of tinder. The best way to learn what works well is to experiment.

Having collected the material, you need to break it down with your hands into separate plant fibres, teasing and fluffing it up until you have a soft, dry ball about the size of a grapefruit.

KINDLING

Though a larger firelighter than tinder, kindling is still small: you should be looking for twigs about as thick as a pencil. It also has to be totally dry. Just as with tinder, you always need far

▲ *Sticks ranging from thin twigs to boughs as thick as a wrist are generally referred to as small bulkwood. They make up most of the wood that is used in a fire once it is lit.*

more than you think – if you gather three or four times as much as you think you will need, that should be enough. Always bear in mind that if you do not select your tinder and kindling carefully, all your fire-making efforts might come to a frustrating halt.

As an alternative type of firelighter, you can try making a "fuzz-stick" (*see below*). This is a larger stick carved in thin slivers down to the dry wood: the slivers should be left attached like many small "branches" on a tree.

SQUAW WOOD

Named after the Native American women who gathered this wood in large quantities, squaw wood ranges in size from the thickness of a pencil to that of a finger. If you don't mind a lot of smoke, you can use this wood when it is slightly damp.

▲ *Bulkwood is used to keep a fire going. Though it burns for a long time, it needs small bulkwood to keep it going, and may be smoky if the fire isn't hot enough.*

SMALL BULKWOOD

This is the kind of wood you will mainly be burning. The thickness ranges from marker-pen size to the thickness of your wrist. This is the most important size, as the wood is large enough to give off the heat you need, but small enough to burn on its own without failing. You will need to get your fire established using this size of wood before you can get larger pieces of bulkwood to burn.

BULKWOOD

This is the type of fuel that is too big to break. You would want to use it only to make a large fire, or to keep the fire burning overnight. Never waste energy trying to cut wood this size – just let the fire break it for you. This size of wood can be wet if you don't mind the smoke.

MAKING A FUZZ-STICK

1 If you have a blade suitable for carving you can make this firelighting aid. Select a dry stick, preferably of birch or another resinous wood.

2 Carve deep cuts into the stick, layering them like the scales on a fish. Don't cut right through the wood, but leave the slivers hanging on it.

3 By carving these "scales" you are essentially enlarging the surface area of the wood. This means the fire has more wood to "get at" to ignite.

Lighting fires using friction

There are many ways to light a fire besides using matches or a lighter, and they have been around a lot longer than these artifical methods of creating a flame. Learning the so-called "primitive" ways will enable you to light a fire when your matches get wet, run out or if you don't have any.

Ancient peoples all over the world used these methods. Their very lives depended on their skill, and it is still truly awesome to watch somebody learn this age-old skill, seeing that look on their face when they first manage to get an ember after hours of trying. It is always a special feeling when the ember forms itself, even after you have started hundreds of fires.

The friction method (which applies to all of the techniques described in this chapter apart from the Arctic fire) depends on the fact that two pieces of wood rubbed together at speed will generate enough heat to produce carbonized particles and sparks, which will ignite a ball of dry tinder. The trick lies in not only getting the correct technique but also having the right mindset. You will probably come to understand this when you learn to make fire, and it is also true of other techniques of survival.

THE FIRE PLOUGH

A simple firelighting technique using the friction method that works quite well in some circumstances is the fire plough. As a sharpened stick is rubbed up and down in the groove of a fireboard, small fragments of wood dust collect at the bottom of the groove, and will eventually ignite into an ember when there is enough heat. You must take care not to scatter the dust by an erratic stroke of the plough. This procedure can be fairly laborious, and the friction techniques described on the following pages are usually preferable if there is an option.

THE DRILL METHOD

The bow drill, hand drill and pump drill (see 314–315, 318–319 and 322–323 respectively) are traditional ways of generating enough friction to create a spark. Each technique relies on a stick being spun at speed in the notch of a "hearth-board" to create embers. The Native Americans have a neat way of describing the process: they tell their children that making a fire resembles making a baby. They liken the drill to the male reproductive organ, while the hearth-board is the female. The ember is created in the notch, like the embryo forming in the womb.

MAKING A FIRE PLOUGH

1 Find a strong stick of hard wood and carve the tip to make a sharp edge like that of a screwdriver.

2 Split a thick branch of softer wood or shave off one side to make a flat fireboard about 60cm/2ft long.

3 With a sharp stone carve a groove about 45cm/18in long for the plough to move along.

4 Place the plough in the groove, and start moving it back and forth. At first nothing will seem to happen.

5 After a while, you will notice smoke coming off the fireboard and plough, and the groove will darken.

6 Wood fibres collect at the bottom and with a lot of speed and pressure, they will ignite into an ember.

SOURCES OF WOOD FOR LIGHTING FIRES BY FRICTION

▲ *Alder is a medium-hard wood, often used for carving reasonably efficient drill sets.*

▲ *Cedar bark makes excellent kindling and the wood is good for making bow drills.*

▲ *Poplar can be used to make successful drill sets, and it is also slow-burning.*

▲ *Elder branches have a soft, pithy centre, which works well to help extend an ember.*

▲ *Stout, woody mullein stalks also have a pithy centre and make good hand drills.*

▲ *Burdock is another large herb with rigid, woody stalks that are good for fire-making.*

DRILL-MAKING MATERIALS

You need medium-hard wood to make a drill, and some of the best species for this purpose are shown above. If you're not sure what kind of wood you have, it's quite easy to test its hardness by running your thumbnail down the length of the stick.

Apart from wood, to make a bow drill you will need a length of cord about 60–90cm/2–3ft long, and you can make this by braiding plant or tree fibres. The best fibres come from stinging nettles stems, but many other plants are also suitable. The dry stems need to be pounded with a rounded stone to separate the fibres, which can then be twisted or braided together.

Another solution is to use spruce roots, which also work extremely well. To find spruce roots, simply dig around the base of a spruce tree. When you come across a root, follow it through the ground, carefully extracting it as you go along. The roots are usually quite close to the soil surface and grow straight out from the tree. When you have collected a few roots, rub them over a branch to get rid of the bark. The roots can be quite long and it is better to use them as single lengths, because they are more likely to break if they are tied in knots.

TESTING WOOD FOR HARDNESS

1 Find a dry stick of the material you intend to use for your bow drill. Cut down the stick to expose a flat area.

2 Run your nail from one end of the stick to the other. You do not have to follow the grain.

3 If the line is crumbly the wood is too soft or rotten. If there is no line or it's only barely visible, it's too hard.

The bow drill

The bow drill is the staple means of lighting a fire by friction. It works on the same principle as all other methods, but is the easiest to use. It is efficient and works even in damp conditions.

SELECTING AND CARVING THE WOOD

To make a bow drill set you will need some suitable pieces of wood from which to make the three carved components, a slightly curved stick (which does not have to be flexible) for the bow, and some cordage. You will also need a knife or stone tool for carving. The set consists of several different parts: a spindle, a hearth-board, a handhold and a bow, and for each of these you should select wood that requires a minimum of shaping.

The first component to carve is the spindle, which should be as long as the distance between the tip of your index finger and the tip of your thumb when you hold your hand outstretched. The top of the spindle needs to have a long point, while the bottom should have a shallow point. The spindle should be perfectly round, and the points need to be sharp and even.

The hearth-board, made from the same wood as the spindle, should be of about the same thickness and twice the width. It should be about 30cm/1ft long so that you can hold it steady with your foot, and should have a flat bottom so that it does not wobble.

The handhold can be made of any material as long as it is as hard or harder than the wood from which the spindle is made. The handhold should fit comfortably in your hand, with a thickness at least that of the drill.

The bow is best made with a slight bend, though a completely straight stick will work. It is best to learn to use the drill with a bow about 1m/3ft long. Once you have mastered the technique, you can try longer or shorter bows: even a bow as little as 20cm/8in long may work.

A piece of cordage is attached to the bow and you have to try to get just the right tension when the spindle is twisted into the cord. It should not be so loose that you can pull the spindle up and down while holding it in your hand, but it should not be so tight that you cannot twist the spindle at all: ideally, you should just about manage to twist the drill with effort. The correct tension will also depend on how flexible your bow is, and the cord is bound to need tightening during use, so you will need to make adjustments. For this reason, you should tie a permanent knot at one end, but a semi-permanent knot that is easily undone at the other.

MAKING A BOW DRILL

1 Gather three pieces of wood: the pieces for the hearth-board and the spindle should be about 2.5cm/1in thick. The handhold should be thicker.

2 First carve the spindle: it needs to be straight, perfectly round and smooth, about 2.5cm/1in in diameter and 20–23cm/8–9in long.

3 Carve or abrade (scrape away) one end to a fairly deep point, about 2.5cm/1in long. This point will become the top of the drill.

4 Abrade the other end into a much shallower point, about 6mm/¹⁄₄in deep. This end will be the bottom.

5 After use, both points may look very similar, so to make sure you remember which is the top, carve a notch.

6 The finished spindle should be straight, with a shorter and a longer point, and a notch around the top.

7 To prepare the hearth-board, carve a small hole a spindle's width from the edge. This is where the bottom end of the spindle will go.

8 Make a similar hole in the handhold, positioning it above the line on the palm of your hand running up from your wrist, clear of your fingertips.

9 Fasten the string to the bow. Use a permanent knot at one end and one that is easily undone at the other, as you may need to tighten it frequently.

10 Twist the spindle into the string, ensuring that the string is between the bow and the spindle (the spindle is on the outside of the bowstring).

11 With your left foot on the hearth-board, wrap your arm around your left leg, and place the spindle in the holes in the hearth-board and the handhold.

12 Start to move the bow back and forth vigorously. The action will drill round impressions in the hearth-board and the handhold.

13 When the whole diameter of the drill has been drilled into the hearth-board, you can stop. By now, there should also be a hole in the handhold.

14 Grease the handhold so the spindle rotates smoothly. The notch will stop you accidentally putting the greased end of the spindle in the hearth-board.

15 Carve or abrade a wedge shaped notch in the hearth-board, nearly, but not quite, reaching the centre of the hole you have drilled.

PREPARING THE BOW DRILL SET
Before you can start making fire you must drill holes to take the spindle in both the hearth-board and the handle. This is done by using the spindle itself to enlarge small guide holes made with the point of your knife or another sharp tool. The drilling action is the same as that used for making fire, and for this you need to practise getting into the right position to make the drill work efficiently.

GETTING INTO POSITION
These instructions are written for a right-handed person – if you are left-handed you will need to reverse them.

Kneel down on your right knee, while placing your left foot over the hearth-board. The arch of your left foot should be right beside the hole where the drill is going to be once it's in place. Your left knee should be bent at a right angle. Now you are ready to twist the spindle into the cord on the

bow so that it is outside the string, meaning that the string is between the spindle and the bow.

Rest your chest on your left knee, and wrap your left arm, holding the handle, around the outside of your thigh and across your shin. Your wrist and thumb pad should be pressing against your leg with the handhold facing down. Position the drill with the top in the handhold and the bottom in the hole on the hearth-board.

THE RIGHT STROKE

The spindle should now be standing perfectly upright between the handhold and the hearth-board. If this is not the case, try to adjust the angle of your left knee slightly until the drill is pointing straight down into the hearth-board. Once your angles are nice and straight, grasp the bow with your right hand.

To get the most out of each stroke, grip the bow as far back as you can. Move it slowly backwards and forwards while keeping the bow parallel with the ground. Once you get a feel for the technique and once your strokes are steady and regular, you can try to speed up a bit with the bow.

If your technique is correct – with the right pressure on the handhold, keeping the spindle steady and vertical and the bow horizontal and going at the right speed – you should start to get some smoke and black dust around the edges of the hole in the hearth-board even if you are not going too fast with the bow. Don't worry if you are not getting any smoke at first. It takes a bit of practice to get it right. The usual problem is not holding the drill steadily enough and at the same time not applying enough downward pressure. You should be spending about 25 per cent of your energy holding your wrist tight against your left leg, 50 per cent pushing down and 25 per cent moving the bow back and forth.

Once there is plenty of smoke, you can increase the speed of the bow a

little while applying more downward pressure. You can stop drilling once the whole diameter of the spindle is in the hearth-board.

COMPLETING THE BOW DRILL

At this point, it is time to grease the handhold to reduce the friction there, and to carve a notch to collect the black dust and eventually the ember.

The hole in the handhold can be greased with the oil from crushed pine needles, animal or vegetable fat, the oil from your skin or hair, or anything else you have available. But don't use water – it will not lubricate the top of the spindle and it will make the wood swell, shrinking the hole and thus creating more friction. Once you have greased the top of the spindle, you must never put the greased end into the hole on the hearth-board because you need friction there.

▲ *Use medium-hard woods for your DIY wood-burning kit, such as hazel, cedar, poplar or sycamore, and look for pieces that require minimal shaping.*

The notch in the hearth-board is important as it will collect all the dust created by the friction, and the size of the notch makes a big difference in performance. It should be a perfect eighth of the hole and should stop just short of the centre of the hole. Divide the circular hole into 16 segments and then carve out the two segments closest to the edge of the hearth-board. Make sure the sides of the notch are smooth.

Now your set is ready to create an ember. At this point you should construct your fire and prepare the tinder to receive the spark. The tinder bundle, made from fine, dry fibres, should be fluffy and in the shape of a shallow bird's nest.

USING A BOW DRILL

1 Place a piece of wood, a leaf or a dry flat stone under the notch in the hearth-board, so that any dust that gathers will not fall on damp ground.

2 Place the spindle in the hole, and start moving the bow at a slow but steady speed, increasing the speed and pressure as smoke starts to build.

3 When you are successful, there will be an ember in the dust in the notch. It may not be visible at first, but there will be sustained smoke from the dust.

▶ *The trick of using a bow drill lies in applying enough pressure with your left arm while holding the spindle steady and upright and ensuring the bow is going at the right speed, level with the ground.*

MAKING AN EMBER

Place the hearth-board with the notch on a piece of dry bark or some thick dry leaves to prevent the hot dust from falling on the ground and getting damp or cooling down. This base will also help you later when transferring the ember to your tinder bundle. Some people like to dig a little hole in the ground underneath the notch to hold the tinder, but this can cause the tinder bundle to get squashed or damp.

It doesn't matter too much whether the notch is facing you or away from you. Check the wind direction and make sure there is enough room to hold your foot down on the hearth-board. Taking up the same position you used to drill the holes, start off again with gentle strokes to warm up the hearth-board. Often it will sound squeaky at this point – this means you are going too fast with the bow or applying too little pressure.

Don't put too much pressure on the spindle just yet. Once the set starts to smoke, you can speed up and apply

more pressure. Continue until there is a lot of smoke coming from the bottom of your hearth-board and until it seems that smoke is coming from below the dust in the notch. Then carefully lift off the drill and very carefully remove the hearth-board to see if you have an ember. You will tell from the smoke – if it continues to pour from the black dust you have an ember. Sometimes you can also see a red glow at this

point. Once you have reached this stage, you can take a breather to allow the ember to grow. You can also help the process by gently wafting a little air towards it with your hand, but be gentle as the ember is only just forming and is very frail.

Once the ember has settled a little and you've had a few seconds rest, carefully pick it up and transfer it to your tinder bundle.

TURNING AN EMBER INTO A FLAME

1 Hold the tinder bundle slightly higher than your face to prevent too much smoke going in your eyes and start blowing on it gently. Once the ember starts to spread into the tinder you can blow a little harder.

2 When the tinder bundle is nearly too hot to hold in your hands, give it all the oxygen you can. The tinder should go up in flames. You don't have a lot of time to place your tinder bundle in the fire before it burns out, but be careful.

3 If you squeeze the bundle too much, you may extinguish the flames. If you are worried that you don't have enough tinder, place the bundle inside the fire as soon as it's glowing well, and blow it into flames there.

The hand drill

Though the technique and materials are different, the hand drill works on the same principle as the bow drill. The hand drill consists of a straight stick, 30cm–1.5m/1–5ft long and as thick as an average pen, and a hearth-board about the same thickness as the drill and twice as wide. This means that the hand drill involves a lot less material and less preparation than the bow drill. The downside is that the hand drill does not work well in damp conditions, whereas the bow drill will work under most circumstances.

Medium-hard woods are needed for the apparatus. The spindle is often made from hollow straight shoots of plants such as elder, mullein or burdock. The hearth-board should be made from woods such as poplar and cedar. This time the spindle is not pointed at the top or bottom. The only preparation it requires is smoothing and the removal of side branches and knots.

MAKING A HAND DRILL

1 To prepare the spindle, select a straight shoot or branch about 1.2cm/^{1}/$_2$in thick.

2 Make sure the stick is perfectly smooth by cutting away any side branches, knots and perhaps even bark.

3 Round the bottom of the spindle to stop it creating excess friction at the side of the hole in the hearth-board.

4 Press the tip of the drill into the hearth-board, about 6mm/^{1}/$_4$in from the edge, to make a round indentation.

5 Carve out the indentation carefully. The resulting hole should be exactly the same diameter as the drill.

6 Holding the hearth-board with one foot, spin the drill slowly between your hands starting at the top of the spindle.

7 Once you are confident the hole has been burnt deep enough to prevent the spindle slipping, stop.

8 Carve a notch in the hearth-board, cutting a segment of one eighth of the circle, which just enters the hole.

9 If the drill is hollow you may cut the notch all the way to the centre. The hand drill set is now ready for use.

▶ *The hand drill method requires minimal preparation but is a reliable technique only in dry or hot regions.*

CREATING AN EMBER

Place the hearth-board on a stable surface and steady it with your foot, as far away from the hole as possible. If you kneel, as with the bow drill, your left arm should be on the inside of your leg. You may be flexible enough to sit, steadying the board with the side of your foot. This gives more space to move your hands, but it may be harder to apply enough downward pressure.

With the spindle in the hole, hold it at the top between your flat palms. While pressing down, move your hands back and forth across the drill to make it twirl. Work slowly and gently until there is plenty of smoke coming from the bottom of the spindle, then speed up and apply more pressure.

Embers produced with the hand drill are generally frail and burn out quickly.

It may help to have an "extender" to hand to help strengthen and enlarge the ember before you place it in the tinder bundle. This can be any dry, fluffy material that helps the ember grow. Good materials include bulrush (cattail) down, shredded cedar bark or pulverized, dead softwood.

USING A HAND DRILL

1 Place the end of the drill in the hole in the hearth-board. Orient the notch so that it is protected from wind.

2 Start by slowly rubbing the stick back and forth between your hands until you notice the first puff of smoke.

3 Your hands will move down the drill; when you reach the bottom, move up as fast as possible for another run.

4 Try to ensure you use the whole hand, including your fingers, so that there are more revolutions per stroke.

5 Once the notch has filled with dust, and smoke pours from it when you stop drilling, you may have an ember.

6 The ember is generally small and can break very easily or run out of fuel. Try to use it as soon as it's made.

The pump drill

In a survival situation you need to get an ember going fast, and this takes energy and muscle power. If you find yourself surviving in a more permanent shelter where there is not much room to move about you can try the pump drill method. The apparatus is harder to make, but it is easier to use in a confined space such as inside a shelter, and will light many fires without too much effort. It can also be used for drilling holes for other purposes.

MAKING THE SPINDLE
For the spindle of the pump drill, you'll need a straight branch about 60cm/2ft long and about 3cm/1¼in in diameter. If the branch is at all bent you'll have to straighten it, or find another branch, otherwise the drill will not work properly.

Clean off all the bark, and abrade the stick so that it tapers slightly: the thicker end will eventually be the bottom of the pump drill. Once this is done, carve or drill a notch in the thicker end of the stick to enable you to insert a stone blade or a chuck later on. The thinner end of the spindle is also notched. It will later hold a string.

MAKING THE FLYWHEEL
The next component to be made is the flywheel. To make the two halves match exactly, make them from a single piece of wood about 7.5cm/3in wide and 45cm/18in long. Drill, burn or carve a hole right through the middle. The hole must be slightly less than the diameter of the spindle at the bottom end. Split the wood in half so you have two matching pieces, each with a hole through the centre.

To weight the flywheel, find two round stones of the same weight. These will be sandwiched between the two half sticks. Carve a few notches in the ends of the sticks to make it easier to tie the rocks securely into place. When tying the pieces together, make sure you line up the central holes perfectly.

Once the flywheel is assembled, you can slide it on to the spindle. If you

have made the holes the correct size, it should fit snugly when it is about 2.5–7.5cm/1–3in from the bottom of the spindle.

THE HANDHOLD
The handle of the pump should be about 60cm/2ft long and 7.5cm/3in wide. You may be able to split a branch to get a plank with these measurements. You need to drill a hole in the centre of this piece, which should be large enough for the handle to slide freely right down the spindle to meet the flywheel. Carve notches at each side of both ends of the handle to take the string.

Now all you need to complete the apparatus is a piece of cordage, which should be about 1m/3ft long. Tie one end of the cord around one end of the handle, securing it in the notches, and the other end to the second set of notches on the other end. Slide the handle down over the spindle, and insert the middle of the cord into the notch you made on the spindle.

PREPARING THE FIRE PUMP
The pump drill can perform a number of functions, but in order to use it to start a fire by friction, it needs to be fitted with a wooden bit that can

▲ *The fire pump is especially useful when you need to make fire regularly while inside a confined space such as a long-term shelter.*

be twirled in a hearth-board. Select a piece of medium-hard wood such as poplar or cedar for this purpose. The bit should be carved to look much like the bottom of a bow drill spindle, though the top end will need to be shaped to fit into the notch you made in the bottom of the pump drill spindle. The diameter of the bit can be a little smaller than that of the bow drill spindle – 12mm/½in or slightly thicker works very well. Insert the bit into the spindle and tie it securely so there is no sideways movement.

Make a hearth-board like that for the bow drill. Carve a little hole into it, and insert the tip of the pump drill. Wind the handle up to twist the cord around the spindle, then push it down. Once it's fully down, the flywheel will take over the motion and bring the handle up automatically. Push down again and keep this motion going until you have drilled a sizable hole into the hearth-board. Carve a notch and you are ready to start lighting fires with your pump drill. The technique of balancing pressure and speed is exactly the same as in the other methods.

MAKING A PUMP DRILL

1 The spindle should be about 1m/3ft long and 2.5cm/1in in diameter. Carve a notch in the top (the thinner end).

2 Drill a hole in the thicker end to hold a chuck, and wrap cord around the spindle just above the hole.

3 Find a piece of wood 7.5cm/3in wide and 45cm/18in long. Drill a hole through the centre then split the stick.

4 Find a piece of wood about 60cm/2ft long for the handle and carve notches in each end to hold the string.

5 Drill a hole in the centre of the handle. It should be large enough for the spindle to move freely through it.

6 To weight the flywheel find two large stones of about 1–1.5kg/2–3lb and several lengths of cordage.

7 Wrap cord around both pieces of the flywheel to reinforce the centre and prevent splits when pressure is applied.

8 Sandwich the two stones between the pieces of wood and tie them in securely to make the flywheel.

9 Slide the flywheel over the thin part of the spindle. It should stick 2.5–5cm/1–2in above the hole in the bottom.

10 Tie a 1m/3ft piece of string around the notches at both ends of the handle.

11 Thread on the handle and insert the string in the notch on the spindle.

12 Twist the handle up to the top then push it down to start the pump action.

Jungle fire

A method that works extremely well in tropical environments is the fire saw, which is usually made from a piece of dead bamboo, about 60cm/2ft long and with a diameter of 4–5cm/1½–2in.

The bamboo is split in half and the hearth-board is prepared by laying one piece flat on a stable, dry surface with the convex side facing up. If you are by yourself, you will need to anchor the hearth-board very securely to the surface it's lying on, otherwise get another person to hold it down. Cut a small hole in the convex surface to keep the saw on one spot.

The saw is prepared by carving off any joints in and outside the stick and scraping one of the split sides to smooth it and even it out. This saw is then placed perpendicular to the hearth-board, with the smoothed edge over the hole.

USING THE FIRE SAW

Just as with the other friction methods, you should start slowly, sawing back and forth over the hearth-board until it starts smoking. The pressure and speed should then be increased until there is a lot of smoke or until you can't go on any longer. The ember will form under the hollow of the hearth-board.

This ember tends to be fairly frail, so be careful to extend it with some dry, fluffy, easily flammable material and be sure to handle it gently.

THE FIRE THONG

Instead of the saw, a piece of dry, flexible rattan about 90–120cm/3–4ft long can be used, though then the hearth-board is held upside down, and you saw upwards. This method, known as the fire thong, is very efficient with a little practice.

FIRE PISTON

Conditions in the jungle can often be too wet to light a fire by friction. An ingenious method developed by indigenous people is a device known as a "fire piston". This rapidly compresses air in a small, very smoothly bored cylinder, which makes it very hot. The end of the piston is hollowed out to hold tinder, and the compressed air gets hot enough to ignite it.

The tube itself, closed at one end, is traditionally made of hardwood, bamboo or even horn. The piston can be made of wound thread, fibre or leather, to ensure a proper seal to create the compression successfully.

MAKING A FIRE SAW

1 Split a length of bamboo in half. One half will become the hearth-board and the other half will be the saw.

2 Using a knife or sharp stone, make a little hole in the convex side of one piece of bamboo, just piercing it.

3 Prepare the saw by cleaning up the edge of the other piece of bamboo. It should be rounded, not too sharp.

4 Hold the saw in the hole, keeping it at a slight tilt so as not to saw both sides of the split at once.

5 Move the saw back and forth while applying a lot of pressure. It should start smoking quite rapidly.

6 When the set is smoking profusely, lift the saw. If the smoke persists, there is an ember under the hearth-board.

Arctic fire

By far the most amazing way to light a fire is by using ice. Being able to create an ember using this fire kit is something special indeed, since it is the only natural method that doesn't depend on generating friction between pieces of wood. In fact, no wood is needed at all, apart from the fuel that is to be used in the fire. In polar regions even the fire may be built using different materials – fuels such as dried dung and animal fat are commonly used in such extreme terrain.

To make an ice lens you'll need a block of ice about 10cm/4in thick and about 5cm/2in long and wide. It should be free of cracks and other imperfections that will distort the lens. Carve the block into a round shape, before carefully carving away the edges to create the lens. Don't carve too much material away from the centre,

but make the edges nearly sharp. Once you are approaching the right shape, put your knife or stone tool down, and continue shaping the lens by using body heat to melt the ice where it is not needed. This will prevent you from accidentally breaking the lens. Test the lens by looking through it at a nearby object, and go on shaping until you achieve a clear magnified image.

MAKING AN EMBER

You'll need some very fine tinder to make an ember with the lens. Crushed bark works well, but only if it's fibrous. Hold the lens between the sun and the piece of tinder and move it back and forth until the light is focused on the tinder. This should start smoking very rapidly. By blowing on it gently you should be able to get an ember in about 30 seconds.

MAKING FIRE FROM ICE

1 The ice needs to be about 10cm/4in across and 5cm/2in thick. Carve a circular shape, then pare the edges.

2 The profile of the ice lens shows its shape clearly. The final shaping is best done by rubbing with the fingers.

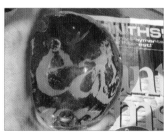

3 You should strive for a clear, magnified image when shaping the lens: test it by looking through it.

4 When you find the lens's focal point by trial and error, it will quickly char a sheet of paper by focusing sunlight.

5 It is better to hold the lens only with gloves after it has been completed, otherwise it will soon melt away.

6 When the sunlight is focused on a piece of tinder, in this case cedar, it will start to smoke in a matter of seconds.

Building a fire

Having decided where you will site your fire and how you will light it, you need to build it using dry, carefully selected fuel so that it lights easily and burns steadily, otherwise all the effort you put into igniting your tinder will be wasted. Different situations require different sorts of fires. However, the tipi fire is probably one of the best constructions to use in a survival situation. It has several advantages:
• maximum heat
• maximum light
• efficient use of fuel
• smoke and sparks travel straight up
• it is resistant to water and snow.

To build the fire you need a shallow fire-pit, which (in damp or dangerously dry conditions) you should line with dried bark, grasses or stones. Then add the fuel, starting with the smallest type of wood, the kindling. Try to fashion a neat pyramid, but be sure to leave an opening near the ground, because that is where the tinder is going to be put as soon as it's alight.

Aim to put the thinner pieces of kindling nearer to the inside and the bigger pieces to the outside of the fire. Do not pack the wood too tightly at this stage. Leave space for oxygen to reach the centre of the fire, and if there is any wind, line up the opening with the direction it is coming from – it will help drive the flames up into the tipi. If you have any available, it is a good idea to add pieces of resinous bark, such as birch bark, which will combust very, very easily.

Next comes the squaw wood, which is built up in the same manner. At this point, you can also add some pieces of small bulkwood to the fire if you wish. The only problem is that the fire may collapse as the smaller wood burns away from underneath the bulkwood. It is important in any case to feed smaller pieces of wood into the bottom of the fire rather than just piling wood on top. This is especially important if you are using bulkwood, otherwise the fire sometimes hollows out, making it hard to keep alight.

MAKING A TIPI FIRE

1 Dig out a shallow pit with sloping sides to keep the embers in the centre.

2 If the ground is damp or extremely dry, line the pit with bark or stones.

3 To contain the fire, place a ring of large rocks around the side.

4 Break a bunch of kindling in half and arrange it in a pyramid shape.

5 Add slightly larger wood but leave an opening to insert the lighted tinder.

6 You can add a few larger pieces of wood at this point, but not too many.

7 Add the tinder as soon as it is alight, because it doesn't burn for long.

8 Once the fire is lit, you can maintain it by adding larger pieces of wood.

Keeping a fire going

There may be many times when you want to ensure that your fire survives through the night, so you don't have to go through the process of relighting it in the morning. There are various ways to make sure that some embers survive all night, but you must be very sure that there is no danger of the fire spreading and getting out of control while you are asleep.

Once you are pretty much ready to go to sleep for the night, you can prepare the fire to last until the morning by adding some large pieces of green wood. The best wood to use

for this would be fresh branches of hardwoods such as oak. However, green wood will cause a lot of smoke, which may be undesirable.

If the fire is sheltered and the smoke will not disturb you, just throwing on a large amount of green wood should make it glow through the night. If the fire is less protected from the wind, you can also throw some soil over the glowing embers once you have placed the green wood on the fire. The soil will prevent too much oxygen from reaching the embers, thereby reducing the speed at which they burn out.

Make sure that the soil does not contain dry leaves, grasses or other such material, because this may flare up unexpectedly.

The next morning, to get the fire going again, all you have to do is carefully remove the soil from the fire. There should be plenty of embers still there, though they may be buried beneath a layer of ash. Use a bit of tinder and plenty of kindling wood to build a small new fire on top of the embers. By blowing at the embers, you should be able to get the fire to light again in a matter of seconds.

DAMPING DOWN A CAMP FIRE

1 While you are getting ready to go to sleep in the evening, leave the fire until it has pretty much burned down. Place a number of thick green sticks on the fire, which will smoulder slowly through the night.

2 Cover the fire with soil, making sure you are not using really wet soil, to reduce the flow of oxygen. In the morning, remove the soil from the fire and carefully scrape the ash away so the embers are exposed.

3 Using some tinder and plenty of kindling, build a small fire over the embers and blow on it to get it going. Once the first flames have started to appear, add more wood, and build your fire up again as usual.

MAKING A MATCH TO CARRY FIRE

1 Collect a good amount of tinder such as bulrush (cattail) down and other small fibres, and find a piece of bark 10cm/4in wide and 30cm/12in long.

2 Roll the tinder into the bark like a cigar. Make sure the tinder is not too tightly rolled, but not too loosely either. A bit of testing is often required.

3 Tie up the bundle with cord and put the ember in the top. The trick is to give it just enough oxygen to let it slowly smoulder down the match.

Building a fire for cooking

A fire for cooking needs to be built in a way that will create plenty of hot embers. When you are roasting meat or cooking food in a vessel such as an earthenware pot, you don't want too many flames. A good bed of hot coals will give a more sustained heat and the temperature will also be more regular, so that your food will cook properly without charring.

Often such a fire is built between two heavy logs, which both contain the fire and provide support for any pots or sticks to rest above the embers. Of course these two logs will burn as well and will eventually have to be replaced. One way round this is to line the inside of the logs with a layer of clay, which will prevent them from burning. The fire will be somewhat hemmed in by the logs, so if there is a prevailing wind, lay them in that direction to ensure a good supply of air.

A tipi fire is initially built between the logs. Once this is lit and burning profusely, thicker squaw wood is added, laying it in the same direction as the two logs. Once these are burning well, more branches are laid crossways and left to burn. The fire will burn down rather quickly, but will leave a lot of embers suitable for cooking on.

From now on, the trick is to keep a good amount of embers in the fire. It helps to add only one stick at a time. This will flare up, but turn into embers

quickly, because there is no additional wood to support the flames. Just keep adding sticks one after the other.

Cooking fires have many other uses. When you light one, be ready to make some glue, strip some spruce roots, or do any other tasks that require a fire without flames. You should light the fire for such activities during the day, as the embers do not provide much light to see by.

HANDLING EQUIPMENT

Apart from some fireproof containers, you also need to make some equipment to get the containers off the fire when the food is ready. Make suitable tools

▲ *The best fire for cooking provides a good bed of embers and should be built with stable supports for bowls and pots.*

before you start cooking, as it can be very frustrating if food or hot water gets lost in the fire because you drop a container or knock it over.

The most useful tool would be a pair of tongs, though separate tools often need to be fashioned for each container you use, since the shapes of cooking pots can vary so much. Try to incorporate features such as handles that sticks can slide through when you are making the pots. See also chapter 12 on Tools and Equipment, 366–385.

COOKING WITHOUT UTENSILS

▲ *Cook fish by laying it out flat on a hot rock, or hang it on a stout log placed next to the fire.*

▲ *Thread meat and vegetables on to straight sticks to make kebabs, then roast them over ash-covered embers so they don't burn.*

▲ *Simple small loaves of unleavened bread are delicious when baked on a flat stone heated by a wood fire.*

CONSTRUCTING A SHALLOW OPEN FIRE FOR COOKING

1 Dig a shallow fire-pit so the embers stay together. Don't make the pit any wider than your cooking pot.

2 Line the pit carefully with either bark or stones. If you use stones, make sure they are collected from a dry area.

3 Place two thick logs on either side of the pit, close enough together to support the pot over the fire.

4 Break a few handfuls of kindling in half and arrange them in the middle of the pit in the shape of a tipi.

5 Leave an opening on one side of the fire so you can place the burning tinder bundle under the wood.

6 Add some slightly larger pieces of wood, again leaving one side open. The fire will now resemble a lean-to.

7 Add small bulkwood if you wish, but take care not to choke the fire.

8 As it is hemmed in, you may need to blow on the fire to get it to light.

9 Once the fire is lit, add squaw wood and small bulkwood to the open side.

10 As the fire takes hold, add larger pieces of wood until a good bed of embers is forming below the fire.

11 Go on adding wood for about half an hour, so that you end up with a good thick layer of embers.

12 After the base of embers is established, keep adding the odd stick, so fresh embers are produced.

Using hot rocks for cooking

As well as cooking your food in or over the fire, you can try an alternative method using rocks, which retain heat well and can be used in various ways. You'll need to gather some large, smooth rocks and place them inside a hot fire that is already well established. Leave them for a few hours, until they are red hot.

CHOOSING THE RIGHT ROCKS
When finding rocks or stones to put in your fire, never collect them from streams, marshes or other waterlogged areas. Always collect them from higher ground where they won't have soaked up a lot of water. When waterlogged rocks are heated, it may be too hard for the expanding water to seep back out, causing the rock to explode. Rocks that appear damp due to rainfall are

usually fine as long as they are collected from a higher elevation. Even then, it's usually a good idea to stay away from them for half an hour when they first go into the fire, just to be safe.

▲ *Tempting though it might be, never remove waterlogged rocks from a stream to use on your fire.*

BOILING WATER
One of the most useful ways of using heated rocks is to boil water. You can use them to heat water stored in containers, such as wooden bowls or animal bladders, that would burn if placed over the fire. A few fist-sized rocks can easily bring several litres of water to the boil. If necessary you can keep it boiling by adding more rocks.

COOKING ON ROCKS
If you can find large flat rocks, you can heat them in the fire until they are red hot and then use them in much the same way as a griddle or frying pan. This technique is most successful if you have some oil or fat to prevent the food sticking to the stone. It can be used to fry or bake flat bread.

If you have two thin flat rocks you can even cook food such as meat or fish between them. This makes the food taste good as well as speeding up the cooking time.

ROCKS AS HEATING DEVICES
Having cooked your meal, you can also use hot rocks to keep you warm. You can place them inside your shelter to warm up the space, or use them as personal body warmers (though you should make sure they are not too hot).

HEATING ROCKS TO BOIL WATER

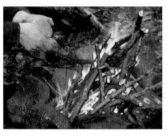

1 Collect dry rocks and place them in a hot fire. Make sure they are placed right in the hottest part of the fire.

2 Keep adding wood, and use your fire as normal. The stones are ready when they appear to be red hot.

3 Take a rock out of the fire with a pair of improvised tongs and carefully immerse it in water. The water should start bubbling immediately.

4 Add more rocks to boil large amounts of water, or to keep the water boiling. Stirring the water will help to distribute the heat of the rocks evenly.

Cooking food in a covered pit

Another great way of cooking is in a pit, heated with rocks from the fire. You simply put your meal in the pit, let it cook throughout the day, and have a nice meal ready for you when you come back home in the evening. The pit needs to be 30–60cm/1–2ft deep, and the hot rocks are put on the bottom. Wait a little to allow the rocks to dry out the pit, otherwise the food may taste rather earthy.

Once the pit has dried out, put a thick layer (about 20cm/8in) of green grass or large edible leaves over the rocks. Place your food in the pit, cover it with more grass or leaves, and fill the pit with debris and soil. All you have to do is dig your food up again a few hours later. If you put in plenty of rocks, it should be thoroughly cooked. It's worth experimenting with this to see just how many hot rocks you need and how long the food should stay in the pit for the ideal meal.

MAKING A COVERED PIT FOR COOKING

1 Collect plenty of rocks, making sure they are not waterlogged, and place them in the fire to heat up.

2 Dig a pit about 60cm/2ft deep and wide enough to place all the food you want to cook in a single layer.

3 Once the rocks are red hot, place them in the bottom of the pit. The more rocks you have, the better.

4 Leave the rocks for a while so that the pit dries out. Cover the rocks with leaves to stop them burning the food.

5 Wrap the food in large edible leaves and place the wrapped food bundles at the bottom of the pit.

6 The heat from the rocks will rise up to cook the food bundles. Large pieces of meat do not need to be wrapped.

7 Cover the food with more grass and edible leaves. Adding a layer of bark will also help to protect it from debris.

8 Fill up the pit with debris and soil. Mark the pit in some way to remind you where you buried your food.

9 Leave the food to cook for 3–7 hours (depending on its size) then dig it up carefully and enjoy your meal.

WATER

Even in ideal circumstances, human beings can survive for only three
to four days without water, and if you are exerting yourself or having
to contend with high temperatures, this time will be much shorter.
So as soon as your shelter is taken care of, you must make sure you
have access to a supply of fresh water. That's easier said than done and if
you don't have a modern water filter, then you will need to purify
the water by boiling it (this, in turn, makes fire more important in
the big scheme of survival). Purification of drinking water could turn out
to be your biggest headache in a survival situation. It is essential, however,
otherwise you might survive other adverse conditions only
to fall prey to waterborne diseases or the chemical pollution that
infiltrates many water sources.

The importance of water

About 60–70 per cent of the human body consists of water, and the brain consists of about 85 per cent water. This means that the average person contains about 50–60 litres/11–13 gallons of water. Clearly, water is therefore very important for survival. Every cell in the body depends upon water in order to function properly. We need a supply of water daily, because we cannot maintain reserves of it in our body as we can with food. Numerous disorders are caused by insufficient water, as well as by drinking water containing micro-organisms or polluted by chemical effluent.

In order to maintain the various bodily functions in a temperate climate, the average person should consume about 3.8 litres/6¹/₂ pints of water a day. In hot climates, or when working hard, the average person may need to consume over 10 litres/17¹/₂ pints of water per day.

WATER LOSS

The table below shows the effects of losing only a moderate amount of water without replenishing it. Looking at this table, it becomes clear that in a temperate climate you would start to feel some unpleasant effects of dehydration after just one day without water. The second row pretty much coincides with the end of a second day without water. This table represents loss of water only in a moderate climate – in extreme situations, the loss of water can be a lot faster.

▲ *Natural caches often contain water but it is important to purify it as the water may have been stagnant for a long time.*

KEEPING FLUID LOSS DOWN

If you can't acquire water immediately, or if the supply is limited, it is clearly important to try to minimize your loss of fluid so that you need to replace less.

Humans have the capability to sweat away as much as 1.5 litres/2¹/₂ pints of fluids per hour when engaged in strenuous exercise in temperate conditions. Couple physical exertion with a hot environment, and you could lose even more. In moderate circumstances, when at rest, the average person sweats about 1 litre/1³/₄ pints per day. This means that by keeping sweating down, you can stop a lot of fluid from being lost from the body.

In a survival situation, you will have no choice but to exert yourself quite

regularly to satisfy your daily needs, and this can cause sweating. However, there are a few ways in which you can reduce this loss of fluid.

The first necessity is to master all the skills you need to survive. Spending only 30 seconds to light a fire using a bow drill set, for example, will cost you a lot less effort, and therefore a lot less sweat, than having to spend 30 minutes to get a fire lit. Mastering survival skills also includes learning to be as efficient as possible when gathering the materials you need, again saving on fluid loss through sweating.

THE EFFECTS OF DEHYDRATION		
Loss of water	**Effects**	**Survival chances**
Up to 4 litres/ 7 pints	Thirst, vague discomfort, impatience, nausea and loss of efficiency.	3 days in moderate climate
Up to 8 litres/ 14 pints	Dizziness, headache, breathing difficulty, tingling in the limbs, increased blood concentration, absence of salivation, purplish discoloration of the skin, indistinct speech and inability to walk.	2 days in moderate climate
Up to 15 litres/ 26 pints	Delirium, spasticity, dimming of vision and death.	1 day in moderate climate

SIGNS OF WATER – SIGNS OF LIFE

▲ *Although rivers are often not visible during the dry season, they may still be running below ground. Patches of vegetation can indicate their courses.*

▲ *Often there is water below the ground at the bottom of deep canyons like this one. This may or may not be confirmed by the presence of vegetation.*

▲ *Coarse vegetation is usually found farther away from the underground water source, while the presence of grasses indicates water just below the surface.*

The second way to prevent excessive sweating is to take care of as many of the tasks requiring physical activity as you can during the cool hours of the day. In extremely hot climates, that may even mean working during the night and resting during the day when it's scorchingly hot.

The third method is the simple precaution of avoiding overheating by removing layers of clothing when you get hot. On the other hand, in some climates adding layers can help keep the heat down. A good example is set by various nomadic desert peoples, who are often covered from head to toe in several layers of loose clothing to keep them cool. Covering the head with a turban or other headdress to protect it from the sun is another example.

A lot of moisture is lost through breathing. Again, keeping your core temperature and expenditure of effort down is one way to prevent excessive loss by this means. Another way to minimize loss of moisture is to focus on breathing through the nose, rather than through the mouth. This might seem extreme, but concentrating on small things like this can make all the difference in a survival situation.

Water is also needed to break down food, so when water is short, avoid eating as far as possible. You should also be careful what you drink. Don't consume alcohol, as it will take more water to break down the alcohol than is added by drinking the alcoholic beverage. Coffee is another liquid to avoid when there is little water available, as it has a diuretic effect.

RATIONING YOUR WATER

A common misconception is that you need to ration water when it is short, much as you would ration food. It is important not to do this. The negative result far outweighs the positive result of saving water for later. Sometimes, dehydration can overcome your body too fast to realize something is wrong. A state of unconsciousness can often occur with little warning when you are dehydrated. There are recorded incidents of people having been found dead due to dehydration even though they had a full water bottle at their side. Even when you are short of water, therefore, it is important to continue to drink as normal.

Don't guzzle what you have, however – take it in sips. Be methodical. If you do become dehydrated and then find a source of water, you should replenish your body fluids slowly, otherwise the stomach may go into convulsions, losing even more fluid by vomiting.

CONSERVING WATER

1 When you do have a supply of water, store it out of the sun to avoid excessive loss by evaporation.

2 Suspending a water bag under a tree will keep it cool. Take only as much as you need, to conserve your supply.

Finding a safe water supply

There are many ways to gather water and the ideal source to look for is clear, fresh, running water. Gathering is the first part of the exercise, for which you need manufactured or natural containers. You should then always filter and purify water, but it is a good idea to get it from the cleanest source.

WHAT TO LOOK FOR

Look for relatively fast-flowing rivers and streams, with healthy vegetation on their banks. In stagnant pools of water, it is generally easier for bacteria and viruses to survive and multiply. It is harder for fast-flowing water to sustain much bacterial growth.

One indication of water quality is to see whether many animals come to drink from it or if they favour a different source. This method is not always foolproof, however, as many wild animals build up a certain amount of resistance to waterborne bacteria and viruses that may cause serious illness in humans. The same is true for water sources frequented by the local human population. It is often the case that Western people become ill after drinking water that local people have been drinking all their lives.

If you find what appears to be a good, clean source, check it out as far upstream as you can. It is possible that an animal carcass or some other pollutant may be located just upstream, making the water unsafe.

▲ *Only when you are absolutely certain the water is safe to drink should you drink straight from a stream.*

DANGERS IN DRINKING WATER

Common infections that may be contracted from unclean water include cholera, hepatitis A and giardiasis.

Cholera is the relatively friendly one. It is a bacterial infection that causes mainly diarrhoea, and is treated by continually replacing lost fluid by drinking clean water. (Continuing to drink infected water will make the situation far worse.) Approximately one in 20 of those infected will have severe symptoms characterized by profuse

watery diarrhoea, vomiting and leg cramps. In these people, rapid loss of body fluids often leads to dehydration and shock. Without treatment, death can occur within hours, and such victims may require fluids to be replaced intravenously.

Hepatitis A is rather less friendly; it is a disease of the liver caused by a viral infection. Symptoms do not always occur but may last for up to two months and include fever, tiredness, loss of appetite, nausea, abdominal discomfort, dark urine and jaundice (yellowing of the skin and eyes). Older people are generally more susceptible to the disease than children. Luckily,

▼ *A watering hole on the African savanna may be a hazardous source of water as it will attract many dangerous creatures who come to drink there.*

▼ *Animals drinking water is not always a sign that it is safe for human consumption: many animals are resistant to infections and diseases that can make humans ill.*

▼ *Some wells have a mechanical method of lifting water while others require you to haul it up manually. Never pollute a well by washing yourself or your equipment near it.*

COLLECTING WATER

▲ *One of the commonest ways of collecting water is by cupping your hands and drinking directly from a stream. Do so only if you know the water is absolutely safe.*

▲ *If you have plenty of containers, rainwater can be collected as it falls and does not need to be purified, though it may contain low concentrations of chemicals.*

▲ *If you have a tarpaulin or poncho, set it up on four poles with a weight in the centre to collect rainwater. Keep one edge low to allow the water to run off into a container.*

the disease is not life-threatening, though medication is often required, and once you have recovered, your body will have made antibodies that prevent a recurrence of the disease.

Giardiasis is caused by a one-celled, microscopic parasite that lives in the intestines and is ingested in water contaminated by sewage. Due to its tough outer shell, it can survive outside the body for a long time. Giardia is currently one of the most common waterborne diseases. Infection can

▼ *For a few days after rain has fallen you can often find water in natural hollows in the landscape.*

cause a variety of intestinal symptoms, which include diarrhoea, greasy stools that tend to float, stomach cramps and nausea. These symptoms may lead to weight loss and dehydration. Symptoms may last from two to six weeks or longer, though some people with giardia have no symptoms at all. The disease is generally treated by alleviating the symptoms and allowing the parasite to be flushed out of the body.

ALWAYS PURIFY

If you find a water source where animals appear to drink, where the water flows fast and cold and no dead animals have been found higher up the

stream, you can be reasonably sure the source is fairly clean of bacterial and viral infections. Even then, you should be sure to purify water for drinking, as any infectious agents will not be apparent until it's too late.

CHECKING FOR CHEMICAL POLLUTANTS

Even when the water is free of viral and bacterial contamination, the source may have been polluted by chemicals. The only ways to minimize the danger of drinking chemically contaminated water are to walk all the way upstream, or to check the plant life in and around the water source carefully.

Ask yourself questions such as: "Are there many algae in the water?" (None could be a bad sign, but so can too many, as some algae thrive on phosphates and the like.) Another question might be: "How healthy do the plants growing around the water source look?" Often, when water is chemically contaminated, it affects the health of the flora around the polluted area. "Are there many healthy looking fish living in the stream?" is another question worth asking yourself.

The problem with chemical pollutants is that many will not "boil" away when the water is purified. Filtering through charcoal and the like may filter out some chemicals, but not others. So if in doubt about pollution, try to find an alternative source before relying on your purifying techniques.

Natural sources of water

In most regions, it is fairly easy to obtain enough water to sustain yourself. In a moderate climate there are generally plenty of rivers and streams from which you can take water. However, if you find yourself in an area where there are no watercourses nearby, or where riverbeds have dried up, you need to know how to locate alternative sources.

NATURAL WATER CACHES
After rain has fallen, you may find water that has collected in natural caches such as hollows in rocks. Ideally, you should use this kind of standing water within a few days of the rainfall. A small cache of water that remains for a long period of time can become the perfect breeding ground for bacteria and viruses.

Useful caches of water can often be found in uneven ground. A good example is where rainwater has collected in little holes and hollows in a rocky surface. These sources will often be fairly safe, but even so you should not neglect to treat any water you collect, just in case of some form of pollutant being present.

It is also important to collect as much water as possible from such sources, as the water may be around for only a day or two. Sometimes it may even disappear within hours.

COLLECTING MORNING DEW
Even where no rain falls, changes of temperature at night result in moisture condensing out of the atmosphere and being deposited on the landscape in the form of dew. In the morning you can collect it by wiping it from vegetation and rocks with an absorbent cloth, then wringing it out into a container.

A very successful Australian native method of collecting this kind of water is to tie absorbent materials to your legs and walk through the grass when there is a layer of dew or raindrops clinging to it. It is possible to gather a large amount of water using this method.

▲ *Water may be found in streams such as this, but make sure it is safe to drink by checking for obvious signs of pollution.*

RAINWATER
An excellent source of drinking water, rainwater has the additional advantage that it is free of bacterial and viral infection. It may, however, contain traces of chemical pollution in heavily industrialized regions.

Rainwater can be gathered using the dew collection method, though it may be easier to collect it while it is actually raining if you have plenty of containers to spread over an area.

COLLECTING DEW

1 If you have some spare clothes made out of material such as cotton, they can be used to collect water. Simply tie the material around your feet.

2 Walk through areas of fairly long grass or other plants, allowing the cloth around your ankles to soak up as much dew as possible.

3 Wring the water out of the soaked material into a bowl. Don't forget to purify it, even though dew is not very likely to contain pollutants.

▲ *Birch sap can be tapped from the trunk and drunk as it is, or boiled down to a sweet liquid not unlike maple syrup.*

▲ *Slow-moving streams are often dangerous to drink from as bacteria and viruses can more easily reproduce in sluggish water.*

▲ *Useful liquid can be found in the fruits of many trees, such as the palm. Coconuts have more liquid inside when unripe.*

GETTING WATER FROM PLANTS

In the jungle a common way of getting water is by retrieving it from water vines, which are easily identified by their round stems, 7.5–15cm/3–6in thick. To produce clear water you simply cut off a piece of stem about 1m/1yd long. If the vine produces a cloudy, bitter liquid, you have picked a different species: don't drink that sap. The liquid from a water vine will have a neutral or fruity taste. The downside

is that it cannot be stored. Some vines irritate the skin, so gather the liquid in a container rather than putting the stem straight to your mouth.

In Australia, the water tree, desert oak and bloodwood grow roots near the surface that can be prised out of the ground. Remove the bark and suck out the moisture or reduce the root to a pulp and squeeze it over your mouth or a container. Green bamboo thickets are an excellent source of fresh water.

Bend a stalk over, tie it down, and cut off the top. Place a container under the cut, and you can collect quite a lot of water in a few hours.

In deserts, most species of barrel cacti contain water. If you cut off the top you can mash the pulp and suck it dry, though it is not edible. However, unless you have a large tool such as a machete, it is impossible to get through the defensive spines and cut the flesh, and doing so will kill the plant.

PLANTS THAT STORE WATER

▲ *This pitcher plant contains fluid that is drinkable in small doses but beware of insects trapped inside: you need to filter and sterilize the fluid first.*

▲ *Succulent desert plants such as aloes and agaves hoard fluid to help them survive periods of drought. The fleshy leaves can be cut or broken off to obtain the liquid.*

▲ *Opuntia microdasys, a prickly pear cactus also known as "bunny ears", has thousands of barbed spikes that can irritate, but contains moisture in its fleshy pads.*

Filtering and purifying water

Whatever water you get, it is a good idea to purify it. You can never tell for sure where the water has been, and what may be in it.

You should start by filtering the water if it contains debris and larger particles. To do this you will need to make some kind of sieve or strainer. A hollow log stuffed with grass can do a good job of removing larger particles from the water, but if you have a sock you can make a finer filter. The first resort is to fill it with grass, as with the hollow log, but if you have access to sand you can use this to fill the sock filter. Start with the finest sand you can find, and fill the sock with coarser and coarser sand until you reach the top.

Suspend the filled sock over a container, pour in the water you have collected, and leave it to filter through.

BOILING WATER
Filtered water may look clean but it is by no means safe to drink. To purify water, you have to boil it (or use a modern filter or purifying agent if you have access to either of these options).

There are different opinions on how long water should be boiled to get rid of bacteria. It is safer to stick to a time of about 15–20 minutes. This may sound like a long time, but you just cannot afford to risk drinking water that is still contaminated.

PURIFYING AGENTS
Modern methods of purifying water include the use of purifying agents such as household bleach, iodine and water-purifying tablets. Modern commercially available filters purify the water as well as filtering it. The purifying agents are used in the following ways:

Bleach: Add 10 drops of household bleach to 4.5 litres/1 gallon of water and mix it well. Then allow it to stand for 30 minutes. A slight smell or taste of chlorine indicates that the water is fit to drink.

Iodine: This can be used in much the same way as bleach.

▲ *Use a sock, filled with sand if possible, to filter silt and debris out of your water before you purify it. Ideally, use fine sand at the bottom and coarser sand at the top.*

Water-purifying tablets: If you use commercial tablets, ensure you follow the package directions. They will make the water taste of bleach, but it will be very safe.

With all these agents, be sure to shake the container so that the purifier reaches every part of the water, to ensure that no bacteria are left behind. Bacteria often lurk in the screw top of a bottle, for example.

FILTERING WATER

1 To filter out pieces of debris and small aquatic creatures floating in water, hollow out a piece of dead wood by burning it almost through.

2 Create a form of sieve or strainer by stuffing the cavity with grass to catch the larger particles. The charcoal on the log will also help to clean the water.

3 Pour the water you have collected through the filter and collect it in a container placed underneath. The water will now need to be purified.

DESALINATING SEA WATER

1 When all you have is salt water, it's possible to make drinking water by distilling it. Bring it to the boil in a fireproof container.

2 Place a clean piece of cloth over the container so it catches all the steam. If you don't have any cloth, you can use moss instead.

3 From time to time, wring out the cloth or mosses and catch the liquid in another container. This water will be pure and ready to drink when cooled.

The problem with some of the above methods is that water treated in this way can make you feel unwell if you drink it over an extensive period of time. Many makers of commercially available tablets will advise you not to use their product continuously for longer than a few weeks. And, of course, tablets and tinctures eventually run out, so use them to extend the time before you have to gather clean water and purify it using more primitive methods.

COMMERCIAL FILTERS
The second option is to use a commercial filter. Such filters are an ideal way to clean large amounts of water over a long period. There are many different types of filters on the market, and many are small enough to fit in your pocket.

Some commercial filters are created chiefly to improve the taste of the drinking water, and particularly to eliminate the undesirable flavour created by chlorination at water treatment plants. For wilderness travel, choose a filter that claims to take care of chemical as well as viral and bacterial contaminants. This will safeguard you against pesticide runoff and other harmful pollutants as well as disease-carrying impurities. Remember that you may need to pack iodine or similar fluids with which to clean the filters.

VITAL SALT

You can't drink salt water, but your body does need a regular intake of salt in order to retain water. So when you desalinate salt water, keep and use the salt that remains behind when the liquid has evaporated.

RESTORING THE TASTE OF BOILED WATER

1 When water has been purified by boiling for 15–20 minutes, it loses its taste. It will be perfectly drinkable, but will simply taste flat.

2 Adding a tiny amount of charcoal greatly improves the taste. You will need to let the water stand for a little while after adding the charcoal.

3 Another way of refreshing the water is to blow air through it using a straw. Alternatively, you can pour the water from container to container.

Further ways to find and treat water

Even in the most inhospitable, apparently arid terrain, it may be possible to find enough water to sustain life.

SEARCH FOR TRAILS

In the desert, it is often worthwhile following local wildlife to their water source, though you should keep in mind that a lot of desert animals do not drink, but get their liquid from the food they eat.

There is an important saying among the natives of desert regions: "The path is wiser than the person who walks it." Animals and native people use the same trails, and these paths often twist and meander across the land. If you come across such a trail it is better to follow it than to walk in a straight line to "cut off a corner". The trails follow courses where there are the least obstacles. Furthermore, they often run from shadow to shadow, and from water source to water source. If you find a well-used trail in the desert follow it, and stick to it.

UNDERGROUND WATER

In a dry region, look for dried-up river beds or canyons where water can be found by digging. Any vegetation will generally lead you in the right direction. The first plants you find will be thorny brush, farthest from the invisible water source; when the vegetation changes to grass-like plants you will be near the underground

▲ Some water filters can be complicated and contain a number of components (as with this tower water filter) and this may cause difficulties in extreme conditions.

▲ The tube of a portable filter goes into the unpurified water and clean water comes out of the spout once the pump is primed.

▲ Purifying agents can be used to eliminate any bacteria in water; their main drawback is their unpleasant taste.

▲ Placing a clear bag over a leafy branch with one corner weighed down will collect water as it evaporates from the leaves and condenses on the bag.

water. A ribbon of vegetation is often the only indication of a streambed in the desert, but it shows that there is water below ground. If the water is very hard to get at, you may be able to reach it with a filter straw, if you are carrying one. This very small, light device enables you to drink directly from an impure water source in an emergency, filtering and purifying the water as you suck it up.

In some deserts indigenous peoples have built extensive waterworks that capture any rainfall that does occur. In the Negev desert in Israel, for instance, there are areas where channels built in the rocks catch any rainwater that runs

down the hills and guide it to deep water pits. These systems are so effective that there will be water in the pits all year round. This may be valuable information if you land in a survival situation in a desert region where such pits exist.

COLLECTING CONDENSATION

An easy way to get water when the temperature is high and there is plenty of vegetation is to "capture" a branch with plenty of leaves, and tie a transparent plastic bag around it. Make sure you choose a tree that is non-poisonous, as the poison may find its way into the water. Then you must

MAKING A SOLAR STILL

1 To desalinate or purify water, build a solar still by digging a pit 60cm/2ft wide and 60cm/2ft deep. (Don't try to use a solar still to procure water in the desert, as it takes too much effort for too little return.)

2 Place an empty container in the middle of the pit to act as a collecting bowl. If you have a plastic tube at least 60–90cm/2–3ft long, place one end in the container, and allow the other end to come out of the side of the pit.

3 Place whatever water and vegetation you have found beside the collecting bowl. Place a sheet of clear plastic over the pit, secured by sand and weighted in the middle. Any condensation that forms will drip into the bowl.

tie one corner of the bag down, so the water doesn't escape near the branch where you tied the bag closed.

After a day, you can often procure a substantial volume of water by this means. Remember to change the location of the bag regularly to prevent leaves drying out completely, thereby stopping the process. A bag placed on a branch in the sun will produce more water than a bag placed in shadow.

The water produced by this method will be absolutely clean and safe to drink without any purification, though you may find that a lot of debris from the branch has dropped into the water. A quick filtering should sort that out.

WATER FROM SNOW AND ICE
In arctic regions, your main source of water may be the snow and ice around you. The snow is always as clean – or as dirty – as rainwater: that is, it may contain chemicals but not micro-organisms, though if it has been lying on the ground for an extended period of time it may have picked up pollutants from the environment. The saying "Never eat yellow snow" is one to be heeded.

Snow should always be pre-melted, as it takes too much of your body's energy to melt it in your mouth or in your stomach. This may not only cause you to lose vital heat, but can also lead

to dehydration, as you cannot get sufficient water into your system quickly enough.

Ice can be a great source of water, though again it will need to be melted. In arctic regions the problem is that a lot of ice is formed from salt water. Ice that is opaque or grey is often formed from salt water. More crystalline ice, with a bluish cast, has little or no salt in it. The water from salt water ice will need to be desalinated for drinking.

Don't forget that ice is no cleaner than the water it was formed from, and will often require purification. Some bacteria and viruses are able to survive for many years in a frozen state.

USING A FILTER STRAW

1 If you find a dried-up watercourse, you can dig down and use a filter straw to obtain the water directly.

2 It is possible to drink water direct from an inaccessible source if you have some kind of filter straw.

3 Before taking water from a pool try to clean the surface of the water or you will clog up your filter.

BUSH TUCKER

When you begin to fend for yourself in the wilderness, it immediately becomes obvious how much is taken for granted in the modern urban environment. The food you normally eat probably comes with very little effort, whereas providing yourself with food in the wild is an activity and a chore that may consume a large part of the day. One thing is for sure: gathering all your food from the wild for a few days will make you appreciate your nourishment a lot more. Seize every opportunity to collect seasonal items such as fruits. When gathering wild edibles, make a mental note of where you spot animals such as rabbits near their burrows. Consider where good trapping areas may lie, such as on an animal trail between its feeding and bedding ground and a water source. Just before dusk is usually a good time to locate them.

Edible plants

Since nearly three-quarters of your balanced diet in the wilderness will come from vegetables and fruit, your chances of survival will be improved by learning to recognize as many edible plants as possible. You also need to be able to recognize suitable plants at any time of the year, as many species look completely different in different seasons. For example, in a long-term survival situation you may be able to identify a tree that you know will bear fruit later in the year.

Some plants completely disappear in the winter except for the roots, which may provide essential nutrition when other foods are scarce. For this reason it can be important to locate particular plants while they are growing during the summer, or to recognize their likely habitat, so you can find the roots when you need them in the winter.

PLANT FOOD

Whenever you gather plants for food, whatever the species, keep the following points in mind:

- The plants should be clean and growing in a healthy looking area. Never collect plants close to roads, quarries and other disturbed areas.
- Never gather more than a third of a particular species in your area. You don't want the species to disappear, and you should keep some for real emergencies.
- When picking leaves and stems, try to find the youngest plants. In general they are easier to digest.
- Go for leaves that haven't been eaten away by other insects or animals. Always try to get the best quality food you can.
- Avoid accidentally gathering parts of other plants that are growing alongside those you are picking.
- Whatever plants you gather, eat them sparingly at first. People react differently to certain plants, and they may disagree with you.

TASTE TEST

Although about 80 per cent of plants are edible, and another small percentage are inedible but not poisonous, the remainder can be very dangerous. To avoid the toxic ones it is vital that you leave alone any plants you don't recognize. However, where there is no other option but starvation, you can do a taste test as a last resort.

Before you begin you should have eaten nothing in the previous eight hours. Divide up the plant so that the leaves, stem, roots, buds and flowers are separate, and test only one part of the plant at a time.

Start by smelling the first part of the plant: if it has a strong or acid odour, don't eat it.

Put the plant part against your skin for about 15 minutes (your elbow will do here). If there is no skin reaction, prepare it in the way you plan to cook it (boiling is a preferred method).

When the plant is cooked, place a small amount against your lip for a few minutes. If no itching or burning sensation occurs, place it under your tongue for about 15 minutes. If no

▶ *Doing a taste test is not recommended, but in an emergency it may be the only way to find edibles if your local knowledge is limited, and you will have to take the risk.*

▲ *Most people are aware of the tasty berries produced by plants such as blackberries and cranberries. However, other parts of the plants, such as the leaves, are also edible.*

burning or itching occurs, chew it well and keep it in your mouth for another 15 minutes. If there is still no irritation, you can swallow it.

Now you should wait for another eight hours to see if you still feel normal. If you start feeling sick or get an upset stomach, try to induce vomiting, and drink plenty of water. If

POISONOUS FUNGI

Fungi are rich in protein, high in vitamins, tasty and free to pick. There are over 1,000 edible species but you must only ever eat those you can definitely identify and know to be safe, as some contain deadly toxins, which can cause symptoms up to 14 hours after eating. It's a tough call when you're desperate for food but it's not worth death by liver failure.

Some poisonous species are easy to confuse with common edible mushrooms. A case in point is the yellow stainer, which will make you very ill, unlike its edible lookalike the horse mushroom (*Agaricus arvensis*). The yellow stainer colours yellow when pressed or cut, whereas the horse mushroom's cap keeps its natural buff colour. You should always make a positive identification before eating any fungus, rejecting any unfamiliar species, and all fungi should be cooked before eating.

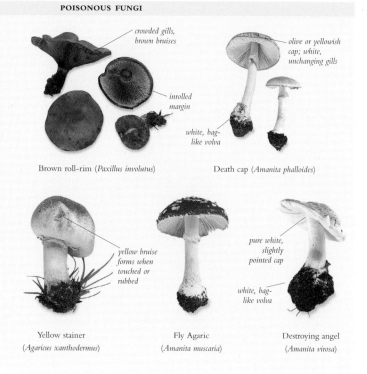

crowded gills, brown bruises

inrolled margin

Brown roll-rim (*Paxillus involutus*)

olive or yellowish cap; white, unchanging gills

white, bag-like volva

Death cap (*Amanita phalloides*)

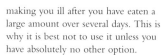

yellow bruise forms when touched or rubbed

Yellow stainer
(*Agaricus xanthodermus*)

Fly Agaric
(*Amanita muscaria*)

pure white, slightly pointed cap

white, bag-like volva

Destroying angel
(*Amanita virosa*)

all stays fine, prepare a little more for eating – you could try a quarter of a portion, for instance. Eat this and wait another eight hours. If there is still no adverse reaction, you can eat this part.

The problem with the test is that certain plants can make you seriously ill with just one leaf, while it is safe to eat others in small amounts, though they carry toxins that gather in your body,

making you ill after you have eaten a large amount over several days. This is why it is best not to use it unless you have absolutely no other option.

While you are learning, your first few meals may be a little bland, but as you gain experience and expand your plant knowledge, you will soon be able to create tasty and satisfying meals in your "wilderness kitchen".

▼ *Pick only the plant you mean to pick: it's easy to grab leaves of a neighbouring plant, which could be dangerous, by accident.*

▼ *Be as picky as you would be when buying vegetables in a shop. Pick only young fresh leaves, and leave the half-eaten ones.*

▼▲ *In temperate climates wild foods such as rowan berries (above) and blackberries (below) are abundant in summer and autumn.*

Wildlife food sources

There is hardly any animal that cannot be eaten. However, for safety reasons it is important always to cook meat and fish thoroughly when you are taking your food from the wild, since this will kill bacteria, parasites and any other harmful organisms residing in the meat.

FISH AND SHELLFISH

If you have the time and energy to make some simple fishing tools or traps (see 356–357), and there is flowing water close at hand, then fishing is a perfect way to get easy food. Fish are often plentiful and all freshwater fish are edible.

If you are on the coast, look in tidal pools and wet sand for marine edibles. Rocks on beaches or reefs leading into deeper water often bear clinging shellfish. Shellfish must always be caught alive, and should be cooked and eaten straight away. Avoid eating mussels in tropical zones in winter as they can be poisonous, and don't collect any fish in polluted areas.

▶ *Though crab meat is delicious, it must be eaten as soon as the crab is caught, as it goes off very quickly.*

▶ *Steam, boil, or bake shellfish in their shells. They make very good stews in combination with greens.*

▼ *Fishing can be an excellent way to gather fresh food. Especially when you can build fish traps that can be left unattended, fishing can be done with a minimum of effort.*

SMALL MAMMALS

If fishing is not an option, then you may need to catch smaller animals such as squirrels and rabbits. Rabbits can be found throughout the world and are relatively easy to catch – a snare or trap (see 354–355) outside a burrow or along a rabbit run is usually enough to catch one. If you can make some tools for hunting, such as a throwing stick (see 358–359) you can get larger animals such as deer this way. The only thing to look out for when getting food from land mammals is the danger an animal

▲ *Snails can be eaten, as long as they are boiled or cooked thoroughly. They are full of calcium, magnesium and vitamin C.*

may pose if it is not hunted correctly, or when it is wounded. Nearly all mammals will fight if they are cornered or protecting their young.

Hunting involves a host of different wilderness skills, including tracking, stalking and camouflage, and these are covered on the following pages. Learn these skills because in a survival situation you won't have the luxury of a rifle or ready-made bow and arrows.

Although most animals can be eaten, not all of them will necessarily be tasty or easily digested. Try to go for young animals, since their meat is usually the most tender. The flesh of some animals, although edible, may have a strong smell that can make it unpalatable. Though you will want to avoid such animals when possible, you should not disregard them as a viable food source.

INSECTS

The same goes for insects. In general, insects carry about 70 per cent of their weight in protein, while regular meat normally consists of about 20 per cent protein. The downside of eating insects is that you have to gather a fair number to get the same amount of meat as you would from, say, a rabbit. However, large quantities of insects can be found

GUTTING AND FILLETING A FISH

1 Insert the point of a knife or a sharp stone into the anal vent and slit the fish up the belly to just behind the gills. Carefully remove the internal organs.

2 Cut through the flesh just below the gills to separate the head, then open out the body and work the flesh away from the bones using your fingers.

3 Pull the head and bones away from the flesh in one piece, severing the spine at the tail end. The bones and head can be used to make stock.

by looking under stones, or in places where a lot of insects live in colonies, such as in rotten wood or anthills.

The only insects that you should steer clear of are adults that sting or bite, hairy or brightly coloured insects, and caterpillars and insects that have a pungent odour. You should also avoid spiders and common disease carriers such as ticks, flies and mosquitoes.

The idea of eating insects is enough to turn most people's stomachs. The best way to eat any unappetizing creature is to cook them in a stew, and try to forget they are even there.

▼ *Most frog species are edible, but avoid brightly coloured ones or those with a cross on their back. Most toads are poisonous.*

FORAGING FOR FOOD

Although you will certainly be making "normal" meals in your camp, you should try to use your energy efficiently and this may mean eating on the move, snacking on local edibles while you are finding materials for your shelter or tools. During the first few days, especially, it will be hard to make time to gather enough food for a proper meal – as long as you drink enough, you shouldn't worry about that. It is then best to feed by nibbling at nettles, berries and whatever else may be easy to find. Only when all

essential tasks have been taken care of should you take time to forage properly for food. If you have been prowling around the area for a few days, you should already have a good idea of where to go for what foods.

If you can source a regular supply of food, try to make your main meal around noon, when it is light enough to cook. In the evening, you can snack on leftovers or items that don't require cooking. Ordering your meals this way is also healthier for your body. A good meal in the morning will raise your energy levels, ready for the coming day.

▼ *Worms may appear unappetizing, but nearly all are edible. Put them in clean water for a few minutes, then mix into a stew.*

▼ *Rodents such as squirrels are abundant and will probably be the main part of your meat diet until you fashion hunting tools.*

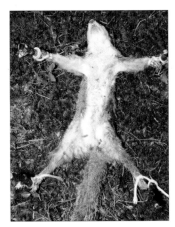

Tracking animals

When you start hunting animals for food the first thing you have to realize is that mammals and rodents – your potential meals – are not evenly spread about the whole wilderness. They gravitate close to where food, water and shelter are available. The middle of a dense forest, for instance, provides no water, light or food, so there will be few animals dwelling there. The edge of a forest is likely to provide food, water and shelter.

TRAILS AND RUNS

To find out which animals live in a particular area you must seek out their trails and runs. These are the most obvious signs of wildlife. Trails are used by many different species and generally lead towards water, food or shelter. Runs are smaller than trails, and are used by a particular animal species. They connect the trails with the shelter areas and sometimes connect water and food areas to the trails as well. Runs often change location, and sometimes a run becomes a trail over time. You can often guess by the width of the run who travels there.

SLEEPING AND FEEDING AREAS

The other signs that can help you establish your "virtual map" of animal life are sleeping, resting and feeding areas. Sleeping areas differ according to

species. Many small animals sleep in burrows, while larger animals often sleep out in the open. If a sleeping area is out in the open you can usually detect the outline of the animal's body on the ground. These areas are often bordered by scrub that is dense enough to stop predators walking through, though not so dense that the animal can't look through the brush. They will have three or more escape routes.

Resting areas have less cover and generally offer animals a good view of their surroundings. They are often found near feeding and watering areas and are infrequently used.

Feeding areas are also likely to be different for different species, but they are often grassy areas with a good variety of plants.

IDENTIFYING SPECIES

Once you have these signs mapped out, you can try to find smaller signs to narrow down the species that live in the landscape. By looking more closely you can often find scat throughout the trails, runs, resting areas and even feeding areas. If there are hoofed animals, you can often find exposed roots and branches on the ground with scrape marks all over them. In feeding areas, you can observe how the grass and other plants are eaten. Rabbits, for instance, neatly scissor through grass,

▲ *A deer lie, or sleeping area, will be used for many nights, until the season changes or the area is threatened repeatedly.*

▼ *Clues such as these scrape marks on a mossy log help you to build a "virtual map" of an area's animal life.*

whereas hoofed animals rip it up, creating jagged breaks. In resting and sleeping areas you will no doubt find hairs belonging to the residents.

Next, you can look for actual animal footprints, narrowing certain runs and feeding areas down even further. Quite often, you won't actually find such clear prints as those shown opposite, but more of an outline. The tracks that you do find, whether they are outlines (compression marks) or full prints, should be combined with all the other information you have found on the trail or run, to give you a clear picture of which animal uses it.

THE COUP DE GRACE

When hunting you should always aim to kill with the first strike. If the animal is only wounded, once you've found it you need to finish it off swiftly. For an animal that's still dangerous, you will probably want to use your weapon again, but the most efficient method if the creature is safe to touch is to slit its throat either side of the windpipe. The best way to put a bird or small animal out of its misery is to break its neck by pulling the head away from the body with a sharp twist.

IDENTIFYING ANIMAL FOOTPRINTS

Being able to read animal footprints is a great survival skill. Footprints reveal the identity of an animal, the direction in which it was heading and when it last used the track – all crucial information when hunting animals for food or keeping out of the way of animals such as bears or wild cats.

▲ **Grey fox**: *front foot 4 x 3.5cm/1⁵/8 x 1³/8in, rear foot 3.8 x 3.2cm /1¹/2 x 1¹/4in.*

▲ **Otter**: *front foot 6.7 x 7.5cm/2⁵/8 x 3in, rear foot 7.3 x 8cm /2⁷/8 x 3¹/8in.*

▲ **Skunk**: *front foot 2.2 x 2.8cm/⁷/8 x 1¹/8in, rear foot 3.8 x 3.8cm /1¹/2 x 1¹/2in.*

▲ **Marten**: *front foot 4.5 x 4.5cm/1³/4 x 1³/4in, rear foot 3.5 x 4cm /1³/8 x 1⁵/8in.*

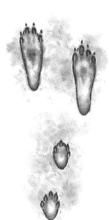

▲ **Hare**: *front foot 3.8 x 2.8cm /1¹/2 x 1¹/8in, rear foot 7.5 x 5cm/3 x 2in.*

▲ **Rabbit**: *front foot 2.2 x 1.5cm/⁷/8 x⁵/8in, rear foot 7 x 2.8cm/2³/4 x 1¹/8in.*

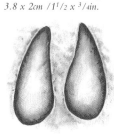

▲ **Weasel**: *front foot 2.8 x 1.2cm/1¹/8 x ¹/2in, rear foot 3.8 x 2cm /1¹/2 x ³/4in.*

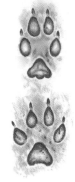

▲ **White tail deer**: *(one foot shown) front foot 7.5 x 4.7cm/3 x 1⁷/8in, rear foot 6.7 x 3.8cm/2⁵/8 x 1¹/2in.*

▲ **Grey wolf**: *front foot 12 x 10.8cm/4³/4 x 4¹/4in, rear foot 11.5 x 10.5cm /4¹/2 x 4¹/8in.*

▲ **Grey squirrel**: *front foot 5 x 3.5cm/2 x 1³/8in, rear foot 6.7 x 3.2cm /2⁵/8 x 1¹/4in.*

▲ **Grizzly bear**: *front foot 14 x 12.5cm/5¹/2 x 5in, rear foot 25 x 14cm /10 x 5¹/2in.*

Stalking animals

In order to get close enough to animals to hunt them, you will have to learn some techniques that enable you to catch them unawares. You won't have a high-powered rifle but a survival bow or throwing stick, and in order to get close enough to kill accurately with one of these, you'll need to approach to within 10–15m/33–50ft. This means you'll need to be able to move quietly and invisibly.

CREEPING LIKE A FOX
First of all, it is important to slow down and become more aware of your surroundings. You can achieve part of that by adopting the "fox walk".

The fox walk is a stalking style that would have been used by our ancestors. The idea is to take each step by leaving your weight on your standing leg, while you feel the ground with your free foot before putting it down. To do this, simply roll your foot from the outside of the foot to the inside, feeling what is beneath your sole. Once you are sure there is nothing sharp or noisy below your foot, you can put it down and move your weight on to your front leg. If there is anything painful or noisy

on the ground, lift the foot back up without putting your weight on it, and try another spot nearby. You need to be just as careful when lifting your feet as when putting them down to avoid cracking twigs or moving stones.

You will find that this method of walking is certainly very slow, but the main advantages are that you don't need to take your eyes off your surroundings to look down at the ground, it is very quiet, and you appear less of a threat to other animals because you are moving so slowly.

WIDE-ANGLED VISION
Animals usually see us before we see them. One reason for this is that we are so noisy and move quite fast. However, the other reason is that animals view their surroundings in a different way. Animals use wide-angled vision and this enables them to see all the movement around them.

The way we see the world is in a series of focused views. We take snapshots of our environment. This means there is a lot we never see at all, because we are focused on something else. However, we also have the ability

▲ *The throwing stick (see 358–359) has the advantage that it is easy to pick up off the ground whenever you enter a survival situation. Carry it with you wherever you go in case you come across an animal that has not noticed you.*

to use our eyes in a less focused way, the way animals do. With practice you should be able to see all the movement that goes on around you, although everything will appear slightly blurred.

THE FOX WALK

1 Carefully lift the foot to be moved off the ground. Keep your balance on the leg that is taking your weight.

2 Move your free foot forward and gently bring it down, rolling it from the outside in over the ground.

3 If the ground is clear, lower your foot and shift your weight forward. Repeat, moving in a slow, fluid motion.

PRACTISING WIDE-ANGLED VISION

1 To learn to see all around you, go to a wide field or into a forest. Hold your hands out in front of you with your fingers pointing in, 30cm/1ft apart.

2 Look at both hands, but also at everything in between them. Slowly move your arms out to your sides, still looking at everything between them.

3 When your hands are at your sides wiggle your fingers, and you should see your hands again. While keeping this "view" slowly drop your hands.

4 Still in the same frame of vision, stretch out your arms again in front of you, but this time hold one hand below the other.

5 Move your arms apart again, one arm up and the other down, while seeing everything in between until you lose sight of your hands.

6 When you drop your arms, you should have a field of view about 180 degrees wide and 80 degrees high. You will instantly spot any movement.

A lot of people, when learning this technique, end up wandering around like zombies because they are trying so hard to retain their wide-angled vision.

Don't forget to move your head around – by doing this you can increase your total angle of view to 360 degrees. so you miss nothing. Then, as soon as you see some interesting movement, focus on it. If it turns out to be nothing of interest, go back into wide-angled vision and move on.

You will see a lot more wildlife on your walks through the wilderness this way, since every little movement will catch your eye.

A NEW WAY OF LISTENING

You can extend your listening skills in the same way as your vision. Follow the steps of the wide-angled vision practice in your head, but use your ears to try to hear everything, rather than just the most obvious sounds.

EXPERIENCING YOUR SURROUNDINGS

These techniques will make you far more aware of your surroundings, and will make it easier for you to spot any wildlife in the area. There is one more layer of awareness you can add to the three already discussed – feeling.

Become aware of the wind caressing your body, feel the muscles move in your legs. Feel the rain falling on your skin and clothes. When you put all these skills together successfully, you will become more attuned to your environment. Rather than just being aware, you will become part of your surroundings, allowing you to sense an animal almost before you see it.

Moving around like this in the wilderness will enable you to get much closer to the local wildlife. To get close enough to hunt them, however, you will need a few more skills: the skills of stalking and camouflage.

STALKING SLOWLY

The basic stalking technique is nearly the same as the fox walk – you feel the ground before you put your weight on it. This time, however, it is much slower. So slow in fact, that it is not noticeable that you are moving at all. An average step would take you about a minute. You might even try to disguise any further movement by moving only when your environment is "moving" – when leaves are rustling in the wind or trees are swaying back and forth. Not only does this method hide your movement, it may also cover up any sounds you make inadvertently. Try to keep your hands either in front of you or behind you to help break up the familiar human shape. In front is generally easier because you can hold your weapon there or use your hands to help lift up your leg.

The two stalks shown below are mainly used when there is plenty of concealing brush between you and the animal. A third method involves lying on the ground on your belly, with your hands beside your shoulders. Lift yourself about 10cm/4in off the ground on your toes and hands and move forward. Then slowly lower your body back down to the ground, move your hands and toes forward, and repeat the action. Any additional movements, such as standing, sitting, getting your weapon ready or swatting a fly, need to be done extremely slowly.

KEEPING YOUR BALANCE

A big problem when moving very slowly is balance. To avoid wobbling, bend your knees slightly while remaining upright. This enables you to keep a tight check on your balance. If you do lose it, try to correct it below the hip. If you correct with your upper body, the movement will surely alert any animals nearby.

STALKING ON ALL FOURS

1 Set out on all fours. Use your hands to feel for noisy material below you.

2 Place your knee exactly on the spot where you have just removed your hand.

3 Use this method to creep up when there is plenty of low brush.

MOVING SILENTLY

1 Make sure that any clothes you are wearing are well tucked in.

2 Ensure your body does not hook into any foliage.

3 Toes will catch in brush if you don't curl them when lifting your feet.

CAMOUFLAGE FOR STALKING

1 Rub white ash, from a cold campfire, into your skin to dull its shine. This will also help to de-scent you.

2 Apply charcoal on areas that would normally not be shadowed. Make the "pattern" as random as possible.

3 Break up your outline further using mud, again creating a random pattern of light and shade.

4 Use leaves growing in the area to "stamp" mud on to your skin.

5 Sprinkle forest debris over the muddy patches while they are still sticky.

6 Try to cultivate a "quiet mind" as you get really close to your prey.

USING CAMOUFLAGE

Camouflage is not about hiding, it is about being "invisible" right out in the open, so you can approach your quarry. If you are hiding behind a tree, it will be hard to launch an arrow or a throwing stick at an animal.

There are two simple ways to camouflage yourself. One is to rub white wood ash all over your body and clothes, then use charcoal to break up your appearance. Apply it to areas that would normally be light, such as right below your eyes and on the bridge of your nose. Use mud to paint different colours on your body. You should finish by rolling through some forest debris to "fluff up" your appearance, breaking your shape up even further. Because you have covered yourself in wood ash, your smell will also be well camouflaged. The second method is a

lot easier. You simply roll in the mud, then in forest litter. Because your smell may not be adequately covered using this method, you may want to rub in some smelly plants. Use only species that grow in the area where you intend to hunt. If you use different plants your smell will still be obvious.

If you camouflage properly and apply good stalking and awareness, you should get almost within touching distance of most animals. To get really close, however, it is important to quieten your mind as well. Animals are very good at picking up your "vibe".

Mammals do not see colours, so even without camouflage you should be able to get close enough for a good shot, provided the animal doesn't smell you. That is, if there are no birds around. Birds do see colour, and birds are also the sentries of the wilderness.

▲ *It is important not to muddy yourself completely, as you will then be making the shape of your body more apparent. Instead, try to create a random pattern.*

Setting animal traps

Before you learn how to set traps, you need to know that it is illegal in most parts of the world to do this unless your life depends on it. This is because a trap can kill an endangered animal as easily as the most abundant species, not to mention the harm it could cause to bigger animals or even to humans.

The traps described here are simple to make, can be used in most situations and are designed to kill quickly and cleanly. There are many types of traps, but these are the most effective. Once you have set a trap, test it to make sure that you will not make an animal suffer unnecessarily. There is no excuse for an animal to limp away from a deadfall or choke to death on a snare.

When setting traps, try to disturb the area as little as possible so as not to warn any animals that something is up. You should also set your traps far apart,

because when one is triggered, all animals in the vicinity will go on high alert. Make sure they are well camouflaged by using wood ash, mud and strong-smelling local plants.

THE FIGURE-4 DEADFALL TRAP

This trap is intended mainly for feeding areas. It is called a "deadfall" trap because it works on the principle that a heavy weight will fall on the head of the animal when it nibbles on the food you place on the bait stick.

The simple trap described here is made of three sticks and looks like a figure 4 when set up. The arrangement is kept in place by the weight, but will collapse when the baited end of the horizontal stick is pushed by the animal. The weight of the deadfall should be about twice the weight of the animal you are trying to catch –

enough to kill it, but not so heavy that the animal will be completely squashed. The trap shown below would be an appropriate size to kill a rabbit.

You can make the trap more effective by placing an "anvil" such as a flat stone underneath. Make sure that the weight does not extend over the upright stick. If it does, it may fall on top of the stick rather than the animal.

Bait the trap with the plant that, from your observation, the intended victim seems to enjoy most. Be wary of importing a plant for bait, as animals may be suspicious of a plant that does not naturally occur in the area.

To force the animal to come in from the right direction, so that it pushes the stick when it eats the bait, you can build some sort of fence around the structure, though it must look natural and not arouse suspicion.

SETTING A FIGURE-4 DEADFALL TRAP

1 Square off the central part of the vertical stick and carve the tip to a flat "screwdriver" shape.

2 Near the end of the horizontal (bait) stick carve an upward-pointing notch to take the end of the diagonal stick.

3 Carve a slot to hold the bait stick against the squared-off section of the upright, at 90 degrees from the notch.

4 Carve a notch in the diagonal stick to take the top of the upright and sharpen the end to fit in the bait stick.

5 To set the trap, apply pressure on the diagonal stick while using the other hand to put the notches into place.

6 Lean a weight (such as a log or rock) on top of the diagonal stick and bait the free end of the horizontal stick.

SETTING A TWO-HOOK SNARE TRAP

1 Carve a notch near the top of a stick and plant it securely in the ground.

2 The second stick, also notched, will be tied to a flexible branch overhead.

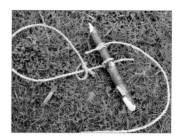

3 The loop the animal will walk into is also tied to the second stick.

4 Tie the second stick to the branch and hook the notches together. The fit should be secure but easy to set off.

5 Make sure the loop will slip easily and is the right size to fit over the animal's head as it walks through.

6 Rest the open loop on sticks or blades of strong grass, about two to four fingers' width above the ground.

THE TWO-HOOK SNARE TRAP

This snare trap is generally used on animal runs, though you can adapt it for use in feeding areas as well. It is important to ensure that the snare is strong enough to break the animal's neck and lift it high enough off the ground to prevent other animals getting at it before you do.

The trap consists of two sticks, each notched so they will hook into each other. One of the hooked sticks is planted firmly in the ground, while the other is tied with a length of cordage to a strong, flexible sapling or branch, which keeps the hooks together under tension. A slipknot loop is tied on to the hook attached to the string and placed over the run so that an animal walking into it will trigger the trap and be lifted up by the branch.

The height of the loop should be such that the animal will walk straight in. For a rabbit, for example, the correct height would be about a hand's width above the ground, while the loop should be about 12.5cm/5in in diameter. By varying the depth of the notches, you can change the sensitivity of the trap, depending on the size of the animal you are trying to catch. What you want to avoid is subjecting the animal to a slow death, so it's important to get the settings right.

Make sure you don't use green wood, since the two branches could fuse together – they can even freeze together during the night. You can increase the tension on the trap by using a number of saplings or branches in a row to compound their power. If there are no flexible branches near the run, you can make a lever and fulcrum by pounding a Y-shaped stick into the ground and tying a long branch over the top. Tie the string to one end of the lever and add a heavy weight to the other.

▼ *A lever and fulcrum can be made from sticks to support the two-hook snare trap when there is no suitable branch nearby.*

▼ *The two-hook trap can be adapted for fish by replacing the noose with fishing line. It must raise the fish well out of the water.*

Fishing techniques

If you are near water, fishing is an excellent way to obtain high-protein food. Fish can be netted, hooked, speared or snared, or even caught by hand. Setting a trap in a stream allows you to get on with other tasks while waiting for the fish to swim into it.

TRAPPING FISH

One of the easiest ways to catch fish is with a snare such as the two-hook trap described on page 355. You can adapt this by using fishing line in place of a noose, arranging it so that the fish is pulled well out of the water.

Another good method is to make a fish pen (*see below*): erect a curved fence to create an enclosure with only one opening facing upriver, then construct a funnel leading into the opening. If the stream is fast-flowing this may be enough to catch fish. In slower water, weave in flexible twigs so that they stick out towards the trap entrance. The sticks will bend aside as a fish swims in, but not when it tries to swim back out again. You can vary the size of fish the trap catches by adjusting the gaps between the fence poles.

MAKING A FISH SPEAR

If you want to catch larger fish and have enough time on your hands to be selective, making a fishing spear is the best option. The spear is made in two parts: a two-pronged spearhead is fitted into a notch in the end of a long, straight shaft. The reason for this is that if you miss the fish and hit the bottom of the stream, the spearhead will simply come out of the notch, whereas if the spear were made in one piece the prongs might break. The spearhead is loosely tied to the shaft so that it can be retrieved if it comes apart.

It is best to use green wood to make the spearhead as it has flexibility and will split without breaking. The stick should be completely straight and about 2.5cm/1in thick. It must be tightly wrapped with cord to stop it splitting too far, and the cord should be made of plant fibre, as sinew will loosen when it is immersed in water.

The prongs of the spear need to be sharp but strong, so that they will stand up to striking stones on the stream bed. On the inner surfaces of the prongs you will need to cut two small "shelves" to support barbs so that once speared the fish can't escape. The best materials for the barbs are sharp stones such as flint flakes or slivers of very hard wood. You can also easily make barbs from the bones of other animals. The barbs must be tied on tightly using fine cordage. If you know how to make pitch glue (see page 382) use it to make the joints between the barbs and wood more secure.

▲ *Spearing a fish requires clear water to spot your prey, stealth in stalking the fish then speed and accuracy in jabbing the spear.*

FISHING WITH A SPEAR

Look for a likely fishing spot – it could be on the outside of bends if it's cool, under shade on a hot, sunny day, in white water, or in shallows. Sit absolutely still, with the tip of the spear in the water, ready to stab a fish when it appears, or try stalking your prey. You'll need to experiment with different spots, times and styles until you are successful.

MAKING A FISH PEN

1 Erect a half-circle of sticks in fast-flowing water where fish are present, making sure the water flows into the opening in the "fence".

2 Create a funnel by planting more sticks to make two fences out to both banks of the stream, leaving a small opening where the fish can swim in.

3 In slower streams, weave some branches through the fences pointing towards the trap, so that the fish can swim in but not back out again.

MAKING A FISHING SPEAR

1 Find a straight stick about 30cm/1ft long and 2.5cm/1in in diameter and clean off any side-branches.

2 Wrap a length of cord made from plant fibre tightly around the central part of the stick.

3 Using a sharp stone, carefully split the stick. The binding will stop the split going further than the centre.

4 Wedge a small twig as far into the centre as possible to push the two "prongs" apart by 5–7.5cm/2–3in.

5 Use more cord to tie the wedge in place, to stop it popping out of the spear when the wood dries a little.

6 Using a knife or a sharp stone, carve the two prongs into long but sturdy points.

7 Carve a small "shelf" on the inside of each prong to support the barbs.

8 Use flint to produce two sharp flakes about 2.5cm/1in long for the barbs.

9 Using fine cordage, tie the barbs into place on the prongs.

10 Carve the other end of the spearhead into a flat plank shape. This will fit into a notch in the spear shaft.

11 Tie a length of string to the spearhead and make a noose on the free end to tie around the spear shaft.

12 Carve a notch in the end of a straight pole 3–3.5m/9–12ft long and fit the spearhead on to the shaft.

Making and using a throwing stick

The first hunting tool you are likely to make and use in the wilderness is a throwing stick, which can be any sturdy stick you can find. It needs to be about 5–7.5cm/2–3in in diameter and about 60cm/2ft long. It can also be made into a quieter, faster weapon by carving the central section in the shape of a wing. You can even carve a non-returning boomerang, which may be accurately thrown over more than 100m/110yd. The principles are the same.

The throwing stick is mainly a tool for the opportunistic hunter. As soon as you are in a situation where food needs to be provided, you can simply pick up a suitable stick and carry it about with you wherever you go. It will be there when a curious animal pokes its head out of the bushes right in front of you. This way of hunting is particularly effective if you move around using the fox walk and wide-angled vision, as described on pages 350 and 351.

THROWING THE STICK

There are two common ways of throwing the throwing stick. The first method is overarm. Though there is less chance of hitting the animal, because the killing zone is only about 7.5cm/3in wide, this technique is very useful when there are many trees between you and the animal, or when you have to deal with high grass that

▲ A throwing stick should be held so the butt end sits in the palm of your hand. It should not extend past your hand, as this could cause the stick to injure you, or the throw to go off course.

would obstruct an underarm throw. One tip to remember is to give a flick with your wrist as you release the stick to give it extra revolutions, increasing the chance of hitting the target.

The second method is the underarm throw. The stick is held with its end in the hand in the same way as before.

▲ Placing your thumb over the end of the stick ensures that it stays in the right spot in your hand. By holding the thumb like this, you can also achieve a throw in which the stick spins a lot while in the air.

This time, however, you are standing sideways and the stick rotates horizontally through the air. This gives you a much better chance of killing the animal because the killing zone is about 60cm/2ft wide, but you can use it only when there is no grass or shrub to block the throw.

MAKING A THROWING STICK

1 Shaping the stick reduces the noise it makes in the air, and makes it fly faster. Find a sturdy but flexible piece of wood (yew in this instance).

2 Carve two sides of the stick, working it down to a wing-like shape. Try to orient any bend along the wing, so it does not affect the flight of the stick.

3 Leave more wood at the ends to provide some extra weight and so that you can easily sharpen the ends without the stick getting too weak.

USING A THROWING STICK OVERARM

1 If you are right-handed, place your left foot forward and hold the stick over your shoulder. Face the target.

2 You can use your elbow to aim roughly at your target. Start to throw the stick forward over your shoulder.

3 Just as you release the stick, give it a little flick with your wrist to produce extra revolutions in its flight.

USING A THROWING STICK UNDERARM

1 Stand sideways to the target, holding the stick at waist level.

2 Bring the stick behind you as you move your body forward.

3 Sink through your knees, resting your non-throwing hand on one knee.

4 Start to throw your hip into the throw as you crouch down.

5 Use your whole body to provide the power for the throw.

6 Flick your wrist just as you release the stick to give it spin.

Skinning and butchering an animal

Once you have managed to trap and dispatch an animal, it is important to hang and skin it as soon as possible. If the skin is left on for too long, the heat inside will spoil the meat rapidly. The internal organs should also be removed; they deteriorate quickly and any spillage of their contents will contaminate the meat.

If you are dealing with a large animal, such as a deer, hang it from a horizontal pole by its front legs and neck. If it is a small animal, such as a rabbit, lay it out on its back and tie all four legs to stakes so it is spread-eagled.

SKINNING THE ANIMAL

After making a small initial cut at the breastbone, insert your fingers to open it out so that there is no danger of puncturing the gut: from now on you can make sure your knife does not cut anything but skin. Push down under the skin with your fingers to create a

▼ *If you are in the wilderness for a long period, a deer provides not only good meat but also buckskin to make warm clothes.*

gap before cutting with your tool. Your cut should go all the way from the head to the reproductive organs.

With a large animal you should complete the skinning process before cutting into the flesh. If you have a small animal you can continue with the butchering, but if you decide to skin it fully now, make sure you are working on as clean a surface as you can prepare: it's amazing how forest debris always manages to get on to the carcass.

To continue the skinning, cut from the initial incision all the way up each leg, as far as you can go. Then finish off by cutting around the reproductive organs and the neck and by carefully cutting around the legs. (The leg tendons, or sinews, can be used in many ways. If you want to keep them, be very careful that you don't sever them when cutting around the legs.) With all cuts complete you can take off the skin. If the animal is spread-eagled, it is best to untie the legs at this point.

Try to avoid using your knife. In fact it is very easy to remove the skin entirely without using a knife, and this will prevent accidental cuts in the skin. If you don't use a knife, there will also be a lot less fat left on the skin, which will need to be removed if you intend to tan the hide. The easiest way is to pull the skin away from the animal with one hand, while you work the fingers of the other hand between the muscles and the skin.

BUTCHERING THE ANIMAL

Once the skin is removed you are ready for the next stage in the process. Carefully cut through the abdominal muscles, starting again at the breastbone. Make sure you do not puncture any internal organs at this point as this would spoil the meat.

Make this cut all the way to the reproductive organs. Now, you need to cut around the reproductive organs and the anus. This can be hard because the hips will be in the way. If you cut any tubes going to the reproductive organs or the anus, tie them off so they won't

▲ *Hang a large animal by its front legs and head so that when the innards are removed they fall between the legs, minimizing the danger of contaminating the meat.*

leak into the meat. Now extend your cut all the way up to the windpipe. Once you reach it, cut through the windpipe and the gullet. If your animal is hanging by the front legs most of the internal organs should now fall out.

Now you can cut out the edible organs – the heart, liver, kidneys and lungs – and store them separately to avoid cross-contamination. Be careful not to puncture the gall bladder when removing the liver, as anything in contact with the gall will be spoiled.

WARNING

Ideally you should wear protective gloves when working with dead animals, as it is very easy to pick up an infection if bacteria from the meat get into small grazes or cuts on your hands. If you cannot get any kind of protection for your hands, try to make sure they are free of wounds and wash them at regular intervals, with soap or a disinfectant if possible.

HOW TO SKIN A DEER

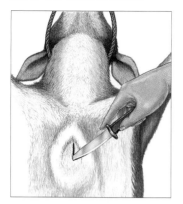

1 Start skinning by making a small, careful incision right over the breastbone to avoid piercing the gut.

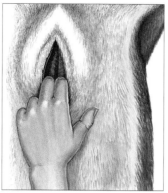

2 Insert two fingers, pointing down, into the incision to widen it and work the skin away from the flesh.

3 Insert your knife or cutting tool between your fingers, and slowly make your way down, cutting only the skin.

4 Stop at the reproductive organs, then do the same working upwards to the neck, starting from the initial cut.

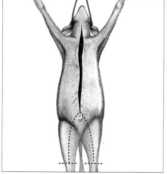

5 Cut through the skin around the hind legs, then cut down the fronts of the legs from the original incision.

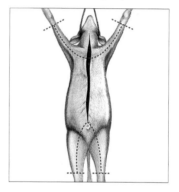

6 Do the same with the forelegs, cutting around the "wrists" and connecting these with the initial cut.

Check the whole carcass carefully for discoloration and other signs of spoilage. While you are working, you may find that a glaze seems to form over the meat. This is perfectly normal, and will even help to preserve it.

If you have not yet skinned a small animal, do so now. Otherwise, remove the legs and head and cook it as it is. For a larger animal, it is easier to cut off the meat while the carcass is hanging. Try to remove all the meat. Some parts, such as the ribs, have very little flesh, so it may be easier to cut the muscle between the ribs, break off the bones and fry them or put the whole ribs in a stew.

7 After cutting around the reproductive organs, anus and neck, you can pull off the skin. Next, deepen the cut on the breastbone until you hit bone.

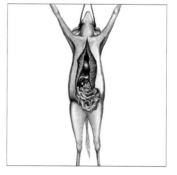

8 Follow the initial cut to open the body. Remove the edible organs and sever the windpipe, gullet and other connecting tubes to free the innards.

Preserving meat and other animal products

No part of an animal you have killed should be discarded. As well as providing fresh meat, the flesh of a large animal can be preserved for future meals, and the non-edible parts can be used to make clothes and tools.

▲ *Antlers (if there are any) can be used for flint-knapping and other skills.*

▲ *The lower jaws of deer make great saws, though the teeth may loosen after a while.*

USEFUL BODY PARTS

The intestines, stomach and bladder should be cleaned out immediately after butchering the animal, as they have many uses. The bundle of tendons should be carefully removed from each leg. Use a knife to open the bundle lengthways, then spread it out to dry.

The head of the animal contains lots of goodies. The liquid in the eyes makes a strong glue when mixed with resin. The tongue can be skinned and kept as meat. Keep the rest of the head intact for now. The brain can be eaten while fresh (within a day), but is better kept for tanning the hide later on.

Hooves should be kept as they can be boiled to make a strong glue. Skim the water they are boiling in to collect neatsfoot oil, used for softening hide.

▲ *Clean and keep all animal bones because many of them can be made into tools.*

▲ *Either rinse animal bones well or bury them for a few weeks to clean them.*

DRYING MEAT

The easiest way to dry meat is in the sun or near a fire, but don't leave the meat too close to the fire, or it will fry, not dry. With bigger pieces of meat, you should remove any fat, which will go off quickly, then cut it into slices no

more than 3mm/^{1}/$_8$in thick. Then you can hang these strips up around a fire or in the hot sun to dry. The meat must be fully dry before you store it. If it crumbles in your hands it may be a little too dry, but make sure that when

you bend the pieces of meat they crack. If they just bend without cracking, they are still too moist.

You can grind up this dried meat and store it for a long time in the intestines you cleaned earlier.

PRESERVING MEAT ON A TRIPOD

1 Find three poles about 120cm/4ft long and tie them together by wrapping cord loosely around the tops, then binding it tightly between them.

2 Place a number of horizontal poles around the frame you have made and bind them to the tripod at suitable heights to dry your strips of meat.

3 Cut the meat into strips as thin as you can get them. Place the tripod over the fire, making sure that the meat is not so close it cooks instead of drying.

Making buckskin for clothes

There is no material better suited to the outdoors than tanned buckskin. If you are to survive a long-term emergency, you may need to know how to make buckskin from animal hides so that you can make warm, durable clothing.

PREPARING THE HIDE

To start the process, make a framework that is about one and a half times larger all round than the hide you are going to treat. The framework should be strong and sturdy as the hide will be stretched on it. Two neighbouring trees make ideal verticals for the frame, and for the horizontals you can lash two strong poles across them.

Punch holes all round the hide so that you can tie it to the frame, but don't make them too close to the edge

as the cords will tear through the hide when it is stretched. Use strong cord for this, and check that the hide is taut.

You will need a sharp tool such as a knife or a sharp flake of stone to scrape the hide. Hold the tool so that the edge is at a right angle to the hide and draw it down while pressing into the surface. Make sure you are always scraping when pressing into the hide: if you stop the movement of the blade while maintaining pressure, you may punch through the hide.

SCRAPING

The purpose of scraping is to remove all the fat and the innermost layer of skin called the subcutaneous tissue (a layer of fat and connective tissue that houses larger blood vessels and nerves). Once the underside of the hide is

▲ *Leave the skin to soak in water mixed with charcoal, a tannic stream or a container of rainwater for a few days to loosen up the hair cuticles and any fatty tissue.*

scraped clean, start on the outer side and scrape off the hair and the outermost layer of skin (the epidermis). If the hair does not want to come off,

PREPARING AND SCRAPING AN ANIMAL HIDE

1 Tie two sturdy poles between two trees to make a frame one and a half times as long and wide as the hide.

2 Puncture holes about 7.5cm–10cm/ 3–4in apart all round the skin, about 2.5cm/1in in from the edge.

3 Tie the skin on to the frame, using a separate cord in each hole so that you can tighten each one when necessary.

4 Using a stone with a straight but not too sharp edge, scrape off all the fatty tissue and remaining flesh from the underside of the hide.

5 Using a very sharp flint, scrape off all the hair. If the skin has been soaked in acidic water it should come off easily. Scrape off the top layer of skin as well.

6 Scrape off any remaining fat on the underside of the hide and continue until the skin appears velvety. Leave the hide to dry out completely.

▲ *Part of the age-old process of making clothes from animal hides. When both sides have been scraped free of flesh, fat and hair, you are left with rawhide. To get buckskin for making clothes, the hide then needs to be tanned.*

then the skin may need to be soaked for a day or two in a stream or a container of water. Don't soak it for too long, or the hide may begin to rot.

When you have scraped both sides you are left with the dermis. Leave this stretched on the frame for a few days to dry out completely. At this point, you have created a fine grade of rawhide, which can be used for a multitude of purposes. To soften it for clothing, the hide needs to be tanned, and for this you can use the brains you saved when butchering the animal.

BRAIN-TANNING

Once the hide is dry, heat up some water and mix in the brains. Massage this mixture deeply into the hide. You can use egg-yolk for this job (if you have found birds' nests) as an alternative to brains, but in either case make sure the entire hide is saturated with the mixture. You can even take the hide off the rack, and soak it in the mixture in a container for a while.

The brains will stop the fibres binding back together to form rawhide, but only if the fibres are stretched apart while they dry. So the secret of soft buckskin is to stretch the fibres while the hide is drying. One way of doing this is to stake the hide out again and poke it with a rounded stick. Or you can hold it in your hands and stretch and pull it out until it is dry. If you can feel hard areas, you can try to give them some extra attention, though you may have to tan these sections again when the hide is completely dry. Once the whole hide is dry and soft, buff it over a tree trunk or a twisted cord to produce a material much like felt.

SMOKING THE HIDE

The next step is to smoke the hide. This is very important to stop your hide reverting to rawhide as soon as it gets wet. Sow the hide together to form a bag. Set a tripod above some embers and suspend the hide over it in such a way that the smoke has to travel through the hide. Now add smoky materials such as pine needles to the embers, and leave it for a few hours. Make sure the embers do not burst into flame, as this would ruin your hide. Once one side is fully smoked, turn the

---

BRAIN-TANNING AN ANIMAL HIDE

1 Having left the skin to dry completely, warm the animal's brains and massage them into the skin.

2 Pull the skin to stretch the fibres, continuing the process uninterrupted until the hide is completely dried out.

3 When the hide is dry and flexible you can soften it further by running it over a taut string or a branch.

bag inside out and smoke the other side. The finished product is buckskin, and is ready to be made into clothes.

You will need to re-smoke the hide once in a while to ensure it stays thoroughly oiled and prevent the fibres going hard again.

THE BENEFITS OF HIDE CLOTHING

Making clothes and other items from what is around you may be essential for long-term survival. Though it takes a lot of work to make a piece of soft buckskin, you will find that leather made this way is much stronger and more durable then modern leather. It is a natural product and therefore helps to mask your smell when stalking. It is also ultra-quiet and one of the best backgrounds for a camouflage pattern.

When making clothes, you can use various materials to sew hides together. Animal tendon could be used, though that would be more applicable in drier regions. You can also use cord made with plant fibres, though you may have to replace some of the seams from time to time. The easiest method is to tie the seams together using small strips of tanned hide made from offcuts. You can also use these for fringing, to help break up your outline in the bush. Make the fringing a little irregular and not too long, or it may snag in brush. The disadvantage of fringing is that it can show up your movements while stalking if you are not careful.

▼ *A small deerskin is easily big enough to make a pair of shoes following this pattern. If you have thick and thin skins, use the thicker skin for the soles.*

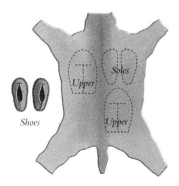

Shoes

TURNING SKINS INTO CLOTHING

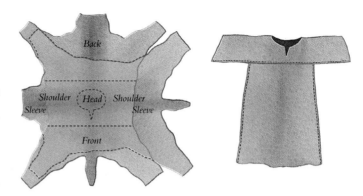

▲ *Two average skins can make an excellent shirt, using them as shown above. This design gives extra material on the shoulders, making the shirt stronger and warmer.*

▲ *This is what the shirt would look like when it is finished. You could add fringing to the sleeves and hems to make your shape less obvious when stalking game.*

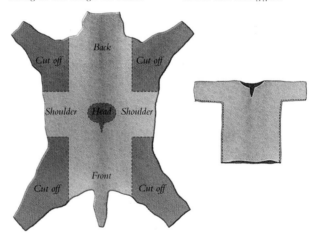

▲ *If you have a large hide, you can cut the whole shirt out in one piece, one half becoming the front and the other becoming the back. Simply fold it at the shoulders and sew up the sides and sleeves.*

▲ *This shirt might feel a little "square" due to the fact that the sleeves are not shaped. It is a good idea to make the shirt very roomy, allowing plenty of material under the arms so you can move in it easily.*

▶ *Basic trousers can be made by taking two hides, cutting out matching shapes according to the pattern shown here and sewing one on top of the other. Make the trousers roomy like the shirt above.*

TOOLS & EQUIPMENT

The fashioning of tools and equipment often signals the end of sheer survival and the beginning of "living". Your existence is no longer a matter of primitive survival: many of the skills required to make tools from materials found in the wild are highly advanced techniques, which most modern people are not able to reproduce without re-learning. The crafts covered in these pages are fundamental to many aspects of wilderness survival, from hunting and gathering to ensuring comfort and rest. Familiarity with even one or two will prove extraordinarily beneficial, should an occasion to practise them for real suddenly present itself.

Basic food bowls and containers

Using fire, you can very quickly turn out wooden bowls and spoons, simply by allowing an ember to burn into the wood in a controlled way.

To make a bowl, start with a thick log about 30cm/12in long (burn it to size if necessary). Split it in half then place an ember right in the centre of the flat side. By gently blowing on it, you can get the fire to spread slowly into the wood and also control the direction in which it burns. If you find you are getting too close to the side or bottom of the log, put some sand or clay over the spot to stop the ember

▼ *The stomach of an animal makes a watertight container and can be used to cook food and boil water in.*

▲ *Bark baskets are relatively easy to make, and can be used to hold a variety of items, such as equipment or edible plants.*

spreading that way. Scrape the surface clean of char regularly, as it will insulate the wood and make the burning process less efficient. If you want to speed up the process – and avoid hyperventilating – it is a good idea to use a straw made from a hollow stem such as elder, reed or bamboo, or the windpipe of an animal. You can use your burned-out bowl as it is, though you may find that food tastes better if you take time to scrape out all the char and sand the inside smooth.

Spoons can be made in exactly the same way as bowls, then carved to make them comfortable to eat with. Wooden utensils hold food particles in the fibres, however, so after washing them it is a good idea to hold them above a flame for a minute or two to sterilize them each time they are used.

▲ *Burning into wood is an easy way to produce containers, and has even been used to produce large items such as canoes.*

BARK CONTAINERS

Great containers can also be made from bark. Many different species, such as birch, cedar and elm, are suitable. Try to take it from trees that have fallen or are on their way out. If you have to take bark from a healthy tree, take a strip from only a third of its circumference to ensure that the tree survives. For best results, soak the bark in water for a few hours.

ANIMAL PRODUCTS

You can use the stomach of an animal to hold food or water. Clean it out, turn it inside out and suspend it from a tripod, or dig a hole in the ground and stake the edges around the pit. It can be used for boiling liquids by adding hot rocks. A bladder will work in the same way, though not for so long.

MAKING A SPOON

1 Light a good fire to make a large pile of embers. If necessary, shorten the stick you want to use in the fire.

2 Using tongs, place an ember on the flattened stick, on the point where you want your depression to form.

3 Hold the ember down and blow at it so that it burns into the wood. Sand out the depression and carve the spoon.

MAKING A BOWL

1 Make a sizeable fire in order to obtain plenty of embers for burning.

2 Split a log in half using a stone wedge and a sturdy branch hammer.

3 Place an ember on the wood, right in the centre of one half of the log.

4 Hold the ember down and blow on it gently. A depression will slowly form.

5 As the depression deepens, add more embers to burn the hole more quickly.

6 If you burn too close to one side, add clay to protect it from the fire.

MAKING A BARK BASKET

1 Select a strip of bark about 60cm/2ft long by 30cm/1ft wide.

2 Score an oval shape in the centre of the bark. Do not pierce the outer layer.

3 Using a sharp stone, punch holes all around the edges of the bark.

4 Bend the basket into shape and stitch the sides together tightly using cord.

5 To reinforce the basket, bind some stems into a ring to fit the rim.

6 Sew the ring into place using the holes you punctured earlier.

Weaving a basket

A basket can serve you in many useful ways, both for collecting and for storing food, and baskets can be made in a wide variety of forms, shapes and sizes. Once you have learned the technique you can use it to make containers of any size you need.

Basketwork allows air to circulate easily, so it is ideal for holding delicate wild foods such as berries and fungi, which deteriorate very quickly if they are carried in airtight containers. Baskets are also useful for storing wild greens or pieces of meat, or for gathering small-scale materials for kindling and tinder in the woods. A very loosely woven basket can also be used for trapping fish or to scoop small fish out of the water by hand.

MATERIALS FOR BASKETS
The function of each basket should dictate its size and shape, and may also influence the material you choose to make it from. Many different materials can be used to weave baskets, as long as they are flexible. The long, slender shoots of willow and hazel are traditionally used for basketry, and would be a very good source if they are growing in your vicinity, but there are plenty of other flexible materials that can also be used, such as pine or cedar shoots, spruce roots or cordage. Long shoots reduce the need to weave in new strands and make it easier to achieve a smooth, even finish.

▼ *A small collection of baskets of various sizes is useful for collecting food and keeping small items of all kinds safe.*

WEAVING A BASKET

1 Gather six flexible willow or hazel twigs to make the ribs of the basket.

2 Split one stick in the centre by inserting a cutting tool and twisting it.

3 Insert one of the other sticks into the split you have just created.

4 Place two more split sticks beside the first, and insert the remaining sticks.

5 Push two strands of weaving material into the splits alongside the three ribs.

6 Tightly weave one of the strands over the first three ribs. Hold at the bottom.

7 Weave the second strand under the first ribs, and over the second three.

8 Repeat to go around the centre three times. Make sure the weave is tight.

9 Now continue to weave between the individual ribs until you feel the base is big enough. Keep the shape circular.

10 Split each rib, right at the edge of the weave, twisting the tool as you bend it up to stop the rib breaking.

11 Repeat to bend all the ribs up, then place three weaving strands to the right side of one of the ribs.

12 Take the first strand and weave it over the first rib. Hold it in place at the bottom of the basket.

13 Weave the second strand under the first rib and over the second. Release the first strand and hold the second.

14 Weave the third strand under two ribs and over one rib. Release the previous strand and hold this one.

15 Continue weaving, following the last step, until the ribs are pointing upwards to your satisfaction.

16 When a strand runs out, lift it up and insert a new one in its place, so that it points in the same direction.

17 When the ribs are pointing up, continue using only two strands, following the weave used for the base.

18 When you have reached the height you want, tuck the ends of the strands into the previous rows.

19 Weave in the ribs if possible, or cut them off, leaving the ends protruding a little so that the weave doesn't slip off.

20 This weaving pattern will produce a strong basket of any size, even if its shape is not completely regular.

Crafting simple pottery

Pottery was the first craft to be developed in most human cultures, and serviceable pots are still made using natural river clay and the simplest of crafting and firing techniques. Your own containers may be crude but they will make effective utensils for cooking and eating.

FINDING THE CLAY

You won't have the luxury of buying ready-made clay in a survival situation but as it's an abundant natural material you should be able to find some to hand. Formed primarily by the weathering of granite, clay can be found all around us and the best way to look for pure, clean clay is by digging in a bend in a river, where the finest particles have settled.

PREPARING THE CLAY

Having gathered your clay, leave it to dry, then grind it to a powder so that you get rid of stones and any other impurities that would spoil the pottery. Once you have a fine clay powder, you should temper it by adding a little harder material, such as ground seashells, sand, powdered eggshells or

▼ *The thumb-pot technique can be used to make vessels such as bowls and lamps.*

crushed pottery fragments. Tempering the clay will prevent the pottery shrinking too much during drying and firing, thereby helping to prevent it cracking. Once the temper is mixed in, you can add water.

Knead the clay thoroughly before you start to shape it to eliminate any air bubbles, which would expand during firing and break the pot. Try to get the consistency of the clay right before you start working with it. The clay should be soft enough for you to move but

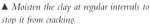

▲ *Moisten the clay at regular intervals to stop it from cracking.*

firm enough so that it does not stick to your hands. You'll soon get an idea of the sort of "give" you need to achieve in order to be able to craft simple pots.

FROM BALL TO BOWL

The pottery bowl described opposite uses a ball of clay about the size of an orange. It is simply shaped using your hands, using a pinching technique. Press in with your thumb as you turn it until you are about 6mm/¹⁄₄in from the bottom, then start pressing outward, working from the bottom up, to form a pot. If the pot gets too big, put it on a flat surface while you thin the sides to a uniform 6mm/¹⁄₄in. Once the pot is finished, leave it to dry for a few days.

Fire your pots after drying to make them more durable. The simplest form of firing, which is still practised by village potters in parts of the world today, is with open fires or with pits using a local source of fuel. The method used here is as basic as it comes. The firing temperature will be low, so your pots will eventually start to disintegrate, but you can easily make more to replace them.

MAKING A POTTERY BOWL

1 To make sure the clay is entirely pure, it is best to dry it and then pound it with a large stone.

2 You can then filter out any debris. Keep pounding until you have a fine clay powder.

3 Mix the powder with a small amount of temper such as crushed shell, adding about one part temper to ten parts clay.

4 Add just enough water to the powdered clay to make it hold together in a ball without breaking.

5 Knead the clay thoroughly, working it between your hands to smooth it and eliminate any air bubbles.

6 After kneading, shape the clay into a ball. For a small bowl you will need a ball about the size of an orange.

7 Press your thumb into the top of the ball, then turn it and repeat.

8 Keep turning and pressing, slowly widening the hole and shaping the pot.

9 Dry for a few days, then burnish the pot with a stone to make it watertight.

10 To fire the clay, place the pot under a thick layer of soil and light a fire on top, or build a fire around the pot.

11 Make sure the flames are well away from the pot at first, and slowly get closer, so it doesn't heat up too quickly.

12 Once the pot is immersed in flames, add more wood and let the fire burn as hot as possible for about three hours.

Making a bow for hunting

A bow is a versatile hunting weapon that will allow you to stalk and kill mammals of any size. The bow described here is designed for short-term survival and is sometimes called a father-son bow, because it actually consists of two bows – a bigger bow with a smaller one tied on to the back. The reason for this construction is that the bow is made from green wood. Though this is easier to carve, it does not have the same strength as a bow made from properly seasoned wood. By adding a second stave, you can achieve a stronger bow with weaker wood.

WORKING WITH THE WOOD

To make the survival bow you will need a branch of a young tree without side branches or knots. The wood should be straight, about 150cm/5ft long with a diameter of 7.5cm/3in.

You will need to split the branch exactly down the centre of the wood as both halves will be used. If you don't manage to salvage two staves from the branch, cut another length and split it to obtain the second stave. In this case it need only be about 120cm/4ft long.

Once you have two staves, select the one that is going to become the "father" or main part of the bow. The side with the bark on will be the back of the bow, and this should never be touched with a knife. The other side, which will face you in the finished bow, is the belly. Measure off a handle

about 7.5cm/3in long in the centre of the bow, then carefully thin both limbs by carving until they start to bend evenly, forming a D-shape.

SHAPING AND TESTING THE BOW

At this point you can carve two notches at the end of each limb, and string a length of cordage between them. This is not the final string and doesn't have to be tight, but you can use it to pull the bow to see the result of your thinning more clearly.

The best way to do this is to make a "tillering-stick" about 75cm/30in long. Carve a notch on top of the stick and further notches every 12.5cm/5in. Sit the handle of the bow on the notch at the top and pull the string down to the first notch. Examine the bend of the bow. If it looks good, pull the string to the next notch. If you find spots that bend more then the rest, you need to thin the bow at either side of that weak spot so it bends evenly again. If parts of the limbs bend less than the rest, you'll need to thin those down a little more. Using this process to test the bow, keep thinning until you reach the last notch.

Now shorten the bowstring so that it is about 15cm/6in away from the handle when the bow is strung and

▲ *Though the "father-son" bow is made from green wood, which is weak, the two bows reinforce each other to give enough power for a kill.*

repeat the process until your bow has a draw of 63–70cm/25–28in. Use the same process to make the shorter bow, which needs a draw of 25–37cm/10–15in. The shorter bow will not need a handle. Once it is tied on to the back of the larger bow it should be "recurved" by pushing in two wedges on each side of the handle and tying them in place. Connect the limbs of the two bows and fit the string back on to the main bow. Each bow should bear a pull of 7–9kg/15–20lb.

FIRING THE BOW

Once you've made your arrows (see pages 376–37) you can use your bow, though its performance will be greatly improved if it is left to dry out for a week or two. Don't expect instant success. Find some open ground (so that you don't lose your arrows), set up a target and start practising. Learn how to load, draw, aim and fire effectively from a range of distances. Once you are hitting the target with confidence it's time to go out and do it for real.

MAKING A SURVIVAL BOW

1 Gather two pieces of straight, flexible green wood, looking for poles without side branches or knots.

2 Split one branch in half using a stone wedge or other splitting tool. Always work away from the "back" of the bow.

3 Unless you have managed to split the branch exactly in half, repeat the procedure with the second stick.

4 The short bow should be about three-quarters the length of the main bow.

5 Carefully carve away to get an even bend along the stave.

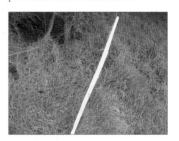

6 With one stave completed, repeat for the second bow.

7 Carve two sets of notches in each end of the larger bow and one set of notches in each end of the smaller bow.

8 Tie the two bows together at the centre, with the belly of the smaller bow touching the back of the larger bow.

9 Insert wedges as close to each side of the handle as possible to "recurve" the smaller bow away from the larger bow.

10 Tie these wedges into place very securely to stop them popping out again when the bow is in use.

11 Tie the tips of the larger bow to those of the smaller bow. Make sure the connection is taut but not too tight.

12 Finally, string the main bow. The bowstring should be 10–12.5cm/4–5in shorter than the large bow stave.

Making arrows

It is best to make a number of arrows at a time, as they are easily broken or lost in use. Look for young shoots to make the shafts as they are firm and straight. Once the bark has been stripped off, the stems should be about 6–10mm/$^1/_4$–$^3/_8$in thick. Cut them to a length of about 70cm/28in. Shoots of hazel, willow and yew all work really well for survival arrows.

If the shafts needs straightening, you can do this by heating the wood over the fire until it is just too hot to touch, then bending it in the opposite direction and holding it in that position until the wood has cooled down. When you let go, the bend should be gone. If it is not, repeat the process.

If you do not have any feathers to use as fletching, you can fletch the arrows with tough leaves, or tie a bunch of pine needles on to the shaft.

STRENGTHENING THE TIP

If you need to use your arrows quickly, you can get away with carving the shaft to a point and fire-hardening the tip after you have finished the fletching. If you have a little time on your hands, it is better to strengthen the tip of an arrow by notching it and inserting an arrowhead. Simple arrowheads can be made of bone or very hard wood, but you can also make arrowheads from stone. In any case, the arrowhead should be tied on securely.

To make it extra strong, coat the arrowhead with pitch glue (see page 382) before you tie it on to the shaft. Now all you have to do is wrap just behind the arrowhead to prevent the shaft from splitting, and wrap the shaft just in front of the notch in the back to prevent the string from splitting the shaft when the arrow is fired.

▲ A "primitive" arrow should be made as straight as any modern arrow, otherwise it may miss the mark.

SHARPENING AND SHAPING A FLINT ARROWHEAD

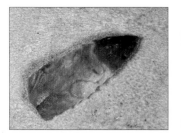

1 When you have found a suitable flake of material, imagine the arrowhead inside to help you shape the stone.

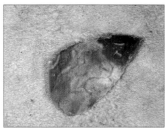

2 It is most important to thin the piece as much as possible while taking as little material as possible off the sides.

3 You should get to the required shape slowly but surely, so that a minimum of material loss is incurred.

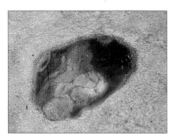

4 When the piece is between 3–1.5mm/$^1/_8$–$^1/_{16}$in thick, it is thin enough for an arrowhead.

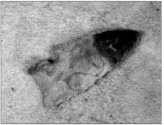

5 Small flakes are removed to create a notch. It is best to make the first notch on the most difficult side of the piece.

6 The second notch is made to match the first. After further sharpening and shaping, the arrowhead is ready for use.

MAKING AN ARROW

1 Find a young branch that is nearly perfectly straight with no side shoots.

2 Carefully strip off the bark. Don't cut into the wood, as that will weaken it.

3 Remove any bends by heating the wood and bending it the opposite way.

4 Cut a notch in one end to fit on to the bowstring, and a deeper notch in the other end to take the arrowhead.

5 To prepare deer sinew for binding the arrow, take a dried leg tendon and pull off long fibres.

6 Chew the fibres to make them supple and sticky: sinew sticks to itself when wet and shrinks and hardens as it dries.

7 When the sinew is soaked through, use it to bind the shaft just behind the notch to prevent splitting.

8 Repeat at the other end. Make sure the wrapping overlaps, because the sinew will stick only to itself.

9 Place a resin-soaked arrowhead in the notch, as deep as it will go. Make sure you orient it straight along the shaft.

10 Melt more pitch glue and mould it over the arrowhead so it "flows" into the shaft, to give smooth penetration.

11 When the glue has nearly set, wrap the arrowhead in place using more sinew to form an unbreakable bond.

12 Use sinew to bind on the fletching to balance the arrow – a half-stripped branch of spruce has been used here.

Making basic stone tools

Being able to make stone cutting tools is an important survival skill in this modern age. We are not allowed to carry knives on public transport, so after a crash, for example, you might find yourself in a survival situation without one. You may also want to learn the techniques out of interest, or as a way of connecting with the past.

The simplest way to produce a cutting tool is by "bipolar percussion". For this you need a rounded pebble about 7.5cm/3in long, preferably fine-grained or even glassy (coarse stone will not produce a sharp edge). Hold it on a stone anvil or pack sand around it to hold it upright. Now smash a heavy

rock with all your strength down on the pebble. If you hit it hard enough, the stone will fracture into long, sharp shards that can be used as emergency cutting tools.

KNAPPING STONE

For more refined tools, a technique called "knapping" is used. Creating a tool from a stone is very much like chess. You have to learn the individual moves and put them all together to remove the right flakes.

Because the flakes you are working on are extremely sharp (obsidian can be 400 times as sharp as surgical steel) it is vital to protect yourself. This means

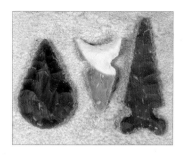

▲ *Arrowheads come in all shapes and sizes, depending on the use of the arrow as well as the skill of the knapper, but their principle task is to reinforce arrows, so beauty comes last. Even a simple flake could do the job.*

FLINT KNAPPING PROCESSES

1 For large pieces of flint, "direct percussion" is used. The "core" is often held on the outside of the leg and the flake is struck off with a stone.

2 When large, thin flakes are needed a "soft hammer" (in this case a piece of antler) is used, and the blow is angled in the direction of the flake.

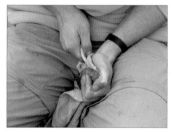

3 The final method, "pressure flaking", is used to remove small flakes with precision, pressing outwards with a fine piece of antler to push the flakes off.

MAKING A WORKABLE KNIFE FROM STONE

1 Select a fine-grained pebble roughly the size of an egg, and a solid hammer stone at least twice as heavy. Steady the pebble on a sturdy rock surface.

2 Keeping your fingers out of the way, or using sand to hold the pebble upright, strike it as hard as you can with the hammer stone.

3 Ideally the pebble will split into a number of sharp-edged flakes. Even if it does not, you will often end up with at least one sharp piece, as here.

▶ *This hammer was produced by "pecking" a groove around a hard stone. A piece of hazel, shaped to fit the groove, forms a handle, which is strengthened with rawhide.*

wearing gloves, and using sheepskin or a large pad of leather when working on your lap. You should also wear safety goggles when practising as splinters may fly towards your eyes. If you take up knapping on a regular basis, make sure you do it in a well-ventilated area, preferably outside. Put down a groundsheet and clean the floor and all surfaces well after knapping so that no sharp debris is left lying around.

From an archaeological point of view, you should dispose of your flakes and chips (known as "debitage") responsibly. Some people bury a glass bottle beneath them to show any future digs that the flakes are not prehistoric.

▼ *Stone tools and arrowheads can be made from different types of stone. The top arrowhead is made from English flint, while the bottom one is of porcelanite.*

PREDICTING HOW STONE WILL FLAKE

There are five main "rules" to help you decide where flakes will come off a stone you are knapping:

- **The angle of the platform** The platform is the surface to which you are going to apply a force to detach a flake. An angle close to, but less than, 90 degrees in relation to the surface where the flake is to come off, gives the best result. An angle far less than this will result in a crushed edge, while more than this will produce nothing at all.
- **Every stone has an imaginary centre line** The centre line divides the mass of the stone in half. If a platform is above the centre line, it is very likely the stone will break when you apply a force. If the stone doesn't break, you could end up with a lopsided item. If it is on or

below the centre line, the flake should travel well without breaking the piece you are working on.

- **The angle of the force applied** With direct percussion the angle of the blow is more than 90 degrees in relation to the platform surface if a hard hammer is used (like a glancing blow). When using pressure flaking, or applying direct percussion with a soft hammer, the force is directed into the stone, following the direction of the flake you want to detach.
- **Flakes love to travel far over convex surfaces** They don't travel over concave surfaces, where they will just break off.
- **Flakes love to follow mass** They travel well along ridges and lumps on the stone.

MAKING A CHOPPER

1 Using a hard hammer, it is possible to create a rough tool such as a chopper in only three steps. Select a hammer stone and a flint nodule (the "core").

2 Flakes are removed by striking the edge of the core with sharp, forceful blows. The control of each blow is more important than its strength.

3 The rules described in the box above will help you predict where the flakes will come off, allowing you to shape the stone just as you want it.

Working with bones and sticks

Once your basic requirements of shelter, warmth, food and water are taken care of, you can use all the natural materials around you to create numerous other artefacts. If you are surviving in the wilderness for a long period you will want to make your life as comfortable as possible. You'll have time to develop your skills and to seek out the best materials for each task.

MAKING BONE TOOLS

The bones of any animals you kill for food should always be cleaned and saved for future use. Bone is soft enough to be shaped with stone, but hard enough to hold a sharp edge or point, so it can be turned into many useful tools, such as needles, fishing hooks, drills and punches. Large bones

and antlers can be used for digging and hammering, or sharpened to make saws and knives.

Bones can be broken up easily by simply smashing them with a piece of rock, although the results may be unpredictable. If you want a specific shape, you can score bone in much the same way as glass to make it break in more predictable patterns. You can then give the bone its final shape using a fine abrading stone.

Bone tools can be extremely sharp. You can prepare an item such as a bone knife or arrowhead for sharpening by rubbing it with hot oil, then heating it in the fire. If you then sharpen the object much as you would sharpen a steel knife, you can get very sharp edges indeed.

BACKRESTS AND MATS

A simple backrest can make life a lot more comfortable, enabling you to relax in front of your fire or sit up in your shelter. You can make one quite easily using stout sticks arranged in a tripod. This will be easy to move around and stable on uneven ground.

You can make your backrest even more comfortable by weaving a grass mat to lay over it and sit on. You could also make a mattress to sleep on. For these you will need a lot of tall grass or long hollow reeds and a lot of cordage. Just keep adding more bundles of grass until you have a mat long enough for your needs. Its width will be decided by the length of the grass, though you can chop off the sides when you have finished if they are too long.

MAKING A KNIFE FROM BONE

1 Large bones, either found or harvested from an animal, can be broken up simply by smashing them with a rock to get shards.

2 Shape the resulting shards into whatever tool you need by using a large rough stone as an abrading block and rubbing the bone across it.

3 For greater precision, score the bone with a stone cutting tool in the rough shape of the object, then carefully "smash" it along the scored lines.

4 When the shaping of the knife is complete, rub hot oil into the bone, and heat the knife over the fire before sharpening the blade.

5 Sharpen the knife pretty much as you would a regular steel blade. Try to find a stone as smooth as possible for this sharpening process.

6 The bone blade can be bound into a notch in the end of another long, smooth bone or a piece of wood to create a handle.

MAKING A GRASS MATTRESS

1 Collect a large amount of long grass or hollow reeds. Start by making a bundle about 7.5cm/3in thick.

2 Split the bundle in half and turn one half over, so half the thicker ends are at each end, to keep the thickness even.

3 Tie the bundle using two or three long cords. Wrap the cord around itself three times to make each knot.

4 The knots provide a flat surface on which you can rest the next bundle. Tie this in using the same knots.

5 Repeat until the mat is the right size. The flat knots square off the bundles, eliminating gaps between them.

6 This method can be used to make mats of any size and shape you want. Trim the ends of the stems if you wish.

MAKING A BACKREST

1 Select three sturdy poles, each 90–120cm/3–4ft long. Make sure they are reasonably straight.

2 With the poles side by side, wrap a good length of cord fairly loosely around one end and knot it.

3 Wind the cord between the sticks to form a "cinch". This is the chance to tighten up your tie as much as possible.

4 When the top is tied securely, place the sticks upright, and bring the middle stick backwards.

5 Tease the two other sticks outwards to form a tripod. Adjust the distances between them to stabilize the structure.

6 Tie on some horizontal bars to give you a sturdy surface to lean against, and tie a grass mat over this frame.

Working with natural resins and oils

Both animal and vegetable products can be used to make glue, which has numerous uses in a survival situation. Apart from its use as food, animal fat is also useful as a lubricant, and can be used as fuel in lamps.

HIDE GLUE

Generally used to glue organic matter together, hide glue is the strongest glue known. The downside is that it stretches when wet, will not withstand heat, and will not glue materials such as stone. It is made from hide scrapings or pieces of rawhide, boiled until they dissolve into a thin liquid. You must use hide glue hot, as it sets fairly quickly on cooling. To reuse it, simply add a little water and heat it up slowly. However, it can be stored for only a few days before it goes off.

PITCH GLUE

The sap from conifers, chiefly spruce and pine, can be made into a good waterproof glue (it is used in the fishing spear project on pages 356-7). The resin seeps out of wounds on the trunks of trees, or can be found in blisters under the bark and scraped off with a stick.

Once you have a container full of resin, place it on the fire. As soon as it begins to melt, you will notice a strong turpentine smell: this is normal. Don't allow the resin to boil as that will reduce the quality of the glue. Make sure you have some sort of lid to hand as well, as it catches fire easily. If you have a large amount of resin, and require very clean glue, strain the liquid as quickly as possible, so it doesn't set while in the filter. For most outdoor projects, however, this is not necessary.

The resin on its own will simply revert to its natural state as it cools. In order to make it set hard and strong you need to add a "temper". Three different substances can be added, all with their own advantages. Powdered charcoal is most often used, because it's

MAKING HIDE GLUE

1 Place the scrapings from a hide in a fireproof container and pour on some water: you will need nine parts water to one part hide.

2 Put the container on the fire and allow it to boil. Fat may rise to the surface, and you should skim this off, but keep it safe.

3 Keep boiling, adding more water as required to stop all the moisture evaporating, until the hide has completely dissolved into a sticky glue.

MAKING PITCH GLUE

1 Collect a sufficient amount of spruce or pine resin in a fireproof container. Try to avoid getting too many little bits of debris mixed in with the resin.

2 Place the container on the fire and allow it to heat up. Keep stirring so that the heat is spread evenly and don't allow it to boil.

3 Mix in some powdered charcoal, wax or dried scat to make the glue set hard when it cools. Allow the liquid to set on sticks or in small clumps for storage.

MAKING AN OIL LANTERN

1 The container for an oil lantern can be made of many different materials. Pictured here are a simple clay bowl and a purpose-made lamp.

2 To render pieces of animal fat into usable lamp oil, heat it in a fireproof container on the fire, skimming off the liquid fat continually.

3 Pour this oil into the container you are using for your lantern. It is important you have rendered the oil well, so it remains liquid.

4 Make a "wick" for the lamp by braiding some plant fibres. The best fibres to use are from the resinous bark of trees such as red cedar and basswood.

5 Place the wick in the oil, making sure a little sticks out at the top. It is helpful to soak the entire wick in the oil for a minute or two to help it catch.

6 Now light the wick. The size of the flame can be adjusted to a certain extent by having more or less wick sticking out of the lamp.

easy to get. Charcoal works well for most purposes, though the glue may become brittle after a while. Beeswax creates a more flexible glue, though it is not so strong and tends to feel a little greasy. The glue also seems to be a little softer when set. A good temper is the dried scat of herbivores such as rabbits or deer, ground into a powder. This makes the strongest and longest-lasting glue, often referred to as "loaded" glue, though it is less hygienic – don't use it to waterproof a cup, for example.

It is hard to judge how much temper to add to the resin to make it set properly. Try about a tenth, then leave a little to set. If it sets hard, it's done. If it stays sticky and soft, add more. Once the temper is added, the glue must be used hot: it will set as it cools down.

It is best to divide the glue up into small portions containing just enough for each project. The reason is that the

more times you re-heat the glue, the less strong and more brittle it becomes. There are many ways of dividing the glue into small portions, but the best is to create "pitch-sticks".

With a container filled with water to hand, take a small stick and dip it into the hot glue as you would dip a candle. Then place the stick with the blob of hot glue in the water to cool it down quickly. Briefly dip the stick into the glue again, so more glue is collected, and cool it again in the water. Keep repeating this until you have as much glue collected on the stick as you want. While the glue is still warm, you can mould it into raindrop or sausage shapes for easier storage.

When you wish to use the glue, you can either heat the object to be glued and touch the pitch-stick against it, or heat up the tip of the pitch-stick so that a drop of hot glue drips on to

the surface of the object. You can improve the bond between the glue and the materials by pre-heating the surfaces to be glued.

OIL LANTERNS

The name would suggest that such lanterns use oil as a fuel. However, research into early societies has revealed that animal fat was often used for lighting. The oil lantern can be made from any container that will not burn. Clay containers are particularly good, because you can make them in any shape to suit your needs, easily creating a spout to support the wick.

The wick is best made from the bark of resinous trees such as red cedar and basswood. Alternatively, natural cordage made from nettles and other fibrous plants also works well. Simply melt the animal fat in the container and light the wick.

Making cordage

You will need cordage, or thread, of varying strengths and thicknesses, for many different purposes in a survival situation, from lashing together the timbers of your shelter to fishing and making snares. It can be made from both plant and animal fibres. The fibres of animal matter such as sinew (the leg tendons) are usually stronger, but plant fibres may be easier to find, and can withstand getting wet, while animal fibres stretch when wet, so your choice of materials will be governed by the jobs you need the cordage to do.

PLANT FIBRES

The inner part of a plant's stem is generally used for making cordage. The stinging nettle is a good plant to choose, but many other species with long, tough stems can be used. Find young, green stems and carefully remove the leaves without damaging the fibres (and without getting stung). Use gloves or a piece of leather to rub the hairs off the stalk, then split it open from on one side only and spread it out. Discard the woody pith from the inside and carefully scrape the outer part off the fibres. These parts of the stem add no strength, and may even make the finished product weaker. Gently roll the fibres between your hands for a while to make them supple.

SINEW AND RAWHIDE

For cordage that needs to have a lot of strength, sinew and rawhide will do the trick. The advantage of such animal matter is that it shrinks when it dries, enabling it to form a very tight binding. The downside is that it loosens up again when it gets wet.

You can use sinew as it comes from the animal, by ripping off fibres as you need them. This works well when making arrows. You don't even need to tie any knots. Wetting the sinew with saliva forms a sticky adhesive that will glue the sinew to itself when wrapped.

If you want to make a long cord out of sinew, you need to prepare it first by separating the fibres. You can do this by pounding the tendons on a wooden surface with a wooden anvil. If you use a stone or metal hammer, you will break the fibres. You may find that it takes a lot of hammering to loosen the fibres. Just try to get into a rhythm.

PREPARING PLANT FIBRES

1 Many different plants can be used to procure fibres for cord – this is blackberry. Pick a stem carefully, choosing the longest you can find.

2 Using a piece of buckskin or some leather gloves, rub up and down the stem to clean off the thorns as well as the leaves.

3 Split the stem in half lengthways (if it is very thick, you may even want to quarter it). Make sure the split goes right through the centre of the stem.

4 You will find a pithy substance inside, which should be scraped out (you can keep it to enlarge an ember when making fire by friction).

5 Break the stem outward. This will split the woody inner part from the bark. Follow this split all down the stem, breaking it again if necessary.

6 Strip off the outer bark by holding a sharp edge perpendicular to the fibre: the inner bark is the only part of the stem you want to use.

MAKING CORDAGE FROM PLANT OR ANIMAL FIBRES

1 For long-lasting cord, it is best to use dried fibres, otherwise they will shrink later, leaving the cord loose.

2 Hold the bunch of fibres between your thumbs and index fingers with your hands about 5cm/2in apart.

3 Twist the fibres away from you with your right hand. This will tighten the fibres together.

4 Keep twisting the fibres in your right hand until they form a loop or kink.

5 Grab the kink between your left thumb and finger.

6 Twist the upper strand away from you; stop just before the fibres kink.

7 Still holding the twisted fibres in your right hand, grab the lower strand between your second and third fingers.

8 Twist your right hand towards you and slide your left hand up the cord to grab the fibres where the strands cross.

9 Release what is now the lower strand and grab the top strand. Twist it away from yourself as you did in step 6.

10 When it is rolled up tight, grab the lower strand again, and twist your hand over. Repeat until the cord is complete.

11 As the fibres run out, add another bundle to the ends of the old one, but avoid splicing both bundles at once.

12 To make a regular cord, ensure that both strands are equally thick, and remain constant in thickness.

THE URBAN LANDSCAPE

Minimizing risk at home and abroad

Since the terror attacks of 9/11, the urban environment has again become the focus of national security strategies. Yet it should be remembered that urban-based aggression is, sadly, as old as the metropolis itself. The interaction between so many groups of people creates an exciting chemistry that simply cannot be matched in suburbs or smaller towns, yet this comes with a certain amount of antagonism. Even though you are not likely to suffer serious attacks from others, many of us have experienced some form of threatening behaviour or petty crime.

RECOGNIZE YOUR STRENGTHS

For this reason, the first of the chapters on The Urban Landscape looks at methods of defending yourself. Many of us are forced, at various times, to navigate the city's byways alone, both above and below ground, and we often feel vulnerable as a result. In fact, as an individual, you are far from helpless. Physical fitness creates an important

▼ *Recent terror attacks have seen air travel and airport security scrutinized by authorities, with new practices introduced.*

advantage: not only the strength to escape or, in certain cases, to fight back, but also a familiarity with physical stress. In a largely sedentary society, it is often the shock of a physical blow that will immobilize the victim as much as an actual injury.

Of equal importance is the ability to anticipate your assailant's actions and respond in the most effective way. This is key to many schools of self-defence and martial arts training. Although your aggressor may appear to have the upper hand, in fact their physical efforts to control you also lay them open to injury – it's about about knowing exactly how, and where, to hit back. From coping with bag-snatching to attempted strangulation or sexual assault, practised defence training could mean the difference between a narrow escape and unthinkable consequences.

SAFETY IN THE HOME

Of course, urban survival is not only about dealing with premeditated attacks. With so many people living in close contact, accidental injury is rife. It is interesting that we often view the home as a fortress, even though this is

▲ *Often, we simply do not recognize hazards in the home. Hot drinks can easily be dragged from surface tops by children.*

where a large proportion of accidents occur. Frustratingly, it's perhaps also the environment we have the most control over. When safeguarding your home, a good place to start is by cleaning out the clutter. Falls, often caused by random objects left lying around, are the biggest killer in the home, and tidying up may also reveal other perils such as frayed electric wiring or slippery spills. More vulnerable family members such as young children or the elderly may need special attention: chapter 14 looks at simple, effective ways to adapt the layout of your home to their physical needs. There is also advice on making your home security-tight against intruders, some of whom may be aggressive towards you, and of minimizing the risk of fire – another big killer.

KEEPING SAFE ON THE MOVE

The chances are that your lifestyle wil require you to travel beyond your home on most days. You can minimize risks by making certain decisions about how you get from A to B, but, in the event of a transport accident, being familiar with certain strategies could

potentially save your life. Whether it is being able to visualize the layout of an aircraft, escaping from an overturned car, or cleanly breaking a safety glass window on a train, your actions in those first few moments are essential to increasing your chances of survival.

Street savviness becomes even more significant when the location is unknown. Many people tend to let their guard down on holiday, which is understandable – it offers a fantastic opportunity to relax. Yet everything is made doubly difficult by the fact that, in all likelihood, a different language is spoken in your destination, so, if things do go wrong – you lose your travel documents for instance, or have a valuable stolen – it becomes much harder to communicate the problem. Invest in a good travel guide and a basic language glossary, so that you at least have more options to explore if you want to report an incident.

As emphasized throughout this book the natural environment should always be respected, especially if it is an unknown quantity. It's a sad fact that people may be caught in a 'rip' at no great distance from heavily crowded beaches. Always appraise every new situation carefully before taking action, and avoid unnecessary risks.

▼ *We all look forward to our holidays, but it is worth keeping in mind any hazards associated with the new environment.*

▲ *Health and safety requirements, and first aid training, are becoming important features of the work place.*

THE WORST CASE SCENARIO

The reality of urban living today is that vigilance is consistently urged upon city dwellers, who are encouraged to report stray packages and monitor out-of-the-ordinary behaviour. Some people feel this has created a culture of mistrust, but a more positive view is that it is teaching the average person to practise greater self-awareness in their daily movements.

If asked to picture our worst case scenario, few of us could come up with anything more terrifying than a hostage situation. Even if attacked in the street, there is a possibility that someone will rush to our aid, whereas being taken captive, and subsequently isolated from all apparent help, presents a much harsher reality. Chapter 16 on Surviving Terrorism and Conflict looks at ways to cope with these extraordinary circumstances, from experiencing a car hijacking to being physically trussed up by captors. You may be vulnerable but you are never helpless. A clear head and the right attitude will put you in a stronger position to help yourself and others who may be held captive with you. As with survival strategies deployed elsewhere in this book, it is vital to use whatever resources you have to give yourself the very best chance of survival and escape.

PRACTISE FIRST AID

In more and more locations, first aid training is becoming mandatory for representatives in schools and in the work place. Of course, when witness to an injury, our instinct is to help, but unless we are clear on technique, the power to do so effectively is severely limited. When a casualty is unconscious or dazed, they may be wholly dependent on the first aider to respond in the best way. Yet the misapplication of aid can be just as damaging as doing nothing. This is why training in the correct procedure – whether treating burns, circulatory shock, skin wounds or spinal injuries – is so important. Some of the most common injuries and illnesses, from broken limbs to the symptoms connected with chemical poisoning, are covered in the final chapter of the book and these techniques could prove useful in just about every terrain described.

DEFENDING YOURSELF

There are two key factors in surviving the hazards of modern urban life. One is to develop an awareness of your environment, establishing good habits in your daily routines and using common sense to minimize risks – for instance, avoiding a deserted underpass in which all the lights have been broken. The second basic rule of survival is that "proper prior preparation prevents pathetically poor performance". In other words, success depends on correct mental and physical training.

Identifying the risk of attack

There are places in the urban landscape that it's obviously best to avoid at certain times, but if you have to be alone in a deserted area you should carry an alarm or a makeshift weapon such as an umbrella or dog lead. Sensible footwear is vital – don't wear shoes that will slip off or cause you to stumble if you need to run.

Prevention is better than cure, but if you do have to resort to self-defence remember that in potentially violent situations stress causes the body to release adrenaline, preparing you for flight or fight. However, this can make your movements less precise. It is only through training in a realistic way that you can learn to respond effectively when faced with danger.

The best way to develop effective skills is to join a martial arts school that concentrates on teaching methods of self-defence rather than developing competitors for sporting events. You need realistic training based on a genuine understanding of the demands of actual fighting, rather than visually impressive sports-based techniques.

AGGRESSIVE BEHAVIOUR

People are creatures of habit and in stressful situations habitual actions and movements tend to dominate. This is true of both attackers and defenders, and surveys of attacks show that various forms of aggressive behaviour can be identified and predicted.

Human predators are not that different from other hunters. Tactics used by aggressors, such as the use of stealth and surprise to isolate and then overpower a victim, often reflect the hunting habits of wild animals.

WHERE TO BE ON YOUR GUARD

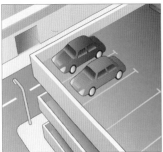

▲ In large car parks, numerous pillars and poorly lit areas make perfect cover for potential attackers, so maintain awareness in such places at all times, especially if they are deserted.

▲ Because you are facing a cash machine it's hard to know what's going on behind you. Glance around whenever possible, and put cash into an inside pocket or handbag immediately.

▲ In a queue it's normal to allow strangers closer proximity than usual. It is best to hold something in your hand, such as a rolled-up newspaper. Drunks can be a particular problem here.

▲ Pickpockets and gropers are the usual problems on public transport. Keep valuables in an inside pocket, ideally zipped. As for gropers, the best tactic is to shout to draw attention to them.

▲ A poorly lit, deserted underpass can be dangerous as there are few escape routes. If you must use it stay close to one wall and check around corners before you turn. Use your eyes and ears.

▲ If you have to stop at lights in an unsafe area, keep the car doors locked and windows up. Look out for anyone approaching the car, and for missiles that could be used to smash a window.

A TYPICAL ATTACK ON A MALE VICTIM

1 The attacker moves in close and attempts to intimidate his opponent by aggressive, loud, insulting language. Often a blank stare will accompany the use of threatening words and gestures.

2 The attacker pushes both hands into the chest, causing the victim to lose balance. He will usually try to push his victim over a chair or other object to increase the effectiveness of the attack.

3 The attacker next grabs his victim by the lapels and pushes him backwards again. By taking control of the victim's balance in this way he is making him vulnerable to further attack.

4 The attacker, now in full control, escalates the attack by delivering a blow to the victim's head with a bottle.

COMMON ATTACKS ON MEN

Studies show that when both assailant and victim are men, the ten most common forms of attack, in order of frequency, are:

1 A push to the chest followed by a punch to the head.

2 A swinging punch to the head.

3 A grab to the front clothing, one-handed, followed by a punch to the head.

4 A grab to the clothing with two hands, followed by a head butt.

5 A grab to the front clothing with two hands, followed by a knee to the groin.

6 A bottle, glass or ashtray to the head.

7 A lashing kick to the groin or lower legs.

8 A broken bottle or glass jabbed into the face.

9 A slash with a knife, usually a short-bladed lock knife or kitchen utility knife. (Hunting/combat-type knives tend to be used in gang violence and sexual assaults.)

10 A grappling-style head lock.

Attacks on women

There are a number of reasons why a woman might be attacked. As well as the obvious rape scenario, a woman could be attacked by a thief intent on taking something valuable, such as a mobile phone or a purse. In these circumstances it is not worth risking your health; let the thief take what they want and escape as quickly as possible. Only fight when the attack is directed at you rather than your property.

SEXUAL ASSAULTS

While strangers may seem to be the greatest threat, statistics prove that this is not the case. In fact most rapes occur in the home: 32 per cent of rape victims are attacked by their partners and another 22 per cent by men known to them.

From a self-defence point of view this means that the natural caution exercised among strangers is relaxed when in the company of friends, so reducing the opportunity for a fast, decisive response. However, it is important to react positively when a situation changes from one of normal affection or social interaction. Rape is an act of violence intended to degrade and humiliate the victim, and in police

▼ *Use your eyes to continuously scan for potential attackers or areas where an attack might come from. Stay away from dark doorways where an attacker could hide.*

interviews rapists often report that they commit the act as much for a sense of power and violence as for sex.

Submission to the rapist's demands is often thought of as a way to minimize the intensity of the attack, but in fact it may serve to encourage the attacker, who rationalizes that the victim is actually enjoying the activity and is, in fact, "asking for it".

The emotional effect of rape can include eating disorders, sleeping disorders, agoraphobia, depression, suicide attempts and sexual difficulties.

On pages 416–418 we cover other sexual assault issues including typical strategies employed by rapists. We also offer advice on how to fend off rapists in various street situations.

▲ *Badly lit car parks are high-risk areas for attacks. Always stay alert when approaching your vehicle and hold your keys ready in your dominant hand as a possible weapon.*

COMMON ATTACKS ON WOMEN

According to police records, these are the five most common forms of attack usd by men against women and girls:

1 The attacker approaches the victim displaying a weapon as a threat. The weapon is then hidden and the victim is led away, often by the attacker holding the victim's right upper arm.
2 The attacker pounces from behind, grabs the victim's head or neck in a lock and drags the victim away to a quiet place, often bushes or a deserted lane.
3 As with 2 above but the victim is grabbed around the waist and carried or dragged away.
4 The attacker pins the victim to a wall with a throat grab (often using the left hand). He issues a threat as in 1, and leads the victim away.
5 The attacker approaches from behind, grabs the victim's hair with his left hand and drags her away to a quiet place.

A TYPICAL ATTACK ON A FEMALE VICTIM

1 The attacker grabs the woman's right arm with his left hand. This initial assault is often accompanied by threatening instructions intended to frighten the victim into compliance.

2 In this case the threat is reinforced by the attacker brandishing a knife.

3 The knife might be partially hidden by being placed along the attacker's forearm. However, the victim can see it clearly, especially if the attacker pulls her in towards the blade.

DOMESTIC VIOLENCE

The victims of domestic violence, which accounts for almost a quarter of all the violent crime reported, are most likely to be women and children. Weapons are less likely to feature in domestic attacks: the victim is more likely to be injured from repeated blows with the hands and feet as well as being thrown into walls and furniture. Attempts at strangulation may also feature in this kind of situation.

Characteristically, this kind of attack is not a single incident, and on average a women will suffer 35 attacks from her partner before reporting the violence to the police. Domestic crime is the most under-reported type of violent crime, with about two-thirds of cases never coming to the authorities' attention.

Learning some basic survival strategies may minimize the chance of attack. On the physical level the ability to fight back will minimize the effects of an attack and may dissuade the attacker from using violence. Training can develop a level of self-esteem improving the victim's view of the world.

PERSONAL ALARMS

For well over a hundred years police officers carried the simplest form of personal alarm, a whistle, which could be heard over surprisingly long distances. Three strong blasts on it would bring speedy assistance.

Tiny modern key-ring whistles make useful personal alarms, but these days the more hi-tech, high-decibel, battery-powered alarm is more likely to be carried in a handbag or pocket. They emit a sound louder than that of a shotgun, and just above the pain threshold. The most practical type has

▲ *This tiny high-pitch siren alarm also has a built-in torch.*

a wrist cord connected to a small pin which, when sharply tugged free, allows a spring-loaded contact to complete an electrical circuit, triggering an ear-splitting siren. The second type, which may be little larger than a lipstick, is activated by pressing a button. This type of alarm is more discreet to carry in a pocket or bag, but it is just as effective.

◀ *A personal alarm can be clipped to a bag or belt hook and activated quickly if an attacker pounces.*

Learning to defend yourself

In a self-defence situation it is the training not only of the body but also of the mind and spirit that can give you an advantage.

TRAINING FOR IMPACT

Your strength and stamina can be improved by correct weight training, and the accuracy and impact of your strikes can be developed by hitting a target. It is best to train for impact without gloves as it is unlikely you will be wearing any protection on your hands if you are attacked. At first hit lightly, aiming for accuracy, but as you

become used to the feeling of hitting you can increase the intensity of your blows. Learn to hit as hard as you can. If you ever have to fight for your life against a stronger, heavier opponent you may have only one opportunity to land a decisive strike. Learn how to do it properly.

By adapting to the stresses of training you are also improving your ability to face the shock of physical confrontation: without becoming masochistic about it, look on the knocks and bruises you receive in the gym as a good investment.

TRAINING WITH A PARTNER

If you train alone, a punch bag is a very useful tool to improve your striking skills, but training is more productive and fun if you have a partner. If you join a martial arts school you will have a ready supply of training partners, but you may be able to recruit a friend or relative who also wants to develop some self-defence skills.

A training partner is very useful if you train with a pair of specialized pads worn on the hands, usually known as focus pads or hook-and-jab pads. By moving the pads around, your partner can simulate an attacker moving in a random way, and you can learn how to hit a moving target. It is very important when training with a partner to hold back a little on the degree of power used in strikes, locks and chokes. It is very easy to injure someone inadvertently through over-enthusiasm or clumsiness. Begin slowly, adding power and speed as your levels of coordination and timing improve.

MARTIAL ARTS FOR SELF-DEFENCE

The best way to learn effective self-defence skills is to join a martial arts club. It is important to find a club that concentrates on training in self-defence methods rather than developing skills aimed at participation in tournaments. The traditions and customs of the martial arts exist to create safe training

IMPROVING YOUR PHYSICAL FITNESS

▲ *Cardiovascular conditioning is necessary to build up stamina and the ability to move quickly. Running outside or on a machine in the gym is an excellent way to develop stamina.*

▲ *Upper body strength is vital. By using a rowing machine grip strength can be improved, and the pulling action duplicates the movements used in grabbing an attacker's hair or flesh.*

▲ *The "pec deck", a piece of equipment found in many gymnasiums, is a useful way of training the muscles of the chest and shoulders.*

▲ *The bench press develops strength in the arms, chest and shoulders. Train as heavily as possible – the increase of strength not stamina is the intent.*

WEIGHT TRAINING

The easiest way to become physically strong is to join a weight training gym, and many sports centres have extensive facilities. If you are a total beginner join a class to learn how to do the exercises correctly and safely. As you gain experience you may want to train at home. As well as barbells and dumbbells you can try lifting heavy things such as large stones, bags of sand, buckets of water or car tyres.

MARTIAL ARTS TRAINING

• **Judo** is a very popular combat sport. Training is based on grappling and makes extensive use of throws and ground fighting. Since its introduction into the Olympics the stress in training has been towards competition skills, but its intensity means that the techniques can be most effective in self-defence. Being thrown hard into a wall, for example, deters most attackers.

• **Karate-do** is primarily a striking art, which concentrates on developing powerful structures and to develop the correct mental attitude towards the training. Each discipline stresses its own skills and approach.

Finding a good club takes a little perseverance. If you know any martial artists you can ask them for their recommendations, explaining clearly what it is you are looking for. Then visit the club and watch the training in progress. Look carefully at the training methods and the way the instructors interact with the members. A bullying, militaristic atmosphere, where questions are not welcome, should be avoided. You may find that the training in this kind of club is not primarily about self-defence but is more a form of personal discipline.

Training methods and traditions in martial arts clubs are often derived from an oriental background, and as a beginner you may find features such as bowing or the wearing of white cotton training clothes a little exotic, but in essence these traditional elements are similar to the rituals found in Western fencing and boxing clubs.

punches, strikes and kicks. Some styles also make use of close-range knee and elbow strikes, throws and locks. Tae kwon do is the Korean version of karate, and specializes in kicking methods.

• **Aikido** is a Japanese martial art. It makes use of circular movements, which are designed to intercept an attack, blend with the movement and throw the attacker. Advanced training in Aikido involves training with weapons such as the *jo* (stick). In a real self-defence situation these techniques can be applied to implements such as walking sticks or umbrellas.

LEARNING TO PUNCH

1 Practise with a focus pad to develop accuracy and impact. Hit with the big knuckles, keeping the wrist straight, and drive the fist in a straight line, as if you were trying to break an attacker's nose or jaw. Keep your balance and use your waist and hips to add drive to the blow, hitting through the target.

• The term **"Kung-fu"** covers a wide range of Chinese martial arts. Some, such as T'ai Chi Ch'uan, are concerned mostly with health, while others such as the Wing Chun and Shaolin styles, are taught as combat methods.

• **Kick boxing** is a form of full-contact competiton fighting in a ring, but can also be very effective in self-defence situations. Tae kwon do also uses kick fighting (plus hand blocking and striking) for effective self-defence.

2 When you apply the punch, your intent should be to hit the fleshy parts rather than the bones, which could damage your hand. A fairly light punch to the throat will cause breathing problems to any attacker, but be careful in training as the neck and throat are very vulnerable to blows.

ELBOW STRIKE

1 Close in, an elbow strike can cause a lot of pain. In training, drive the elbow round and into the focus pad, aiming to land with the point of the elbow. Pull the other hand back to rotate the waist and simulate pulling an attacker into the strike.

2 The strike leaves the attacker's groin wide open for a follow-up kick or knee attack. Never rely on a single technique – be ready to exploit any weakness or hesitation on the attacker's part. Your survival may depend on this, especially if the attacker is bigger than you.

HAND SLAP

1 An open hand slap inflicts a surprising level of pain and shock. In training, focus on using the hand like a whip and slap down or sideways, hitting with the palm and not the fingers. Keeping the wrist a little loose gives a whiplash effect.

2 If the slap is aimed at the neck, try to hit in and slightly downwards to damage the throat. The best target for this kind of strike is the eyes. An assailant will almost certainly lift the hands to the face if the eyes have been heavily slapped. Take advantage of this to kick the attacker's groin or knees.

KNEE JERK

1 The knee is a very effective weapon, and is often used when an attacker has seized you and pulled you close. When training the knee on the focus pads, hold on to your training partner to simulate the correct range and the feeling of being close to an attacker.

2 The groin is a natural target, but many men will reflexively pull back if they sense an attack coming. By driving upwards it is often possible to hit the solar plexus. Other targets include the kidneys and the large muscles on the thighs. Try to augment the strike by gouging the eyes or biting the ear.

ROUNDHOUSE KICK

1 The roundhouse kick makes use of the whipping motion of the hips and the supporting leg. Use your instep to hit the groin, knees or thigh. With a lot of training this technique can even be used against the head, but in general it is safer to select a target from the waist downwards.

2 A very effective way to use a roundhouse kick is to strike against the back of an attacker's knee. As well as causing pain and slowing him down there is a strong possibility that this strike will cause him to stumble and fall. If this happens follow up your kick with a stamp to the ankle or groin.

GROIN KICK

1 A direct kick to the groin can drain an attacker of strength and aggression very quickly. Use the knee like a hinge and snap the lower leg directly to the target, aiming to hit with the instep of the foot. When practising this move, drive the kick upwards into the focus pad to develop maximum power and penetration. A male attacker who is kicked hard in the groin will usually bend forwards, covering his groin with his hands, leaving the eyes, throat and neck exposed to a powerful strike to any of those targets.

EFFECTIVE FIRST BLOWS

Ideally, the first blow should be decisive, allowing you to escape as quickly as possible. However, a number of factors could limit the effectiveness of your initial strike. The attacker may have been drinking alcohol or taking drugs, which will dull his response to pain. He may be wearing heavy clothing that absorbs some of the force of your blows, or your strike may be inaccurate.

It is therefore important to follow up as quickly as possible with a number of blows, all intended to cause as much pain and disorientation as possible. Aim at the eyes, groin, joints and other vulnerable parts. When training on a heavy bag try to keep going in bursts of 20–30 seconds; this will build stamina, fighting spirit and the skill to switch targets quickly. As soon as the attacker backs away, run towards somewhere safe.

Using improvised weapons

Because of the fear of attack some people habitually carry a knife or some other weapon. Although they may see it as a perfectly acceptable thing to do as they intend to use the weapon for self-defence only, the police in most countries would regard this as an illegal act, which could lead to arrest and punishment.

However, the law does accept that at times the use of force, even if it proves lethal, is justified if the action is reasonable in the prevention of an attack against yourself or another person. The key word is "reasonable". It would not be reasonable, for example, if having driven off an attacker you then pursued him and jammed your pen into his eye. On the other hand, if you performed the same act because you were being attacked and believed your life was in danger, it would probably be seen as reasonable, especially if your attacker was armed.

Within the boundaries set by the law it is perfectly possible to make use of items in your possession that are not usually thought of as weapons to defend yourself. These might include an umbrella or rolled newspaper, a bunch of keys, a belt or dog lead, the contents of a handbag – such as a comb (especially if it is made of steel or is pointed), credit cards, hairsprays and deodorants, a lighter, and pens and pencils – or the handbag iteslf, particularly if it is heavy.

IMPROVING YOUR STRIKES

As with all other aspects of effective self-defence it is important to practise your responses in order to develop efficient technique. If you make a target from a bundle of rolled-up newspapers taped together you can improve significantly your striking and targeting skills. Hang the bundle at about head height and practise delivering fast, hard and accurate blows at the centre line of the target.

NEWSPAPER OR MAGAZINE

1 A tightly rolled magazine or paper is surprisingly rigid and can be used to deliver powerful blows to the throat and face. The windpipe, eyes and mouth are especially vulnerable to this.

2 The magazine needs to be readily accessible, so it could be carried in the side of a bag, placed in such a way that the dominant hand (in this case the right hand) can grab it quickly.

3 Once the attacker has tried to take control of you as a victim, pull the magazine out of the bag and strike towards the attacker's neck or face.

4 Grab the hair or throat and pull the head towards the magazine as it moves up. Stab inwards, driving in with all the power of your shoulders and hips.

BUNCH OF KEYS

1 A bunch of keys can be used to deliver a very painful strike to the face. Keep the keys in the pocket nearest to your dominant hand, and if you feel you might be entering a dangerous place make sure that the pocket does not contain anything else that might prevent you getting to the keys quickly.

2 Pull the keys out and step backwards to create some space. This will also tend to unbalance the attacker if he has already made contact.

3 Drive the keys towards the attacker's eyes with a strong raking movement. A natural follow-up technique in this situation would be a knee to the groin.

UMBRELLAS

Umbrellas can be used in several different ways as an effective improvised weapon. A long rolled umbrella, held in either one or both hands, can be used to block someone attacking you with a weapon. Alternatively the tip can be rammed into the attacker's face with the intention of hitting the eyes, nose or teeth. Even a short umbrella, when open, can be used to distract an attacker while setting him up for a counter-attack such as a kick to the groin.

AEROSOL SPRAYS

Hair spray or deodorant can be used as an effective way to interfere with an attacker's vision. As with the rolled magazine and the keys, the aerosol needs to be carried in such a way that it can be brought into use quickly with the dominant hand. When transferring it to somewhere handy, make sure you remove its cap, if it has one, so that you don't lose the element of surprise by having to fumble with it at the crucial moment – speed and surprise are key in self-defence.

Once the attack begins, seize the initiative by stepping forwards and spraying into the attacker's eyes and mouth. Don't be afraid also to use the container as a striking weapon against the eyes, nose and mouth. The likelihood is that your attacker will recoil in pain or surprise, exposing his groin to attack from your knee or foot. Take the first opportunity to run to safety that you can.

Frontal attack

Most attacks from the front you will, by definition, see coming. That is to your advantage, giving you crucial moments to take in the situation and switch into survival mode.

Preparation for surviving a real attack must involve a physically vigorous approach. In training, the partner who is playing the part of an attacker must attempt to duplicate as closely as possible the actual situation likely to be faced to allow the defender to develop realistic responses. This is not simply about technique – a spirited attitude is very important. A man attacking a woman, for example, will generally be stronger and heavier than his intended victim. It is vital for the defender to respond with total commitment and decisiveness and to keep on resisting, even if some pain is involved.

A study of victims of attempted rape found that those women who were used to engaging in a contact sport were better able to resist an attack and avoid being raped. This kind of habitual experience teaches that physical contact, even if it involves being hurt or knocked down, is not the worst thing that can happen, so it can be helpful in an attack.

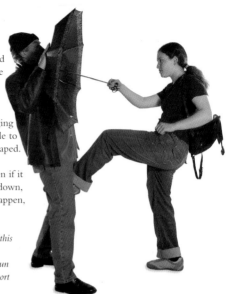

▶ *Use a weapon of opportunity (in this case an umbrella) to continue your counter-attack. As soon as possible run away towards a well-lit area and report the attack to the police.*

TAKING CONTROL OF A FRONTAL ATTACK

1 The attacker makes his initial approach and contact by taking hold of the defender's right wrist.

2 The attacker raises his other hand as a threat. You should see this as an attempt to force your compliance by invading your personal space with a threatening gesture.

3 Break free from the attacker's grasp and slap his hand away to the side. Simultaneously, with your other hand grab his raised finger and bend it back with the aim of snapping it. If possible use a twisting action as you bend the finger back. Spitting in the assailant's eyes will also help to distract him momentarily.

4 Continue the defence by driving your knee into his groin. Meanwhile, you should scream as loudly as possible to attract attention, intimidate the attacker and add strength to your attack.

5 Follow through with a right elbow to the face, aiming at the nose, the throat or the temple.

6 Step backwards and pull the attacker on to your rising right knee aimed at the face, throat or other target.

7 Continue to attack with your right foot, this time by stamping as hard as possible against the attacker's knee.

8 By now he may be doubled up. Step in and deliver a dropping elbow strike to the neck or face.

9 Drive the attacker into the ground to create space to escape, or hit him with an improvised weapon such as a bag.

Attack from behind

Any kind of attack from the rear is likely to be very successful as it makes the best use of surprise and the shock of impact and minimizes the possibility of the victim using the hands and feet in defence.

A person using a cash machine is in a situation where they are vulnerable to an attack from behind, and this approach is also often used by potential rapists targeting women and girls. As an attack from the rear is based on surprise the best defence is to stay alert to the possibility of such an attack. If you have to walk on your own along a poorly lit pavement at night, walk facing the

traffic so a car cannot pull up behind you and catch you unawares. If you think someone is following you, cross the road more than once. If you are still afraid get to the nearest place where other people are – a take-away or somewhere with lights on – and call the police. Scan your surroundings continuously to minimize the possibility of an attacker approaching from a blind spot – even if it is unlikely to occur it is sensible to be aware.

Most attacks from behind will involve some grappling as the attacker is likely to wrap his arms around your upper body or grab and pull your hair.

It is important to maintain your balance and to try to destroy the attacker's balance while causing him pain. Tactics such as stamping on the foot or knee while clawing at his groin work well.

COUNTERING A REAR ATTACK

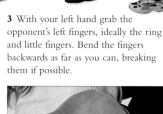

2 Drive your elbow backwards into the attacker's ribs as hard as possible. As you make this strike you should feel as if you are trying to smash completely through the attacker's body in order to generate sufficient force.

3 With your left hand grab the opponent's left fingers, ideally the ring and little fingers. Bend the fingers backwards as far as you can, breaking them if possible.

1 The attacker attempts to grab you with a bear hug. At the moment of contact step forward as far as possible and lift your arms to minimize the attacker's advantage of strength.

▶ *If you can break the attacker's fingers you will make it virtually impossible for him to strike or grab you with his damaged hand. In addition, a relatively small slap to his broken fingers will cause intense pain.*

4 Step away from the attacker's right hand, pivoting at an angle to expose his centre line. Maintain the pressure on the fingers.

5 Push forwards using both hands to apply more leverage to the fingers; if possible apply a twisting, wrenching motion to the finger joints.

6 Reach with the right hand to grab the attacker's hair, and pull the head backwards and down while maintaining leverage on the fingers of the left hand.

7 Stamp on the back of the attacker's left knee with your right foot. Drive down with your full weight, smashing his knee joint on to the ground.

8 Once you have succeeded in getting the attacker to the ground, maintain your holds on him as you shift your body weight forwards.

9 Now push the attacker away from you and down on to the ground. Escape as quickly as possible.

KEEPING THE ADVANTAGE

As you drive forwards take any opportunity that comes by to deliver strikes to the perpetrator's body.

Attacks with knives and other weapons

While a fist or foot can inflict lethal injuries, there is no doubt that the chance of being badly hurt or killed is greatly increased when an attacker makes use of a weapon. Many objects can be used as weapons but experience has shown that the most commonly carried weapon is a knife.

The number of attacks using knives has risen over the past few years, and some authorities believe that a knife culture is growing, particularly among young men. The claim is often made that they carry knives for self-defence, but it is also clear that blades can be and are used to attack anyone perceived as a danger or – more prevalent – as a target for theft or racial violence.

DEFENCE AGAINST AN EDGED WEAPON

Knives or broken bottles, glasses and ashtrays can cause horrific wounds. Certain arteries are more vulnerable to attack than others, because they are nearer the surface of the skin, or are not protected by clothing or equipment. It is important to protect these areas from attack – the neck, with its jugular vein and the carotid artery, is one such area.

The most frightening thing about a knife attack is knowing that you might be cut, stabbed or even killed. Such fear is potentially paralysing. In order to regain any degree of control over the situation, you need to accept that you might get hurt.

Trying to disarm a determined attacker is very difficult. But showing that you are not one to freeze with fear is enough to put some attackers sufficiently off-guard to enable you to escape. If you are forced to defend yourself, keep it simple – and whatever you do, don't rush a person with a knife. The most likely place you will be cut is across the face or abdomen. Keep circling your attacker and at a safe enough distance to avoid being slashed – keep sucking your stomach in. If you can, find something to use as a defensive weapon such as a chair. Grab a coat or belt to use as a striking,

entangling device, or throw the loose change from your pocket directly at the attacker's eyes as hard as you can.

USING A KNIFE

Extreme circumstances might arise in which you are forced to wield an attacker's knife to save yourself or another victim in an attack. The heart or stomach are the best targets if they are unprotected. The psychological effect of receiving even a slight wound in the stomach is such that it is likely to throw an attacker into confusion.

If you are attacked in your own home, say by a burglar armed with a baseball bat, don't be tempted to pick up a kitchen knife and use it to threaten the attacker. You are just inviting the burglar to take it from you and to use it against you.

BLUNT WEAPONS

Weapons such as sticks, coshes, iron bars, hammers and similar objects can cause terrible injuries. A hammer smashed down on an arm can easily break it while the same blow to the head can fracture the skull and cause massive brain damage. Try to sway, duck and dodge out of the way. If you are knocked to the ground, keep rolling, shielding your skull with both hands and your ears with your wrists.

GUNS

The golden rule when faced by someone with a gun in a robbery is to do exactly what they tell you to do. If they say "Freeze," do just that. Many prospective robbers will carry a weapon precisely to scare you and may not even know how to use the gun properly. You are peripheral to their main plan, which is almost certainly to steal rather than murder. By remaining as inconspicuous as you can, you represent less of a threat and there is therefore less reason for them to escalate the crime. You also cannot guarantee whether they are a good shot or not and the last thing you want to do is panic your attacker into shooting.

▲ *A selection of combat knives designed to cause maximum injury. Always remember that a knife with a 7.5cm/3in blade is long enough to penetrate the heart. It is illegal in most countries to carry a knife as a weapon for self-defence so don't be tempted to do so, and it can always be turned against you.*

But what if this is nothing to do with theft and you are the intended victim? What if your attacker has been stalking you and is trying to force you into their car at gunpoint?

Some would argue that you should acquiesce on the basis that if you cooperate you might be able to talk the attacker round. Others say that you should play the odds and that the first few seconds of an attack offer you the greatest chance of escape and survival – by refusing to cooperate and making a scene you might just buy that crucial second that allows you to run.

If you do decide to run for your life, try to quickly put some distance between yourself and the attacker. Keep low and run in a zig-zag fashion to put them off their shot. If you can put some obstructions between you, such as a line of cars, trees or a fence then so much the better.

BEING ATTACKED WITH A KNIFE

1 If your attacker is armed the best defence is, of course, to run away as quickly as you can, but in some circumstances this may be impossible.

2 As the attacker slashes, sway back out of range, keeping your arms close to your body. Do not flap your arms wildly as they may be cut.

3 As the attacker slashes towards your face lift both arms to protect your face and neck. Do not expose the vulnerable inner wrists to the blade.

4 As you lift the arms to shield your face, don't raise them passively but smash them into the attacker's arm to cause injury or possibly loosen his grip on the knife.

5 When the slash has missed its target, grab the attacking arm strongly to put the weapon under control and drive your elbow into the attacker's ribs or face. Once you have established control over the knife arm do not give it up under any circumstances. This is your best protection against being cut.

6 Push the attacker's elbow straight up and push your weight into him to put him off balance. Turn the knife towards his ribs. Drive forward with all your weight to push the blade into his body. If he falls, back off as quickly as possible and escape.

DEFLECTING A STABBING ATTACK

1 The attacker has grabbed you with his left hand and raised the knife to stab down towards your head or neck.

2 Move inwards to intercept the stabbing arm and deflect the blade with your forearm.

3 Grab the wrist holding the knife and extend the arm while clawing at his eyes. Push him backwards off balance.

4 As you push him back, sweep his supporting leg away from under him with your foot, causing him to fall. Try not to lose control over the hand holding the knife.

5 Use both hands to control the wrist holding the knife. Twist the point of the knife towards the attacker.

6 Drop your full weight on to the handle of the knife, forcing the blade into the attacker's chest. Escape as quickly as possible.

BEING THREATENED WITH A GUN

1 When faced with someone holding a gun the best piece of advice is to obey the attacker's instructions. If it is a robbery give him what he wants. Your life is worth more than a watch, money or a car.

2 If you are convinced that the attacker will shoot you whatever happens, you have no choice but to defend yourself. Sweep the gun to the side to get out of the way of the muzzle.

3 If the weapon goes off at this point you will be shocked by the noise, but you must hang on to either the weapon or the attacker's wrist.

4 Attack the elbow of the arm holding the gun.

5 Your aim is to get both hands controlling the arm holding the gun. Stamp-kick the attacker's knee as hard as you can to distract him as you make a move to get possession of the gun. Maintain forward momentum at all times to dominate the situation.

6 Pull the gun out of the attacker's hand, and back away as quickly as possible. At this point you might be tempted to use the weapon but you would almost certainly be found guilty of attempted murder, unless the attacker produced another weapon, such as a knife, in which case shooting him would be seen as reasonable.

Strangulation

Because the neck lacks any form of bony protection and contains the spinal cord, major blood vessels and the windpipe, it is extremely vulnerable to damage by being compressed. A victim will initially experience severe pain, quickly followed by unconsciousness and brain death. Pressure to the throat can affect blood flow to the brain and stop the heart beating. It takes only about 15kg/33lb of force to close the trachea; you can become unconscious in seconds. This form of attack is often directed by men against women and strangulation is frequently a feature of domestic abuse.

STRENGTHENING THE NECK

Weight training can be used to strengthen the muscles of the neck and shoulders, as can exercises such as shrugs and shoulder presses and those involving the head harness.

DEFENDING AGAINST STRANGULATION 1

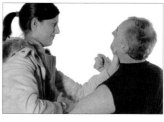

3 Spitting directly into the attacker's eyes will make him blink, leaving him vulnerable to further attack.

1 The attacker attempts to grab your throat with the left hand, intending to throttle you.

2 Push down on the attacker's elbow joint as hard as possible while punching him in the throat with the other fist.

4 Drive the left hand upwards while grabbing the hair with the right hand to pull the head back strongly. Use a jerking action to damage the neck.

5 Stamp on the back of the attacker's leg, driving the knee into the ground. Commit your full weight to the stamp to do as much damage as possible.

6 Drive his head to the ground with your palm. If he begins to get up kick his groin or stamp on the back of his ankle. Escape as quickly as possible.

DEFENDING AGAINST STRANGULATION 2

1 The attacker reaches for your throat with his right hand.

2 Parry the attacker's hand and begin to apply upward pressure to his elbow.

3 Push the arm up and over to unbalance the attacker.

DEFENDING AGAINST STRANGULATION 3

1 The attacker approaches with his right hand reaching towards the throat.

2 The attacker seizes your throat and starts to squeeze.

3 ◀ Pull your head a little to the side, drop your chin and then push forwards, simultaneously attacking with a punch, slap or grab to the groin, intended to force the attacker to back away.

4 ▶ Pivot to the outside, sliding your left forearm across the attacker's throat and pulling him off balance. Step backwards as quickly as possible while pulling the attacker to the ground. As soon as he is down you can use a stamp to prevent any further attack.

THE COUNTER-ATTACK

Do not stamp on the attacker's face or head as it could be considered unreasonable force; a stamp to the arm or hand, or to the knee or ankle, is usually acceptable.

ATTEMPTED STRANGULATION FROM BEHIND

1 The attacker approaches from behind, giving him the advantage of surprise.

2 The attacker wraps his left arm around your throat and begins to apply pressure.

3 Lean forwards and pull the attacker's left arm down as hard as possible to reduce the pressure on the throat.

4 Maintaining control of the arm, pivot in a clockwise motion away from the attacker, wrenching his arm as hard as possible outwards.

5 Step in with your heel behind his nearer leg while delivering a strike to his face with your right hand. A strike with the heel of the hand to the jaw or throat is very effective, especially if it is accompanied with a clawing action directed at the attacker's eyes.

6 Push the attacker backwards over your leg to throw him off balance and drive him to the ground. Once he is down continue to counter-attack with a stamp to the body or groin. Don't assume that because the attacker is on the ground they have ceased to be a threat. Move away quickly so the perpetrator cannot reach out and grab your legs and pull you to the ground.

Head butt

A head butt can be a devastating form of attack if it lands on the nose, eye or cheekbone, and is often the favoured method of those skilled at heading a football. Its effect can be maximized by pulling the victim on to the strike, and the target area is stabilized by gripping the victim's clothing with both hands. If a head butt lands cleanly it can easily cause a knockout, concussion and damage to the soft tissues of the face. It can also lead to permanent eye damage or even brain damage.

Defending against a head butt requires fast reaction to the initial grab.

DEFENDING AGAINST A HEAD BUTT

1 The attacker has grabbed you to set you up for a head butt. Often the grab is so strong that the victim's head suffers a degree of whiplash. It is important to train the muscles of the neck to minimize the effects of being grabbed and jerked into a blow.

2 As the attacker drives his head forwards towards your face, lift your elbow in such a way that the point of the elbow meets the attacker's face. This will stop the head butt and cause some damage to the soft tissues of the attacker's face.

3 Drive the heel of your right hand directly into the attacker's jaw or throat, pushing the head backwards. A claw hand attack to the eyes can be delivered at the same time to further weaken and disorient the attacker.

4 Drop your body weight and jerk the attacker's arm downwards as strongly as possible with the aim of damaging the elbow joint. If space permits you should step backwards or to the side to maximize the leverage you are exerting on the arm.

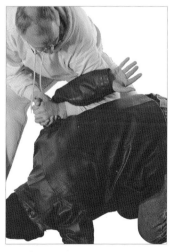

5 Twist the attacker's arm up and around, forcing it up his back and wrenching his shoulder. This will force his head downwards, where it is vulnerable to strikes with the knee or foot. If the attacker manages to retain his balance, ram him into a wall.

6 Grab the attacker's open fingers with both hands and pull sideways strongly to damage the joints of the hand. You do not need a lot of strength to do major damage in this way. The attacker will then be unable to use his hand to grab or strike you.

Bag snatching

A bag swinging on a long strap over the shoulder is an attractive proposition for an opportunistic thief. A safer and more discreet way to wear a bag is on a short strap under the arm, tight to the body – not that this will deter the determined mugger.

A common approach by bag snatchers is to move rapidly towards the victim from the rear, grab the bag and run away as quickly as possible. In some cases the thief will use force or the threat of force to obtain the bag. Some victims have been injured by the attacker pushing them to the ground or into a wall when the bag is grabbed. In the case of a frail victim, the consequences of the attack may far outweigh the value of the possessions that have been lost.

If an attacker makes a serious threatening gesture with a knife to intimidate you and force you to comply, let the bag go. It is not worth getting stabbed or slashed in order to keep your possessions. If possible back away while keeping your eyes on the attacker. Try to remember details of his build and appearance to report to the police later. Write down your impressions as soon as you can and get details of any witnesses.

To minimize the effect of having your bag stolen do not carry all your valuables in one place. If you

▶ *A thief intent on snatching a bag is likely to aproach from behind and simply grab it, catching the victim unawares.*

THEFT THROUGH A CAR WINDOW

1 If you see the attacker approaching the window turn on the engine. Ideally drive away, but if that is not possible, make sure the door is locked.

2 As the attacker reaches through the open window grab his arm with both hands and pull it into the car as hard as you can.

3 Try to pull on his arm with enough force to smash his face and neck against the door frame of the car. If possible twist the arm to maximize damage.

4 Throw your weight against his elbow joint, jamming his shoulder into the front of the window. Attack his fingers and twist or break as many as possible.

have to carry a large amount of cash, put most of the larger denomination notes in an inside pocket of your jacket. Do not display large amounts of money if shopping or taking money out of a cash dispenser; this will advertise to a bag snatcher that you are worth robbing.

If you become involved in a struggle with a bag snatcher, scream at the top of your voice. A street thief depends on speed and surprise so if you can slow him down or attract the attention of others he will be neutralized.

BAG SNATCHING FROM A CAR
Even if you are sitting in it, a stationary car with an open window is an open invitation to an opportunistic thief. Whether you are parked or stuck in a traffic queue, a thief can easily reach in and grab a bag on the seat, so get wise and keep valuables out of sight.

If you spot the thief's movements in time you may be able to take action by grabbing his arm. Meanwhile, sound your horn continuously to attract attention from passers-by. Other possible responses would be to use a demister aerosol as a spray into the attacker's face, or to use a pen or pencil as a spike to gouge his arm or hand.

DEALING WITH A STREET THIEF

1 The attacker approaches from behind and attempts to grab the handbag, which is worn in such a way that it cannot be released quickly.

2 As soon as you are aware of the attacker's intentions, pivot to the side and deflect his arm. Pull the arm to the side a little to disturb his balance and reach up and grab either his hair or the hood of his jacket.

COUNTER-ATTACK STRATEGIES

When there is a large difference in weight between attacker and victim it is very important to react with great speed and ferocity. Like a mongoose fighting a large snake, the victim has to rely on speed and counter-attacks to the vulnerable areas of the attacker's body. Punching the stomach or chest, for example, is less effective than clawing the eyes or landing a heavy strike on the testicles or throat.

Ideally, attack the knee joints to hamper the attacker's ability to move quickly. This will remove his advantages of weight and reach, and prevent him chasing you when you escape. A stamp on the back of the ankle should damage the Achilles tendon and prevent any fast movement with that leg.

3 Pull his head back while stamping on his knee joint.

4 Smash the attacker's knee on to the ground. While he is down move away as quickly as possible to a safe place.

Sexual assaults

Although anyone can be a target for a rapist, many victims are under the age of 18, and most rapists use physical force to intimidate and subdue their victims. Although there is a belief that rapes are mostly unplanned attacks committed by strangers, the great majority of rapists are known to their victims and the assault itself is a result of a plan worked out well in advance.

A group attack is possibly the most dangerous situation you could encounter. The most important thing is to maintain as much distance as possible. Ideally, run away as fast as you can to a well-lit, populated area.

RAPE STRATEGIES
A potential rapist will often use one of the following approaches:
• **Gaining the victim's confidence** Usually the rapist openly approaches the victim and asks for help in some way. Once within range he becomes more aggressive and threatening. An attacker using this approach may

pretend to be a police officer, a door-to-door-salesman or a driver giving a lift to a hitch-hiker. This is the commonest tactic when the rapist is a stranger.
• **Sudden attack** The rapist hides in some kind of cover and suddenly attacks without warning.
• **Stealth attack** The rapist breaks into where the victim is sleeping.

Rapists try to control their victims through physical intimidation, verbal threats, the display of a weapon (usually a knife) and physical force. Often the victim is so frightened or shocked that little force is required to make them compliant. The rapist depends on this, so disrupt his plan by shouting and resisting his attack to attract attention.

Heavy drinking can make victims very vulnerable to attack. Their physical skills are impaired to such a point that it may be impossible to make use of either fight or flight, and the memory is so disrupted that it may be difficult to remember details that could help convict the attacker.

SEXUAL HARASSMENT
Though not usually as serious as rape, sexual harassment at work is a threat to your peace of mind and self-esteem and laws exist to protect employees from this kind of thing. It may take a variety of forms, from inappropriate comments about your appearance to a fellow employee trying to touch you in unwelcome ways. You should make it very clear that you do not welcome such comments or behaviour. Do not apologize for your reaction or try to present a friendly smiling exterior. Make it very clear from the outset, ideally in front of witnesses, that you will not accept any form of harassment.

If this does not work keep a record of all the incidents and report them to your employer. By law they have to take action against the offender. If, as a last resort, the continued behaviour necessitates physical action on your part, you may need to prove that your action was justified as the result of an unresolved situation.

FRONTAL ATTACK

1 Reach up and seize the attacker's clothing, or if he has long hair or earrings, pull on them forcefully.

2 As the attacker's head is moving down, drive your knee in an upward motion into his groin.

3 As the attacker falls forwards push his head backwards. Continue to counter-attack with a clawing action at the eyes.

SEXUAL ATTACK ON THE GROUND

1 When walking along a quiet lane, an attacker approaches from behind and quickly moves in to grab you.

2 He uses his weight and strength to push you to the ground, straddling you and pushing on your shoulders or arms.

3 The attacker does not have control of your legs. Hook your foot around one of his ankles.

4 The ankle hook, seen here in close-up, gives the purchase you need to roll to the side, pushing hard with the arms and driving your leg against the ankle.

5 Once you have managed to dislodge the attacker, use your arms if possible to throw him into a wall to maximize the effect of the escape.

6 Drive your knee into the attacker's groin, then break free and run to a populated area. Contact the police as quickly as possible.

FENDING OFF A GROUP OF ATTACKERS

1 If confronted by a threatening group, shout as loudly as possible to attract attention and to show clearly that you will not simply accept the situation.

2 If the group persists and advances towards you, a belt with a heavy buckle, or a dog lead or chain, makes a useful weapon of opportunity.

3 A belt can be swung in fast arcs to keep attackers as far away as possible. Keep it in motion as they advance, while backing away as fast as you can.

ATTACK AGAINST A WALL

1 The attacker is hiding on a corner watching you as you approach.

2 He moves towards you quickly, pushing you back against a wall.

3 Respond instantly by driving a knee into his groin, stomach or thigh.

4 Move your head to one side and with all your weight and strength pull the attacker's face into the wall.

5 Push the attacker away from you on to his back. As he falls shout at the top of your voice and keep watching him.

6 Stamp on his groin and then run away as quickly as possible and move into a crowded area.

INAPPROPRIATE TOUCHING 1

1 Respond to the initial contact by trapping the attacker's hand to prevent further movement and raise your elbow in preparation for a response.

2 Drive the elbow directly into the attacker's face, aiming at the nose, lips, or eyes. Shout loudly to add power to the strike and inhibit the attacker.

3 Counter-attack by driving a knife hand into the attacker's groin. Stand up and move away, pushing the attacker as hard as possible in the other direction.

INAPPROPRIATE TOUCHING 2

1 The attacker approaches from behind. Typically, this could be an approach to someone sitting at a desk.

2 He places his hands on the defender's shoulders and leans forward, as if he is about to speak quietly.

3 Respond by grabbing one or more of the attacker's fingers with your dominant hand (in this case the left).

4 Twist and pull the finger causing the attacker's head to drop and at the same time prepare a counter-attack with the other hand.

5 Slam the heel of your hand directly upwards into the attacker's chin, forcing his head back. This will create enough space for you to stand and move away.

SURVIVAL IN THE HOME

When did you last review the security of your home and its possessions? How would you guard against intruders in your house? Could you fall victim to a gas leak or carbon monoxide poisoning? Is your home a potential fire trap? If a fire did break out, would you know how to get everyone out safely? In order to correctly assess the dangers in your home, you should be asking yourself questions like these, and also looking at the needs of individual family members. Your home may feel like a refuge, but this does not automatically make it a safe environment.

Safety in the home

One in three of all accidents happen in our own homes, the place where we feel safest and at our most comfortable. Our houses are filled with hazards – from faulty electrical appliances to ill-fitting carpets or sticking-out nails in the floorboards. Even a hot pan of soup can cause a serious injury. Most of these accidents are preventable, so making our homes safe must be a prime consideration. The majority of home accidents involve children. So, if you have children or if children may visit your house, home safety is all the more important.

Most of us love our homes, and we feel secure and safe when we are in them. However, although we may feel protected from the dangers of the outside world, our home environments are actually filled with all kinds of potential hazard. In fact, domestic accidents are what keep many country's accident and emergency departments busy. On average, more people are killed every week in domestic accidents than die in road traffic accidents. A large number of these accidents are due to a combination of carelessness, ignorance and human frailty – and most of them are preventable.

HOME HAZARDS

Almost anything has the potential to be a hazard. For example, accidents suffered by elderly people are most commonly a result of them putting their slippers on to the wrong feet, and then attempting to walk in them. Trousers are another unsuspected hazard, especially in the elderly and less physically able. Simply sitting down before attempting to put on a pair of trousers cuts down the chance of an accident. Naked feet are also vulnerable – stepping on broken glass or dropping something on your foot can cause a nasty injury.

AVOIDING ACCIDENTS

Many of the accidents that occur in the home can be prevented by taking a few simple precautions.
• Don't leave toys lying around.
• Don't leave plastic bags within easy reach of children.
• Don't smoke in bed.
• Don't leave shoes in people's way.
• Don't leave flexes trailing or hanging in any part of the house.
• Don't allow pets on the stairs – they may become trip hazards.
• Don't ever put a mat at the top or bottom of stairs.
• Don't place anything on a table with an overhanging cloth if you have children.
• Don't hang a mirror or toys over a fire.
• Don't put plants on the television – it will be hazardous when you water them.
• Repair or throw away rickety, unstable ladders.

A TIDY HOME

Messy houses are without a doubt more dangerous than immaculate ones. Falls – the number one killer in the home – are much more likely to occur if the floor is covered with clutter. Glossy magazines strewn across a sitting room floor can be as slippery as a sheet of ice, and a bean bag lying in a hallway is difficult not to trip over. Children's toys left scattered across the floor are another major source of injury common in the home.

Keeping a house clear of mess is obviously a good idea, but continually tidying away – especially after very young family members – is not always possible. The best policy is to have a place for everything and to make sure that, even if it will be several days before you can clean and tidy the house fully, all walkways are kept as free of clutter as possible. Communicate this house rule to other family members so that it is put into practice.

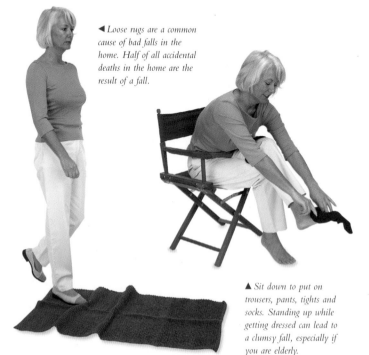

◀ *Loose rugs are a common cause of bad falls in the home. Half of all accidental deaths in the home are the result of a fall.*

▲ *Sit down to put on trousers, pants, tights and socks. Standing up while getting dressed can lead to a clumsy fall, especially if you are elderly.*

CAUSES OF ACCIDENTS IN THE HOME

- Falls: 50 per cent.
- Accidental poisoning from taking medicines: 20 per cent.
- Fires: 10 per cent.
- Other, miscellaneous causes, including DIY: 20 per cent.

STAIRWAYS

It is particularly important to keep the stairs absolutely clear. Leaving objects on the stairs to be taken up (or down) later on, when you get around to it, is a major hazard. A vacuum cleaner left at the top of the stairs while you are dusting a room, for example, is easily tripped over, and a trailing cable from the item to a plug will only increase the chance of injury.

Stair carpets wear out quickly and may develop lethal holes or tags. Repair any damage as soon as possible. Fitting stair gates helps to protect children from falls. These gates need to be secured at the top and bottom of the stairs to be effective. There are two main kinds: screw-fitting and pressure-

fitting. The latter come equipped with stoppers that mean they need not be screwed into the adjacent walls.

PREVENTING FIRE HAZARDS

Cracked plugs, loose flexes, old wiring, furniture placed too close to the fire and unguarded fires are all common factors in house fires. Fire is one of the most serious hazards in the home, and yet one of the most preventable. Smoke alarms cut deaths from fires by 60–80 per cent, but even people who install smoke detectors often fail to maintain them by checking the batteries.

SAFETY IN THE BATHROOM

Some 90 per cent of accidents in the home that involve electricity happen in the bathroom. The chief hazards here are the combination of water and electricity, water itself and medicines left within reach of young children. Getting in or out of the bath is another hazard. It is a common cause of falls, particularly among elderly people, but these can be minimized by choosing a bath with side grips and placing a non-slip mat on the base. Children love bathtime but should always be supervised – leaving them alone could have fatal results. See also the guidelines to bathing in the section Safety for children and the infirm, 424–425.

▲ *Never leave toys or shoes lying around on the floor because they are a common cause of falls in the home.*

▲ *Protect toddlers from falling down stairs by fitting gates with the appropriate locking devices at the top and bottom of each flight of steps.*

All medicines should be kept in a medicine cabinet – this is particularly important if children live in the house or are likely to come to visit. The cabinet should be safely screwed to a wall, well out of the reach of children.

▲ *Always keep the stairs free of appliances, cables, toys and pets to reduce the chance of an accidental fall.*

Safety for children and the infirm

A few simple precautions taken when planning and designing a kitchen will prevent a lot of the problems that occur in this part of the house. In addition, laying down some basic kitchen rules may serve a useful purpose in protecting you and other house-dwellers from avoidable hazards.

GUARD AGAINST BURNS

- Keep counters and tabletops clear of appliances unless they are in daily use. Even then, it may simply be safer to put them away.
- Buy appliances with coiled flexes since these are neater and more difficult to catch hold of by accident. Avoid long flexes.
- Remember that tablecloths have dangling edges that are very tempting to small children wandering past.
- Don't try to drink your coffee or tea with a small child in your lap; they may wriggle and cause you to spill it.
- Make a habit of always using the back rings on the hob, and of turning the handles of pots and pans away from the edge of the cooker.
- Oven doors can get very hot. The time around opening the oven door and getting the food out can be an especially dangerous one.

▲ *Ensure that flexes and cables are kept to the back of kitchen worktops to prevent a child from pulling down a heavy appliance.*

▲ *Use the back burners on a hob in preference to the front ones and turn handles away from the edge.*

- Burning oil is one of the biggest hazards in a kitchen. If you deep-fat fry a lot, you should seriously consider buying an electric fryer.
- Putting a shelf above your cooker is never a good idea. As you stretch over the cooker to reach it, you may burn yourself. If the shelf is made of wood or contains flammable objects, it will also increase the risk of fire.
- Leaving the gas on and unlit for more than 10–15 seconds can result in a fireball, which will burn you and whoever is beside or near you. If you can smell gas, but cannot see anything left on that is causing it, get out of the house immediately and call the emergency 24-hour number for your local gas authority.

PREVENT SKIDS AND FALLS

- Try to wash floors in the evenings when everyone is settled and out of the kitchen.

- Keep drawers and doors closed when not in use.
- Always wipe up immediately any grease and food spills, and wipe the patch with a dry cloth afterwards.
- Keep the floor clear of obstacles.

MINIMIZE HAZARDS

- Cupboard locks prevent a child gaining access to harmful substances such as household bleach.
- Never leave wiring exposed; if wiring starts to fray, stop using the appliance until it is repaired. Every plug socket should be at least 1m/3 ft from any water supply.
- Lacerations from careless chopping are common. Use a proper chopping board and cut with all your fingers above the blade of the knife.
- Store plastic bags, knives and matches out of sight and reach of children.
- Do not be tempted to use chipped glasses and crockery.

BATHING BABIES AND YOUNG CHILDREN

At bathtime, babies and children up to the age of five years should always be supervised by an adult. Young babies should always be bathed in a baby bath or on a specially shaped foam insert for a normal bath. For toddlers and older children, make sure you do not overfill the bath and avoid using slippery bath foams.

It is essential that you test the temperature of the water before your baby or child is immersed. For a baby, use your elbow – the water should feel just warm.

TEENAGERS AND BATHING

Favourite teenage pursuits may include soaking in the bath for several hours at a time, and bathing while listening to music. Make sure they know the dangers of dragging a sound system into the bathroom using an extension lead. Water is a great conductor of electricity, so electric shocks in the bath are usually fatal.

Teenagers should also be made aware that falling asleep in the bath and bathing after they have consumed alcohol or illegal drugs is potentially very dangerous.

OLDER PEOPLE

Fatigue, reduced mobility and lapses in concentration or memory can lead to the elderly having accidents in the bathroom. They may run a bath that is too hot and scald themselves, slip and have a nasty fall or fall asleep in the bath, making drowning a possibility.

To minimize these risks, make sure that the bathroom of an elderly person is as safe as possible. You should install

SAFETY IN THE BATHROOM

- Turn down the hot water thermostat to 40°C/105°F .
- Make sure that all bathroom lights have pulley switches; do not use wall-mounted switches.
- Have a non-slip floor. Avoid rugs and mats in the bathroom, and don't leave towels on the floor.

a bath with hand grips in the sides and place a non-slip mat in the bath, to reduce the risk of a fall when getting in and out of the bath. Elderly people should wear a call alarm to enable them to raise the emergency services in the event of an accident.

▲ *Many people, and women in particular, enjoy spending time soaking in the bath, but it is important to be aware of hidden dangers such as falling asleep in the water.*

▼ *Child safety gadgets such as these are a worthwhile investment for the home.*

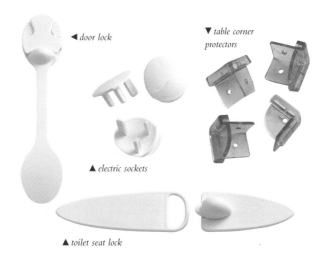

◀ *door lock*

▼ *table corner protectors*

▲ *electric sockets*

▲ *toilet seat lock*

Making your garden safe

The garden can be an oasis of calm in a busy life. However, ponds, bonfires, barbecues, and even plants can all present hazards, particularly if children are around. To ensure your garden is a safe haven for everyone, you'll need to take a few sensible precautions. Choose water features that are child-friendly, fence off a swimming pool, and make sure that paths are easy to negotiate. Check that children and pets are out of the way before you start to mow, and store garden tools and implements in a locked shed with all garden chemicals.

A little forward planning and common sense will go a long way towards preventing accidents in the garden. Many accidents happen when a child or elderly person is visiting a garden that has not been made safe for them. Small children, including those from neighbouring houses, often go wandering. Your elegant ornamental pond with its shimmering goldfish may be a fatal attraction for them.

CARE WITH CHEMICALS
Lock away garden chemicals in a dark, dry and cool place, out of reach of children and animals. Follow the instructions for use exactly and do not decant chemicals into other bottles;

▲ *Do not underestimate the climbing abilities of a toddler; this type of gate has been designed to keep out horses not children.*

keep them in their original containers so you know what they are. Minimize chemicals in the garden: for example, rather than using slug pellets, use environmentally-friendly methods such as egg shells, copper, or dishes of beer sunk into the soil.

WATER SAFETY
Garden ponds are a major hazard for children. They have interesting things floating on the surface that invite curious children to lean over and grab at them. They are also usually placed at ground level, so are easy for a toddler to fall into.

Covering the water with wire netting can give a false sense of security since they could still fall in if they landed on top of it. Placing a sturdy cover over the pond is the safest option. If you really want a water feature but have children, install one in which the water cascades out of a container to drain into a bed of stones rather than into a pool of water. All swimming pools should be fenced off.

▶ *A pond can be converted into a sandpit to provide children with an extra play area. When not in use, a sturdy cover (see below right) will help to keep the sand clean.*

◀ *Children are curious to explore their environment through taste and touch. A pond is particularly inviting – but is a potentially fatal hazard.*

▲ *Place plastic containers or flowerpots on top of your garden canes, to protect your eyes when you are bending down near them.*

ELECTRICITY IN THE GARDEN

- All electric garden tools should be plugged into residual current circuit breakers, so that the current switches off instantly if there is an accident.
- When using electric tools, keep the cable over your shoulder and well away from lawnmower blades and hedge trimmers.
- Keep children out of the garden when you are mowing the lawn or using other electrical equipment.
- Water conducts electricity, so great care should be taken when using the two together in a water feature. Many of the pumps available for water features are completely sealed and will automatically switch off if the system fails in any way.
- Exterior lights are designed to be used safely in the garden. If you are unsure, get an electrician to install or check them.

USING LADDERS SAFELY

Accidents on ladders are common but almost entirely avoidable. Make sure that all the rungs are safe before climbing up a ladder. Do not place it so that you have to lean over or stretch up to do the job – move the ladder or use a taller one if necessary. When pruning trees, use two ladders with a plank between them. If you are using a ladder up against the side of the house, ask someone to secure it from below.

TIPS ON GARDEN SAFETY

- Steps should be well lit. They should have a handrail if elderly people are to use them.
- Moss gathers on patios and can be slippery. Wash surfaces with diluted bleach to get rid of it.
- Nylon line trimmers throw up stones and other potentially dangerous things, including irritants from plant sap. Wear goggles, long-sleeved shirts and trousers when using them.
- Get into the habit of wearing heavy boots and thick gloves when you are working in the garden.
- To stop canes from poking your eyes, place film canisters, plastic bottles or flowerpots over the top of them.
- Keep all garden tools tidy and store them in a locked shed. Lock away petrol, kerosene and chemicals.
- Ensure that a clothesline is not positioned at children's neck level.

CHILDREN AND PLANTS

Few children die from eating poisonous garden plants. However, they can become ill with stomachache and diarrhoea. It is best to discourage young children from eating any flowers, fruit or foliage, rather than teach them which ones to avoid.

Certain toxic plants are best kept out of the garden altogether since they are very poisonous in small amounts. These include laburnum, foxgloves, monkshood, woody nightshade and deadly nightshade. Others, such as yew, could be fenced off. Cut back trailing plants, such as thorny brambles and roses, if they could trip a child, tear clothes, scratch the skin or harm the eyes if caught across the face.

▲ *Foxgloves are poisonous and have no place in a garden where young children play.*

▲ *One rule of DIY safety is not to overstretch. These steps are too low.*

▲ *Yew is a common toxic plant. Fence off dangerous plants and trees.*

Guarding against break-ins

The best way to check how easy your home would be to break into is to imagine you have lost your keys and then try to find a way in, causing least damage and noise. You may be surprised at how easy it would be – and you can guarantee that a burglar will be better at it than you.

WINDOW LOCKS

For many burglaries windows are the primary point of entry, as even when locked they are often less secure than doors. Toughened glass or double glazing acts as a deterrent, as the last thing a thief needs is the sound of breaking glass to alert the neighbours, but of course if you don't bother to shut and lock every window in the house, a burglar won't even need to consider a forced entry.

On all but the most modern factory-made double-glazed units, a window is usually secured by just one central catch. Frequently, judicious use of a garden shovel in one corner is all that is needed to distort the frame enough to allow the burglar to release the latch.

▲ *A small safe, available from stationery chain stores, is a cheap and secure way of storing documents and valuables.*

IMPROVING YOUR HOME SECURITY

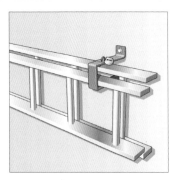

▲ *If you have to keep a ladder outside your home, secure it with a locking bracket to prevent thieves using it to gain access to your upper windows.*

▲ *Shut and lock all the upper floor windows when the house is empty, as your neighbours may not have secured their ladders even if you have.*

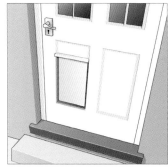

▲ *If you have a catflap in a door, you should be sure never to leave a key in the lock. An additional lock at the top of the door will improve security.*

▲ *The first two places a burglar will check are under the front doormat and under a nearby plant pot, just in case you have left a spare key there.*

▲ *If intruders should manage to break into your house, you will make their job very easy if you keep all your valuables and documents together.*

▲ *If you are going away, you can make the house look occupied by using time switches in a few rooms to turn lamps and radios on and off.*

▲ *A battery-powered alarm on the wall opposite the stairs will give you warning of intruders prowling downstairs at night.*

To counter this, cheap and simple surface-mounted secondary locks at the corners most likely to be pried open can be fitted by anyone who can wield a screwdriver. Incidentally, your home insurance company will probably give a discount if extra window locks are fitted, but they will only pay out if you actually keep them locked.

SECURING DOORS

The front door to the property is usually the most secure, and therefore is not such an inviting entry point for the burglar. However, if the door is secured only by a single latchkey lock, it becomes a more tempting target, as this can often be "sprung" from the outside using a flexible blade or possibly even a credit card. If the door is fitted with a secondary mortise lock, or a deadlock, the thief will think twice. Not only is it much more difficult – and noisy – to force this type of lock, but should a burglar get in through a window, it precludes the option of nonchalantly walking out of the front door with your valuables at the end of the job.

Rear or side doors, often less visible from the street, are usually an easier way in than the stout front door. As well as having less substantial locks, they are often part-glazed. As the family tends to use a secondary door frequently for access to the garden or garage, it may be left unlocked, or with

▲ *Even if you don't actually have a burglar alarm fitted, a dummy box on the front of your home can work as a deterrent.*

the key in the lock. Bolts may well be fitted top and bottom, but how many people bother to close them?

There are many ways of retrieving a key from the inside of a lock, but if a catflap is fitted the job is easy. Larger flaps, designed for dogs, can even be used by young or skinny burglars to access the property silently, unless they are fitted through thick walls rather than thin door panels. Even if the catflap in an outer door allows access only to a porch or conservatory, breaking into it can allow the burglar to get out of sight and earshot of neighbours and passers-by, and then to work at leisure in forcing locked doors or windows into the main building.

▼ *Some sliding glass doors can be lifted off their rails from outside, but fitting a secondary lock will prevent this.*

OUTBUILDINGS AND LADDERS

Even if you secure all your ground floor doors and windows, your home is vulnerable if you leave tools in an unlocked shed or garage, and have an unsecured ladder in the garage or garden. Would your neighbours question a "workman" or "window cleaner" working on your first-floor windows? Lock, and alarm, sheds and outhouses, and secure a ladder on a proper rack with a substantial padlock. These can be purchased very cheaply from good hardware stores.

DETERRING THE BURGLAR

Thieves will always go for the property of least resistance, so if a burglar alarm box is clearly visible, the side gate is padlocked to prevent anyone sneaking round the back, and there is flimsy trellis on top of the boundary wall, they will not waste time but will seek another target. They do not like gravel driveways either, as these make a silent approach very difficult. However, if you are stupid enough to leave a key under the doormat or an obvious plant pot, a burglar will be in and out in a trice.

Don't make the burglar's job any easier by leaving house or car keys openly visible from outside, as it takes only seconds to snatch them through a letterbox or prised window frame with a collapsible fishing rod. Your insurers probably won't pay up if you lose your car, or thieves break in, with keys that you obligingly left for them.

▼ *If a latch lock such as this is your only form of lock on external doors, add a mortise deadlock for extra security.*

Enhancing your security

Stout locks are likely to deflect a thief's attention away from your home, but at all times you should be aware of situations that make your home more vulnerable to intruders. There are also further steps you can take to protect your property, particularly at night, when a break-in could result in an attack on you or your family.

SECURITY LIGHTING

The careful positioning of security lights on the outside of the property, activated by movement sensors, will provide a great deterrent at night. For maximum effect, lights must be positioned to illuminate the most likely entry points, and they should not be mounted in such a way that they dazzle neighbours and passers-by while allowing the intruder to work unseen behind blinding light.

If you have a garden around your home, bushes that obscure doors and vulnerable windows from view are useful to the burglar. Chop them down. (Conversely, a thorny hedge on the boundary can be a good deterrent.)

PREPARING FOR THE WORST

If, in spite of your security measures, an intruder does manage to get in at night, bolts on the inside of your bedroom door will give you a few extra seconds to telephone for help; your mobile phone should be in the bedroom with you, rather than charging up in another room, in case the intruder cuts the telephone line.

You should also consider keeping a torch by your bedside, preferably a large, multiple-battery, police-style one that can double as a defensive weapon.

VULNERABLE SITUATIONS

▲ You are offering a sneak thief an open invitation if you leave the front door open while you return to your car to unload your shopping bags.

▲ An open garden door could allow your property to be burgled while your back is turned: and your insurers may refuse to settle your claim for any loss.

▲ Don't leave keys hanging neatly together where a burglar can help himself – especially if they include spare sets of keys for your neighbours' houses.

▲ Leafy shrubs growing too near your home can provide cover for a thief to hide behind while forcing an entry through a window or door.

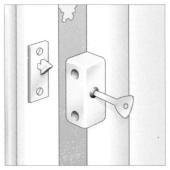

▲ Window locks are only effective if you lock them and remove the key. If you leave windows open at night make sure they cannot be used to gain entry.

▲ Even if tools and ladders are not in full view, an experienced thief will know where to look and will use them if they are not locked up securely.

▲ *Don't let in strangers at the door: use a spyhole or, failing that, a door chain to check the visitor's ID before you open the door.*

Levels of permissible force when dealing with intruders vary from country to country, so be aware of the law in this respect.

USING AN ALARM AT NIGHT

Finally, forewarned is forearmed. If you have a burglar alarm with a zone facility, set the downstairs circuit each evening when you go to bed. In addition to possibly scaring off the intruder, the alarm will alert you that somebody is prowling around on the ground floor and should give you time to telephone for help, get dressed, and prepare to confront an intruder who ventures upstairs.

A battery-operated stand-alone room alarm, positioned to cover the stairs, is a cheap alternative warning system if your house is not alarmed.

SECURITY CHECKLIST

Most burglaries are committed by opportunist thiefs when a house or flat is empty, more often during the evening or at night. Good security is about deflecting a thief's attention away from your house in the first place and reducing their chances of entry if they do decide to burgle you.

Around the home
- Install security lighting.
- Secure ladders, put away tools and keep garages and sheds locked.
- Don't make it easy for the intruder to slip into the garden – padlocked side gates, flimsy trellis and gravel drives are good deterrents.
- Trim back any plants or hedges near to the house that a burglar could hide behind.
- Never leave a spare key in a convenient hiding place outside – thieves know where to find them.

In the home
- Have a burglar alarm professionally installed and regularly serviced.
- Fit window locks to all downstairs windows and any others that are easy to reach. Keep them locked and their keys out of sight.
- Secure all outside doors with mortise deadlocks. Fit mortise bolts to the top and bottom of doors.
- Fit a door viewer and door chain

and use these every time someone calls. If you live in a flat, consider having a phone-entry system fitted to the main door of the building.
- Make sure that window and door frames are sufficiently strong to withstand forced entry.
- Keep your house keys safe and away from doors and windows.
- Rest easier at night by having a means of securing your bedroom door if you hear an intruder and your mobile phone and a defensive weapon to hand.

When you go away
- Keep curtains open during the day.
- Use timer switches to turn on some lights when it gets dark.
- Cancel newspapers and other deliveries when you go on holiday.
- Cut the grass before you go away.
- Ask a neighbour to keep an eye on your house – do the same for them when they go away.

If you are burgled
- If you return home and see or hear sounds of a break-in, don't go in – call the police immediately.
- If you are in the house and hear a prowler, phone the police if you can. You are allowed to use reasonable force to protect yourself or others from an intruder.

▲ *Put a bolt on your garden gate, and padlock it so that the thief can't use that route to remove larger valuables such as televisions and antiques.*

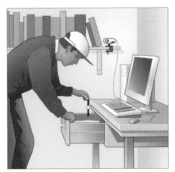

▲ *If a burglar does get into your home, a video camera connected to your computer can help identify him – but only if he doesn't steal the computer too.*

▲ *Keep a mobile phone, torch and other emergency aids handy in your bedroom. A bolt on the door could give you a breathing space if an intruder comes upstairs.*

Dealing with an intruder

The average burglar aims to sneak in and out of the home while the occupants are at work or on holiday, as confrontation leading to possible recognition is the last thing a thief wants. That said, if you return unexpectedly and surprise an intruder he is not likely to apologize, raise his hands, and wait quietly for the police to arrive. If you return home to find your window prised open or your front door damaged, never charge in alone or unprepared. Leave that to the police, who should be only a phone call away. You have no way of knowing if the intruder is still inside the building, or how many people are involved.

▲ *If you find an unarmed intruder in the house, don't be the one to escalate the situation. Give him the opportunity to back off, while standing your ground and showing that you are prepared to defend yourself.*

TYPES OF INTRUDER
If anything, you are more likely to encounter a sneak thief than a professional burglar. Opportunists, who are highly likely to be drug addicts looking for easy pickings to fund their habit, can be more dangerous than career burglars, as they are more desperate and therefore more likely to

take chances. Should the unsuspecting householder interrupt them in the act, they are just as likely to strike out in the hope that surprise is still on their side.

Of course, there are unscrupulous types who are prepared to bully and bluster their way into a home to commit their crime, usually picking on vulnerable members of society such as the elderly or infirm. The simple precaution of checking the identity cards of callers purporting to be from public utility companies, and making use of a stout safety chain fitted to the door when answering calls, should stop this type of intruder in his or her tracks. If they do become difficult or aggressive, a panic alarm carried in your pocket or mounted by the door can be used to attract the attention of passers-by and should be enough to deter such intruders. Unlike burglars, who are predominantly male, confidence tricksters can be of either gender, often hunt in pairs, and tend to rely on their smart appearance to talk their way into your home.

BREAK-INS AT NIGHT
The home is the place where people feel most relaxed, and therefore it is where they are probably at their most vulnerable and least ready to deal with a confrontational situation. At night, the householder is even more

vulnerable, especially if the intruder breaks or sneaks in while the occupants are asleep. Even if you are wearing nightclothes, you will still feel naked when confronted by a masked stranger, dressed in black and carrying a weapon. Should he walk into your bedroom armed with a gun or a knife, he will definitely have the upper hand. If this face-to-face meeting is in the dark, your fear will be heightened.

DECIDING HOW TO REACT
In such circumstances, many people assume that it is acceptable to use any means available to defend themselves, their family and their property, but in stable societies the law usually dictates that any force used has to be in proportion to the strength of the attack.

The official advice is to try to avoid a violent confrontation if you discover a burglar in your home, though in fact your basic instinct may be to lash out and drive the intruder out. If you do decide to tackle a burglar, you must be confident that you can win the fight and that you can do so without putting your own freedom in jeopardy.

REASONABLE FORCE

Should an intruder attack you in your home, you are likely to be within your rights if you pick up an item such as a frying pan, umbrella or golf club to defend yourself. Likewise if the attacker is wielding a hefty blade it is probably OK to parry this with a kitchen knife, but a court is unlikely to be sympathetic if you use more force than a court decides is necessary to deter the burglar or intruder.

One way of ensuring both is to prepare for the possibility of such a situation by joining a self-defence class. This way you will not only learn the necessary skills, but also build up your confidence in your own physical abilities. It is sometimes suggested that taking up a martial art can be useful, but these specialist skills can be lethal; always bear in mind that if you kill or seriously injure an intruder in this way, you could be punished for making unreasonable use of force.

If you decide to take the submissive route, particularly if you are female, the intruder may take violent advantage of this, whereas a show of bravado and confidence may well cause him to flee. Only you can make this split-second decision, based on your reading of the situation at the time. It is, however, worth bearing in mind that the intruder does not know for sure what lies in store and how a householder will react if or when they discover him, so his nerves are going to be on edge. A sudden loud noise, such as the sound of a personal alarm, could be enough to frighten him off the premises. Likewise, if he has broken in at night, a burst of bright light from a high-powered torch shone in his eyes may temporarily blind and disorient him.

If a confrontation does develop, your positive mental attitude and confident body posture may well be enough to allow you regain control of the situation, but you should remember that if the attacker calls your bluff he is unlikely to fight clean. On the other hand, a screaming and pummelling woman with right on her side, however small and slight, can be enough to scare off a burly intruder twice her weight if

▲ *In self-defence, the palm strike is very effective. Cock your wrist and curl your fingers and thumb in. Aim for the jaw for maximum impact.*

he is unprepared for the onslaught. In many situations, the thief or assailant will simply try to escape if "caught on the job". Let him go. Property is replaceable, your life is not.

TACKLING A BURGLAR

1 ◄ Remember, if you can avoid a fight do so because property is not worth risking a life for. But if you believe you or a family member are at risk then go for a lunge from behind.

2 ► A rugby-style tackle is an effective way to bring someone who is moving away from you to his knees.

3 ▼ Drive your shoulder into the intruder's legs while gripping around his knees and squeezing until he falls. The intruder will quite possibly be disoriented by being tackled in such a decisive way.

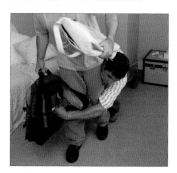

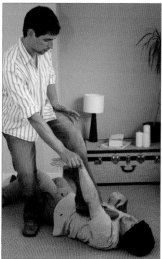

4 ◄ Once on the ground you must immobilize the intruder and at the same time shout at the top of your voice for help if you haven't already done so.

5 ▼ Only confront the intruder with a weapon as a last resort.

Fire in the home

Although fire is the single greatest killer in the home environment, the vast majority of home fires would be easily avoided by taking some basic precautions. The kitchen is the most dangerous room in the house and is the seat of most daytime fires, but if a member of the household is a smoker, the chances of being involved in a night-time fire increase dramatically. Unguarded candles, the least technological way of lighting a room and a favourite in romantic or party settings, also pose a high risk of fire, as do the many electrical appliances used around the home. Awareness of potential fire risks is half the prevention battle, and most of the following advice is really just common sense.

SMOKE ALARMS

If a fire does break out, a functioning smoke alarm should give the occupants a few extra vital minutes to organize an escape, call the fire service, and possibly even attempt to bring the fire under control. At night, a smoke alarm will save lives, as smoke and gases produced by a fire can silently kill sleeping occupants before they become aware that their home is ablaze.

▼ *In less than 60 seconds a small fire can fill your home with smoke. Firemen have breathing apparatus – you don't so get out fast. If any closed door feels warm when touched, do not open it - the fire is on the other side. Go to the windows instead.*

Ceiling-mounted smoke alarms are cheap and easy to fit, though they are as much use as a chocolate fireguard if their batteries are not checked regularly.

AVOIDING FIRE

Prevention is always better than cure, so when deep frying, which is the largest single cause of kitchen fires, never fill the pan more than one third full, and never ever leave it unattended.

To extinguish a pan fire, turn off the heat source and throw a fire blanket, or a damp towel, over it to extinguish the flames. Never throw water on an oil fire, as that will make the flames flare up and spray burning oil outside the pan, igniting other combustibles. A small fire blanket, suitable for tackling most accidental fires in the kitchen, is an inexpensive necessity often overlooked. If you tackle a pan fire yourself, remember that cooking fat retains its temperature for a long time,

▲ *A domestic fire at night can be a killer, though it is usually the smoke rather than the flames that proves lethal.*

▼ *If someone's clothes catch fire, roll them on the floor and smother the flames using a blanket or rug or large coat. Keep low at all times as it's easier to breathe. Go to the window and wait for the fire brigade.*

▲ *Carbon monoxide is a silent killer – gas-fired central heating boilers and water heaters should be checked and serviced annually.*

and it may well reignite if you remove the blanket too soon. Vacate the premises and summon the fire service.

The easiest precaution to take against fires caused by cigarettes is to ban smoking completely inside the house. Unlike cooking fires, which flare up quickly, most cigarette fires start gradually, sometimes hours after a smouldering end has fallen unnoticed into upholstery or bedclothes.

The precautions needed to prevent electrical fires are simple: switch off and unplug appliances when not in use, and never overload wall sockets. Even when an appliance is switched off, it may still be drawing power from a live wall socket unless physically unplugged. Televisions left on standby mode and, to a lesser extent, video recorders and digital boxes

◄ *Pull, Aim, Squeeze, Sweep (PASS) is a good tip to remember. Aim low, point the extinguisher at the base of the fire and sweep from side to side.*

are all potential time bombs if they develop an electrical fault or there is a power surge during an electrical storm. Bad wiring or overloaded sockets, usually identifiable through the plugs being overly hot, should be remedied immediately. If you are not actually using a particular appliance, unplug it, and if you hear crackling, smell plastic burning or see lights flickering, find the cause. Make sure that any cables running on the floor do not get trapped or pinched by furniture, and that any long cables drawing a lot of power are not coiled, as both circumstances can cause wires to overheat and ignite out of the blue.

ESCAPING FROM A FIRE

If fire does break out, your first priority is to get everybody out as fast as possible. Do not stop to dress properly or collect valuables. Most fire deaths are caused by inhalation of smoke and noxious gases rather than burns. Furnishings, once ignited, burn with incredible intensity and very quickly produce dense toxic fumes. To survive this you not only have to get out very quickly, but you also need to stay as close to the floor as possible, as that is where any oxygen will be.

Do not assume that the air at head height is breathable if it is free of smoke, as some by-products of building fires are virtually clear. The first you will know about them is when they burn your throat and lungs, as you try to take your last gulping breaths. Burning plastics and upholstery rapidly

▼ *Blocking any gaps by the door helps to keep fumes out of the room you are in and may deprive a fire of oxygen.*

▲ *Smoke alarms are essential survival tools in the modern home, giving you precious time to escape. Battery life and location – at least one ceiling-mounted alarm on each floor – are critical.*

produce thick clouds of acrid smoke, and even at ground level you may find breathing difficult. A wet cloth over your mouth and nose will act as a temporary respirator; even a dry handkerchief or shirt tail may keep out larger toxic particles. You will need to remember the layout of the room to find your exit route, as even if it is not dark you will be blinded by the smoke.

Once clear of danger outside, alert any neighbours and call the fire service. Do not go back in. Material possessions can be replaced, but your life cannot.

▼ *If you have to escape from an upper floor try to find ways to lower yourself to safety rather than jumping, to reduce the height of your fall.*

Gas leaks

The most common cause of damage, injury and even death in the home is undoubtedly fire. However, gas incidents, though much less common, can be equally deadly. In most of the Western world, bottled or mains gas provides the fuel for the bulk of our heating and hot water systems, as it is more efficient and more ecologically sound than coal and oil. In the past, domestic gas was derived from coal and was a smelly substance, but modern natural gas is odourless and so has to have a smell added to alert us to leaks.

Gas, like water, will always find any leaks in pipes, joints and appliances. Unlike water, it is highly explosive, so it is imperative that you are both familiar with its artificial smell, and you attend to any leakage immediately. Do not try to repair a gas leak yourself, as this is a highly skilled job that can be very dangerous if tackled by a novice.

If you smell gas you should immediately open windows to vent the building and get outside as quickly as possible. The main supply valve, whether you are using bottled or mains gas, is usually located outside the building, next to the meter if you are on a mains supply, and should be turned off if at all possible. If you don't know where your gas valve is, go and check now!

Once you are clear of the building, hopefully having been able to vent it and turn off the supply, contact the service provider or the emergency services. Gas leaks can cause massive damage and those responsible for

▲ *Check your vents have not got clogged up with growing plants.*

prevention would much rather be called out before the explosion, even if it is a well-intentioned false alarm, than have to pick up the pieces afterwards.

CARBON MONOXIDE POISONING
It is not only the gas supply that can be potentially dangerous in a domestic situation. The by-products of combustion can also poison the occupants if gas appliances such as heaters and stoves are not working efficiently and properly vented.

Carbon monoxide is a silent killer that works by first inducing sleep before poisoning the body. Even if the poisoning is not fatal it can cause permanent neurological damage. The gas is odourless, tasteless and colourless, so a special detector is necessary to check for its presence.

To ensure that your home is safe, all gas appliances should be checked and serviced at least once a year, particularly after having lain unused for any length of time, and flues must never be blocked or obstructed. Birds' nests, and even ivy or other creeping plants growing on outside walls, can very easily block a flue during the summer months, turning the home into a death trap when the heating system is fired up again in the autumn.

The first signs of carbon monoxide poisoning are unexpected drowsiness and headache, and first aid for an unconscious victim is access to fresh air and artificial respiration.

DEALING WITH A GAS LEAK

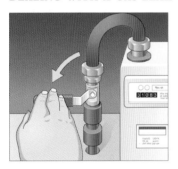

1 If you smell gas, turn off the mains supply by the valve near the meter.

2 Open all the windows to ventilate the building and disperse escaped gas.

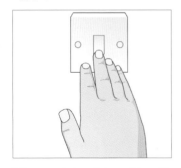

3 Do not switch on lights as this could create a spark and ignite the gas.

4 Report a leak immediately to the gas supplier or the emergency services.

Flooding

Water leaks in the home can cause untold damage. The primary causes are burst pipes during the thaw after a winter freeze, overflowing baths and faulty washing machines. Water spreads at an alarming rate and it does not take long for it to permeate into the fabric of a building. Burst mains pipes can be disastrous as the high flow rate can undermine foundations, but even an upstairs bath left overflowing for five minutes is likely to short-circuit the

▼ *If your home is prone to flooding, keep a supply of sandbags, ready-filled, with which to create barriers in front of doorways.*

electrical supply and damage the ceiling below to such an extent that a complete replacement is necessary.

NATURAL FLOODS
If you are one of those living in an area prone to natural flooding, the risks are of a totally different order. You should be alert to flood warnings and familiar with local plans for dealing with such a disaster. Simple precautions like having sandbags ready-filled and heavy duty

▼ *If you do not know where the main stopcock for your home's water supply is located, go and check it out right now.*

▲ *Freak weather can quickly cause flooding in low-lying residential areas: is your home in a vulnerable situation?*

plastic on hand to block doors may help, but if your home is subjected to a major flood, follow the advice of your local authority and emergency services.

If you have to leave your home, do not be tempted to walk through flowing flood water. Even if it does not appear to be very deep it may have a deceptively fast current that could sweep you off your feet, and there may well also be dangerous debris below the surface that could cause serious injury.

After drowning, electrocution is the second most common cause of death following a flood: stay well away from power cables and do not attempt to use electrical equipment that has been wet. You should also check for gas leaks in case the pipework has been damaged. A flood is likely to contaminate your water supply, so if you are at risk from flooding it is sensible to keep an emergency supply of bottled water.

Emergency escape

In a fire or gas emergency, it is imperative that you get yourself and any other occupants out of the building as quickly as possible. In a domestic situation you should·be well aware of your primary escape route, but if fire is barring your way, you will need to seek an alternative. Despite what you may have seen in television dramas and on the cinema screen, the staircase is usually of sufficiently robust construction to survive the early stages of a house fire, and in most multiple occupancy buildings it will be reinforced and protected to afford a safe escape route. In some circumstances, however, especially if fire doors have been left open, use of the staircase may not be possible and you may need to use a window instead.

ESCAPING THROUGH A WINDOW
If window locks are fitted, the key should be kept in a place where it is easy to find, especially in the dark and when under duress. However, if you are in an unfamiliar room and cannot undo the catches, you may have no option but to break the glass. Double-glazed window units, or those with strengthened anti-burglar glass, will not break easily. (If you have windows of this kind, it might make sense to mount a safety hammer on the window frame in case the key cannot be found in an emergency.)

Be aware of glass shards, and wrap your arm with thick clothing for protection. If no hammer is available to break the glass, a small and heavy hard object, such as a bedside lamp or a metal ornament, can be used; if you

ESCAPING FROM A BUILDING

1 If you are trapped in a room and cannot open a window, put a heavy object in a pillowcase or a sock and use it as a hammer to shatter the glass.

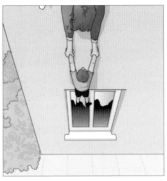

2 To reduce the severity of injuries, the strongest person should lower the lighter occupants from upper windows, rather than letting them jump out.

3 As the last one out, you should lower yourself from the ledge to reduce your fall, remembering to bend the knees before impact then go into a roll.

1 If using an improvised rope to escape, such as knotted sheets or garments, tie it securely to an immovable object that will bear your weight.

2 If no structural anchor points are available, a strong bed frame can be effective as it is too large to be pulled through the window.

3 Grip the improvised rope between your insteps and use arm-over-arm movements to descend quickly – even a short rope will reduce your fall.

PARATROOPER ROLL

1 This roll was devised to prevent injury when hitting hard ground at speed, and it is easy to learn. The legs must be slightly bent at knees and hips.

2 As you hit the ground, absorb the initial impact through your bent legs then roll over on to your thigh and shoulder, swinging the legs over.

3 Keeping the knees and heels together and the lead arm tucked in will spread the impact of the fall throughout the body, saving your ankles and legs.

REVERSE BREAK ROLL

1 If you have no lateral speed, you will take the full-on impact with your legs. You must convert this force into rotational energy before it impacts your spine. Keep your legs bent before impact.

2 Immediately roll backwards as your legs compress, and strike the ground as hard as you can with your arms. This reduces the impact to your spine and adds to your rotational momentum.

3 Make sure you are rolling backwards and not simply falling flat on your back. Continue to roll over backwards.. This is the safest and least impactful way to absorb the energy of the fall.

put this inside a pillowcase and swing it around your head first, the striking power can be increased markedly.

Escape from ground floor room windows is pretty straightforward, and even from those on the floor above the drop should not kill you unless you fall on your head or land on sharp objects, such as spiked railings.

ESCAPING FROM UPPER FLOORS

Do not just stand on a ledge and jump, but try to find a way of lowering yourself gently. To break your fall, push a mattress out through the window if possible, followed by bedding and anything else that will cushion your fall. When it looks likely that staying in the room will be more hazardous than

risking the fall, drop children and the infirm out of the window, sliding them out feet first and lowering them as far as possible by the wrists before letting go directly over the improvised cushioning. If you have made enough noise, the neighbours may by now be there to catch or steady those dropped.

Ideally, a knotted escape rope or rope ladder should be available if the window is two or more storeys above ground floor, but few householders give much thought to providing these. An alternative would be to make an improvised rope by knotting sheets or other suitable items together to stretch from window to ground, but this is not a particularly quick fix. If you do have time to do it, make sure you tie the

rope to something that will bear your weight. If necessary, push the bed in front of the window: as it is wider than the frame, it should provide an anchor.

GETTING DOWN STAIRS

If escape through a window is not feasible, and the smoke-filled staircase is the only option, a well-soaked jacket with sleeves tied at the bottom will retain pockets of breathable air. Any remaining oxygen in the corridors and on staircases will be at ground level or close to the steps, so keep low and move slowly. Running fast and upright will probably cause you to inhale poisonous and damaging gases, but taking time without dallying will help conserve your breath.

Emergency home shelter

If a natural disaster hit your area, or your town was suddenly on the frontline of a combat zone, or if international terrorism unleashed a weapon of mass destruction on your doorstep, could you shelter and feed yourself and your family until normality returned?

An ordinary house will keep you safe from the elements in the depth of winter, but when shells and bombs start exploding all around, or if terrorists detonate a "dirty" bomb to contaminate your town, it won't hold up particularly well. However, if you had a strongpoint in the most structurally sound part of the house, and could retreat there with stocks of food and water, you and your loved ones might just make it through. Unless warring forces were to

▶ *Maintain a plentiful stock of candles and matches in case the power supply is cut off during an emergency.*

dig in for a battle of attrition, the fighting would probably pass you by quite quickly, and the contamination caused by a terrorist attack could be even shorter lived, so the ability to build a basic shelter and the availability of enough emergency supplies to last you just a few weeks, could enable you to survive.

SELECTING A SURVIVAL SPACE

In a conventional two- or three-floor urban home, the space beneath the stairs usually offers the best structural protection. In the case of a bombardment, this can be reinforced by removing the internal doors from their hinges and nailing them over the stair treads. The space under the stairs will be cramped and claustrophobic, but unless the house takes a direct hit, it should provide adequate shelter. Line the floor, and the walls where possible, with mattresses and you will have a snug refuge.

Apartment dwellers will probably not have the luxury of an under-stairs cupboard, so they will have to identify the room that seems structurally the strongest, preferably one without windows, in which to build a shelter. Tables sited in the

▲ *Terrorist attacks have led manufacturers to produce inexpensive emergency escape masks and smoke hoods for the general public.*

corner of the room, with doors and mattresses on top and on the open sides, can be used to construct a compact refuge, but only if the table legs are strong enough to take the weight. If they are not, lean the doors against the wall at an angle of more than 45 degrees to give a triangular shelter, and stack mattresses on top for additional protection.

IMPROVISED SHELTERS

▲ *The strongest part of many houses is the space under the stairs. It may be cramped and too small for long-term use, but it could save your life.*

▲ *A windowless bathroom can provide a safe retreat in a crisis and is easy to seal against gas attack. Fill the bath with water in case the supply is cut.*

▲ *Failing any other shelter, a mattress and doors stacked around a sturdy table make a survival capsule that offers some protection from explosion and shrapnel.*

▲ *Women's tights secured with a rubber band over the filter tap or stop-cock will act as a makeshift filter for some pollutants.*

EMERGENCY SUPPLIES

There is no point in having an emergency shelter in your home unless you also have the basics to support life for days, if not weeks. The one constraining factor in assembling your supplies will be storage space. If you are lucky enough to be using a large cellar as your shelter, stocking it with supplies for several weeks will not be a problem.

Water is the primary concern, as humans cannot live for much more than three or four days without water, but if the water is contaminated it could be a double-edged sword. It makes sense to keep at least a few days' supply in large sealed containers in your shelter all the time, with plenty of

▼ *Check the contents of your first-aid kit: you may want to add items you use regularly, such as basic painkillers.*

empty ones ready to be filled in times of crises and before the supply is cut off. Water filters and/or purification tablets should also be stocked in case the crisis lasts longer than expected. A "volcano" kettle in which to boil water efficiently will also come in handy, as will candles for light; candles also provide a little bit of warmth and can be used to heat tinned food. A wind-up radio and torch, which do not need batteries, are also useful to have in your shelter. In a civil defence scenario, radio will be used by the authorities as the primary method of broadcasting information about the emergency.

Adequate stocks of foodstuffs that don't deteriorate are also a necessity, in or close to your shelter. Tinned meat, fish and beans, which can be eaten without preparation, are far preferable to dried foodstuffs that will need scarce fuel and water for reconstitution, but dried soups are cheap and use up little storage space and they can perk up the spirits by providing a warm and nourishing drink when you are cold and downhearted.

If there is a threat of nuclear or biological contamination, temporarily tape up doors, windows and ventilators to the room in which your shelter is located, but remember that you will exhaust your air supply very quickly. When a candle flame starts to die, you will have to pull back the tape and take your chances.

▲ *In an emergency, the radio will be the primary method used by the authorities to inform the public: if you don't have a wind-up radio stock up with spare batteries.*

HOME SURVIVAL ESSENTIALS

- Drinking water
- Canned food, or other food that does not need cooking or refrigeration
- Can opener
- Candles
- Matches
- Cooker or kettle
- Wind-up radio
- Wind-up torch (flashlight)
- First-aid kit and any essential medication
- Covered bucket
- Clothing and blankets

▼ *Ordinary duct tape is adequate for sealing around doors and windows to protect against chemical or biological agents.*

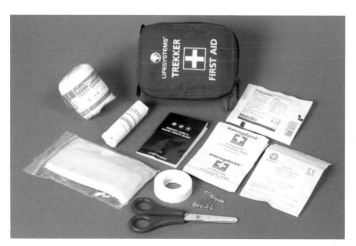

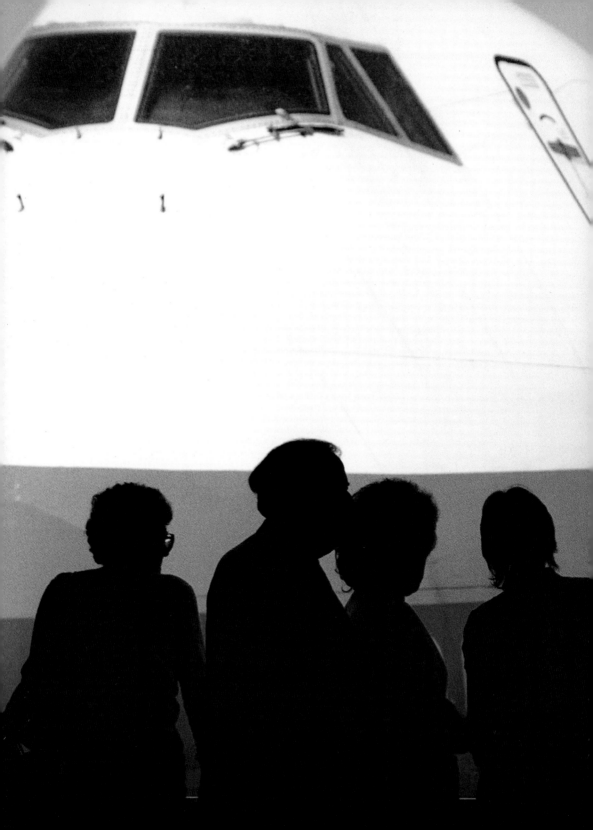

SURVIVING ON THE MOVE

We are often at our most vulnerable when travelling from one place to another. When walking, driving or cycling we can control the pace of our progress but need to be ready to cope with the careless actions of other road users, extreme weather or the mechanical failure of a vehicle. On public transport we must be watchful for our personal safety and that of our possessions, and cope with delays and diversions. World travel brings the remote yet awful possibilities of air crashes, shipwrecks and terrorist attack. Yet the spirit of adventure defies all these risks, and with the right approach and preparation we are right to regard travel as one of the greatest of life's experiences.

Safeguarding yourself and your possessions

There's an old adage that packing for a journey is not about what to take, but what to leave behind. Most irregular travellers have a lot of luggage, and this can be an enormous burden, not just in terms of weight, but as items to keep an eye on, to worry about losing, and to attract unwanted attention.

PROTECTING VALUABLES
Dress down when travelling, and do not flaunt money or wear jewellery, other than perhaps a wedding ring. Do not carry a laptop or camera in an obvious-looking bag. Use a money belt or a more obscure hiding place on your person for carrying money and

documents while travelling. You should also carry medicines and other essentials on your person in case you lose your luggage.

If you are staying in a high-risk area it may be worth using a wire luggage protector to prevent anyone from slashing your bag in the street. Another common technique of street thieves is to cut the shoulder strap before grabbing the bag. This is very difficult to combat because the aggressor is holding a knife and is ready to use it. Make yourself look like a difficult target in everything you do, but if someone does take you on, let the bag go. It's just a bag.

▲ *Arriving in an unfamiliar city can be disorienting. For your first night, it's worth splashing out on a hotel in a central, safe location while you get your bearings.*

BAGS ON PUBLIC TRANSPORT
As well as the risk of theft, you should be wary of your luggage being tampered with for criminal purposes. Always lock your luggage or tie zips shut, and use labels that cannot be read by casual bystanders, allowing unwanted access to your identity. You might want to use a business address for added security.

Do not accept letters, parcels or gifts from strangers and do not leave your luggage unattended, even for a minute. If you see unattended luggage in an airport, train, or bus station, report it and then stay away from it.

For a small fee, many airports will shrink-wrap your bag in plastic. This not only prevents tampering but also saves wear and tear on your luggage.

FINDING SAFE ACCOMMODATION
What is safe? An expensive hotel, probably. But people come into such places to steal from the rich. Seek advice from travel agents, even if you do not plan to book with them, from people who have attempted a similar trip before, or better still from trusted locals. If you arrive somewhere by accident rather than design, ensure the provision of basic essentials like water, warmth and shade, then take time to consider what the local threats and opportunities might be before choosing somewhere to stay.

SECURING PERSONAL BELONGINGS

1 If you wear a money belt, it should not be visible in any way: keep it securely tucked under your clothing.

2 Put your trousers on over the belt, and tuck in your shirt. This way it will not be exposed by your movements.

1 In areas where luggage crime is rife, protect your baggage with a wire mesh cover like this one, which can be placed over the entire bag.

2 Close the mesh cover and secure it with a lock. You can then use the cable to fasten it either to your person or to an immovable object.

Surviving city streets

The greatest danger facing you as a road user, whether you are walking, cycling or driving, is everybody else. In a busy city street you may be preoccupied by the possible threat of malicious intent, but more prevalent than that is the danger of accidents.

As always, anticipation is the key. Keep an eye out for drivers nodding off at the wheel, reading maps while driving or using their phones. Be aware that cycles often go unseen by motorists, and that older and smaller cars often have poor levels of grip and limited braking ability. Avoid trouble by ensuring that your vehicle is in good condition and keeping your fuel topped up so that you don't have to stop where you might prefer not to. Keep a secret weapon (such as a rape alarm or pepper spray) in the door pocket.

ROAD RAGE

The phenomenon of road rage is increasingly common as roads become busier, and drivers unable to cope with daily pressures experience extreme stress and frustration when confronted by situations they cannot control. It is a serious problem because the affected driver is at the controls of an extremely dangerous projectile – a motor vehicle.

If you are an innocent victim of road rage you must protect yourself. Most importantly, do not make eye contact

▲ *Keeping safe on a busy street depends on staying alert, reacting quickly and anticipating the actions of other people.*

with an angry driver, but get away as quickly as possible. Take the next easy turn and choose an alternative route.

If an enraged driver follows you, do not go home: go straight to the police. If a driver gets out of his car and comes over, lock the doors and windows, and ignore him even if he attacks the car. It's far better that he should take his anger out on the car than on you.

CAR JACKING

With car security systems getting more sophisticated, thieves are turning to the weakest link in the system – the driver. Car jackings at traffic lights or in filling

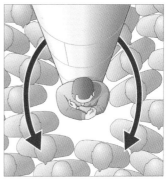

▲ *In the event of a crowd surge, say at an emergency exit, if you can find a pillar or similar structure seek refuge behind this.*

stations are increasingly common. If the car jacker's motivation is to steal your car, the best thing to do is let them. Don't resist, and get away safely. If they are trying to force you to drive, you are probably in less danger of personal injury as they need your cooperation and you have some degree of control.

HITCHHIKERS

There is a significant risk to a driver picking up any stranger, and those who look as though they really need a lift are sadly more likely to turn out to be difficult or dangerous. The safest course is simply not to pick up hitchers.

SURVIVING BEING HIT BY A CAR

1 When you realize a car is bound to hit you, jump just high enough to avoid the front of the car and land on the bonnet (hood).

2 Curl up on impact, drawing up your legs out of harm's way and protecting your head with your arms in case it hits the windshield or roof of the car.

3 Your secondary impact may be with the windshield or roof, or with the road, but in each case your injuries will probably be less than in a direct hit.

Coping with dangerous road situations

You can run into trouble on any road journey, and of course, you cannot influence when and where things could go wrong beyond ensuring adequate preparation and maintenance of your own vehicle and keeping the fuel tank topped up. Tell someone where you are going and when you expect to arrive, and always carry a mobile (cell) phone: the bane of modern life is also an invaluable lifesaver.

The number 112 is the international emergency telephone number and can be used in any country on any digital network. Due to the nature of cellular systems the success of such calls cannot be guaranteed, so you should also check for local emergency numbers. When you get through, if you are a woman travelling alone be sure to tell them so because rescue services give priority to women in this position.

MOTORWAYS

If you break down or have an accident on the motorway (freeway) and have to pull over, get out on the side away from the traffic and move away from your vehicle. It is quite common for inattentive drivers to crash into a stationary vehicle in this situation.

Telephone a recovery service or the emergency services as appropriate, but stay well away from the road while you wait for them to arrive. For advice on how to treat victims of road accidents, see page 506.

BLIND BENDS

If you come to rest just around a blind bend there is the danger of a collision as other road users come around the corner. Alert other drivers by placing a warning device 150m/165yd up the road from your vehicle. Stay away from the vehicle. If you have no warning device, wait 150m/165yd up the road yourself, to warn drivers to slow down.

TUNNELS

If you break down inside a tunnel it is best to get out of the vehicle but you may feel there is no safe space where you can wait for rescue. Most tunnels, however, have alcoves in the walls at regular intervals that enable you to shelter from passing traffic. Make sure you are not wearing loose clothing that could snag on a passing vehicle.

There may be emergency phones in the tunnel, but if not you may have to walk out of it to summon help. Mobile

Many road accidents are caused by drivers falling asleep at the wheel on long journeys. The received wisdom is that you should not drive for more than two hours at a stretch, so leave early and build in time for breaks. Particularly vulnerable times are when you've been on the road for five or six hours (even if breaks have been taken); when you are driving when you would otherwise be asleep; and an hour after meals. Learn to recognize the symptoms (yawning, blinking and increasingly erratic driving), open a window and find a place to stop so that you can wake yourself up properly.

phones often work in major tunnels because aerials have been installed in the tunnel for that purpose.

INNER CITY BACKSTREETS

If you break down in a dangerous area there may be a threat from the local inhabitants. The best way to deal with an immediate threat is to stay in your

GETTING OUT OF A SUBMERGED CAR

1 Act immediately if your car ends up in water. Get out of the car by any means possible. Turn the lights on and try to escape via a window or sunroof.

2 Wind down a side window in order to escape through it. If you have electric windows, they may well not be functioning – stay calm.

3 If you cannot open a side window by conventional means, try to smash it. Use a strong pointed object like a fire extinguisher or a wheel brace.

BREAKING DOWN ON A RAIL CROSSING

1 Don't tempt fate if your car becomes immobilized on the tracks. Assume that a train is approaching, even if you can't see or hear one.

2 Get any passengers out of the car immediately and make sure they retreat to a safe distance away from the crossing.

3 Use the emergency telephone by the crossing at once to inform the train operator or police that there is an obstruction on the line.

---

car and avoid eye contact or aggressive behaviour. If there is no immediate threat, lock the vehicle, leave all personal items out of sight, and make your way to safety, arranging for the recovery of the vehicle only when you have ensured your own personal safety.

REMOTE AREAS

If you break down in the middle of nowhere, you may be tempted to try to walk to safety. If you can positively identify somewhere you know to be within range that will afford you safety and help, then do so – otherwise, you should stay with the vehicle and attempt to attract the attention of a passing motorist. Do not risk getting lost or injured or running out of food, water and energy by setting off on a hike that has no definite goal. Your vehicle will afford you excellent protection from most dangers in a wilderness area.

ON A BEACH OR NEAR WATER

If you are planning to leave your vehicle anywhere near water you must allow for the tidal variation. Just because others have parked by the sea does not mean the rising tide will not swamp your car – locals may be parking there only temporarily. Obtain a tide table or ask for advice before leaving the car for long.

Surface conditions can also change with the incoming tide. You may park on sand that seems solid enough to drive over, but as the sea approaches or recedes, the surface may become softer or more powdery, making it impossible to drive away.

CLIFFTOPS AND SLOPES

If you park on a clifftop, or on any slope, the security of your parking brake is paramount. You don't want your car to roll away, causing accident or injury or leaving you with no means of escape. Selecting "park" in an automatic vehicle or first gear with a manual transmission is an excellent precaution. However, if you have concerns about the brake, do not rely on the gearbox alone. Place chocks on the downhill side of the wheels, or if against a kerb or similar, turn the front wheels so that the vehicle will jam against it if it moves downhill.

4 If you can't smash the window, kick it as hard as you can, starting at the corners, the weakest spots. You could also try to kick out the windshield.

5 If all else fails, try to open a door. This will only be possible when the car is nearly full of water, with the inside and outside pressure almost equal.

Dealing with mechanical failure

Breaking down in a vehicle can leave you stranded and vulnerable, but a mechanical failure while you are driving can be very scary indeed, and you need to know what action to take to minimize the risks to yourself and others on the road.

FAILING BRAKES

When you make your regular inspection under your car before driving, always check to see if the brakes are leaking. It is tempting to carry on using a car with a poor hand (parking) brake, but you should keep it in good order as it's your best line of defence if the driving brakes fail.

In the event of catastrophic brake failure you can downshift to slow the car. Many steeply inclined roads have "escape lanes" for brake failure. If you are lucky enough to be on such a road then use the escape lane. If you have to stop urgently, the hand brake will do it, but be gentle and brake only while travelling in a straight line or you will spin. Other techniques to consider are slowing down using the friction of banks of snow, hedges or ditches against the side or underside of the vehicle, but unless you have practised this before

▲ *You can plug a hole caused by a nail using rubber plug material (available from tyre repair mechanics). Reinflate the tyre or spray latex foam tyre repair gunk (available from most auto shops) through the valve, which mends and reinflates it temporarily.*

the likely outcome is that you'll lose control or the car will turn over. If you are travelling in a convoy and can communicate with another driver, it is possible to get a vehicle ahead of you to slow you down using the power of their brakes. However, this technique is only to be tried by very calm and brave drivers.

CRUISE CONTROL FAILURE OR STUCK THROTTLE

If the engine will not slow down, *do not* press the clutch or select neutral unless your life depends on it, because

the vehicle may instantly over-rev and destroy the engine. Instead, switch off the ignition immediately. The car will decelerate straight away, if anything slightly more so than normal. Brakes and steering will still work normally. If extreme circumstances dictate that you need to accelerate again, turn the ignition back on.

Some older or diesel-powered cars may not respond to being switched off – in this case the brakes are all you have, but it is still worth trying to fight the motor with these before you admit defeat and trash the engine.

STEERING FAILURE

This typically happens in one of two ways. If the steering wheel pulls off its spline, you can try to jam it back on again – it doesn't matter in what position it goes on as long as it does. If this fails, or the steering rack under the car breaks or fails, you must try to stop as quickly as possible. If you do not have anti-lock brakes you can try to lock up all the wheels by braking too hard: this will make the car understeer instead of following the errant front wheels and in an extreme case you may decide that would be a safer option.

PUNCTURE

By far the most common failure to occur while driving is a tyre puncture. If this happens you will hear a muffled flapping sound, sense vibration through the steering, and possibly feel a change of attitude (the way the vehicle sits on the road). High-speed punctures can be extremely dangerous. Put your hazard lights on, brake and stop immediately – not at the next convenient place, but right now.

If you can bring the vehicle to a stop within a few seconds of the puncture happening, you should be able to change the tyre or even repair it. If you drive on it for any distance at all you'll probably damage the wheel itself. This means that when you do stop you may not be able to remove it from the hub to fit the spare.

WHAT TO DO IF YOUR BRAKES FAIL

1 Don't switch off the engine. Shift down through the gears if you can. This will slow the vehicle down considerably, while allowing you to maintain good grip and control.

2 Once the car has slowed down to a speed of under 40kph/25mph try using the hand (parking) brake to bring it to a halt. Keep a tight grip on the steering wheel while applying the hand brake.

REINFLATING A TYRE

In extreme cases, you can reinflate a punctured tyre using lighter fuel and a match. If the tyre is still correctly seated, knock the "bead" (the stiff bit round the tyre edge that sits against the rim) off the rim on one side. For this you will need a lever such as a crowbar or very large screwdriver and a lot of strength. You could also use some sort of pipe to extend your leverage. If, on the other hand, the tyre has already peeled off the rim you need to lever it back on but make sure the bead on one side is unseated.

Squirt a small quantity (approximately half a cupful) of lighter fuel inside the tyre rim and spin the tyre to spread the fuel around inside. Ignite the fuel with a match or lighter, making sure that you keep your hands away from the rim so that your fingers don't get crushed. If it works there will be a loud explosion and the tyre will be inflated, possibly a little over-inflated. This technique can also be used to re-seat a tyre that has peeled off the rim.

Warning: This is an extremely dangerous procedure. Do this only in a life-threatening emergency.

▲ *In an extreme emergency you can reseat a tyre with lighter fuel and a lighter or match, but it is a dangerous procedure.*

JUMPSTARTING A VEHICLE

1 With the donor vehicle's engine running, connect a cable to the positive terminal of its battery. Keep the other end of the cable well away from the bodywork of the vehicle.

2 Connect the other end of this cable to the positive terminal on the vehicle you want to start. Connect the other cable to the negative terminal or another bare metal part (earth point).

3 Finally, connect the other end of the second cable to the donor car's negative terminal or an earth point. Turn on the engine, which should now start. Disconnect the cables in reverse order.

WHAT TO DO IF YOUR THROTTLE STICKS

1 If your engine will not slow down you can control the car by turning the ignition off and on as required, but do not use the clutch if you have one as this could damage the engine.

2 If there is an escape lane or a safe run-off area, use it to get off the road and out of danger to yourself and other road users, and bring the vehicle to a halt.

3 You may be able to slow the vehicle down by friction against verges, hedges, snow banks or other soft objects, but beware bouncing off them into danger or turning the vehicle over.

Getting out of a skid

The secret of skid control is to practise. You can read and hear about it all you like, but you will not be able to do it adequately unless you have tried it before. However, a few attempts on a "skid pan" to acquaint yourself with the basics are enough to give you a good chance of controlling even extreme angles of slide.

The word "skid" is used to describe any kind of slide in which the wheels are not gripping the road, of which there are many. The most common are wheelspin and brakeslides, where excessive amounts of throttle or braking respectively have caused the wheels to lose traction. These do not necessarily cause any change of direction, however, and simply easing off the pedal will solve the problem. Cornering slides, which are more challenging to control, come in three main types.

UNDERSTEER

In an understeer (sometimes called push or scrub), the front wheels do not have enough grip and the car does not turn into the corner as much as is required. It can be caused by excessive speed or braking, and it is very difficult to stop a car understeering. You can jump on the power or ease off the steering – the former adds to your already excessive speed, the latter may take you off the road or into the path of oncoming traffic.

The most common accident caused by this happens when the driver continues to turn the steering in an attempt to make the car respond, and then the front wheels suddenly grip. The car then responds to the steering and may dart to the inside of the corner or make a sudden transition to an oversteer or even a spin.

HOW TO CONTROL A FRONT SKID

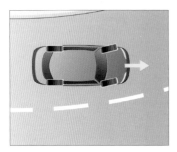

1 In an understeer, the front wheels of the car continue to plough straight ahead, so that the vehicle does not turn into the corner.

2 Reduce the amount you have turned the front wheels to regain grip and control. You will inevitably run wide of your desired path round the corner.

3 Once you have regained grip and control you can correct your course and turn the vehicle in the direction you originally intended to go.

HOW TO CONTROL A REAR SKID

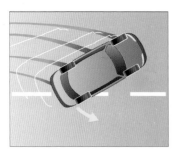

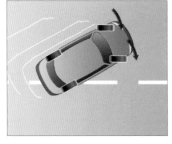

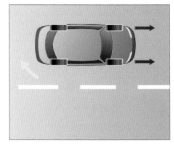

1 When the rear of the vehicle loses traction in a corner it will turn more than you intended, and could even spin right round.

2 Turn the steering in the opposite direction (opposite lock) until the front of the car is back under your control, albeit at a rather extreme angle.

3 Bring the steering back smoothly to the centre as the car approaches the right direction: keep steering the front irrespective of what the back is doing.

OVERSTEER

This kind of skid occurs when the rear wheels lose traction in a corner. The rear of the vehicle will run wide, causing the car to turn more than the driver intended. In extreme cases it may spin right around. The cause is usually excessive power application in a rear-wheel drive car, but it can also occur due to overbraking while cornering and can be caused deliberately by applying the hand (parking) brake in mid-corner (when it is known as a hand-brake turn).

If oversteer occurs accidentally the remedy is to turn the steering wheel towards the outside of the bend. Ease off whichever pedal caused the offending slide. In extreme cases you will end up with the front wheels pointing the opposite way they do in a normal cornering situation. Turning the steering wheel the opposite way from normal cornering practice is called "opposite lock".

If your car has four-wheel drive or is exceptionally well balanced you can sometimes experience all four wheels sliding in a corner ("four-wheel drift"). The same basic rules apply: ease off the throttle or brake as applicable and apply opposite lock if necessary.

Most modern cars, especially those with front-wheel drive, are designed to have a slight tendency to understeer. This is because understeer is thought to be safer for drivers who do not have

the necessary skills to control slides. Ironically, understeer is a nightmare for a skilful driver whereas oversteer is fairly controllable as long as it happens predictably.

SLIPPERY ROAD SURFACES

In ice or snow (or at very high speeds on other surfaces), the car will slide around no matter how well you drive. The trick here is to maintain a slight oversteer situation and never let the car understeer. To learn the various tricks to achieve this in different types of vehicle – front-, rear- and four-wheel drive – you may have to go on a specialist driving course. In snow, using chains or lowering your tyre pressures to about 0.7bar/10psi can really help, but you must be able to reinflate them subsequently for normal driving. On ice, narrow tyres are better, and studs or chains are best.

SWAYING TRAILERS

Trailers, caravans and horseboxes can cause all kinds of problems if you don't drive sympathetically. A trailer can cause snaking (swinging wildly from side to side) if you try to slow down too quickly, especially going downhill – the only solution is to accelerate slightly, which can be alarming to the uninitiated. At lower speeds, attempting to corner too quickly can cause the rig to jackknife and the trailer to roll over or hit the towing vehicle.

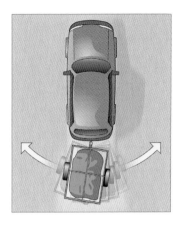

▲ *Too much weight at the back of a trailer may cause sway, which can lead to loss of control. In this case keep the steering straight – do not try to steer out of the slide.*

Even if you keep your tyres at the correct air pressure and check the treads and side walls regularly, there is always the chance of a blowout to one of your trailer's tyres. This is a highly dangerous situation, particularly if there is other traffic and you panic. Whatever you do, don't automatically slam on the brakes or try to stop suddenly. Apply the brakes gradually, and if the trailer tries to go sideways let off the brakes and accelerate a little. This will jerk the trailer back into line. Continue like this until you have slowed right down and it is safe for you to pull off the road.

ESCAPING FROM A CAR THAT IS UPSIDE DOWN

1 Push yourself up using your hands against the roof to take the weight off the seat belt buckle, otherwise you will not be able to release it.

2 If the doors won't open you may need to smash the nearest window with a heavy object. Use your arms to pull yourself through it.

3 Be aware of the danger of broken glass in the window frame, in the car and on the ground as you make your escape from the vehicle.

Fire in a vehicle

Most vehicle fires start either in the engine compartment (as a result of a fuel or oil leak), under the dashboard, or because a cigarette has fallen on to a seat. Many vehicles also catch fire when parked in tall grass and left while the engine is hot – this can ignite combustibles under the vehicle.

If you drive a motorhome or tow a caravan, you have to be doubly careful, because these vehicles contain propane tanks, which provide another source of fuel for fire. They are also prone to electrical fires because of their complex wiring harnesses. Make sure you have a smoke and/or gas detector.

USING A FIRE EXTINGUISHER

Different kinds of fire extinguishers are available, but an ABC (powder) extinguisher is the most versatile. Get a big, heavy one, to avoid the horror of the extinguisher running out, but also because it makes a very useful escape tool and weapon.

To put out a fire, sweep the extinguisher back and forth across the base of the fire until it is out. Don't spray at the flames – that won't put the fire out and will waste the contents of the extinguisher.

If you have a fire in a seat, put out the fire but then pull the seat out of the vehicle. The upholstery will probably still be smouldering: open it up to extinguish the fire, or discard the seat.

ENGINE FIRES

Fire may result from a fuel line leaking on to a hot manifold. Inspect fuel pipes frequently and replace them if they look cracked. If your engine is on fire, turn off the ignition immediately to shut down the fuel pump.

Putting out an engine fire safely takes two people, one to use the extinguisher, the other to open the bonnet (hood). It's important to get the bonnet open fast. Once the fire burns through the release cable there'll be no way to get it open. The fire will flare up as the fresh air hits it, so be ready to start spraying immediately. Don't try to put out an engine fire by spraying through the radiator or wheel arches – this won't work. You have to get at the source of the flames.

▲ *If your engine is on fire, try not to lift the bonnet (hood) more than necessary. Aim the extinguisher at the base of the fire.*

CONE OF DANGER

If you're fighting a vehicle fire, stay out of the cone-shaped danger zone, which is directly behind a vehicle with the fuel tank in the usual position at the back. If the tank explodes it sends a blast over this area that can be lethal for 15–30m/50–100ft. Some vehicles have the fuel tank at the front or side – don't assume the danger zone is the back.

Most danger is associated with petrol, not diesel fuel, which is difficult to ignite. Petrol will explode at the slightest exposure to heat, flame or sparks. So get everyone well away from a petrol-driven car.

WHAT TO DO WHEN A CAR IS ON FIRE

1 A dashboard fire can spread quickly into the engine or fuel system. Put it out at once or abandon the vehicle.

2 Prepare your fire extinguisher according to the instructions while you are standing safely outside the vehicle.

3 Reach into the car quickly and aim the extinguisher at the base of the fire. Spray until all the flames are out.

Drivers' survival strategies

If you break down in a remote area, or are stranded in severe weather, you may have to wait a long time for rescue. Your vehicle will give some protection from the elements, but in extreme cold keeping warm will be a priority.

MAKING A FIRE

Use a mirror or a car light reflector as a burning glass, or use a pair of glasses or binoculars to focus the sun's rays on to some tinder or dry leaves.

If there is no sun, use your car battery and jump leads, or any batteries and wire you have. If the batteries are small hold two together, positive to negative, and attach two pieces of wire to the positive and negative terminals at each end. Touch the free ends of wire to a bit of wire wool. It will spark up really well. If you have no wire wool touch the ends of the wires together to draw a spark. A small amount of fuel will help if your tinder isn't good.

If you have a petrol engine running and don't want to mess about, grip one of the plug leads with a gloved or well-insulated hand and pull it off the plug. Holding it near the plug or any metal part of the engine will make a big spark to light a handful of tinder. (If your insulation isn't good you'll get a very invigorating electric shock which will also warm you up.) Crucially, don't overlook the car's cigarette lighter.

DIGGING A CAR OUT OF SNOW

Dig the snow away from the vehicle's exhaust pipe before you start your engine, and dig through the snow to the middle of the underbody to allow any leaks from the exhaust system to vent. Without proper ventilation,

▲ *In extremely cold conditions you can light a small fire under a diesel engine to keep it warm if you are stranded. Never try this with a petrol vehicle, and be very careful the fire doesn't lick at wiring or rubber hoses or seals.*

deadly gases can quickly build up in the passenger compartment.

Clearing ice and snow from the windows and lights is a good start. Don't forget to clear snow from the bonnet and roof, or it will quickly blow on to your front and rear windows again.

If digging and spreading sand or gravel near the wheels doesn't give you enough grip to get moving, try rocking the car with quick movements forward and backwards. You can use the weight of the car to push it out of the icy depressions the tyres have settled in: be gentle with the throttle, ease forward, then rock back, until you are clear.

BEING SEEN

The colour of your vehicle may make it difficult to see: for instance, a white car in snow or a green one on grass. Put something brightly coloured on it such as a jumper or scarf so you will be seen and rescued.

◀ *Use blankets or coats to insulate your engine compartment to retain heat – either to keep you warm or to stop the engine freezing overnight.*

LONG JOURNEY ESSENTIALS

- Car/driving documents
- Map
- Mobile (cell) phone with emergency numbers
- Torch (flashlight)
- Extra batteries for torch
- First-aid kit
- Spare tyre, inflated to recommended pressure
- Jump leads
- Tow rope
- Road flares or warning triangles
- Ice scraper and de-icer
- Container for fuel
- Basic tool kit including adjustable spanners, cutters, some wire and duct tape
- Blanket or sleeping bag
- Waterproof clothing and gloves
- Extra washer fluid
- Bottled water/protein bars
- Shovel

Choosing a safe seat

Whenever you use public transport, whatever type of vehicle you are travelling in, your "What if?" survival attitude should equip you to choose the safest place to sit, based on experience and observation. Here are some tips to help you decide where and how to sit.

TRAINS AND BUSES

It is safer not to choose a seat at a table. In the event of a collision or a sudden stop, you could be severely injured by being thrown forward into the table, and you could also be hit by other passengers, or objects on the table, flying into you. It is safer to choose a seat where you are protected both ahead and behind by your own seat and the one in front of you. On the other hand, you need to bear in mind that on long journeys you are more at risk from discomfort – and in an extreme case from suffering deep-vein thrombosis (DVT) – than from being involved in an accident, so it may be more important to choose a comfortable seat with leg room and where you can get up and move around. If you have a choice of

forward- or rear-facing seats it is probably safer to be rear-facing, but this would depend on the nature of any accident and other factors may affect your decision.

A seat next to an emergency exit should always be your first choice. This is probably even better than being next to the main exit, since you will be in control of it, and first out of the door. Also, on aircraft and coaches such seats usually have more legroom than the rest of the seating. On airlines,

▲ Public transport is statistically far safer than travel by car, with air travel being 27 times safer than cars in terms of fatalities.

emergency exit row seats are allocated to passengers capable of operating the doors, which rules out the elderly and infirm and children. By contacting the airline, you might be able to secure an exit row seat in advance. If the airline policy is not to allocate them until the day of departure, arrive early and see if you can get transferred.

▼ In a train with three cars, the middle one is probably the safest since it cannot be struck directly in a collision. In a longer train, consider being nearer the rear, though not in the last two cars.

▶ In a single-carriage train, sitting close to an exit will mean you are first in the queue for any quick escape needed.

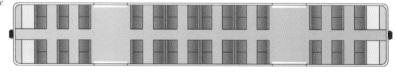

▶ Take care when leaving a train on an open line – you could get hit by a passing train.

▲ *Before boarding many types of public transport your belongings may be searched or X-rayed. Be ready to demonstrate that drinks are harmless and electrical equipment is what it appears to be.*

SEAT BELTS AND RESTRAINT SYSTEMS

If there are seat belts, use them whenever you are in your seat. In an accident in any form of transport a seat belt can improve your chances of survival considerably.

Do not get up from your seat as soon as a vehicle comes to a halt. This is a common cause of injury – when a vehicle stops it will actually have moved forward on its suspension, especially if it has rubber tyres. A second or so later it will rock back. If

▼ *On a bus sit on the inside aisle so that you are able to make a quick escape and also are less likely to be hurt by flying glass.*

you get up too soon, you could be thrown forward or to the floor by the unexpected movement.

As with all survival considerations, the most important thing is to think at all times about the likely outcome of an accident. Some experienced travellers, when in Third World countries, prefer to travel on the roof of a bus rather than inside. They say this is safer in low-speed accidents (which are the most common), more comfortable and healthier than being crammed in with other travellers and their livestock; in addition, it enables them to keep an eye on their luggage, which is stored on the roof and may otherwise be stolen at bus stops. This way of travelling may not be for you, but extreme circumstances sometimes require extreme measures, so you should at least be open to such options.

STORING LUGGAGE SAFELY

Most people prefer to keep their luggage close by them for security and convenience, but it is also true to say that loose luggage can be a significant danger to passengers in the event of an impact. The overhead lockers or racks are the best places for items of hand luggage that you won't need during the journey, but don't try to stow very heavy items overhead as they could become dangerous missiles in a collision. Those items you would need in an emergency should be stored about your person as far as possible.

STRANGERS ON PUBLIC TRANSPORT

Other people are the bane or joy, depending on your attitude, of travel by public transport. You'll experience the full range of human behaviour, from the travelling companion who simply talks too much when you want to sleep or be alone to threatening, drunk or abusive passengers. It's also possible that they might try to steal from you. Try to appear confident but not aggressive when dealing with fellow passengers, using firm but non-threatening body language with open hand gestures.

Women in particular may be vulnerable to unwanted attention of a sexual nature, and this attention can become uncomfortable and/or escalate into confrontation or in extreme cases sexual assault. Rule number one is never to travel alone – but this is not much consolation if you have no choice. Try to keep within sight of other passengers or the driver, and form bonds with people you feel you can trust. Finally, keep a secret weapon handy, such as a rape alarm or pepper spray (but be certain that whatever you carry does not contravene local laws), to be used as a last resort.

▼ *In an aircraft, there is no evidence that any one part of the plane is safer in a crash, though being close to an emergency exit is clearly beneficial in terms of evacuation.*

▶ *In a plane, the seats over the wing are the strongest and most stable but close to fuel tanks.*

▼ *The seats at the back are noisier and the plane moves more in turbulence.*

▼ *If you have to vacate a bus by a rear window be wary of passing traffic.*

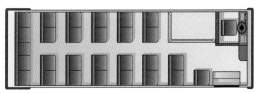

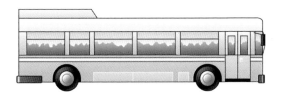

▼ *Seats at the front are preferred by most, but are usually the first place to sustain damage in a crash.*

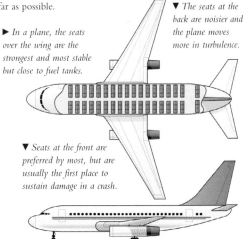

Transport accidents on land

Accidents on buses or trains generally leave you in a less extreme type of environment than those in air or water, but unfortunately they are a lot more common. Many of us are likely to be involved in one or more during our lives, in particular when travelling by road. Preparation and premeditation is key, as in all survival scenarios.

Count the number of seat rows to the exits, familiarize yourself with the operation of emergency doors, and take note of the position and instructions for any glass-breaking devices supplied. Simple things like carrying a small torch (flashlight) and a mobile (cell) phone on your person, and considering your exit strategy from the moment you get on board, will always pay dividends if things go wrong.

ROAD TRAFFIC ACCIDENTS

The best protection you can have in a road accident is a seat belt. If the vehicle is fitted with them, wear one at all times, even when stationary. Once the vehicle has come to rest after an accident, release your seat belt and get yourself and others out and to safety as

▼ *Escalating congestion on the roads means that the chances of accidents and breakdowns are constantly increasing. We have to be prepared for any scenario.*

quickly as possible, unless you suspect someone has a serious spinal injury. Anyone injured in this way should not be moved until medical help arrives unless their life depends on it.

If you do not have a seat belt you should adopt the brace position – placing your hands on your head with your arms against the back of the seat in front of you – if you believe an accident is imminent. This will reduce the likelihood of injury.

ESCAPING FROM A VEHICLE

When you need to get out of a vehicle after an accident you may have to operate the doors yourself. The emergency exits may have releases on the inside, outside, or both. On some buses and trains they can simply be forced open by hand in the event of a power failure.

If you can't leave by a door you may need to break a window. Many public transport vehicles have small devices for breaking glass stowed at intervals along the passenger compartments. When you get on board, make sure you know where the nearest one to your seat is located, and read the instructions. The devices vary in type and operation and you won't be able to break the strong safety glass of the vehicle's windows by any other means.

▲ *Without their underground train systems, many of the world's capital cities would grind to a halt. Accidents on them are rare, but when they happen they present the rescue services with major problems in terms of access and communications.*

LEAVING A MOVING VEHICLE

If you realize you have to get out of a vehicle while it is still moving, keep to the following rules. Look in the direction of travel before you jump to make sure you aren't going to hit a lamp post or something similar. Aim to hit the ground as if running and then roll, protecting your head with your arms. If you have practised jumping off moving things such as swings, roundabouts, bicycles or skateboards you will do it better. Jumping off a vehicle travelling at more than about 50kph/30mph is probably not worth the risk of injury unless staying on board means almost certain death.

Warning: This is an extremely dangerous procedure. Do this only in a life-threatening emergency.

FIRE AND SMOKE

If there is a fire on a public transport vehicle the compartment will quickly fill with smoke from burning carpets, seat foam and plastic fixtures. Luckily, you counted the number of seat rows between you and the nearest exits, and

with the aid of your torch you can crawl to an exit along the floor beneath the worst of it. Wrapping a scarf around your face will help.

ELECTRIC TRAINS AND TRAMS

Having left the train you need to negotiate the tracks. These may be electrified, so do not touch them. Look out for any conductive debris that could also give you a shock. Some electric vehicles get their current from overhead wires. Look out for these, either on top of the vehicle, or brought down by the accident.

UNDERGROUND STATIONS

If you need to escape from an underground train you will arrive on the tracks in a tunnel. If trains are still running you are in great danger. There may be alcoves at intervals in the wall, in which you can shelter from passing trains. Face outwards and keep any loose clothing or hair under control. A passing train could suck items out of the alcove and snag them.

If you don't know the direction of the nearest station, see if there is a breeze in the tunnel. The nearer station is more likely to be downwind. Once in the station, get above ground and out of danger. If there has been a fire, do not use lifts (elevators) or escalators.

▲ *Standing too near the edge of a platform carries the twin dangers of trains passing at high speeds and the possibility of falling on to the live rail.*

It is usually better to use stairs anyway as fewer people may try this way. Those who habitually use a route are unlikely to shake off the habit in an emergency.

If you are already in a lift and it stops, force the doors manually to see if you are near enough to a floor to clamber out. If not, you may be able to

escape through a hatch in the top and climb to a floor. Both actions are very dangerous, particularly if the lift starts again, so use the stop switch on the control panel before you try. Unless you are in immediate danger it is better to wait for rescue. Most lifts have a bell or phone with which to signal for help. This may not work after an electrical failure, but try it first. You can signal by shouting or banging metallic objects on the floor: this sound will carry a long way in a lift shaft.

BREAKING A SAFETY GLASS WINDOW

1 Follow the instructions to open the box containing the hammer – usually by smashing a glass cover. Use an object such as a book if possible.

2 Remove the tool and tap it firmly against the window near the corner. Make sure you break both panes if the window is double-glazed.

3 Use a bag or coat to enlarge the hole until it is big enough to use as an escape route. Remove the glass to the bottom of the pane to avoid injuries.

When things go wrong in the air

Most people fear flying more than any other common form of transport, despite being perfectly aware that it is in fact one of the safest. This is partly due to lack of familiarity – you probably fly less often than you take a car, train or bus. But another factor is the lack of control you have over your environment. In almost no other mode of transport do you have so little influence – you don't get to choose when to travel or where to sit, and you are told what to do at every stage.

You can make yourself feel much better about flying simply by being proactive about the things you can control, and in doing so you can dramatically improve your chances of survival if the unthinkable did happen.

IN-FLIGHT BRIEFING AND SAFETY CARD

If you are apprehensive about flying, the safety briefing can make matters worse by putting in your mind the idea that you are likely to experience serious turbulence, loss of cabin pressure, a crash landing and being lost at sea – all of which are very unlikely to occur. Even so, you should listen to

▼ *Members of a fire crew carry a victim away from the scene of a serious accident. The foam from their chemical extinguishing equipment can be seen all around them.*

and concentrate on the safety briefing. It is important. Read the card that explains what to do in the case of an accident. Not only will this make any emergency action less of a shock to you but you will understand what everyone else is doing, and why.

The in-flight briefing and safety card will tell you where your lifejacket is stowed. It is usually under your seat – make sure you really understand how to access it. They will also explain how in the event of loss of cabin pressure, oxygen masks will drop down from the panel above you.

The ordinary person requires supplemental oxygen at altitudes above 3,000m/10,000ft, and either aircraft must have pressurized cabins or everyone must use oxygen masks. As a result, passenger aircraft must carry emergency oxygen supplied via masks in case the cabin pressurization system fails or the plane is punctured by accident. This supply provides the necessary time for the pilot(s) to descend safely to an altitude where supplemental oxygen is no longer needed. Loss of cabin pressurization by a bullet or other puncture isn't catastrophic, as portrayed in the movies, and the loss of a door or window does not destroy the aircraft.

▲ *This plane has veered off the runway at speed and the undercarriage has collapsed on the grass, but the passengers inside may have come to no harm at all.*

FAMILIARIZATION

When you board an aircraft, familiarize yourself with everything around you. In the event of an incident it is the cabin crew's job to open emergency exits and to deploy fire extinguishers, but it can't hurt for you to make sure you know how they work. The nearest crew member might be injured in the incident, or wrestling with a passenger who is less calm than yourself.

AIR RAGE

Extreme behaviour by unruly passengers, often called air rage, can put crew members and other passengers at risk. The reasons for such aggression could include excessive alcohol consumption, a ban on smoking, claustrophobia, the tedium of a long flight, psychological feelings of loss of control and problems with authority.

Cabin crews are trained to deal with this, but in the event that you become involved, maintain eye contact and passive, open body language and attempt to calm the troublemaker. Do not escalate the conflict.

TURBULENCE AND WIND SHEARS

Sometimes the aircraft can be jerked around violently by atmospheric conditions. The pilot will usually give you some warning of this but sometimes that isn't possible so it's a good idea to be prepared for it at any time during the flight.

Make sure that anything you put in the locker above you is correctly stowed and check that the locker is shut properly after each time it is opened. Minimize the chances of something falling on you.

Don't drink too much so that you need to go to the toilet frequently or at inconvenient times. Put your seat belt on whenever you are in the seat, not just when the seat belt light is on.

PREPARING FOR THE WORST

The worst-case scenario worth considering is that you have to exit the aircraft in an emergency. The trick here is to know how many rows of seats there are between you and each of the exits. Once you have found your seat, look around and identify the emergency exits, and count the number of seat-backs between your seat and each one of the exits. This knowledge could save your life in the case of smoke, fire or power outage, since you will be one of the minority of people who will be able to find the exits blind. Anything in your possession that would be absolutely essential for your continued well-being outside the aircraft (such as medication or an inhaler) should be carried in your pockets or otherwise on your person at all times. That way you won't need to stop to grab your carry-on luggage.

In the case of smoke or fire you need to be out of the plane within 90 seconds or you won't be capable of being proactive any more. Pulling some clothing across your face as a mask can help minimize inhalation problems, especially if you can wet it first.

▶ *On water the slides may be used to get passengers out, but afterwards they will be deployed as rafts. They remain tethered to the aircraft until all people and supplies are out, or the plane is in danger of sinking.*

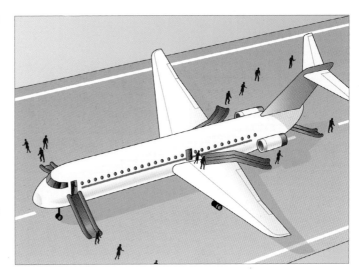

DEEP VEIN THROMBOSIS

One danger you face on a commercial airliner is deep vein thrombosis (DVT), especially if you are overweight, unfit, drink too much alcohol, or have a history of vascular problems. Blood clots form, especially in the legs, and cause pain and swelling; they may later be life-threatening if they become dislodged and block a blood vessel in the lung. Contrary to urban myth the condition is not confined to flying, and can occur whenever you sit still for many hours at a time. To avoid it, just

▲ *In an emergency, escape slides are deployed from every exit and passengers are moved quickly away from the aircraft.*

go for a stroll up the aisle every hour, and do mild flexing exercises with your legs while seated.

Current medical thinking is that "flight socks" can reduce the risk, and these are available from airlines and travel stores. DVT is extremely rare and, while you should take precautions even if you're not in a high risk group, you shouldn't worry about it unduly.

Surviving an air emergency

If an emergency develops while you are on board an aircraft, make sure you have your jacket on with all essential items in your pockets. Any non-essential carry-on baggage should be left behind if you eventually have to evacuate the plane.

Ideally you should be wearing roomy, comfortable clothes that give you freedom of movement, and cover your arms and legs fully. Natural fibres give the best protection. Shoes should be low, with straps or laces to keep them on your feet in an emergency.

Fasten your seat belt and adopt the brace position. Make sure you have remembered how many rows of seats there are between you and each exit, and glance at all the passengers around you, to take in who is who and try to form an impression of how they will react if you have to get out.

EMERGENCY LANDING IN WATER

If the aircraft is forced to come down in the sea, do not inflate lifejackets or rafts until they are outside the plane. Get yourselves and all emergency equipment off the aircraft as soon as possible, remembering that fresh water is possibly the most important thing to have with you in a survival situation. Retain a line from the aircraft to the raft until everything you need is aboard

EMERGENCY IN THE AIR

▲ If the plane loses oxygen pressure, oxygen masks will drop down automatically. Secure your own mask so that you can breathe normally before helping others in difficulty.

▲ When you hear the words "Brace! Brace!" adopt the position shown here, with your hands on your head against the back of the seat in front of you.

▲ If fire breaks out after a crash landing, crawl beneath the smoke and fumes towards the nearest emergency exit, which you should have identified earlier.

USING AN EMERGENCY EXIT

1 Emergency exits are opened by pulling a handle in the direction indicated. Do not attempt to operate it until the aircraft is stationary.

2 The door may open, or come right off. Make sure the way is clear before deploying a slide or other apparatus, and before attempting to make an exit.

3 Remove your shoes as they can damage slides. Jump into the centre of the slide, fold your arms across your chest and keep your feet together.

or the aircraft starts to sink – be ready to release the line and paddle away as the aircraft goes under.

If you have more than one life raft it helps to tie them together with 8–10m/25–30ft of line. If you can deal with it, linking swimmers together in this way is a good idea too.

If you need to search for missing people, think primarily about the wind direction and which way you, the aircraft and they might be blown by it. Any current is irrelevant because you are all in that, but wind affects different flotsam in differing ways.

Be careful about trimming and balancing your raft, but have a strategy for righting it and containing your important supplies if it should capsize for any reason.

The drier you are the better, as immersion can have adverse effects later on. If it is cold, think about ways to keep warm as soon as possible – if you deal with more pressing matters first and get cold you will probably not warm up again. If it is warm, you need to consider the consequences of sunburn or dehydration – get under cover or keep your skin covered. If you are swimming, face away from the sun or try to improvise some face covering with clothing. Obviously wear a hat and sunglasses if you have them.

Activate any rescue transmitters you may have as soon as possible. Try the radio as well if you have one. Remember that search aircraft and ships have difficulty spotting survivors, especially small rafts or swimmers. Do anything you can to increase your visibility. Keep mirrors handy, use the radio when you can, and be prepared to use the mirrors and/or marker dye if an aircraft or ship is sighted.

SURVIVING A CRASH LANDING

If fire breaks out in the aircraft after a crash landing, crawl beneath the smoke, following the floor lights if they still work and counting the seats to the exit, having identified the nearest one earlier. Go over or around anyone in your way. The chances are that some of these passengers will be lost, or just slow. That isn't your problem – don't wait in line.

If escape slides are being deployed, don't sit down to slide, just jump into the middle of the chute. Cross your arms across your chest to minimize the risk of snagging on something or injury to yourself or someone else.

Once you are out of the aircraft, stay well away from it until the engines are cooled and spilt fuel has evaporated. Check the injured and administer whatever help you can. Get out of the

wind or rain – improvise some kind of shelter as a priority. Make a fire if you need one, and make hot drinks if you can. Get communications equipment operative if possible and begin broadcasting. Having done this, relax, give yourselves a chance to get over the shock and leave any further planning and operations until later.

WAITING FOR RESCUE

After you have rested, recover all useful supplies and organize them. Remember that water is the most important thing. Determine your position as best you can and include it in any radio broadcast – if it is based on any assumptions, transmit those too.

If you bailed out of the aircraft, try to get back to it, as it will be found before you are. If it is cold you can use the aircraft for shelter while you try to build a better, warmer shelter outside. Do not cook inside the plane.

If it's hot, the plane will be too hot to use as a shelter. Instead, make a shade shelter outside using parachutes or blankets as an awning. Leave the lower edges 50cm/20in off the ground to allow the air to flow.

Conserve the power of any electrical equipment, and sweep the horizon with a signal mirror or light at regular intervals, even if you are broadcasting.

IN THE EVENT OF A CRASH LANDING

1 The pilot will attempt to make a survivable landing no matter how severe the situation: an ideal approach angle may not be achievable.

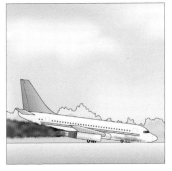

2 Whether the aircraft impacts nose or tail first there is a significant risk of the fuselage snapping, endangering the lives of the passengers.

3 The fuselage is most likely to break near the middle, and this may be accompanied almost immediately by fire in this and other areas.

Abandoning ship

Preparation is everything if you are to survive a shipwreck. Know where the lifesaving equipment is and know how to lay your hands on essential supplies: water is the most important, but also food, clothing and communications gear. If you do find yourself without a proper raft or life preserver you will need to seek out the largest floating item available, then try to transfer essential items to it.

Follow the instructions of the crew where possible. Once in the water, be rational about getting away from the ship. If it is not going to sink or explode immediately, stay with it, tethered if necessary, until all useful supplies have been recovered or it appears to be too dangerous to stay.

BURNING OIL

If fire breaks out and there is burning fuel on the surface of the water, try to make your way upwind. Burning oil is easily blown and does not spread upwind. It may be necessary to dive under narrow stretches of burning fuel, and you will need to deflate your life preserver to do this. If you have to surface among the flames, you can try to thrash your arms as you do so – this may make a break in the fire while you

get a breath, but you should regard this as a last resort as the fire will have extracted the oxygen from the affected area and the super-hot air inside a fire can burn your lungs and kill you.

You can breathe the air in a life-preserver if it was inflated by mouth. Although it is exhaled air, it still

▲ *Follow the instructions of the crew on when to abandon ship. If you are lucky, the rescue services may arrive in time.*

contains enough oxygen to breathe a couple more times. But beware automatically inflated vests – they are usually full of carbon dioxide.

IMPROVISING FLOTATION AIDS

▲ *Knot the ankles of a pair of trousers. Swing them by the waistband over your head then pull the waistband under water to trap air in each leg.*

▲ *Cushions and pillows can be used as flotation devices. Some of those found on board ship may be specifically designed for this purpose.*

▲ *If you have no flotation aids (don't take off the trousers you are wearing), try to tread water as little as possible to conserve your energy.*

SURVIVING IN THE WATER

Don't swim if you can help it. Float on your back using as much additional buoyancy (from a life preserver, or air trapped in clothes or cushions) as you can, and save your energy. Swim only if you can be certain from experience that you are capable of swimming to relative safety. Save energy by keeping your head submerged except when you need to breathe. Even if you are a strong swimmer you may find it very difficult in the sea. Previous practice swimming in rough seas is a great help.

Swimming, even gently, reduces your survival time, and strips the heat away from your body incredibly quickly. If you stay still you will warm up a thin layer of water around you, and particularly inside your clothes. Every time you move you exchange this warm water for cooler, and lose a bit more heat and hence energy. For this reason, keep as many clothes on as possible. If you have a bag (a bivvy bag or plastic survival bag, even a bin bag), getting inside this will trap water around you and dramatically improve your chances. Being a big orange blob is also a great deterrent to one of our greatest fears in the water – sharks (*see following pages*).

▲ *If there is burning oil on the water, swim upwind from it.*

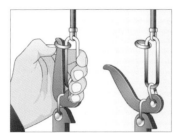

◄ *The best place to be if your sailing craft is capsized or swamped is close to the boat so that rescuers can find you more easily.*

EVACUATION PROCEDURES

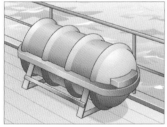

1 In addition to orthodox lifeboats, most ships have cylinder-shaped "throwover" life rafts complete with emergency survival kit.

2 In order to launch the life raft, the lashings securing the two halves of the cylinder must first be released.

3 After securing the "painter" (the rope attached to the life raft) to a point on the boat, ensure all is clear below then throw the life raft overboard.

4 Pull out the entire length of the painter and then, when it is taut, give the painter a hard tug. This will start the inflation process.

5 Ideally bring the life raft alongside the boat and enter without getting wet, having first removed shoes and any sharp objects.

6 After everyone has boarded the raft, cut the painter, look for survivors who had to jump and paddle away from the sinking vessel.

Survival at sea

When you have to survive on minimal supplies you must first look after what you have – that means firstly your life raft. Any boat will stay drier with the weight near the centre, though it will pitch and roll less with the weight distributed. In rough conditions a sea anchor off the bow can help you stay stable and facing oncoming waves, but it also slows your downwind progress. In hot climates deflate the raft a little in the morning to stop it bursting.

FOOD AND WATER

Use any supplies wisely. You can go for weeks without food, but only days without water. Drink as little as you

▲ *If you have some stiff wire you may be able to create a hook using any tools you have aboard. Tie the hook on to any thin string or line you can find. Try to bait the hook with something, but you may even be lucky with just a bare hook.*

can to keep yourself hydrated and if it is hot try to minimize perspiration by wetting your hair and clothes with sea water, provided this does not irritate your skin. Rain, old (bluish) ice, and the bodily fluids of sea creatures are all sources of water at sea. Do not drink salt water under any circumstances.

If you have no food, you'll have to catch some, and the primary food sources are fish, birds, and plankton. Plankton can be filtered from the sea with a cloth and are an excellent source of protein and carbohydrate if all spiny material and stinging tentacles can be removed, though you may ingest a lot of salt water with them and you should test them for toxicity.

It's easy to improvise hooks and line for small fish. Failing a line, you can

▲ *Sharks are greatly feared, but remember that only a few shark attacks are recorded around the world each year, and not all of those are fatal. You cannot swim anywhere near as fast as a shark, but they find it hard to stop or change direction quickly – especially large ones, so you may be able to get out of the way, especially downwards as the shark can't see ahead or below once it's jaws are open. If you are attacked and have a knife, go for the eyes or gills – the most sensitive areas – or gouge with your fingers. With a bit of luck it will be scared off.*

try to make a spear, but don't try to spear anything big. Birds are hard to catch but may be speared or lassoed after enticing them to land on the boat. Most seaweed is edible, while coral is always poisonous and inedible.

USING A DINGHY AS A LIFE RAFT

1 If possible attach a righting line running from gunwale to gunwale under the dinghy, which you can use to turn the boat if it capsizes.

2 Tie yourselves and your equipment into the boat if necessary, leaving your tethers long so that you will not be trapped under the boat if it capsizes.

3 You may be able to improvise a sail using a tarpaulin or even a shirt, which can move a small boat quite well and may also provide a little shade.

Jellyfish often have stinging tentacles, and in particular the Portuguese man-of-war and box jellyfish can cause death if the contact is prolonged and prolific. Jellyfish stings can be treated with vinegar except for a sub-group of the Portuguese man-of-war whose sting is made much worse by it, so it is safer not to use vinegar on man-of-war stings. Pluck off all the tentacles, apply vinegar if appropriate, and if possible treat with ice until the pain subsides.

▲ *Sharks are careful hunters and will avoid what they see as a huge target with lots of limbs. If you group together, face outwards and stay calm, there is every chance that sharks will ignore you.*

▲ *If you can see an attacking shark, you do have a good chance of defending yourself if it's not too big. Kick with your feet or punch with a stiff arm, using the heel of your hand to ward the shark off.*

To find out if something is okay to eat, you'll need to adapt the taste test outlined on page 344 as you won't have the means to cook the food.

SHARKS

If you're with a group of people and stranded in the sea near sharks, the best advice is to bunch together and face outward. Sharks are scared by strong, regular movements and loud noises so if one is close by try slapping the water with cupped hands.

If you are alone, try to float in a horizontal rather than a vertical position: this will slightly reduce the risk of attack because the shark may see you as a live target, not an easy sick or dead one. Swim rhythmically and don't panic. Sharks have highly developed

senses of smell and can detect blood and waste matter from a great distance. Twilight is the most dangerous time, followed by darkness. Few attacks happen in full daylight. They rarely attack brightly coloured things but they see contrasts particularly well, even tan lines. Shiny objects can also look like a small fish-like target to a hungry shark.

OTHER HARMFUL CREATURES

Many species of fish have sharp defensive spines that can puncture your skin, and a small number of these are venomous. Any spines should be viewed with caution. Fish such as the stonefish and greater weaver hide on the seabed in shallow water and can be trodden on by the unwary. Other spiny fish can be accidentally hooked and

sting you when you try to handle them. If in doubt, cut them loose as the venom can be fatal in some cases. If you are injured, remove the spines and flush the wound immediately. Apply very hot water and then hot compresses to try to kill the toxin with heat.

Although it is a small risk, some fish can give you a powerful electric shock if touched. These are electric rays, found at the bottom of temperate and tropical seas, and electric eels, found in tropical rivers. If you get close to one in water, a tingling sensation may warn you of the electrical energy.

Don't take any risks at all with snakes in or near water. There are thousands of different varieties, mostly harmless, but some are extremely venomous and fatal if they bite you.

CATCHING FOOD WITH A SEA ANCHOR

1 Tie a shirt or a similar piece of cloth over the mouth of a sea anchor to act as a sieve before deploying the anchor in the normal way.

2 While the sea anchor is in use the improvised sieve will collect plankton and other small creatures as well as fragments of seaweed.

3 Sort through the marine material you have collected each day and try it out for edibility adapting the taste test described on page 344.

Survival at the seashore

Many accidents and emergencies take place at the water's edge and it is as well to be familiar with the basic skills that can help you survive them, or to understand how your rescuers will act to help you.

There is a lot you can do to help yourself: you should be able to swim at least 50m/51.5yd in your underclothes, and to stay afloat indefinitely without wasting energy. You should also understand the basics of wave action, rip currents and tides.

▶ *The priority if you are in difficulty is to stay afloat, while alerting others to your predicament by waving and shouting.*

SWIMMER–SWIMMER RESCUE

1 A lifeguard or other strong swimmer may attempt a rescue by swimming if they are sure they won't get into the same predicament themselves.

2 The rescuer will swim to the victim as quickly as possible: this man is equipped with a towed float, which will not impede his movements.

3 The exhausted victim is carried ashore by two rescuers: the float has been tied round his waist to keep him afloat and aid the rescue.

CARRYING AN INJURED PERSON

1 Resuscitation is the priority but if rescuers suspect a spinal injury they will carry the victim ashore very carefully while supporting the neck and head.

2 The injured person is lowered to the ground as soon as the shore is reached so that resuscitation can be started in a safe environment.

3 Once breathing is restored the rescuers stabilize the victim to prevent movement and possible further injury until specialist help arrives.

LIFEGUARD RESCUE

1 A lifeguard may effect a rescue using a large, buoyant surfboard, enabling them to get to the victim quickly while maintaining good visual contact.

2 The victim can use the board as support while recovering while their state is assessed by the lifeguard, who stays on board to give stability.

3 The victim can be helped on to the board and paddled ashore by the lifeguard, which is quicker and easier than towing a swimmer.

4 If necessary the victim, who is probably exhausted, can be helped ashore by more rescuers.

5 The rescuers will check the victim over and make sure their condition is stable and not deteriorating.

6 If necessary the victim will be placed in the recovery position and checked for vital signs until medical help arrives.

RIP CURRENTS

1 When waves break on the shore a significant amount of water is pushed up the beach; as this falls back it may gradually build up a sandbar.

2 When the pressure of the returning water creates a channel through the sandbar, it all flows out in one spot. This powerful outflow is called a rip.

3 A distinct flattening of the waves often indicates a rip. Swim directly across it: don't try to make for the beach until you are out of the rip.

Travelling abroad

In spite of the fact that worldwide travel is now an essential part of so many people's lives, whether for leisure or business, there is still a widespread belief that abroad is inherently dangerous, and that a citizen cannot expect the same reasonable treatment from foreign locals that could be relied upon at home. In fact the opposite is more likely to be true.

The biggest danger you face when travelling abroad is probably your own disorientation and the difference between your preconceptions about a place and what is actually happening. You need to approach any situation with the same common sense you would utilize at home, without allowing your lack of knowledge of a foreign culture to flood your mind with irrational fears.

PASSPORTS AND VISAS

You need a passport to travel to most foreign countries and a visa to remain in many. Check on the restrictions before you even begin to arrange a trip, either with the embassy of your destination country or by consulting a professional travel service. You may, for example, need a passport that has at least six months left to run in order to enter certain countries.

On arrival in a foreign country, some travellers become paranoid about their passports, carrying them everywhere as if they were a lifeline. By carrying your passport you run the risk of losing it and having to go through a lot of bureaucracy to get a replacement. In some places foreign passports are quite sought after and you would not want to make yourself a target. Hotels in many countries require you to submit your passport when checking in: instead of arguing, hand it over – it will be more secure in

◄▲ *Legal self-defence sprays can shoot out a thick slimy goo that sticks to an attacker giving you time to react and escape. A bright difficult-to-remove UV dye helps identify the attacker days later. The rapid foaming spray (above) blocks an attacker's view and stains the face in a personal attack.*

▲ *As a visitor in a foreign city, you should not forget to take all the normal precautions you would at home to safeguard yourself and your possessions.*

the hotel safe. The exception to this rule is when your day's itinerary involves crossing a border – if you leave your passport behind you won't be able to complete your trip. This happens in many European ski resorts, for instance, so check before you go out for the day.

On the same note, e-tickets are much safer than paper travel documents, because you can't lose them. All you have to do is get yourself to your point of departure. Leave photocopies and details of any documents you do need to carry, such as air tickets, traveller's cheques and credit or debit cards, at home with a family member or a friend. Make additional copies for yourself and keep them separately from your documents. Consider setting up a web-based internet account and emailing such details to yourself so that you can access them from an internet café in extremis.

Make some effort to understand the monetary system in the country you are visiting, not just the currency and exchange rate with your own but the relative wealth of the local people. Carrying the equivalent of two years'

CHOOSING SAFE TRANSPORT

The safest mode of travel depends on where you are. In parts of many US cities, for instance, it is not safe to walk around, while in some parts of Europe driving is the most dangerous option. You'll see many people in Chinese and Indian cities riding bicycles, but it's not recommended for non-locals. In most countries air travel is advanced and safe, but there are still places you could be taking your life in your hands by getting on a plane. You should always accept expert advice and be prepared to adapt to the local conditions.

average salary around with you in case you need to buy a drink is a great way to get unwanted attention, even in fairly safe and civilized countries.

CULTURAL DIFFERENCES

It is amazing that you can get by knowing only the English language in so many places in the world. However, this is not a reason to be complacent if you are an English speaker. There are a

▼ *It's best to plan excursions in advance through reputable travel agencies or guides. Find out the duration of the excursion and how to get back to your accommodation on your return. Don't join an excursion if the transport looks dangerously overloaded.*

few language issues to consider whenever you visit a foreign country.
• Even if you stand no chance of being able to learn the language, knowing how to say "yes", "no", "please" and "thank you" goes a really long way.
• Consider whether the local language is going to be impossible to read as well as understand. If it is written in a non-Roman alphabet, you aren't even going to be able to read road signs and basic information unless you do some homework before you go.
• From the point of view of safety (or just comfort), differences in body language can be more important than the spoken word. In many ways people are the same the world over, and you

▲ *Normal modes of transport in a foreign country may be very different from what you are used to: in this Chinese industrial city many motorcycles are in fact taxis.*

will of course be able recognize something as basic as a threat or a smile. However, there can be major cultural differences and knowing about these can save you from causing offence or, at worst, from putting yourself at risk. Most good travel guides will give you the information you need on customs and cultural differences in the country you are visiting, so do your homework and find out about appropriate clothing before you go, whether any types of dress are compulsory or advisable (particularly if you are a woman) and whether certain behaviour is illegal or frowned upon.
• Knowing something about what is safe to eat is also a good idea. If the locals eat it, it's probably OK, but you may have a lower resistance to local toxins and bacteria than they do, so stick to food that has been well prepared and cooked.
• Many countries have specific local health problems that you might be vulnerable to. Malaria is a common example. While locals may not take any precautions at all, you need to check before you go whether you are at risk, and obtain the correct medication and inoculations from your doctor.

SURVIVING TERRORISM & CONFLICT

The terrorist strikes out of the blue, when least expected, and almost invariably anonymously. He or she seldom wears a uniform and often takes the coward's way out by planting a bomb and sneaking away before either a timer or remote signal triggers devastation. Even more deadly and effective is the increasingly prevalent, fanatically driven suicide bomber, a development which calls for even more alertness and vigilance in public places and spaces.

Being street smart

Terrorism is usually defined as being the unlawful use of, or the threatened use of, violence against the state or the general public as a politically motivated means of coercion. The 11 September 2001 terrorist attack by Al Qa'eda on the World Trade Center and Pentagon has had a marked affect on both American perceptions of international terrorism and the face of global politics, with the subsequent invasions of Afghanistan and Iraq being just the tip of the iceberg in what President George W. Bush labelled the "War Against Terror". Although 9/11 is seen as the ultimate terrorist act, terrorism is not of course a recent phenomenom. Countries such as Britain and Spain have been victim to prolonged and indiscriminate terror attacks arising respectively from the Northern Ireland "troubles" and the Basque separatist movement. Elsewhere around the globe over the last three or so decades, those seeking to overthrow the state in places as diverse as Zimbabwe, Sri Lanka, Lebanon, the Balkans, Peru, Chechnya and Sierra Leone, to name but a few, have used the bomb and gun as their political tool.

Inevitably, it is the innocent civilian who pays the price. Western holiday destination spots such as Bali and Egypt have also become bombers' targets and there are obvious considerations to be made when planning a vacation – not least checking with government alerts.

SUICIDE BOMBERS

While the United Nations tries to agree on a definition of "terrorism", city dwellers have to go on living with the real and present danger of the bomber strapped with explosives or carrying them in a backpack walking into the crowd, martyring themselves and taking countless innocent lives with them. Survival against this type of terrorist is not easy, should you be unlucky enough to cross their path, but if you have good powers of observation and are alert to the tell-tale signals, you may just survive.

Bombs, or to be more precise improvised explosive devices, are favoured methods of terror delivery. (Kidnappings and hostage-taking are also part of their arsenal and these are dealt with on later pages.) In times of heightened tension, government offices, military establishments, recruitment offices, power and water supply networks, airports and stations all become terrorist targets, and should be avoided where possible.

Anniversaries that are in some way related to the separatists' struggle are obvious magnets for those wishing to either heighten awareness of their

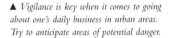
▲ *Vigilance is key when it comes to going about one's daily business in urban areas. Try to anticipate areas of potential danger.*

cause, or to create fear and outrage among the public; the 1987 IRA bomb attack on a Remembrance Sunday service in Enniskillen, which killed 11 and injured more than 60, being just one example of the latter. Through simply being aware of places where and times when the terrorist might be tempted to attack, and altering your plans to avoid these, you greatly reduce your chances of being caught up in such terrorist actions.

▲ *CCTV and identity cards will not stop the fanatical terrorist but they can help in the prevention of future outrages.*

▲ *Police around the world are armed now as a matter of routine which makes lethal outcomes more likely.*

▶ *Public spaces such as rail terminals are obvious targets for indiscriminate terrorist activity and you need to use your powers of observation to spot anything suspicious.*

PUBLIC AWARENESS

Could the Madrid railway bombings of March 2004 have been foreseen? With Spain's support for the Coalition invasion of Iraq in March 2003 and the chance to sway the result of forthcoming elections, the populace and the authorities should have been on heightened alert. More to the point, those in the carriages where the bombs were left unattended in luggage might have realized the potential danger and taken action before it was too late.

On 7 July 2005, after a four-year respite from terrorist bombings, due to the changed political climate in Northern Ireland, London was plunged back into chaos by a series of suicide bombs. This was a tactic never seen before in Britain – though it had been anticipated – and one that is harder to both detect and foil. This time the bombers did not leave unattended packages, but stayed with their lethal devices, dying themselves in the blast. They escaped detection by not standing out. Over 50 innocent civilians died after three bombs, carried in rucksacks, were detonated almost simultaneously in the cramped confines of underground railway carriages across the capital, and a fourth exploded on a city centre bus just under an hour later. At the time Britain was hosting the G8 international political summit, ensuring maximum attention for the terrorists' cause. Exactly two weeks later, an unsuccessful copy attack failed.

WHAT YOU CAN DO

Be street smart. Use your powers of deduction and observational skills to keep you alert to possible terrorist dangers, blending in with your surroundings. What police and military close-protection and undercover operatives dub "playing the grey man", is one of the most important skills to master. If the terrorist can neither single you as a potential target nor mark you out as deserving special

attention, your chances of survival increase dramatically. Don't stand out. Don't be the hero. Don't switch off to

your surroundings. It is probably only you that holds the key to personal survival in a terrorism setting.

SEARCHING FOR CAR BOMBS

1 Check the wheel arches and around the underside where a sandwich box-sized device can be concealed. Memorize what the underside of your car looks like.

2 Check for signs of tampering – such as a forced door or marks or damage around the lock – and peek inside the interior for anything out of place.

3 A mirror on a pole (with a torch attached for checking in the dark), either improvised or a bought one, will help you see into vehicle recesses.

4 Do not assume that just because you cannot see a foreign object under your vehicle it is safe. Before opening the door, check the interior.

Being taken prisoner or hostage

The high profile cases of aid workers and contractors kidnapped in Iraq, Afghanistan and Pakistan once again drew international attention to the methods used by terrorist groups to publicize their cause and how to protect foreign nationals in high-risk countries. To the committed terrorist, seizing an innocent charity worker is a sure way to attract the attention of the international media and in recent years terrorist organizations around the world have shown themselves to have very little or no regard for human life. If you are taken hostage by a terrorist group the situation is extremely grave.

A kidnap for ransom is big business for criminals with or without political leanings. To the gangster, a foreign businessman or engineer employed by a wealthy company can be just as tempting a target as someone who works for a bank vault.

Terrorists and criminals or, to be more specific, their foot soldiers, are not always the most logical or intelligent of people, so you do not need to belong to a high-risk group to be a potential kidnap victim. Mistakes of identity are easily made, or not even worried about, so it is essential that you try at the very least not to look like a

vulnerable target, and also that you take basic precautions to make it harder for kidnappers to seize you. Once again, become the grey man or woman so that you do not stand out from the crowd, and keep your wits about you for potential danger.

EARLIEST ESCAPE ESSENTIAL

If you are taken prisoner, you must attempt to escape at the earliest opportunity. The longer your captors have you, the less your chances are of getting away from them. During the initial lift, you will most likely be simply bundled into a vehicle by one

KIDNAP SCENARIO

1 Those who work with large sums of cash, such as bank employees and payroll staff, and their families, can be potential robbery kidnap victims.

2 If kidnapped outside of the home, a get-away will be needed for the victim. Unless death or serious injury seems likely, try not to go quietly and easily.

3 The best time to escape captivity is immediately on capture while everything is still fluid and out in the open. Seize any opportunity you can.

4 If your captors are distracted, hit out and run. At this stage you are probably too valuable for them to seriously hurt you. Try to escape being incarcerated.

5 Once you know there is no chance of escape, try to befriend and take an interest in your captors. Such bonding might save your life.

6 When your captors are in total control, be submissive to survive; don't be confrontational. Bide your time until an escape plan presents itself.

or two assailants and driven speedily away. Unless you are very switched-on, this part of the operation will pass in a confusing blur, but it offers your first chance of escape. As they throw or drag you through one door, try to use your body's momentum and the power of your limbs to burst out of the opposite door – the chances are that they won't have locked it so that the team can make a quick escape if they run into trouble during the pick-up.

A van offers better rear-door options. Try to burst out through the rear doors as soon as you are lifted, as a broken shoulder and a few cracked ribs is probably a better option than weeks in captivity, or worse. Just try to work out which door of the two opens first before you hit the other one and find that it is secured in such a way that even an elephant would have trouble bursting out.

BUNDLED INTO THE BOOT

Up to now, we have assumed that you are conscious when thrown into the vehicle and that your captors are merely planning on hooding, gagging and binding you once they have you in the back. If they knock you out during the pick-up, the chances are that you will already be trussed up like a turkey by the time you come around, but if they merely throw you into the boot or trunk of a saloon, you may still have a chance. Your captors will have needed to use quite a large car for the boot to be big enough to fit an adult in speedily, and these days most large cars have a cable release to let the driver pop it open from the inside, so see if you can detect such a device running into the inner lock mechanism.

If there is no cable release, it may also be possible to spring the lock from the inside using a tyre lever or even the pressed metal stand for a warning triangle to pry the jaws apart. Chances are that either of these, which are carried as standard in many countries, could be stowed on brackets or in compartments to keep them out of the way and out of view when not needed. Hopefully your kidnappers have not spotted them either.

ESCAPING A LOCKED CAR

1 If you have to kick out a safety glass windscreen, remember the glass won't fall out or separate into pieces. It's held together by laminated plastic layers.

2 To kick out a broken windscreen in one piece brace yourself against the seat. Use a bag, coat or book to protect your feet as your legs strike through the glass.

3 Strike any of the other windows with a hard metal object near the edge of the glass. They will smash quite easily. Avert your eyes or cover them.

4 Clean off the broken shards from the edges of the frame with your chosen tool to avoid serious injury while you are making your escape.

JUMPING ON THE MOVE

If you really believe your life is in peril and the vehicle is speeding away, you will have to jump while travelling at speed. First try to pull the handbrake before opening the door suddenly and pushing yourself out at an angle away from the direction of the car. You will be moving at the same speed as the car so jump where you think you can hit grass or soft ground or undergrowth. Protect your head as much as possible by wrapping your arms around it and keep rolling away in a tucked-in position. (Try to adopt the Paratrooper Roll position shown on page 439.) If you have escaped injury get away fast to avoid re-capture by zig-zagging between any parked vehicles and buildings.

Warning: This is an extremely dangerous manoeuvre and should only be attempted in a truly life-threatening situation.

IF TAKEN HOSTAGE

- Keep calm – your captors will be in a highly emotional state and the situation will be very volatile.
- Don't become aggressive.
- Reassure others if they are showing signs of strain.
- Make yourself useful to your captors as much as possible by helping with other hostages.
- Get rid of any documents that may make the captors single you out.
- Keep your mind alert and look for chances to escape all the time.
- Listen to your captors grievances – don't try to argue politics.
- Talk about your family and show pictures if possible to make yourself more of an individual and less of a victim.

Survival in captivity

Once your captors have brought you to the place where they intend to hold you captive, possibly the first of many places that will be used, your chances of escape will diminish considerably. Here, unlike while they have you in transit, they will be in complete control of you and will no doubt have done their best to ensure that escape is difficult, if not impossible. That does not mean that they will not have made mistakes, and you will probably now have plenty of time to allow your brain to work out where they may have gone wrong, but unless you think that you are worth no more to them alive than dead, it is probably still well worth trying to make a run for it at the earliest opportunity.

EARLIEST ESCAPE ATTEMPT

By making an early escape attempt, you will not only test the resolve of your captors, but may well glean additional information for future attempts. On the other hand, you are likely to receive blows in return at best, or a severe beating at worst. Only you will know if you have the strength of will to take

▲ *Conventional handcuffs are not easy to escape from, but with practice you should be able to slip your hands over your posterior to bring them to the front of the body.*

this. Just remember that every bit of information that you gain on the routine of your captors and the layout outside your immediate prison, could affect how and when you eventually

▼ *Always check the obvious. Don't assume that just because a window has a lock, that it is functional, or that it cannot be forced to give a quiet and simple escape route.*

▲ *Make use of your observational skills to identify captor routines and spot potential escape routes or methods. Don't merely wait for rescue, as it may not come.*

escape. If the room outside your prison door is living accommodation for a large group of armed men, chances are that you will not be going out that way, but if there is only one guard sitting on a chair outside the door and you determine that there is a door or window to the outside world in the room or corridor, you could well be onto an escape route.

GAINING THEIR SYMPATHY

Let's assume that you are of some worth, be that political or financial, to your captors and that they have no reason to torture you for information or pleasure. Ideologically and culturally you could be worlds apart, but your jailers are still human beings, so you should try to find ways of gaining their sympathy and even bonding with them. Anything that will make your life in captivity easier or increase the chances of you escaping should be tried. Do not assume that your government or employer will pay a ransom or make political concessions to those holding you captive, as to do so would be seen as a sign of weakness and would just

▼ *When left on your own, explore all possible escape routes. Try to find a potential way out that can be concealed while you are working on it.*

NYLON CABLE TIES

These days, it is likely that your captor will use cable ties to bind you as they are light and easy to use. They bind the wrists and ankles tighter than cord, are near impossible to break, and cut into the skin if you struggle. You can loosen them by releasing the ratchet lock, but you'll need an accomplice to do so.

lead to more kidnappings. Do not bank on anyone coming to your rescue for a long time, if ever, as you will almost certainly be on your own.

MENTAL AND PHYSICAL TOOLS

Prepare yourself mentally for a long and boring wait, but use your time wisely to find a way out of your predicament. Remember that your mind is the one place that the kidnappers cannot see. To describe every potential way of escaping from a room would take a whole book, and most methods would be of little relevance to your particular situation. That you are reading this book suggests that you are intelligent enough to have read many books and newspaper reports where actual escapes were mentioned, and you are bound to have seen films where the hero breaks out from incarceration. Use your mind to draw parallels with your predicament and discover that chink in their armour that will rid you of your captors.

HOSTAGE SITUATIONS

Terrorism is usually behind most hostage situations, though occasionally a bank robbery may go wrong and the crooks decide to use those in the building as bargaining tools. Either way, if caught up in a situation like this you will be faced with dangerous and possibly unstable captors. As with a kidnapping, grab any opportunity to escape in the initial confusion, but if that is not possible you must try to keep alert.

If your captors are negotiating with the authorities for either political concessions or the opportunity to

escape themselves, there may be times when it is in their interest to release captives. The obvious ones in such a situation are children, women, the aged and the infirm. If you can, convince your captors that you are ill by feigning the symptoms of heart trouble or food poisoning or missing your medication – all can work in your favour. The last thing captors need if using hostages as a bargaining tool are dead or dying prisoners, so if you act convincingly you might just get away with it.

BOUND AND TIED

1 If rope is used to secure your wrists, you have a good chance of loosening and untying it. Tense your fists to gain a degree of looseness.

3 Broad fabric, electrical or gaffa tape is stronger than rope when in tension and if twisted, but carefully nick the edge first and you might tear it laterally.

Play the sympathy card in terms of "understanding" their cause and listen to their grievances. It is often the best way of getting past their guard.

If your captors are terrorists and you belong to a religious or national grouping that they consider to be the enemy, you must try to mask this. Simple things like adopting a fake accent to hide your English or American one could be enough to throw them off the scent. It is the inconspicuous hostage that is most likely to survive.

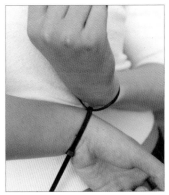

2 Given time alone, and with your hands brought to the front for access, ropes can be loosened further and knots unpicked by using your teeth.

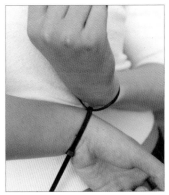

4 A pair of nylon ties is the worst wrist binding to escape from as the thin material cuts into the flesh when put under tension. They need to be cut.

Transport hijacks

Planes, coaches and trains pose an obvious target for terrorists as they provide large numbers of hostages packed into a small, mobile and controllable area. With the notable exception of the 9/11 attack on the World Trade Center and the Pentagon, where the terrorists killed themselves and everyone else on board the aircraft, almost every transport hijack has seen captives being taken primarily for publicity purposes, with most eventually being either released or rescued. However, with an increase in the use of suicide bombers by terrorist organizations, and the willingness of those bombers to take the lives of their captives at the same time, one can no longer afford to just sit back and wait for the men in black to come to the rescue. Any chance to escape must be seized if you want to survive.

SKYJACKING

Escape from an aircraft in flight is virtually impossible, so if it is clear that the hijackers intend taking your and their lives at some point, you have absolutely nothing to lose in attempting to overpower them. This is exactly what happened on Flight 93, the fourth aircraft hijacked on 11 September 2001, and although those who struck out against the terrorists did not succeed in turning the tables, their

heroic attempt did prevent the hijacked aircraft from reaching its intended target and taking countless more lives.

If you are caught up in such a situation, you will have to identify fellow passengers both mentally and physically fit enough to back you up and positioned in the aircraft where they can help you take out all captors at the same time. On many scheduled flights these days, there will be at least one sky marshal aboard, but the hijackers may well have identified and neutralized him or her, so don't bank on help from that direction.

▲ *High value performance cars and expensive 4x4 SUVs make attractive targets for thieves. The easiest way to steal one is to wait for the owner to appear with the keys.*

Unless you have smuggled your own self-defence weapon aboard, you will have to try to identify cabin fittings or items of passenger baggage that could be surreptitiously concealed for use as a weapon. Anything from handbag or camera straps, which could be used as garrottes, to bits of aircraft trim that could be turned into improvised stabbing or slashing weapons, should be

---

CARJACK ESCAPE

1 A hooded criminal with a weapon climbs into the passenger seat and attempts to carjack your car with you in the driving seat. Think quickly.

2 As the driver, you are actually in control. When travelling at a reasonable speed release his belt, if he is wearing one, and step violently on the brakes.

3 Taken by surprise, he should either hit the dashboard or be temporarily incapacitated by the air bag, and you can exit the vehicle quickly.

▲ *An evocative memorial near Shanksville, Pennsylvania, USA, where Flight 93 crashed on 11 September 2001. A National Memorial is being built there to honour the dead. The 40 passengers learned on mobile phones that they were one of four suicide attacks. They decided to fight and nearly succeeded in overcoming their captors.*

▲ *A "close protection" team practises ambush drills on a live-fire range. A high value business target or a contractor working in a conflict zone may need their services.*

▼ *In a "close protection" situation, your bodyguards will run you through possible scenarios and evasive action drills. Pay close attention if you wish to survive.*

identified; even that bottle of duty free spirits could become a cosh. In life or death situations like this, necessity is the mother of invention.

LIKELY SCENARIOS

In most cases the hijackers will gather all captives in one large group, usually at the back of the aircraft, coach or railway carriage, where they pose less threat of coming to the aid of the pilot or driver. Due to the close confines and high seat backs, this could work to your favour by allowing you to communicate with fellow plotters. When you are moved you may have the chance to secure an aisle seat from where you can launch your attempt to overpower the hijackers – assuming that you didn't get the chance to do so during the move itself. Try to stay alert at all times to any opportunities.

Once the aircraft is on the ground, or the coach or train is stationary, it makes sense to try to make a mad dash for freedom as soon as you can. Unless you have loved ones on board, make your move. If you can get to an emergency escape door and open it (instructions are on that aircraft seat pocket card that nobody bothers to read), a broken ankle or two caused by the jump to freedom might just save

your life, and if you roll under the aircraft fuselage when you hit the ground, the hijackers won't be able to shoot you. Escape from a coach or train can be easier, as a sharp hit on the glazing with an escape hammer or any other suitable heavy pointed implement, will give you instant access to the outside world – you just have to be quick and fit enough to take the opportunity when it presents itself.

The most dangerous time for hostages held captive in any mode of transport is the moment when the

security forces try to effect a release, as the smoke, stun bombs and panic bring on a tirade of lethal bullets, while the terrorists may also decide to trigger explosive devices.

If you see your captor is about to trigger explosives, tackling him or her might just be your only chance of survival. However, if this is not an apparent risk try to keep alert, look out for the security forces and their instructions, keep still and avoid any sudden movement that could attract shots in your direction.

Bombs and explosives

The bomb, be it placed in a car, a waste bin, an abandoned suitcase, or strapped to a fanatic's body, is the classic terrorist weapon. Unfortunately, if you happen to be at the wrong place at the wrong time and get caught up in an bomb attack, your survival will very much be determined by where you are sitting or standing at the time impact. Bombers usually strike with little or no warning, or worse, they give a warning that is actually intended to drive victims into the killing zone of the weapon of mass terror.

BEING FOREWARNED

The only ways to guarantee survival from bomb attacks are to be aware of potential targets and therefore avoid them, and to be constantly alert for suspicious packages and individuals. In Israel, where the constant strife between Palestinians and Israelis has seen countless suicide bomb attacks resulting in massive loss of life, police, soldiers and security guards are trained to watch for suspicious signs that could identify the bomber as he or she approaches. Either excess shiftiness and heavy sweating, or a state of euphoria, can betray the potential suicide vest wearer, but so too can the more obvious visual clues such as an excessively bulky torso when the rest of the person is conventionally proportioned. Many Israeli security personnel have lost their lives by spotting a bomber before they reached the intended target and forcing an early trigger, thereby saving countless other innocent lives by their sacrifice.

The suitcase or sports bag bomb, left in an airport, railway station, coach station or even aboard a railway train, is the classic low-risk but high-casualty weapon used by terrorists around the globe. Observation, and avoiding the places where such bombs may be left, are the keys to survival in such cases. If you see unattended luggage or a suspicious package on public transport or in airport or station terminal rest room, give it as wide a berth as possible

and report it to someone in authority. Never, ever, move it or open it to see what is inside, as the clued-up bomb maker will almost certainly have built in some form of anti-handling device.

MOVE ON TO SAFETY ZONES

We cannot avoid being in places that the terrorist may choose as a target, but we can certainly increase our chances of survival by passing through as quickly as possible. At airports, for example, check in early to avoid queues and the need to loiter on the public side. Once you have checked in your hold baggage, move straight through to the departure lounge, where all hand luggage will have been security screened and the chances of a terrorist incident are reduced.

THE DANGER OF FLYING GLASS

In a bomb blast away from the epicentre the vast majority of injuries are caused by flying shards of glass. If you have to spend any length of time in an area at high risk of bomb attack, try to keep well clear of windows and large glazed areas. Normally it is best to position yourself in a corner, facing entrances or doors, from where you can observe everything that is going on around you. However, if you feel exposed and vulnerable, particularly if there is a lot of glazing around, sit with

▲ *The UK has had considerable experience of dealing with modern terrorist attacks since the IRA campaigns in the 1970s.*

your back towards the potential threat area so that at least your eyes are protected, as they are the part of you most likely to be severely injured if on the periphery of the blast area.

▼ *A few sticks of explosive in a backpack – self-detonated or activated by a timing device – is all that is needed to bring a city to its knees and cause appalling injuries.*

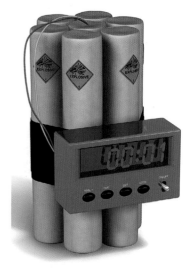

► *In the event of a blast, cover your mouth and nose as emergency protection and get out of the vicinity fast, as another blast might be detonated.*

▲ *Discreetly armoured cars like this Range Rover afford good protection against bullet and blast, but they cost as much as a small home.*

▲ *If you spot a suspicious package or case on a train, don't touch it. Call the authorities and don't be afraid to halt the service.*

SECONDARY DETONATIONS

Very often an initial bomb attack will be followed up with a second blast either to blow up security forces responding to the incident, or kill and maim those missed by the first bomb who are now gathered as a larger target in a muster area. Should you be caught up in a terrorist bomb attack, don't hang around on the periphery or allow yourself to be corralled into a holding area. Get as far away from the scene as you can, as fast as possible, keeping your wits about you and your eyes peeled for potential follow-up attacks.

▲ *The world's underground train systems are particularly vulnerable to terrorist attack. Stay alert and report anything unusual.*

IF A BOMB GOES OFF

1 In the event of a blast away from the epicentre, turn away immediately to protect your eyes and vital organs from flying glass and shrapnel.

2 Throw yourself flat on the floor with your head away from the seat of the blast as shrapnel tends to spread out in an upwards direction.

3 Use your arms to protect your highly vulnerable ears and eyes (the aircraft safety position) if trapped in a confined space with a bomb.

Toxic gases and poisons

The spectre of Weapons of Mass Destruction (WMD) in Iraq has brought the subject of toxic gases, biochemical weapons and other poisons into the public eye, but these nasties have actually been around for the best part of a century. During World War I between 1914 and 1918, both sides used and suffered from poison gas attacks, but in the main these were not used against civilian targets. Then, in the late 1980s, when Saddam Hussein wiped out the population of a Kurdish town in a chemical attack, the topic came into the public eye. During the Iran–Iraq war in the 1980s, both sides had claimed that the other used chemical weapons on the battlefield but, just like with the war itself, few outside the region paid much attention.

It was only when Saddam invaded Kuwait in 1990 that the international community started to panic about the chemical and biological weapons that they believed he was capable of using. This fear rumbled on through the last decade of the 20th century, and when the predominantly Anglo-American

invasion of Iraq took place in 2003, it was the neutralizing of the WMD that was cited as being the driving force. It has now been admitted that no WMD have been found in Iraq, though the fear is that they or their constituent parts may have fallen into the hands of terrorists.

The same can be said for missing stocks of chemicals from the defunct Warsaw Pact days, and periodically the mass media in Europe and America

▲ Minute quantities of toxic, chemical or biological substances can contaminate thousands in minutes. In response, emergency respirators are now much more widely available

runs a scare story on this. The only major use of this type of weapon in a terror attack was when a Japanese religious sect released a quantity of sarin nerve gas on the Tokyo subway in 1995, killing 12 people and affecting over 5,000 others. The chemical used in this incident turned out to be an impure strain which the group had manufactured themselves.

DEADLY AND INVISIBLE AGENTS

Chemical and biological agents of the type likely to be used by terrorists cannot easily be detected before they affect you, and normally the first symptoms are breathing difficulties or vision problems. The one thing which might just save you is the immediate donning of a respirator when you see others beginning to be affected, but even then, there is no guarantee that your model will be proof against the threat, as each chemical or biological agent has its own individual characteristics and general purpose

▼ Specialist decontamination units should eventually take care of any survivors, but it is only through your own efforts that you will be one of those survivors.

▲ *A decontamination team moves into action. The threat of chemical or biological attack by terrorists is very real.*

▲ *A trauma victim (role player) in the aftermath of a terrorist attack.*

masks can only guard against a limited range. However, any protection has to be better than none.

EMERGENCY RESPIRATORS

Since the outbreak of suspected anthrax attacks in the USA following the 9/11 terrorist outrage in New York, Washington and Pennsylvania, and a heightened awareness of how easily terrorists could obtain or manufacture basic chemical or biological weapons, relatively affordable pocket-sized emergency respirators have become available for civilian purchase. As competition kicks in their price is

dropping. If you are a regular passenger on mass transit systems, or if you frequent large public indoor events that could possibly be a tempting target for the terrorist, carrying one of these lightweight masks makes sense.

Some extremist political activist groups, seeking everything from regime change to the stopping of fur wearing or the performing of abortions, have turned away from the letter bomb to the chemical terror attack through the post. Usually some form of odourless powder is used, as sending liquids by mail is much harder. In almost every case, terrorist attacks like these turn out to be well-prepared hoaxes.

Government advice to anyone who may be a possible target for chemical attack, or who deals with mail in a

high-risk industry, is simply to be aware, to not disturb and to clean up afterwards. Awareness of suspicious packages is the first priority, followed by gently opening all mail, with an opener rather than fingers, in a manner that will not disturb the contents.

Once the package is open, preferably on a clear flat surface, it's important not to shake or pour out the contents, nor should one blow into the envelope, as airborne contamination can be the killer. Finally, it's important to clean your hands after dealing with mail, as the second most common form of chemical poisoning is ingestion through the skin.

▼ *Should you fall victim to a chemical or biological attack with no protection to wear, get out into the open as quickly as possible, and fight the urge to panic.*

▼ *By keeping upwind of others who have become contaminated, you will reduce the chances of inhaling or ingesting more poison. But a mask is a must to survive longer term.*

▼ *Attempting to wash off any contaminant – fire hoses are the obvious choice at public venues – will lessen its effects and prolong your chances of survival.*

War zones

Since the end of the Cold War, when the political balance between the American and Soviet superpowers broke down, the world has become a much more unstable place. Nowhere was this more noticeable than in the former Yugoslavia, right in the heart of Europe, where centuries-old hatred boiled to the surface and civil war pitted neighbours who had lived in harmony for nearly half a century against one another in the ultimate battle for survival. Most people think of war as being waged by one government upon another, but in reality it is more often ethnic or religious differences that bring about wars, many being civil wars rather than wars between nations.

WAR ZONE SURVIVAL
Survival in a war zone, where you not only have to avoid the enemy but also battle against mother nature when the infrastructure collapses around you, depends primarily on three basics:
• You must have the abilities to adapt as conditions deteriorate around you.

▼ *As thunder follows lightning, so a blast and shockwave will follow the initial explosive flash, so keep down and brace yourself.*

• You need to be able to construct a refuge that you and your loved ones can retreat to, certainly for days and maybe for weeks on end as the battlefront hopefully passes by.
• You have to build and maintain stocks of water, food and essentials to get you through the hardest times. The very fact that you are reading this book probably means that you are probably someone with a grasp of that first basic – the ability to adapt.

▲ *Ship and ferry hijacks are on the increase. Here Scandinavian and Dutch special forces recapture a hijacked ship during a maritime counter-terrorism exercise.*

WAR ON YOUR DOORSTEP
While there will be some who have the ideal base for a refuge in the form of a cellar, the vast majority of the population of the developed world are town or city dwellers and that will probably not be an option. In such circumstances it will be necessary to turn one room, preferably the one with the fewest outer walls and windows, into a refuge with both sleeping accommodation and emergency water and food stocks.

A survival cell should be constructed in one corner of the room, ideally the one farthest from outside walls and closest to a stairway where the structure will be stronger. You will need to improvise some overhead protection against falling rubble caused by nearby explosions, so under the stairs is a sensible option if there is sufficient space. The survival cell should be your main sleeping area, and it is also where your emergency water and medical supplies should be kept. If the fighting gets close, or if your locality is subject to bomb or artillery attack, you should retreat there immediately.

It is essential that adequate stocks of basic, non-perishable foodstuffs are stocked in your refuge, but stocks of drinking water are more important. The human body is remarkably resilient and can survive for weeks on little or no food, but without drinking water you will last only a few days.

In towns and cities, the two first major casualties of war tend to be power supplies and piped water, mainly because power stations are key targets for attackers, and the water supply relies on electricity to pump it out to homes and businesses. Limited emergency water can be kept in the bath, protected by a tarpaulin or board, but even if you seal around the plug with silicone before filling it to avoid any leakage, one bath of water is unlikely to last for long. As time passes you will have to use precious fuel supplies to boil the water to ensure it is still safe to drink. Maintaining stocks of bottled drinking water, preferably in 50-litre plastic containers or larger, is a good idea.

▼ *In addition to constantly training with each other police and military counter-terrorist teams regularly exchange information and techniques internationally.*

It is also sensible to maintain a large stock of basic long-life foodstuffs in your refuge, especially high-protein canned meat, fish and beans. Do not be tempted to store too much low-bulk dehydrated foodstuffs, or things like pasta and oats which require water for their preparation, as you will need to use valuable drinking water and fuel to make a meal. In peacetime cold beans or beef stew may not seem too appetizing, but if you are stuck in your survival cell for days at a time, as fighting rages all around, you will look forward with great anticipation to mealtimes of cold canned food.

▶ *Breathable, warm, windproof and waterproof gear is essential when the power supplies are cut off. A feather-down duvet will provide good insulation.*

▲ *Curfews are commonly set for dusk to dawn so security forces can keep a lid on terrorism or insurgency. You must not go outside at such times as you are putting yourself in unnecessary danger.*

Survival in the workplace

To the terrorist, the commercial world can sometimes be a better target than the civilian population. Society cannot easily function without bureaucracy, banks and big business, so the public servant, bank employee and business executive can easily find themselves in the front line. In recent years every "direct action" group, from animal rights activists and anarchists through to religious fundamentalists, has attacked businesses and the symbols of Western capitalism either to publicize their cause, to create a climate of fear in society at large, or to hammer home their political stance, so the laboratory technician, the office worker and even the counter assistant in the burger bar can also find themselves at risk.

If anarchists are attacking where you work, it is most likely to be during a public order crisis and the assault will probably be overt and aimed primarily at the premises, so your personal survival should not be too much of an issue. Just take off your work uniform and leave quietly by the side entrance. However, if political activists or religious fundamentalists pick on you, the attack is likely to be less overt.

LETTER BOMBS
The letter or parcel bomb and, to a lesser extent, hazardous substances such as toxins or biochemical agents, are the primary method of attack, and must be guarded against if you work for a high-risk commercial or government target.

▲ *The 6m/20ft tall cast iron "cross" found in the rubble of the World Trade Center was adopted by rescue workers as a symbol of faith.*

Usually, it will be the post-room worker or the secretarial assistant who falls victim to these devices, but if you open your own mail you must be aware of the potential threat.

Often bomb or hazardous-substance attacks against businesses involve carefully constructed hoax packages, as the fear of attack is often just as effective as the real thing, and the dangers of losing public sympathy by maiming or killing the wrong victim are less. Even so, the stress and trauma of opening a package and finding it contains a fake bomb or a mysterious powder along with a warning message is not a pleasant experience.

With the spread of the internet since the late 1990s, anyone with a grudge and the most basic technical skills can learn how to build a cheap and effective improvised explosive device from easily sourced components, so the threat has never been greater. To the anti-vivisectionist attacking pharmaceutical company employees, the political activist attempting to disrupt government departments or even the disgruntled former employee seeking revenge, the bomb delivered by

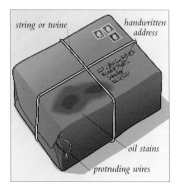

◀ *The parcel bomb has long been a method of attack for separatist and animal rights terrorists. Incorrectly addressed labels, twine bindings or odd bulges can be warning signs.*

string or twine

handwritten address

oil stains

protruding wires

post is an anonymous and effective weapon. The last thing that most terrorists want is to be easily traced, so they will try to leave as few clues as possible on the packaging.

If the address is handwritten – and in most cases it will be as setting up computer-printed address labels can leave incriminating evidence – the writer will almost certainly try to disguise their handwriting, but the human eye and brain can usually easily spot this, so the first line of defence is to read the label. The device will also have been packaged so that it does not go off in transit and it is unlikely to be timer-driven due to the vagaries of the postal system, so handling it unopened should be safe. If it looks suspicious or feels suspicious, simply back off and call in the experts. It is better to be an embarrassed survivor than a dead fool!

LESSONS FROM 9/11
Since 9/11, businesses – especially in high-rise buildings – have taken risk assessment much more seriously with routine "major incident" evacuations and fire drills being timed and assessed. The 9/11 outrage was perpetrated by

terrorists, but it could just as easily have been a terrible accident (after all, a B-25 bomber had crashed into the 78th floor of the Empire State Building on 28 July 1945) and it was one which was actually foreseen when the building was originally designed. Back in those days, wide-bodied jets had yet to take to the skies, so the designers underestimated the size of the aircraft that eventually tested their foresight, but even so they provided sufficient means of escape for all survivors beneath the impact-affected floors to escape. What they could not factor in was that some people failed to get out at the first sign of trouble, resulting in them perishing when the towers eventually collapsed.

The Twin Towers had already been the subject of a major bomb attack by the same group, which caused several deaths and badly damaged the

FREEFALL

You sometimes hear that you should jump immediately before an elevator crashes, so you would be "floating" at the second of impact. Chances are your freefall will be slowed by the compression of air at the bottom of the shaft as it fell (like a piston compresses air in a bicycle pump). The air pressure would slow the elevator down. Also many cable elevators have built-in shock absorbers at the bottom of the shaft – to cushion the impact. Either try to cling on to a ledge as shown or lie flat on the floor so that no single part of your body takes the brunt of the blow.

lower floors, so people working there could have realized they were a potential terrorist target. When the first plane struck, with such devastating consequences and igniting several floors, many workers in both the neighbouring tower and on the lower, unaffected floors of the first tower, remained in their offices rather than following the well-documented emergency evacuation plans. Instead of looking to their personal survival, they waited either to be told what to do, or assumed that the emergency services would have the matter in hand.

OFFICE SAFETY

Remember that it is down to you as the individual to make your own risk assessment before trouble strikes, and have a plan to ensure your survival. Just in case that fateful day comes (and bear in mind that we could just as easily be talking of a building fire or a natural disaster as a terrorist attack), you should be well aware of how to get out by both the fastest route and by at least one secondary one should your first choice be unusable. In an emergency, you cannot count on the electricity and lighting supplies being maintained, as back-up systems could well be taken out by the incident, so make sure you know how to escape in the dark as well.

It makes sense to work as close to your emergency escape route as possible, so try to engineer this if at all

▲ *Check your company has fully implemented evacuation procedures in the event of a terrorist incident.*

possible. Time is precious in an emergency situation, and if you have to fight your way through a packed open-plan office with dozens of terrified workmates, you will already be at a disadvantage. If you have a say in the matter, opt for having your workplace near the emergency exit.

By their very nature, internal fire escapes tend to be the strongest parts of buildings, being either in the central core, or at the corners or ends of buildings where they form a self-standing structural feature. This is another good reason to have your workplace sited near them. If a vehicle bomb is used against the building, these are the areas most likely to suffer the least structural damage and subsequent collapse, thereby increasing your chances of survival.

Be aware that after blast trauma, flying glass presents the major injury hazard to most people. Even a bomb exploding several hundred metres away against a totally unrelated target will cause most windows in the vicinity to shatter, with terrifying results. It is tempting to sit near windows so that the view will break up the monotony of office life, but should the terrorist strike nearby, that view may well be the last thing you see.

LIFE-SAVING
FIRST AID

Understanding first aid, and how to apply it, is a vital life skill for extreme
survival and crucial in serious emergencies. If you know the basic
techniques you can sustain a victim of an accident or sudden emergency
until professional help arrives on the scene. At home or on a crowded
street, the support you give can mean the difference between life and
death, and if you are in a remote or dangerous environment you'll be
much farther away from paramedics, so you really
need to know what to do.

First-aid essentials and assessment

When someone has been injured, first aid is literally the very FIRST assistance you give. First aid help can cover an extremely varied range of scenarios – from simple reassurance after a small accident to dealing with a life-threatening emergency. In every case, a speedy response is crucial. Emergency workers refer to the first hour after an accident as the golden hour: the more help given within this period, the better the outcome will be for the injured person.

THE GOALS OF FIRST AID
- To keep the person alive. The ABC of life support – Airway, Breathing and Circulation – constitutes the absolute top priority of first aid.
- To stop the injured person's condition getting worse.
- To promote their recovery.
- To provide reassurance and comfort to the person.

In any emergency, the first essential is for you to stay calm. The second requirement is to assess the situation promptly and accurately. Once you

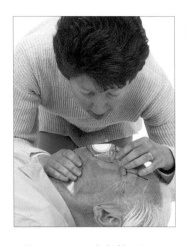

▲ *You can use a mouth shield to give mouth-to-mouth resuscitation. If you do not have one, placing a handkerchief over the person's mouth gives some protection.*

understand the problem you should follow the DRSABC sequence, which is designed to help you prioritize your actions and minimize risks to you and the injured person:

1 **Danger: Your assessment should have alerted you to any potential hazards. Now you should:**
- Keep yourself out of any danger.
- Keep bystanders out of danger.
- Make safe any hazards, if you can do so without endangering yourself or others. Only in extreme circumstances should you move the injured person away from danger.

2 **Response: Try to establish the responsiveness level.**
- If the person appears unconscious or semi-conscious, speak loudly to them – as in "Can you hear me?".
- If this fails to get a response, tap them firmly on the shoulders.

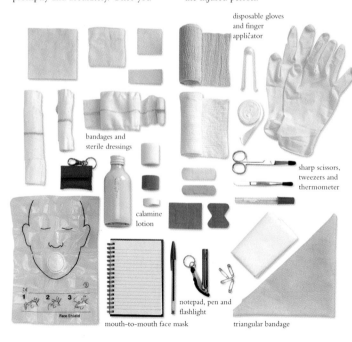

disposable gloves and finger applicator

bandages and sterile dressings

calamine lotion

sharp scissors, tweezers and thermometer

notepad, pen and flashlight

mouth-to-mouth face mask

triangular bandage

◀ *A first-aid kit, packed in a watertight box, should contain adhesive and sterile dressings in various sizes, gauze dressings and pads, tubular and roller bandages, safety pins, a thermometer, scissors and surgical gloves. Pen, paper and a torch are useful.*

3 Shout: If no response to step 2:
- Shout out loudly to anyone in the area for help with the situation.

4 Airway: Now determine whether the airway (the passage from the mouth to the lungs) is clear enough to allow proper breathing.
- Check the mouth and remove any visible obvious obstructions, such as food, at the front of the mouth only.
- Tilt the person's head back gently to prevent the tongue from falling back and blocking the airway. Place a hand on the forehead/top of head and two fingers under the jaw. Tilt back gently until a natural stop is reached.

5 Breathing: Is the person breathing?
- LOOK to see if the chest is moving.
- LISTEN for breathing sounds – put your ear against their mouth.

- FEEL for expired air by placing your cheek or ear close to their face.
- CHECK for other signs of life – body warmth, colour, ability to swallow.
- If these checks are negative, the casualty is probably not breathing. Now CALL THE EMERGENCY SERVICES. Ideally, get someone else to do this.
- Without delay, start artificial respiration procedures (giving two breaths): see next page.

6 Circulation: Look for signs of a working circulation.
- Check for breathing, coughing or any movement.
- Never waste time trying to find a pulse unless you are trained to do so.
- If there are no signs of a circulation, start cardiac massage (chest compressions) if trained to do so.

GETTING HELP
Phoning the emergency services is free on all kinds of phone. If the person is inside a building, ask someone to stand outside to guide the ambulance. If you are in a building and it's dark outside, switch on any outside lights. Tell the emergency services:
- Whether the person is conscious and breathing – information you will have if you have followed DRSABC.
- Your location and phone number.
- Your name.
- What the problem is and what time it happened.
- Number of victims, their sex and age.
- Report any hazards, such as ice on the road or hazardous substances.
- Don't hang up the telephone until the authorities tell you to do so.

FIRST-AID ASSESSMEMT

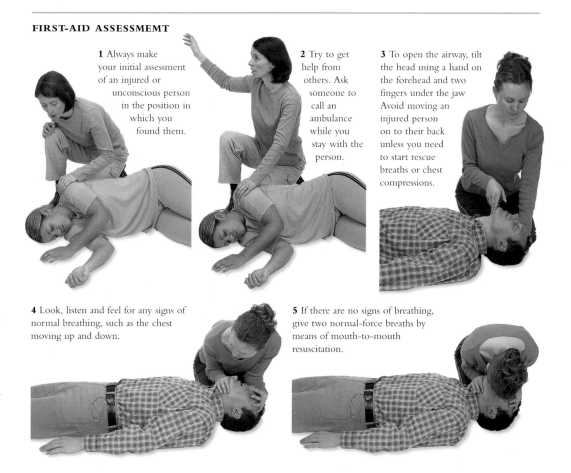

1 Always make your initial assessment of an injured or unconscious person in the position in which you found them.

2 Try to get help from others. Ask someone to call an ambulance while you stay with the person.

3 To open the airway, tilt the head using a hand on the forehead and two fingers under the jaw Avoid moving an injured person on to their back unless you need to start rescue breaths or chest compressions.

4 Look, listen and feel for any signs of normal breathing, such as the chest moving up and down.

5 If there are no signs of breathing, give two normal-force breaths by means of mouth-to-mouth resuscitation.

Rescue and resuscitation

Cardiopulmonary resuscitation (CPR) is the technique of providing basic life support using chest compressions and artificial ventilation (mouth-to-mouth respiration or rescue breathing). CPR is needed after a cardiac arrest: that is, when the heart suddenly stops beating and circulation ceases. A person who has had a cardiac arrest is unresponsive to voice or touch, is not breathing and has no pulse.

After only 3–4 minutes without oxygen, the brain can suffer irreversible damage and this can be fatal, so you should act swiftly. In most cases, a little knowledge and training can definitely save lives. If CPR is started within seconds of the cardiac arrest, the victim has a significantly improved chance of surviving.

In normal circulation, the heart pumps blood to the lungs where it absorbs oxygen and gives up carbon dioxide. The blood then returns to the heart, and the oxygenated blood is sent to all parts of the body, including the

brain. The brain controls all body functions, including those of the heart and lungs, and the working of these three organs is closely linked. If any one fails, it does not take long for the other two organs to fail too.

▲ *Never jump in the water when dealing with a potential drowning. Hand the person something to hold on to. If nothing is available, lie down and extend your arms so that they can haul themselves up to the safety of the bank.*

RESCUE BREATHING

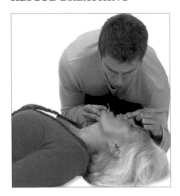

1 This is also known as mouth-to-mouth respiration. Maintaining the head tilt and pinching the nose, open your mouth wide and take a deep breath. Put your mouth against the injured person's mouth and make a tight seal with your lips around their mouth, so that when you breathe out no air escapes around the sides.

2 Breathe out steadily into the person's mouth, making this breath last for about 2 seconds. If you are in the correct position, you will see their chest rising as you breathe out. If you do not think you are getting air into their lungs on this first attempt, reposition the person's head, keeping the airway open, and try again.

3 Check for circulation signs: breathing, coughing or movement. If there are signs of circulation, continue giving rescue breaths until the paramedics arrive. Every 10 breaths (about once a minute), pause and spend a few seconds checking to see that there are still signs of a circulation. If there are no circulation signs, start cardiac compressions.

RESPONSIVENESS

You must assess an injured person's responsiveness before acting. Their level of consciousness may be anything from fully alert to a deep coma. If they have any level of response, they don't need to be resuscitated, but it is very important that their airway is kept clear and that you can see signs of breathing and circulation.

HOW CPR WORKS

Keeping the person's airway open, breathing for them and doing chest compressions means that an oxygenated blood supply will continue to reach their brain. This can "buy" really valuable time by keeping the brain alive until more specialized help becomes available to restore the circulation.

If someone has stopped breathing, their brain will soon be deprived of oxygen and there will be a build-up of toxic carbon dioxide in the blood. You can breathe for them by artificial ventilation, but if the heart has stopped as well, you must give chest compressions to help move the oxygenated blood around the body.

CHEST COMPRESSIONS

The blood is kept circulating by the use of external chest compressions. By pressing down on the breastbone, blood is forced out of the heart and into the rest of the body. When the pressure is released, the heart fills up with more blood, ready for the next compression. The procedure is done at a rate of 80–100 compressions per minute.

For cardiac compressions to be effective, the person should be lying flat on their back on a firm surface such as the floor or the ground. It's vital that you learn the correct technique from a trained first-aider. If done incorrectly heart massage may not work, and you may also cause damage to surrounding structures, such as the ribs or liver. Never practise compressions on conscious volunteers, as you may cause harm. Always use a first-aid dummy.

To find the compression site, run the fingers of the hand nearer the person's waist along the lower ribs until they meet the breastbone at the centre of the ribcage. Keeping your middle finger at this notch, place your index finger over the lower end of

the breastbone. Place the heel of the other hand on the breastbone and slide it down to lie beside the index finger. The heel of your hand is now on the compression site.

DROWNING

Knowing what to do in a near-drowning incident can definitely save life: it is the third commonest cause of accidental death.

Drowning causes death by suffocation, usually because water enters the lungs and rapidly causes respiratory failure. "Dry drowning" occurs when a small amount of water makes the upper airways go into spasm.

Remember that the victim may have swallowed a lot of water as well as inhaling it. If they vomit, they may inhale the swallowed water into their lungs. To avoid this, try to keep their head lower than the rest of their body when you take them out of the water.

If the victim is not breathing, and the water is shallow enough for you to stand, start rescue breaths in the water. If their heart has stopped, remove them from the water and start CPR.

CHEST COMPRESSIONS

1 Adopt a position where you are kneeling at right angles to the person halfway between their shoulders and waist. Check for a circulation by looking for breathing, coughing or movement. If there are no signs of circulation, perform 15 chest compressions and then give two breaths via mouth-to-mouth.

2 Locate the compression site and place the heel of one hand over it. Place the heel of the other hand on top with fingers interlaced. Place your shoulders over your hands to concentrate pressure at the compression site. Compress the chest wall by 4–5cm/1^1/$_2$–2in. Release the pressure without lifting your hands or bending your elbows.

3 You must continue in cycles of two breaths to 15 chest compressions until expert aid arrives, because the person's circulation is unlikely to resume functioning without advanced techniques such as defibrillation – you are just keeping things going until help arrives with specialized equipment.

Moving an injured person

There are good reasons for leaving an injured person in place until more skilled personnel arrive. Injuries to the spine, especially to the neck, are possible after accidents and falls, and further movement can cause serious damage to the spinal cord. You may have to use some movement to deal with an injury, but the golden rule after an accident is not to move an injured person unless they are in danger, need to be resuscitated, or are unconscious and must be put into the recovery position.

▲ *In the recovery position the thigh is at right angles to the hip, as shown, and the person is completely stable. The knee acts as a prop and prevents them rolling forwards.*

EVALUATING RELATIVE RISKS

Never move an injured person if there is any chance that they could have a spinal injury, especially in the neck area. Sometimes, however, you will have no choice in the matter – the person may not be breathing and the airway must always take first priority. See pages 500–501 for advice on how

to approach this. Very rarely, it may be vital to move the injured person into a safer environment, perhaps because of fire or the danger of gunfire or explosion, or even drowning.

If you have to move someone on your own, you must know how to move people without causing further

injury or endangering yourself, keeping your back straight and the weight close to your body. Otherwise, doing nothing may be wiser – it is a question of weighing up the relative perils. Also, think laterally: it may be easier to remove the danger from the person than the other way around. For instance, if an accident victim is lying in a busy street, park your vehicle so that others will drive around the incident area.

MOVING SOMEONE WITH HELP

It is much easier and less likely to cause further injury if two or more people help to move someone. If the injured

▼ *Cradle carry. This method works particularly well with children and helps them to feel reassured and safe. Never attempt this lift on someone unless they are a great deal lighter than you, as you may damage your back; there is also the danger of dropping the person and causing further injury.*

▼ *Piggyback. Use this only in a severe emergency and if confident of your strength. With your back to the person, bend forward and get them to put both arms over your shoulders. Pull them on to your back and grasp their thighs. If you can, take hold of their hands. Try to keep your knees slightly bent while walking.*

▼ *Two-hand seat. This can be done with a minimum of two helpers. Squatting on either side of the casualty, each helper should cross their arms across the back of the injured person. Holding on to the casualty's clothes, they should then pass their hands under the casualty's knees and grip each other's wrists. Remaining close to the casualty, they should then lift, keeping knees bent and backs straight to reduce risk of injury to themselves.*

▲ *Use the upturned hem of a jacket as an improvised sling for an injured arm. Leave the hand exposed to check circulation.*

person is unconscious or immobilized, you can try a fore and aft carry. This can also be used if the person is conscious, but should be avoided if the arms, shoulders or ribs are injured. With an unconscious or immobile victim and two helpers, the stronger should take the upper body and the other the legs. Make sure you synchronize your actions and move in the same direction. Move slowly and carefully and watch out for any obstacles such as steps or stairs.

If there is an immediate risk to life, such as fire or water, that outweighs the danger of movement, very carefully roll

the victim away from the danger with as many helpers as possible supporting and controlling the body to minimize damage. All helpers must act in sync when rolling the victim.

If four helpers are available and you have a blanket or piece of cloth, a blanket lift provides a safe, supportive method – except when spinal injury is suspected. With the injured person on their side, and the blanket edge rolled up lengthways, position the roll against their back. Move them over the rolled edge, on to their other side. Roll up the other long edge of the blanket. Two helpers on either side grasp the rolls firmly with both hands to lift the person, with head and neck supported.

THE RECOVERY POSITION

Placing an injured person in the recovery position means that they are in a secure pose that ensures an open airway and also allows any fluid to drain from their mouth.

Kneeling to one side of the person, straighten out the arms and legs. Place the lower arm nearest to you at right angles to their body, elbow bent with the palm uppermost. Bring the furthest arm up and over the chest, and place the person's hand against their face, palm facing outward. Holding this hand in place against their cheek, pull up their leg on the same side, so that the knee is bent and the foot is flat on the ground. Begin to pull this leg towards you.

▲ *If you are in a very remote location and have to move someone with a fractured leg, you may need to splint it. Add extra padding around the limb and keep movement to a minimum.*

Continuing to support their hand against their face, pull them by the leg towards you, until their bent knee touches the ground. Check the airway, tilting their head back to keep it open. You may need to adjust the hand under their cheek, so that it is in the correct position to keep the airway open. Adjust the bent leg so that the thigh is at right angles to the hip and the position is completely stable. The knee acts as a prop to prevent the person from rolling forward.

If you need to leave an injured person to get help, this is a safe position, but check on their breathing and circulation as soon as you return.

MOVING AN UNCONSCIOUS CASUALTY WITH HELP

If the casualty is unconscious or immobilized as a result of their injuries, and there are at least two of you to help, you can attempt a fore and aft carry. This can also be used if the person is conscious, but should be avoided if you suspect that the arms, shoulders or ribs may be injured.

The stronger of the two helpers should take the upper body, and the other person should support the legs. Make sure you synchronize your actions and move in the same direction. Move slowly and watch out for any obstacles such as steps or stairs.

If four helpers are available, and you have a blanket or a large piece of cloth to hand, a blanket lift provides a safe, supportive method of transporting an unconscious casualty, except when spinal injury is suspected, in which case it should be avoided. Remember that if there is an immediate risk to life, such as fire or water, that outweighs the danger of movement, very carefully roll the victim away from the danger with as many helpers as possible to support and control the different areas of the body. The log roll technique is explained on pages 500–501.

▲ *The fore and aft carry. Lock your arms around the casualty's chest and move only when you are sure that the second helper is supporting the legs.*

Dressing wounds

Even minor wounds can become infected and cause real problems with the victim's health. However, most bites, grazes and cuts heal without too much trouble and are easily treated. It is important that you are aware of the type of wound sustained so that you can carry out the appropriate first aid. Some wounds, such as puncture wounds, are more likely to cause damage to the underlying tissues and organs, and really need professional assessment by medical personnel.

TYPES OF WOUND

There are two main types of wound: closed and open. Closed wounds are usually caused by a blunt object, and vary from a small bruise to serious internal organ damage. A bruise the size of the injured person's fist would cause substantial blood loss.

Open wounds range from surface abrasions to deep puncture wounds. A laceration is a wound with jagged edges, which may cause heavy bleeding. As the object causing the wound may be very dirty, the risk of subsequent infection is high. Incisions are clean-edged cuts, such as those caused by a knife or broken glass, and may be deep. The wound may look relatively harmless, but there can be considerable damage to underlying tendons, nerves, blood vessels and even organs. Deep incisions may be

life-threatening, especially if the injury is around the chest or abdomen, and bleeding from incisions can take some time to stop.

Puncture wounds can be tricky to assess, as the size of the external wound gives no clue to how deep it goes (and the extent of tissue damage). Professional assessment may be needed.

All bites carry a high risk of infection, with human bites almost invariably becoming infected – a doctor should see any human bite at all, in case antibiotics are needed.

Guns can inflict many types of wound, and bleeding can be external and internal. Handguns, low-calibre rifles and shotguns fire fairly low-velocity projectiles, which usually stay in the body, while high-velocity bullets from military weapons often leave entry and exit wounds. High-velocity bullets create powerful shock waves that can break bones and cause widespread damage.

The cutting or tearing off of body parts needs urgent help. Keep the severed part dry and cool and take it to hospital along with the person, as reattachment may be possible.

BASIC FIRST AID FOR MAJOR WOUNDS

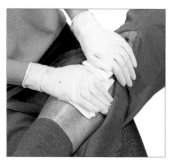

1 Expose the whole of the wound to assess the injury. Do not drag clothing over the wound, but cut or lift aside the clothing.

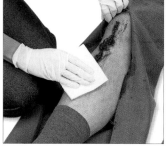

2 Using a gauze pad, clear the surface of the wound of any obvious debris such as large shards of glass, lumps of grit or mud.

3 Control bleeding with direct pressure and then by elevating the limb.

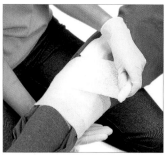

4 Once bleeding is controlled, apply a bandage to the wound.

FIRST AID FOR MINOR WOUNDS

Avoid touching the wound, in order to prevent infection. Find out how and where the wound was caused. Wash it

BANDAGING A LIMB

1 Place the tail of the bandage below the injury and work from the inside to the outside, and from the furthermost part to the nearest.

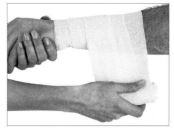

2 Roll the bandage around the limb and start with two overlapping turns. Cover two-thirds of each turn with the new one. Finish with two overlapping turns.

3 Once you've finished, check the circulation; if the bandage is too tight, unroll it and reapply it slightly looser.

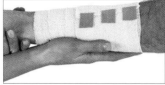

4 Secure the end with pieces of adhesive tape or tie the ends of the bandage using a reef knot.

under running water, or with bottled or boiled water. Dry the wound and apply a sterile adhesive dressing (plaster or Band-aid). For wounds that extend over a larger area, it may be better to use a non-adhesive dressing, sterile dressing and bandage. The wound must be kept clean and dry for the next few days.

A wound needs to stay fairly dry: wounds kept damp are more likely to become infected and can take longer to heal. If a dressing becomes wet, it should be changed for a dry one. Small wounds, grazes and blisters respond well to exposure to the air – provided dirt is unlikely to get into them.

INFECTED WOUNDS

Sometimes a wound becomes infected despite having been cleaned and dressed correctly. Some people are more vulnerable to infection, including those with diabetes, or with a compromised immune system.

You may notice the first signs of infection in and around a wound within hours, but it frequently takes longer to manifest itself. The infection may not surface until a day or two after the injury. Pain, redness, tenderness and swelling are all signs of infection. The person may also experience fever and notice pus oozing from the wound.

Infection may spread under the skin (cellulitis) and/or into the bloodstream (septicaemia). Suspect cellulitis if there is redness and swelling beyond the wound site. The glands in the armpits, neck or groins may be tender, and there may be a red line going up the limb towards the glands. Suspect septicaemia if the person feels unwell, with a fever, thirst, shivering and lethargy. These conditions require medical treatment. Tetanus can contaminate the tiniest of wounds, so immunization must be kept up to date.

Cover an infected wound with a sterile bandage. Leave the surrounding area visible, so that you can monitor signs of spreading infection. Elevate and support the area if possible and get medical help for the injured person as soon as possible.

DRESSING A WOUND WITH AN EMBEDDED OBJECT

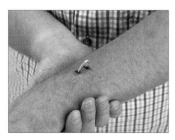

1 Do not try to remove this kind of embedded object as you may cause further damage. Your aim is to deal with bleeding and protect the area from infection, and to get aid promptly.

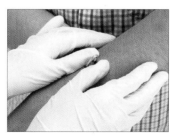

2 If the wound is bleeding, apply pressure to the surrounding area with your hands. Never apply pressure directly on to an embedded object. Elevating the wounded part will also help.

3 Place padding around the object. If possible, as it would be here, build this padding up until it is as high as the embedded object, ready to bandage over smoothly.

Bone fractures

In the short term, the various methods used to deal with fractures focus on preventing the fracture from becoming worse. This is all you can hope to achieve in a wilderness situation, without proper medical expertise or equipment. The general idea is to immobilize the fracture and the joints above and below it, and this can be done either by cradling the affected limb or by surrounding it with padding.

Moving a fracture can cause severe pain, as well as damage to surrounding tissue and structures, and possibly further complications, such as shock, from bleeding or from bone penetrating through skin, nerves or blood vessels. Before dealing with a fracture, check that there are no other injuries that require more immediate treatment.

HAND OR ARM IMMOBILIZATION
This can be used on a fracture to the normally rigid bone of the hand or arm. Use your own hands and arms to cradle the injured limb in order to stop all movement. This method is most appropriate when medical help is expected to arrive fairly quickly, or when no other equipment or first aid materials of any kind are available.

If you are dealing with a simple fracture to an arm, and you are confident that bending the limb will not cause further damage, it will be more secure and convenient to put the arm in a broad arm sling in order to prevent movement, rather than to hold it. Have a sling in your first aid kit.

USING PADDING AND BOXES
These props are used mostly for leg fractures, though they are also suitable for arm fractures when bending the elbow to put the arm in a sling would cause further damage.

For this method, hold the fractured limb still, then roll large, loose sausage shapes from sweaters, towels or sleeping bags, and place gently against the limb. Fill any gaps beneath the limb, such as from a bent knee, with just enough padding material to provide support without moving the limb at all. Finally, place backpacks, boxes or other heavy items on either side of the limb to hold the padding in place.

This method is ideal if you can leave the injured person where they are until medical help arrives because it frees you as the first aider to concentrate on taking care of them.

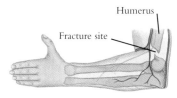

▲ *Fractures of the humerus above the elbow are common in children, whereas adults are more likely to fracture the shoulder end of this bone.*

SYMPTOMS OF A FRACTURE

- The injured person may have a visible history of impact or trauma at the fracture site.
- Bone may be penetrating the skin.
- Swelling, bruising or deformity may be visible at the fracture site. These may worsen over time.
- The person may feel pain on moving the limb.
- The person may feel numbness or tingling in the injured area.
- There may be additional wounds at or near the fracture site.
- The person may have heard the bones crack or grate against one another at the time of impact.

APPLYING A SLING FOR A SIMPLE ARM FRACTURE

1 Ask the person to keep the arm still. Support the fracture and apply light padding, such as folded bubble wrap or a small towel (nothing too bulky).

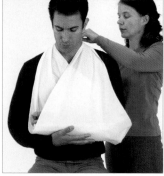

2 The fracture should be immobilized completely. Apply a broad arm sling as shown, keeping the light padding in place within the sling.

3 Tie a second bandage across the chest to stabilize the sling and prevent movement when the person is in transit to hospital. Seek medical help.

COMMON FRACTURE TYPES

Simple or closed fracture
There is a clean break in the bone, with no displacement of the bone and no penetration of the skin.

Compound or open fractures
The broken ends of the bone stick out through the skin. The chance of infection is much higher.

Greenstick fracture
The fracture is on only one side of the bone, and the unbroken side bends over like a pliable young tree branch. This type of fracture is common in children.

Comminuted fracture
The bone is splintered at the fracture site, and smaller fragments of bone are found between two main fragments.

Fracture dislocation
The bone breaks or cracks near an already dislocated joint.

Avulsion fracture
A ligament or muscle attached to a bone has ripped off, taking a piece of the bone with it.

SPLINTS
Rigid supports for fractures are rarely used by medical professionals today, but they are useful if you are in a remote location when the accident occurs, and may have a long wait for professional help, or are forced to move the patient to reach a safe area. Improvised examples of splints include ice axes and shovel handles, or even sturdy, stripped tree branches. Add extra padding around the limb, using sweaters or towels, and fix the padding in place with tied bandages, scarves, rope or whatever equivalent you have available. As always with a fracture, your aim is to keep movement to an absolute minimum.

COMPOUND FRACTURES
When you are dealing with a compound or open fracture, it is important to prevent blood loss and reduce the chance of infection at the fracture site, as well as immobilizing the area. Seek medical help or contact the emergency services urgently, if you can. While you wait, place a clean dressing or sterile pad over the wound site and apply hard pressure, using your hands, to either side of the protruding bone to control the bleeding. Do not press on the protruding bone.

Build up padding alongside the bone sticking out of the skin, and secure the dressing and padding with a bandage, but do not do so if it causes any movement of the limb and never bandage tightly. Monitor the person's condition as there is a risk of shock.

If you are forced to move the injured person to get medical help, you may have to splint the fracture. Add extra padding around the limb and fix in place with tied bandages. Try to keep all movement to a minimum.

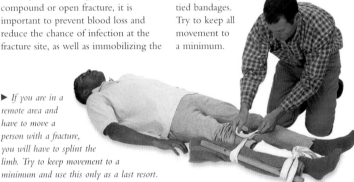

▶ *If you are in a remote area and have to move a person with a fracture, you will have to splint the limb. Try to keep movement to a minimum and use this only as a last resort.*

USING PADDING TO SUPPORT A LOWER LEG FRACTURE

 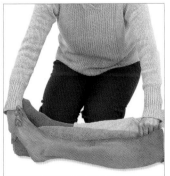 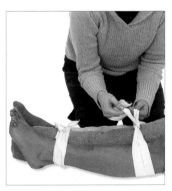

1 Help the person to lie down, then contact the emergency services. Feel the foot and lower leg for warmth and to check the person senses your touch.

2 Place soft padding in the middle of both legs, extending it well above the knee. The foot should be supported in the position in which it was found.

3 If you are forced to move the person yourself, secure the padding in place with bandages, placed well above and below the site of the fracture.

Managing spinal and neck injuries

The golden rule with spinal injuries (and neck injuries) is that the casualty must not be moved unless it is vital to do so. People with head injuries of any kind often have spinal injuries as well. The spinal cord, housed within the vertebrae, is commonly damaged at the mobile parts of the backbone such as the neck and lower back. Road accidents, rugby and diving are notorious causes of spinal injuries; other causes include falling from a height, being thrown from a horse, and impact to the head and/or face.

FIRST AID FOR SPINAL INJURY IN AN UNCONSCIOUS PERSON

1 Keep the casualty still, in the position in which they are found. Hold the head still, as shown here, in its current position. Ask others to support the rest of the body using hands and blankets, coats or towels. Continue to keep the casualty as still as possible. If the casualty is already on their back, and the airway is clear, with nothing in the mouth and no signs of possible bleeding or vomiting, keep them in that position. If the tongue is falling back and blocking the airway, bring it forward by pushing up at the angles of the jaws, as explained earlier. Do not use a head tilt unless absolutely necessary to clear the airway.

▼ *Using the "log roll" – for draining the mouth or resuscitation.*

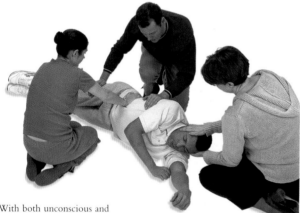

2 With both unconscious and conscious casualties, blood, vomit or other substances in the mouth or throat can block the airway (listen for gurgling). Only if this is a risk, make sure that they are in a position that allows these to drain out of the mouth. If you need to move them for this, be gentle, keep movement minimal, and keep the head still as you do so. Use a "log roll" to turn them from their back on to their side, as explained on the opposite page.

3 If the breathing or heartbeat stops, and the person is not already on their back, you must turn them on to their back to perform rescue breaths or CPR. Use the "log roll" technique, so that there is no change in the spine or head position.

4 ▶ To resuscitate, one person holds the head still while another performs resuscitation, as shown right.

Suspect a spinal injury if a person:
- Has suffered a significant impact/fall.
- Is unconscious after a head injury.
- Has fallen from a height and injured their face or head.
- Says that their neck hurts.
- Holds their neck in an odd position.
- Has any paralysis (loss of movement and sensation), loss of sensation or tingling or numbness in their arms and/or legs.
- Is confused and uncooperative.
- Has lost bowel and bladder control.
- Has difficulty breathing, with only small amounts of movement in the abdomen.
- Is lying flat on their back with arms stretched above the head, or with arms and hands curled to the chest.

FIRST AID FOR A SUSPECTED NECK INJURY

- Don't try to straighten or pull on the neck. Keep it in the position found, and as still as possible.
- Ask a helper to get some towels or clothing and place these rolled-up items either side of the neck, all the time keeping it still.
- Monitor their breathing and pulse and if either stop, be prepared to start resuscitation procedures. If they vomit, "log roll" them on to their side.

THE "LOG ROLL" TECHNIQUE

If you absolutely must move a casualty with a spinal injury you should only use the "log roll" technique. By moving them "as one piece", with everyone in synchronicity, you avoid their head twisting on their shoulders or their body rotating on their pelvis. This minimizes the chances of any of the spinal vertebrae moving and causing more damage. There should be a minimum of four people, ideally six, present to carry out this technique. One person should be in charge of the head and should dictate everyone else's movements. There should always be one helper at the casualty's feet. The other helpers are positioned along the body at close intervals and act as a team. To be absolutely safe, the log roll needs training and team practice.

1 To move someone from their back on to their side (if they want to vomit or if blood, vomit or other substances are blocking their mouth or throat): cross their arms over in front. Then, while one person supports the head, the other people stagger themselves along the body, gently straighten out the limbs and prepare to make the "log roll".

FIRST AID FOR A CONSCIOUS SPINAL INJURY CASUALTY

- Reassure the casualty. Unless there is an urgent reason to move them, such as breathing difficulties, do not do so. Call the emergency services promptly.
- Ask the casualty to keep absolutely still. Kneel behind their head and hold the head completely still, in the position in which you found it.
- Support the head at all times and ask someone to help monitor their breathing and circulation until medical help arrives.

PREVENTING NECK/ SPINAL INJURIES

Most spinal injuries occur in men aged 18 to 30 – the "risk-takers". Certain simple measures can prevent many such injuries:
- Always wear proper protective clothing when participating in a sport.
- Never dive into water until you know the depth, especially in tidal waters.
- Never dive into a swimming pool unless the water is at least 2.7m/ 9ft deep.
- Wear a seat-belt in any vehicle, and a padded jacket on a motorbike.

2 The head is supported all the time, and the helpers must hold the body and legs steady. The casualty's head, body and toes must align and all face in the same direction. Once turned on to their side, keep them there, perfectly still, until professional help arrives. Only move them (on to their back again) if they stop breathing or their heart stops and resuscitation becomes necessary.

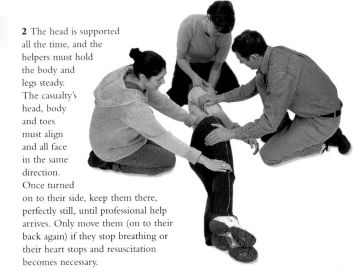

Burns, shock and extreme temperatures

Time is of the essence when giving first aid for burns. A major priority in all burn cases is to cool the skin. This not only eases the pain, but also reduces the amount of damage done to the skin, so that it will heal faster and scar less. However, be careful about making the person too cold and causing hypothermia. If in doubt, cover them with a coat or light blanket.

Run cold water over the burn site for at least 10 minutes, preferably from a gently running tap. If the burn is on a hand or arm, remove watches, rings, or bracelets, as the burn may cause swelling of tissues. Reassure the victim and phone the emergency service if necessary. If you think the burns are deep or cover a large proportion of the body, watch them carefully and be ready to deal with signs of further problems, such as shock.

Skin damage allows potential infection to enter, so burns must be covered. Dry dressings, even non-fluffy ones, tend to stick to burns, so the best

options are: wet sterile dressings or dampened clean handkerchiefs, clean plastic bags, or clear food wrap film.

WHAT NOT TO DO WITH BURNS

Here is a summary of major things to avoid when dealing with burns:
- Do not remove anything that is stuck to the burn – you may damage the skin further.
- Do not touch the wound and risk introducing infection.
- Do not put any fat, lotions, or ointments on a burn.
- Do not burst any blisters that form. While the skin is intact it continues to protect from infection, and provides an element of pain relief.
- Do not give anything to eat or drink if the burn is severe, unless you are a long way from hospital.

SHOCK

Physiological or circulatory shock is a serious condition caused by a sudden and dramatic drop in blood pressure, and without swift medical attention it can be life-threatening. It can be caused by any illness or injury that causes too little blood to circulate, depriving the body of oxygen, leading to the pale, cold, collapsed state that typifies shock. A common cause of

▲ *A large fire may cause life-threatening burns over a large part of the body, together with damage from inhalation of fumes.*

shock is excessive loss of body fluids, which may be due to blood loss after a serious accident or fluid loss caused by extensive burns. In reaction to the reduced circulation of blood, the body directs blood to vital areas such as the heart and lungs, and away from the skin. This makes the skin cold and pale. Adrenalin (epinephrine) is released as

▼ *Someone who appears confused or clumsy may be suffering from hypothermia. Get them into shelter and wrap them warmly.*

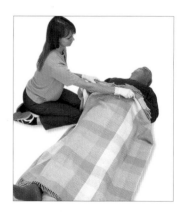

FIRST AID FOR SHOCK

- If the person is unconscious, check DRSABC. Start resuscitating, if necessary.
- If the person is unconscious but breathing, put them in the recovery position. Stop any heavy bleeding.
- If the person is conscious, lay them down and calm them.
- Call the emergency services.
- Check the body for fractures, wounds and burns. Deal with these as necessary; make sure any heavy bleeding is controlled.
- Unless you think the legs may be fractured, place them on a low, padded support so that the legs are higher than the heart.
- Cover the person with a blanket and try to keep them reassured.
- Do not give anything to eat or drink. Moisten an uncomfortably dry mouth with a wet cloth.

FIRST AID FOR HYPOTHERMIA

Basic principles
• Prevent further heat loss
• Get urgent help
• Rewarm the person – gradually
• Follow DRSABC

Keep movement of the person to a minimum, and be very gentle. Sudden movement can cause heart problems.

If outdoors
Keep the victim in shelter. Replace wet clothing with dry, ideally warmed (e.g. from dry, warm bystanders). Cover the person's head and insulate them against cold from the ground. Wrap them in something warm such as a sleeping bag or plastic bags (leave the face uncovered), or ideally a survival bag.

If indoors
Rewarm gradually in a generally warm room. Replace any cold, damp clothing. If the victim is alert enough to eat or drink, give hot, sweet fluids (no alcohol) and a little high-calorie food. Do not: heat up the body too fast, apply direct heat (hot-water bottles, sitting someone against a radiator), massage or rub the skin, or get the victim to exercise.

▼ *If someone is dehydrated but can still ingest water without vomiting, encourage them to sip slowly and keep them calm.*

an emergency response and this causes a rapid pulse and sweating. As the blood flow weakens further, the brain begins to suffer from lack of oxygen, leading to nausea, dizziness, blurred vision, and confusion. If blood circulation is not restored rapidly, the person will start gasping for breath and will soon lose consciousness.

HYPOTHERMIA
Caused by cold, hypothermia occurs when the body's core temperature drops below 35°C/95°F. It commonly occurs in cold, exposed outdoor conditions, such as in mountainous regions, at the scene of traffic accidents, or as a result of immersion in cold water. Temperatures do not have to be freezing. It is more likely to occur in wet and windy conditions.

Diagnosis can be difficult, and unconscious sufferers may be mistaken for dead. However, due to the body's reduced need for oxygen when very cold, even prolonged resuscitation efforts have been successful.

HEAT EXHAUSTION
Due to excessive loss of water and salt from profuse sweating, heat exhaustion often occurs after heavy exertion and on hot days. If not treated promptly, heat exhaustion can prove fatal or develop into heatstroke.

HEATSTROKE
A very serious condition, heatstroke is often fatal. It may start as heat exhaustion, but if the body does not cool down, its heat-regulating mechanism fails, and body tissues start to heat up. Muscles and major organs begin to break down. Heatstroke tends to happen mainly in a very hot environment or with a fever.

Certain people are more vulnerable to heatstroke, such as the disabled and infirm, those with diabetes, the obese, and alcoholics. Some drugs, especially anti-depressants, diuretics, and sedatives, can increase susceptibility.

A person suffering from heatstroke needs urgent medical attention. While waiting for the emergency services, follow DRSABC, then move the

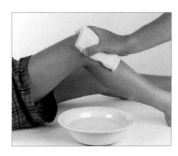

▲ *A cool, damp compress can be used in the treatment of minor burns and will give some comfort to the victim.*

person out of the sun to a cool place. Remove excessive clothing. Lay them flat unless they have heart problems. In this case, sit them up. Watch for breathing problems.

To cool the person down, sponge the skin with cool water or spray with water and put them near a fan.

HEAT CRAMPS
These may happen after excessive exertion or exertion in very hot weather. They occur as a result of loss of salt and water from sweating. People may also feel sick and dizzy. First-aid treatment involves moving the sufferer to a cool place and giving them fluids with added sugar.

FIRST AID FOR HEATSTROKE

Follow DRSABC and call the emergency services if necessary or if the condition seems severe.
• Place the person in a cool place with a fan.
• Sponge the skin with tepid water.
• Give them cool water to drink.
• Do not give salt – this can cause dehydration if used incorrectly. A medical adviser will tell you what to give, or recommend an oral rehydration solution.
• If the person cannot drink because of nausea or vomiting, or there is no improvement after 1 hour, call a doctor or the emergency services.

Treating alcohol and drug poisoning

Alcohol in moderate amounts is easily detoxified by the liver; but in very large quantities alcohol becomes a poison that the body can no longer deal with – and it can prove fatal. The same doesn't go, however, for many illicit drugs. Even relatively small amounts of a substance such as cocaine or fumes from glue can result in severe effects on the body. Emergency medical treatment is vital, especially if a child has taken alcohol or a drug because children absorb the toxins much more quickly than adults.

Taking illicit substances and drinking large quantities of alcohol is socially acceptable in some parts of society, but such practices are potentially dangerous and lead to medical crises, serious accidents and even fatalities.

ALCOHOL POISONING

When drunk in sufficient quantities, alcohol can poison the system. Consumption of half a litre (1 pint) of a spirit, such as vodka, is enough to cause severe alcohol poisoning. Alcohol-related risks include:
• Depression of the central nervous system, most seriously the brain.
• Widening of blood vessels, making the body lose heat and increasing the risk of hypothermia.

SIGNS AND SYMPTOMS OF ALCOHOL INTOXICATION

It is usually fairly obvious when someone is intoxicated with alcohol, but similar symptoms may be caused by a head injury or a diabetic hypoglycaemic (low blood sugar) condition.
• A smell of alcohol on the breath.
• Empty bottles or cans nearby.
• Flushed and warm skin.
• Actions are aggressive or passive.
• Speech and actions are slow and become less coordinated.
• Deep, noisy breathing.
• Low level of consciousness; an intoxicated person may often slip into unconsciousness.

HOW TO DEAL WITH ALCOHOL INTOXICATION

1 Check that they are rousable by shaking them and shouting their name, if you know it. If they respond but fall back into unconsciousness, keep a regular watch on them until they start to come around.

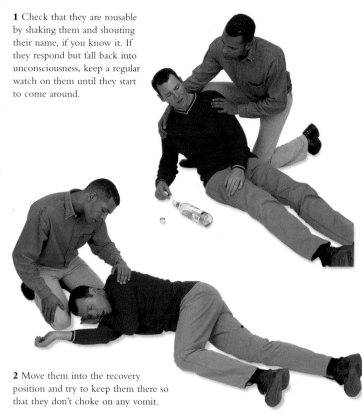

2 Move them into the recovery position and try to keep them there so that they don't choke on any vomit.

3 Phone the emergency services and do not leave them until the ambulance arrives. Once conscious, you could give them some water to drink.

ARE YOU DRINKING TOO MUCH ALCOHOL?

If you regularly drink more than the recommended safe limit of alcohol, you could be putting your health at risk. Any of the following may indicate a potential problem with alcohol.
• Regular, excessive consumption.
• Not being able to stop drinking once you have started.
• Days off because of hangovers.
• Drinking in the morning.
• Not being able to recall what happened the previous night.
• Friends commenting on your excessive drinking.
• Injury to yourself and others because of drinking.

POISONING VIA SOLVENT ABUSE

Children and adolescents are the main solvent abusers – they may inhale fumes from glue, paint, lighter fuel, cleaning fluids, aerosols and nail polish to "get high". All such solvents depress breathing and heart activity, and may cause respiratory and cardiac arrest. Signs and symptoms are as follows:
• The casualty has a dry throat and cough.
• Their chest feels tight and they may be breathless.
• They have a headache.
• They feel nauseous and may vomit.

FIRST AID FOR SOLVENT ABUSE POISONING

• If the casualty has stopped breathing or their heart has stopped beating, start resuscitation immediately.
• If unconscious but their ABC (airway, breathing and circulation) is normal, place them in the fresh air in the recovery position.
• Phone the emergency services.
• Check their ABC regularly.
• Often, the casualty starts to "come round" quickly and may seem normal after 20 minutes. Stay with them until help arrives.

◄ *Children and teenagers are the main abusers of solvents – whether it be sniffing glue, propellants from aerosols or lighter fuel. When dealing with a casualty of solvent abuse, it's vital to maintain their breathing and circulation and get them to hospital as soon as possible.*

• They have hallucinations – they "hear voices" or "see things".
• Their breathing becomes faster and more laboured as fluid builds up in their lungs.
• They become drowsy and confused and eventually may lose consciousness altogether.
• They have episodes of fits (convulsions), which may lead to coma and eventually to death.

ILLICIT DRUGS

Illicit stimulant drugs include Ecstasy, cocaine, amphetamines and LSD. If you suspect someone has taken any of these drugs, watch out for the following:
• Excitable and hyperactive behaviour.
• Sweating.
• Shaking hands.
• Hallucinations.
   These drugs can occasionally be fatal. Ecstasy interferes with the brain's ability to control body temperature, which can rise to over 42°C (107.6°F) and cause heat exhaustion. Ecstasy-

takers often drink lots of water to try to combat this sensation, which can cause kidney malfunction and abnormal heart rhythms. Cocaine's main effects are on the heart rate – with the potential to lead to abnormal rhythms and even cardiac arrest.
   Opiate drugs such as heroin and codeine may depress the respiratory system, causing breathing to stop. Rapid recovery occurs if a particular drug is given intravenously, but this must be done urgently, by trained medical personnel.

FIRST AID FOR ILLICIT DRUG POISONING

• Do not try to make the casualty vomit.
• Place them in the recovery position.
• Phone the emergency services.
• Check their ABC and monitor their breathing every 10 minutes.

Treating the victims of road accidents

The most common site for people to have a road accident is within two miles of their own home – perhaps because of fatigue or because drivers exercise less care when on their home turf. Other common causes of road accidents include inexperience and carelessness by young and newly qualified drivers, being distracted by children in the back and driving while under the influence of alcohol. The best way to avoid accidents is to drive not only safely but also watchfully, so that you can compensate for the mistakes of others on the road.

Roads around the world are becoming increasingly busy. Although there are stringent laws governing road safety in many countries, most of the accidents are caused by human error – 95 per cent are somebody's fault, rather than simply an unlucky twist of fate. Perhaps surprisingly, most road traffic accidents happen in daylight; less surprisingly, these often occur in the rush hours: 7–9 a.m. and 3–7 p.m.

WHY ACCIDENTS HAPPEN

Alcohol is a big factor in many accidents. It affects multiple aspects of driving ability – decision-making, self-criticism, balance, coordination, touch, sight, hearing and judgement to name a few. It is best not to drink at all if you are planning on driving rather than trying to stick to a general "safe limit" that may not be safe for a particular individual at all.

Inexperienced and young drivers, especially men, often drive without enough thought for road safety or their responsibility as drivers. This is why those under 20 years old have to pay large amounts for their car insurance – and can then be a hazard on the road.

Older drivers can be a danger to themselves and others if their eyesight and reaction speeds are failing, particularly if they do not have any insight into their condition. When travelling as a group, lack of concentration caused by chatting to

others in the car, turning to reprimand children or talking on a cellphone can also cause an accident.

Tiredness is a major killer. Its incidence is probably underestimated because no one can know the exact details of what has gone on before a fatal car crash. Planning regular breaks, being aware of times when you are likely to feel drowsy (for example, just after lunch or between the hours of 2 a.m. and 6 a.m.) and stopping for a nap or a coffee if tiredness hits can all help to prevent a tragedy.

Motorways are particularly hazardous because the monotony of driving on long, straight roads and the lack of gear changing can cause the driver to feel tired or be inattentive. But fatigue and

▲ *Always carry a warning triangle in your car. Place this near the stationary vehicle to warn approaching drivers of an accident.*

◀ *Make sure that the casualty is in a safe place – move them if necessary – then call the emergency services for help.*

lack of concentration can also cause accidents on urban and suburban roads. Most road accidents occur within two miles of the driver's own home.

WHAT TO DO IN A CAR ACCIDENT

If you witness a road accident, be aware that stopping could jeopardize your own safety. Check all your mirrors before pulling up at the scene. Stay calm and ensure that your car is visible and that the accident scene is protected from oncoming traffic. Switch on your hazard lights as soon as you have stopped the vehicle.

If the accident has happened on a bend, try to warn approaching drivers by using a hazard warning triangle or asking another driver to flag the cars down. Watch out for broken glass and metal. Make sure that your handbrake is on and that your car is safe to leave.

On motorways, the speed that vehicles travel at may well make stopping to help too hazardous. If this is the case, drive on and use a telephone to summon help.

FIRST AID FOR ROAD TRAFFIC CASUALTIES

- People are often trapped in cars after accidents. This should not stop you from initiating first-aid measures. You can still protect and open the airway on a casualty in the upright position.
- Make the area safe. Move people to safety if possible. But do not move anyone who is injured, or whom you suspect is injured, unless they are in further danger.
- Telephone the emergency services with precise details of your location.
- Stop heavy bleeding.
- Instigate CPR if needed.

TO REDUCE THE RISK OF FIRE

Turn off the damaged car's engine and, if possible, disconnect the car battery. Stop people from smoking at the scene, and cover any fuel spillage with soil or sand. For more advice on dealing with road transport accidents safely, see pages 456–7.

▲ *A casualty slumped forward in the driver's seat should be moved so their airway is opened, even if spinal injury is a possibility.*

▲ *To clear the airway of a casualty who is still in the car, tilt their jaw slightly upwards and remove any blood or vomit. Then use the resuscitation techniques.*

MOTORCYCLE ACCIDENTS

Motorcyclists are 24 times more likely to be killed or injured for every kilometre or mile travelled compared with car drivers. This is partly because they are often inexperienced, young drivers, and partly because they are in a more physically vulnerable situation.

▲ *When dealing with any roadside casualty, assume that there may be a neck/spinal injury and handle with great care. Wherever possible, treat the casualty in the position found.*

Index

Acknowledgements

The publishers would like to thank the following individuals for their valuable contributions to this book:

Text contributors: Nick Banks (navigation), Colin Drake (physical fitness), Beverley Jollands (nutrition) Bill Mattos (kayaking and canoeing), Will Patterson (cycling), Debra Searle and Hayley Barnard at SHOAL Projects Ltd www.debrasearle.com. (introduction and accompanying photographs; one image also appears on the jacket).
Text advisors: Peter Tipling, Dr Bill Turner, J. Evans, Mrs A. Funnel.
Advice and assistance: Malcolm Creasey, Sue Dowson, Andy Middleton, David Williams.
Anthonio Akkermans would like to thank Gillian and Reuben, Ofer Israeli, Shomeri Hagan, Allan "Bow" Beauchamp, Tom Brown and the instructors at the Tracker school for teaching these skills.
Harry Cook would like to thank Sheila Cook and the members of Hexham Sijinkai Karate-do Club: Katie Khudarieh, Katy Cook, Sheila Cook, Catriona Moreland, Malcolm Wilson, Lucy Anne Donnelly. Thanks are also due to Lisa Henderson.

Models for photography: S. Atkins, Nikki Ball, Doncaster Scout Group, Joe O'Brian, Tattiana Cotts, Tim Denson, Robert Driskel, Gabby Footner, Mr and Mrs Gibson, Gary and Loretta Harper, Matthew Harrison, Alison Martin, Bill Mattos, Lynn Milner, Andy Parritt, Paul Ross, Alastair Stewart, Mike and Luke Waldock.

Equipment: Julian McIntosh at Safariquip, The Stones, Castleton, Derbyshire (tel: 01433 620 320) (camping and walking equipment), Holmfirth Cycles, Bradshaw Road, Honley, Huddersfield, Yorkshire (tel: 01484 661672) (cycles and cycling equipment), Andrew Morrison (additional camping items). Also Brian Turner and his wife at Kazan Budo Ltd (Martial Arts supplies - http://www.kazanbudo.com and Bellingham Fitness Centre (gym, models, props and lunches for the self-defence shoots).

PICTURE CREDITS
All the photography in this book is by Martyn Milner and Helen Metcalfe (Helen is at Nookie Xtreme Sports Equipment http://nookie.co.uk),

except for the following:
t = top; c = centre; b = bottom;
l = left; r = right
Alamy 9tl, 458tr, 462tr, 473tr, 479tl, 486tr
Corbis: 167, 170
Simon Dodd: 17b, 24t, 127tl, 127tc, 127tr, 131b, 473tr, 479tl, 486tr
Peter G. Drake: 12tr, 13 (both), 16b, p19b, 20b, 22, 24b, 25 (both), 27 (both), 28, 29 (both), 33b, 38, 39 (both), 41b, 42, 43tl, 44/5; 48 (both), 50 (both), 52, 54, 56, 66t, 68 (both), 69tl, 69tc, 69tr, 70 (both), 71t, 71br, 75 (both), 76bl, 81tl, 81tr, 81cl, 94t, 98t, 105t, 108t, 108br, 109br, 119tl, 119tr, 122 (both), 123tl, 125 (both), 130b, 162t, 164, 165 (all), 166 (all), 168t, 169 (both), 170b, 171b, 172 (all), 173 (all), 177bc, 177br, 184 (both), 185 (both), 186, 187 (both), 188, 189tl, 189bl, 189br, 190bl, 191tl, 204bl, 205tr, 205br, 210bl, 211br, 212 (both), 213t, 216t, 218r, 223t, 232bl, 234br, 235 (both), 238b, 239tl, 239tc, 241bl, 241br, 245tr, 245bc, 242bl, 242br, 250tr, 250br, 110t, 258t, 263 Istock 265tr, 267tl, 268tl, tr, 269tr, 434tr, 435tr, 437bl, 453tr, 456bl, 458bl, 463tl, 472tr, 480tr, 480bt, 484bl, 485tr, 488/9
Mick O'Connell: p52br, p53b

Sciene Photo Library: 264bl, 265cl, cr, bl, bt, 266bl, 268b, 482tr
Thanks also to: Rob Bicevskis for his help on the images of making fire with a lens of ice, Peter Bull Art Studio for the footprints, skinning, tanning and hiding step illustrations, Peter Drake for supplying charts and African bushcraft photographs, Tim Gundry for shooting the self-defence sequences, Mick Kalakoski for the snow shelter images, Tunde Morakinyo at the Iroko Foundation for the jungle photographs, Bob Morrison's Military Scene for the military and biological pictures, Patrick Mulrey for the disaster scenario illustrations, Jean-Philippe Soulé www.jpsviewfinder.com for the palm shelter pictures, Mark Wood for shooting the first aid sequences, Ray Wood and Mark Duncalf for shooting the rock climbing sequences.